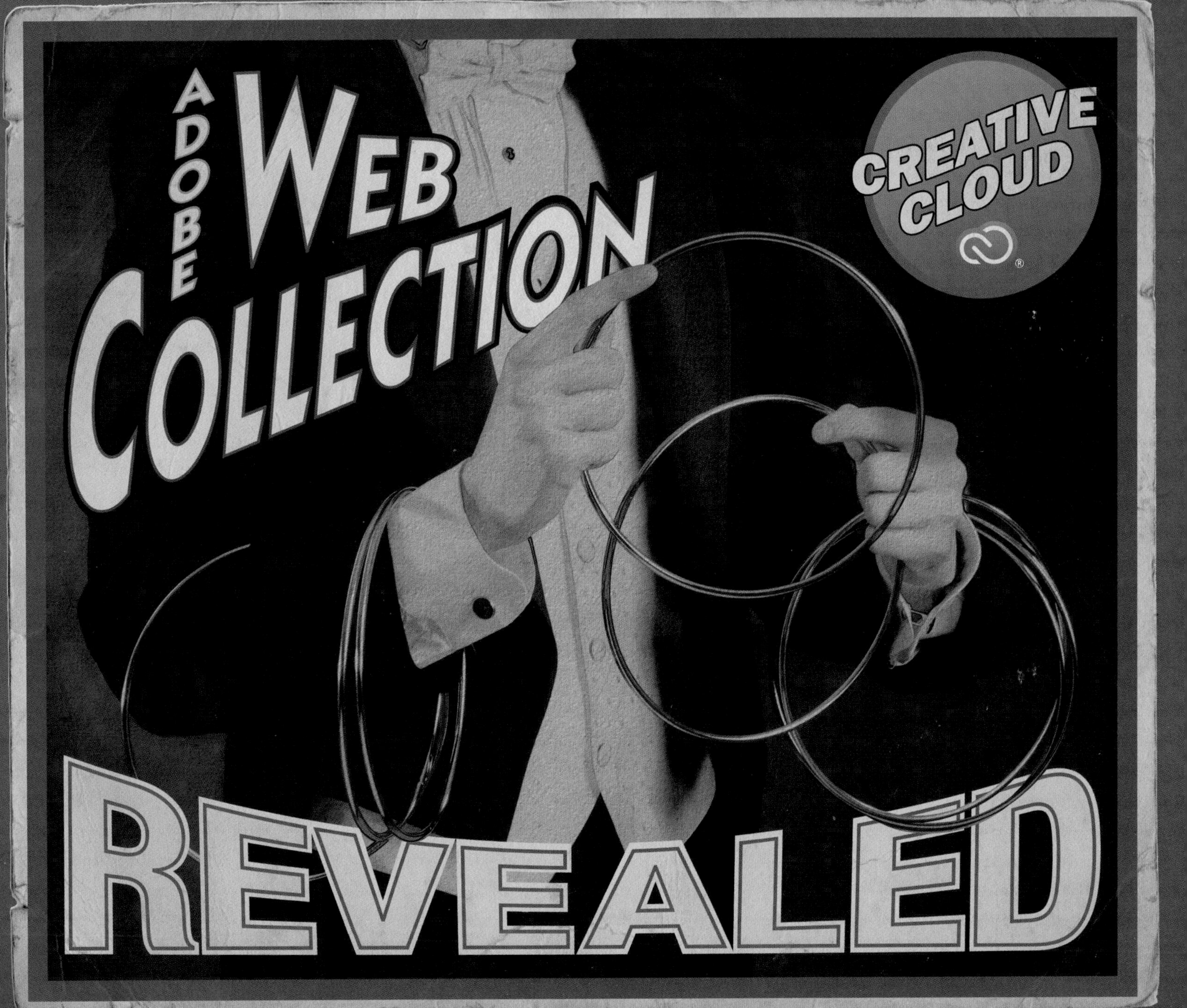
ADOBE
WEB
COLLECTION
CREATIVE CLOUD
REVEALED

Australia • Brazil • Mexico • Singapore • United Kingdom • United States

CENGAGE
Learning·

The Web Collection Creative Cloud Revealed
Sherry Bishop, Jim Shuman, Sasha Vodnik

Product Director: Kathleen McMahon

Senior Product Manager: Jim Gish

Content Developer: Megan Chrisman

Senior Marketing Manager: Eric La Scola

Senior Content Project Manager:
   Jennifer Goguen McGrail

Developmental Editors: Barbara Clemens, Ann Shaffer

Technical Editors: John Freitas, Jeff Schwartz,
   John Shanley, Danielle Shaw

Managing Art Director: Jack Pendleton

Manufacturing Planner: Julio Esperas

IP Analyst: Amber Hosea

Senior IP Project Manager: Kathy Kucharek

Production Service: Integra Software Services Pvt. Ltd

Text Designer: Liz Kingslein

Proofreader: Harold Johnson

Indexer: Alexandra Nickerson

Cover Image: Cengage Learning

For product information and technology assistance, contact us at **Cengage Learning Customer & Sales Support, 1-800-354-9706**

For permission to use material from this text or product, submit all requests online at **www.cengage.com/permissions.**

Further permissions questions can be emailed to **permissionrequest@cengage.com.**

Library of Congress Control Number: 2014954895

ISBN: 978-1-305-26362-8
ISBN-10: 1-305-26362-6

Cengage Learning
20 Channel Center Street
Boston, MA 02210
USA

Cengage Learning is a leading provider of customized learning solutions with office locations around the globe, including Singapore, the United Kingdom, Australia, Mexico, Brazil, and Japan. Locate your local office at **www.cengage.com/global**.

Cengage Learning products are represented in Canada by Nelson Education, Ltd.

To learn more about Cengage Learning Solutions, visit **www.cengage.com**.

Purchase any of our products at your local college store or at our preferred online store **www.cengagebrain.com**.

Printed in the United States of America

Print Number: 01   Print Year: 2015

Revealed Series Vision

The Revealed Series is your guide to today's hottest digital media applications. For years, the Revealed Series has kept pace with the dynamic demands of the digital media community, and continues to do so with the publication of six new titles covering the latest Adobe Creative Cloud products. Each comprehensive book teaches not only the technical skills required for success in today's competitive digital media market, but the design skills as well. From animation, to web design, to digital image editing and interactive media skills, the Revealed Series has you covered.

We recognize the unique learning environment of the digital media classroom, and we deliver textbooks that include:

- Comprehensive step-by-step instructions
- In-depth explanations of the "why" behind a skill
- Creative projects for additional practice
- Full-color visuals for a clear explanation of concepts
- Comprehensive online material offering additional instruction and skills practice

With the Revealed series, we've created books that speak directly to the digital media and design community—one of the most rapidly growing computer fields today.

—The Revealed Series

New to This Edition

The latest edition of *The Web Collection Creative Cloud Revealed* includes many exciting new features, some of which are:

- In Dreamweaver, New Fluid Grid Layouts
- CSS Designer
- Adobe Edge Web Fonts
- Element Quick View
- In Flash, coverage of how to create and publish HTML5 Canvas content and how to repurpose existing Flash documents as HTML5 Canvas documents
- In Edge, creating basic and interactive animations with Edge Animate
- Testing web documents on mobile devices with Edge Inspect
- Incorporating HTML5 Canvas documents and Edge Animate compositions into Dreamweaver documents
- Exporting symbols from Flash Professional and importing them into Edge Animate

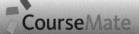

A CourseMate is available to accompany *Adobe Web Collection Creative Cloud Revealed*, which helps you make the grade!

This CourseMate includes:

- An interactive eBook, with highlighting, note-taking, read-aloud, and search capabilities
- Interactive learning tools including:
  - Chapter quizzes
  - Flash cards
  - Crossword puzzles
  - And more!

Go to login.cengagebrain.com to access these resources.

AUTHOR'S VISION

This book introduces you to Dreamweaver, a fascinating tool to create rich and exciting websites. Although the world of technology moves more quickly than we sometimes like, we are in a particularly exciting time with the Adobe Creative Cloud. With HTML5 and CSS3, we are challenged to learn more efficient, sleeker methods for designing sites.

Many talented and creative individuals created this text for you. Our Content Developer, Megan Chrisman, guided and directed the team from start to finish. She listens to others, correctly assesses each situation, and makes timely and appropriate decisions. We appreciated these talents as we worked through an aggressive schedule.

Barbara Clemens, my Development Editor, is an example of so many things I value: joy, kindness, patience, and determination. We have worked together on the Dreamweaver book for many years and I appreciate her more with each new edition. She can pull deep inside me to bring out my best. Thank you for all these years of dedication, Barbara.

The legal information about copyright in Chapter 7 was based on content from the book *Internet Surf and Turf Revealed: The Essential Guide to Copyright, Fair Use, and Finding Media* by my good friend, Barbara Waxer, author of the Can I Use It blog, www.barbarawaxer.com.

John Shanley is our Dreamweaver Technical Editor for both Mac and PC. He had a daunting job, juggling two sets of files as he carefully tested each step to make sure that the end product was as error-free as possible. He gave exceptional feedback as he reviewed each chapter.

Suwathiga Velayutham, Senior Project Manager, Jennifer Feltri-George, Senior Content Project Manager, and Jack Pendleton, Managing Art Director, managed the layout and kept the production schedule on track. We thank them for keeping up with the many details and deadlines. The work is beautiful.

Harold Johnson quietly worked behind the scenes to ensure that all grammatical and punctuation errors were corrected. He also provided valuable insight on the accuracy of content specifics. Harold has been on our team for many editions and I always feel good knowing he will be reviewing my work.

Thanks also to Jim Gish, Senior Product Manager. He embraced the Revealed books with enthusiasm and provided us with excellent resources to produce books that make us all proud. I would also like to express my gratitude to others who have worked on this book during the last 13 years: Jane Hosie-Bounar, Nicole Pinard, Rebecca Berardy, Ann Fisher, Barbara Waxer, Marjorie Hunt, Karen Stevens, Jeff Schwartz, Ashlee Wetz, and Joe Villanova.

I would also like to extend my appreciation to the Adobe Dreamweaver beta team. My participation in the beta process is always a positive, energizing experience. The Dreamweaver engineers clearly dedicate themselves to meeting and exceeding designer and developer needs and expectations. Kirsti Aho was the first Adobe visionary with whom I had the pleasure to work, beginning in the Macromedia Dreamweaver days.

Thanks to the Beach Club in Gulf Shores, Alabama, beachclubal.com, for being such a delightful place to visit. Several photographs of their stunning property appear in The Striped Umbrella website. They also generously provided several new photographs for this edition that added beauty to the page designs. Thank you, also, to each of you that allowed us to use images of your websites and to Pleasure Island Parasail LLC for a small video clip.

Typically, your family is the last to be thanked. My husband, Don, supports and encourages me every day. Our travels with our children and grandchildren provide happy memories for us and content for the websites.

Thank you to each student and instructor using this book as you travel along your educational path, and for making this book a part of your journey.

—Sherry Bishop

Writing a textbook on an application development and animation program is quite challenging. How do you take such a feature-rich program like Adobe Flash Professional CC and put it in a context that helps users learn? My goal is to provide a comprehensive, yet manageable, introduction to Adobe Flash Professional CC—just enough conceptual information to provide the needed context—and then move right into working with the application. My thought is that you'll get so caught up in the hands-on activities and compelling projects that you'll be pleasantly surprised at the level of Flash skills and knowledge you've acquired at the end of each chapter.

Being an author can be a somewhat lonely endeavor unless you have a team providing the support that I have found with Delmar and Cengage Learning. What a delight it has been to be a part of such a creative and energetic publishing team. The Revealed Series is a great format for teaching and learning Flash and I would like to thank Jim Gish, who provided the vision for the series. I am indebted to two individuals that I have had the joy of working with for the first time, Megan Chrisman and Ann Shaffer. Megan used her management skills to guide this book through the incredibly complex publishing process and Ann applied her expertise as a Developmental Editor to make sense of my writing while providing the encouragement that helped me over the inevitable authoring hurdles. Thanks Ann and Megan! I also want to give a heartfelt thanks to my wife, Barbara, for her patience, support, and use of her remarkable artwork. This book is dedicated to our new twin grandchildren, Masato and Sayuri, who bring us such joy!

—Jim Shuman

I've been excited about the Adobe Edge suite since it was first announced, and I was thrilled to create an introduction to Edge Animate and Edge Inspect, and to show how Edge Animate works with Dreamweaver and Flash Professional. Thanks to Jim Gish for the invitation to join the team, and to Sherry Bishop and Jim Shuman for collaborating with me to create solid educational material. I'm also thankful to Megan Chrisman, who organized our efforts. Ann Shaffer and Mary Pat Shaffer provided incredibly helpful editorial feedback and helped me to strengthen the explanations, illustrations, and steps. Thanks also to Jennifer Goguen McGrail and Suwathiga Velayutham for laying everything out and making it look great, and to Jeffrey Schwartz, Danielle Shaw, and John Freitas for meticulously testing all the steps and letting me know what needed fixing before the book went out the door.

Finally, thanks to my husband, Jason Bucy, for his love, support, and help in navigating the balancing act that's a fundamental part of an author's life.

—Sasha Vodnik

Introduction to The Web Collection Creative Cloud—Revealed

Welcome to *The Web Collection: Adobe Dreamweaver CC, Flash CC, and Edge Animate CC—Revealed.* This book offers creative projects, concise instructions, and coverage of basic Dreamweaver, Flash, Edge Animate, and Creative Cloud integration skills, helping you to create polished, professional-looking websites and art work. Use this book both in the classroom and as your own reference guide. It also includes many of the new features in the 2014 release of Creative Cloud.

This text is organized into fifteen chapters, as well as a special introductory section covering Adobe's Creative Cloud features. In these chapters, you will learn many skills, including how to move amongst the Creative Cloud applications, which provide familiar functionality from one application to the next.

Understanding the relationship between Flash Professional and Edge Animate

Flash Professional has long been used to create animations for the web, as well as to generate vector-based web assets. Flash is a widely-used tool in game development and in the creation of mobile apps using the AIR (Adobe Integrated Runtime) technology. In addition, Flash can save projects as HTML5 Canvas documents. Although the HTML5 Canvas format currently supports only a subset of Flash features, the resulting files render in all mobile browsers.

Edge Animate is a new tool designed to provide a graphical interface for creating animations using only HTML, CSS, and JavaScript. Edge Animate saves all compositions as .html files, meaning that they play in browsers by default, with no publishing or exporting required. Edge Animate currently supports only a fraction of the Flash feature set.

Both Flash and Edge Animate have a number of use cases, some overlapping and some distinct. For maximum flexibility and employability, students studying web animation, mobile apps and game development should learn the basics of both programs. We are pleased to introduce you to both applications in this book.

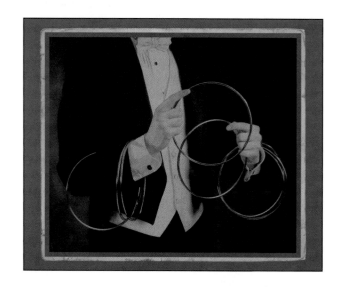

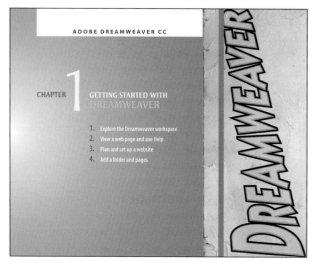

ADOBE DREAMWEAVER CC

CHAPTER 1 GETTING STARTED WITH DREAMWEAVER

1. Explore the Dreamweaver workspace
2. View a web page and use Help
3. Plan and set up a website
4. Add a folder and pages

What You'll Do

A What You'll Do figure begins every lesson. This figure gives you an at-a-glance look at what you'll do in the chapter, either by showing you a file from the current project or a tool you'll be using.

Comprehensive Conceptual Lessons

Before jumping into instructions, in-depth conceptual information tells you "why" skills are applied. This book provides the "how" and "why" through the use of professional examples. Also included in the text are tips and sidebars to help you work more efficiently and creatively, or to teach you a bit about the history or design philosophy behind the skill you are using.

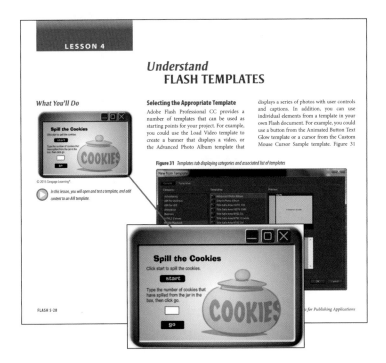

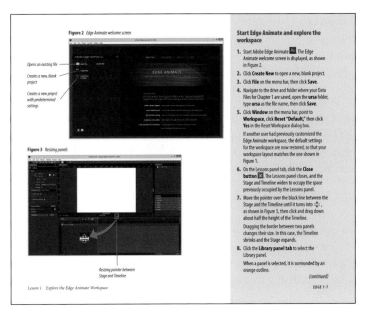

Step-by-Step Instructions

This book combines in-depth conceptual information with concise steps to help you learn Adobe Dreamweaver, Adobe Flash, and Adobe Edge Animate. Each set of steps guides you through a lesson where you will create, modify, or enhance a Creative Cloud file. Step references to large colorful images and quick step summaries round out the lessons. The Data Files for the steps are provided on Cengage Brain. For information on how to access Cengage Brain, see "Read This Before You Begin."

Projects

This book contains a variety of end-of-chapter materials for additional practice and reinforcement. The Skills Review contains hands-on practice exercises that mirror the progressive nature of the lesson material. The chapter concludes with four projects: two Project Builders, one Design Project, and one Portfolio Project. The Project Builders and the Design Project require you to apply the skills you've learned in the chapter. The Portfolio Project encourages students to address and solve challenges based on the content explored in the chapter in order to create portfolio-quality work.

In this project you will customize an interactive game based on the RPG Game Collisions Flash template. The template allows the player to use the mouse and/or keyboard controls to direct an object (a head) with the goal of collecting money and artifacts. Feedback is provided to the player as the game progresses. You start by opening and saving the template, then make changes to the various objects to customize the app.

1. Open the Templates tab in the New Document dialog box, display the Sample Files Category, then open the RPG Game Collisions template.
2. Save the document as **customGame.fla**.
3. Test the application in the Flash Player window, play the game and study how it works.
4. Close the Flash Player window.
5. Import GameBackground.png to the Library.
6. Choose New Symbol from the Insert menu, then create a movie clip with the name **GameBg**. The new symbol is displayed in the Edit window.
7. Drag the GameBackground.png image from the Library and center it on the Stage.
8. Click Scene 1 to return to the main Timeline.
9. Lock all layers except for the Worldboard layer, click frame 1 of the Worldboard layer, then click the Worldboard (green checkered background) on the Stage to select it.
10. Click Modify on the menu bar, point to Symbol, then click Swap Symbol.
11. Select the GameBg symbol and click OK.

12. Reposition the GameBg object so that it is behind the money in both the upper-left and lower-right corners of the Stage as shown in Figure 45.
Note: The gameBackground.png image was originally created with the same dimensions as the Worldboard object.
13. Lock the Worldboard layer and unlock the WorldObjects layer.
14. Display the Library panel, then double-click the WallSquare icon to display the WallSquare image in the Edit window.
Note: The brown WallSquare image is used to fill the vertical and horizontal bars on the Stage.
15. Click Layer 1 to select it, then click the square.
16. Use the Properties panel to change the color to a blue gradient.
17. Click Scene 1 to display the main Timeline with the Stage and notice the vertical and horizontal bars are now a blue gradient color.
18. Display the Library panel, then double-click the WaterSquare icon to display it in the Edit window.
19. Click Layer 1 to select it, then click the square.
20. Use the Properties panel to change the color to a green gradient, then display the main Timeline with the Stage.
21. Display the Gold movie clip in the Edit window.
22. Rename Layer1 **gold** and lock the layer.
23. Add a layer above the gold layer and name it **dollarSign**.
24. Click frame 1 on the dollarSign layer, then use the Text tool to type a dollar sign ($) with a green color and a size of 18pt.

25. Center the dollar sign over the gold object.
26. Display the main Timeline with the Stage.
27. Test the application in the Flash Player window, then close the Flash Player window.
28. Save and close the application.

Figure 45 *Completed Project Builder 2*

What Instructor Resources Are Available with This Book?

The Instructor Resources are Cengage's way of putting the resources and information needed to teach and learn effectively into your hands. All the resources are available for both Macintosh and Windows operating systems. These resources can be found online at **http://login.cengage.com**. Once you log in or create an account, search for the title under "Add a product to your Instructor Resource Center" using the ISBN. Then select the instructor companion site resources and click "Add Selected to Instructor Resource Center."

Instructor's Manual

The Instructor's Manual includes chapter overviews and detailed lecture topics for each chapter, with teaching tips.

Sample Syllabus

The Sample Syllabus includes a suggested syllabus for any course that uses this book.

PowerPoint Presentations

Each chapter has a corresponding PowerPoint presentation that you can use in lectures, distribute to your students, or customize to suit your course.

Data Files for Students

To complete most of the chapters in this book, your students will need Data Files, which are available online. Instruct students to use the Data Files List at the end of this book. This list gives instructions on organizing files.

To download the Data Files for this book:

1. Open your browser and go to http://www.cengagebrain.com
2. Type the author, title, or ISBN of this book in the Search box. (The ISBN is listed on the back cover.)
3. Select the book title in the list of search results.
4. In the book's main page, click the Free Materials tab, and then click the Access Now button.
5. Select a chapter and then click the Data Files link on the left.

Solutions to Exercises

Solution Files are Data Files completed with comprehensive sample answers. Use these files to evaluate your students' work. Or distribute them electronically so students can verify their work. Sample solutions to all lessons and end-of-chapter material are provided, with the exception of some Portfolio Projects.

Test Bank and Test Engine

Cengage Learning Testing Powered by Cognero is a flexible, online system that allows you to:

- author, edit, and manage test bank content from multiple Cengage Learning solutions
- create multiple test versions in an instant
- deliver tests from your LMS, your classroom, or wherever you want

Start right away!

Cengage Learning Testing Powered by Cognero works on any operating system or browser.

- No special installs or downloads needed
- Create tests from school, home, the coffee shop—anywhere with Internet access

What will you find?

- Simplicity at every step. A desktop-inspired interface features drop-down menus and familiar, intuitive tools that take you through content creation and management with ease.
- Full-featured test generator. Create ideal assessments with your choice of 15 question types (including true/false, multiple choice, opinion scale/likert, and essay). Multi-language support, an equation editor and unlimited metadata help ensure your tests are complete and compliant.
- Cross-compatible capability. Import and export content into other systems.

BRIEF CONTENTS

FLASH

EDGE ANIMATE

INTEGRATION

CREATIVE CLOUD: GUIDE TO USING CREATIVE CLOUD

CHAPTER 1: GETTING STARTED WITH DREAMWEAVER

CHAPTER 2: DEVELOPING A WEB PAGE

CHAPTER 3: WORKING WITH TEXT AND CASCADING STYLE SHEETS

CHAPTER 3: CREATING ANIMATIONS

CHAPTER 1: INTEGRATING ADOBE CC WEB COLLECTION

Data Files

To complete the lessons in this book, you need the Data Files. To download the Data Files for this book:

1. Open your browser and go to http://www.cengagebrain.com
2. Type the author, title, or ISBN of this book in the Search box. (The ISBN is listed on the back cover.)
3. Select the book title in the list of search results.
4. In the book's main page, click the Free Materials tab, and then click the Access Now button.
5. Select a chapter and then select the Data Files link on the left.

Your instructor will tell you where to store the files as you work, such as the hard drive, a network server, or a USB drive. The instructions in the lessons will refer to "the drive and folder where you store your Data Files" when referring to the Data Files for the book.

For Dreamweaver: When you copy the Data Files to your computer, you may see lock icons that indicate that the files are read-only when you view them in the Dreamweaver Files panel. To unlock the files, right-click on the locked file name in the Files panel, then select Turn off Read Only.

Adobe Creative Cloud Updates

As new updates are posted to Creative Cloud, you have the choice of updating or continuing to use your existing version. If you decide to keep your existing version until you finish using this book, your screens and menus should stay consistent with the book figures and instructions. If you decide to update to a newer version, read the What's New? material after you have downloaded the new version to determine what has changed. The changes may not affect the book figures and instructions very much at all, or they could affect them significantly. Visit www.cengage.com to find resources for Adobe Creative Cloud updates.

Approach

The text allows you to work at your own pace through step-by-step tutorials. A concept is presented and the process is explained, followed by the actual steps. To learn the most from the use of the text, you should adopt the following habits:

- Proceed slowly: Accuracy and comprehension are more important than speed.
- Understand what is happening with each step before you continue to the next step.

- After finishing a skill, ask yourself if you could do it on your own, without referring to the steps. If the answer is no, review the steps.

Icons, Buttons, and Pointers

Symbols for icons, buttons, and pointers are shown in the step each time they are used. Icons may look different in the files panel depending on the file association settings on your computer.

Fonts

The Data Files contain a variety of commonly used fonts, but there is no guarantee that these fonts will be available on your computer. In a few cases, fonts other than those common to a PC or a Macintosh are used. If any of the fonts in use is not available on your computer, you can make a substitution, realizing that the results may vary from those in the book.

Windows and Mac OS

The Adobe programs in this book work virtually the same on Windows and Mac OS operating systems. In those cases where there is a significant difference, the abbreviations (Win) and (Mac) are used.

Dreamweaver CC
Intended Audience

This text is designed for the beginner or intermediate user who wants to learn how to use Dreamweaver. The book is designed to provide basic and in-depth material that not only educates, but also encourages you to explore the nuances of this exciting program. These chapters are written for the Dreamweaver CC June 2014 release.

General

Throughout the initial chapters, students are given precise instructions regarding saving their work. Students should feel that they can save their work at any time, not just when instructed to do so.

Skills Reference

As a bonus, a Power User Shortcuts table is included at the end of chapters. This table contains the quickest method of completing tasks covered in the chapter. It is meant for the more experienced user, or for the user who wants to become more experienced. (Please note: If you are using a mini keyboard, your keyboard shortcuts may differ.)

Images vs. Graphics

Many times these terms seem to be used interchangeably. For the purposes of this book, the term *images* is used when referring to pictures on a web page. The term *graphics* is used as a more encompassing term that refers to non-text items on a web page such as photographs, logos, navigation bars, Flash animations, graphs, background images, and drawings. You may define these terms in a slightly different way, depending on your professional background or business environment.

System Preference Settings

The learning process will be much easier if you can see the file extensions for the files you will use in the lessons. To do this in Windows 7, open Windows Explorer, select Organize, select Folder and Search Options, select the View tab, then uncheck the Hide extensions for known file types box. In Windows 8, open Windows Explorer, select the View tab, and then select the File name extensions check box in the Show/Hide group. To do this for a Mac, go to Finder, select the Finder menu, and then select Preferences. Select the Advanced tab, then select the Show all file extensions check box. The figures in the book were taken using the Windows setting of Smaller. If you want to match the figures exactly, change your system to match this setting. It is located in the Control Panel, Appearance and Personalization, Display dialog box. Personalization, Display dialog box.

Creating a Portfolio

The Portfolio Project and Project Builders allow you to use your creativity to come up with original Dreamweaver designs. It is a good idea to create a portfolio in which you can store your original work.

Microsoft Windows System Requirements

- Intel® Pentium® 4 or AMD Athlon® 64 processor
- Microsoft Windows 7 with Service Pack 1, Windows 8, or Windows 8.1
- 1 GB of RAM

- 1 GB of available hard-disk space for installation; additional free space required during installation (cannot install on removable flash storage devices)
- 1280 × 800 display with 16-bit video card
- Java™ Runtime Environment 1.6 (included)
- Internet connection and registration are necessary for required software activation, membership validation, and access to online services.*

Mac OS

- Multicore Intel processor
- Mac OS X v10.7, v10.8, v10.9
- 1 GB of RAM
- 1 GB of available hard-disk space for installation; additional free space required during installation (cannot install on a volume that uses a case-sensitive file system or on removable flash storage devices)
- 1280 × 1024 display with 16-bit video card
- Java Runtime Environment 1.6

- QuickTime 7.6.6 software required for HTML5 media playback
- Internet connection and registration are necessary for required software activation, membership validation, and access to online services.*

*This product may integrate with or allow access to certain Adobe or third-party hosted online services ("Online Services"). Online Services are available only to users 13 and older and require agreement to additional terms and Adobe's online privacy policy. Online Services are not available in all countries or languages, may require user registration, and may be discontinued or modified in whole or in part without notice. Additional fees or subscription charges may apply.

Memory Challenges

If, instead of seeing an image on an open page, you see an image placeholder with a large X across it, your RAM is running low. Try closing any other applications that are running to free up memory.

Building a Website

You will create and develop several websites named The Striped Umbrella, Blooms & Bulbs, TripSmart, and Carolyne's Creations in the lesson material and end of unit exercises in this book. Because each chapter builds from the previous chapter, it is recommended that you work through the chapters in consecutive order. Your screens should match the figures in The Striped Umbrella and Blooms & Bulbs sites, as these sites are built with specific instructions. The TripSmart and Carolyne's Creations sites are built with less specific instructions to encourage individual creativity. Your screens will probably not match the figures for those sites.

Websites Used in Figures

Each time a website is used for illustration purposes in a lesson, where necessary, a statement acknowledging that we obtained permission to use the website is included. Sites whose content is in the public domain, such as federal government websites, are acknowledged as a courtesy.

Flash CC
Intended Audience

This book is designed for the beginner or intermediate user who wants to learn how to use Adobe Flash CC. The book is designed to provide basic and in-depth material that not only educates, but encourages you to explore the nuances of this exciting program.

Microsoft Windows System Requirements

- Intel Pentium 4 or Intel Centrino, Intel Xeon, or Intel Core Duo (or compatible) processor
- Microsoft Windows 7 with Service Pack 1 (64 bit), Windows 8 (64 bit), or Windows 8.1 (64 bit)
- 2 GB of RAM (4 GB recommended)
- 4 GB of available hard-disk space for installation; additional free space required during installation (cannot install on removable flash storage devices)
- 1024 × 900 display (1280 × 1024 recommended)
- QuickTime 7.7.x software recommended

Mac OS System Requirements

- Multicore Intel processor
- Mac OS X v10.7 (64 bit) or v10.8 (64 bit), or v10.9 (64 bit)
- 2 GB of RAM (4 GB recommended)
- 4 GB of available hard-disk space for installation; additional free space required during installation (cannot install on removable flash storage devices)
- 1024 × 900 display (1280 × 1024 recommended)
- QuickTime 10.x software recommended

Projects

Several projects are presented at the end of each chapter that allow students to apply the skills they have learned in the unit. Two projects, Odyssey Adventure Tours and the Portfolio, build from chapter to chapter. You will need to contact your instructor if you plan to work on these without having completed the previous chapter's project.

Edge Animate

Intended Audience

This book is designed for the beginner or intermediate user who wants to learn how to use Adobe Edge Animate CC, and includes an introduction to Edge Inspect CC. The book is designed to provide basic and in-depth material that not only educates, but encourages you to explore the nuances of these exciting programs.

Microsoft Windows System Requirements

- Intel® Pentium® 4 or AMD Athlon® 64 processor
- Windows® 7, Windows 8, and Windows 8.1 operating system
- 1GB of RAM
- 200MB of available hard-disk space for installation
- 1280 × 800 display with 16-bit video card

Mac OS System Requirements

- Multicore Intel processor
- Mac OS X v10.7, v10.8, or v10.9 operating system
- 1GB of RAM
- 200MB of available hard-disk space for installation
- 1280 × 800 display with 16-bit video card

Edge Inspect

The Edge Inspect Google Chrome browser extension requires at least Chrome 14, though the latest version of Chrome is recommended.

GUIDE TO USING
CREATIVE CLOUD

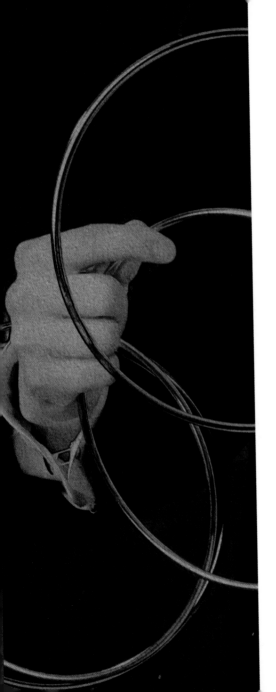

GETTING STARTED WITH
CREATIVE CLOUD

Introduction

With the introduction of Adobe Creative Cloud in 2012, Adobe introduced a new way to purchase, use, and upgrade its products. All Adobe applications and tools are now available under an online Creative Cloud account. Instead of purchasing a group of related products, you purchase a monthly or yearly subscription that gives you instant access to all Adobe applications, tools, and services, including Creative Cloud services such as file sharing and file storage. The applications remain active and available as long as the subscription is kept current. In May 2013 Adobe announced that they would no longer offer new versions of the Creative Suite except by subscription through Creative Cloud.

Creative Cloud lets you work from anywhere on any device, and share your work with others. When product updates are available, they can be automatically downloaded and installed seamlessly at no additional cost, giving Creative Cloud users unlimited access to the latest versions of all Adobe applications. From this point forward, we will refer to Adobe applications as Adobe apps.

Creative Cloud: Apps and Services

In addition to serving as the hub that gives you access to all Adobe apps, Creative Cloud accounts include other services. For instance, you can use Creative Cloud to store your files, share files to collaborate with others, host up to five websites, post an online portfolio of your creative work, and view inspiring videos showcasing creative work by other professionals using Adobe products.

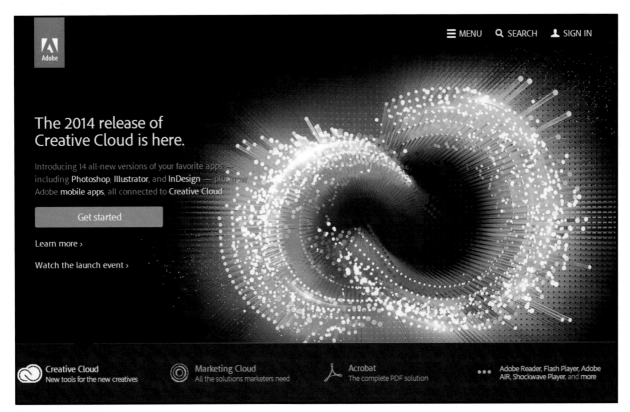

Source: Adobe Systems, Inc.

Explore
CREATIVE CLOUD

What You'll Do

Source: Adobe Systems, Inc.

 In this lesson, you will view the Creative Cloud desktop app and the Creative Cloud website Files panel.

Signing up for a Creative Cloud Account

To use Creative Cloud apps and services, you must have an Adobe ID. An Adobe ID is an email address and password you use to download free trials, purchase Adobe products, and access Creative Cloud. There is no charge for creating an Adobe ID. If you don't have one, you can create one on the Adobe website at www.adobe.com. Select Sign In on the opening screen, then select

Get an Adobe ID under the Sign in button, as shown in Figure 1.

Signing in to Creative Cloud

Once you have an Adobe ID, you use it to sign in each time you use a Creative Cloud app. Signing in to one app, such as Dreamweaver, automatically signs you in to all other tools you have downloaded when you open them. You can stay signed in when you exit apps, but

Figure 1 *Adobe ID sign-in page*

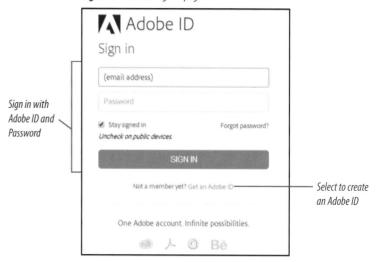

Sign in with Adobe ID and Password

Select to create an Adobe ID

Source: Adobe Systems, Inc.

you will only be able to access Creative Cloud on two active devices. To access Creative Cloud on a third device, you must sign out of Creative Cloud on one of the active devices.

Using the Creative Cloud Desktop App

To use Creative Cloud apps and services, you can begin by downloading the Creative Cloud desktop app from one of these Adobe websites: www.adobe.com/downloads.html or creative.adobe.com/products/creative-cloud. (Remember that websites, by their nature, are easily and frequently updated. If a specific link does not work, you can always search the site to find the current location for the content.) The Creative Cloud desktop app is a small dashboard that runs in the background as you use the Adobe apps. Figure 2 shows the Home panel in the Creative Cloud desktop app. The panels take you to the various parts of Creative Cloud: Home, Apps, Assets, and Community. The area below the panels lists your recent Creative Cloud installations and updates. Figure 2 shows four fonts added, updates to Creative Cloud, Photoshop CC, Bridge CC, InDesign CC (2014), and Photoshop CC (2014), and the installation of Flash Professional CC and Mobile Device Packaging (2014) (your list will differ). The links next to each activity can help you learn more: The View tutorials link next to the Flash Professional CC and Mobile Device Packaging (2014) notice provides tutorials that introduce you to those apps. When you select the name of an updated app, such as Photoshop CC (2014), you will be directed to the Adobe website with information about what is new in this release of the app.

The desktop app has three other panels: Apps, Assets, and Community, which let you download and install new apps, share files, add fonts, and share creative works with other members of the Creative Cloud community.

Figure 3 shows the Apps panel, which is divided into two sections. The upper section

Figure 2 *Creative Cloud desktop app Home panel*

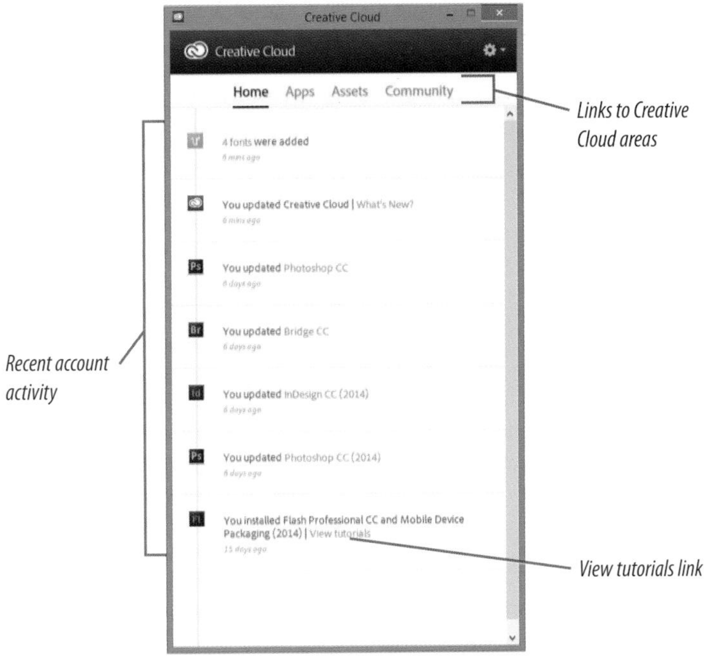

Figure 3 *Creative Cloud desktop Apps panel*

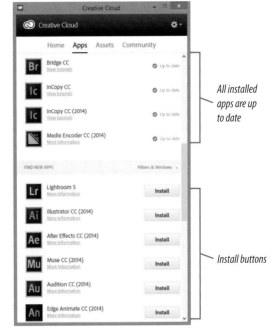

Links to Creative Cloud areas

Recent account activity

View tutorials link

All installed apps are up to date

Install buttons

lists your currently-installed apps. It also tells you if your apps are up to date and provides a link that lets you update any apps that are not current. Each app name includes a link that lets you view tutorials or more information for that app. The lower Find New Apps section lists all available apps, with an Install button next to each one. Select the Install button to download and install any apps you would like to use.

The Assets panel lets you work with your Creative Cloud files, in conjunction with the Creative Cloud website: As you create files, save them to the Creative Cloud Files folder on your local computer, and create a copy on the Creative Cloud website. Then when you save a file on your computer, it will be automatically synced (updated) to the copy on the website. You will be able to either view your files in the Creative Cloud Files folder on your computer, or view the online versions on the Adobe website, using any other computer or device. When you sync your files to the website, your Creative Cloud files will be available to you anywhere.

The Assets panel also has an Open Folder button that lets you view the files on your computer, as well as a View on Web button that lets you view your online files (also known as your remote files). The Creative Cloud website provides learning resources, including tutorials on Creative Cloud products.

You might want to keep both the Creative Cloud website and the Creative Cloud desktop app open when you are downloading files and folders or working with online services. When you are simply working within an app, such as Dreamweaver, it is not necessary to keep either open, as an Internet connection is not required for the Creative Cloud apps to run.

Navigating the Creative Cloud Website

After you go to the Creative Cloud website by logging in at creative.adobe.com, you see the central dashboard, a navigation bar at the side of the screen, shown in Figure 4. The central dashboard has three main sections: Apps, Assets, and Community. The bottom of the dashboard displays a Sign out button. At the

Figure 4 *Creative Cloud dashboard*

Source: Adobe Systems, Inc.

Central dashboard   *Sign out button*   *Manage account*   *Your name with a Manage Account button to access your plan and app settings.*   *Links to menu, site search, and Adobe web site*

top right corner of the page are links that let you access a main product menu, search the site, and go to the Adobe website, also shown in Figure 4. The next three lessons discuss some of the resources in these sections.

The central dashboard also displays a Manage account button under your name, which gives you access to your plan, profile, and application settings, as shown in Figure 5. You can check your account status, your subscription renewal date, billing information, and transaction history. You can also edit your profile settings such as your password and address.

Figure 5 *Account settings*

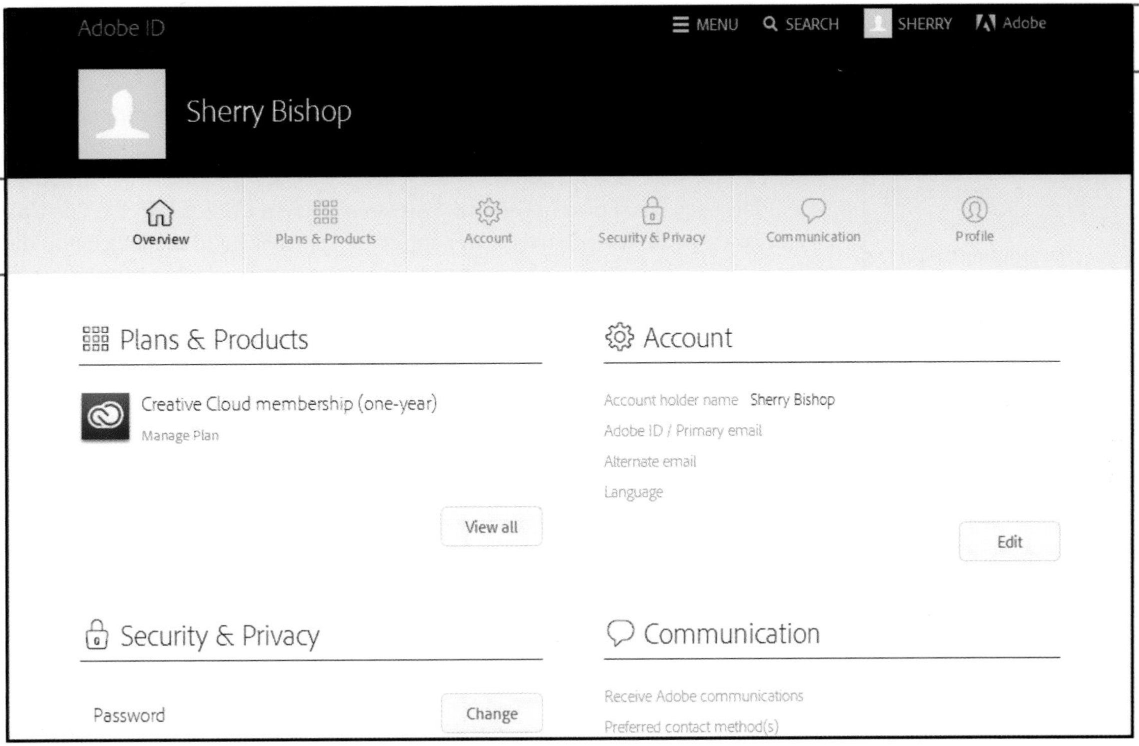

Links to menu, search, the central dashboard, and the Adobe website

Menu for plan and account settings

Source: Adobe Systems, Inc.

Manage Creative
CLOUD FILES

What You'll Do

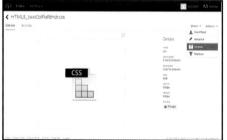

Source: Adobe Systems, Inc.

 In this lesson, you will explore the menu options available in the Actions menu in the Files window.

Accessing Creative Cloud Files

When you first log into the Creative Cloud website, you access your file storage by selecting the Files link listed under the Assets group on the central dashboard. When you select this link, the Creative Cloud Files window opens, as shown in Figure 6. You can also access your files with the CC desktop app by selecting Files, View on the Assets panel. A Creative Cloud account comes with 20 GB of online storage, and you manage your online files on this page. You can view, share, move, and rename your files and folders; you can also create new folders, upload files, search your files and folders, and archive files.

Uploading Files

It is a good idea to use folders to organize your online files. To create a folder in your Creative Cloud online storage area, select the Actions menu, select Create Folder, enter a folder name, then select Create Folder. To add files from your computer to a Creative Cloud folder, select the folder where you want to store the file, select the Actions menu, then select Upload. In the File Upload dialog box, navigate to the location of the files you want to upload, then select them and select Open. The upload will begin immediately and your uploaded file will be listed in your Creative Cloud Files list, in the location you selected. See Figure 6.

QUICK TIP

If you don't see the right column shown in Figure 6, select the small icon to the right of the Actions menu to show it. Select it again to hide this information if you would rather use that space for your files and folders.

Figure 6 *Uploaded folders and files are listed in the Files window*

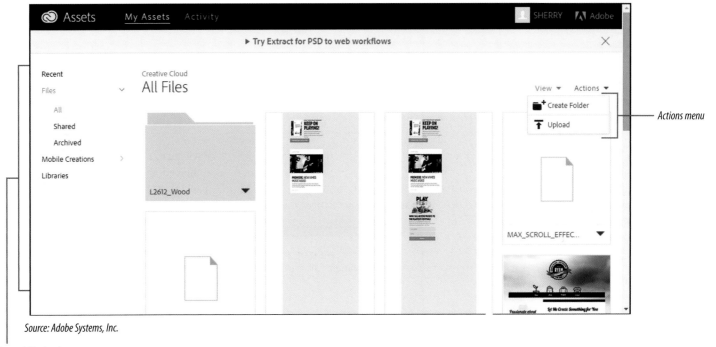

Source: Adobe Systems, Inc.

Folders and files listed

Actions menu

Working with Files

Once you have uploaded files to your account, you can share them with others by selecting a file and sending a link to it using the Share drop-down menu, as shown in Figure 7. The Send Link command lets you email a link to your documents to others so they can view and download them.

If you want to send someone else a link to your file, first select the file, then select the Send Link command in the Share menu. Next, select the Create Public Link button in the Send Link dialog box. Enter the email address for the person you want to send the link, and select the Send Link button. Your contact will then be sent a public link within the Adobe website to view your file. There is also an Allow File Download button you can select if you want the viewer to have the ability to download your file. Select the Remove Public Link button to delete the link.

You can also download, rename, archive, or replace files using the Actions drop-down menu, as shown in Figure 8. You must select a file before you see these menu options.

If you decide to delete a file, you must move it to the Archives first. To delete a file, select the file you want to delete in the Creative Cloud Files list, select the Actions menu, then select Archive, as shown in Figure 8. A dialog box will open to confirm you want to archive the file. Select the Archive button to confirm or the Cancel button to cancel the action.

Figure 7 *Share menu options*

Selected file

The Share menu option with a file selected

Source: Adobe Systems, Inc.

Figure 8 *Archive option in the Actions menu*

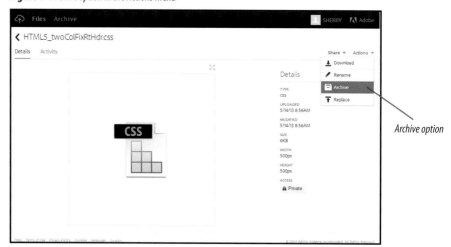

Archive option

Source: Adobe Systems, Inc.

After you have archived a file, select Archive on the menu bar at the top of the Creative Cloud Files window to view your archived files. Select the check box to the left of the file you want to delete, then select Permanently Delete to delete the file, as shown in Figure 9. A dialog box will open to verify that you want to delete the file. Select Permanently Delete to delete the file. To restore an archived file, select Restore. A dialog box asks you to confirm that you want to restore the file; select the Restore button to restore the file to the active file list. To return to your files list, select Files on the menu bar at the top of the Creative Cloud Files window.

Figure 9 *Archive options*

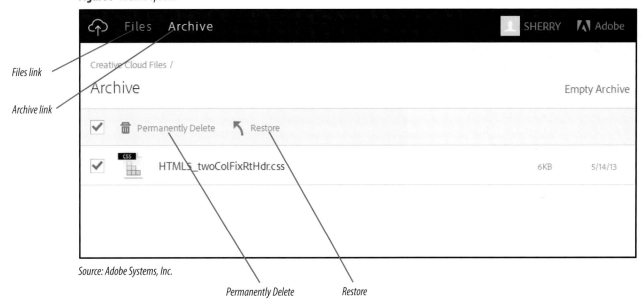

Files link

Archive link

Source: Adobe Systems, Inc.

Permanently Delete

Restore

Download Creative Cloud
APPS AND SERVICES

What You'll Do

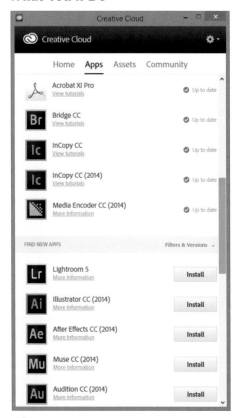

In this lesson, you will explore the apps and services provided in Creative Cloud.

Using the Desktop Apps Window

Your Creative Cloud subscription gives you access to a collection of apps and services. The collection includes familiar products such as Dreamweaver, Flash, Edge, and Photoshop, but also includes additional services and apps such as Adobe Typekit and Behance. Each app clearly documents

Figure 10 *Creative Cloud desktop apps*

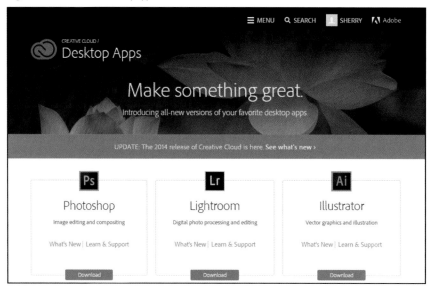

Source: Adobe Systems, Inc.

its new features, so as you upgrade to new versions, you can quickly see what has changed in each app.

To access Adobe apps, select Desktop in the Apps section of the central dashboard, which takes you to the creative.adobe.com website location: www.adobe.com/creativecloud/ catalog/desktop.html with the Creative Cloud apps listed, as shown in Figure 10. Each app is listed with What's New and Learn & Support links, along with a Download button, shown in Figure 11.

To download a Creative Cloud app, select the Download button below the product name. A window opens, and, depending on the app, may ask you questions about your skill levels before it begins downloading. You can also download apps with the Creative Cloud Desktop with either a Try or Install button.

Figure 11 *Options for exploring and downloading an app*

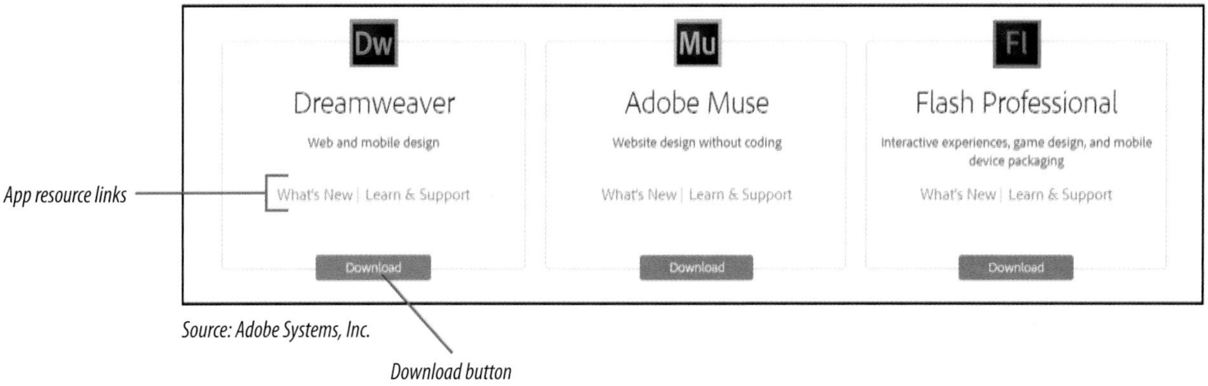

App resource links

Source: Adobe Systems, Inc.

Download button

Viewing Your Creative Cloud Apps

To view your downloaded apps, open the Creative Cloud desktop app, then select the Apps panel, shown in Figure 12 (Windows). Mac users will see the Apps panel with a slightly different appearance, and it only appears when you select the Creative cloud icon in the Mac menu bar. The Windows Apps panel remains open unless it is minimized or closed. These behaviors can be turned on and off in the Preferences settings. A notification appears to the right of each app name to tell you whether an update is available, or if the app is currently up to date. The Find New Apps section lists apps that are available to download, so you can also download and install apps from the Creative Cloud desktop app in addition to the Creative Cloud download center.

Incorporating Type into Your Project with Typekit

Type is an essential part of any creative project, so Creative Cloud includes Typekit, a type repository that gives you access to over a thousand font families that you can use in your web or print projects. Typekit, founded in 2008 and acquired by Adobe in 2011 to make fonts accessible and universal, is a library of high-quality fonts called Adobe Edge Web Fonts that can be used in any application that uses fonts. Your Adobe subscription provides the license to use these fonts, so you don't have to be concerned about font licensing or compatibility. In Dreamweaver, when you download and apply a font to web page content, JavaScript is added to the page head

Figure 12 *Creative Cloud desktop app with the Apps tab selected (Win)*

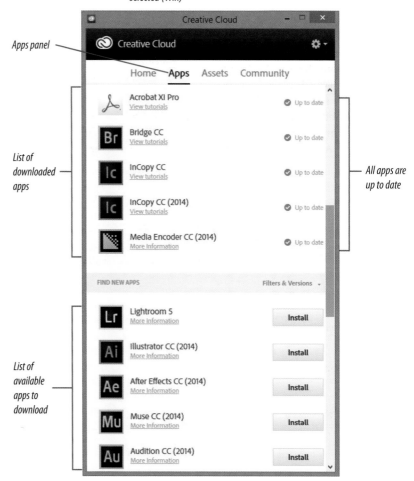

Apps panel

List of downloaded apps

All apps are up to date

List of available apps to download

section to direct the browser to access the font from the use.edgefonts.net website and apply it to the content.

You can access Typekit through the Typekit website, typekit.com, or through the Creative Cloud desktop app Fonts link in the Assets panel using the Turn Typekit On button the first time you use this feature, then the Add Fonts from Typekit button each subsequent time. The fonts are seamlessly integrated into Creative Cloud apps. Any Typekit font that you download will be available in the Font menus in your apps. For instance, if you are inserting type into a project in Photoshop, your Typekit fonts will be available in the Font-Family menus in the Character and Character Styles panels. When you select the Add Fonts from Typekit button on the Fonts panel, Typekit opens.

The Typekit dashboard makes it easy to browse the font libraries, shown in Figure 13, then save and organize the fonts you select. A search text box helps you locate fonts quickly. On the right side of the screen, filters let you select appropriate fonts, such as by classification (Serif, Script, Decorative), platform (Web or Desktop use), use (Paragraphs or Headings), or properties (such as weight or width). The Typekit dashboard also lets you enter sample text so you can see how a font will look using text from your project. In Figure 13, Dreamweaver has been entered as sample text.

Figure 13 *Browse Fonts tab on the Adobe Typekit site*

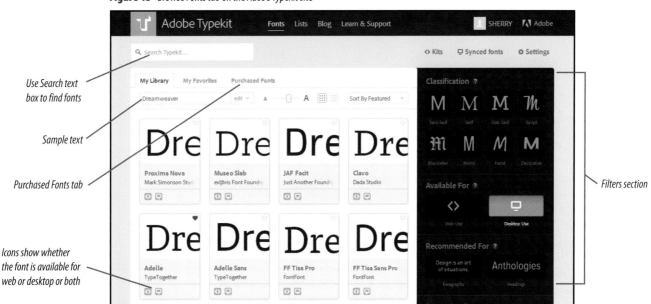

Source: Adobe Systems, Inc.

After filtering and viewing samples, select the font you want to use. You can then view the available weights and styles of that font, such as bold and italic, as well as specimens. You can also test the font by entering text of your choice, and view samples in various browsers. Once you have selected a font you would like to save, point to the font, then select the Use fonts command to sync your selected fonts to your Creative Cloud account. You can store up to 100 fonts for desktop use. Be aware, however, that each font style counts as a separate font. For instance, Adelle Regular, Adelle Bold, and Adelle Italic count as three fonts.

If the font you have selected is your first font, you need to create a new kit, then sync it to your desktop via Creative Cloud. Your new fonts will then be listed in your Creative Cloud account, as shown in Figure 14.

To use a font on a Dreamweaver website, add the font family to an existing one or create a new one. You then publish and embed the website with the JavaScript that is automatically added to the page head content. To use a font for a print project, apply the font to selected text from the application Font menu. For instance, fonts added from Typekit are automatically added to the list of available fonts in both the Edit, Fonts menu and the Fonts list in the Character panel in InDesign.

If you are not a Creative Cloud subscriber, you can still subscribe to Typekit, but you will need to pay a subscription fee.

Using Behance to Share Your Work

Creative Cloud also features Behance, an online service that lets you share and track your creative work with others. An Adobe

Figure 14 *Synced Adelle font listed on the Creative Cloud desktop app*

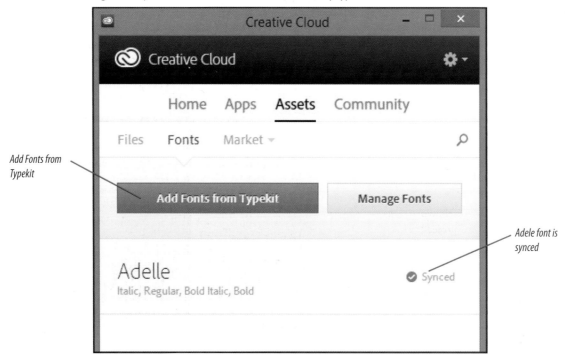

Add Fonts from Typekit

Adele font is synced

subsidiary, Behance offers a professional portfolio site for your work called ProSite, which provides you with a URL to publish your work. Behance is also available as an iPhone and Android app, together with a Creative Portfolio app that can be used without an Internet connection.

To access Behance using the Adobe desktop app, select the Community panel. Or you can open the Behance site at www.behance.net. If you are logged into an Adobe app, you will automatically be logged in to the website. If you are using the Community panel in the desktop app, you'll see the the Behance dashboard tabs, My Activity, My Work, and Discover Work. The My Activity tab shows activites posted for people you are following; My Work and Discover Work let you access your portfolio of creative work, and follow other Behance members' work. (Notice the tab names vary slightly between the desktop app Community panel and the Behance website.) An **Add Work button** lets you upload your work to your portfolio. On the Behance website, you can select **Discover** to explore work posted on Behance, as shown in Figure 15. You may filter by schools, tools used, colors, or galleries.

After selecting a project to view, as shown in Figure 16, you can see the entire project, other projects by the same artist, and see how many users have viewed, appreciated (liked), and commented on the work. You can also message the artist and share the project using social media choices.

Figure 15 *Behance website*

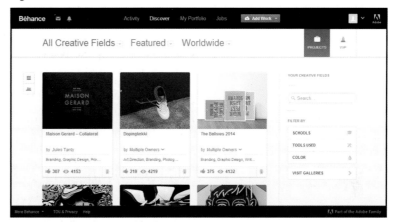

Source: Adobe Systems, Inc.

Figure 16 *Viewing a project posted on Behance*

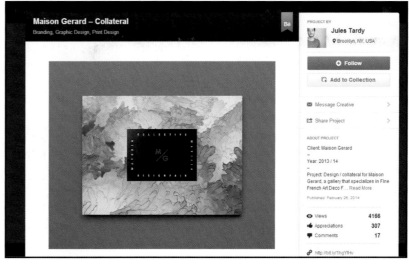

Source: Adobe Systems, Inc.

View Additional
LEARNING TOOLS

What You'll Do

Source: Adobe Systems, Inc.

 In this lesson, you will explore additional Adobe Creative Cloud resources.

Using the Learning Resources

To learn more about Creative Cloud products and services, select the Menu link on the top of the Creative Cloud page, then select the Learn & Support link on the new page that opens, as shown in Figure 17. You can then select Learn at your level to view tutorials, Contact support to contact customer support, or Ask the community to browse postings from Adobe community members. When you select the Learn at your level link, you will see listings for all Adobe apps, with comprehensive video tutorials for each one. You can either watch them or follow along to complete the work as you go. Each tutorial includes data files you can use to work through the tasks. Figure 18 shows the introductory page for an Edge

Figure 17 *The Learn & Support page*

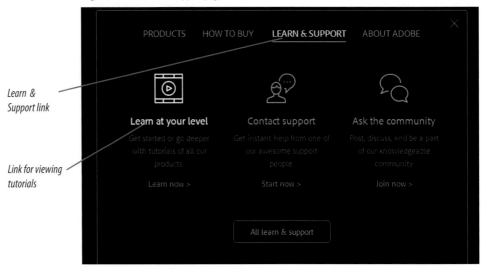

Source: Adobe Systems, Inc.

Animate CC video tutorial. The tutorial layout is simple and easy to use. Each lesson begins with a short paragraph; then you can either watch the video lesson or download the data files and work along with the videos.

Viewing Learning Content with Adobe TV

The Learn & Support page also lets you view many of the presentations delivered through Adobe TV. At the bottom of the Learn & Support page, select All learn & support, then select the Adobe TV link in the More learning section to access a library of videos and training materials. The menu at the top of the page has links to Products, Channels, Shows, Translations, and My Library, as shown in Figure 19. Take the time to browse through some of the videos offered and you will find a wealth of information.

Figure 18 *Edge Animate CC video tutorial*

Source: Adobe Systems, Inc.

Figure 19 *Adobe TV*

Source: Adobe Systems, Inc.

Find and Use
ADOBE ADD-ONS

What You'll Do

Source: Adobe Systems, Inc.

In this lesson, you will view the Adobe Marketplace and explore Adobe Add-ons.

Identifying and Locating Adobe Add-ons

One of the exciting developments in the evolution of Creative Cloud is the introduction of the new Adobe Add-ons website. This website is a marketplace for products and resources developed for Creative Cloud, designed for both producers and end users. Producers are people who can use the site to sell, share, and promote products they have developed for an Adobe product, such as an interactive menu bar for Dreamweaver or a new brush tip for Photoshop. They can either distribute their products for a set price, by subscription, or at no charge. End users are people looking for new, exciting ways to use Adobe products. They can search, purchase, and install new tools or content for Adobe apps.

The Adobe Add-ons website, shown in Figure 20, has been redesigned to become a richer environment for both producers and end users.

Using Adobe Add-ons for Dreamweaver

To browse through add-ons from Dreamweaver CC, use the Window, Browse Add-ons command. This command opens the Adobe Add-ons website, where you should already be signed in. You can filter add-ons by product, such as Dreamweaver, Photoshop, or Muse, and according to whether they are free or paid. For example, you can show only free add-ons for Photoshop or all add-ons for Dreamweaver. You will notice that some add-ons are compatible with more than one Adobe product. You can also sort available add-ons according to how recently they were created, by title, by price (high to low or low to high), or by rating, and you can search for a specific add-on. Figure 21 shows some Dreamweaver featured add-ons. These listings will change frequently as new add-ons are created and added to the site.

Figure 20 *Adobe Add-ons website*

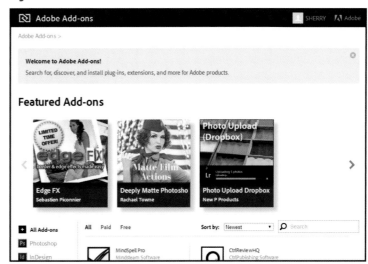

Source: Adobe Systems, Inc.

Figure 21 *Dreamweaver Featured Add-ons*

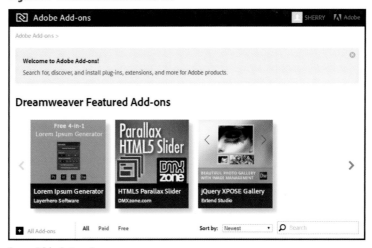

Source: Adobe Systems, Inc.

One free Dreamweaver Add-on, Advanced CSS Menu Light by Ajatix, creates CSS drop-down menus. After selecting the link to Advanced CSS Menu Light, you are directed to a page of product information, ratings and reviews, notes, and where to find it, as shown in Figure 22. The product information includes the platforms that support it and the product versions that it supports.

Select the Free button to download the app, then after the app downloads, you will see a green check mark beside a label "Acquired" as shown in Figure 23.

When you select the Where to find it link, you see instructions on how to locate the Add-on after you have installed it. When you

Figure 22 *Exploring the Advanced CSS Menu Light Add-on*

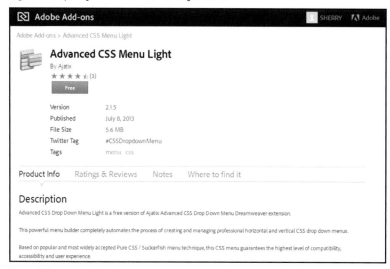

Source: Adobe Systems, Inc.

Figure 23 *An acquired Add-on*

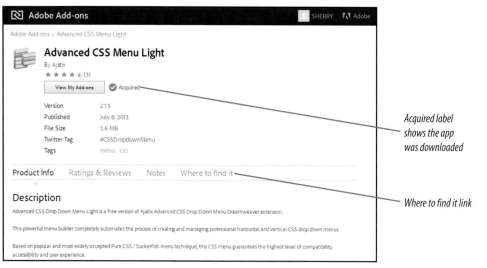

Acquired label shows the app was downloaded

Where to find it link

Source: Adobe Systems, Inc.

Getting Started with Creative Cloud

are ready to create your CSS menu bar, follow the instructions, then choose a theme for your menu bar, as shown in Figure 24. After choosing a theme, use the New Menu dialog box to add each menu item, link, and target to build the menu bar.

Other examples of Add-ons for Dreamweaver include shopping carts, image galleries, search pages, form designers, slideshows, and Google analytics tools. Table 1 lists some other possibilities for Add-ons you might find helpful. Take some time browsing the list of Add-ons and explore those that might be useful to you. Each Add-on includes a logo of the Adobe app(s) that it is designed to be used with.

The Adobe Add-ons site is constantly evolving so it can continue to match the talents of producers with the needs of users and the capabilities of Adobe Creative Cloud apps. Add-ons that prove to be popular with users can even be incorporated into an app's interface. This is exactly what happened with the Advanced CSS Menu Light Add-on. It is now conveniently listed under the Dreamweaver Insert, Ajatix menu as Advanced CSS Drop Down Menu Light.

Figure 24 *Choosing a menu-bar theme*

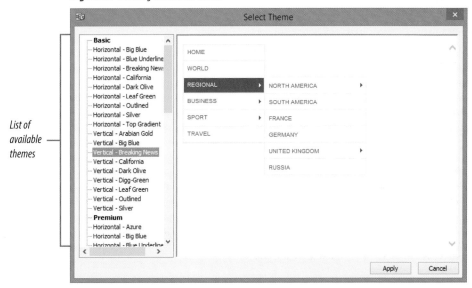

List of available themes

Source: Adobe Systems, Inc.

TABLE 1: ADOBE ADD-ON EXAMPLES AND USES			
Name of Add-on	**Add on to**	**Used To**	**Cost**
HTML5 Data Bindings	Dreamweaver	Connect to your data	Free
DMXzone Bootstrap	Dreamweaver	Create a site layout	Free
Taster	Photoshop InDesign Dreamweaver Illustrator Premier Pro InCopy	Insert 20 web-sized textures for backgrounds	Free
HTML5 Image Gallery	Dreamweaver	Images	Charge
Toolkit for CreateJS	Flash	Create assets for HTML5 projects	Free
Light Date Picker Calendar	Dreamweaver	Insert a calendar into a form	Charge
EAN Barcode Generator	InDesign	Make EAN-8 & EAN-13 barcodes	Free

CHAPTER **1**

GETTING STARTED WITH DREAMWEAVER

1. Explore the Dreamweaver workspace
2. View a web page and use Help
3. Plan and set up a website
4. Add a folder and pages

GETTING STARTED WITH
DREAMWEAVER

Introduction

Adobe Dreamweaver CC is a web development tool that lets you create dynamic web pages containing text, images, hyperlinks, animation, sounds, video, and interactive elements. You can use Dreamweaver to create individual web pages or complex websites consisting of many web pages. A **website** is a group of related web pages that are linked together and share a common interface and design. Dreamweaver lets you create design elements such as text, forms, rollover images, and interactive buttons, or import elements from other software programs. You can also save Dreamweaver files in many different file formats, including XHTML, HTML, JavaScript, CSS, or XML, to name a few. **XHTML** is the acronym for eXtensible HyperText Markup Language, the current standard language used to create web pages. You can still use **HTML** (HyperText Markup Language) in Dreamweaver; however, it is no longer considered the standard language. You use a web browser to view your web pages on the Internet. A **web browser** is a program, such as Google Chrome, Apple Safari, Mozilla Firefox, or Microsoft Internet Explorer, used to display web pages.

Using Dreamweaver Tools

Creating a robust website is a complex task. Fortunately, Dreamweaver has an impressive number of tools that can help. Using Dreamweaver design tools, you can create dynamic and interactive web pages without writing a word of code. However, if you prefer to write code, Dreamweaver makes it easy to enter and edit the code directly and see the visual results of the code instantly. Dreamweaver also contains organizational tools that help you work with a team of people to create a website. You can also use the Dreamweaver management tools to help you manage a website. For instance, you can use the **Files panel** to create folders to organize and store the various files for your website, and to add pages to your website.

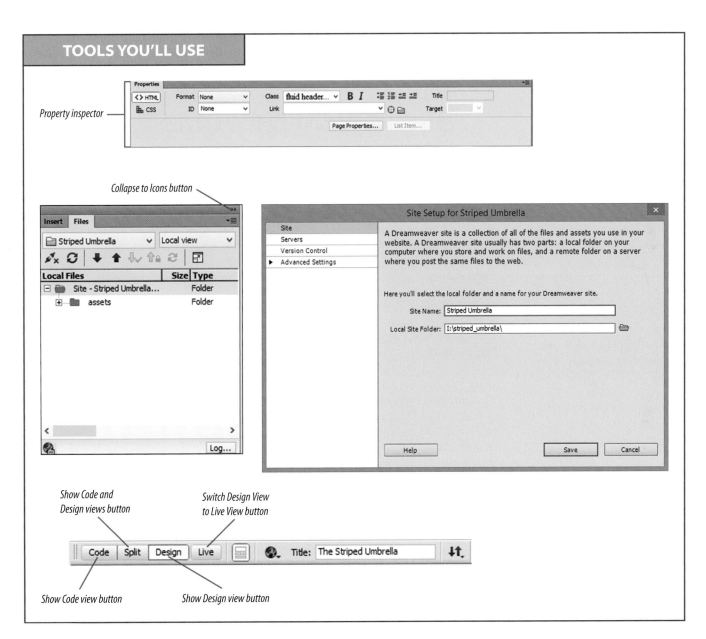

Property inspector

Collapse to Icons button

Show Code and Design views button

Switch Design View to Live View button

Show Code view button

Show Design view button

Explore the
DREAMWEAVER WORKSPACE

What You'll Do

 In this lesson, you will start Dreamweaver, examine the components that make up the Dreamweaver workspace, and change views.

Examining the Dreamweaver Workspace

The first time you start Dreamweaver, you are offered several video tutorials to help you learn new features. You can watch as many as you like, then select Done to begin using Dreamweaver.

QUICK TIP

To return to the list of videos later, select Help on the Menu bar, then select New Feature Videos.

After you start Dreamweaver, you see the **Dreamweaver workspace**, the screen that includes all of the menus, panels, buttons, inspectors, and panes that you use to create and maintain websites. It is designed to give you easy access to all the tools you need to create web pages. Refer to Figure 1 as you locate the components described below.

After you open or create a new file, you see the **Document window**, the large area in the Dreamweaver program window where you create and edit web pages. The **Menu bar** (also called the **Application bar**), located above the Document window, includes menu names,

a Workspace switcher, and other application commands. The Menu bar appears on either one bar or two bars, depending on your screen size and resolution. To choose a menu command, select the menu name to open the menu, then select the menu command. The Insert panel appears on the right side of the screen. The **Insert panel**, sometimes called the Insert bar, includes eight categories of buttons displayed through a drop-down menu: Common, Structure, Media, Form, jQuery Mobile, jQuery UI, Templates, and Favorites. Selecting a category in the Insert panel displays the buttons and menus for inserting objects associated with that category. For example, if you select the Structure category, you find buttons for using div tags to create blocks of content on pages; for inserting lists; and for inserting HTML5 elements such as headers and footers.

QUICK TIP

The Insert panel drop-down menu also lets you hide or display any panel's button labels. To hide labels and show only icons, select Hide Labels. To display them, select Show Labels.

The **Document toolbar** contains buttons and drop-down menus you can use to change the current work mode, preview web pages, add a title, and use file-management options. One of the buttons on the Document toolbar, the Switch Design View to Live View button, is used to view the current page in Live view.

Live view displays an open document as if you were viewing it in a browser, with interactive elements active. When you switch to Live view, Manage Hidden Elements and Live view

Options buttons are added to the Document toolbar.

One additional toolbar does not appear by default: the Standard toolbar. The **Standard toolbar** contains buttons you can use to execute frequently used commands that are also available on the File and Edit menus such as Cut, Copy, Paste, and Save. To display or hide the Document or Standard toolbars, right-click an empty area of an open toolbar, then select the toolbar name you wish to display or hide. You can also use the View > Toolbars menu.

The **Related Files toolbar** is located below an open document's filename tab and displays the names of any related files. **Related files** are files that are linked to a document and are necessary for the document to display and function correctly. An external style sheet, which contains formatting rules that control the appearance of a document, is a good example of a related file. The **Coding toolbar** contains buttons you can use when working directly in the code and is not visible unless you are in Code view. When visible, it appears on the left side of the Document window.

Figure 1 *Dreamweaver CC workspace*

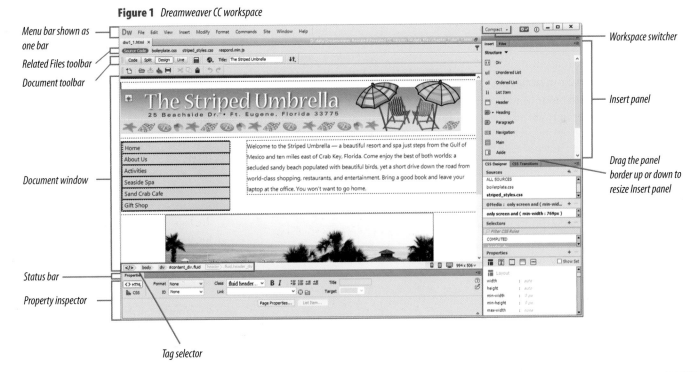

Menu bar shown as one bar

Related Files toolbar

Document toolbar

Document window

Status bar

Property inspector

Tag selector

Workspace switcher

Insert panel

Drag the panel border up or down to resize Insert panel

The **Property inspector**, sometimes referred to as the **Properties pane**, located at the bottom of the Dreamweaver window, lets you view and change the properties (characteristics) of a selected object. The Property inspector is context sensitive, which means it changes according to what is selected in the Document window. The **status bar** is located above the Property inspector. The left side of the status bar displays the **tag selector**, which shows the HTML tags used at the insertion point location. The right side displays icons used for displaying the open page as viewed in a mobile, tablet, or desktop device. The far right side of the status bar shows the Window Size pop-up menu, used to change the page view or edit the default window size settings. You can also change the page orientation to landscape or portrait.

A **panel** is a tabbed window that displays information on a particular topic or contains related commands. **Panel groups** are sets of related panels that are grouped together. A collection of panels or panel groups is called a **dock**. To view the contents of a panel in a panel group, select the panel's tab. Panels are docked on the right side of the screen by default. You can undock or "float" them by dragging the panel tab to another screen location. To collapse or expand a panel group, double-click the panel tab, as shown in Figure 2. When you first start Dreamweaver, the Insert, Files, CSS Designer, and CSS Transitions panels are expanded by default, with the Insert and CSS Designer panels selected. You can open panels using the Window menu commands or the corresponding shortcut keys.

QUICK TIP

The Collapse to Icons button ▸▸ above the top panel lets you collapse all open panels to icons to enlarge the workspace.

Working with Dreamweaver Views

A **view** is a particular way of displaying page content. Dreamweaver has three working views. **Design view** shows the page similar to how it would appear in a browser and is primarily used for designing and creating a web page. **Code view** shows the underlying HTML code for the page; use this view to read or edit the underlying code.

QUICK TIP

You can also split Code view to enable you to work on two different sections of code at once. To change to Split Code view, select View on the Menu bar, then select Split Code.

Show Code and Design views is a combination of Code view and Design view. Show Code and Design views is the best view for **debugging** or correcting errors because you can immediately see how code modifications change the appearance of the page. The view buttons are located on the Document toolbar. If you want to switch to the same view for all open documents, hold down the Ctrl key (Win) or Command key (Mac) while you select a view button.

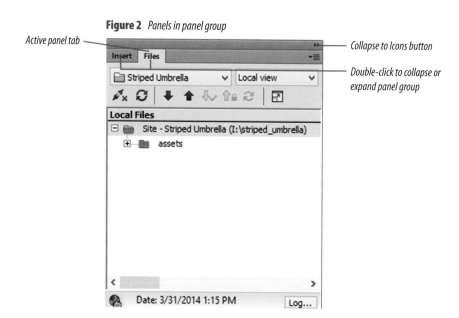

Figure 2 *Panels in panel group*

Active panel tab

Collapse to Icons button

Double-click to collapse or expand panel group

Figure 3 *Starting Dreamweaver CC (Windows)*

Select Adobe
Dreamweaver CC

Start Dreamweaver (Windows)

1. On the Windows start screen, select the **down arrow** or swipe to your screen that lists all installed programs.

2. Select **Adobe Dreamweaver CC**.

TIP You can right-click a program name, then create a tile by selecting Pin to Start.

or

3. Select the **Adobe Dreamweaver CC tile**, as shown in Figure 3.

You started Dreamweaver CC for Windows.

Viewing and Editing Pages in Live view

When you view your web pages in Dreamweaver, the page elements appear similarly to the way they will appear on the web, but not exactly. To get a better idea of how they will look, you can use the Switch Design View to Live View button on the Document toolbar. This button directs the open document to appear as it would in a browser, with interactive elements active. One recent improvement in Live view is the ability to directly edit page elements in Live view. For instance, you can now use the Insert panel in Live view to either drag and insert or select and insert a new element onto the page. To directly edit text and add or delete page elements such as images in Live view, you must select the Hide Fluid Grid Layout Guides button on the Document toolbar before you can begin editing.

Start Dreamweaver (Macintosh)

1. Select **Finder** in the Dock, then select **Applications**.

2. Select the **Adobe Dreamweaver CC folder**, then double-click the **Adobe Dreamweaver CC application**, as shown in Figure 4.

TIP Once Dreamweaver is running, you can add it to the Dock permanently by [control]-clicking the Dreamweaver icon, selecting Options, then selecting Keep in Dock.

You started Dreamweaver CC for Macintosh.

Figure 4 *Starting Dreamweaver CC (Macintosh)*

Source: Apple Inc.

Using In-App and In-Product Messages

When you start Dreamweaver the first time, you are asked whether you are a new user or a current user. Depending on how you respond, pop-up messages will appear when a "trigger" is activated to guide or suggest tips for boosting productivity. These pop-ups are called In-app and In-product messages. **In-app messages** apply to Dreamweaver workflow content. **In-product messages** apply to Dreamweaver integration with other Creative Cloud apps content. Selecting a pop-up will close it. In-app and In-product messages will only appear once if the you follow the directions given in the pop-ups. If you do not want to use these pop-ups, you can disable them by deselecting the Show In-app help check box in the Preferences dialog box Accessibility category. You can also reset the In-app help to display pop-ups that you have viewed by selecting the Reset button next to the Show In-app help check box.

Figure 5 *Code view for new document*

Show Code view button | Show Code and Design views (Split) button | Show Design view button | Switch Design View to Live View button | Menu bar may be displayed as two bars | Select to collapse all panels to icons

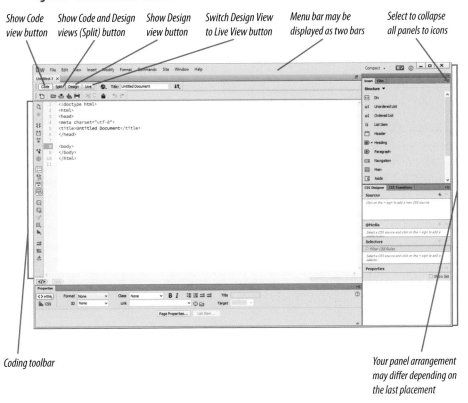

Coding toolbar

Your panel arrangement may differ depending on the last placement

---

Change views and view panels

1. Select **HTML** in the Create New category on the Dreamweaver Welcome Screen.

   The Dreamweaver Welcome Screen provides shortcuts for opening files and for creating new files or websites.

   TIP If you do not want the Dreamweaver Welcome Screen to appear each time you start Dreamweaver, remove the check mark next to Show Welcome Screen in the General category in the Preferences dialog box.

2. Select the **Show Code view button** `Code` on the Document toolbar.

   The default code for a new document appears in the Document window, as shown in Figure 5.

   TIP The Coding toolbar is available only in Code view and in the Code window in Split view.

3. Select the **Show Code and Design views button** `Split` on the Document toolbar.

4. Select the **Show Design view button** `Design` on the Document toolbar.

   (continued)

5. Select the **Insert panel tab**, then compare your screen to Figure 6.

   Your Insert panel may have a different category selected.

6. Select the **Files panel tab** to display the contents of the Files panel.

7. Double-click **Files** to collapse the panel group.

8. View the contents of the CSS Designer panel.

9. Drag the **blank area** next to the CSS Designer panel tab to the middle of the document window.

   The panel group is now in a floating window. The CSS Designer panel looks like more than one panel because it is divided into four panes: Sources, @Media, Selectors, and Properties.

   (continued)

Figure 6 *Displaying a panel group*

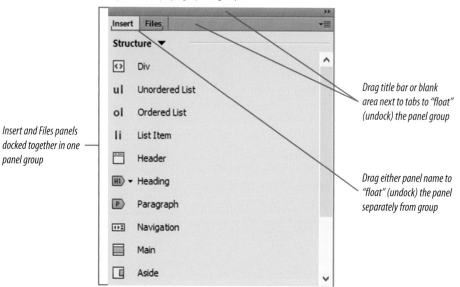

Insert and Files panels docked together in one panel group

Drag title bar or blank area next to tabs to "float" (undock) the panel group

Drag either panel name to "float" (undock) the panel separately from group

Choosing a Workspace Layout

The Dreamweaver interface is an integrated workspace, which means that all of the document windows and panels appear in a single application window. By default, each open document appears as a tab below the document toolbar. To view a tabbed document, select the tab with the document's filename. The **Workspace switcher**, a drop-down menu in the top right corner on the Menu bar, lets you change the workspace layout. The default layout is Compact, where the panels are docked on the right side of the screen. The other workspace layout is Expanded. The Expanded layout increases the width of the panels to allow the CSS Designer panel to flow into two columns. To change the workspace layout, select the Workspace switcher, then select the desired layout. You can also rearrange the workspace using your own choices for panel placement and save the workspace with a unique name using the "New Workspace" and "Manage Workspaces" commands on the Workspace switcher. The Reset 'Current view' option resets the workspace layout to return to the default positions on the screen for the selected view.

Figure 7 *Docking a panel group*

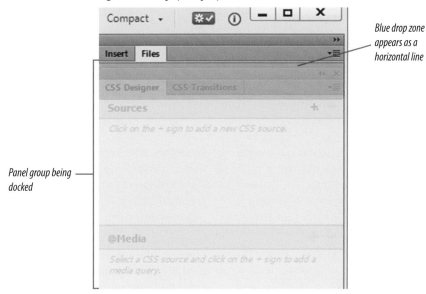

Blue drop zone appears as a horizontal line

Panel group being docked

10. Drag the **panel title bar** back to its original position, then drop it to dock the panel group below the Insert panel.

    Release the mouse only when you see the blue drop zone. The blue drop zone is a heavy blue line that appears when the panel is in the correct position to be docked. See Figure 7. If the blue drop zone appears as a box, releasing the button adds the panel to the boxed panel group.

    TIP   If you have rearranged the panels from their original positions and want to reset them back to their default positions, select the Workspace switcher drop-down menu, then select Reset 'Current view'.

11. Select the **Workspace switcher**, then select **Reset 'Compact'**.

12. Select **File** on the Menu bar, then select **Close** to close the open document.

You viewed a new web page using three views, opened panel groups, viewed their contents, undocked a panel group, then docked a panel group.

Using and Editing Keyboard Shortcuts

Most chapters in this book include a table titled Power User Shortcuts. These tables list keyboard shortcuts that relate to the chapter steps you use in that chapter. To see all of the Dreamweaver keyboard shortcuts, select Edit on the Menu bar (Win) or Dreamweaver on the Menu bar (Mac), then select Keyboard Shortcuts. The Keyboard Shortcuts dialog box opens and displays commands grouped by location; select the Commands list arrow to display a different location. You can add or delete keyboard shortcuts by selecting the Add item or Delete item buttons. You can also change a keyboard shortcut by selecting a current shortcut in the commands list, entering a new key sequence in the Press key dialog box, then selecting the Change button.

View a Web Page AND USE HELP

What You'll Do

In this lesson, you will open a web page, view several page elements, and access the Help system.

Opening a Web Page

After starting Dreamweaver, you can create a new website, create a new web page, or open an existing website or web page. The first web page that appears when users go to a website is called the **home page**. The home page sets the look and feel of the website and directs users to the rest of the pages in the site.

Viewing Basic Web Page Elements

There are many elements that make up web pages. Web pages can be very simple and designed primarily with text, or they can be media-rich with images, sound, and movies, creating an enhanced interactive web experience. Figure 8 shows a web page with text and graphics that work together to create a simple and attractive page.

Most information on a web page is presented in the form of text. You can type text directly onto a web page in Dreamweaver or import text created in other programs. You can then use the Property inspector to format text so that it is attractive and easy to read. Text should be short and to the point to engage users and prevent them from losing interest and leaving your site.

Hyperlinks, also known as **links**, are images or text elements on a web page that users select to display another location on the page, another web page on the same website, or a web page on a different website.

Images add visual interest to a web page. However, the saying that "less is more" is certainly true with images. Too many images cause the page to load slowly and discourage users from waiting for the page to download. Many pages have **banners**, which are images that appear across the top or down the side of the screen that can incorporate a company's logo, contact information, and links to the other pages in the site.

Menu bars, also called navigation bars, are bars that contain multiple links, usually organized in rows or columns. Sometimes menu bars are used with an image map. An **image map** is an image that has been divided into sections, each of which serves as a link. The way that menu bars and other internal links are used on your pages is referred to as the **navigation structure** of the site.

Rich media content is a comprehensive term that refers to attractive and engaging images, interactive elements, video, or animations. Some of this content can be created in Dreamweaver, but much of it is created with other programs such as Adobe Edge Animate, Fireworks, Photoshop, or Illustrator.

Getting Help

Dreamweaver has many excellent Help features that are comprehensive and easy to use. When questions or problems arise, you can use the commands on the Help menu to find the answers you need. Selecting the Dreamweaver Help menu displays a list of help features including information on what's new in the current version and new feature videos. You also use the Help menu to sign in and out, manage your Creative Cloud account, and check for updates. To access context-specific help, select the Help button on the Property inspector. For example, if you select an image, then select the Help button on the Property inspector, you will be see help about inserting and editing images.

The Help & Support command on the Help menu (and on the Dreamweaver startup screen) opens the Learn & Support / Dreamweaver Help web page. The Search text box at the top of the page lets you enter a keyword to search for a specific topic.

Figure 8 *Common web page elements*

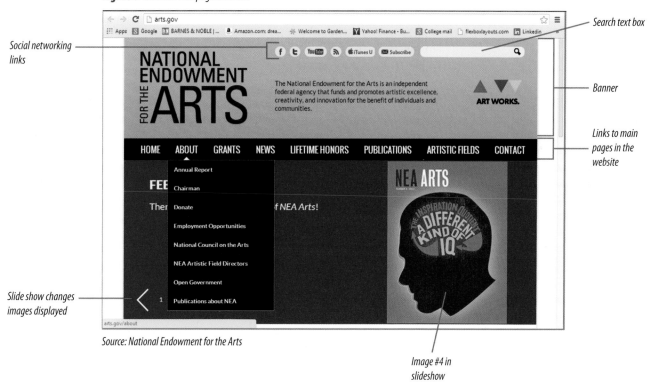

Social networking links

Search text box

Banner

Links to main pages in the website

Slide show changes images displayed

Image #4 in slideshow

Source: National Endowment for the Arts

Open a web page and view basic page elements

1. Select **File** on the Menu bar, then select **Open**.

2. Navigate to the drive and folder where you store your Data Files, then double-click the **chapter_1 folder** (Win), or select the **chapter_1 folder** (Mac).

3. Select **dw1_1.html**, then select **Open**. You may not see the .html file extension if the option for hiding file extensions for known file types is selected on your operating system.

TIP If you want your screen to match the figures in this book, make sure the Document window is maximized.

4. Select **Window** on the Menu bar, then select **Hide Panels** to temporarily hide the panels and the Property inspector.

   If In-app help messages appear, just read and close them. Refer to the sidebar on page 8 for more information.

   Hiding the panels gives you a larger viewing area for your web pages. You can also press [F4] to show or hide the panels.

   Note to Mac users: On the newest Mac OS, the F-keys are assigned to system functions. (F1=monitor brightness and F4=widgets) You can change this in your system preferences. Newer keyboards have an "FN" or "fn" key that can be used in conjunction with the F-keys so that they function "normally."

5. Locate each of the web page elements shown in Figure 9.

TIP Because you are opening a single page that is not in a website with access to the other pages, the links will not work.

(continued)

Figure 9 *Viewing web page elements (Windows)*

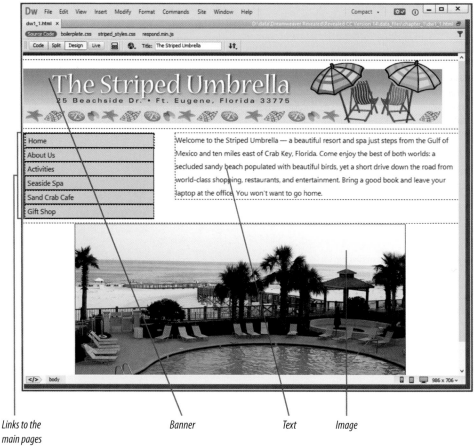

Links to the main pages in the website   *Banner*   *Text*   *Image*

Figure 9 *Viewing web page elements (Macintosh)*

Banner

Links to
the main
pages in the
website

Text

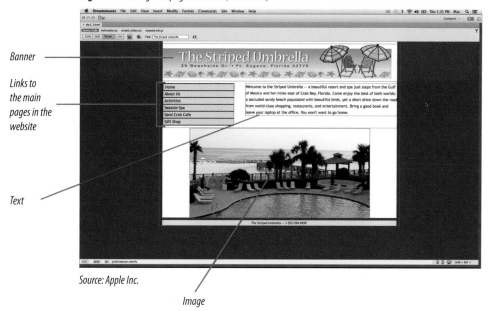

Source: Apple Inc.

Image

6. Press **[F4]** to show the panels.

7. Select the **Show Code view button** `Code` to view the code for the page.

8. Scroll to view all the code, if necessary, then select the **Show Design view button** `Design` to return to Design view.

   TIP To show and highlight the code for a particular page element, select the page element in Design view, then select the Show Code view button.

9. Select **File** on the Menu bar, then select **Close** to close the open page without saving it.

   TIP You can also select the Close button (the X) on the filename tab to close the page.

You opened a web page, located several page elements, viewed the code for the page, then closed the page without saving it.

Use Dreamweaver Help

1. Close any open files to display the Dreamweaver Welcome Screen.

2. Select **Help** on the menu bar, select **Help and Support**, then select **Dreamweaver Online Help**; or select the **Help & Support link** in the Learn column, as shown in Figure 10.

   The Learn & Support / Dreamweaver Help page opens from the Adobe website.

3. Select the **Dreamweaver CC (June 2014)** link under Help PDFs in the left column.

   The Adobe Dreamweaver CC Help pdf file opens in a new browser window.

4. Scroll down to the Contents page, then select the **Dreamweaver workflow and workspace link** under the Chapter 2: Workspace and workflow heading, as shown in Figure 11.

   The Dreamweaver workflow and workspace content appears.

5. Scroll down to browse through the content, then close the browser tab to return to the Learn & Support / Dreamweaver Help page.

(continued)

Figure 10 *Learning resources on the Welcome Screen*

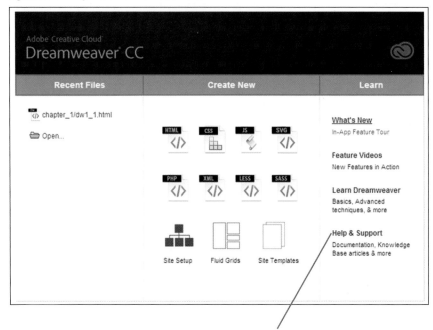

Help and Support link

Figure 11 *Viewing the table of contents*

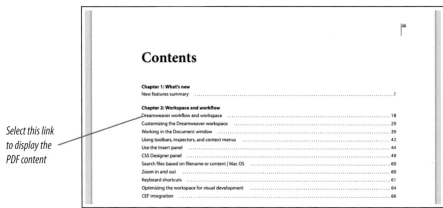

Select this link to display the PDF content

Source: Adobe Systems, Inc.

Figure 12 *The Learn & Support / Dreamweaver Help site*

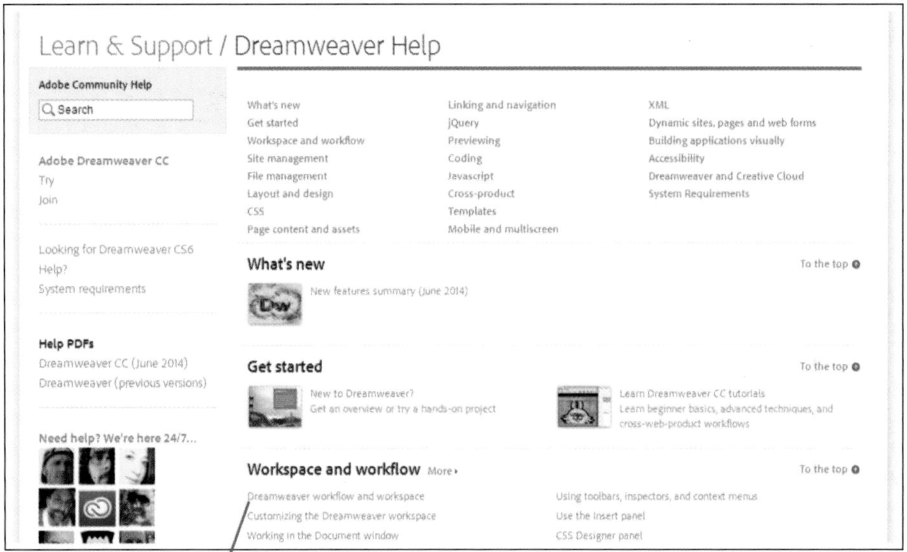

Source: Adobe Systems, Inc.

Select this link
to display the
HTML content

6. Scroll down the Learn & Support / Dreamweaver Help page, then select the **Dreamweaver workflow and workspace link** in the first column under Workspace and workflow, as shown in Figure 12.

   This content covers the same topics as the PDF help file, except these topics are organized and presented in live HTML files.

7. Select the **Back button** on your browser toolbar to return to the Learn & Support / Dreamweaver Help screen, then close Dreamweaver Help to return to Dreamweaver.

You used Adobe Help to read information about Dreamweaver.

Learning New Features in Dreamweaver CC

The right column in the Dreamweaver Welcome Screen is divided into four sections: What's New, Feature Videos, Learn Dreamweaver, and Help & Support. This content provides valuable learning materials for both the new Dreamweaver user and the experienced Dreamweaver user who just wants to find out what features have changed in the current version. Take the time to watch the In-App Feature Tour and the New Features in Action videos to help you get up to speed quickly. The Learn Dreamweaver link takes you to a library of Dreamweaver CC tutorials, complete with data files. The Help & Support link takes you to the Learn & Support / Dreamweaver Help page, which includes Dreamweaver CC manuals that are both PDFs and web-based. You can also read about top issues and participate in Dreamweaver forums and blogs.

Plan and Set Up
A WEBSITE

What You'll Do

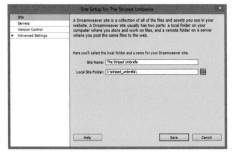

In this lesson, you will review a website plan for The Striped Umbrella, a beach resort and spa. You will also create a local site folder for The Striped Umbrella website, and then set up the website.

Understanding the Website Development Process

Creating a website is a complex process. It can often involve a large team of people working in various roles to ensure that the website contains accurate information, has an attractive design, and works smoothly.

Figure 13 illustrates the phases in a website development project.

Planning a Website

Planning is probably the most important part of any successful project. Planning is an essential part of creating a website,

Figure 13 *Phases of a website development project*

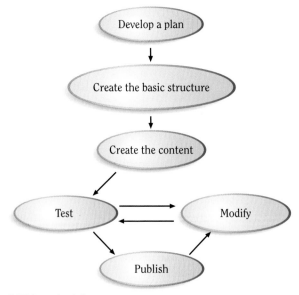

© 2015 Cengage Learning®

and is a continuous process that overlaps the subsequent phases. To start planning your website, you need to create a checklist of questions and answers about the site. For example, what are your goals for the site? Who is the audience you want to target? Teenagers? Children? Sports enthusiasts? Senior citizens? How can you design the site to appeal to the target audience? What content is appropriate for the target audience? What content is relevant to the purpose of the website? The more questions you can answer about the site, the more prepared you will be when you begin the developmental phase. Because of the public demand for up-to-date information, your plan should include not just how to get the site up and running, but how to keep it current. Table 1 lists some of the basic questions you need to answer during the planning phase for almost any type of website. From your checklist, you should create a statement of purpose and scope, a timeline for all due dates, a budget, a task list with work assignments, and a list of resources needed. You should also include a list of deliverables, such as page prototypes and art for approval. The due dates for each deliverable should be included in the timeline.

Planning the Basic Structure

Once you complete the planning phase, you need to determine the structure of the site by creating a wireframe. A **wireframe**, sometimes referred to as a storyboard, is an illustration that represents every page in a website. Like a flowchart, a wireframe shows the relationship of each page in the site to all the other pages. Wireframes also show how each page element is to be placed on each page. Wireframes are helpful when planning a website, because they allow you to visualize how each page in the site links to others. They are also an important tool to help the client see how the pages will look and work together. Make sure that the client and all other interested stakeholders approve the wireframe before the site construction actually begins.

Wireframes range from very simple (known as low-fidelity wireframes) to interactive and multidimensional (known as high-fidelity wireframes). You can create a simple

TABLE 1: WEBSITE PLANNING CHECKLIST	
Question	**Examples**
1. Who is the target audience?	Seniors, teens, children
2. How can I tailor the site to reach that audience?	Specify an appropriate reading level, decide the optimal amount of media content, use formal or casual language
3. What are the goals for the site?	Sell a product, provide information
4. How will I gather the information?	Recruit other employees, write it myself, use content from in-house documents
5. What are my sources for media content?	Internal production department, outside production company, my own photographs
6. What is my budget?	Very limited, well financed
7. What is the timeline?	Two weeks, one month, six months
8. Who is on my project team?	Just me, a complete staff of designers
9. How often should the site be updated?	Every 10 minutes, once a month
10. Who will update the site?	Me, other team members

© 2015 Cengage Learning®

wireframe by using a pencil and paper or by using a graphics program on a computer, such as Adobe Illustrator, Adobe Fireworks, or Microsoft PowerPoint. To create more complex wireframes that simulate the site navigation and user interaction, use a high-fidelity wireframe program such as Adobe InDesign, Adobe Muse, ProtoShare, Microsoft Visio, or Adobe Photoshop.

The basic wireframe shown in Figure 14 shows all the The Striped Umbrella website pages that you will create in this book. The home page appears at the top of the wireframe, and it has four pages linked to it. The home page is called the **parent page**, because it is at a higher level in the web hierarchy and has pages linked to it. The pages linked below it are called **child pages**. The Activities page, which is a child page to the home page, is also a parent page to the Cruises and Fishing pages. You can refer to this wireframe as you create the

actual links in Dreamweaver. More detailed wireframes also include document names, images, text files, and link information. Use your wireframe as your guide as you develop the site to make sure you follow the planned site structure.

In addition to creating a wireframe for your site, you should also create a folder hierarchy on your computer for all of the files that will be used in the site. Start by creating a folder with a descriptive name for the site, such as the company name. This folder, known as the **local site folder**, will store all the pages or HTML files for the site. Traditionally, this folder has been called the **root folder** and many people still use this term; in this book we will call it the local site folder. Then create a subfolder, often called **assets** or **images**, in which you store all of the files that are not pages, such as images and sound files.

After you create the local site folder, you are ready to set up your site. When you **set up** a site, you use the Dreamweaver Site Setup dialog box to assign your site a name and specify the local site folder. After you have set up your site, the site name and any folders and files it contains appear in the **Files panel**, the panel you use to manage your website's files and folders. Using the Files panel to manage your files ensures that the site links work correctly when the website is published. You also use the Files panel to add or delete pages.

Creating the Web Pages and Collecting the Page Content

This is the fun part! After you create your wireframe, obtain approvals, and set up your site, you need to gather the files you'll need to create the pages, including text, images, buttons, video, and animations. You will import some of these pages from other software programs, and some you will create in Dreamweaver. For example, you can create text in a word-processing program and import or paste it into Dreamweaver, or you can create and format text in Dreamweaver.

Images, tables, colors, and horizontal rules all contribute to making a page attractive and interesting, but they can increase file size.

Figure 14 *The Striped Umbrella website wireframe*

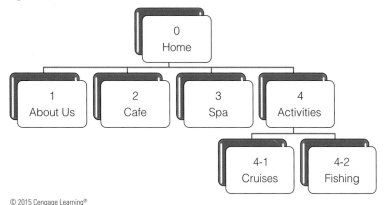

© 2015 Cengage Learning®

In choosing your page elements, carefully consider the file size of each page. A page with too many graphic elements might take a long time to load, which could cause visitors to leave your site.

Testing the Pages

Once all your pages are completed, you need to test the site to make sure all the links work and that everything looks good. It is important to test your web pages using different browser software. The four most common browsers are Mozilla Firefox, Google Chrome, Apple Safari, and Microsoft Internet Explorer. Test your site using different versions of each browser, because older versions may not support the latest web technology. Websites today are viewed with a variety of devices, screen sizes, and screen resolutions, so you should test your site using a variety of sizes, including mobile, tablet, and desktop. Some users may have small monitors, while others may have large, high-resolution monitors. Also consider connection download time. Although most people use high-speed connections with cable modems or DSL (digital subscriber line), some in rural areas still use slower dial-up modems. Testing is a continuous process, for which you should allocate plenty of time.

Modifying the Pages

Modifying and testing pages in a website is an ongoing process. After you create a website, you'll probably find that you need to keep changing it, especially when information on the site needs to be updated. Each time you make a change, such as adding a new button or image to a page, you should test the site again.

Publishing the Site

Publishing a website refers to the process of transferring all the files for the site to a **web server**, a computer that is connected to the Internet with an IP (Internet Protocol) address, so that it is available for viewing on the Internet. A website must be published so that Internet users can view it. There are several options for publishing a website. For instance, many **Internet Service Providers (ISPs)** provide space on their servers for customers to publish websites, and some commercial websites provide limited free space for their users. Although publishing happens at the end of the site development process, it's a good idea to set up web server access in the planning phase. Use the Files panel to transfer your files using the Dreamweaver FTP capability. **FTP (File Transfer Protocol)** is the process of uploading and downloading files to and from a remote site.

Managing a Project with a Team

When working with a site development team, it is especially important to define clear goals for the project and a list of objectives to accomplish those goals. Your plan should be finalized after conferring with both the clients and other team members to make sure that the purpose, scope, and objectives are clear to everyone. Establish the **deliverables**, or products that will be provided to the client at the product completion such as new pages or graphic elements, and a timeline for their delivery. You should present the web pages at strategic times in the development process to your team members and to your clients for feedback and evaluation. Analyze all feedback objectively, incorporating both the positive and the negative comments to help you make improvements to the site and meet the clients' expectations and goals.

A common pitfall in team management is **scope creep**. Scope creep means making impromptu changes or additions to a project without corresponding increases in the schedule or budget. Proper project control and communication between team members and clients can minimize scope creep and achieve the successful and timely completion of a project.

Select the location for your website

1. Open or expand the Files panel if necessary to view the contents.

   TIP If the Background File Activity dialog box opens, select Close. It is just indicating the status of any current file activity.

2. Select the **drive or folder** that is currently displayed in the pop-up menu in the Files panel to display a menu of storage locations. See Figure 15.

3. Navigate to and select the **drive or folder** (or subfolder) in the list where you will store your folders and files for your websites.

   You will store all of the folders and files you create inside this drive or folder.

   You selected the drive or folder where you will create your website.

Figure 15 *Selecting a drive in the Files panel*

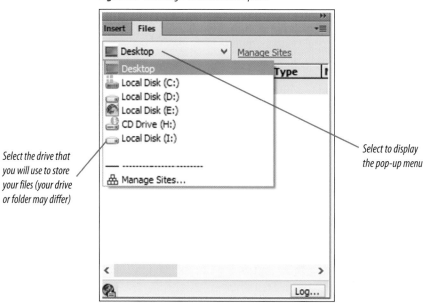

Select the drive that you will use to store your files (your drive or folder may differ)

Select to display the pop-up menu

Understanding IP Addresses and Domain Names

To be accessible over the Internet, a website must be published to a web server with a permanent IP address. An **IP address** is an assigned series of numbers, separated by periods, that designates an address on the Internet. To access a web page, you can enter either an IP address or a domain name in the address text box of your browser window. A **domain name** is a web address that is expressed in letters instead of numbers and usually reflects the name of the business represented by the website. For example, the domain name of the Adobe website is www.adobe.com, but the IP address is 192.150.16.117.

Because domain names use descriptive text instead of numbers, they are easier to remember. Compare an IP address to your Social Security number and a domain name to your name. Both your Social Security number and your name are used to refer to you as a person, but your name is much easier for your friends and family to use than your Social Security number. You can type the IP address or the domain name in the address text box of the browser window to access a website. The domain name is also referred to as a **URL** or Uniform Resource Locator.

Figure 16 *Creating a local site folder using the Files panel*

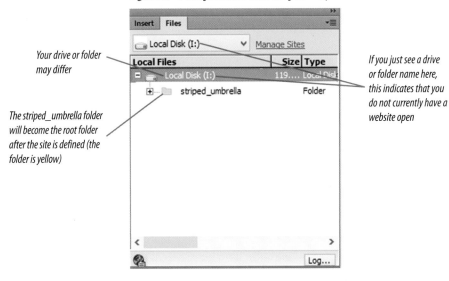

Your drive or folder may differ

If you just see a drive or folder name here, this indicates that you do not currently have a website open

The striped_umbrella folder will become the root folder after the site is defined (the folder is yellow)

Figure 17 *Viewing an open website in the Files panel*

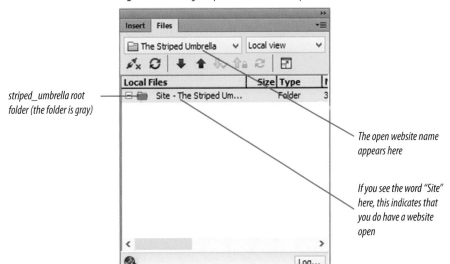

striped_umbrella root folder (the folder is gray)

The open website name appears here

If you see the word "Site" here, this indicates that you do have a website open

Create a local site folder

1. Verify that the drive or folder where you want to store your site is selected in the Files panel, right-click (Windows) or control-click (Macintosh) the **drive or folder**, then select **New Folder**.

2. Type **striped_umbrella** to rename the folder, then press **[Enter]**.

   The folder is renamed striped_umbrella, as shown in Figure 16. You have not created a website yet. You have just created the folder that will serve as the local site folder after you set up the site.

   The folder color is currently yellow (Mac users will see blue folders), but after you set up the site in the next section, it will change to gray. Notice the difference between Figure 16 and Figure 17. In Figure 16, you have only created the local site folder, not the website, and the color of the folder is yellow. In Figure 17, The Striped Umbrella website has been created and is open, so the local site folder is gray.

You created a new folder to serve as the local site folder for The Striped Umbrella website.

Set up a website

1. Select **Site** on the Menu bar, then select **New Site**.
2. Select **Site** in the category list in the Site Setup for Unnamed Site dialog box (if necessary), then type **The Striped Umbrella** in the Site name text box.

TIP You can use uppercase letters and spaces in the site name because it is not the name of a folder or a file.

3. Select the **Browse for folder button** 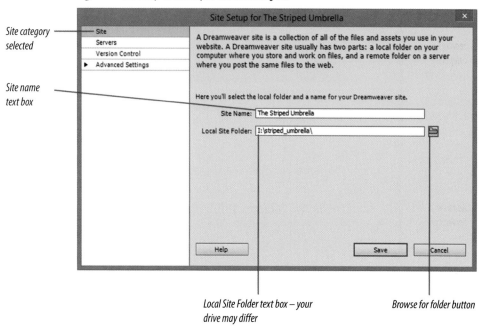 next to the Local Site Folder text box, in the Choose Root folder dialog box, navigate to and select the **drive and folder** where your website files will be stored, then select the **striped_umbrella folder**.
4. Select **Select Folder** (Win) or **Choose** (Mac). See Figure 18.

You created a website and set it up with the name The Striped Umbrella. You then told Dreamweaver the folder name and location to use for the local site folder.

Figure 18 *Site Setup for The Striped Umbrella dialog box*

Site category selected

Site name text box

Local Site Folder text box — your drive may differ

Browse for folder button

Understanding the Process of Publishing a Website

Before publishing a website so that web users can access it, you should first create a **local site folder**, also called the **local root folder**, to house all the files for your website, as you did on page 1-23. This folder usually resides on your hard drive. Next, you need to gain access to a remote server. A **remote server** is a web server that hosts websites and is not directly connected to the computer housing the local site. Many Internet Service Providers, or ISPs, provide space for publishing websites on their servers. Once you have access to a remote server, you can then use the Servers category in the Site Setup dialog box to enter information such as the FTP host, host directory, login, and password. After entering this information, you can then use the Put File(s) button in the Files panel to transfer the files to the designated remote server. Once the site is published to a remote server, it is called a **remote site**.

Figure 19 *Adding a server for Remote Access for The Striped Umbrella website*

Servers category

Add new Server icon

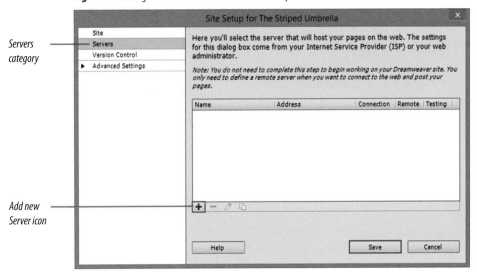

Figure 20 *Entering server information for The Striped Umbrella website*

Enter Server name here

Choices for publishing a website

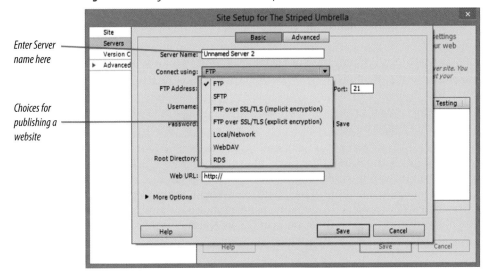

Set up web server access

1. Select **Servers** in the Category list, then select the **Add new Server icon** ✛ , as shown in Figure 19.

   TIP If you do not have the information to publish your website, skip step 2 and continue to step 3. You can specify this information later.

2. Select the **Connect using: list arrow**, choose the method you will use to publish your website, as shown in Figure 20, enter any necessary information in the Site Setup for The Striped Umbrella dialog box based on the setting you chose, then select **Save**.

   TIP Your network administrator or web hosting service will give you the necessary information to publish your website.

3. Select **Save** to close the Site Setup dialog box.

You set up the remote access information to prepare you for publishing your website.

Add a Folder
AND PAGES

What You'll Do

In this lesson, you will use the Files panel to create a new folder and new pages for the website.

Adding a Folder to a Website

After setting up a website, you need to create folders to organize the files that will make up the site. Creating a folder called **assets** is a good beginning. There is nothing magic about the word "assets," though. You can name your folder anything that makes sense to you, as long as you follow proper folder naming conventions such as avoiding the use of spaces. You can use the assets folder to store all non-HTML files, such as images or sound files. Many designers name this folder "images" and use additional folders to store other types of supporting files. After you create the assets folder, it is a good idea to set

---

DESIGNTIP

Creating an Effective Navigation Structure

When you create a website, it's important to consider how your users will navigate from page to page within the site. A menu bar, or navigation bar, is a critical tool for moving around a website, so it's important that all text, buttons, and icons used in a menu bar have a consistent look across all pages. If you use a complex menu bar, such as one that incorporates JavaScript, it's a good idea to include plain text links in another location on the page for accessibility. Otherwise, users might become confused or lost within the site.

A navigation structure can include more links than those included in a menu bar, however. For instance, it can contain other sets of links that relate to the content of a specific page and which are placed at the bottom or sides of a page in a different format. No matter which navigation structure you use, make sure that every page includes a link back to the home page. Don't make users rely on the Back button on the browser toolbar to find their way back to the home page. It's possible that the user's current page might have opened as a result of a search and selecting the Back button will then take the user out of the website.

---

it as the default location to store the website images. This saves a step when you import new images into the website.

Creating the Home Page

The **home page** is the first page that users see when they visit your site. Most websites contain many other pages that all connect back to the home page. The home page filename usually has the name index.html (.htm), or default.html (.htm).

Adding Pages to a Website

Websites might be as simple as one page or might contain hundreds of pages. When you create a multi-page website, you can begin by adding blank pages and saving them in the website folder structure within the local site folder. Once you add and name all the website pages, you can then add text and graphics to each one. This method enables you to set up the navigation structure of the website at the beginning of the development process and view how each page is linked to others. When you are satisfied with the overall structure, you can then add content to each page. This is strictly a personal preference, however; you can also add and link pages as you create them, and that will work fine, too.

You have a choice of several default document types you can generate when you create new HTML pages. The default document type is designated in the Preferences dialog box. HTML5 is the default document type when you install Dreamweaver, but you can change it to any other document type. We will use HTML5 as our standard document type for the files we create in each lesson.

Using the Files Panel for File Management

You should use the Files panel to add, delete, move, or rename files and folders in a website. It is important that you perform these file-maintenance tasks in the Files panel rather than in Windows Explorer (Win) or in the Finder (Mac). Working outside of Dreamweaver, such as in Windows Explorer, can cause linking errors. You cannot take advantage of the simple, yet powerful, Dreamweaver site-management features unless you use the Files panel for all file-management activities. You can use Windows Explorer (Win) or the Finder (Mac) only to create the local site folder or to move or copy the local site folder of a website to another location. If you move or copy the local site folder to a new location, you will have to set up the site again in the Files panel, as you did in Lesson 3 of this chapter.

Setting up a site is not difficult and will become routine for you after you practice a bit. If you are using Dreamweaver on multiple computers, such as in labs or at home, you will have to set up your sites the first time you change to a different computer. Use Creative Cloud to sync your site files when you work with your files on more than one device. See the Creative Cloud introduction at the beginning of this book for more information on syncing.

Add a folder to a website (Windows)

1. Right-click **Site - The Striped Umbrella** in the Files panel, then select **New Folder**.

2. Type **assets** in the folder text box, then press **[Enter]**.

TIP To rename a folder, select the folder name, pause, click once, when highlighted, type the new name and press [Enter].

3. Compare your screen to Figure 21.

You used the Files panel to create a new folder in the striped_umbrella folder and named it "assets".

Add a folder to a website (Macintosh)

1. Press and hold **[control]**, select the **striped_umbrella folder**, then select **New Folder**.

2. Type **assets** in the new folder name text box, then press **[return]**.

TIP To rename a folder, select the folder name, pause, click once, when highlighted type the new name and press **[return]**.

3. Compare your screen to Figure 22.

You used the Files panel to create a new folder in the striped_umbrella folder and named it "assets".

Figure 21 *The Striped Umbrella site in Files panel with assets folder created (Windows)*

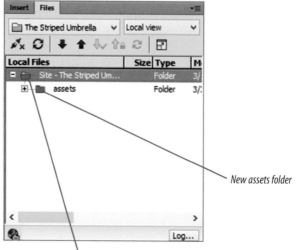

New assets folder

Local site folder for
The Striped Umbrella
website

Figure 22 *The Striped Umbrella site in Files panel with assets folder created (Macintosh)*

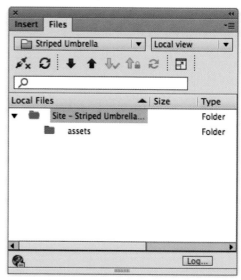

Source: Apple Inc.

Figure 23 *Site Setup for The Striped Umbrella dialog box with the assets folder set as the default images folder*

Local Info in the Advanced Settings category

Default Images folder text box

Browse for folder button

Site Setup for The Striped Umbrella

| Site |
| Servers |
| Version Control |
| ▼ Advanced Settings |
| Local Info |
| Cloaking |
| Design Notes |
| File View Columns |
| Contribute |
| Templates |
| jQuery |
| Web Fonts |
| Edge Animate Assets |

Default Images folder: I:\striped_umbrella\assets\

Links relative to: ⦿ Document ◯ Site Root

Web URL: http://

Enter the Web URL if you don't have a remote server defined. If you have a remote server defined, Dreamweaver uses the Web URL specified in the server settings.

Change the Remote server's Web URL

☐ Case-sensitive links checking

☑ Enable Cache

The cache maintains file and asset information in the site. This speeds up the Asset panel and link management features.

Help   Save   Cancel

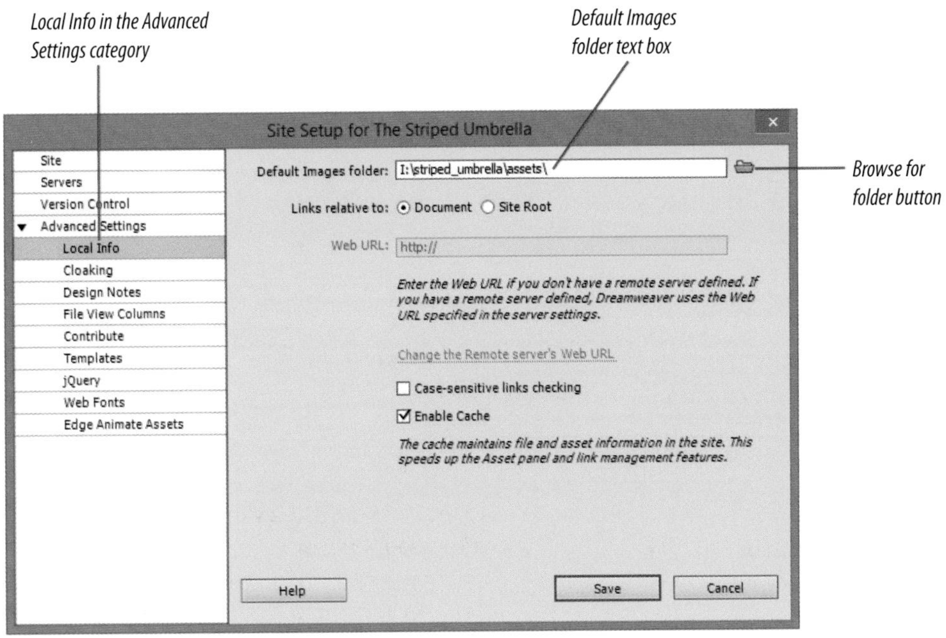

Set the default images folder

1. Select the **Site pop-up menu** in the Files panel, select **Manage Sites**, then select the **Edit the currently selected site button** ✐.

2. Select **Advanced Settings** in the category list in the Site Setup dialog box, then select **Local Info** if necessary.

3. Select the **Browse for folder button** 📁 next to the Default Images folder text box.

4. If necessary, navigate to your striped_umbrella folder, double-click the **assets folder**, then select the **Select Folder** (Win) or double-click the **assets folder** (Mac).

   Compare your screen to Figure 23.

5. Select **Save**, then select **Done**.

You set the assets folder as the default images folder so that imported images will be automatically saved in it.

Create the home page

1. Open **dw1_2.html** from the drive and folder where you store your Data Files.

2. Select **File** on the Menu bar, select **Save As**, navigate to your striped_umbrella folder, select **dw1_2.html** in the File name text box (Win) or select **dw1_2** in the Save As text box (Mac), then type **index**.

   Mac users should be careful not to remove the .html extension.

3. Select **Save**, then select **No** when asked to update links.

   As shown in Figure 24, the drive where the local site folder is stored, the local site folder name, and the page's filename appear on the title bar (Win), to the right of the document tab. This information is called the path, or location of the open file in relation to other folders in the website.

   The banner image is no longer visible because although you saved the .html file under a new name in the website's local site folder, you have not yet copied the related files into the website's local site folder. The banner image is still linked to the Data Files folder. You will fix this in the next set of steps.

   Two cascading style sheet files and a javascript file are linked to this page to provide the formatting. Since you have not yet copied these files into the local site folder, the page appears with unformatted text. If you select a related file's tab, a warning appears above the Document window telling you that the file is not in the correct folder. You will also fix this in the next set of steps.

   You opened a file, then saved it with the filename index.html.

Figure 24 *index.html saved in the striped_umbrella local site folder*

Banner will not be visible because the path to it is inside one of the cascading style sheets; until it is copied to the site, it will not be visible

Path for file (Win)   Root folder   File renamed index.html

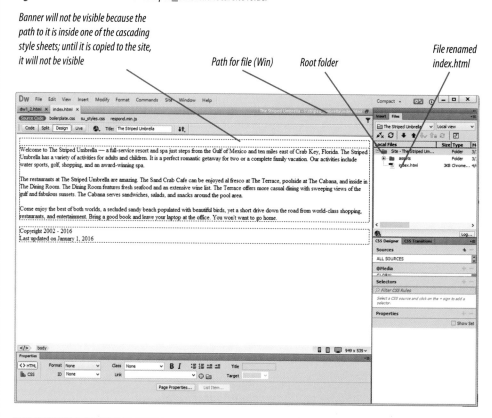

Related and Dependent Files for The Striped Umbrella Website

Files linked to an HTML page, and necessary to make the page display or work correctly, are called **dependent files**. Files that are used as images, background images, videos, etc, are stored in the website and are listed in the Assets panel. Files that are used for styling the content or enabling functions such as Javascript are called **related files**. They are stored in the website and can be opened and edited from the Related files toolbar. Both the terms dependent files and related files are also collectively referred to as supporting files. The supporting files for The Striped Umbrella site are listed in Table 2 on the next page.

Figure 25 *The index page with related files' formatting applied*

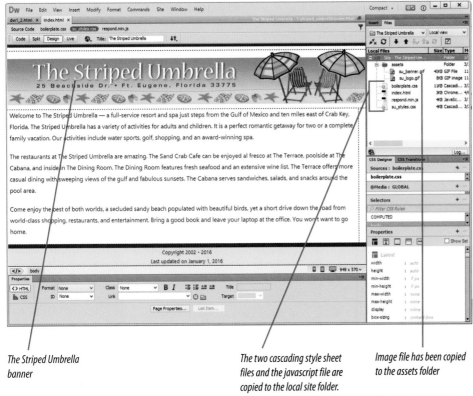

The Striped Umbrella
banner

The two cascading style sheet
files and the javascript file are
copied to the local site folder.

Image file has been copied
to the assets folder

TABLE 2: SUPPORTING FILES FOR THE STRIPED UMBRELLA WEBSITE	
File Name	**Function**
su_banner.gif	The image background for the banner
su_logo.gif	The image background for the mobile banner
boilerplate.css	Provides styles for the page; automatically generated
su_styles.css	Provides custom formatting; automatically generated; user assigns name
respond.min.js	Provides code for displaying the page on different sized media; automatically generated

© 2015 Cengage Learning®

Lesson 4   Add a Folder and Pages

Saving files in the site folder

1. Open your file management program, browse to the chapter_1 data files folder, then select and copy the files **boilerplate.css**, **respond.min.js**, and **su_styles.css** to your striped_umbrella local site folder.

   The index page contains links to these three files. Even though they are listed on the Related files toolbar, until they are copied to the same folder as the index page, they will be broken links and will not work when the site is published.

2. Repeat Step 1 to copy the **su_banner.gif** and **su_logo.gif** file from the Data Files chapter_1/assets folder to the striped_umbrella/assets folder.

   Now that the related files are copied to the website folder, the page formatting is applied, as shown in Figure 25.

3. Return to Dreamweaver, double-click the **assets folder** in the Files panel to expand it if necessary, then notice that all files are now listed in the Files panel.

   Don't concern youself now with the details of how this works. We will learn more about cascading style sheets as we go.

TIP Until you copy all supporting files needed to a website local site folder, the related HTML file will appear without complete formatting.

You copied the linked related files for The Striped Umbrella index page to the local site folder.

Add pages to a website (Windows)

1. Select the **plus sign** to the left of the assets folder (if necessary) to open the folder and view its contents, su_banner.gif and su_logo.gif.

TIP If you do not see a file listed in the assets folder, select the Refresh button ↻ on the Files panel toolbar.

2. Right-click The Striped Umbrella **local site folder**, select **New File**, type **about_us** to replace untitled, then press **[Enter]**.

   Each new file is a page in the website. This page does not have page content or a page title yet.

TIP If you create a new file in the Files panel, use care to make sure the .html file extension is not deleted or that the file does not end up with a double file extension.

3. Repeat Step 2 to add five more blank pages to The Striped Umbrella website, naming the new files **spa.html**, **cafe.html**, **activities.html**, **cruises.html**, and **fishing.html**.

TIP Make sure you add the new files to the site folder, not the assets folder. If you accidentally add them to the assets folder, just drag them to the site folder.

4. Select the **Refresh button** ↻ on the Files panel to list the files alphabetically, then compare your screen to Figure 26.

5. Select **File**, **Save**, to save the index.html file, if necessary. Close both open files, select **File** on the Menu bar, then select **Exit**.

TIP If you are prompted to save changes to the dw1_1.html file, select No.

You added the following six pages to The Striped Umbrella website: about_us, activities, cafe, cruises, fishing, and spa.

Figure 26 *New pages added to The Striped Umbrella website (Windows)*

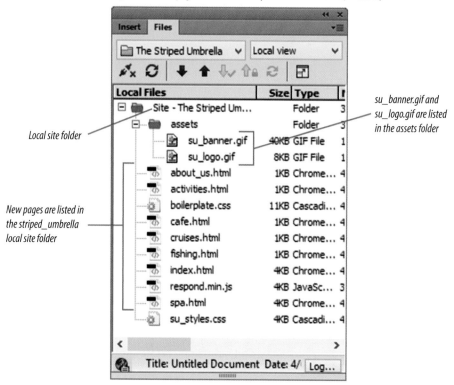

Local site folder

su_banner.gif and su_logo.gif are listed in the assets folder

New pages are listed in the striped_umbrella local site folder

Adding Page Titles

When you view a web page in a browser, its page title appears in the browser window page tab. (The page title is different from the filename, the name used to save the page on a computer.) The page title reflects the page content and sets the tone for the page. It is especially important to use words in your page title that are likely to match keywords users might enter when using a search engine. Search engines compare the text in page titles to the keywords typed into the search engine. When a page tab displays "Untitled Document," the designer has neglected to give the page a title. This is like giving up free "billboard space" and looks unprofessional. You'll learn more about page titles in Chapter 2.

Figure 27 *New pages added to The Striped Umbrella website (Macintosh)*

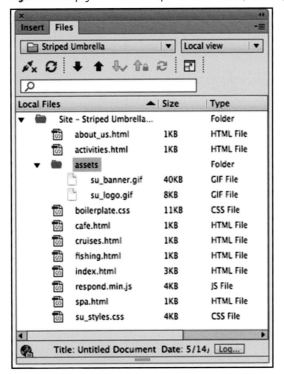

Source: Apple Inc.

POWER USER SHORTCUTS	
To do this:	**Use this shortcut:**
Open a file	[Ctrl][O] (Win) or ⌘ [O] (Mac)
Close a file	[Ctrl][W] (Win) or ⌘ [W] (Mac)
Create a new file	[Ctrl][N] (Win) or ⌘ [N] (Mac)
Save a file	[Ctrl][S] (Win) or ⌘ [S] (Mac)
Get Dreamweaver Help	[F1]
Show/Hide panels	[F4]
Switch between Code view and Design view	[Ctrl][`] (Win) or [command] [`] (Mac)

© 2015 Cengage Learning®

Add pages to a website (Macintosh)

1. Select the **triangle** to the left of the assets folder to open the folder and view its contents.

   TIP If you do not see a file listed in the assets folder, select the Refresh button 🔄 on the Files panel.

2. [control]-click the **striped_umbrella local site folder**, select **New File**, type **about_us** to replace untitled, then press **[return]**.

   TIP If you create a new file in the Files panel, use care to make sure the .html file extension is not deleted or that the file does not end up with a double file extension.

3. Repeat Step 2 to add five more blank pages to The Striped Umbrella website, naming the new files **spa.html**, **cafe.html**, **activities.html**, **cruises.html**, and **fishing.html**.

   TIP Make sure to add the new files to the site folder, not the assets folder. If you accidentally add them to the assets folder, just drag them to the site folder.

4. Select the **Refresh button** 🔄 to list the files alphabetically, then compare your screen to Figure 27.

5. Select **File**, **Save**, to save the index.html file, then close both open files.

6. Select **Dreamweaver** on the Menu bar, and then select **Quit Dreamweaver**.

   TIP If you are prompted to save changes, select No.

You added six pages to The Striped Umbrella website: about_us, activities, cafe, cruises, fishing, spa.

Explore the Dreamweaver workspace.

1. Start Dreamweaver.
2. Create a new HTML document.
3. Change the view to Code view.
4. Change the view to Code and Design views.
5. Change the view to Design view.
6. Collapse the panels to icons.
7. Expand the panels.
8. Undock the Files panel and float it to the middle of the document window. Dock the Files panel back to its original position.
9. View the Insert panel.
10. Close the page without saving it.

View a web page and use Help.

1. Open the file dw1_3.html from the location where you store your Data Files.
2. Locate the following page elements: a banner, an image, and text.
3. Change the view to Code view.
4. Change the view to Design view.
5. Use the Dreamweaver Online Help command to search for information on docking panels.
6. Display and read one of the topics you find.
7. Close the Learn & Support / Dreamweaver Help window.
8. Close the page without saving it.

Plan and set up a website.

1. Use the Files panel to select the drive and folder where you store your website files.
2. Create a new local site folder in this folder or drive called **blooms**.
3. Create a new site called **Blooms & Bulbs**.
4. Specify the blooms folder as the local site folder.
5. Use the Servers Info category in the Site Setup for Blooms & Bulbs dialog box to set up web server access. (*Hint*: Skip this step if you do not have the necessary information to set up web server access.)
6. Select Save to close the Site Setup dialog box.

Add a folder and pages.

1. Create a new folder in the blooms local site folder called **assets**.
2. Edit the site to set the assets folder as the default location for the website images.
3. Open the file dw1_4.html from where you store your Data Files, save this file in the blooms local site folder as **index.html**, then select No to updating the links.
4. In your file manager, locate the data files bb_styles.css, boilerplate.css, respond.min.js, blooms_banner.jpg, blooms_banner_tablet.jpg, and blooms_logo.jpg.
5. Copy the blooms_banner.jpg, blooms_banner_tablet.jpg, and blooms_logo.jpg files to the website assets folder, then copy the two style sheet files and the javascript file to the website local site folder.
6. Return to the index page and verify that the banner background is displayed and the styles are applied.
7. Create seven new pages in the Files panel, and name them: **plants.html**, **workshops.html**, **newsletter.html**, **annuals.html**, **perennials.html**, **water_plants.html**, and **tips.html**.
8. Refresh the view to list the new files alphabetically, then compare your screen to Figure 28.
9. Close all open pages.

Figure 28 *Completed Skills Review*

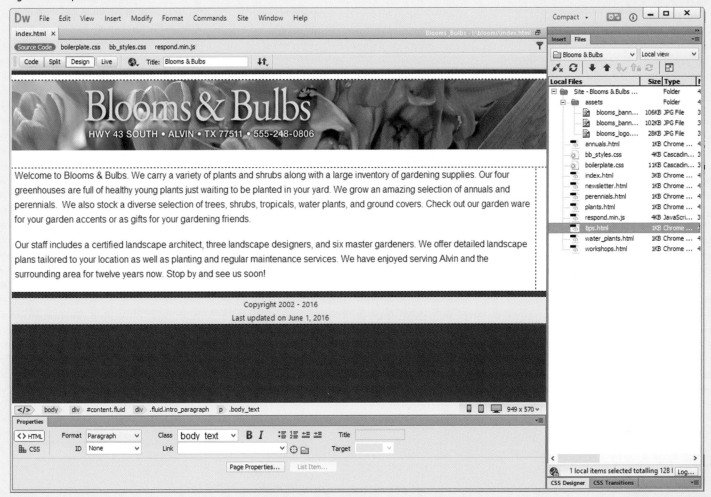

You have been hired to create a website for a travel outfitter called TripSmart. TripSmart specializes in travel products and services. In addition to selling travel products, such as luggage and accessories, they organize trips and offer travel advice. Their clients range from college students to families to vacationing professionals. The owner, Thomas Howard, has requested a dynamic website that conveys the excitement of traveling.

1. Using the information in the preceding paragraph, create a wireframe for this website, using either a pencil and paper or a program such as Microsoft Word. Include the home page with links to four child pages named **catalog.html**, **newsletter.html**, **services.html**, and **tours.html**. Include two child pages under the tours page named **egypt.html** and **argentina.html**.

2. Use either your file manager or the Dreamweaver Files panel to create a new local site folder named **tripsmart** in the drive and folder where you store your website files.

3. Start Dreamweaver, if necessary, then create a site with the name **TripSmart**. Set the tripsmart folder as the local site folder for the site.

4. Create an assets folder and set it as the default location for images.

5. Open the file dw1_5.html from where you store your Data Files, then save it in the tripsmart local site folder as **index.html**. (Remember not to update links.)

6. Locate the following files from your Chapter 1 data files folder: tripsmart_banner.jpg, tripsmart_logo.gif, boilerplate.css, respond.min.js, and tripsmart_styles.css.

7. Copy the two image files to the site assets folder, then copy the two style sheet files and javascript file to the local site folder.

8. Create six additional pages for the site, and name them as follows: **catalog.html**, **newsletter.html**, **services.html**, **tours.html**, **egypt.html**, and **argentina.html**. Use your wireframe and Figure 29 as a guide.

9. Refresh the Files panel.

10. Close all open pages.

Figure 29 *Completed Project Builder 1*

Getting Started with Dreamweaver

Your company has been selected to design a website for a catering business called Carolyne's Creations. In addition to catering, Carolyne's services include cooking classes and daily specials available as take-out meals. She also has a retail shop that stocks gourmet treats and kitchen items.

1. Create a wireframe for this website that includes a home page and child pages named **shop.html, classes.html, catering.html,** and **recipes.html**.

Create two more child pages under the classes.html page called **children.html** and **adults.html**.

2. Use your file manager or the Dreamweaver Files panel to create new local site folder for the site in the drive and folder where you save your website files, then name it **cc.**

3. Create a website with the name **Carolyne's Creations**, using the cc folder for the local site folder.

4. Create an assets folder for the site and set the assets folder as the default location for images.

5. Open dw1_6.html from the where you store your Data Files then save it as **index.html** in the cc folder.

6. Copy the files cc_banner.jpg, cc_banner_tablet.jpg, and cc_logo.gif from the data files folder to the cc/assets folder.

7. Copy the files boilerplate.css, cc_styles.css, and respond.min.js from the data files folder to the local site folder.

8. Using Figure 30 and your wireframe as guides, create the additional pages shown for the website.

9. Refresh the Files panel to sort the files alphabetically.

10. Close all open pages.

Figure 30 *Completed Project Builder 2*

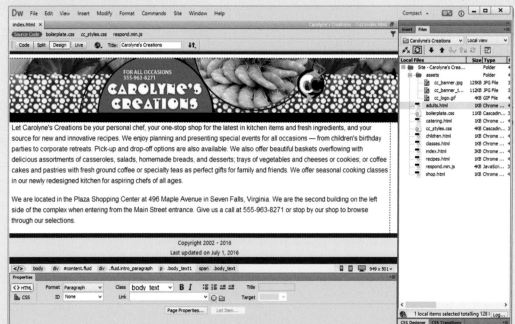

Figure 31 shows the Department of Defense website, a past selection for the Adobe Site of the Day. To visit the current Department of Defense website, connect to the Internet, then go to www.defense.gov. The current page might differ from the figure because dynamic websites are updated frequently to reflect current information. The main navigation structure is under the banner. The page title is United States Department of Defense (defense.gov). You have not yet learned how to create a new page with a Fluid Grid Layout, so you can either create a simple HTML page now and convert it to a Fluid Grid Layout later, or use one of your website index pages as a template.

Go to the Adobe Dreamweaver CC Showcase at www.adobe.com/products/dreamweaver/showcase.html, then visit one of the sites listed. (After you select the PDF associated with a site, you will see a link to the site listed.) Explore the site and answer the following questions:

1. Do you see page titles for each page you visit?
2. Do the page titles accurately reflect the page content?
3. Is the navigation structure clear?
4. How is the navigation structure organized?
5. Why do you think this site was featured?

Figure 31 *Design Project*

Source: United States Department of Defense

The Portfolio Project will be an ongoing project throughout the book, in which you will plan and create an original website without any Data Files supplied. The focus of the site can be on any topic, organization, sports team, club, or company that you would like. You will build on this site from chapter to chapter, so you must do each Portfolio Project assignment in each chapter to complete your website. When you finish this book, you should have a completed site that would be an excellent addition to a professional portfolio.

1. Decide what type of site you would like to create. It can be a personal site about you, a business site that promotes a fictitious or real company, or an informational site that provides information about a topic, cause, or organization.
2. Write a list of questions and answers about the site you have decided to create.
3. Create a wireframe for your site to include at least four pages. The wireframe should include the home page with at least three child pages under it.
4. Create a local site folder and an assets folder to house the assets, then set up your site using the local site folder as the website local site folder and the assets folder as the default images folder.
5. Create a blank page named **index.html** as a placeholder for the home page.
6. Begin collecting content, such as pictures or text to use in your website. You can use a digital camera to take photos, use a scanner to scan pictures, or create your own graphics using a program such as Adobe Photoshop, Adobe Edge Animate, or Adobe Fireworks. Gather the content in a central location that will be accessible to you as you develop your site.

CHAPTER 2 DEVELOPING A
WEB PAGE

1. Create head content and set page properties
2. Create, import, and format text
3. Add links to web pages
4. Use the History panel and edit code
5. Modify and test web pages

DEVELOPING A
WEB PAGE

Introduction

The process of developing a web page requires a lot of thought and planning. Besides developing the page content, you also need to write descriptive head content. Head content does not appear on the page but in the HTML code; it contains information search engines use to help users find your website. Next, choose the page background and text colors using style sheets. Then add the page content, style it attractively, and add links to let users navigate between the site pages. Finally, to ensure that all links work correctly and are current, test them regularly. You will learn about each of these processes as you work through this book.

Understanding Page Layout

Before you add content to a page, consider the following guidelines for laying out pages:

Use white space effectively. A room with too much furniture makes it difficult to appreciate the individual pieces. The same is true of a web page. Too many text blocks, links, animations, and images can be distracting. Consider leaving white space on each page. **White space**, which is not necessarily white, is the area on a page with no content.

Limit media elements. Too many media elements, such as images, video clips, or sounds, can result in a page that that looks too cluttered and takes too long to load. Users might leave your site before the entire page finishes loading. Use media elements only if they serve a purpose.

Keep it simple. Often the simplest websites are the most effective and are also the easiest to create and maintain. A simple, well-designed site that works well is far superior to a complex one that contains errors.

Use an intuitive navigation structure. Make sure your site's navigation structure is easy to use. Users should always know where they are in the site and be able to easily find their way back to the home page. If users get "lost," they might leave the site rather than struggle to find their way around.

Apply a consistent theme. To help give your website pages a consistent appearance, consider designing your pages using a common theme. Consistency in the use of colors and fonts, the placement of the navigation links, and the overall page design gives a website a unified look and promotes greater ease of use and accessibility. Style sheets and pre-developed page layouts called **templates** can make this easier.

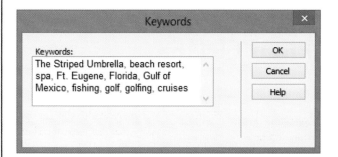

Keywords

Keywords:

The Striped Umbrella, beach resort, spa, Ft. Eugene, Florida, Gulf of Mexico, fishing, golf, golfing, cruises

OK
Cancel
Help

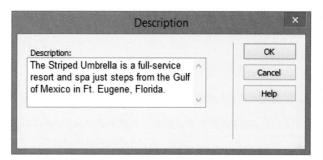

Description

Description:

The Striped Umbrella is a full-service resort and spa just steps from the Gulf of Mexico in Ft. Eugene, Florida.

OK
Cancel
Help

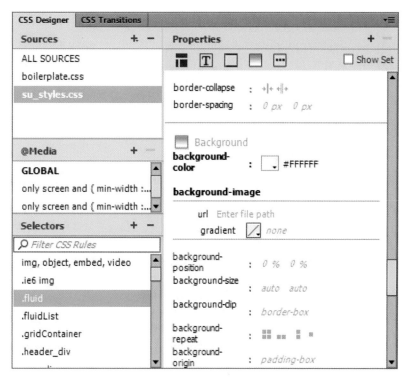

CSS Designer CSS Transitions

Sources   + −

ALL SOURCES
boilerplate.css
su_styles.css

@Media   + −

GLOBAL
only screen and { min-width :...
only screen and { min-width :...

Selectors   + −

Filter CSS Rules

img, object, embed, video
.ie6 img
.fluid
.fluidList
.gridContainer
.header_div

Properties   + −

☐ Show Set

border-collapse   :
border-spacing   :   0 px   0 px

Background
background-color : ☐ #FFFFFF

background-image

url   Enter file path
gradient   none

background-position   :   0 %   0 %
background-size   :   auto   auto
background-clip   :   border-box
background-repeat   :
background-origin   :   padding-box

Create Head Content and
SET PAGE PROPERTIES

What You'll Do

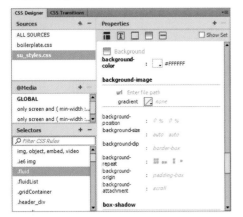

In this lesson, you will learn how to enter titles, keywords, and descriptions in the head content section of a web page. You will also change the background color for a web page.

Creating the Head Content

A web page is composed of two distinct sections: the head content and the body. The **head content** includes the page title that appears in the title bar of the browser and some important page elements, called meta tags, that are not visible in the browser.

Meta tags are HTML codes that include information about the page, such as keywords and descriptions. Meta tags are read by screen readers for users who have visual impairments. **Keywords** are words that relate to the content of the website. For instance, the words "beach" and "resort" would be appropriate keywords for The Striped Umbrella website. A **description** is a short paragraph that describes the content and features of the website. Search engines find web pages by matching the title, keywords, and description in the head content of web pages with keywords that users enter in search engine text boxes. Therefore, it is important to include concise, useful information in the head content. The **body** is the part of the page that appears in a browser window. It contains all the page content that is visible to users, such as text, images, and links.

QUICK **TIP**

Don't confuse page titles with filenames, the names used to store files on the server.

Setting Web Page Properties

When you create a web page, begin by choosing properties that control the way the page appears in a browser, such as the **background color**, the color that fills the entire page. The background color should complement the colors used for text, links, and images on the page. You can also use a background image to fill an entire page or a section of a page, called a CSS layout block. A **CSS layout block** is a section of a web page that is defined and formatted using a Cascading Style Sheet, a set of formatting characteristics you can apply to text, links, and other page elements. For example, the best way to set a page background color is to modify the background-color code in a style sheet. You will learn more about CSS as you work through each chapter. If you use the Page Properties dialog box to set page properties such as the background color, Dreamweaver automatically creates a style that modifies the HTML tag to include the properties you added.

A strong contrast between the text color and the background color makes it easier for users to read your text. One of the Web Content Accessibility Guidelines (WCAG), Version 2.0, from the World Wide Web Consortium (W3C) states that contrast makes it easier for users to see content. You can choose a light background color with dark text, or a dark background color with light text. A white background with dark text, though not terribly exciting, provides good contrast and is easiest for most users to read.

Another design decision you need to make is whether to change the **default font** and **default link colors**, which are the colors used by the browser to display text, links, and visited links. The default color for **unvisited links**, or links that the user has not clicked yet, is blue. Unvisited links are usually simply called **links**. The default color for **visited links**, or links that have been previously clicked, is purple. You change the text and link colors in the CSS Designer panel. You can choose colors from the color picker, as shown in Figure 1.

Choosing Colors to Convey Information

Before 1994, colors appeared differently on different types of computers. In 1994, Netscape developed the first web-safe color palette, a set of colors that appears consistently in all browsers and on Macintosh, Windows, and UNIX platforms. The evolution of video cards has made this less relevant today, but use of appropriate colors is an important factor in creating accessible pages. Be sure

to use only colors that provide good contrast on your pages. Dreamweaver lets you choose from three color notation schemes: RGBa, HEX, and HSLa. You can use any of the three notations to name a color. You will use HEX values to specify your color choices in the exercises in this book. You select colors using the color picker, shown in Figure 1. You can also type color values directly in your style sheet code in Code view.

Another WCAG guideline states that color should never be the only visual means of conveying information. For example, don't refer to a page object solely by the color, like the "red" box.

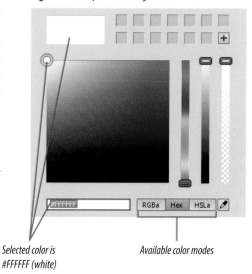

Figure 1 *Color picker showing color modes*

Selected color is #FFFFFF (white)

Available color modes

DESIGN TIP

Making Pages Accessible

Not all of your users will have perfect vision and hearing or full use of both hands. There are several techniques you can use to ensure that your website is accessible to individuals with disabilities. These techniques include using text alternatives for any non-text content, making text readable and understandable, and providing ways to help users navigate through the site easily. Adobe provides information about website compliance with Section 508 accessibility guidelines. To learn more, visit the Adobe website at www.adobe.com/accessibility/. Here you will find suggestions for creating accessible websites, an explanation of Section 508 and **VPAT** (Voluntary Product Accessibility Template). VPAT is a document that lists how an app such as Dreamweaver CC complies with Section 508 provisions and information on how people with disabilities use assistive devices to navigate the Internet.

The World Wide Web Consortium (W3C) provides the Web Content Accessibility Guidelines (WCAG) 2.0 as the standard for designing sites that are accessible to users of all abilities. These guidelines are published at www.w3.org. To learn the rationale behind creating accessible web sites, go to http://www.webaim.org and locate the article called "Constructing a POUR Website"; **POUR** stands for Perceivable, Operable, Understandable, and Robust. The WebAIM site also has a free tool called the **WAVE** (Web Accessibility Evaluation Tool). Simply type in a URL or upload a file to test for accessibility.

Edit a page title

1. Start Dreamweaver, select the **Site list arrow** on the Files panel, then select **The Striped Umbrella** if necessary.

2. Double-click **index.html** in the Files panel to open The Striped Umbrella home page.

   The page title The Striped Umbrella appears in the Title text box in the Document toolbar.

3. Click after the end of The Striped Umbrella text in the Title text box in the Document toolbar, press **[Spacebar]**, type **beach resort and spa, Ft. Eugene, Florida,** press **[Enter]** (Win) or **[return]** (Mac), then click in the title text box.

   Compare your screen with Figure 2. The new title is better, because it incorporates the words "beach resort" and "spa" and the location of the resort—words that potential customers might use as keywords when using a search engine.

TIP To view hidden text in the Title box, click in the title and scroll using the left and right keyboard arrow keys.

You opened The Striped Umbrella website, opened the home page, and changed the page title.

Figure 2 *The new title appears in the Title text box*

Click in the title and scroll
with an arrow key to see
the rest of the title

DESIGNTIP

Designing Appropriate Content for Your Target Audience

When you begin developing the content for your website, you need to decide what content to include and how to arrange each element on each page. Design the content with the target audience in mind. What is the age group of your audience? What reading level is appropriate? Should you use a formal or informal tone? Should the pages be simple, consisting mostly of text, or rich with images and media files? Evaluate the font sizes, the number and size of images and animations, the reading level, and the amount of technical expertise necessary to navigate your site, and make sure they fit your audience. Usually, the first page that your audience will see when they visit your site is the home page. Design the home page so that users will understand your site's purpose and feel comfortable finding their way around your site's pages.

To ensure that users do not get "lost" in your site, design all the pages with a consistent look and feel. You can use templates and Cascading Style Sheets to maintain a common look for each page. **Templates** are web pages that contain the basic layout for each page in the site, such as the location of a company logo or a menu of buttons.

Figure 3 *Insert panel displaying the Common category*

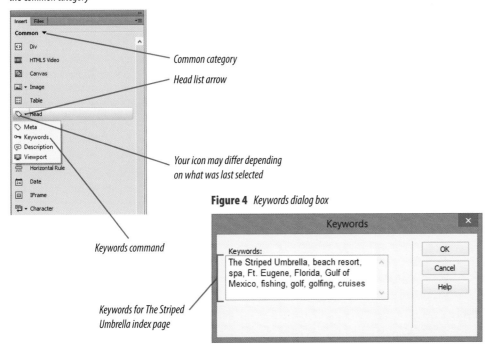

Common category

Head list arrow

Your icon may differ depending on what was last selected

Keywords command

Keywords for The Striped Umbrella index page

Figure 4 *Keywords dialog box*

Enter keywords

1. Select the **Insert panel list arrow**, then on the dropdown menu, select the **Common category** (if it is not already selected).

2. Select the **Head list arrow**, as shown in Figure 3, then select **Keywords**.

TIP Some buttons on the Insert panel include a list arrow indicating that there is a menu of choices available. The button that you selected last will appear on the Insert panel until you select another.

3. Type **The Striped Umbrella**, **beach resort**, **spa**, **Ft. Eugene**, **Florida**, **Gulf of Mexico**, **fishing**, **golf**, **golfing**, **cruises** in the Keywords text box, as shown in Figure 4, then select **OK**.

You added keywords relating to the resort to the head content of The Striped Umbrella home page.

DESIGNTIP

Entering Keywords and Descriptions

Search engines use keywords, descriptions, and titles to find pages based on search terms a user enters. Therefore, it is important to anticipate the search terms your potential users would use and include these words in the keywords, description, and title. Many search engines display page titles and descriptions in their search results. Some search engines limit the number of keywords that they will index, so make sure you list the most important keywords first. Keep your keywords and descriptions short and concise to ensure that all search engines will include your site. To choose effective keywords, many designers use focus groups to learn which words potential customers or clients might use. A **focus group** is a marketing tool that asks a group of people for feedback about a product, such as the impact of a television ad or the effectiveness of a website design.

Enter a description

1. Select the **Head list arrow** on the Insert panel, then select **Description**.

2. In the Description text box, type **The Striped Umbrella is a full-service resort and spa just steps from the Gulf of Mexico in Ft. Eugene**, **Florida**.

   Your screen should resemble Figure 5.

3. Select **OK**.

4. Select the **Show Code view button** `Code` on the Document toolbar, then click on the page to deselect the text, if necessary.

   The title, keywords, and description tags appear in the HTML code in the document window, as shown in Figure 6. The code in Figure 6 has been collapsed between lines 10 and 27 to display the title, keywords, and description tags. Your line numbers may differ, but should all fall between the <head> tags.

TIP You can enter and edit the title tag and the meta tags directly in the code in Code view.

5. Click the **Show Design view button** `Design` to return to Design view.

You added a description of The Striped Umbrella resort to the head content of the home page. You then viewed the page in Code view and located the head content in the HTML code.

Figure 5 *Description dialog box*

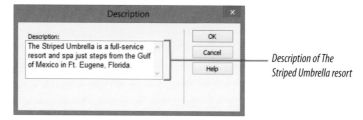

Description of The
Striped Umbrella resort

Figure 6 *Head content displayed in Code view*

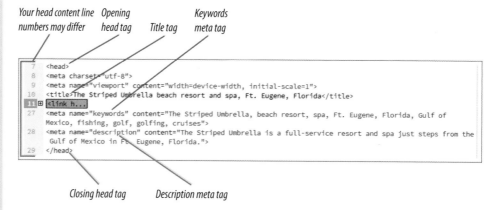

Your head content line numbers may differ · Opening head tag · Title tag · Keywords meta tag

Closing head tag · Description meta tag

Using Descriptions for POWDER Authentication

A website description can be stored in an XML file to provide POWDER authentication. **XML** stands for Extensible Markup Language, a type of file that is used to develop customized tags to store information. **POWDER** is the acronym for **Protocol for Web Description Resources**. This is an evaluation system for web pages developed with the World Wide Web Consortium (W3C) that provides summary information about a website. Examples include the date the site was created, the name of the person or company responsible for the content on the site, and a description of the content. It is designed to help users determine if a site would be considered a trustworthy resource of value and interest. It replaces the previous system called PICS, or Platform for Internet Content Selection.

Figure 7 *Resizing the CSS Designer panel*

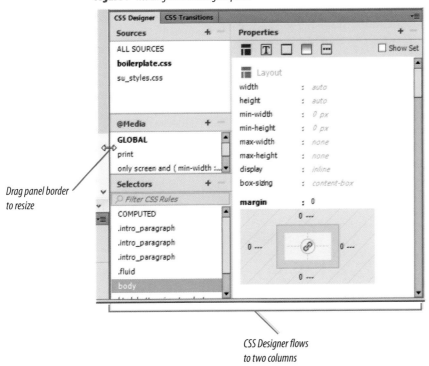

Drag panel border
to resize

CSS Designer flows
to two columns

Expand the CSS Designer panel

1. Place the pointer over the CSS Designer panel group title bar, then drag it to the Document window to float it.

2. Place your pointer over the left side of the panels, then drag to increase the width of the panels until the CSS Designer panel flows into two columns, as shown in Figure 7.

   It is much easier to use CSS Designer if you spread it over a two-column layout. There will be no instructions in this book to dock the CSS Designer, but you may keep it docked if you prefer.

   TIP Resize any docked panels in Dreamweaver by dragging a left panel border to the right or left to decrease or increase the width of the panels.

3. Select the Files panel tab if necessary, then notice that with the CSS Designer panel floated, the Files panel can show all of the website files without scrolling.

   The Insert panel also has room to show all commands without scrolling.

   (continued)

Understanding CSS Designer

The new CSS Designer panel lets you create and set properties for styles used to position and format page content across a website. Depending on the size of the Dreamweaver program and Document windows, CSS Designer will appear in one or two columns. The two-column layout is easier to use. The CSS Designer panel is divided into four panes: Sources, @Media, Selectors, and Properties. The Sources pane lists the style sheet files used to format the website pages. The @Media pane lists the device categories that could be used to view the pages, such as mobile and tablet sizes. The Selectors pane lists the selectors that are included in the style sheet highlighted in the Sources pane and @Media pane. The Properties pane lists the properties of the highlighted selector in the Selectors pane.

---

4. Select **su_styles.css** in the Sources pane, then select **.fluid** in the Selectors pane.

The Properties pane now displays the properties and values for the .fluid style. The .fluid style is used to position and format the page content, including the page background.

5. Scroll down the Properties pane in the right column until you see the Background category, then select the **Set background color box** next to the background-color property, as shown in Figure 8.

The color picker opens, as shown in Figure 9, and you see that the current background color is white. The color value for white is shown as a hexadecimal: #FFFFFF.

(continued)

Figure 8 *The background-color value for the .fluid style*

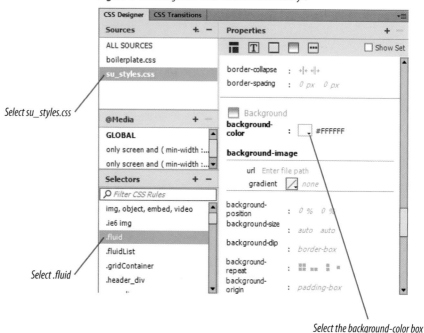

Select su_styles.css

Select .fluid

Select the background-color box

Understanding Hexadecimal Values

Each color is assigned a **hexadecimal RGB value**, a value that represents the amount of red, green, and blue present in the color. For example, white, which is made of equal parts of red, green, and blue, has a hexadecimal value of FFFFFF. This is also called an RGB triplet in hexadecimal format (or a **hex triplet**). Each pair of characters in the hexadecimal value represents the red, green, and blue values. The hexadecimal number system is based on 16, rather than 10 in the decimal number system. Because the hexadecimal number system includes only numbers up to 9, values after 9 use the letters of the alphabet. "A" represents the number 10 in the hexadecimal number system. "F" represents the number 15. The hexadecimal values can be entered in the code using a form of shorthand that shortens the six characters to three characters when the color is represented by three repeating numbers. For instance: FFFFFF become FFF; 0066CC becomes 06C. The number value for a color is preceded by a pound sign (#) in HTML code.

Figure 9 *The color picker*

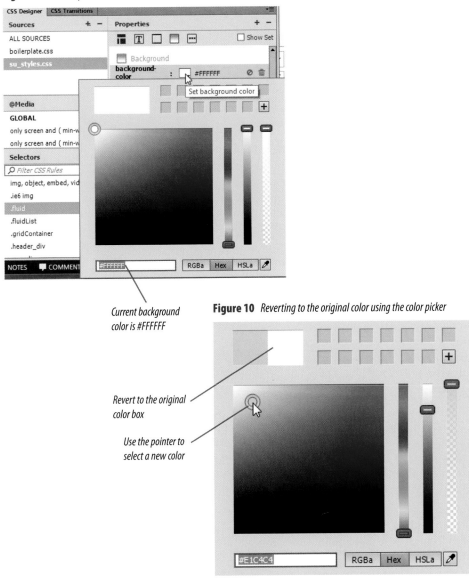

Current background
color is #FFFFFF

Figure 10 *Reverting to the original color using the color picker*

Revert to the original
color box

Use the pointer to
select a new color

6. Select a different color in the color picker, then click in the Document window to close the color picker.

   The page background changes to the new color you selected.

7. Select the **Set background color box** again, then type **#FFFFFF** in the Color value text box.

   The page background changes back to white.

TIP You can also use the Revert to the original color box, as shown in Figure 10, to change a color back to the original color as long as you do not close the color picker after you select the new color.

8. Click in the Design view window to close the color picker.

9. Select **boilerplate.css** in the CSS Designer Source pane, select **GLOBAL** in the @Media pane, then select **body** in the Selectors pane.

10. Select the **background-color property** in the Properties pane, select the **Remove CSS Property button** 🗑, select **File** on the Menu bar, then select **Save All** to save your work.

    Removing this property will allow the .fluid selector's white page background property to format the background.

TIP When making changes to related files, such as a style sheet, use the File, Save All command to be sure all files that may have been changed are saved.

You edited the .fluid selector in the su_styles.css file to add a white page background, then removed the page property in the boilerplate.css file to prevent a potential style conflict.

Create, Import,
AND FORMAT TEXT

What You'll Do

In this lesson, you will create a new page to replace the blank spa page, enter and format text, import text, set text properties, and check the spelling on the Striped Umbrella home page.

Creating and Importing Text

Most information in web pages is presented in the form of text. You can type text directly on a page in Dreamweaver, import, or copy and paste it from another software program. (Macintosh users do not have the option to import text. They must open a text file, copy the text, then paste it into an HTML document.) When using a Windows computer to import text from a Microsoft Word file, it's best to use the Import Word Document command. Not only will the formatting be preserved, but Dreamweaver will generate clean HTML code. **Clean HTML code** is code that does what it is supposed to do without using unnecessary instructions, which take up memory.

When you format text, it is important to keep in mind that your site users must have the same fonts installed on their computers as the fonts you use. Otherwise, the text might appear incorrectly. To avoid font compatibility and accessibly issues, you can use TypeKit, a company acquired by Adobe in 2011, that provides access to web fonts through the Adobe Creative Cloud. TypeKit offers fonts called Adobe Edge Web fonts through a subscription-based service that can be read correctly by all browsers and devices. TypeKit

is part of your Creative Cloud subscription. Creative Cloud users have access to most of the fonts on TypeKit at no additional charge.

> **QUICK TIP**
>
> To learn more about TypeKit, go to typekit.com.

If text does not have a font specified, the default font on the user's computer will be used to display the text. Keep in mind that some fonts might not appear the same on both a Windows and a Macintosh computer. The way fonts are **rendered** (drawn) on the screen differs because Windows and Macintosh computers use different technologies to render them. If you are not using embedded fonts, it is wise to stick to the standard fonts that work well with both systems. Test your pages using both operating systems.

Formatting Text Two Ways: HTML vs. CSS

Because text is more difficult and tiring to read on a computer screen than on a printed page, you should make the text in your website attractive and easy to read. One way to do this is to format text by changing its font, size, and color. Previously web designers used the Property inspector to apply formatting attributes, such as font type, size, color, alignment, and indents. This created HTML tags in the code that directed the way the fonts would appear in a browser. **Tags** are the parts of the code that specify the appearance for all page content when viewed in a browser.

Today, the accepted method is to create Cascading Style Sheets (CSS) to format and place web page elements. **Cascading Style Sheets** are sets of formatting attributes that you use to format web pages to provide a consistent presentation for content across the site. Cascading Style Sheets make it easy to separate page content from the page design. The content is placed in the body section on web pages, and the styles are placed in either an external style sheet file or in the page head content. Separating content from design is preferable because editing content and formatting content are two separate tasks. So when you use CSS styles, you can update or change the page content without disturbing the page formatting.

You can apply some formatting without creating styles by using the Bold and Italic HTML tags. You can also use HTML heading tags, which determine the relative size and boldness of text, and which help to show the importance of text relative to the rest of the text on the page.

To apply CSS or HTML formatting, you use the Property inspector, which has a panel for each method: the CSS Property inspector and the HTML Property inspector. You display them by clicking the CSS or the HTML button on the left side of the Property inspector. Some coding options are unique to each one and some are available on both. For instance, HTML heading tags are only available on the HTML Property inspector. Font tags are only available on the CSS Property inspector. Regardless of which Property inspector you use, CSS styles will be created when you format page objects.

Because CSS is a lot to learn when you are just beginning, we are going to begin by using a few HTML tags for formatting. Then in Chapter 3, we will use the preferred method, CSS.

Changing Fonts

You can format your text with different fonts by choosing a font combination from the Font list in the CSS Property inspector. A **Font-combination** is a set of font choices that specify which fonts a browser should use to display the text on your web page. Font combinations ensure that if one font is not available, the browser will use the next one specified in the font combination. For example, if text is formatted with the font combination Arial, Helvetica, sans serif, the browser will first look on the user's system for Arial. If Arial is not available, then it will look for Helvetica. If Helvetica is not available, then it will look for a sans-serif font to apply to the text. Using fonts within the default settings is wise, because fonts set outside the default settings might not be available on all users' computers. Remember that TypeKit has greatly expanded your font choices with the ability to embed new fonts into web pages.

Changing Font Sizes

There are two ways to change the size of text using the Property inspector. When the CSS option is selected, you can select a numerical value for the size from 9 to 36 pixels (or type a smaller or larger number). Or you can use a size expressed in words from xx-small to larger, which sets the size of selected text relative to other text on the page. Font sizes are not available on the HTML Property inspector.

Formatting Paragraphs

The HTML Property inspector lets you format blocks of text as paragraphs or as different sizes of headings. To format a paragraph as a heading, click anywhere in the paragraph, and then select the heading size you want from the Format list in the HTML Property inspector. The Format list contains six different heading formats. Heading 1 is the largest size, and Heading 6 is the smallest size. Browsers display text formatted as headings in bold, setting them off from paragraphs of text. It is considered good practice to use headings because they give users an idea of the importance of the heading relative to other text on the page. Text with a level 1 heading would be at a higher importance level than text with a level 2 heading. You can also align paragraphs with the alignment buttons on the CSS Property inspector and indent paragraphs using the Blockquote and Remove Blockquote buttons on the HTML Property inspector. It is better practice, however, to use styles to align text.

Enter text

1. Position the insertion point directly after "want to go home." at the end of the paragraph, press **[Enter]** (Win) or **[return]** (Mac), then type **The Striped Umbrella**.

   Pressing [Enter] (Win) or [return] (Mac) creates a new paragraph.

   TIP If the new text does not assume the formatting attributes as the paragraph above it, click the Show Code and Design views button Split , position the insertion point right after the period after "home", then go back to the page in Design view and insert a new paragraph.

2. Press and hold **[Shift]**, press **[Enter]** (Win) or **[return]** (Mac), then type **25 Beachside Drive**.

   Pressing and holding [Shift] while you press [Enter] (Win) or [return] (Mac) creates a line break. A line break places a new line of text on the next line down without creating a new paragraph. Line breaks are useful when you want to add a new line of text directly below the current line of text and keep the same formatting.

3. Add the following text below the 25 Beachside Drive text, using line breaks after each line:

   Ft. Eugene, Florida 33775

   555-594-9458

4. Compare your screen with Figure 11. Your lines may wrap differently depending on your Document window size.

   You entered text for the address and telephone number on the home page.

Figure 11 *Entering the address and telephone number on The Striped Umbrella home page*

Come enjoy the best of both worlds, a secluded sandy beach populated with beautiful birds, yet a short drive down the road from world-class shopping, restaurants, and entertainment. Bring a good book and leave your laptop at the office. You won't want to go home.

Pressing [Enter] (Win) or [return] (Mac) creates a new paragraph

The Striped Umbrella
25 Beachside Drive
Ft. Eugene, Florida 33775
555-594-9458

Single-spaced lines created by using line breaks

TABLE 1: HTML FORMATTING TAGS	
HTML tag	**Represents**
<p> </p>	Opening and closing paragraph tag
 	Line break tag (does not require a closing tag)
<em> </em>	Opening and closing italic (emphasis) tag
<strong> </strong>	Opening and closing bold tag
<u> </u>	Opening and closing underline tag

© 2015 Cengage Learning®

Using Keyboard Shortcuts

When working with text, the keyboard shortcuts for Cut, Copy, and Paste are useful. These are [Ctrl][X] (Win) or ⌘ [X] (Mac) for Cut, [Ctrl][C] (Win) or ⌘ [C] (Mac) for Copy, and [Ctrl][V] (Win) or ⌘ [V] (Mac) for Paste. You can view all Dreamweaver keyboard shortcuts using the Keyboard Shortcuts dialog box, which lets you view existing shortcuts for menu commands, tools, or miscellaneous functions, such as copying HTML or inserting an image. You can also create your own shortcuts or assign shortcuts that you are familiar with from using them in other software programs. To view or modify keyboard shortcuts, select the Keyboard Shortcuts command on the Edit menu (Win) or Dreamweaver menu (Mac), then select the shortcut key set you want. Each chapter in this book includes Power User shortcuts, a list of keyboard shortcuts relevant to that chapter.

Figure 12 *Formatting the address on The Striped Umbrella home page*

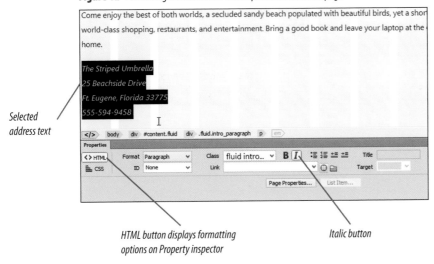

Selected
address text

HTML button displays formatting
options on Property inspector

Italic button

Figure 13 *Viewing the HTML code for the address and phone number*

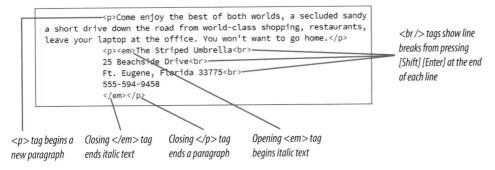

*
 tags show line
breaks from pressing
[Shift] [Enter] at the end
of each line*

*<p> tag begins a
new paragraph*

*Closing </em> tag
ends italic text*

*Closing </p> tag
ends a paragraph*

*Opening <em> tag
begins italic text*

Format text

1. Select the entire address and telephone number, then select the **HTML button** <> HTML in the Property inspector (if it is not already selected) to change to the HTML Property inspector, as shown in Figure 12.

2. Select the **Italic button** *I* in the Property inspector to italicize the text, then click after the text to deselect it.

3. Select the **Show Code view button** Code to view the HTML code, as shown in Figure 13.

   It is always helpful to learn what the HTML code means. Refer to Table 1 to locate some basic HTML formatting tags. As you edit and format your pages, read the code to see how it appears for each element. The more familiar you are with the code, the more comfortable you will feel with Dreamweaver and web design. A strong knowledge of HTML is a necessary skill for professional web designers.

4. Select the **Show Design view button** Design to return to Design view.

5. Save your work.

You changed the Property inspector options from CSS to HTML, then formatted the address and phone number for The Striped Umbrella by changing the font style to italic.

Add an image to a new page

1. Select **File** on the Menu bar, select **Save As**, then type **spa** in the File name text box.

2. Select **Save**, then select **Yes** (Win) or **Replace** (Mac) to overwrite the existing blank spa page.

   The new spa page is identical to the index page. You will replace the content from the index page with content for the spa page. Meanwhile, the formatting will remain identical to give a consistent look between these two pages.

3. Close the index page, select all of the text on the spa page except the address lines, phone number, and footer, then delete it. See Figure 14.

4. Place the insertion point in front of the first address line, select the **Insert panel menu**, select **Common** if necessary, select the **Image list arrow**, then click **Image**.

5. Browse to and open the Chapter 2 data files assets folder, select **sea_spa_logo.png**, select **OK** (Win) or **Open** (Mac), then verify that sea_spa_logo.png has been copied to the assets folder in the Files panel.

   The logo appears on the page, as shown in Figure 15.

   TIP You can also drag an image from the Files panel onto the page if it is already saved in the local site folder.

6. With the logo selected, type **The Sea Spa logo** in the Alt text box on the Property inspector, as shown in Figure 15.

   You will learn more about accessibility attributes for images in Chapter 4.

   (continued)

Figure 14 *Creating a new HTML document from an existing page*

The only remaining text is the
address information and the footer

Figure 15 *Inserting an image on a page*

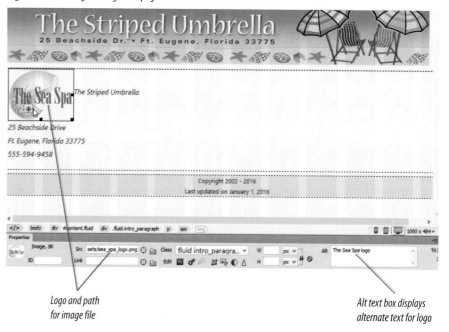

Logo and path
for image file

Alt text box displays
alternate text for logo

Figure 16 *Image file added to the Striped Umbrella assets folder*

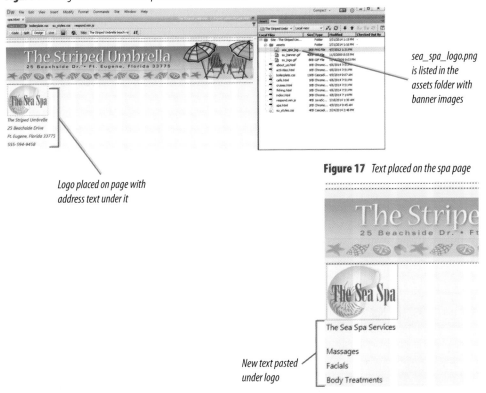

sea_spa_logo.png is listed in the assets folder with banner images

Logo placed on page with address text under it

Figure 17 *Text placed on the spa page*

New text pasted under logo

7. Click to place the insertion point to the immediate right of the logo image, press **[Enter]** (Win) or **[Return]** (Mac) to force the text under the image, if necessary, then save your work.

A copy of the sea_spa_logo.png file appears in the assets folder, along with the banner images, as shown in Figure 16.

You created a new file from the index page file to replace the blank spa file, then deleted existing text and inserted the spa logo under the banner image, which automatically saved it in the site assets folder.

Copy and paste text

1. Open your file management program, navigate to the **chapter_2 folder** from the location where you store your Data Files, then open the file **spa.txt**.

Notepad (Win) or TextEdit (Mac) opens to display the text file.

2. Select all of the text, copy it, then close Notepad (Win) or TextEdit (Mac).

3. Return to Dreamweaver, click to place the insertion point to the right of the spa logo, then press **[Enter]** (Win) or **[return]** (Mac) to create a paragraph break.

4. Select **Edit** on the Menu bar, then select **Paste**.

The text is pasted under the spa logo, as shown in Figure 17.

You copied text and pasted it on the spa page.

Choosing Filenames for Web Pages

When you choose a name for a web page, you should use a short, simple descriptive name that reflects the contents of the page. For example, if the page is about your company's products, you could name it products.html. You should also follow some general rules for naming web pages, such as naming the home page index.html. Most file servers look for the file named index.html or default.html to use as the initial page for a website. Do not use spaces, special characters, or punctuation in filenames for files or folders that you will use in your site. Use underscores rather than spaces for readability; for example: use sea_spa_logo.png rather than sea spa logo.png. Just to be totally safe for all file servers, use only letters, numbers, or underscores in file or folder names. Many designers also avoid the use of uppercase letters.

Set text properties

1. Scroll up the page and select the text **The Sea Spa Services**.

2. Select the **Format list arrow** in the HTML Property inspector, then select **Heading 1**.

   The Heading 1 format is applied to the paragraph. Even a single word is considered a paragraph if there is a paragraph break (also known as a hard return) after it. The HTML code for a Heading 1 tag is <h1>. The tag is then closed with </h1>. For headings, the level of the heading tag follows the h, so the code for a Heading 2 tag is <h2>.

3. Select the text **Massages**, **Facials**, and **Body Treatments**, select the **Format list arrow** in the HTML Property inspector, select **Heading 2**, then click outside the heading to deselect the text.

   The H1 and H2 tags make the text a little large for the page, but it is more in keeping with semantic markup to begin with level 1 headings and work down. Semantic markup means coding to emphasize meaning. You can change the size of the text for each heading using style sheets if you want to change the default settings. We will do this in Chapter 3.

4. Click after the word "Treatments", if necessary, select the **Show Code and Design views button** Split on the Document toolbar, then compare your screen to Figure 18.

   The word "Massages" after the words "Body Treatments" may be in a different position on your screen. Figure 18 was sized down, so your page will be wider than the figure shows.

   (continued)

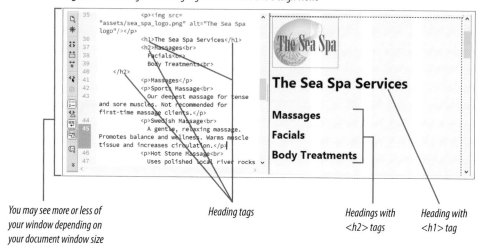

Figure 18 *Viewing the heading tags in Show Code and Design views*

You may see more or less of your window depending on your document window size

Heading tags

Headings with <h2> tags

Heading with <h1> tag

Importing and Linking Microsoft Office Documents (Windows)

Adobe makes it easy to transfer data between Microsoft Office documents and Dreamweaver web pages. When importing a Word or Excel document, select File on the Menu bar, point to Import, then select either Word Document or Excel Document. Select the file you want to import, then select the Formatting list arrow to choose among importing Text only; Text with structure (paragraphs, lists, and tables); Text, structure, basic formatting (bold, italic); or Text, structure, full formatting (bold, italic, styles) before you select Open. The option you choose depends on the importance of the original structure and formatting. Always use the Clean Up Word HTML command from the Commands menu after importing a Word file.

You can also create a link to a Word or Excel document on your web page. To do so, browse to locate the Word or Excel document you want to add as a link, then drag the file name to the location on the page where you would like the link to appear. (If the document is located outside the site, you can browse for it using the Site list arrow on the Files panel, File Explorer, or Mac Finder.) Next, select the Create a link option button in the Insert Document dialog box, then save the file in your site root folder so it will be uploaded when you publish your site. If it is not uploaded, the link will be broken.

Figure 19 *Check Spelling dialog box*

Select "Change" to
correct spelling

Checking for Spelling Errors

It is important to check for spelling and grammatical errors before publishing a page. A page that is published with errors will likely cause the user to judge the site as unprofessional and carelessly made, and to question the accuracy of the page content. If you have text in a word processing file that you plan to import into Dreamweaver, check the spelling in the word processor first. Then check the spelling in the imported text again in Dreamweaver. This allows you to add words such as proper names to the Dreamweaver dictionary so the program will not flag them again. Select the Add to Personal button in the Check Spelling dialog box to add a new word to the dictionary. Even though you might have checked a page using the Check Spelling feature, you still must proofread the content yourself to catch usage errors such as misuse of "to," "too," and "two."

TIP If your <h1> tag is before the image tag rather than before "The Sea Spa Services" heading, cut and paste it to match the code in Figure 18.

You applied two heading formats, then viewed the HTML code.

Check spelling

1. Select the **Show Design view button** Design to return to Design view.

2. Place the insertion point in front of the text "The Sea Spa Services".

    It is a good idea to start a spelling check at the top of the document because Dreamweaver searches from the insertion point down. If your insertion point is in the middle of the document, you will receive a message asking if you want to check the rest of the document. Starting from the beginning saves time.

3. Select **Commands** on the Menu bar, then select **Check Spelling**.

    The word "masage" is highlighted on the page as a misspelled word and suggestions are listed to correct it in the Check Spelling dialog box, as shown in Figure 19.

4. Select **massage.** in the Suggestions list if necessary, then select **Change**.

    The word is corrected on the page. If the Check Spelling dialog box highlights "exfoliating" select Ignore. If it stops on any other correctly spelled words, select Ignore.

5. Select **OK** to close the Dreamweaver dialog box stating that the Spelling Check is completed.

6. Save and close the spa page.

You checked the spa page for spelling errors.

Add Links
TO WEB PAGES

What You'll Do

 In this lesson, you will open the home page and add links to the About Us, Spa, Cafe, and Activities pages. You will then insert an email link at the bottom of the page.

Adding Links to Web Pages

Links, or hyperlinks, provide the real power for web pages. Links make it possible for users to navigate all the pages in a website and to connect to other pages anywhere on the web. Users are more likely to return to websites that have a user-friendly navigation structure. Users also enjoy websites that have interesting links to other web pages or other websites.

To add links to a web page, first select the text or image that you want to serve as a link, and then, in the Link text box in the Property inspector, specify a path to the page to which you want to link.

When you create links on a web page, it is important to avoid **broken links**, or links that cannot find their intended destinations. You can accidentally cause a broken link by typing the incorrect address for the link in the Link text box. Broken links can also be caused by companies merging, going out of business, or simply moving their website addresses.

In addition to adding links to your pages, you should provide a **point of contact**, or a place on a web page that provides users with a means of contacting the company. A common point of contact is a **mailto: link**, which is an email address that users with questions or problems can use to contact someone at the company's headquarters.

Using Menu Bars

A **menu bar**, or **navigation bar**, is an area on a web page that contains links to the main pages of a website. Menu bars are usually located at the top or side of each page in a website and can be created with text, images, or a combination of the two. Menu bars are the backbone of a website's navigation structure, which includes all navigation aids for moving around a website. To make navigating a website as easy as possible, you should place menu bars in the same position on each page. The web page in Figure 20 shows a menu bar that contains a set of main links with additional links that appear when a user moves a mouse pointer over each main link (known as a **rollover**). HTML5 includes code to identify a navigation section of a page with the <nav> HTML tag. You can create a simple menu bar by typing text representing each of your site's pages at the top of your web page, formatting the text, and then adding links to each of the text references. It is always a good idea to provide plain text links like this for accessibility, regardless of the type of navigation structure you choose to use. For example, if you use Javascript for your navigation links, it is a good idea to include a duplicate set of text with links to the same pages. Most websites have links at the bottom of each page for accessing company contact information, copyright, and terms of use statements.

Following WCAG Accessibility for Navigation

The WCAG guidelines list ways to ensure that all users can successfully and easily navigate a website. It states: "Provide ways to help users navigate, find content, and determine where they are." Suggestions include limiting the number of links on a page, using techniques to allow users to quickly access different sections of a page, and making sure that links are readable and easily distinguishable.

Figure 20 *The CIA website*

Source: Central Intelligence Agency

Create a menu bar

1. Open **index.html**.

2. Place the insertion point in front of the word "Welcome" in the first paragraph.

3. Select the **Structure category** in the Insert panel, then select **Navigation**.

   The Insert Navigation dialog box opens.

4. Select the list arrow in the Class list box, then select **intro_paragraph**.

   The intro_paragraph style is the same style used in the three paragraphs.

5. Verify that the Insert as Fluid Element check box is checked, as shown in Figure 21, then select **OK**.

   A new section is created on the page, as shown in Figure 22. This section will be coded as an HTML5 navigation element.

6. Select the placeholder text if necessary, then type Home - About Us - Spa - Cafe - Activities, as shown in Figure 23.

TIP Be careful not to delete the HTML tags around the placeholder text. Backspace over the placeholder text if necessary to prevent deleting the tags, even leaving one letter as a temporary placeholder, then deleting it.

TIP An asterisk after the filename in the title bar indicates that you have altered the page since you last saved it. After you save your work, the asterisk no longer appears.

You inserted code to identify an HTML5 navigation element.

Figure 21 *The Insert Navigation dialog box*

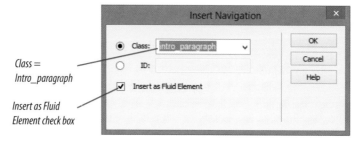

Class = Intro_paragraph

Insert as Fluid Element check box

Figure 22 *Viewing the navigation placeholder text*

This is the content for Layout Nav Tag "intro_paragraph"

Welcome to The Striped Umbrella — a full-service resort and spa just steps from the Gulf of Mexico and ten miles east of Crab Key, Florida. The Striped Umbrella has a variety of activities for adults and children. It is a perfect romantic getaway for two or a complete family vacation. Our activities include water sports, golf, shopping, and an award-winning spa.

Placeholder text

Figure 23 *HTML5 links added to page*

Home - About Us - Spa - Cafe - Activities

Welcome to The Striped Umbrella — a full-service resort and spa just steps from the Gulf of Mexico and ten miles east of Crab Key, Florida. The Striped Umbrella has a variety of activities for adults and children. It is a perfect romantic getaway for two or a complete family vacation. Our activities include water sports, golf, shopping, and an award-winning spa.

New navigation text

Figure 24 *Selecting text for the Home link*

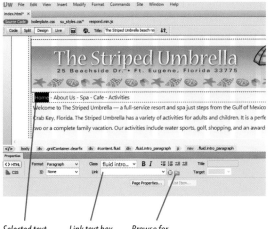

Selected text   Link text box   Browse for
File button

Figure 25 *Select File dialog box*

Striped Umbrella
local site folder

index.html page

Relative to: menu
box

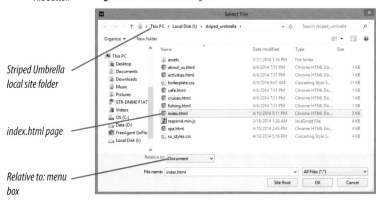

Figure 26 *Links added to menu bar*

Menu bar
with links
added

Add links to web pages

1. Double-click **Home** to select it, as shown in Figure 24.

2. Select the **Browse for File button** 📄 next to the Link text box in the HTML Property inspector, then navigate to the striped_umbrella local site folder if necessary.

3. Verify that the link is set **Relative to Document** in the Relative to: list.

4. Select **index.html** as shown in Figure 25, select **OK** (Win) or **Open** (Mac), then click anywhere on the page to deselect Home.

TIP   Your file listing might differ depending on your view settings.

Home now appears in blue with an underline, indicating it is a link. If users select the Home link, a new page will not open, because the link is on the home page. It might seem odd to create a link to the same page on which the link appears, but this will be helpful when you copy the menu bar to other pages in the site. Always provide users a link to the home page.

5. Repeat Steps 1–4 to create links for About Us, Spa, Cafe, and Activities to their corresponding pages in the striped_umbrella site folder.

6. When you finish adding the links that link to the other four pages, deselect all, then compare your screen to Figure 26.

You created a link for each of the five menu bar elements to their respective web pages in The Striped Umbrella website.

Create an email link

1. Place the insertion point after the last digit in the telephone number, then insert a line break.

2. Select **Email Link** in the Common category on the Insert panel to insert an email link.

3. Type **Club Manager** in the Text text box, type **manager@stripedumbrella.com** in the Email text box, as shown in Figure 27, then select **OK** to close the Email Link dialog box.

TIP If the text does not retain the formatting from the previous line, use the Edit, Undo command to undo Steps 1–3. Switch to Code view and place the insertion point immediately to the right of the telephone number, then repeat the steps in Design view.

4. Save your work.

The text "mailto:manager@stripedumbrella.com" appears in the Link text box in the HTML Property inspector. See Figure 28. When a user clicks this link, a blank email message window opens in the user's default email software, where the user can type a message.

TIP You must enter the correct email address in the Email text box for the link to work. However, you can enter any descriptive name, such as customer service or Bob Smith in the Text text box. You can also enter the email address as the text if you want to show the actual email address on the web page.

You inserted an email link to serve as a point of contact for The Striped Umbrella.

Figure 27 *Email Link dialog box*

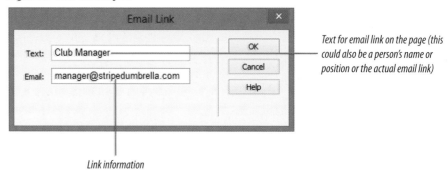

Text for email link on the page (this could also be a person's name or position or the actual email link)

Link information

Figure 28 *mailto: link on the Property inspector*

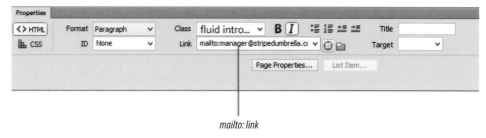

mailto: link

Figure 29 *The Assets panel URLs category*

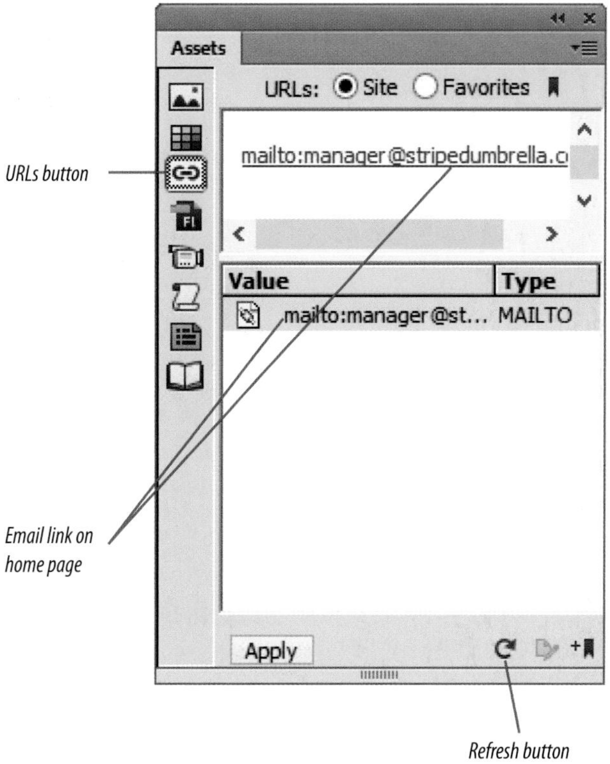

URLs button

Email link on
home page

Refresh button

View the email link in the Assets panel

1. Select **Window** on the Menu bar, then select **Assets**.

   The Assets panel opens.

2. Select the **URLs button** ⊖ to display the URLs in the website.

3. Click the **Refresh button** ⟳ at the bottom of the Assets panel, if necessary, to view the code for the link, then compare your screen to Figure 29.

   URL stands for **Uniform Resource Locator**. The URLs listed in the Assets panel show all of the **external links**, or links pointing outside of the website. An email link is outside the website, so it is an external link. You will learn more about URLs and links in Chapter 5. The links you created to the site pages are internal links (inside the website), and are not listed in the Assets panel.

4. Close the Assets panel.

You viewed the email link on the home page in the Assets panel.

Use the History
PANEL AND EDIT CODE

What You'll Do

In this lesson, you will use the History panel to undo formatting changes you make to the menu bar. You will then use the Code Inspector to view the HTML code for the menu bar, then change the font size for the code. You will also insert a date object and then view it using Code and Design views.

Using the History Panel

Throughout the process of creating a web page, you will make mistakes along the way. Fortunately, you have a tool named the History panel to undo your mistakes. The **History panel** records each editing and formatting task you perform and displays them in a list in the order in which you completed them. Each task listed in the History panel is called a **step**. You can drag the **slider** on the left side of the History panel to undo or redo steps, as shown in Figure 30. You can also click in the bar to the left of a step to undo all steps below it. You click the step to select it. By default, the History panel records 20 steps. You can change the number of steps the History panel records in the General category of the Preferences dialog box. However, keep in mind that setting this number too high will

require additional memory and could affect Dreamweaver's performance.

> **QUICK TIP**
>
> Another quick way to undo and redo steps is with the keyboard shortcuts [Control][Z] (undo) and [Control][Y] (redo). The Mac shortcuts are [command][Z] and [command][Y]. However, if you clear the History panel you are also resetting the memory for keyboard shortcuts to that point, so [Control][Z], etc will no longer work for the steps you performed.

Viewing HTML Code in the Code Inspector

If you enjoy writing code, you occasionally might want to make changes to web pages by writing the code rather than using the panels and tools in Design view. Often it is actually easier to make editing or formatting

---

Understanding Other History Panel Features

Dragging the slider up and down in the History panel is a quick way to undo or redo steps. However, the History panel offers much more. It has the capability to "memorize" certain tasks and consolidate them into one command. This is a useful feature for steps that you perform repetitively on web pages. The History panel does not show steps performed in the Files panel or any program-wide changes, such as editing preferences or changing panel arrangements.

corrections in the code. You can view the code in Dreamweaver using Code view, Code and Design views, or the Code Inspector. The **Code Inspector**, shown in Figure 31, is a separate window that displays the current page in Code view. The advantage of using the Code Inspector is that you can see a full-screen view of your page in Design view while viewing the underlying code in a floating window that you can resize and position wherever you want.

You can add advanced features, such as JavaScript functions, to web pages by copying and pasting code from one page to another using the Code Inspector. A **JavaScript** function is a block of code that adds dynamic content such as rollovers or interactive forms to a web page. A rollover is a special effect that changes the appearance of an object when the mouse moves over it.

Figure 30 *The History panel*

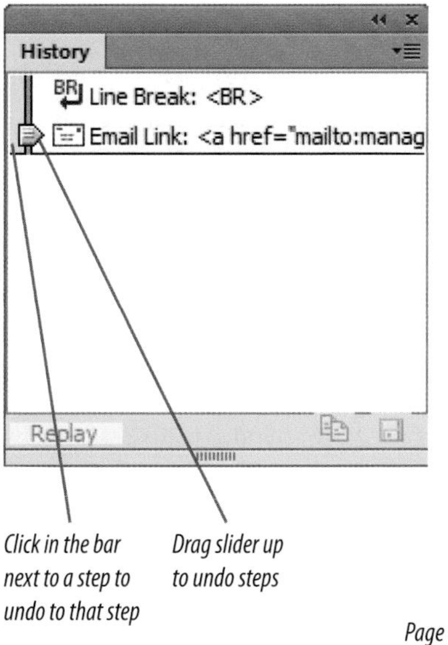

Figure 31 *The Code Inspector*

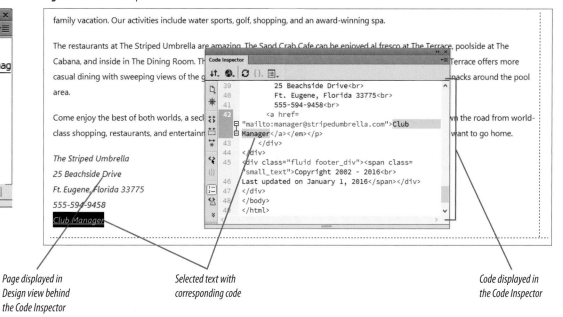

Click in the bar next to a step to undo to that step

Drag slider up to undo steps

Page displayed in Design view behind the Code Inspector

Selected text with corresponding code

Code displayed in the Code Inspector

Use the History panel

1. Select **Window** on the Menu bar, then select **History**.

   The History panel opens and displays steps you have recently performed.

2. Select the **Panel options button**, ≡ select **Clear History**, as shown in Figure 32, then select **Yes** to close the warning box.

3. Select the **five links** in the menu bar on the index page.

   The Property inspector shows the properties of the selected text.

4. Select the **Bold button B** on the Property inspector, select the **Italic button *I***, then compare your Property inspector to Figure 33.

5. Drag the **slider** on the History panel up to the top of the panel, as shown in Figure 34.

   The two steps in the History panel appear gray, indicating that these steps have been undone. The menu bar links are no longer bold or italicized.

6. Right-click (Win) or Control-click (Mac) the **History panel title bar**, then select **Close** to close the History panel.

   You formatted the menu bar made some formatting changes to it, then used the History panel to undo the changes.

Figure 32 *Clearing the History panel*

You may see different steps depending on your keystrokes

Panel options button

Clear History command

Figure 33 *Property inspector settings for menu bar*

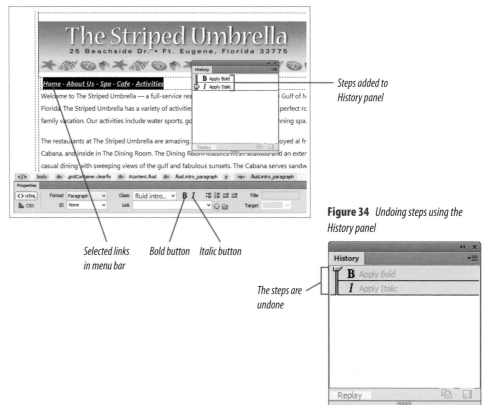

Steps added to History panel

Selected links in menu bar

Bold button   Italic button

Figure 34 *Undoing steps using the History panel*

The steps are undone

Figure 35 *Viewing the View Options menu*

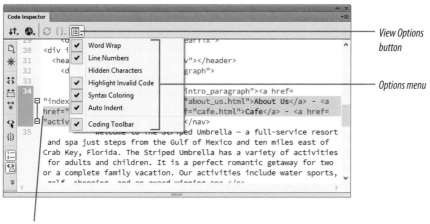

View Options button

Options menu

Code for menu bar

Use the Code Inspector

1. Select the links in the menu bar if necessary, select **Window** on the Menu bar, then select **Code Inspector**.

   Because the menu bar links on the page are selected, the corresponding code is highlighted in the Code Inspector.

   TIP You can also press [F10](Win) or [fn][option][F10] (Mac) to display the Code Inspector.

2. Select the **View Options button** 🔲 on the Code Inspector toolbar to display the View Options menu, then if **Word Wrap** is unchecked, select it once to activate it.

   The Word Wrap feature forces text to stay within the confines of the Code Inspector window, allowing you to read without scrolling sideways.

3. Repeat Step 2 to activate Line Numbers, Highlight Invalid Code, Syntax Coloring, Auto Indent, and Coding Toolbar as shown in Figure 35.

You viewed code in the Code Inspector and set code viewing options.

POWER USER SHORTCUTS	
To do this:	**Use this shortcut:**
Select All	[Ctrl][A] (Win) or ⌘ [A] (Mac)
Copy	[Ctrl][C] (Win) or ⌘ [C] (Mac)
Cut	[Ctrl][X] (Win) or ⌘ [X] (Mac)
Paste	[Ctrl][V] (Win) or ⌘ [V] (Mac)
Line Break	[Shift][Enter] (Win) or [Shift][return] (Mac)
Show or hide the Code Inspector	[F10] (Win) or [fn][option][F10] (Mac)
Preview in browser	[F12] (Win) or [fn][option][F12] (Mac)
Check spelling	[Shift][F7] (Win) or [fn][Shift][F7] (Mac)

© 2015 Cengage Learning®

View HTML5 nav tags

1. Locate the beginning tag for the menu bar, <nav class="fluid intro_paragraph">, as shown in Figure 36.

   The nav tag was added to the menu bar when you used the Insert panel to add a Navigation element in the Structure category. The nav tag is an HTML5 tag that tells screen readers that the text following the opening tag provides navigation links for the site. You will learn more about links and navigation in Chapter 5. Before we look at it, let's change the size of the font for better readability.

2. Select **Edit** on the Menu bar (Win) or **Dreamweaver** (Mac), then select **Preferences**.

3. Select **Fonts** in the Category column, select the **drop-down Size menu** next to Code view, then select **12pt (Medium)**, as shown in Figure 37.

4. Select **Apply**, select **Close** to close the Preferences dialog box, then notice how much easier it is to read the code now, as shown in Figure 38.

   The increased font size will also apply to Code view.

5. Close the Code Inspector.

You read information about the menu bar nav code, then increased the font size for the Code Inspector and Code view.

Figure 36 *Viewing the menu bar code in the Code Inspector*

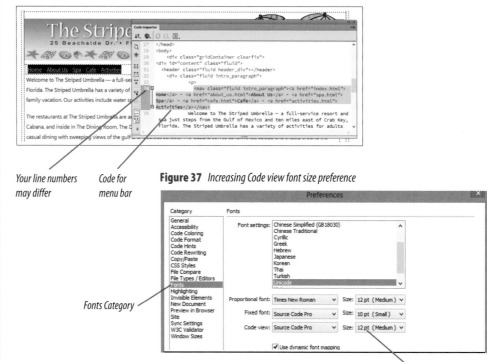

Your line numbers may differ

Code for menu bar

Figure 37 *Increasing Code view font size preference*

Fonts Category

Change font size to 12 pt (Medium)

Figure 38 *The Code inspector with increased font size*

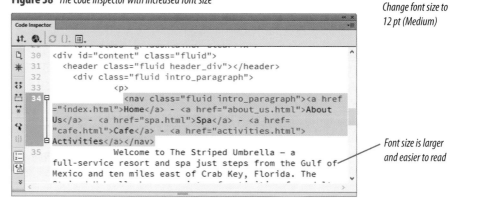

Font size is larger and easier to read

Developing a Web Page

Figure 39 *Insert Date dialog box*

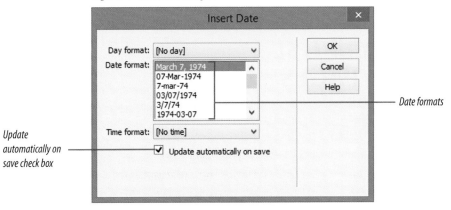

Date formats

Update automatically on save check box

Figure 40 *Viewing the date object code*

Code for date object (deselect the text to see the yellow highlighting)

```
46   Last updated on
47       <!-- #BeginDate format:Am1 -->April
11, 2014<!-- #EndDate -->
48   </span></div>
49   </div>
50   </body>
51   </html>
```

Insert a date object

1. Scroll down the page, if necessary, to select **January 1**, **2016**, then press **[Delete]** (Win) or **[delete]** (Mac).

2. Select **Date** in the Common category in the Insert panel, then select **March 7**, **1974** if necessary in the Date format list.

3. Check the **Update automatically on save check box**, as shown in Figure 39, select **OK**, then deselect the text.

4. Change to Code and Design views.

   The code has changed to reflect the date object, which is set to today's date, as shown in Figure 40. (Your date will be different.) The new code is highlighted with a light yellow background, indicating that it is a date object, automatically coded by Dreamweaver, rather than a date that has been manually typed on the page by the designer or developer.

5. Return to Design view, then save all files.

You inserted a date object that will be updated automatically when you open and save the home page.

Using Smart Design Principles in Web Page Layout

As you view your pages in the browser, take a critical look at the symmetry of the page. Is it balanced? Are there too many images compared to text, or vice versa? Does everything "heavy" seem to be on the top or bottom of the page, or do the page elements seem to balance with the weight evenly distributed between the top, bottom, and sides? Use design principles to create a site-wide consistency for your pages. Horizontal symmetry means that the elements are balanced across the page. Vertical symmetry means that they are balanced down the page. Diagonal symmetry balances page elements along the invisible diagonal line of the page. Radial symmetry runs from the center of the page outward, like the petals of a flower. These principles all deal with balance; however, too much balance is not good, either. Sometimes it adds interest to place page elements a little off center or to have an asymmetric layout. Color, white space, text, and images should all complement each other and provide a natural flow across and down the page. The **rule of thirds**—dividing a page into nine squares like a tic-tac-toe grid—states that interest is increased when your focus is on one of the intersections in the grid. The most important information should be at the top of the page where it is visible without scrolling, or "above the fold," as they say in the newspaper business.

Modify and Test
WEB PAGES

What You'll Do

In this lesson, you will preview the home page in the browser to check for typographical errors, grammatical errors, broken links, and overall appearance. After previewing, you will make slight formatting adjustments to the page to improve its appearance.

Testing and Modifying Web Pages

Testing web pages is a continuous process. You never really finish a website, because there are always additions and corrections to make. As you add and modify pages, you must test each page as part of the development process. The best way to test a web page is to preview it in Live view or in a browser to make sure that all text and image elements appear the way you expect them to. You should also test your links to make sure they work properly. You need to proofread your text to make sure it contains all the necessary information for the page with no typographical or grammatical errors. Designers typically view a page in a browser, return to Dreamweaver to make necessary changes, and then view the page in a browser again. They repeat this process many times before the page is ready for publishing. In fact, it is sometimes difficult to stop making improvements to a page and move on to another project. You need to strike a balance among quality, creativity, and productivity.

Testing a Web Page Using Different Browsers and Screen Sizes

Because users access the Internet using a wide variety of computer systems, it is important to design your pages so that all browsers and screen sizes can display them well. You should test your pages using different browsers and a wide variety of screen sizes to ensure the

DESIGNTIP

Using "Under Construction" or "Come Back Later" Pages

Many people are tempted to insert an unfinished page as a placeholder for a page that they intend to finish later. Rather than have real content, these pages usually contain text or an image that indicates the page is not finished, or "under construction." You should not publish a web page that has a link to an unfinished page. It is frustrating for users to click a link for a page they want to open only to find an "under construction" note or image displayed. You want to make the best possible impression on your users. If you cannot complete a page before publishing it, at least provide enough information on it to make it "worth the trip."

best view of your page by the most people possible. Most web users today use a screen resolution above 1024 by 768. Very few users use a resolution below this, so design your pages for this higher resolution. However, you'll also need to accommodate users who will view your pages with laptops, tablets, and cell phones, so make sure your pages look good at these sizes, as well. To view your page using different screen sizes, select the Mobile size, Tablet size, and Desktop size buttons on the status bar.

To view your pages using several different browsers, select the Preview/Debug in Browser button on the Document toolbar, select Edit Browser List, then use the Add button to add additional browsers installed on your computer to the list. You can also designate which browser to use as the default browser, the browser which opens when you press the F12 key. Remember also to check your pages using Windows and Macintosh platforms. Some page elements such as fonts, colors, table borders, layers, and horizontal rules might not appear consistently in both.

Using Style Sheets for Responsive Design

Most websites today are written using responsive design. **Responsive design** means using style sheets to control how pages look on different devices. For instance, you might design a page with a different banner when it is viewed on a desktop than on a mobile device, as shown in Figure 41.

With the Dreamweaver Fluid Grid Layouts, you can use percents rather than specific measurements to control how large or small page elements appear. **Fluid Grid Layouts** is a tool that uses a combination of style sheets and page elements that work together to adapt page content to flexible column grid layouts: one for mobile devices, one for tablet devices, and one for desktop devices. It is poor design practice not to provide pages that can be viewed and navigated easily whatever size screen is used.

Style sheets are used with **Media Queries** to identify which device is calling up the page, then apply the appropriate code for optimum viewing. When Fluid Grid Layouts and Media Queries are used to create pages, the designer can determine the values to use for each layout: Mobile, Tablet, and Desktop. One style sheet controls the styles for all three devices by providing separate sets of styles for each device. You will build on your understanding of responsive design as you go through each chapter.

Figure 41 *Comparing a desktop design to a mobile design*

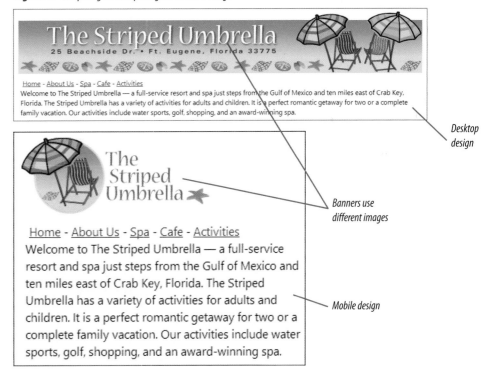

Desktop design

Banners use different images

Mobile design

Modify a web page

1. Select the **Desktop size button** 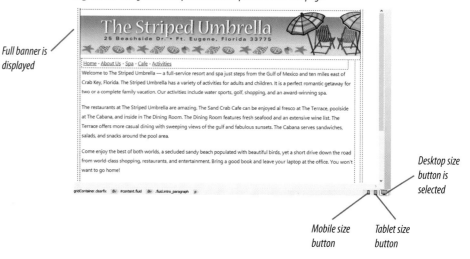 on the status bar to see how the page would appear on a desktop computer using the default desktop settings, as shown in Figure 42.

   A user viewing this page on a desktop will see the full Striped Umbrella banner.

2. Replace the period after the last sentence, "You won't want to go home." with an exclamation point.

3. Select the **Tablet size button** on the Status bar.

   Scroll up if necessary, then notice the page width is narrower and the banner does not display the rightmost umbrella and chair.

4. Select the **Mobile size button** .

   The banner is replaced with a smaller version, as shown in Figure 43.

5. Return to Desktop size, then save your work.

You viewed the home page using three different window sizes and made a simple edit.

Figure 42 *Using the Desktop size button to preview the index page*

Full banner is displayed

Desktop size button is selected

Mobile size button

Tablet size button

Figure 43 *Using the Mobile size button to preview the index page*

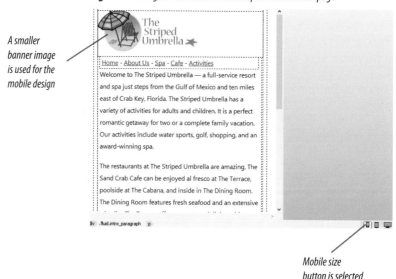

A smaller banner image is used for the mobile design

Mobile size button is selected

Figure 44 *Viewing The Striped Umbrella home page in the Firefox browser*

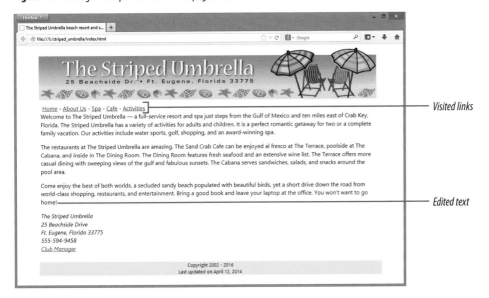

Visited links

Edited text

1. Select the **Preview/Debug in browser button** 🌐 on the Document toolbar, then choose your browser from the menu that opens.

   The Striped Umbrella home page opens in your default browser.

2. Select each link on the menu bar, then after each selection, use the Back button on the browser toolbar to return to the home page.

   Pages with no content at this point will appear as blank pages. Compare your screen to Figure 44. The links in Figure 44 have all been selected, which made them visited links. So they appear in purple rather than blue, the color of unvisited links.

3. Close your browser window, then close all open pages in Dreamweaver.

You viewed The Striped Umbrella home page in your browser and tested each link on the menu bar.

DESIGN TIP

Choosing a Window Size

Today, most users use a screen resolution of 1024 × 768 or higher. Because of this, more content can be displayed at one time on a computer monitor. People tend to use their "screen real estate" in different ways. Some people might use their whole screen to view pages on the Internet. Others might choose to allocate a smaller area of their screen to the browser window. The ideal web page will not be so small that it tries to spread out over a larger screen size or so large that the user has to use horizontal scroll bars to read the page content. The WCAG guideline 1.4.8 states that " … Text can be resized without assistive technology up to 200 percent in a way that does not require the user to scroll horizontally to read a line of text on a full-screen window." Achieving the best balance and meeting accessibility guidelines is one of the design decisions that you must make during the planning process.

Create head content and set page properties.

1. Open the Blooms & Bulbs website.
2. Open the index page.
3. Edit the page title on the Document toolbar so it reads **Blooms & Bulbs - Your Complete Garden Center**.
4. Insert the following keywords: **garden, plants, nursery, flowers, landscape, bulbs, Blooms & Bulbs, Alvin, Texas**.
5. Insert the following description: **Blooms & Bulbs is a premier supplier of plants, trees, and shrubs for both professional and home gardeners**.
6. Switch to Code view to view the HTML code for the head content, then switch back to Design view.
7. Increase the width of the CSS Designer panel to display it across two columns.
8. Select bb_styles.css in the Sources pane, then select .fluid in the Selectors pane.
9. Scroll to find and select the set background color box, then experiment with a different color for the page background.
10. Return the background color to #FFFFFF (white), then save all files.

Create, import, and format text.

1. Create a new paragraph after the second paragraph of text and type the following text, inserting a line break after each line.
    Blooms & Bulbs
    Highway 43 South
    Alvin, Texas 77511
    555-248-0806
2. Verify that the HTML button is selected in the Property inspector, and select it if it is not.
3. Italicize the name, address and phone number lines.
4. Change to Code view to view the formatting code for the italicized text.
5. Return to Design view, then save your work.
6. Save the index page as **tips.html**, overwriting the original blank tips page.
7. Close the index page, select all of the text on the page except the address and phone number lines and footer, then delete it.
8. Place the insertion point in front of the first address line, then use the Image command on the Insert panel to insert the file butterfly.jpg. from the folder where you store your Data Files.
9. With the logo selected, add appropriate alternate text, place the insertion point to the right of the logo, then enter a paragraph break.
10. Open your file management program, navigate to the chapter_2 folder from the location where you store your Data Files, then open the file gardening_tips.txt.
11. Select all of the text, copy it, then close Notepad (Win) or TextEdit (Mac).
12. Return to Dreamweaver, click to place the insertion point to the right of the butterfly logo.
13. Paste the copied text at the insertion point, then save your work.
14. Select the Seasonal Gardening Checklist heading, then use the Property inspector to apply a Heading 1 format.
15. Select the Basic Gardening Tips heading, then apply the Heading 1 format.
16. Place the insertion point at the top of the document, then check the page for spelling errors.
17. Make any necessary corrections, save your work, then close the tips page.

Add links to web pages.

1. Open the index page.
2. Place the insertion point in front of the word "Welcome" in the first paragraph.
3. Use the Structure category in the Insert panel to insert a Fluid Element Navigation element with the Class intro_paragraph.
4. Select the placeholder text if necessary, then type **Home - Featured Plants - Garden Tips - Workshops - Newsletter**. (*Hint*: Be careful not to delete the tags for the menu bar. Backspace over the placeholder text if necessary to prevent deleting the div itself, even leaving one letter as a temporary placeholder, then deleting it.)
5. Use the Property inspector to link Home on the menu bar to the index.html page in the Blooms & Bulbs website.
6. Link Featured Plants on the menu bar to the plants.html page.
7. Link Garden Tips on the menu bar to the tips.html page.
8. Link Workshops on the menu bar to the workshops.html page.
9. Link Newsletter on the menu bar to the newsletter.html page.
10. Create a line break after the telephone number and then use the Insert panel to create an email link, with **Customer Service** as the text and **mailbox@ bloomsandbulbs.com** as the email address. (*Hint:* If your text does not retain the formatting from the previous line, reapply the settings.)

11. Save your work.
12. View the email link in the Assets panel, refreshing it if necessary, then view the Files panel.

Use the History panel and edit code.

1. Open the History panel, then clear its contents.
2. Select the five links in the menu bar.
3. Use the HTML Property inspector to make the link text bold and italic.
4. Use the History panel to remove the bold and italic formatting.
5. Close the History panel.
6. Open the Code Inspector and verify that Word Wrap is selected.
7. View the code for the menu bar links in the Code Inspector, then close the Code Inspector.
8. Delete the current date in the Last updated on statement on the home page and replace it with a date using the March 7, 1974 format that will update automatically when the file is saved.
9. Examine the code for the date at the bottom of the page to verify that the code that forces it to update on save is included in the code. (*Hint:* The code should be highlighted with a light yellow background if it is not selected, or a blue background if it is selected (Win) or gray (Mac).)
10. Return to Design view, then save your work.

Modify and test web pages.

1. View the index page with the Tablet size and Mobile size settings, then return to Desktop size.
2. View the page in your browser. (If you see a message about allowing blocked content, select Allow.)

3. Verify that all links work correctly, then close the browser.
4. On the home page, add the text "**We are happy to deliver or ship your purchases.**" to the end of the first paragraph.

5. Save your work, then view the pages in your browser, comparing your pages to Figure 45 and Figure 46.
6. Close your browser, use Code view to delete any extra spaces between page elements, then save and close all open pages.

Figures 45 & 46 *Completed Skills Review, home page and tips page*

You have been hired to create a website for TripSmart, a travel outfitter. You have created the basic framework for the website and are now ready to format and edit the home page to improve the content and appearance.

1. Open the TripSmart website, then open the home page.
2. Enter the following keywords: **TripSmart, travel, trips, vacations, Fayetteville, Arkansas,** and **tours**.
3. Enter the following description: **TripSmart is a comprehensive travel service. We can help you plan trips, make travel arrangements, and supply you with travel gear.**
4. Change the page title to **TripSmart - Serving all your travel needs.**
5. Use the Insert panel to add an HTML5 menu bar with a class selector name of your choice above the first paragraph with the following text: **Home**, **Catalog**, **Services**, **Tours**, and **Newsletter**. Between each item, use a hyphen with a space on either side to separate the items.
6. Replace the date in the last updated statement with a date that will update automatically on save.
7. Add a paragraph break after the last paragraph, then type the following address, using line breaks after each line:
   TripSmart
   1106 Beechwood
   Fayetteville, AR 72704
   555-848-0807

8. Insert an email link in the line below the telephone number, using **Contact Us** for the text and **mailbox@tripsmart.com** for the email link.
9. Italicize TripSmart, the address, phone number, and email link.
10. Link the menu bar entries to index.html, catalog.html, services.html, tours.html, and newsletter.html.
11. View the HTML code for the page, then return to Design view.
12. Save your work.
13. View the page in Mobile size, Tablet size, and Desktop size, then test the links in your browser window.
14. Compare your page to Figure 47, close the browser, then close all open pages.

Figure 47 *Completed Project Builder 1*

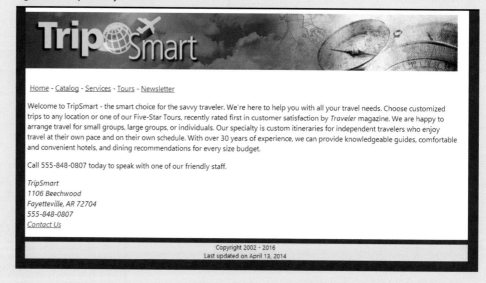

Home - Catalog - Services - Tours - Newsletter

Welcome to TripSmart - the smart choice for the savvy traveler. We're here to help you with all your travel needs. Choose customized trips to any location or one of our Five-Star Tours, recently rated first in customer satisfaction by *Traveler* magazine. We are happy to arrange travel for small groups, large groups, or individuals. Our specialty is custom itineraries for independent travelers who enjoy travel at their own pace and on their own schedule. With over 30 years of experience, we can provide knowledgeable guides, comfortable and convenient hotels, and dining recommendations for every size budget.

Call 555-848-0807 today to speak with one of our friendly staff.

TripSmart
1106 Beechwood
Fayetteville, AR 72704
555-848-0807
Contact Us

Copyright 2002 - 2016
Last updated on April 13, 2014

Your company has been selected to design a website for a catering business named Carolyne's Creations. You are now ready to add content to the home page and apply formatting options to improve the page's appearance, using Figure 48 as a guide.

1. Open the Carolyne's Creations website, then open the home page.
2. Edit the page title to read **Carolyne's Creations: Premier Gourmet Food Shop**.
3. Add the description **Carolyne's Creations is a gourmet food shop. We offer cooking classes, take-out meals, and catering services. We also have a retail side that stocks gourmet items and kitchen accessories.**
4. Add the keywords **Carolyne's Creations, gourmet, catering, cooking classes, kitchen accessories, take-out, Seven Falls, Virginia.**
5. Place the insertion point in front of the sentence in the second paragraph beginning "Give us a call" and type **We also have a pick-up window on the right side of the building for take-out orders**.
6. Add the following address below the second paragraph using line breaks after each line:
   Carolyne's Creations
   496 Maple Avenue
   Seven Falls, Virginia 52404
   555-963-8271
7. Enter another line break after the telephone number and type **Email**, add a space, then add an email link using **Carolyne Kate** for the text and

carolyne@carolynescreations.com for the email address.

8. Insert a Navigation element, add text to serve as links to the website's main pages, then create links from each menu bar element to its corresponding web page. See Figure 48.
9. Replace the date that follows the text "Last updated on" with a date object using a format of your choice

that will automatically update on save, then save your work.

10. Save your work, view the completed page in Mobile size, Tablet size, Desktop size, and in your default browser, then test each link.
11. Close your browser.
12. Close all open pages.

Figure 48 *Completed Project Builder 2*

Fernando Padilla is looking for a durable laptop case that he can use for the frequent trips he takes with his laptop. He is searching the Internet looking for one that is attractive, strong, and that provides quick access for removing the laptop for airport security. He knows that websites use keywords and descriptions in order to receive "hits" with search engines. He is curious about how they work. Follow the steps below and write your answers to the questions.

1. Connect to the Internet, then go to **www.sfbags.com** to view the WaterField Designs website's home page, as shown in Figure 49.
2. View the page source by selecting View on the Menu bar, then selecting Source (Internet Explorer) or Tools > Web Developer > Page Source (Mozilla Firefox).
3. Can you locate a description and keywords? If so, what are they?

4. How many keyword terms do you find?
5. Is the description appropriate for the website? Why or why not?
6. Look at the numbers of keyword terms and words in the description. Is there an appropriate number?

7. Use a search engine such as Google at www.google.com, then type the words **laptop bag** in the Search text box.
8. Click a link in the list of results and view the source code for that page. Do you see keywords and a description? Do any of them match the words you used in the search?

Figure 49 *Design Project*

Source: *Waterfield Designs*

In this assignment, you will continue to work on the website you defined in Chapter 1. In Chapter 1, you created a wireframe for your website with at least four pages. You also created a local site folder for your site and an assets folder to store the site asset files. You set the assets folder as the default storage location for your images. You began to collect information and resources for your site and started working on the home page. You have not yet learned how to create a new page with a Fluid Grid Layout, so you can either create a simple HTML page now and convert it to a Fluid Grid Layout later, or use one of your website index pages as a template.

1. Think about the head content for the home page. Add the title, keywords, and a description.
2. Create the main page content for the home page.
3. Add the address and other contact information to the home page, including an email address.
4. Consult your wireframe and design the menu bar.
5. Link the menu bar items to the appropriate pages.
6. Add a last updated on statement to the home page with a date that will automatically update when the page is saved.
7. Edit the page content until you are satisfied with the results. You will format the content after you have learned to use Cascading Style Sheets in the next chapter.
8. Verify that all links, including the email link, work correctly.
9. When you are satisfied with the home page, review the checklist questions shown in Figure 50, then make any necessary changes.
10. Save your work.

Figure 50 *Portfolio Project*

Website Checklist

1. Does the home page have a page title?
2. Does the home page have a description and keywords?
3. Does the home page contain contact information, including an email address?
4. Does the home page have a menu bar that includes a link to itself?
5. Does the home page have a "last updated on" statement that will automatically update when the page is saved?
6. Do all paths for links and images work correctly?
7. Does the home page look good using at least two different browsers and screen resolutions?

CHAPTER 3 WORKING WITH TEXT AND CASCADING STYLE SHEETS

1. Create unordered and ordered lists
2. Create a Cascading Style Sheet and apply, edit and add rules
3. Understand related files and media queries
4. Add Adobe Edge Web fonts
5. Use coding tools to view and edit rules

WORKING WITH TEXT AND
CASCADING STYLE SHEETS

Introduction

Most web pages depend largely on text to convey information. Dreamweaver provides many tools for working with text that you can use to make your web pages attractive and easy to read. These tools can help you format text quickly and make sure it has a consistent look across all your web pages.

Using Cascading Style Sheets

You can save time and ensure that all your page elements have a consistent appearance by using **Cascading Style Sheets (CSS)**. CSS are sets of formatting instructions, usually stored in a separate file, that control the appearance and position of text and graphics on a web page or throughout a website. CSS are a great way to define consistent formatting attributes for page elements such as paragraph text, lists, and table data. You can then apply the formatting attributes to any element in a single document or to all of the pages in a website.

Formatting Text as Lists

If a web page contains a large amount of text, it can be difficult for users to digest it all. You can break up the monotony of large blocks of text by dividing them into smaller paragraphs or by organizing them as lists. You can create three types of lists in Dreamweaver: unordered lists, ordered lists, and definition lists.

Lists are also excellent for creating simple navigation bars. You can format list items to look like buttons by applying styles to assign background colors to each list item. You can even create rollover effects for list items by having the background color change when the user rolls the mouse over them. This technique gives your links a more professional look than plain text links. Cascading Style Sheets are indeed a powerful tool. This chapter will focus on using Cascading Style Sheets to format text.

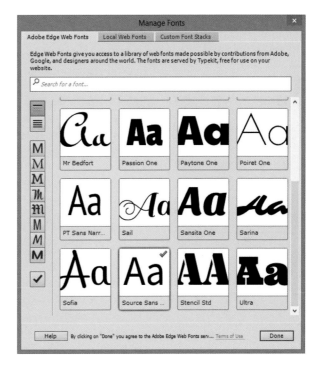

Create Unordered AND ORDERED LISTS

What You'll Do

Body Treatments

- Salt Glow
  Imported sea salts are massaged into the skin, exfoliating and cleansing the pores.
- Herbal Wrap
  Organic lavender blooms create a detoxifying and calming treatment to relieve aches and pains.
- Seaweed Body Wrap
  Seaweed is a natural detoxifying agent that also helps improve circulation.

Call The Sea Spa desk for prices and reservations. Any of our services can be personalized according to your needs. Our desk is open from 7:00 a.m. until 9:00 p.m. Call 555-594-9458, extension 39.

Questions You May Have

1. How do I schedule Spa services?
   Please make appointments by calling The Club desk at least 24 hours in advance. Please arrive 15 minutes before your appointment to allow enough time to shower or use the sauna.
2. Will I be charged if I cancel my appointment?
   Please cancel 24 hours before your service to avoid a cancellation charge. No-shows and cancellations without adequate notice will be charged for the full service.
3. Are there any health safeguards I should know about?
   Please advise us of medical conditions or allergies you have. Heat treatments like hydrotherapy and body wraps should be avoided if you are pregnant, have high blood pressure, or any type of heart condition or diabetes.
4. What about tipping?
   Gratuities are at your sole discretion, but are certainly appreciated.

In this lesson, you will create an unordered list of spa services on the spa page. You will also copy and paste text with questions and format them as an ordered list.

Creating Unordered Lists

Unordered lists are lists of items that do not need to appear in a specific sequence, such as a grocery list, which often lists items in a random order. Items in unordered lists are usually preceded by a **bullet**, a small dot or similar icon. Unordered lists that contain bullets are sometimes called **bulleted lists**. Although you can use paragraph indentations to create an unordered list, bullets can often make lists easier to read. To create an unordered list, first select the text you want to format as an unordered list, then use the Unordered List button in the HTML Property inspector to insert bullets at the beginning of each paragraph of the selected text.

Formatting Unordered Lists

In Dreamweaver, the default bullet style is a round dot. To change the bullet style to a different symbol, use Cascading Style Sheets. You can create a rule to modify the <ul> tag

Figure 1 *Using CSS to format all lists in a website*

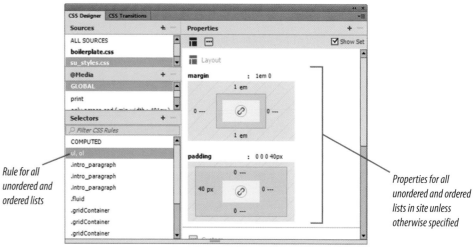

Rule for all unordered and ordered lists

Properties for all unordered and ordered lists in site unless otherwise specified that will apply to all lists in a website, as shown in Figure 1 or you can create a rule for a particular unordered list, such as a list of navigation elements, shown in Figure 2. You will learn about Cascading Style Sheets in the next lesson.

Creating Ordered Lists

Ordered lists, which are sometimes called **numbered lists**, are lists of items that are presented in a specific sequence and that are preceded by sequential numbers or letters. An ordered list is appropriate for a list in which each item must be executed according to its specified order. A list that provides numbered directions for driving from Point A to Point B or a list that provides instructions for assembling a bicycle are both examples of ordered lists.

Formatting Ordered Lists

You can format an ordered list to show different styles of numbers or letters by using Cascading Style Sheets, as shown in Figure 3. You can apply numbers, Roman numerals, decimals, lowercase letters, or uppercase letters to an ordered list.

Creating Definition Lists

Definition lists are similar to unordered lists but have a hanging indent and are not preceded by bullets. They are often used with terms and definitions, such as in a dictionary or glossary. To create a definition list, select the text to use for the list, select Format on the Menu bar, point to List, and then select Definition List.

Figure 2 *Using CSS to format navigation elements as an unordered list*

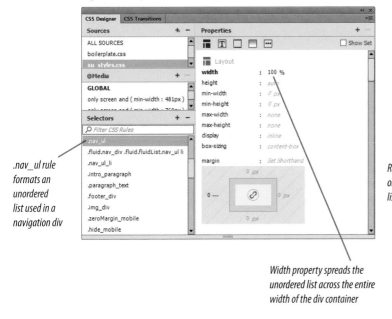

.nav_ul rule formats an unordered list used in a navigation div

Width property spreads the unordered list across the entire width of the div container

Figure 3 *Using CSS to format ordered lists in a website*

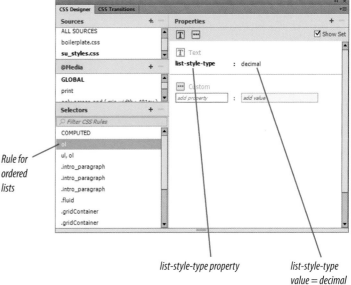

Rule for ordered lists

list-style-type property

list-style-type value = decimal

Create an unordered list

1. Open the spa page in The Striped Umbrella website.

2. Select the three items and their descriptions under the Massages heading.

3. Select the **HTML button** <> HTML in the Property inspector to switch to the HTML Property inspector if necessary, select the **Unordered List button** ≔ to format the selected text as an unordered list, click anywhere to deselect the text, then compare your screen to Figure 4.

    Each spa service item and its description are separated by a line break. That is why each description is indented under its corresponding item, rather than formatted as a new list item. You must enter a paragraph break to create a new list item.

4. Repeat Step 3 to create unordered lists with the three items under the Facials and Body Treatments headings, being careful not to include the contact information in the last paragraph on the page as part of your last list.

TIP Pressing [Enter] (Win) or [return] (Mac) once at the end of an unordered list creates another bulleted item. To end an unordered list, press [Enter] (Win) or [return] (Mac) twice.

(continued)

Figure 4 *Creating an unordered list*

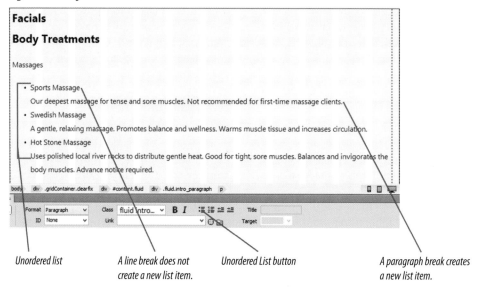

Unordered list

A line break does not create a new list item.

Unordered List button

A paragraph break creates a new list item.

Coding for the Semantic Web

You may have heard the term "semantic web." The word "semantics" refers to the study of meanings of words or sentences. So the term "semantic web" refers to the way page content can be coded to convey meaning to other computer programs such as search engines. One example is to use the <em> tag which means "emphasis" rather than the <i> tag which means "italic" to show emphasis. Another example would be to use font size attributes such as <small> or <medium> rather than using font size attributes expressed in pixels. Cascading Style Sheets are used to define the appearance of semantic tags. For instance, you can specify the attributes of the <h1> heading tag by choosing the Selector Type: Tag (redefines an HTML element) rules in the New CSS Rules dialog box. CSS and semantic coding work together to enhance the meaning of the page content and provide well-designed pages that are attractive and consistent throughout the site. An ideal website would incorporate semantic coding with external style sheets to format all website content. This approach will enable "Semantic Web" programs to interpret the content presented, make it easier for web designers to write and edit, and enhance the overall experience for site users.

Working with Text and Cascading Style Sheets

Figure 5 *Viewing the three unordered lists*

Massages

- Sports Massage
  Our deepest massage for tense and sore muscles. Not recommended for first-time massage clients.
- Swedish Massage
  A gentle, relaxing massage. Promotes balance and wellness. Warms muscle tissue and increases circulation.
- Hot Stone Massage
  Uses polished local river rocks to distribute gentle heat. Good for tight, sore muscles. Balances and invigorates the body muscles. Advance notice required.

Facials

- Revitalizing Facial
  A light massage with a customized essential oil blend that moisturizes the skin and restores circulation.
- Gentlemen's Facial
  A cleansing facial that restores a healthy glow. Includes a neck and shoulder massage.
- Milk Mask
  A soothing mask that softens and moisturizes the face. Leaves your skin looking younger.

Body Treatments

- Salt Glow
  Imported sea salts are massaged into the skin, exfoliating and cleansing the pores.
- Herbal Wrap
  Organic lavender blooms create a detoxifying and calming treatment to relieve aches and pains.
- Seaweed Body Wrap
  Seaweed is a natural detoxifying agent that also helps improve circulation.

Call The Sea Spa desk for prices and reservations. Any of our services can be personalized according to your needs. Our desk is open from 7:00 a.m. until 9:00 p.m. Call 555-594-9458, extension 39.

Figure 6 *HTML tags in Split view for unordered lists*

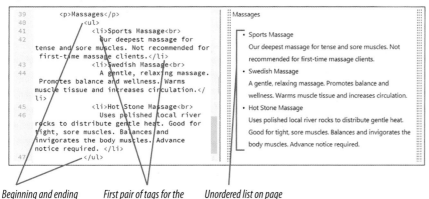

Beginning and ending tags for unordered list   *First pair of tags for the first list item in the list*   *Unordered list on page*

5. Save your work, then compare your page to Figure 5.

6. Position the insertion point to the left of the first item in the first unordered list, then select the **Show Code and Design views button** Split on the Document toolbar to view the code for the unordered list, as shown in Figure 6.

   A pair of HTML tags surrounds each type of element on the page. The first tag in each pair begins the code for a particular element, and the last tag ends the code for the element. For instance, the tag <ul>begins the unordered list, and the</ul>tag ends it. The tags <li>and</li> surround each item in the list.

   TIP Depending on your Document window size, you may have to scroll to locate the code for the unordered list.

7. Select the **Show Design view button** Design on the Document toolbar.

You opened the spa page in Design view and formatted three spa services lists as unordered lists. You then viewed the HTML code for the unordered lists in Show Code and Design views (Split view).

Lesson 1   Create Unordered and Ordered Lists

Create an ordered list

1. Place the insertion point at the end of the last paragraph after the words "extension 39", then press **[Enter]** (Win) or **[return]** (Mac).

2. Open your file management program, browse to the location where you store your Data Files, then open **questions.txt**. Select all, copy, then paste the copied text on the page at the insertion point location.

   The inserted text appears under the last paragraph.

3. Select the text beginning with "How do I schedule" and ending with the last sentence of the pasted text.

4. Select the **Ordered List button** ½≡ in the HTML Property inspector to format the selected text as an ordered list.

5. Deselect the text, delete any unwanted paragraph returns before the contact information, then compare your screen to Figure 7.

You pasted text on the spa page. You also formatted selected text as an ordered list.

Figure 7 *Creating an ordered list*

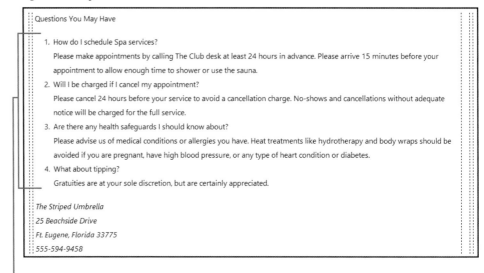

Ordered
list items

Figure 8 *Formatting a list heading*

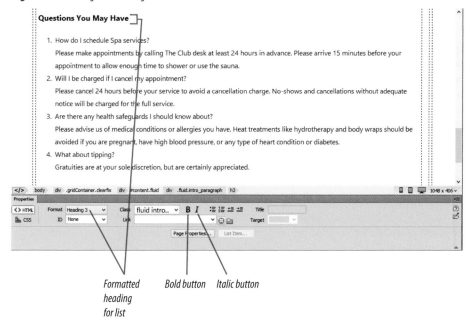

Formatted
heading
for list

Bold button   Italic button

Format an ordered list heading

1. Place the insertion point in the heading "Questions You May Have," then use the HTML Property inspector to apply the **Heading 3** format, as shown in Figure 8.

TIP You could show emphasis by using the Bold button **B** or the Italic button *I* on the HTML Property inspector, as shown in Figure 8, but using the heading code shows the significance (semantics) of the phrase more clearly. It shows that the phrase is a heading related to the text that follows it. The three headings on the page are formatted with three different heading tags that indicate their order of importance on the page: Heading 1 first, then Heading 2, followed by Heading 3.

2. Save your work.

You formatted the "Questions You May Have" heading.

Create a Cascading Style Sheet and APPLY, EDIT AND ADD RULES

What You'll Do

 In this lesson, you will create a Cascading Style Sheet file for The Striped Umbrella website. You will also create a rule named list_headings and apply it to the list item headings on the spa page.

Understanding Cascading Style Sheets

Cascading Style Sheets (CSS) are made up of sets of formatting attributes called **rules**, which define the formatting attributes for page content. Rules can then be used to point to an HTML element and "style" it with the formatting attributes defined in the rule. Style sheets are classified by where the code is stored. The code can be saved in a separate file (an **external style sheet**), as part of the head content of an individual web page (an **internal or embedded style**), or as part of the body of the HTML code (an **inline style**). External CSS are saved as files with the .css extension and are stored in the website's directory structure. Figure 9 shows external style sheets named su_styles.css and boilerplate.css listed in the Files panel. External style sheets are the preferred method for creating and using styles.

CSS are also classified by their type. A **Class type** can be used to format any page element. An **ID type** and a **Tag type** are used to redefine an HTML tag. A **Compound** type is used to format a selection. In this chapter, we will use the class type and the tag type, both stored in an external style sheet file.

Using CSS Designer

You use buttons on the CSS Designer panel to create, edit, and apply rules. To add a rule, use the Sources pane to select the style sheet to which you want to add the new rule. Each rule you create is added to the selected style sheet. The tag generated by a rule is called a selector. A **selector** "selects" HTML elements and applies the rule to style the HTML element. Next, select the Add Selector button at the top of the Selectors pane, then either accept the default name in the New Selector text box that appears (based on the location of the insertion point) or type a different selector name. Once you add a new selector to a style sheet, it appears in a list in CSS Designer. To apply a selector, select the HTML element to which you want to apply the selector, and then choose a rule from the Targeted Rule list in the CSS Property inspector. You can apply CSS rules to elements on a single web page or to all of the pages in a website. When you edit a rule, such as changing the font size it specifies, all page elements formatted with that rule are automatically updated. Once you create an external CSS, you should attach it to the remaining pages in your website.

Use CSS Designer to manage your styles. The Properties pane displays properties for a selected rule at the bottom of the panel, or a second column when CSS Designer is expanded to two columns. You can easily change a property's value by selecting an option from a drop-down menu to the right of the property name.

Understanding the Advantages of Using Style Sheets

You can use CSS styles to save an enormous amount of time. Being able to define a rule and then select and apply it to page elements on all the pages of your website means that you can make hundreds of formatting changes in a few minutes. In addition, style sheets create a more uniform look from page to page and they generate cleaner code. Using style sheets separates the content itself from the way the content is presented. By separating the two processes, you can concentrate on either editing the content or modifying the design without affecting the other. Pages formatted with CSS styles are more compliant with current accessibility standards than those with manual formatting. When you create a Fluid Grid Layout page, a style sheet is automatically generated to define the rules, properties, and values used to position page elements for displaying the page in a Mobile, Tablet, or Desktop size. You will learn more about using style sheets for page layout in Chapter 5.

QUICK TIP

For more information about CSS terminology and the relationships between CSS selectors and Cascading Style Sheets, visit www.w3.org/Style.

Understanding CSS Code

You can see the properties for a CSS rule by looking at the style sheet code. A CSS rule consists of two parts: the selector and the declaration. As you learned earlier, a selector is the name of the tag to which the style declarations have been assigned. A selector consists of the selector's name, followed by declarations using the format [property]: [value]. When there is more than one property, each property is separated by a semicolon. For example, Figure 10 shows the code for an unordered list that will be used for styling navigation bar elements. The width property is set to 100% and the margin-left property to zero. In this example, the selector name is .nav_ul. There are two properties in this selector: width and margin-left. The property(s) and value(s) together comprise the declaration.

When you create a new external CSS file, you will see the file name listed as a related files document in the Related Files toolbar at the top of the Document window. Select the file name to open the contents of the file in the Document window. As you make changes to the CSS file, be sure to save it.

Figure 9 *Cascading Style Sheet files created in striped_umbrella site root folder*

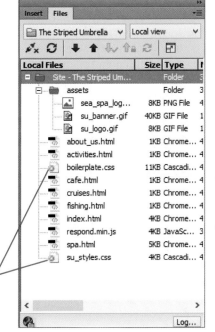

Cascading Style Sheet files

Figure 10 *Viewing the selector and declaration for an unordered list rule*

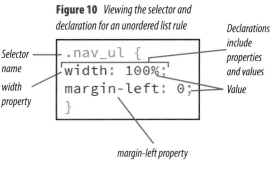

Selector name

width property

Declarations include properties and values

Value

margin-left property

Create a Cascading Style Sheet and add a rule

1. Select the **CSS button** in the Property inspector to switch to the CSS Property inspector, as shown in Figure 11.

2. If the CSS Designer panel is not open, select **Window** on the Menu bar, then select **CSS Designer** to open it or select the **CSS Designer panel tab**.

3. Resize the CSS Designer panel to display it in two columns, select the **Add CSS Source button** in the Sources pane, then select **Create a New CSS File**, as shown in Figure 12.

   The Create a New CSS File dialog box opens.

   TIP You can also choose to attach an existing style sheet file or create internal styles directly in the page code.

4. Select **Browse**, navigate to the striped_umbrella site root folder, type **headings** in the File name text box in the Save Style Sheet File As dialog box, as shown in Figure 13, select **Save**, then select **OK** to close the Create a New CSS File dialog box.

   The new style sheet file named headings.css is saved in the local site folder.

   (continued)

Figure 11 *CSS Property inspector*

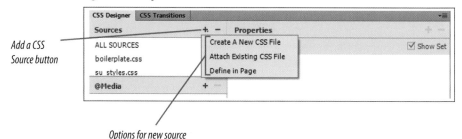

CSS button

Options in the Property inspector change depending on whether the HTML or CSS button is selected

Figure 12 *Adding a new source for CSS rules*

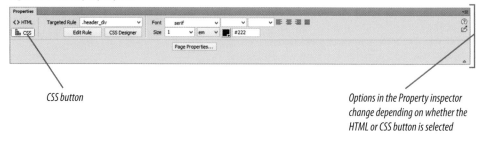

Add a CSS Source button

Options for new source

Figure 13 *Save Style Sheet File As dialog box*

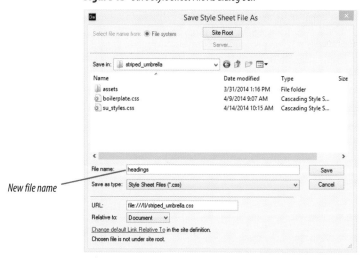

New file name

Working with Text and Cascading Style Sheets

Figure 14 *CSS Designer with .list_headings rule listed in the headings.css file*

Select headings.css —

.list_headings selector —

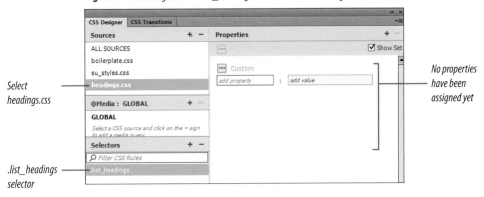

No properties have been assigned yet

Figure 15 *CSS Designer with properties and values displayed for .list_headings rule*

Text button —

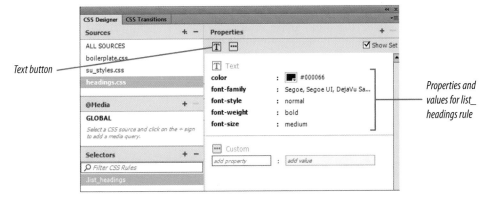

Properties and values for list_ headings rule

5. Select **headings.css** in the Sources pane, then select the **Add Selector button** ➕ in the Selectors pane.

6. Replace the placeholder selector name with **.list_headings**, compare your screen with Figure 14, then press **[Enter]** (Win) or **[return]** (Mac).

   The .list_headings selector appears in the Selectors pane. It is the only selector in the new headings.css style sheet. Next, you define the rule properties

   TIP Class selector names are preceded by a period in the code and in the CSS panel.

7. Uncheck the **Show Set check box** in the Properties pane, if necessary, to view all properties (set and not set).

8. Select the **Text button** ⊤ in the Properties pane, then select and assign values to the following properties: color to **#000066;** font-family to **Segoe, Segoe UI, DejaVu Sans, Trebucket MS, Verdana, sans serif;** font-style to **normal**, font-weight to **bold**; and font-size to **medium**.

9. Select the **Show Set check box** to see only the properties and values you selected in Step 8, compare your screen to Figure 15, then save all files.

   If you don't see the properties listed, select the Text button on the Properties toolbar. These are all text properties.

You created a Cascading Style Sheet file named headings.css and a rule named .list_headings within the style sheet.

Apply a rule

1. Place the insertion point anywhere in the paragraph heading "Massages," select the **Targeted Rule list arrow** in the Property inspector, then select **.list_headings**, as shown in Figure 16. Notice the new style sheet, headings.css, appears in the Related Files toolbar.

2. Repeat Step 1 to apply the list_headings rule to each of the spa services unordered list headings, place the insertion point anywhere in the document to deselect the text, then compare your screen to Figure 17.

TIP You can use the keyboard shortcut [Ctrl][Y] (Win) or [Command][Y] (Mac) to repeat the previous action.

You applied the list_headings rule to each of the Spa Services category headings.

Figure 16 *Applying a CSS rule to selected text*

Rule applied

headings.css appears on the Related Files toolbar

Select to apply list_headings rule to selected text

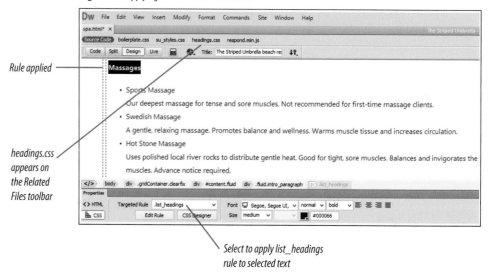

Figure 17 *Unordered list with list_headings rule applied*

list_headings rule applied to each of the Spa Services categories

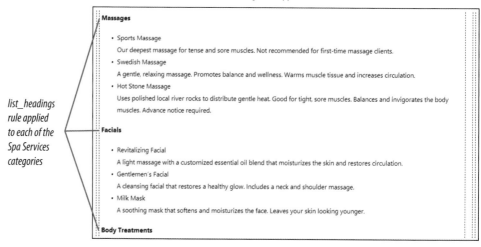

Working with Text and Cascading Style Sheets

Figure 18 *Editing a rule*

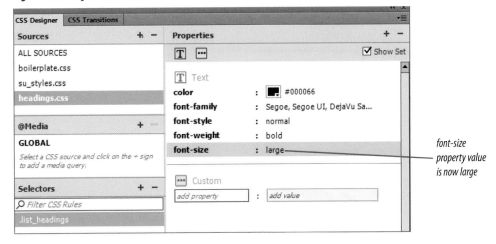

font-size property value is now large

Figure 19 *Viewing the changes made to the list_headings rule*

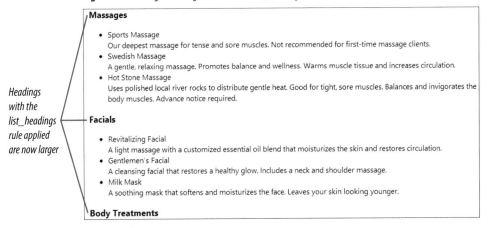

Headings with the list_headings rule applied are now larger

Massages

- Sports Massage
  Our deepest massage for tense and sore muscles. Not recommended for first-time massage clients.
- Swedish Massage
  A gentle, relaxing massage. Promotes balance and wellness. Warms muscle tissue and increases circulation.
- Hot Stone Massage
  Uses polished local river rocks to distribute gentle heat. Good for tight, sore muscles. Balances and invigorates the body muscles. Advance notice required.

Facials

- Revitalizing Facial
  A light massage with a customized essential oil blend that moisturizes the skin and restores circulation.
- Gentlemen's Facial
  A cleansing facial that restores a healthy glow. Includes a neck and shoulder massage.
- Milk Mask
  A soothing mask that softens and moisturizes the face. Leaves your skin looking younger.

Body Treatments

Edit a rule

1. Select **headings.css** in the Sources pane if necessary, select **.list_headings** in the CSS Designer Selectors pane.

   The rule's properties and values appear in the Properties pane.

2. Select the **medium value** in the font-size property, select **large**, as shown in Figure 18, then compare your screen to Figure 19.

   All of the text to which you applied the list_headings rule is larger, reflecting the changes you made to the list_headings rule.

TIP If you position the insertion point in text that has a class CSS rule applied to it, that rule is displayed in the Targeted Rule text box in the CSS Property inspector or the Class text box in the HTML Property inspector.

3. Select **File** on the menu bar, then select **Save All** to save the spa page and the style sheet file.

You edited the list_headings rule to change the font size to large. You then viewed the results of the edited rule in the unordered list.

View code with the Code Navigator

1. Point to the Massages heading, then [Alt]-click (Win) or [Command] [Option]-click (Mac) to display the Code Navigator.

A window opens, as shown in Figure 20, with a list of the three style sheets in the local site folder that have been used to style the page. The rules used in each style sheet are listed under each file name. The boilerplate.css file provides the overall basic structure for the page. The headings.css file only has one rule, .list_headings, the rule you created to style the headings in the three unordered lists. The su_styles.css file provides code for modifying the page content to display on mobile, tablet, and desktop devices.

TIP [Control][Alt][N] (Win) or [Command][Option][N] (Mac) also opens the Code Navigator.

2. Position the mouse pointer over the list_headings rule name until you see a box with the rule's properties, as shown in Figure 21.

TIP You can disable the Code Navigator by selecting the Disable check box as shown in Figure 21.

You displayed the Code Navigator to view the properties of the list_headings rule.

Figure 20 *Viewing the style sheet file names in the Code Navigator*

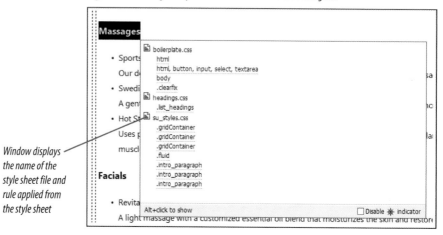

Window displays the name of the style sheet file and rule applied from the style sheet

Figure 21 *Viewing the rule properties and values in the Code Navigator*

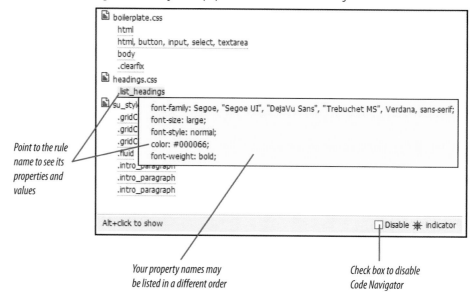

Point to the rule name to see its properties and values

Your property names may be listed in a different order

Check box to disable Code Navigator

Figure 22 *Using Code and Design views to view rule properties*

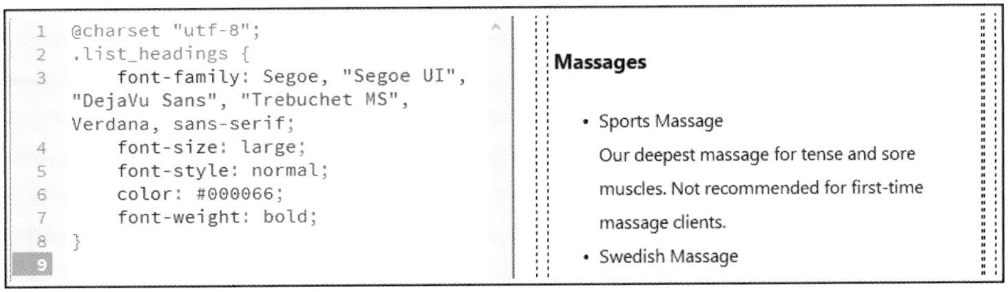

```
1  @charset "utf-8";
2  .list_headings {
3      font-family: Segoe, "Segoe UI",
   "DejaVu Sans", "Trebuchet MS",
   Verdana, sans-serif;
4      font-size: large;
5      font-style: normal;
6      color: #000066;
7      font-weight: bold;
8  }
9
```

Massages

- Sports Massage

  Our deepest massage for tense and sore

  muscles. Not recommended for first-time

  massage clients.

- Swedish Massage

Figure 23 *Editing a rule in Code view*

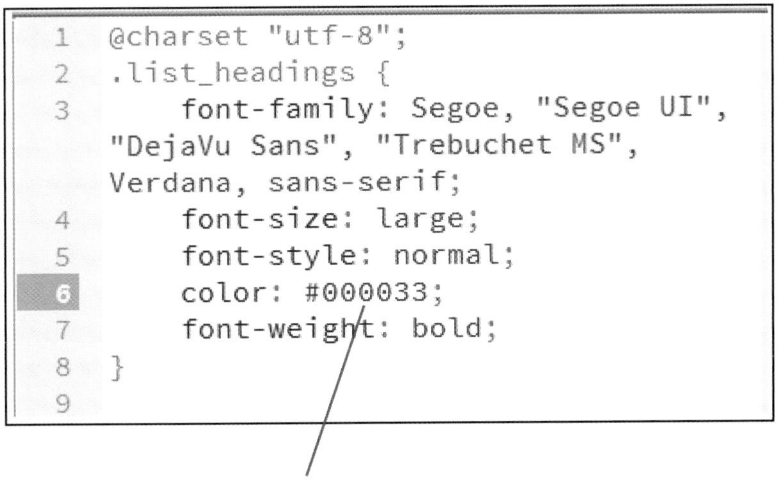

```
1  @charset "utf-8";
2  .list_headings {
3      font-family: Segoe, "Segoe UI",
   "DejaVu Sans", "Trebuchet MS",
   Verdana, sans-serif;
4      font-size: large;
5      font-style: normal;
6      color: #000033;
7      font-weight: bold;
8  }
9
```

Replace color "000066" with "000033"

Use the Code Navigator to edit a rule

1. Select **.list_headings** in the Code Navigator. The document window splits into two panes. The left pane displays the code for the CSS file and the right section displays the HTML page in Design view, as shown in Figure 22.

   Your properties may be listed in a different order. The order of the code in Code view matches the order in which the properties were added.

TIP The default setting for Show Code and Design views in Dreamweaver CC splits the two windows vertically, rather than horizontally. To view the two windows split horizontally on the screen, select View on the Menu bar, then select Split Vertically to uncheck the option and split the screens horizontally.

2. Type directly in the code to replace the color "000066" with the color "000033" as shown in Figure 23.

TIP You can also edit the rule properties in the CSS Designer Properties pane.

3. Save all files.

4. Select the **Show Design view button** Design .

   The font color has changed in Design view to reflect the new shade of blue in the rule.

You changed the color value in the .list_headings color property.

Add a tag selector to an existing style sheet

1. Select **.headings.css** in the CSS Designer Sources pane, then select the **Add Selector** button + in the Selectors pane.

2. Type **h1** in the Selector Name text box, or type **h** and select **h1** out of the code hints list, as shown in Figure 24, then press [**Enter**] (Win) or [**return**] (Mac).

   The h1 rule is listed in the Selectors pane.

   When you create a rule to modify an HTML tag, you do not type a period in front of the rule name. The tag is the rule name.

3. Deselect the **Show Set check box** in the Properties pane if necessary.

   When a rule does not have properties assigned, there is nothing to show in the Properties pane when Show Set is selected. Unchecking the Show Set check box displays a list by category of all property names available to use to format a rule.

4. Select the **Text button** 🅃 in the Properties pane.

   A list of text properties and their default values appears in the Properties pane.

   (continued)

Figure 24 *Creating a tag selector*

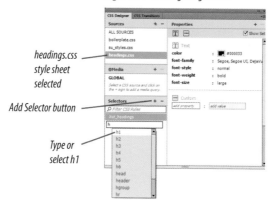

headings.css style sheet selected

Add Selector button

Type or select h1

Figure 25 *CSS Rule Definition for h1 in heading.css*

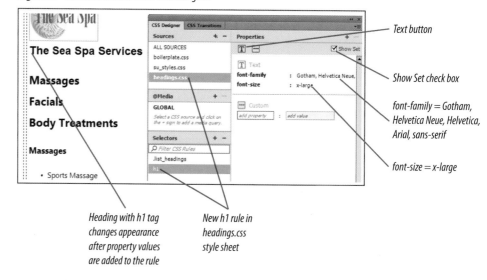

Text button

Show Set check box

font-family = Gotham, Helvetica Neue, Helvetica, Arial, sans-serif

font-size = x-large

Heading with h1 tag changes appearance after property values are added to the rule

New h1 rule in headings.css style sheet

Figure 26 *Viewing the h2 headings with new rules applied*

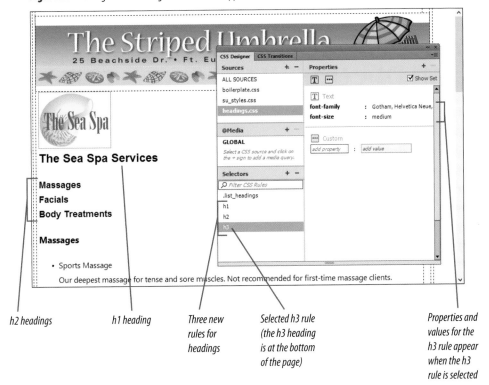

h2 headings

h1 heading

Three new
rules for
headings

Selected h3 rule
(the h3 heading
is at the bottom
of the page)

Properties and
values for the
h3 rule appear
when the h3
rule is selected

5. Select the **font-family value** (default font), then select **Gotham, Helvetica Neue, Helvetica, Arial, sans-serif**.

6. Select the **font-size value** (medium), then select **x-large**.

    The Sea Spa Services heading on the page changes in appearance to reflect the new h1 properties specified in the new rule.

7. Select the **Show Set** check box to display only the properties you have assigned to the h1 tag, as shown in Figure 25.

8. Repeat Steps 1 through 7 to create a new tag selector that redefines the h2 tag with a font-family of **Gotham, Helvetica Neue, Helvetica, Arial, sans-serif** and a font-size of **large**.

9. Repeat Steps 1 through 7 to create a new tag selector that redefines the h3 tag with a font-family of **Gotham, Helvetica Neue, Helvetica, Arial, sans-serif** and a font-size of **medium**.

10. Save all files, then compare your screen to Figure 26.

You added three tag selectors to your style sheet that modify the appearance of the h1, h2, and h3 tags.

Transitioning to a Real-World Work Process

As you learn Dreamweaver throughout the chapters in this book, you practice its many features in a logical learning sequence. You will develop an understanding of both current concepts like CSS3 and older, but still used, features such as HTML formatting and embedded styles. Once you learn Dreamweaver and start using it to create your own websites, you would ideally format all pages with rules from one external style sheet. You would move all of the embedded styles in the predesigned CSS layouts to the external style sheet because the embedded styles on each page would be redundant. After you have worked through this book, you should have the skills and understanding to design sites built entirely and efficiently with CSS.

Understand Related Files and
MEDIA QUERIES

What You'll Do

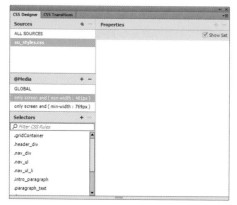

In this lesson, you will add a rule to a Cascading Style Sheet. You will then attach the style sheet file to the index page and apply one of the rules to text on the page.

Understanding External and Embedded Style Sheets

When you are first learning about CSS, the terminology can be confusing. In the last lesson, you learned that external style sheets are separate files in a website, saved with the .css file extension. You also learned that CSS can be part of an HTML file, rather than a separate file. These are called internal, or embedded, style sheets. Some external CSS files are created by the web designer. Other external CSS files are created by Dreamweaver, such as the boilerplate.css file, generated when a new Fluid Grid Layout page is first created. Embedded style sheets are created automatically in Dreamweaver if the designer does not create them, using default names for the rules. The code for these rules resides in the head content for that page. These rules are automatically named style1, style2, and so on. You can rename the rules as they are created to make them more recognizable for you to use, for example, paragraph_text, subheading, or address. Embedded style sheets apply only to a single page, although you can copy them into the code in other pages or move them to an external style sheet. Remember that style sheets can be used to format much more than

text objects. They can be used to set the page background, link properties, or determine the appearance of any page element. Figure 27 shows the Related Files toolbar, showing the names of the style sheets used to format the open Striped Umbrella spa page. Selecting the file name in the Related Files toolbar opens the file in the Document window, as shown in Figure 27.

When you have several pages in a website, you will probably want to use the same styles for each page to ensure that all your elements have a consistent appearance. To attach a style sheet to another document, select the **Add CSS Source button** in the CSS Designer Sources pane, then select **Attach Existing CSS File** to open the Attach Existing CSS File dialog box, make sure the Add as Link option is selected, browse to locate the file you want to attach, and then select OK. The rules contained in the attached style sheet will appear in CSS Designer and you can use them to apply rules to all page elements. External style sheets can be attached, or linked, to any page. Style sheets are extremely powerful; if you decide to edit a rule, the changes will automatically be made to every object on every page that it formats.

Understanding Related Page Files

When an HTML file is linked to a Cascading Style Sheet or other files necessary to display the page content, these files are called **related files**. When a file that has related files is open in the Document window, each related file name is displayed in the Related Files toolbar above the Document window. When an HTML document has a linked CSS file but the CSS file is not available, the page file will appear in the browser, but will not be formatted correctly, because the link is broken. It takes both the HTML file and the CSS file working together to display the content properly. When you upload HTML files, remember also to upload all related page files. Other examples of related page files are Flash player, video files, and JavaScript files.

When an HTML file with a linked CSS file is open in Dreamweaver, the name of the CSS file appears in the Related Files toolbar. When you select the CSS filename, the screen changes to Split view, with the right side displaying the open HTML page in Design view and the left side displaying the CSS file. If you select "Source Code," the first filename listed on the Related Files toolbar, the code for the top level document (open HTML file) will appear on the left side of the Document window. You can edit both Code view windows by typing directly in the code.

Understanding Fluid Grid Layout Code

When a web page is opened in a browser, the style sheet detects the device being used using **Media queries**. Media queries act as traffic policemen. When they detect a mobile device, they direct the device to use the code for mobile devices; when they detect a tablet device, they direct the tablet to use the code for tablets, and so forth. Each set of codes is designed for optimum viewing on each device.

Figure 27 *Viewing an open style sheet file using the Related Files toolbar*

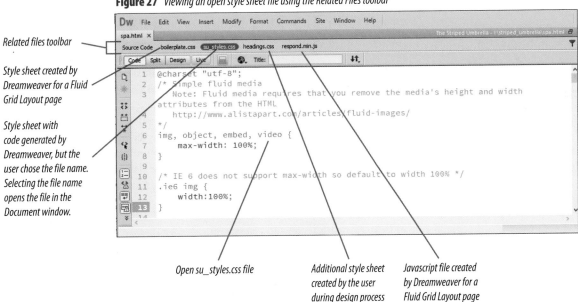

Related files toolbar

Style sheet created by Dreamweaver for a Fluid Grid Layout page

Style sheet with code generated by Dreamweaver, but the user chose the file name. Selecting the file name opens the file in the Document window.

Open su_styles.css file

Additional style sheet created by the user during design process

Javascript file created by Dreamweaver for a Fluid Grid Layout page

Examining Media Queries code

1. With the spa page open, select the **su_styles.css** file name on the Related Files toolbar.

The code for the su_styles.css file opens in the Document window, as shown in Figure 28. Since the file is open in the Document window, the only style sheet file listed in CSS Designer now is su_styles.css, as shown in Figure 29.

TIP The code in Figure 28 was resized to increase readability. Your lines may wrap differently.

2. Scroll to locate the comment line (in light gray text) "/* Mobile Layout: 480px and below. */" (on or around line 45).

The lines of code following this comment are applied when a mobile device reads the page.

TIP Figure 28 was captured with several blocks of code collapsed to point out the beginnings of each different device section, since the entire file is too long to fit on the page. To quickly locate the referenced code, use the Find command.

3. Scroll to locate the comment line (in light gray text) "/* Tablet Layout: 481px to 768 px. Inherits styles from: Mobile Layout. */" (on or around line 123).

The lines of code following this comment are applied when a tablet device reads the page.

4. Scroll to locate the comment line (in light gray text) "/* Desktop Layout: 769px to a max of 1232px. Inherits styles from: Mobile Layout and Tablet Layout. */" (on or around line 165).

The lines of code following this comment are applied when a desktop device is reading the page.

(continued)

Figure 28 *Viewing the styles for each device in the su_styles.css file*

Comment tells you that this code begins the code for mobile devices

Comment tells you that this code begins the code for tablet devices

Comment tells you that this code begins the code for desktop devices

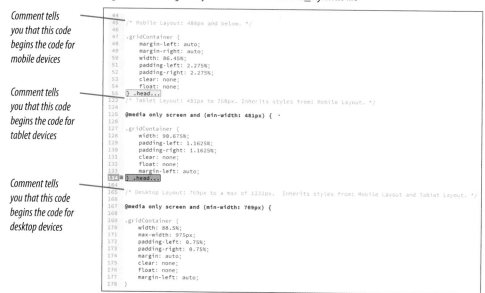

Figure 29 *Viewing CSS Designer with the su_styles.css file selected in the Related Files toolbar*

su_styles is the only file listed in CSS Designer

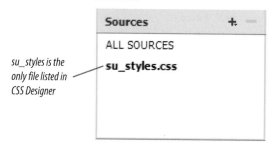

Figure 30 *Viewing the selectors for Tablet devices*

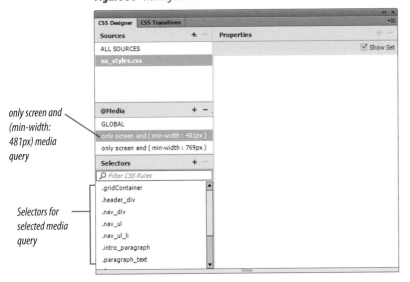

only screen and (min-width: 481px) media query

Selectors for selected media query

5. Select **su_styles.css** in the Sources pane if necessary, then select **only screen and (min-width: 481px)** in the @Media pane.

   The selectors for Tablet size devices are listed in the Selectors pane, as shown in Figure 30. When you select a Media Query, the selectors for that query appear in the Selectors pane.

6. Select **only screen and (min-width: 769px)** in the @Media pane.

   The selectors for Desktop size devices appear in the Selectors pane.

7. Select **Global** in the @Media pane.

   Selectors that are used globally for all devices and those used for Mobile size devices are listed in the Selectors pane.

8. Return to Design view.

You viewed the su_styles.css media queries and their selectors in CSS Designer.

Media Queries and Inherited Styles

When media queries are used in style sheets, it is important to understand how they work. You learned that each section of the code contains styles for different media devices. However, not every style is used with the same properties and values for every device. Rather, styles can be customized for each device.

Any style listed in the Global section applies to the page regardless of what device is used. The styles that apply to mobile devices are also included as global selectors. The global styles are **inherited**, or applied to every other device unless otherwise specified. For instance, the global style for a heading might be a medium-size font used for mobile devices. To specifiy a larger heading font for tablet devices, that same style name can be redefined in the media query section for tablet devices. It can be specified even larger for desktops to use by redefining it in the desktop media query section. Another example: you can start with a global style to use a small banner in a mobile device, a wider banner in a tablet device, and an even wider banner in a desktop device by using a background image property for a header div.

Add Adobe Edge
WEB FONTS

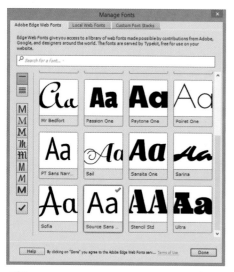

In this lesson, you will add an Adobe Edge Web Font to your list of available fonts to use in The Striped Umbrella website.

Choosing Fonts

There are two classifications of fonts: sans-serif and serif. Sans-serif fonts are fonts without any extra decorative strokes (serifs). They are often used for small blocks of text such as headings and subheadings. The headings in this book use a sans-serif font. Examples of sans-serif fonts include Arial, Verdana, and Helvetica. Serif fonts are more ornate and contain small extra strokes at the tops and bottoms of the characters. Serif fonts are considered easier to read in larger blocks of text and printed material, because the extra strokes lead your eye from one character to the next. Examples of serif fonts include Times New Roman, Times, and Georgia. The text you are reading now is in a serif font. Many designers feel that a sans-serif font is preferable when the content of a website is primarily intended to be read on the screen, but that a serif font is preferable if the content will be printed. When you choose fonts, keep in mind the amount of text each page will contain and whether most users will read the text on-screen or print it. A good rule of thumb is to limit each website to no more than three font variations.

Using Adobe Edge Web Fonts

With Adobe's purchase of Typekit in 2011, access to fonts for web page design changed dramatically. Previously, you specified font families for font-face properties, a user's device searched for the fonts in its system files, then applied the first one it found to the page text. An example of a font-family is Segoe, Segoe UI, DejaVu Sans, Trebuchet MS, Verdana, sans-serif. In this example, a device would first look for the Segoe font, then work down the list looking for each font name. If none of the fonts listed were found, the user's device would apply a default sans-serif. These fonts were hosted locally, meaning the user's device located the fonts in the device system and applied the formatting.

With Typekit, you are provided with an extensive library of Adobe Edge Web Fonts that is available to use free of charge with a Creative Cloud subscription. **Typekit** is a repository of over a thousand font families that you can use both in web and print projects. Once you choose a font family, those fonts are integrated into the Dreamweaver font menus for instant access. Typekit fonts are stored on the Creative Cloud with embedded instructions in the page code for each device calling up the page, as shown in Figure 31. Adobe Edge Web Fonts are hosted remotely, meaning that a remote website (Adobe Typekit) locates the fonts and applies the formatting.

To add an Adobe Edge Web Font to a website, click the current font family list, select the font-family property value list box, select Manage Fonts, then in the Manage Fonts dialog box, select the Adobe Edge Web Fonts tab, as shown in Figure 32. You can then search for a font, or use the font categories in the toolbar on the left side of the page to filter fonts as you browse through the font library.

Adding an Adobe Edge Web Font to a Page

Once you select a new Adobe Edge Web font, you will see it listed in the Dreamweaver menus that allow you to choose fonts. Select a selector's property in your style sheet for which you want to specify a font, then select the Adobe Edge Web font from the font list. The code will then be embedded in the head content of the page and will be used to format text styled by that selector. For more about Typekit, see the Creative Cloud introduction at the front of this book.

Figure 31 *Embedded Adobe Edge Web Fonts code*

```
30    <script src=
      "http://use.edgefonts.net/source-sans-pro:n2:default.js"
       type="text/javascript"></script>
31    </head>
32    <body>
```

Figure 32 *The Manage Fonts Dialog box*

Adobe Edge Web Fonts tab

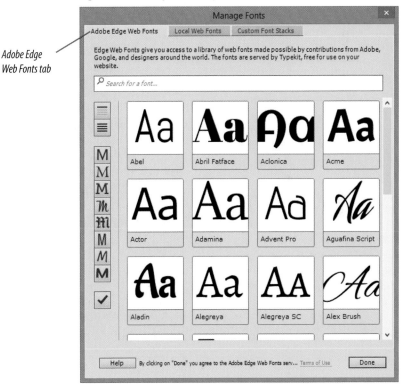

Add an Adobe Edge Web font

1. Select **headings.css** in the CSS Designer Sources pane, then select **h1** in the Selectors pane.

2. Select the **font-family list box**, then select **Manage Fonts**.

3. Select the **Adobe Edge Web Fonts** tab if necessary, then select the **List of fonts recommended for Headings** button 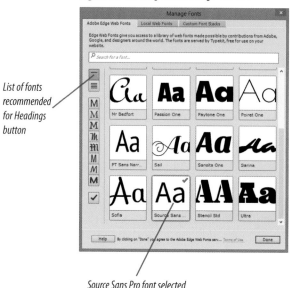.

4. Scroll down and select the **Source Sans Pro** font, as shown in Figure 33, then select **Done**.

   The font is added to your list of available fonts, but was not changed in the property value.

5. Select the **font-family list box** again, then select **source-sans-pro**.

   The h1 font-family property value is now source-sans-pro and The Sea Spa Services heading changes to the font source-sans-pro, as shown in Figure 34. Notice also that a font-weight and a font-size value were added when you chose the font. (Refresh the CSS Designer panel by toggling the Show Set checkbox if you don't see them listed.)

TIP To see the font exactly as it will appear in a browser, use Live view to view the page.

You selected an Adobe Edge Web font for the h1 tag in the headings.css style sheet.

Figure 33 *Selecting an Adobe Edge Web font*

List of fonts recommended for Headings button

Source Sans Pro font selected

Figure 34 *Viewing the Edge Web font value for the h1 tag*

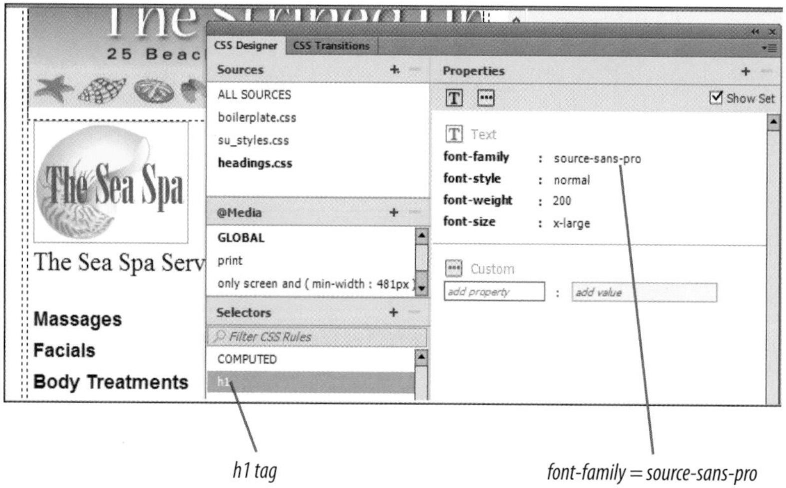

h1 tag

font-family = source-sans-pro

Working with Text and Cascading Style Sheets

Figure 35 *Correcting script errors*

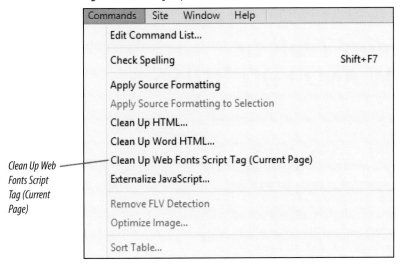

Clean Up Web
Fonts Script
Tag (Current
Page)

View the embedded code for an Adobe Edge Web font

1. Change to Code view, select **Commands** on the Menu bar, then select **Clean Up Web Fonts Script Tag (Current Page)**, as shown in Figure 35, if necessary.

   This command updates the script tag to add new fonts recently selected, as shown in Figure 36.

2. Return to Design view, then save all pages.

You used the Clean Up Web Fonts Script Tag (Current Page) command on the spa page to locate and correct any errors found in the code.

Figure 36 *Adobe Edge Web Fonts script tag added to head section*

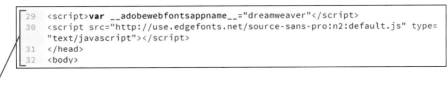

```
29  <script>var __adobewebfontsappname__="dreamweaver"</script>
30  <script src="http://use.edgefonts.net/source-sans-pro:n2:default.js" type=
    "text/javascript"></script>
31  </head>
32  <body>
```

Script added to spa
page to link font

Use Coding Tools to
VIEW AND EDIT RULES

What You'll Do

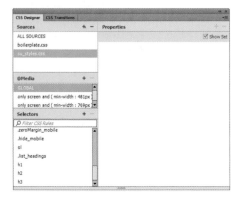

 In this lesson, you will collapse, then expand the code for the index page to view the code for the embedded and external styles. You will then move embedded styles to the external style sheet file.

Coding Tools in Dreamweaver

In Code view, you can see the Coding toolbar, shown in Figure 37. It contains a number of handy tools that help you navigate through and view your code in different ways. It has buttons that expand or collapse code, buttons for changing the way the code is displayed, and buttons for inserting and removing comments. The Coding toolbar appears on the left side of the Document window. Although you cannot move it, you can hide it, using the Toolbars command on the View menu in Code view.

As you learned in Chapter 2, you can customize the way your page code appears in Code view. You can wrap the lines of code, display or hide line numbers and hidden characters, or highlight invalid code so you can fix it. You can also have different code types appear in different colors, indent lines of code, and display syntax error alerts. In Chapter 2, you viewed these options using the View Options button on the Code Inspector toolbar. You can also view and change them on the Code View options menu under the View menu on the Menu bar.

Figure 37 *Coding toolbar*

Show Code Navigator — Open Documents

Collapse and expand buttons

Code selection buttons

Code viewing buttons

Code options buttons

Code formatting buttons

Using Coding Tools to Navigate Code

As your pages get longer and the code more complex, it is helpful to collapse sections of code, much as you can collapse and expand panels, folders, and styles. Collapsing code lets you temporarily hide code between two different sections of code that you would like to read together. To collapse selected lines of code, you can select the minus sign (Win) or the triangle (Mac) next to the line number. You can also use the Collapse Full Tag or Collapse Selection buttons on the Coding toolbar. This will allow you to look at two different sections of code that are not adjacent to each other.

Adding comments is an easy way to add documentation to your code, which is especially helpful when you are working in a team environment and other team members will be working on pages with you. For example, you might use comments to communicate instructions like "Do not alter code below this line." or "Add final schedule here when it becomes available." Comments are not visible in the browser.

Using Code Hints to Streamline Coding

If you are typing code directly into Code view, Dreamweaver can speed your work by offering you code hints. **Code hints** are lists of HTML tags that appear as you type, similar to other auto-complete features that you have probably used in other software applications. As you are typing code, Dreamweaver will recognize the tag name and offer you choices to complete the tag simply by double-clicking a tag choice in the menu, as shown in Figure 38. You can also add your own code hints to the list using JavaScript. Code hints are stored in the file CodeHints.xml.

Converting Styles

You can also convert one type of style to another. For instance, you can move an embedded style to an external style sheet or an inline style to either an embedded style or a style in an external style sheet. To do this, select the style in Code view, right-click the code, point to CSS Styles, then select Move CSS Rules. You can also move styles in the CSS Styles panel by selecting the style, right-clicking the style, and choosing the action you want from the shortcut menu.

Figure 38 *Using code hints*

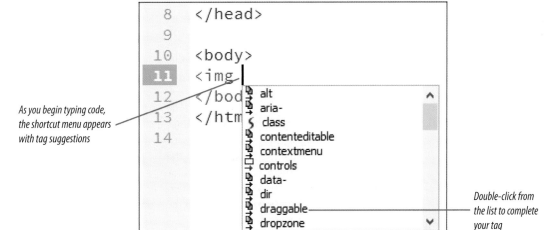

As you begin typing code, the shortcut menu appears with tag suggestions

Double-click from the list to complete your tag

Collapse code

1. Verify that the spa page is open, then select **Source Code** in the Related Files toolbar to change to Split view.

2. Scroll up the page, if necessary, to display the code that begins the head section (<head>).

   The code will probably be on or close to line 7 in the head section.

3. Select this line of code, then drag down to select all of the code down to and including the ending tag for the head section (</head>) on or around line 31, as shown in Figure 39.

   TIP If your code is in a slightly different order, scroll to find the meta tags to select them.

4. Click the **minus sign** (Win) or **vertical triangle** (Mac) in the first or last line of selected code to collapse all of the selected code.

   You can now see code above and below the collapsed code section as shown in Figure 40. The plus sign (Win) or horizontal triangle (Mac) next to the line of code indicates that there is hidden code. You also see a gap in the line numbers where the hidden code resides.

   You collapsed a block of code in Code view to be able to see two non-adjacent sections of the code at the same time.

Figure 39 *Selecting lines of code on the index page to collapse*

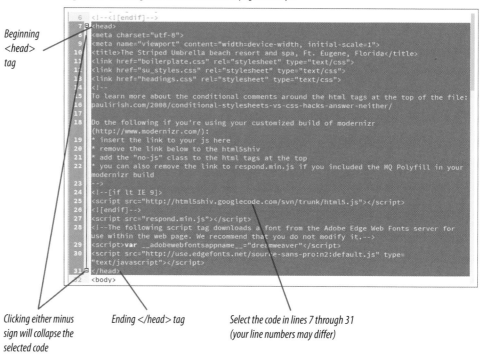

Beginning <head> tag

Clicking either minus sign will collapse the selected code

Ending </head> tag

Select the code in lines 7 through 31 (your line numbers may differ)

Figure 40 *Collapsed code in Code view*

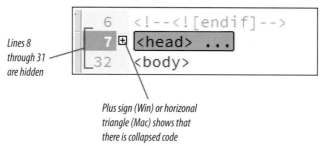

Lines 8 through 31 are hidden

Plus sign (Win) or horizonal triangle (Mac) shows that there is collapsed code

Working with Text and Cascading Style Sheets

Figure 41 *Expanded code for index page*

```
 6    <!--<![endif]-->
 7 ⊟  <head>
 8    <meta charset="utf-8">
 9    <meta name="viewport" content="width=device-width, initial-scale=1">
10    <title>The Striped Umbrella beach resort and spa, Ft. Eugene, Florida</title>
11    <link href="boilerplate.css" rel="stylesheet" type="text/css">
12    <link href="su_styles.css" rel="stylesheet" type="text/css">
13    <link href="headings.css" rel="stylesheet" type="text/css">
14    <!--
15    To learn more about the conditional comments around the html tags at the top of the file:
16    paulirish.com/2008/conditional-stylesheets-vs-css-hacks-answer-neither/
17
18    Do the following if you're using your customized build of modernizr (http://www.modernizr.com/):
19    * insert the link to your js here
20    * remove the link below to the html5shiv
21    * add the "no-js" class to the html tags at the top
22    * you can also remove the link to respond.min.js if you included the MQ Polyfill in your modernizr build
23    -->
24    <!--[if lt IE 9]>
25    <script src="http://html5shiv.googlecode.com/svn/trunk/html5.js"></script>
26    <![endif]-->
27    <script src="respond.min.js"></script>
28    <!--The following script tag downloads a font from the Adobe Edge Web Fonts server for use within the web page. We
      recommend that you do not modify it.-->
29    <script>var __adobewebfontsappname__="dreamweaver"</script>
30    <script src="http://use.edgefonts.net/source-sans-pro:n2:default.js" type="text/javascript"></script>
31 ⊟  </head>
32    <body>
```

Code is expanded again

Expand code

1. Click the **plus sign** (Win) or **horizontal triangle** (Mac) on line 7 to expand the code.

2. Compare your screen to Figure 41, then click in the page to deselect the code.

   All line numbers are visible again.

You expanded the code to display all lines of the code again.

POWER USER SHORTCUTS	
To do this:	**Use this shortcut:**
Switch views	[Ctrl][`] (Win) or [control][`] (Mac)
Indent text	[Ctrl][Alt][]] (Win) or ⌘ [option][]] (Mac)
Outdent text	[Ctrl][Alt][[] (Win) or ⌘ [option][[] (Mac)
Align Left	[Ctrl][Alt][Shift][L] (Win) or ⌘ [option][shift][L] (Mac)
Align Center	[Ctrl][Alt][Shift][C] (Win) or ⌘ [option][shift][C] (Mac)
Align Right	[Ctrl][Alt][Shift][R] (Win) or ⌘ [option][shift][R] (Mac)
Align Justify	[Ctrl][Alt][Shift][J] (Win) or ⌘ [option][shift][J] (Mac)
Bold	[Ctrl][B] (Win) or ⌘ [B] (Mac)
Italic	[Ctrl][I] (Win) or ⌘ [I] (Mac)
Refresh	[F5]

Move style from one style sheet to another

1. Return to Design view, then open CSS Designer if necessary.

2. Select **headings.css** in the Sources pane.

3. Select **.list_headings**, as shown in Figure 42, then drag and drop it on top of **su_styles.css** in the Sources pane.

   The .list_headings rule is moved from the headings.css file to the su_styles.css file, as shown in Figure 43.

4. Repeat step 3 to move the h1, h2, and h3 rules to the su_styles.css file.

   All rules have been moved out of the headings.css file and it is no longer needed.

5. Select **headings.css** in the Sources pane, then select the **Remove CSS Source button** — in the Sources pane.

   The headings.css file is no longer listed as a source in the Sources pane.

   (continued)

Figure 42 *Selecting the .list_headings rule to move to a different style sheet*

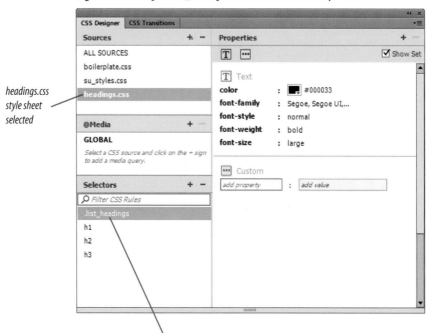

headings.css style sheet selected

Select the .list_headings selector

Figure 43 *The .list_headings rule is not listed*

The list_headings style has been moved to the su_styles.css file and no longer appears in the headings.css file

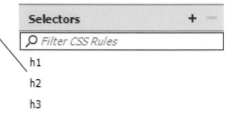

The Evolution of CSS3

The use of Cascading Style Sheets has evolved over the years from CSS Level 1 to the present CSS Level 3. Cascading Style Sheets revisions are referenced by "levels" rather than "versions." Each new level builds on the previous level. CSS Level 1 is obsolete today. CSS Level 2 is still used, but CSS Level 3 is the latest W3C (World Wide Web Consortium) standard. With CSS3, several properties are available that promote website accessibility such as the @font-face rule. For more information about CSS3, go to www.w3.org/TR/CSS/.

Working with Text and Cascading Style Sheets

Figure 44 *Selecting the code to move*

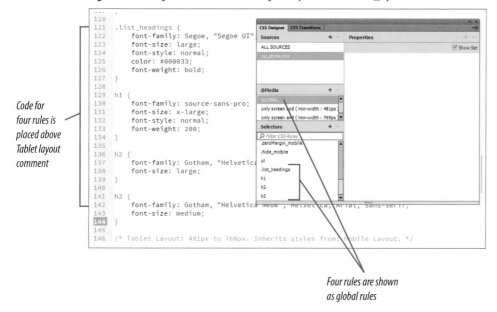

```
206
207 .list_headings {
208     font-family: Segoe, "Segoe UI", "DejaVu Sans",
    "Trebuchet MS", Verdana, sans-serif;
209     font-size: large;
210     font-style: normal;
211     color: #000033;
212     font-weight: bold;
213 }
214
215 h1 {
216     font-family: source-sans-pro;
217     font-size: x-large;
218     font-style: normal;
219     font-weight: 200;
220 }
221
222 h2 {
223     font-family: Gotham, "Helvetica Neue", Helvetica,
    Arial, sans-serif;
224     font-size: large;
225 }
226
227 h3 {
228     font-family: Gotham, "Helvetica Neue", Helvetica,
    Arial, sans-serif;
229     font-size: medium;
230 }
231
```

The four rules are selected and ready to moved to the global styles section of the style sheet

Figure 45 *Viewing the four rules moved to the global styles section of the su_styles.css file*

```
120
121 .list_headings {
122     font-family: Segoe, "Segoe UI"
123     font-size: large;
124     font-style: normal;
125     color: #000033;
126     font-weight: bold;
127 }
128
129 h1 {
130     font-family: source-sans-pro;
131     font-size: x-large;
132     font-style: normal;
133     font-weight: 200;
134 }
135
136 h2 {
137     font-family: Gotham, "Helvetica
138     font-size: large;
139 }
140
141 h3 {
142     font-family: Gotham, "Helvetica Neue", Helvetica, Arial, sans-serif;
143     font-size: medium;
144 }
145
146 /* Tablet Layout: 481px to 768px. Inherits styles from: Mobile Layout. */
```

CSS Designer   CSS Transitions

Sources   +   —   Properties
ALL SOURCES   ☑ Show Set
su_styles.css

@Media   +   —
GLOBAL
only screen and (min-width : 481px
only screen and (min-width : 769px)

Selectors   +   —
🔍 Filter CSS Rules
.zeroMargin_mobile
.hide_mobile
ol
.list_headings
h1
h2
h3

Code for four rules is placed above Tablet layout comment

Four rules are shown as global rules

6. Select **su_styles.css** on the Related files toolbar, then scroll to the bottom of the file to locate the code for the four styles that you just moved from the headings.css file, then select those lines of code, as shown in Figure 44.

7. Right-click the selected code, then select **Cut**.

8. Scroll to place the insertion point above the comment "/* Tablet Layout: 481px to 768px. Inherits styles from: Mobile Layout. */", right-click, then select **Paste**.

   The code for the four styles now is categorized as GLOBAL codes that can be used for all devices, as shown in Figure 45.

9. Switch to Code view on the Spa page, scroll to find the link in the head section to the headings.css file, then delete it.

10. Delete the **headings.css** file in the Files panel.

11. Return to Design view, then save and close all open files.

You moved three embedded rules to the su_styles.css style sheet. You then moved the code from the bottom of the style sheet to the global styles section of the code. Finally, you deleted the headings.css source, which was now empty.

Create unordered and ordered lists.

1. Open the Blooms & Bulbs website.
2. Open the tips page.
3. Select the text items below the Seasonal Gardening Checklist heading and format them as an unordered list. (*Hint*: There are no paragraph breaks between each item. To correct this, enter a paragraph break between each line, then remove any extra spaces.)
4. Select the lines of text below the Basic Gardening Tips heading and format them as an ordered list. (Refer to the Step 3 hint if each line does not become a separate list item.)
5. Save your work.

Create a Cascading Style Sheet and apply, edit, and add rules.

1. Create a new CSS file named **headings.css**.
2. Create a new global selector in the headings.css style sheet named **.bullet_term**.
3. Choose the following text properties and values for the .bullet_term selector: color: #333333; font-weight: bold; font-size: medium.
4. Apply the bullet_term rule to the names of the seasons in the Seasonal Gardening Checklist: Fall, Winter, Spring, and Summer.

5. Edit the bullet_term rule by changing the font size to large.
6. Create a new global selector to modify the h1 tag in the headings.css file with the following property and value: font-size = large.
7. Save your work.

Understand related files and media queries.

1. Select the bb_styles.css file in the Related files toolbar.
2. Change to Code view, then locate each block of code that lists the global, tablet, and desktop selectors.
3. Return to Design view.

Add Adobe Edge Web fonts.

1. Select the headings.css in the CSS Designer Sources pane, then select h1 in the Selectors pane.
2. Select the font-family list box in the Properties pane, then select Manage Fonts.
3. Select the font Lobster Two from the list of fonts recommended for headings.
4. Set the lobster-two font for the h1 font-family value.
5. Use the Clean Up Web Fonts Script Tag (Current Page), then save your work.
6. View the tips page in Live view to view the new h1 font.

Use coding tools to view and edit rules.

1. Open the index page, then change to Code view.
2. Display the code for the head section of the page.
3. Collapse all of the selected code.
4. Expand the code.
5. Use CSS Designer to attach the headings.css file to the index page, then select headings.css in the CSS Designer Sources pane.
6. Select the .bullet_term selector, then drag and drop it to bb_styles.css in the Sources pane.
7. Repeat Step 6 to move the h1 rule to the bb_styles.css file.
8. Select headings.css in the Sources pane, then delete it as a source in the Sources pane.
9. Select bb_styles.css on the Related files toolbar, scroll to the bottom of the file to locate the code for the two styles that you just moved from the headings.css file, then select and cut those lines of code.
10. Scroll to place the insertion point above the comment "/* Tablet Layout: 481px to 768px. Inherits styles from: Mobile Layout. */", right-click, then paste the code you just cut.
11. Go to the tips page code and remove the link to the headings.css file if you find one there, then select and delete the headings.css file in the Files panel.
12. Check the code for the index and tips page for a link to the headings.css file. If you see one, delete it and save the page.
13. Save all open files, change to Design view, compare your pages to Figures 46 and 47, then close all open files.

Figure 46 & 47 *Completed Skills Review*

Home - Featured Plants - Garden Tips - Workshops - Newsletter

Welcome to Blooms & Bulbs. We carry a variety of plants and shrubs along with a large inventory of gardening supplies. Our four greenhouses are full of healthy young plants just waiting to be planted in your yard. We grow an amazing selection of annuals and perennials. We also stock a diverse selection of trees, shrubs, tropicals, water plants, and ground covers. Check out our garden ware for your garden accents or as gifts for your gardening friends. We are happy to deliver or ship your purchases.

Our staff includes a certified landscape architect, three landscape designers
plans tailored to your location as well as planting and regular maintenance
surrounding area for twelve years now. Stop by and see us soon!

Blooms & Bulbs
Highway 43 South
Alvin, TX 77501
555-248-0806
Customer Service

Copyright 2002 - 201
Last updated on April 17

We have lots of tips we would like to share with you as you prepare your gardens this season. Remember, there is always something to be done for your gardens, no matter what the season. Our experienced staff is here to help you plan your gardens, select your plants, prepare your soil, assist you in the planting, and maintain your beds. Check out our calendar for a list of our scheduled workshops. Our next workshop is "Attracting Butterflies to Your Garden." All workshops are free of charge and on a first-come, first-served basis! They fill up quickly, so be sure to reserve your spot early.

Seasonal Gardening Checklist

- **Fall** – The time to plant trees and spring-blooming bulbs. Take the time to clean the leaves and dead foliage from your beds and lawn.
- **Winter** – The time to prune fruit trees and finish planting your bulbs. Don't forget to water young trees when the ground is dry.
- **Spring** – The time to prepare your beds, plant annuals, and apply fertilizer to established plants. Remember to mulch to maintain moisture and prevent weed growth.
- **Summer** – The time to supplement rainfall so that plants get one inch of water per week. Plant your vegetable garden and enjoy bountiful harvests until late fall.

Basic Gardening Tips

1. Select plants according to your climate.
2. In planning your garden, consider the composition, texture, structure, depth, and drainage of your soil.
3. Use compost to improve the structure of your soil.
4. Choose plant foods based on your garden objectives.
5. Generally, plants should receive one inch of water per week.
6. Use mulch to conserve moisture, keep plants cool, and cut down on weeding.

Use Figure 48 as a guide to continue your work on the TripSmart website that you began in Project Builder 1 in Chapter 1, and continued to work on in Chapter 2. (Your finished pages will look different if you choose different formatting options.) You are now ready to create some rules to use for the text on the newsletter and index pages.

1. Open the TripSmart website.
2. Open dw3_1.html from where you store your Data Files and save it in the tripsmart site folder as **newsletter.html**, overwriting the existing newsletter.html file and not updating the links.
3. Create an unordered list from the text beginning "Be organized." to the end of the page except for the contact information.
4. Create a new CSS file named **headings.css.**
5. Create a new selector in the headings.css style sheet named **.list_terms**.
6. Choose properties and values of your choice for the .list_terms selector.
7. Apply the .list_terms rule to each of the item names in the list such as "Be organized."
8. Close the dw3_1.html page, then save the newsletter page and the style sheet.
9. Select the headings.css file in the CSS Designer Sources pane, then create a tag selector to format the h1 tag with properties and values of your choice. If you like, you can choose an Edge Web font.

10. Apply the h1 format to the Ten Tips for Stress-Free Travel heading, use the Clean Up Web Fonts Script Tag (Current Page) if you used an Edge Web font, return to Design view, then save your work.
11. View the newsletter page in Live view to view the new h1 font.
12. Move the two selectors in the headings.css file to the tripsmart_styles.css file, being sure to place them above the comment "/* Tablet Layout: 481px to 768px. Inherits styles from: Mobile Layout. */".
13. Select and delete the headings.css file in the Files panel.
14. Delete the headings.css source in the CSS Designer Sources pane, then save and preview the newsletter page in your browser, using Figure 48 as an example.
15. Close your browser, then close all open files.

Figure 48 *Sample Project Builder 1*

Our staff recently conducted a contest to determine ten top travel tips for stress-free travel. We compiled over forty great tips, but the following were selected as the winners. We hope you will find them useful for your next trip!

Ten Tips for Stress-Free Travel

- **Be organized.**
  Make a list of what you want to pack in each bag and check it as you pack. Take this inventory with you in the event your bags are lost or delayed. Then use the list again when you repack, to make sure you haven't left anything behind.
- **Carry important information with you.**
  Keep your important travel information in easy reach at all times. Include a list of your flight numbers, confirmation numbers for your travel and hotel reservations, and any car rentals. And don't forget printouts of your itinerary and electronic tickets. Remember to bring your passport, and keep a photocopy of it in another piece of baggage. Be sure to have copies of prescriptions, emergency phone numbers, telephone numbers and addresses of friends and relatives, complete lists of medications, and credit card information. It's not a bad idea to email this information to yourself as a backup if you will have email access.
- **Pack smartly.**
  You know the old saying: lay out everything on your bed you plan to take with you, then remove half of it. Pack the remainder and carry your bags around the block once to make sure you can handle them yourself. If in doubt, leave it out! Use packing cubes or zip-top bags to organize your personal items, such as underwear and socks. Make distinctive-looking luggage tags with your name and address for easy identification, and be sure to include the same information inside your luggage.

Working with Text and Cascading Style Sheets

In this exercise, you continue your work on the Carolyne's Creations website that you started in Project Builder 2 in Chapter 1, and continued to build in Chapter 2. You are now ready to add a page to the website that will showcase a recipe. Figure 49 shows a possible solution for the page in this exercise. Your finished pages will look different if you choose different formatting options.

1. Open the Carolyne's Creations website.

2. Open dw3_2.html from the location where you store your Data Files, save it to the website site folder as **recipes.html**, overwriting the existing file and not updating the links. Close the dw3_2.html file.

3. Format the list of ingredients on the recipes page as an unordered list.

4. Create a new CSS Styles file named **headings.css**, then add a new tag selector rule that defines the properties for a Heading 1 rule and another one that defines the properties for a Heading 2 rule, using appropriate formatting options. Use Adobe Edge Web fonts if you like.

5. Apply the <h1> format to the "Caramel Coconut Pie" heading and the <h2> rule to the "Ingredients" and "Directions" headings, then save your work.

6. Move the two new selectors to the cc_styles.css file, then delete the headings.css source in the CSS Designer Sources pane, and also in the Files panel.

7. Save all open files, then preview the page in the browser.

8. Close your browser, then close all open pages.

Figure 49 *Sample Project Builder 2*

Home | Shop | Classes | Catering | Recipes

Caramel Coconut Pie

This is one of our most requested desserts. It is simple, elegant, and refreshing. It is easy to make in advance, because you keep it frozen until just before serving. It makes two pies — one to eat and one to give away!

Ingredients:

- ¼ cup butter
- 7 oz. dried coconut
- ½ cup chopped pecans
- 1 package (8 oz.) cream cheese, softened
- 1 can (14 oz.) sweetened condensed milk
- 1 container (16 oz.) whipped topping, thawed
- 1 jar (12 oz.) caramel ice cream topping
- 2 pie shells (9 in.), baked

Directions:

Melt butter in large skillet. Add coconut & pecans; cook until golden brown, stirring frequently. Set aside. Combine cream cheese & milk. Beat until smooth, then fold in whipped topping. Layer ¼ of cream cheese mixture into each pie shell. Drizzle ¼ of caramel topping on each pie. Sprinkle ¼ of coconut & pecan mixture evenly on each pie. Repeat layers. Cover & freeze until firm. Let stand at room temperature for 5 minutes before serving.

This recipe was contributed by Cosie Simmons.

Charles Chappell is a sixth-grade history teacher. He is reviewing educational websites for information he can use in his classroom.

1. Connect to the Internet, then navigate to the Library of Congress website at www.loc.gov. The Library of Congress website is shown in Figure 50.

2. Which fonts are used for the main content on the home page—serif or sans-serif? Are the same fonts used consistently on the other pages in the site?

3. Do you see ordered or unordered lists on any pages in the site? If so, how are they used?

4. Use the View > Source (IE) or the Tools > Web Developer > Page Source (Firefox) command to view the source code to see if a style sheet was used.

5. Do you see the use of Cascading Style Sheets noted in the source code?

Figure 50 *Design Project*

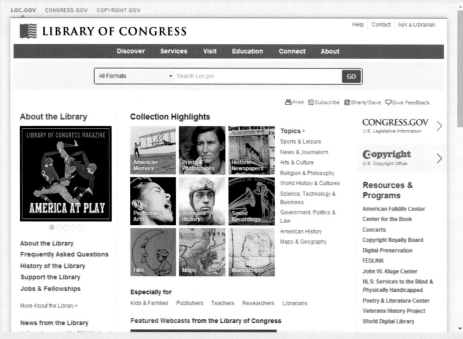

Source: Library of Congress

In this assignment, you will continue to work on the website that you started in Chapter 1, and continued to build in Chapter 2. No Data Files are supplied. You are building this site from chapter to chapter, so you must do each Portfolio Project assignment in each chapter to complete your website.

You continue building your website by designing and completing a page that contains a list, headings, and paragraph text. During this process, you will develop a style sheet and add several rules to it

1. Consult your wireframe and decide which page to create and develop for this chapter.
2. Plan the page content for the page and make a sketch of the layout. Your sketch should include at least one ordered or unordered list, appropriate headings, and paragraph text. Your sketch should also show where the paragraph text and headings should be placed on the page and what rules should be used for each type of text. You should plan on creating at least two CSS rules.
3. Create the page using your sketch for guidance.
4. Create a Cascading Style Sheet for the site and add to it the rules you decided to use. Apply the rules to the appropriate content.
5. Attach the style sheet to the index page you developed in Chapter 2.
6. Preview the new page in a browser, then check for page layout problems and broken links. Make any necessary corrections in Dreamweaver, then preview the page again in the browser. Repeat this process until you are satisfied with the way the page looks in the browser.
7. Use the checklist in Figure 51 to check all the pages in your site.
8. Close the browser, then close all open pages.

Figure 51 *Portfolio Project*

Website Checklist
1. Does each page have a page title?
2. Does the home page have a description and keywords?
3. Does the home page contain contact information?
4. Does every completed page in the site have consistent navigation links?
5. Does the home page have a last updated statement that will automatically update when the page is saved?
6. Do all paths for links and images work correctly?
7. Is there a style sheet with at least two rules?
8. Did you apply the rules to all text blocks?
9. Do all pages look good using mobile, tablet, and desktop sizes?

CHAPTER 4 ADDING IMAGES

1. Insert and align images using CSS
2. Enhance an image and use alternate text
3. Insert a background image and perform site maintenance
4. Add graphic enhancements

ADDING IMAGES

Introduction

The majority of web page information appears in the form of text. But pages are much more interesting if they also include images that enhance or illustrate the information. A well-designed web page usually includes a balanced combination of text and images. Dreamweaver provides many tools for working with images that you can use to make your web pages attractive and easy to understand.

Using Images to Enhance Web Pages

Images make web pages visually stimulating and more exciting than pages that contain only text. However, you should use images with an eye on both the purpose of each page and the overall design plan. There is a fine balance between using too many images that overwhelm the user and not providing enough images to enhance the text. There are many ways to work with images so that they complement the content of pages in a website. For instance, a research website would probably need few graphics other than charts, because the content emphasis would be on text. A photographer's website, on the other hand, would be rich in high-quality photographs to display the photographer's expertise. You can use specific file formats used to save images for websites to ensure maximum quality with minimum file size.

Graphics Versus Images

Two terms that designers sometimes use interchangeably are graphics and images. For the purposes of discussion in this text, we will use the term **graphics** to refer to the appearance of most non-text items on a web page, such as photographs, logos, menu bars, animations, charts, background images, and drawings. Files for items such as these are called graphic files. They are referred to by their file type, or graphic file format, such as JPEG (Joint Photographic Experts Group), GIF (Graphics Interchange Format), or PNG (Portable Network Graphics). We will refer to the actual pictures that you see on the pages as images. But don't worry about which term to use. Many people use one term or the other according to habit or region, or use them interchangeably.

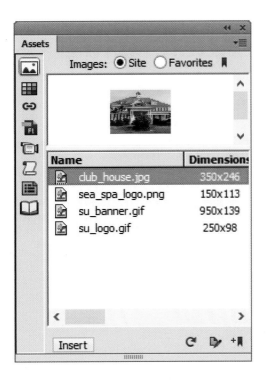

Insert and
ALIGN IMAGES USING CSS

What You'll Do

In this lesson, you will insert an image on the about_us page in The Striped Umbrella website. You will then adjust the alignment of the image on the page to make the page more visually appealing.

Understanding Graphic File Formats

When you choose graphics to add to a web page, it's important to use graphic files in the appropriate file format. Keep in mind the different types of devices that may be used to view the pages, such as tablets or other mobile devices. The three primary graphic file formats used in web pages are **GIF** (Graphics Interchange Format), **JPEG** or **JPG** (Joint Photographic Experts Group), and **PNG** (Portable Network Graphics). GIF files download quickly, making them ideal to use on web pages. Though limited in the number of colors they can represent, GIF files have the ability to show transparent areas. JPG files can display many colors. Because they often contain many shades of the same color, photographs are often saved in JPG format. Files saved with the PNG format can display many colors and use various degrees of transparency, called **opacity**. The PNG format gives greater color depth when designing for mobile devices.

Understanding the Assets Panel

When you add a graphic to a website, Dreamweaver automatically adds it to the Assets panel. The **Assets panel** displays all the assets (images, videos, audio files) in a website. The Assets panel contains eight category buttons that you use to view your assets by category. These include Images, Colors, URLs, SWF, Movies, Scripts, Templates, and Library. To view a particular type of asset, click the appropriate category button.

The Assets panel is divided into two panes. When you select the Images button, the lower pane displays a list of all the images in your site and is divided into five columns. Resize the Assets panel to see all five columns, by dragging a side or corner of the panel border.

The top pane displays a thumbnail of the selected image in the list. You can view assets in each category in two ways. You can use the Site option button to view all the assets in a website, or you can use the Favorites option button to view those assets that you have designated as **favorites**, or assets that you expect to use repeatedly while you work on the site. You can use the Assets panel to add an asset to a web page by dragging the asset from the Assets panel to the page or by using the Insert button on the Assets panel.

Aligning Images

When you insert an image on a web page, you need to position it in relation to other page elements such as text or other images. Positioning an image is also called **aligning** an image. By default, when you insert an image in a paragraph, its bottom edge aligns with the baseline of the first line of text or any other element in the same paragraph. When you first place images on a page, they do not include code to align them, so they appear at the insertion point, with no other page elements next to them. You add alignment settings using CSS. By adding a new rule to modify the <img> tag, you can add an alignment property and value. If you use an external style sheet, the <img> tag will apply globally to all images on pages with a link to the style sheet. If you want to align some images differently than others, create specific rules for each device when using fluid grid layouts. However, as you create these rules, remember the rules of inheritance: tablet and desktop selectors inherit global (mobile) properties, but if you modify the tablet properties, the desktop selectors then inherit the tablet properties, unless you specify otherwise, as shown in Figure 1.

Selecting Images for a Responsive Design

It is important to visualize how your images will look when displayed in multiple devices. Experiment with the images you select by using the Mobile, Tablet, and Desktop size buttons to see how they will look on the finished page. One way to allow for attractive placement of images is to avoid setting specific sizes for image heights and widths on a page. If you do set image sizes, use percents so the image can adjust proportionally to the screen size. Still another method is to specify different images for each device. The Striped Umbrella website has a different image used as the banner background for the mobile size page. The tablet size page uses the same banner image as the desktop size, but not all of the umbrellas on the right side of the banner are visible when the window width is reduced to tablet size. Try each of these methods and see which best fits your design needs.

Figure 1 *Rules of inheritance for selectors*

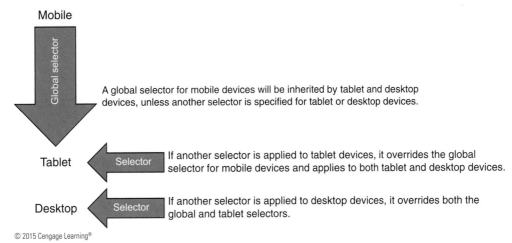

© 2015 Cengage Learning®

Insert an image

1. Open The Striped Umbrella website, then open dw4_1.html from the drive and folder where you store your Data Files.

   Notice that the page is not formatted, as shown in Figure 2. This is because the page cannot find the style sheet. The style sheet is in the local site folder, but not in the Data Files folder. When you save the file without updating links, the link to the style sheet will find the style sheet and apply the selectors to the page elements. If you update links, the link to the style sheet will be broken and the page will remain unformatted.

2. Save the file as **about_us.html** in the local site folder, select **Yes** (Win) or **Replace** (Mac) to overwrite the existing file, select **No** to Update Links, then close dw4_1.html.

   The new about_us page is now formatted with the website style sheets since the link to the su_styles.css file can now find the file in the local site folder.

3. In the Property inspector, select the **HTML button** <> HTML , if necessary, then apply the Heading 1 tag to the text "Welcome guests!"

4. Place the insertion point before "When" in the first paragraph, switch to Code view to place your insertion point before the opening <p> tag for the first paragraph, if necessary, return to Design view, select the **Images list arrow** in the Common category in the Insert panel, then select **Image** to open the Select Image Source dialog box.

   (continued)

Figure 2 *The about_us page before the CSS file is linked to apply formatting*

Welcome guests!

When you arrive at The Striped Umbrella, check in at The Club House. Look for the signs that will direct you to registration. Our beautiful club house is the home base for our registration offices, The Sand Crab Cafe, and The Sea Spa. Registration is open from 8:00 a.m. until 6:00 p.m. Please call to make arrangements if you plan to arrive after 6:00 p.m. The cafe and spa hours are both posted and listed in the information packet that you will receive when you arrive. The main swimming pool is directly behind The Club House. A lifeguard is on duty from 8:00 a.m. until 9:00 p.m. The pool area includes a wading pool, a lap pool, and a large pool with a diving board. Showers are located in several areas for your use before and after swimming. We also provide poolside service from the cafe for snacks and lunch.

Text is not yet formatted since the links to the style sheets cannot find the style sheets to apply the styles

Figure 3 *Striped Umbrella about_us page with the inserted image*

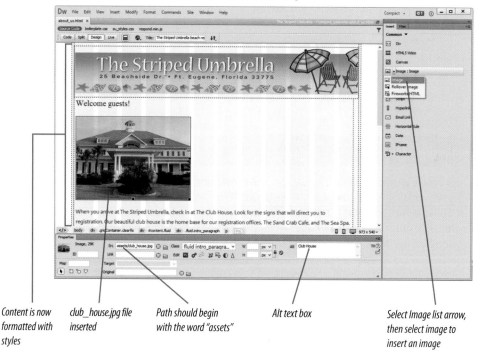

Content is now formatted with styles

club_house.jpg file inserted

Path should begin with the word "assets"

Alt text box

Select Image list arrow, then select image to insert an image

Figure 4 *Image files for The Striped Umbrella website listed in Assets panel*

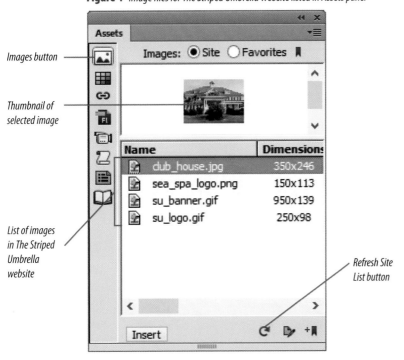

Images button

Thumbnail of selected image

List of images in The Striped Umbrella website

Refresh Site List button

5. Navigate to the assets folder in the drive and folder where you store your Data Files, double-click **club_house.jpg**, type the alternate text **Club House** in the Alt text box in the Property inspector, open the Files panel if necessary, then verify that the file was copied to your assets folder in the striped_umbrella site root folder.

6. If the text appears on the same line as the image, place the insertion point before "When" again, press **[Enter]** (Win) or **[return]** (Mac), then select the club house image.

   The paragraph now begins under the club house image, as shown in Figure 3.

7. Open the **Assets panel**, select the **Images button** in the Assets panel (if necessary), then select the **Refresh Site List button** in the Assets panel to update the list of images in The Striped Umbrella website.

   The Assets panel displays a list of all the images in The Striped Umbrella website, as shown in Figure 4. If you don't see the new image listed, press and hold [CTRL] (Win) or ⌘ (Mac) before you select the Refresh Site List button.

8. Close the Assets panel.

You inserted one image on the about_us page and verified that it was copied to the assets folder of the website.

Organizing Assets for Quick Access

Your can organize the assets in the Assets panel in two ways, using the Site and Favorites options buttons. The Site option lists all of the assets in the website in the selected category in alphabetical order. But in a complex site, your asset list can grow quite large. To avoid having to scroll to search for frequently used items, you can designate them as Favorites. To add an asset to the Favorites list, right-click (Win) or [control]-click (Mac) the asset name in the Site list, and then select Add to Favorites. When you place an asset in the Favorites list, it still appears in the Site list. To delete an asset from the Favorites list, select the Favorites option button in the Assets panel, select the asset you want to delete, and then press [Delete] or [Backspace] (Win) or [control][delete] (Mac), or the Remove from Favorites button on the Assets panel. If you delete an asset from the Favorites list, it still remains in the Site list. You can further organize your Favorites list by creating folders for similar assets and grouping them inside the folders.

Create a global class selector for images

1. Open CSS Designer and expand the width to display two columns, if necessary.

2. Select **su_styles.css** in the Sources pane, then select **GLOBAL** in the @Media pane.

   You are creating a new global rule that will apply to all images that you want to control the float, or position in relation to other page elements next to them. Remember that global rules are used to style page elements for the mobile size display and are inherited by the tablet and desktop size devices unless otherwise specified.

3. Select the **Add Selector button** ➕ in the Selectors pane, then type **.img_float** in the selector name text box and press **[Enter]** (Win) or **[return]** (Mac).

   TIP When you add a new class selector, remember to type a period before all class selector names.

4. Select the **.img_float** selector in the Selectors pane if necessary, then uncheck the **Show Set** check box in the Properties pane if necessary.

5. Select the **Layout button** ▥ in the Properties pane, if necessary, then scroll down to select the **none button** ◻ beside the float property, as shown in Figure 5.

   (continued)

Figure 5 *Selecting the float property for the .img_float selector*

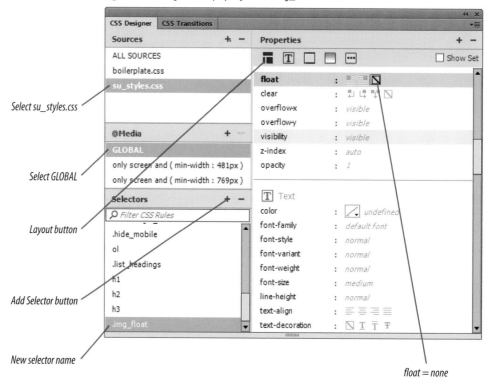

Select su_styles.css

Select GLOBAL

Layout button

Add Selector button

New selector name

float = none

Figure 6 *Viewing only the GLOBAL .img_float selector's set properties*

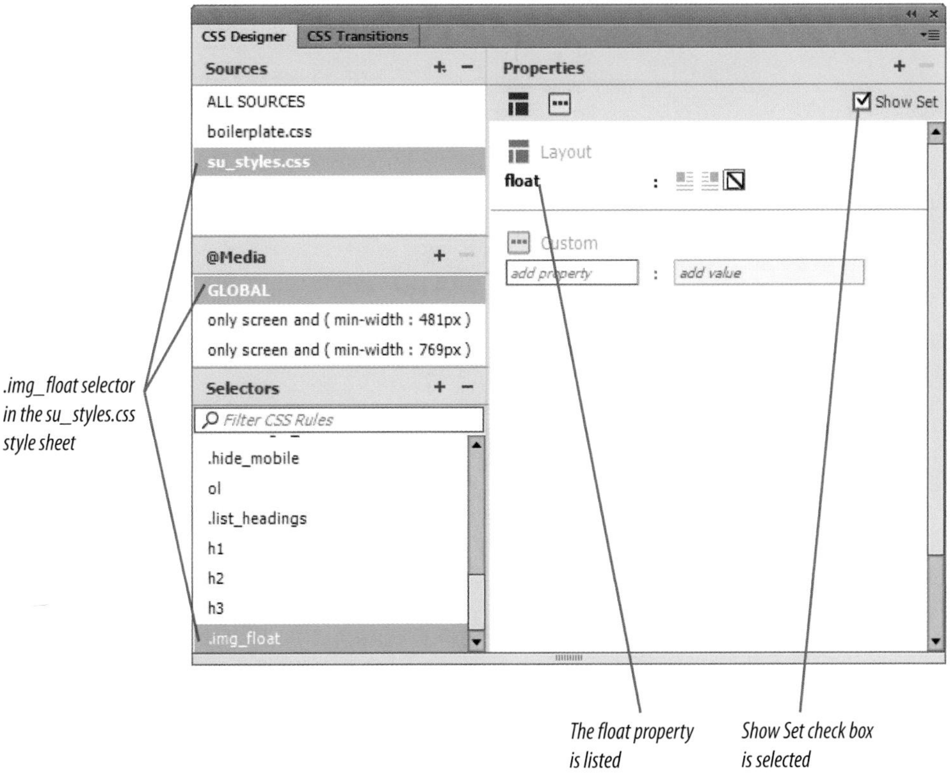

.img_float selector in the su_styles.css style sheet

The float property is listed

Show Set check box is selected

The default value for the float property is none. The float property is used to force other page elements to display to the right or to the left of another page element. The none value means that no other page element will appear beside an image with this selector applied. The left value means an image styled with this selector will "float" to the left of other page elements if space is available. The right value means an image styled with this selector will "float" to the right of other page elements if space is available.

6. Select the **Show Set check box** to see the new selector, as shown in Figure 6, then uncheck it again.

 The Show Set check box allows you to quickly see only the properties that have been set for a selector.

7. Save all files.

You added a global selector named .img_float to set the float property to none selector.

Create a tablet size selector for images

1. Select **su_styles.css** in the Sources pane, then select **only screen and (min-width : 481px)** in the @Media pane.

   You are going to modify the .img_float selector for viewing on a tablet size device.

2. Select the **Add Selector button** ➕ in the Selectors pane, then type **.img_float** in the selector name text box and press **[Enter]** (Win) or **[return]** (Mac) twice.

3. Select the **.img_float** selector in the Selectors pane if necessary, then uncheck the **Show Set** check box in the Properties pane if necessary.

4. Select the **Layout button** ▦ in the Properties pane if necessary, then scroll down to select the **left button** ▤ beside the float property, as shown in Figure 7.

   An image styled with this selector will "float" to the left of other page elements when viewed on a tablet-size or desktop-size device. The global .img_float selector will no longer apply to images with this selector when they are viewed on a tablet-size or desktop-size device, because this selector will now take precedence. Desktop devices will inherit the tablet selector properties and values unless otherwise specified.

   (continued)

Figure 7 *Selecting the float property for the tablet size img selector*

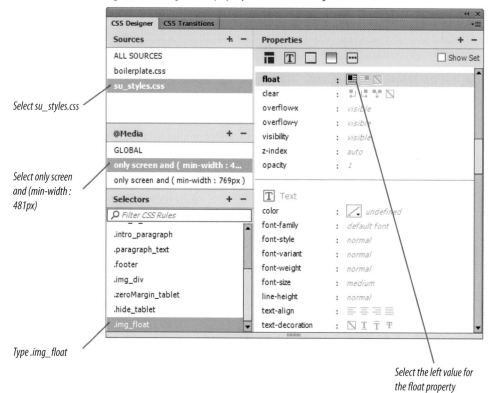

Select su_styles.css

Select only screen and (min-width : 481px)

Type .img_float

Select the left value for the float property

Figure 8 *Viewing the tablet size img selector's set float property*

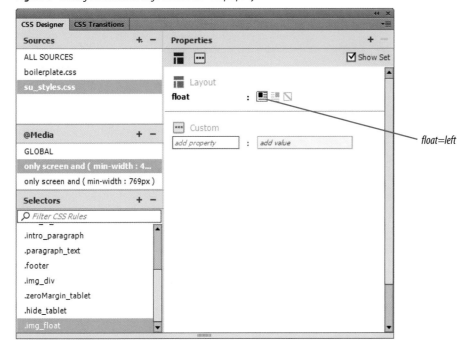

float=left

5. Select the **Show Set check box** to see the new selector, as shown in Figure 8, then uncheck it again.

   The Show Set check box allows you to quickly see only the properties that have been set for a selector.

6. Save all files.

You set the float property to left for the tablet size img selector.

Apply a selector and view the pages in three device sizes

1. On the about_us page, select the **club house** image if necessary, select the **Class list arrow** on the Property inspector, then select **img_float**, as shown in Figure 9.

   The img_float selector is applied to the club house image. The paragraph of text moves up and to the right of the club house image.

2. Select the **Mobile size** button 📱 on the Status bar.

   The paragraphs of text are below the club house image when viewed in mobile size, as shown in Figure 10, because the img_float global selector has a float value of none.

   (continued)

Figure 9 *Applying the img_float selector to the club house image*

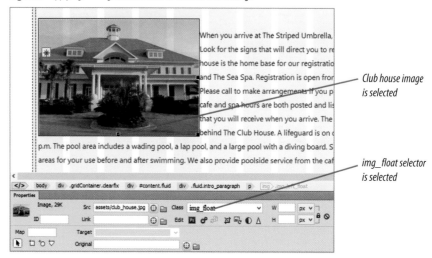

Club house image is selected

img_float selector is selected

Figure 10 *Viewing the about us page in mobile size*

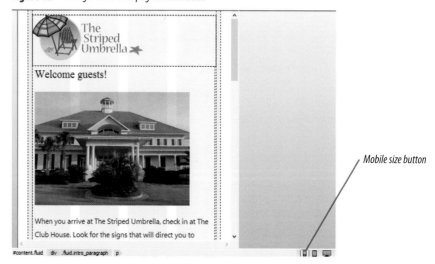

Mobile size button

Figure 11 *Viewing the about us page in tablet size*

Figure 12 *Viewing the about us page in desktop size*

Tablet size button

Desktop size button

Figure 13 *Viewing the two new rules in the su_styles.css file*

Mobile rule

Tablet rule

```
45   /* Mobile Layout: 480px and below. */
46   .gridC...
145  .img_float {
146      float: none;
147  }
148
149
150
151  /* Tablet Layout: 481px to 768px. Inherits styles from: Mobile Layout. */
152  @media...
191  .img_float {
192      float: left;
193  }
194
195
196  }
197
198  /* Desktop Layout: 769px to a max of 1232px.  Inherits styles from: Mobile L
```

3. Select the **Tablet size** button ☐ on the Status bar.

   The first paragraph of text floats up to the right side of the image when the screen is wider, as shown in Figure 11, because the tablet size img_float selector has a float value of left.

4. Select the **Desktop size** button 🖥 on the Status bar.

   With the inherited tablet size img_float selector, the first paragraph of text floats up to the right side of the image with longer lines of text filling the empty space when the screen is wider, as shown in Figure 12.

5. Select **su_styles.css** in the Related Files toolbar, then scroll to locate the two image_float rules.

   Each rule is in a separate section of the file, as shown in Figure 13: one in the mobile layout (global) section of code, and one in the tablet layout section of code. Because the desktop layout inherits the tablet size img_float selector, it does not have an img_float selector listed.

   The two sections of code have been collapsed to show each of the rules in the same figure.

6. Return to Design view.

You applied the img_float selector to the club house image, then viewed the results in three device sizes.

Enhance an Image and
USE ALTERNATE TEXT

What You'll Do

In this lesson, you will use CSS to add borders to images, add horizontal and vertical space to set them apart from the text, and then add or edit alternate text for each image on the page.

Enhancing an Image

After you place an image on a web page, you have several options for enhancing it, or improving its appearance. To make changes to the image itself, such as removing scratches from it, or erasing parts of it, you need to use an external image editor such as Adobe Fireworks or Adobe Photoshop.

QUICK TIP

You can copy a Photoshop PSD file and paste it directly into Dreamweaver. After inserting the image, Dreamweaver will prompt you to optimize the image for the web. Watch the video "Extract from PSDs" in the New Feature Videos list for more information.

You can use Dreamweaver to enhance how images appear on a page. For example, you can modify the brightness and contrast, add borders around an image or add horizontal and vertical space. **Borders** are frames that surround an image. Horizontal and vertical space is blank space above, below, and on the sides of an image that separates the image from text or other elements on the page. Adding horizontal or vertical space is the same as adding white space, and helps images stand out on a page. You add horizontal and vertical space with the CSS margin properties and add borders with the CSS borders properties. The Department of Transportation website,

DESIGNTIP

Resizing Graphics Using an External Editor

Each image on a web page takes a specific number of seconds to download, depending on the size of the file. Larger files (in kilobytes, not width and height) take longer to download than smaller files. It's important to use the smallest acceptable size for an image on a page. If you need to reduce the file size, use an external image editor to do so, instead of resizing it in Dreamweaver. Decreasing the size of an image using the H (height) and W (width) settings in the Property inspector does not reduce the file size or the time it will take the file to download. Ideally you should use images that have the smallest file size and the highest quality possible, so that each page downloads as quickly as possible.

as shown in Figure 14, uses horizontal and vertical space around the images to help make these images more prominent. Adding horizontal or vertical space does not affect the width or height of the image. You can also add spacing around web page objects by using "spacer" images, or transparent images that act as placeholders.

Using Alternate Text

One of the easiest ways to make your web page user-friendly and accessible to people of all abilities is to use alternate text. Alternate text is descriptive text that appears in place of an image while the image is downloading or not displayed. **Screen readers**, devices used by persons with visual impairments to convert written text on a computer monitor to spoken words, can "read" alternate text aloud and make it possible for users to have an image described to them in detail. You should also use alternate text when inserting form objects, text displayed as graphics, buttons, frames, and media files. Without alternate text assigned to these objects, screen readers will not be able to read them.

One of the default preferences in Dreamweaver is to prompt you to enter alternate text whenever you insert media on a page. You can set alternate text options in the Accessibility category of the Preferences dialog box. You can program some browsers to display only alternate text and to download images manually. Earlier versions of some browsers used to show alternate text when the pointer was placed over an image, such as Internet Explorer versions before version 8.0.

The use of alternate text is the first checkpoint listed in the Web Content Accessibility Guidelines (WCAG), Version 2.0, from the World Wide Web Consortium (W3C). The 12 WCAG guidelines are grouped together under four principles: perceivable, operable, understandable, and robust. The first guideline under perceivable states that a website should "Provide text alternatives for any non-text content so that it can be changed into other forms people need, such as large print, Braille, speech, symbols, or simpler language." To view the complete set of accessibility guidelines, go to the Web Accessibility Initiative page at w3.org/WAI/. You should always strive to meet these criteria for all web pages.

Figure 14 *Department of Transportation website*

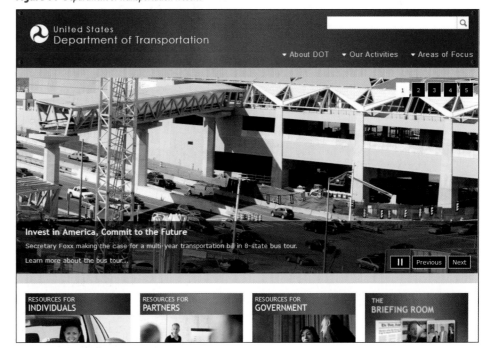

Source: *United States Department of Transportation*

Add a border

1. Select **su_styles** in the CSS Designer Sources pane, select **GLOBAL** in the @Media pane, then select **img_float** in the Selectors pane.

   Since the image property you are going to create will apply to all device-size layouts, it can be defined once in the GLOBAL media selector. The tablet and desktop size layouts will inherit this image property.

2. Select the **Border button** ☐ in the Properties pane, then select the **All sides button** ▭ .

3. Select the **width value** text box, then select **thin**.

4. Select the **style value** text box, then select **solid**.

5. Select the **default color text box** ▨, use the Color picker to select a **dark gray color**, then compare your screen to Figure 15.

   Your color value will probably have a different HEX value.

6. Select the **Mobile size button** ▯ on the Status bar, select the **Tablet size button** ▭ , then select the **Desktop size button** ▭ .

   The thin gray border surrounds the image in each layout, as shown in Figure 16, since the image border property was inherited by the tablet and desktop layouts.

   You edited the img_float global selector by adding a border.

Figure 15 *The img_float border values in the CSS Designer Properties pane*

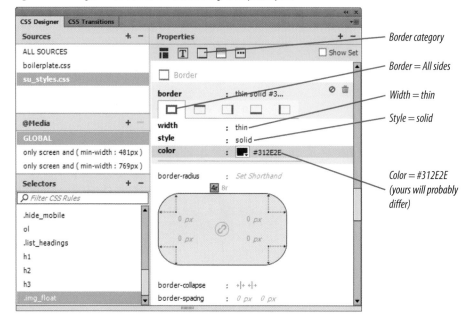

Border category
Border = All sides
Width = thin
Style = solid
Color = #312E2E
(yours will probably differ)

Figure 16 *Viewing the image_float border in the Desktop-size layout*

Thin border frames image

Adding Images

Figure 17 *Setting the margin property value for the img_float selector*

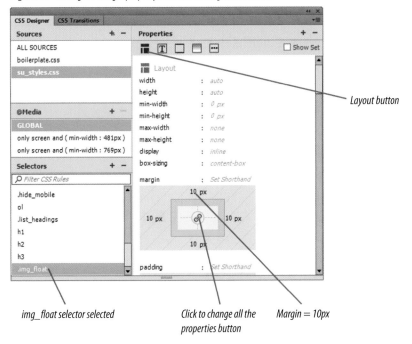

img_float selector selected

Click to change all the properties button

Margin = 10px

Layout button

Figure 18 *Viewing the image with a border and margins*

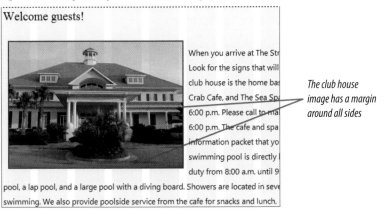

The club house image has a margin around all sides

Add horizontal and vertical space

1. With the img_float global selector selected in the Selectors pane, select the **Layout button** , then select the **Click to change all the properties button** in the middle of the margin properties diagram.

2. Select the **top margin property**, then type **10px**, then press [Enter] (Win) or [return] (Mac) as shown in Figure 17.

    By selecting the Click to change all the properties button, the 10 px margin is applied to all four sides of the image, as shown in Figure 18. The text is easier to read, because it is not so close to the edge of the image. Since you made these changes to the global img_float rule, they will also be inherited by the tablet and desktop size devices.

TIP If you don't want to set the same margin value to all sides, deselect the Click to change all the properties button, then select and change each value independently.

3. Save all files.

You added horizontal and vertical spacing to the img_float selector with the margin property.

Edit image settings

1. Select the **club house image** on the about_us page.

   The club_house image is a jpg, which is an appropriate format to use for photographs. You can tell the image is selected when you see selection handles around it.

2. Select the **Edit Images Settings button** ⚙ in the Property inspector, then select the **Preset list arrow**, as shown in Figure 19.

   You can use the Image Optimization dialog box to save a copy of the image in a different file format. File property options vary depending on which graphics format you choose. When you choose a different file format, then edit and save it, the program creates a copy and does not alter the original file. The current image file size shown at the bottom of the dialog box is 23 K.

3. Choose the **JPEG for Photos (Continuous Tones)** preset, then notice that the file size that appears at the bottom of the dialog box has increased only slightly.

   You can also use the Quality slider to change the file size after you have selected a format and preset.

4. Select **OK** to save the changes and to close the Image Optimization dialog box.

5. Navigate to the website assets folder in the Save Web Image dialog box, then select **Save** to save the about_us.jpg image.

You experimented with the format settings in the Image Optimization dialog box, then saved the image with the JPEG for Photos (Continuous Tones) preset.

Figure 19 *Choosing a Preset in the Image Optimization dialog box*

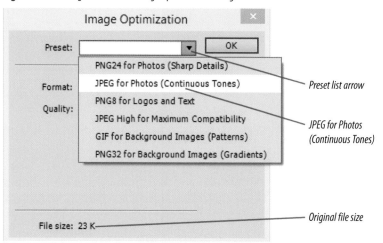

Integrating Photoshop CC with Dreamweaver

Dreamweaver has many ways to integrate with Photoshop CC. For example, you can copy and paste a Photoshop PSD file directly from Photoshop into Dreamweaver. Dreamweaver will prompt you to optimize the image by choosing a file format and settings for the web. Then it will paste the image on the page. If you want to edit the image later, select the image, then select the Edit button in the Property inspector to open the image in Photoshop. (The appearance of the Edit button will change according to the default image editor you have specified.)

Photoshop users can set Photoshop as the default image editor in Dreamweaver for specific image file formats. For Windows users, select Edit on the Menu bar, select Preferences, select File Types/Editors, select Photoshop in the Editors list, then select Make Primary. If you don't see Photoshop listed, select the Add Editor button, then browse to select Photoshop. For Mac users, select Preferences, select File Types/Editors, select Photoshop in the Extensions list, then select Make Primary. If you don't see Photoshop listed, select the Add Extension button, then browse to select Photoshop. You can also edit an image in Photoshop and export an updated Smart Object instantly in Dreamweaver. A **Smart Object** is an image layer that stores image data from raster or vector images. Search the Adobe website for a tutorial on Photoshop and Dreamweaver integration. Fireworks is another commonly used default image editor. Use the same steps to select it rather than Photoshop.

Adding Images

Figure 20 *Alternate text setting in the Property inspector*

Alt text box

Figure 21 *about_us page viewed in browser*

1. Select the club house image, select **Club House** in the Alt text box in the Property inspector (if necessary), then type **The Striped Umbrella Club House** as shown in Figure 20.

2. Save your work.

3. Preview the page in your browser, compare your screen to Figure 21, then close your browser.

You edited the alternate text for the club house image.

POWER USER SHORTCUTS	
To do this:	**Use this shortcut:**
Switch views	[Ctrl][`] (Win) or ⌘ [`] (Mac)
Insert image	[Ctrl][Alt][I] (Win) or ⌘ [option][I] (Mac)
Refresh	[F5] (Win) or Refresh [fn][F5] (Mac)

© 2015 Cengage Learning®

Displaying Alternate Text in a Browser

There is a simple method you can use to force alternate text to appear in a browser when a mouse is held over an image. To do this, add a title tag to the image properties using the same text as the alt tag. Example: <img src="assets/club_house.jpg" alt="The Striped Umbrella Club House" title="The Striped Umbrella Club House" class="img_float" /> This method will work in Internet Explorer and Mozilla Firefox.

Insert a Background Image and
PERFORM SITE MAINTENANCE

What You'll Do

In this lesson, you will insert a background image using an internal style. You will then move the internal selector to the su_styles.css style sheet. Last, you will edit the header background-image repeat value.

Inserting a Background Image

You can insert a background image on a web page to provide depth and visual interest to the page, or to communicate a message or mood. **Background images** are image files used in place of background colors. Although you can use background images to create a dramatic effect, you should avoid inserting them on web pages where they would not provide the contrast necessary for reading page text. Even though they might seem too plain, standard white backgrounds are usually the best choice for web pages. If you choose to use a background image on a web page, it should be small in file size. You can choose a single image that fills the page background, or you can choose a tiled image. A **tiled image** is a small image that repeats across and down a web page, appearing as individual squares or rectangles.

When you create a web page, you can use either a background color or a background image, unless you want the background color to appear while the background image finishes downloading. You can also use background images for some sections of your page and solid color backgrounds for other sections. The NASA home page shown in Figure 22 uses a night sky image for the page background, but individual sections have solid blue or white backgrounds. The banner has a dark night sky background, so NASA used white or light blue text to provide contrast. The stars in the background tie in well with the rest of the page design and help to set a dramatic mood.

Background images or background colors are inserted using CSS. To add them to a single page, use the Modify > Page Properties dialog box, which adds an internal rule to modify the body tag. To use them as a global setting for the entire site, create an external rule to modify the <body> tag.

Managing Images

As you work on a website, you might find that you have files in your assets folder that you don't use in the website. To avoid accumulating unnecessary files, it's a good idea to look at an image first, before you place it on the page, and copy it to the assets folder. If you inadvertently copy an unwanted file to the assets folder, you should delete it or move it to another location. This is a good website management practice that will prevent the assets folder from filling up with unwanted image files.

Removing an image from a web page does not remove it from the assets folder in the local site folder of the website. To remove an asset from a website, if you have a lot of files, it is faster to locate the file you want to remove in the Assets panel. You then use the Locate in Site command to open the Files panel with the unwanted file selected. If you don't have many images in your site, it is faster to locate them in the Files panel. You can then use the Delete command to remove the file from the site. If you designate frequently used image files as favorites, you can locate them quickly in the Assets panel by selecting the Favorites option.

It is a good idea to store original unedited copies of your website image files in a separate folder, outside the assets folder of your website. If you edit the original files, resave them using different names. Doing this ensures that you will be able to find a file in its original, unaltered state. You may have files on your computer that you are currently not using at all; however, you may want to use them in the future. Storing currently unused files helps keep your assets folder free of clutter. Storing copies of original website image files in a separate location also ensures that you have back-up copies in the event that you accidentally delete a file from the website.

QUICK TIP

You cannot use the Assets panel to delete a file. You must use the Files panel to delete files and perform all file management tasks.

Creating a Website Color Palette

With monitors today that display millions of colors, you are not as limited with the number of colors you can use, and you may choose to select any color you feel fits the website design and accessibility standards. You can use the eyedropper tool in the Color picker to pick up a color from a page element, such as the background of an image. To do this, select a color box from a value in the CSS Designer properties pane, then place the pointer over a color on the page. Select the color, and this color will then replace the previous color in the color box and apply it to the page element. If you are designing pages that will be displayed with a web device such as a mobile phone, be aware that many of these devices have more limited color displays and, in these cases, it might be wise to use standard colors.

QUICK TIP

To see the colors used in your site, click the Colors button on the Assets panel.

Figure 22 *NASA website*

Source: NASA

Insert a background image

1. Select **Modify** on the Menu bar, then select **Page Properties** to open the Page Properties dialog box.

2. In the Appearance (CSS) category, select **Browse** next to the Background image text box, navigate to the assets folder in the chapter_4 Data Files folder, then double-click **water.jpg**.

3. Select **OK** to close the Page Properties dialog box, then select the **Refresh** ↻ to refresh the file list in the assets folder in the Files panel. The water.jpg file is automatically copied to The Striped Umbrella assets folder.

   The white page background is replaced with a muted image of water, as shown in Figure 23. The color of the water is close to the shades of blue in the website banner, so the image fits in well with the other page colors. It doesn't interfere with the text because the body of the page is behind the container div where the content appears, and the container div has a white background.

4. Expand the CSS Designer panel if necessary, select **<style>** in the Sources pane, select **body** in the Selectors pane, select the **Show Set check box** in the Properties pane, then compare your screen to Figure 24.

   Since you used the Modify > Page Properties command to set the image background, Dreamweaver created an internal <body> rule that tells the browser to use the water.jpg file as the page background for that one page.

You created an internal style to apply an image background to the about_us page. You then viewed the CSS Designer panel. It now includes two external style sheets and an internal style sheet.

Figure 23 *The about_us page with a background image*

The water image only flows behind the container div, so does not affect contrast

Figure 24 *CSS Designer with the new embedded body rule added*

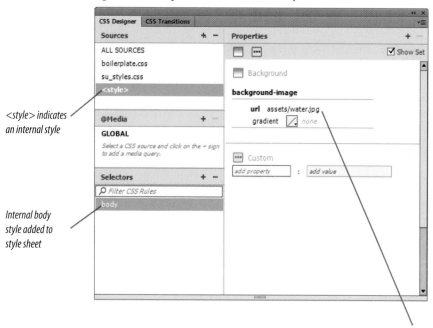

<style> indicates an internal style

Internal body style added to style sheet

Background image = assets/water.jpg

Adding Images

Figure 25 *The <style> source in the CSS Designer panel with no selectors listed*

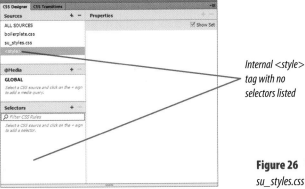

Internal <style> tag with no selectors listed

Figure 26 *Viewing the <body> selector in the su_styles.css source in the Sources pane*

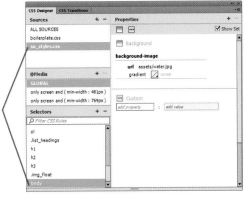

body selector is now in the su_styles.css file

Understanding HTML Body Tags

When you set page preferences, it is helpful to understand the HTML tags that are being generated. Sometimes it's easier to edit the code directly, rather than use menus and dialog boxes. The code for the page background color is located in the head section. If you want to change the page properties, you add additional codes to the body tag. Adding a color to the background will add a style to the page; for example, "body { background-color: #000000, }". If you insert an image for a background, the code will read "body { background-image: url(assets/water.jpg); }".

Move an internal selector to an external style sheet

1. Open the spa page.

   If you see a message above the Document window reminding you that Web Fonts are only visible in Live view; you can close the message. The water background is not behind the page content, because the internal background-image selector only applies to the about_us page.

2. Switch back to the about_us page, select **<style>** in the CSS Designer Sources pane, select **body** in the Selectors pane, as shown in Figure 24, then drag the body selector to su_styles.css in the Sources pane.

   You can only see the body selector in the Selectors pane when the about_us page is open and before you move it to su_styles.css, since it is an internal style for that page only.

3. Select **<style>** in the Sources pane, as shown in Figure 25, then select the **Delete key**.

   Since you moved the only selector in the internal style sheet, you no longer have a need for it.

4. Select **su_styles.css** in the Sources pane, select **GLOBAL** in the **@Media pane**, then scroll to and select **body** in the Selectors pane.

5. Select the **Show Set check box** if necessary, then compare your screen to Figure 26.

   You see the background-image property and value in the Properties pane.

(continued)

---

6. Switch back to the spa page.

   The spa page now has the water image as a page background, as shown in Figure 27.

7. Open the index page.

   The index page now has the water image as a page background, as shown in Figure 28.

8. Save your work.

You moved the internal body selector to the su_styles.css file, then viewed the spa and index pages to see that the body selector was now applied to those pages.

Figure 27 *The spa page with the water background image*

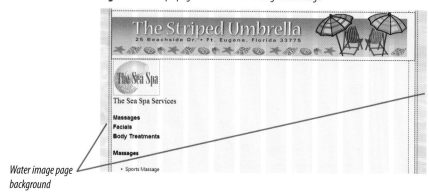

Water image page background

Figure 28 *The index page with the water background image*

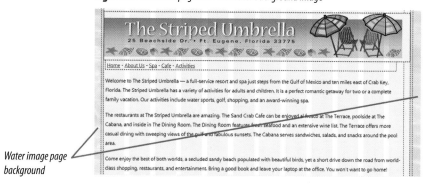

Water image page background

Using Color in Compliance with Accessibility Guidelines

Web Content Accessibility Guidelines (WCAG), Version 2.0, from the World Wide Web Consortium (W3C), states that a website should not rely on the use of color alone. This means that if your website content depends on your user correctly seeing a color, then you are not providing for those people who cannot distinguish between certain colors or do not have monitors that display color. Be especially careful when choosing color used with text, so you provide a good contrast between the text and the background.

If you are typing in the code or in a text box, it is better to reference colors as numbers, rather than names. For example, use #FFFFFF instead of "white." Using style sheets for specifying color formats is the preferred method for coding. For more information, see the complete list of accessibility guidelines listed on the W3C website, www.w3.org.

Adding Images

Figure 29 *Changing the value for the background-repeat property*

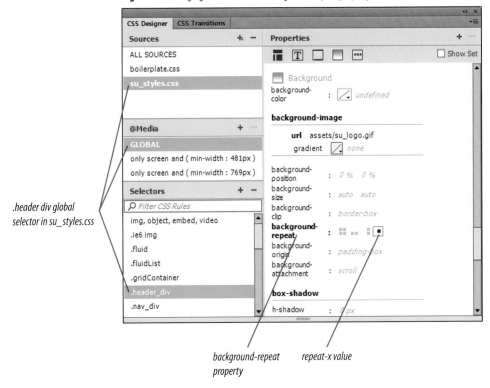

.header div global selector in su_styles.css

background-repeat property

repeat-x value

Figure 30 *Viewing the revised background image on the about us page*

Banner extends to fill header div now

Edit a background-image selector

1. Select **su_styles.css** in the CSS Designer Sources pane, select **GLOBAL** in the @Media pane, then select **.header_div** in the Selectors pane.

   The .header_div selector formats the header block.

2. Uncheck the Show Set check box, if necessary, select the **Background button** in the Properties pane, then select the **no-repeat value** next to the background-repeat property, as shown in Figure 29.

3. Select **only screen and (min-width: 481ps)** in the @Media pane, select **.header_div** in the Selectors pane, then change the background repeat value to **repeat-x**.

   Changing from the no-repeat to repeat-x value will fill in the white space at the right side of the header div in the tablet and desktop sizes.

4. Save all files, then preview the about_us page in your browser.

   The banner image background fills the header, as shown in Figure 30.

5. Preview the spa and index pages to verify that the banner on those pages also fills the header div.

6. Close the spa and index pages.

You edited the .header_div global selector in the su_styles.css style sheet, then viewed the revised pages in the browser.

Add Graphic
ENHANCEMENTS

What You'll Do

In this lesson, you will use a small image to link to a larger image and add a favicon to a page.

Adding a Link to a Larger Image

Sometimes designers want to display a small image on a page with an option for the user to select it to display a larger image. You frequently see this practice on retail sites with multiple items for sale. It is done both to conserve space and to keep the page size as small as possible. These sites will display a **thumbnail image**, or small version of a larger image, so that more images will fit on the page. Another technique is to link from one image to a second image that incorporates the first image. For example, a furniture site may create a link from an image of a chair to an image of the chair in a furnished room. An additional enhancement is often added to allow users to select the larger image to magnify it even more.

To accomplish this, you need two versions of the same image using an image editor such as Photoshop: one that is small (in dimensions and in file size) and one that is large (in dimensions and in file size.) After you have both images ready, place the small image on your page, select it, then link it to the large image. When a user selects the small image in a browser, the large image opens. Another option is to place the large image on a new web page so you can also include additional descriptive text about the image or a link back to the previous page.

Adding Favicons

In most browsers today, when you add a web page to your favorites list or bookmarks, the page title will appear with a small icon that represents your site, similar to a logo, called a **favicon** (short for favorites icon). This feature was introduced in Microsoft Internet Explorer 5. Most browsers now also display favicons in the browser address bar. Favicons are a convenient way to add branding, or recognition, for your site. To create a favicon, first create an icon that is 16 pixels by 16 pixels. Second, save the file as an icon file with the .ico file extension in your site root folder. Do not save it in a subfolder such as an assets or images folder.

> **QUICK TIP**
>
> There are plug-ins available for Photoshop that will save files with an icon file format, or you can search the Internet for programs that will generate icons.

Third, add HTML code to the head section of your page to link the icon file. The browser will then find the icon and load it in the address bar when the page loads.

Figure 31 shows a favicon in the Department of Education website. Notice that the favicon is displayed on the page tab. The design of the favicon ties in with the large logo at the top of the page. This is an attractive touch to complete a well-designed site.

Adding a No Right-Click Script

On most websites, users are able to save an image on a page by right-clicking an image, then selecting Save on the shortcut menu. If you would like to prevent viewers from having this option, you can add a **no right-click script**, or JavaScript code that will not allow users to display the shortcut menu by right-clicking an image. To do this, locate JavaScript code that will add this option and copy and paste it into the head content of your page. To locate JavaScript code, use a search engine to search the Internet with a term such as "no right-click script." You will find scripts that prevent

users from saving any image on the page, or all content of any kind on the page. Some scripts return a message in the browser such as "This function is disabled," and some do not return a message at all. These scripts will keep many users from saving your images, but they will not stop the most serious and knowledgeable perpetrators.

You can also protect website images by inserting the image as a table, cell, or CSS block background and then placing a transparent image on top of it. When a user attempts to save it with the shortcut menu, they will only save the transparent image.

Figure 31 *U. S. Department of Education website*

Favicon displayed on the page tab

Favicon is a smaller version of the logo used on the page

Source: U. S. Department of Education

Use an image to link to another image

1. Place the insertion point at the end of the last paragraph after the word "beachwear", insert a paragraph break, insert the image **map_small.jpg** from the assets folder where you store your Data Files, then type **Map to The Striped Umbrella** in the Alt text box in the Property inspector.

2. Select the map_small image, click the **Browse for File button** 📁 next to the Link text box in the Property inspector, navigate to the assets folder in the drive and folder where you store your Data Files, select **map_large.jpg**, then click **OK**.

    The small map image now links to the large map image, so users can select the small version to view the large version.

3. Place the insertion point after the last paragraph, insert a paragraph break, type **Select the map below to view a larger image.**, then compare your screen to Figure 32.

4. Save your work, then preview the page in your browser.

5. Select the **small map image** to view the large map image in a separate window, use the Back button to return to the about_us page, then close the browser.

6. Open the Files panel if necessary, and verify that both map images were copied to the assets folder, as shown in Figure 33.

You inserted a small image on the page and linked it to a larger image.

Figure 32 *The about_us page with an image linking to a larger image*

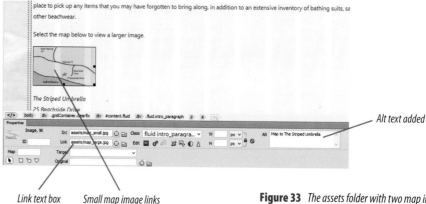

Alt text added

Link text box

Small map image links to large map image

Figure 33 *The assets folder with two map images added*

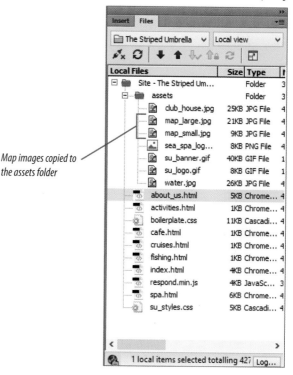

Map images copied to the assets folder

Figure 34 *Copying the favicon.ico file in the data files folder*

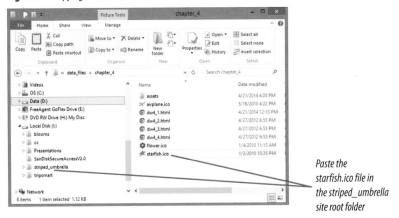

Paste the
starfish.ico file in
the striped_umbrella
site root folder

Figure 35 *Adding code to link the favicon*

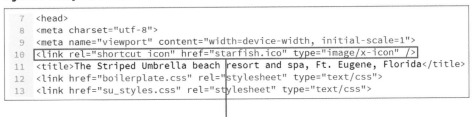

```
7   <head>
8   <meta charset="utf-8">
9   <meta name="viewport" content="width=device-width, initial-scale=1">
10  <link rel="shortcut icon" href="starfish.ico" type="image/x-icon" />
11  <title>The Striped Umbrella beach resort and spa, Ft. Eugene, Florida</title>
12  <link href="boilerplate.css" rel="stylesheet" type="text/css">
13  <link href="su_styles.css" rel="stylesheet" type="text/css">
```

Type this code above the <title> tag

Figure 36 *Viewing a favicon in the Firefox browser*

Starfish favicon

Insert a favicon on a page

1. Open File Explorer (Win) or Finder (Mac), then browse to the chapter_4 folder in the drive and folder where your Data Files are stored.

2. Right-click the file **starfish.ico**, copy it, browse to your site root folder, (not the assets folder) then paste the **starfish.ico** file into the site root folder, as shown in Figure 34, then close File Explorer (Win) or Finder (Mac).

3. Switch to Code view in Dreamweaver, insert a blank line above the line of code for the page title, then insert this code directly above the <title> tag: `<link rel="shortcut icon" href="starfish.ico" type="image/x-icon" />` as shown in Figure 35.

4. Save your work, then preview the about_us page in the browser.

    The favicon will appear on the page tab in browsers that use tabbed pages, as shown in Figure 36.

    TIP Internet Explorer may not display the favicon until the website is published to a server.

5. Copy the code for the favicon link, then paste it into the code for the index and spa pages.

6. Save your work, close all open pages, then exit Dreamweaver.

You copied a favicon to the site root folder, then added code to the About Us page to direct browsers to display the favicon in the title bar when the page is viewed in a browser. Then you copied the code to link the favicon to the index and spa pages.

Insert and align Images using CSS.

1. Open the Blooms & Bulbs website, open dw4_2.html from the drive and folder where you store your Data Files, then save it as **plants.html** in the Blooms & Bulbs website, overwriting the existing plants.html file. Do not update links.
2. Close dw4_2.html.
3. Select the heading "Featured Spring Plant: Roses!" and use the HTML Property inspector to apply the Heading 1 format.
4. On the plants page, change to Code view and verify that the Adobe Edge Web font code is in the head section.
5. If it is not, open the tips page, change to Code view, copy the code for the Edge Web font in the head section, close the tips page, then paste the code you copied in Step 4 to the head section in the code for the plants page.
6. In Design view, place the insertion point in front of the first paragraph that begins with "Who", then insert the file rose.jpg from the assets folder in the drive and folder where you store your Data Files.

TIP Switch to Code view to verify that your insertion point is before the opening <p> tag for the first paragraph.

7. Refresh the Files panel to verify that the image was copied to the assets folder.
8. Add a new global class selector to the bb.styles style sheet named **.img_float**. (Remember to type the period in the selector name.)
9. Set the float property to none.
10. Add a new class selector named **.img_float** in tablet media with the float property set to left.
11. Select the rose image on the page, then apply the img_float selector to it.
12. Save all files, then view the page in mobile, tablet, and desktop views. Notice that the text does not wrap (falls below) the image in mobile view, but wraps around the image in tablet and desktop views.

Enhance an image and use alternate text.

1. Edit the img_float global selector to add a border to all sides of an image with the following settings: Style=solid; Width=thin; Color=#333333.
2. Edit the global img_float margin property to add a 10 px margin to all sides.
3. Add the alternate text "**Rose bloom**" to the rose image.
4. Save your work.

Insert a background image and perform site maintenance.

1. Use the Modify menu to insert the lady_in_red.jpg file as a background image from the assets folder where you store your Data Files.
2. Save your work.
3. Preview the web page in your browser, then close your browser.
4. Move the <body> tag code from the internal style sheet to the bb.styles.css file, then remove the <style> source in the CSS Designer Sources pane.
5. Save your work, verify that the image page background appears on the index and tips pages, then close the index and tips pages.
6. View the colors used in the site in the Assets panel.
7. Edit the desktop size .header_div selector to set the background-repeat value to repeat-x, then save your work.

Add graphic enhancements.

1. Insert the file two_roses.jpg from your Data Files assets folder at the beginning of the second paragraph.
2. Create a new global class selector in bb_styles.css named **.img_float_right**.
3. Use the same properties you used for the .img_float global class selector.
4. Repeat Steps 2 and 3 to add a tablet class selector named **.img_float_right** with the float set to right.
5. Apply the .img_float_right selector to the two_roses image, then add appropriate alternate text.
6. Use the Link text box on the Property inspector to link the two_roses image to the two_roses_large.jpg file in the assets folder where you store your Data Files.
7. Add the sentences **You must see a close-up of these beauties! Select the image to enlarge it**. at the end of the last paragraph.

8. Save your work, preview the page in the browser, then select the two_roses image to view the larger version of the image.

9. Use the Back button to return to the plants page, then close the browser.

10. Open File Explorer (Win) or Finder (Mac), browse to the folder where you store your Data Files, then copy the file flower.ico.

11. Paste the file flower.ico in the blooms site root folder.

12. Close File Explorer (Win) or Finder (Mac), then switch to Code view for the plants page.

13. Insert a blank line above the title tag, then type this code directly above the <title> tag:

    ```
    <link rel="shortcut icon"
    href="flower.ico" type="image/
    x-icon" />
    ```

14. Verify that you entered the code correctly, copy the new line of code, then switch back to Design view.

15. Paste the same code you typed in Step 13 to the index and tips pages, then save all files.

16. Preview the plants, tips, and index pages in mobile, tablet, and desktop views, and the browser, compare your screen to Figure 37, then close the browser.

17. Figures 38a, 38b, and 38c on the next two pages show the plants page in the mobile, tablet, and desktop sizes.

18. Close all open files.

Figure 37 *Completed Skills Review viewed in a browser*

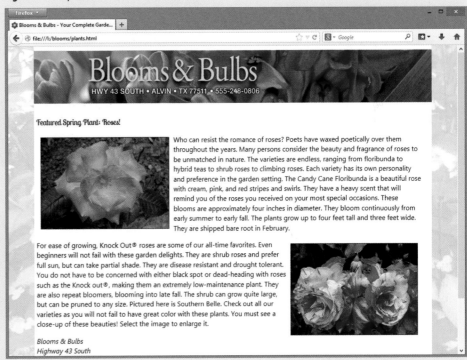

Figure 38a *Mobile view*

Featured Spring Plant: Roses!

Who can resist the romance of roses? Poets have waxed poetically over them throughout the years. Many persons consider the beauty and fragrance of roses to be unmatched in nature. The varieties are endless, ranging from floribunda to hybrid teas to shrub roses to climbing roses. Each variety has its own personality and preference in the garden setting. The Candy Cane Floribunda is a beautiful rose with

Figure 38b *Tablet view*

Featured Spring Plant: Roses!

Who can resist the romance of roses? Poets have waxed poetically over them throughout the years. Many persons consider the beauty and fragrance of roses to be unmatched in nature. The varieties are endless, ranging from floribunda to hybrid teas to shrub roses to climbing roses. Each variety has its own personality and preference in the garden setting. The Candy Cane Floribunda is a beautiful rose with cream, pink, and red stripes and swirls. They have a heavy scent that will remind you of the roses you received on your most special occasions. These blooms are approximately four inches in diameter. They bloom continuously from early summer to early fall. The plants grow up to four feet tall and three feet wide. They are shipped bare root in February.

For ease of growing, Knock Out® roses are some of our all-time favorites. Even beginners will not fail with these garden delights. They are shrub

Figure 38c *Desktop view*

Featured Spring Plant: Roses!

Who can resist the romance of roses? Poets have waxed poetically over them throughout the years. Many persons consider the beauty and fragrance of roses to be unmatched in nature. The varieties are endless, ranging from floribunda to hybrid teas to shrub roses to climbing roses. Each variety has its own personality and preference in the garden setting. The Candy Cane Floribunda is a beautiful rose with cream, pink, and red stripes and swirls. They have a heavy scent that will remind you of the roses you received on your most special occasions. These blooms are approximately four inches in diameter. They bloom continuously from early summer to early fall. The plants grow up to four feet tall and three feet wide. They are shipped bare root in February.

For ease of growing, Knock Out® roses are some of our all-time favorites. Even beginners will not fail with these garden delights. They are shrub roses and prefer full sun, but can take partial shade. They are disease resistant and drought tolerant. You do not have to be concerned with either black spot or dead-heading with roses such as the Knock out®, making them an extremely low-maintenance plant. They are also repeat bloomers, blooming into late fall

Adding Images

Use Figures 39a, 39b, and 39c. as guides to continue your work on the TripSmart website that you began in Project Builder 1 in Chapter 1, and continued to work on in Chapters 2 and 3. You are now ready to begin work on the destinations page that showcases one of the featured tours to Egypt. You want to include some colorful pictures on the page.

1. Open the TripSmart website.
2. Open dw4_3.html from the drive and folder where you store your Data Files and save it in the tripsmart site root folder as **tours.html**, overwriting the existing tours.html file and not updating the links. Close the dw4_3.html file.
3. Apply the Heading 1 format to the "Destination: Egypt" heading.
4. Insert statues.jpg from the assets folder in the drive and folder where you store your Data Files to the left of the sentence beginning "We have a really special", then add appropriate alternate text.
5. Insert nile.jpg from the assets folder in the drive and folder where you store your Data Files to the left of the sentence beginning "To provide the finest", then add appropriate alternate text.
6. Create one or more new rules in the tripsmart_styles.css file to add alignment, spacing, and borders of your choice to each new image.
7. If you would like, use the existing rules in the style sheet to add any additional formatting to the page to enhance the appearance or copy any rules from other websites that you would like to reuse.

8. Copy the file airplane.ico from the folder where you store your data files to your site root folder.
9. Add appropriate code to the head content to link the favicon to the page, then copy the code to the index and newsletter pages.
10. Save your work, then preview the tours, index, and newsletter pages in your browser and in mobile, tablet, and desktop sizes.
11. Close your browser, then close all open files.

Figure 39a *Mobile view*

Figure 39b *Tablet view*

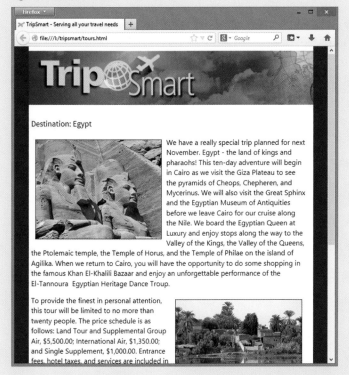

Figure 39c *Desktop view*

In this exercise, you continue your work on the Carolyne's Creations website that you started in Project Builder 2 in Chapter 1, and continued to build in Chapters 2 and 3. You are now ready to add a new page to the website that will display featured items in the kitchen shop. Figures 40a, 40b, and 40c show a possible solution for this exercise. Your finished page will look different if you choose different formatting options.

1. Open the Carolyne's Creations website.
2. Open dw4_4.html from the drive and folder where you store your Data Files, save it to the site root folder as **shop.html**, overwriting the existing file and not updating the links.
3. Insert peruvian_glass.jpg from the assets folder in the drive and folder where you store your Data Files, in a location of your choice on the page, and add appropriate alternate text.
4. Add a rule to the cc_styles style sheet that adds alignment and spacing to the Peruvian glass image, then apply the new selector to the glass image.
5. Apply the Heading 1 format to the page heading "June Special: Peruvian Glasses".

6. If you would like a different mobile banner, replace cc_logo.gif with cc_banner_mobile.jpg in the global .header_div selector only. (*Hint:* It is the background image.)
7. Save the shop page, then preview it in the browser and mobile, tablet, and desktop sizes.
8. Close your browser, then close all open pages.

Figure 40a *Mobile view*

Figure 40b *Tablet view*

Figure 40c *Desktop view*

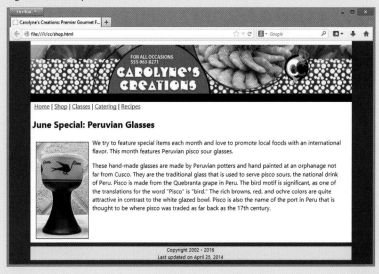

Patsy Broers is working on a team project to design a website for her high school drama department. She has been assigned the task of gathering images to add interest and color.

1. Connect to the Internet, then navigate to the National Oceanic and Atmospheric Administration at noaa.gov, shown in Figure 41.
2. Do you see a favicon used on the page?
3. Are any of the images on the page used as links to other images or pages?
4. Is a background image used for any of the page objects?
5. How do the images, horizontal and vertical spacing, color, and text work together to create an attractive and interesting experience for viewers?

Figure 41 *Design Project*

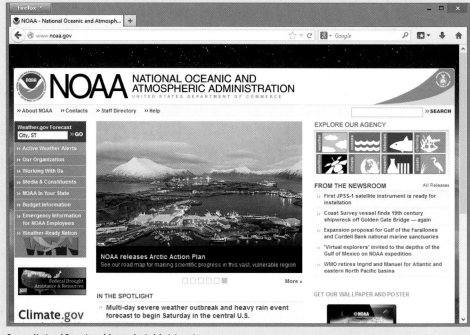

Source: National Oceanic and Atmospheric Administration

In this assignment, you will continue to work on the website that you started in Chapter 1, and continued to build in Chapters 2 and 3. No Data Files are supplied. You are building this site from chapter to chapter, so you must do each Portfolio Project assignment in each chapter to complete your website.

You continue building your website by inserting appropriate images on a page and enhancing them for maximum effect.

1. Consult your wireframe and decide which page to create and develop for this chapter.
2. Plan the page content and make a sketch of the layout. Your sketch should include several images and a background color or image.
3. Create the page using your sketch for guidance.
4. Access the images you gathered, and place them on the page so that the page matches the sketch you created in Step 2. Add a background image if you want, and appropriate alternate text for each image.
5. Create rules in your style sheet to position and format your images.

6. Identify any files in the Assets panel that are currently not used in the site. Decide which of these assets should be removed, then delete these files.
7. Preview the new page in a browser, then check for page layout problems and broken links. Make any necessary corrections in Dreamweaver, then preview the page again in the browser, mobile, tablet, and desktop sizes. Repeat this process until you are satisfied with the way the page looks in the browser.
8. Use the checklist in Figure 42 to check all the pages in your site.
9. Close the browser, then close the open pages.

Figure 42 *Portfolio Project checklist*

Website Checklist
1. Does each page have a page title?
2. Does the home page have a description and keywords?
3. Does the home page contain contact information?
4. Does the home page have a last updated statement that will automatically update when the page is saved?
5. Do all paths for links and images work correctly?
6. Do all images have alternate text?
7. Are there any unnecessary files you can delete from the assets folder?
8. Is there a style sheet with at least two selectors?
9. Did you apply the selectors to all text?
10. Did you use selectors to position and format images?
11. Do all pages look good using at least two different browsers and mobile, tablet, and desktop sizes?

© 2015 Cengage Learning®

CHAPTER **5** **WORKING WITH LINKS AND NAVIGATION**

1. Create external and internal links
2. Use IDs to navigate to specific page locations
3. Create, modify, and copy a menu bar
4. Create an image map
5. Manage website links
6. Incorporate Web 2.0 technology

WORKING WITH LINKS
AND NAVIGATION

Introduction

What makes websites so powerful are the links, or hyperlinks, that connect one page to another within a website or to any page on the Web. Although you can enhance a website with graphics, animations, movies, and other features to make it visually attractive, the links you include are a site's most essential components. Links that connect the pages within a site are important because they help users navigate between the pages of the site. If it's important to keep users within your site, link only to pages within your website and avoid including links to external sites. For example, e-commerce sites only link to other pages in their own site to discourage shoppers from leaving.

In this chapter, you will create links to other pages in The Striped Umbrella website and to other sites on the Web. You will insert a menu bar, and check the site links to make sure they all work correctly. You will also learn about Web 2.0 and social networking, an area of the Internet that has exploded over the years. **Social networking** refers to the grouping of individual web users who connect and interact with other users in online communities. **Online communities**, or virtual communities, are social websites you can join, such as Facebook and Twitter, where you can communicate with others by posting messages or media content such as images or videos. You will learn about how you can connect your website to these communities.

Understanding Internal and External Links

Web pages contain two types of links: internal links and external links. **Internal links** are links to web pages within the same website, and **external links** are links to web pages in other websites or to email addresses. Both internal and external links have two important parts that work together. The first part of a link is displayed on a web page, for example, text, an image, or a button that is used for a link. The second part of a link is the **path**, or the name and location of the web page or file that users select to open the target for the link. Setting and maintaining the correct paths for all of your links is essential to avoid having broken links in your site, which can cause a user to leave the site.

Insert

Structure ▼

- ⟨⟩ Div
- ul Unordered List
- ol Ordered List
- li List Item
- ▢ Header
- H1 ▾ Heading
- P Paragraph
- ◁▷ Navigation
- ▢ Aside
- ▤ Article

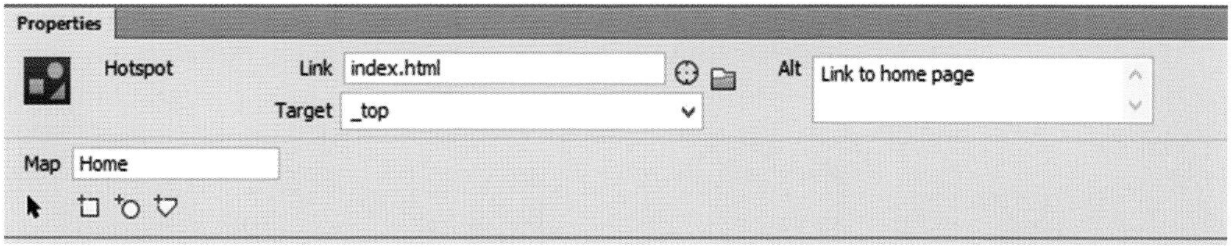

Properties

Hotspot   Link index.html   Alt Link to home page

Target _top

Map Home

Properties

⟨⟩ HTML   Format None   Class fluid header...   **B** *I*   Title

CSS   ID banner   Link   Target

Page Properties...   List Item...

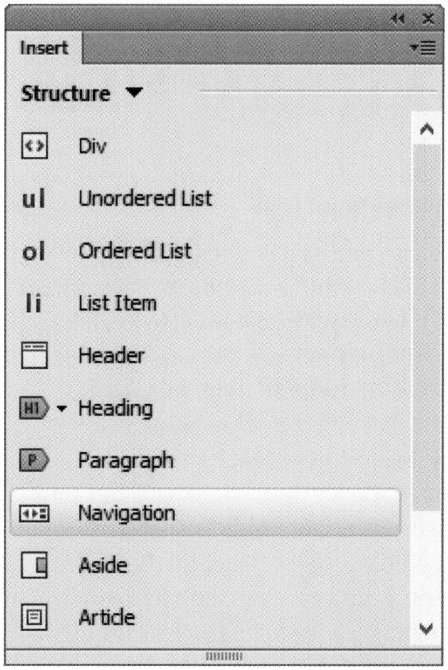

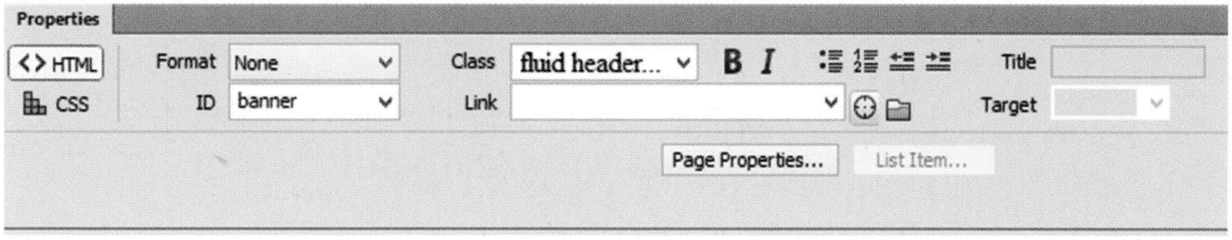

Create External and INTERNAL LINKS

What You'll Do

In this lesson, you will create external links on The Striped Umbrella activities page that link to websites related to area attractions. You will also create internal links to other pages within The Striped Umbrella website.

Creating External Links

If one of the objectives of your site is to provide users with additional research sources for information not provided within the site, external links are one way to meet that objective. To create an external link, first select the text or object that you want to serve as a link, then type the absolute path to the destination web page in the Link text box in the Property inspector. An **absolute path** is a path used for external links that includes the complete address for the destination page, including the protocol (such as http://) and the complete **URL** (Uniform Resource Locator), or address, of the destination page. When necessary, the web page filename and folder hierarchy are also part of an absolute path. Figure 1 shows an example of an absolute path showing the protocol,

URL, and path, which in this case is a single folder name. Paths can contain several folder levels and a file name, depending on how the destination page is stored on the server. An example of the code for the external link to the United States Army website would be <a href="http://www.army.mil"> The United States Army website</a>.

Creating Internal Links

Each page in a website usually focuses on an individual information category or topic. You should make sure that the home page provides links to each major page in the site, and that all pages in the site contain numerous internal links so that users can move easily from page to page. To create an internal link, you first select the text element or image that you want to use to make a link, and then use the Browse

Figure 1 *An example of an absolute path*

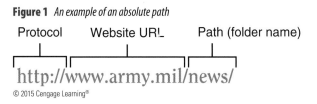

© 2015 Cengage Learning®

for File button next to the Link text box in the HTML Property inspector to specify the relative path to the destination page. A **relative path** is a type of path that references web pages and media files within the same website. Relative paths include the filename and folder location of a file. An example for the code for a relative internal link would be <a href="news.html">News</a>.

Figure 2 shows an example of a relative path. Table 1 describes absolute and relative paths. Relative paths can either be site-root relative or document-relative. The internal links that you will create in this lesson will be document-relative. You can also use the Point to File button in the HTML Property inspector to select the file you want to link to, or drag the file you want to use for the link from the Files panel into the Link text box in the Property inspector.

You should take great care in managing your internal links to make sure they work correctly and are timely and relevant to the page content. Design the navigation structure of your website so that users are never more than a few clicks or taps away from the page they are seeking.

Figure 2 *An example of a relative path*

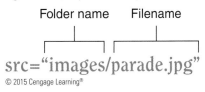

© 2015 Cengage Learning®

TABLE 1: DESCRIPTION OF ABSOLUTE AND RELATIVE PATHS		
Type of path	**Description**	**Example**
Absolute path	Used for external links and specifies protocol, URL, and filename of the destination page	http://www.yahoo.com/recreation
Relative path	Used for internal links and specifies location of file relative to the current page	spa.html or assets/heron.gif
Site Root-relative path	Used for internal links when publishing to a server that contains many websites or where the website is so large it requires more than one server	/striped_umbrella/activities.html
Document- relative path	Used in most cases for internal links and specifies the location of a file relative to the current page	cafe.html or assets/heron.gif

© 2015 Cengage Learning®

Create an external link

1. Open The Striped Umbrella website, open dw5_1.html from the drive and folder where you store your Chapter 5 Data Files, then save it as **activities.html** in the striped_umbrella local site folder, overwriting the existing activities page, but not updating links.

2. Close the dw5_1.html page.

   The page code picks up the links to the style sheet from the website now and formats the page, but the links to the images are broken because these images have not yet been copied to the website assets folder.

3. Select the first broken image link, select the **Browse for File button** 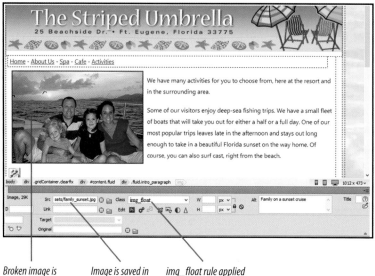 next to the Src text box, then select **family_sunset.jpg** in the Data Files assets folder to save the image in your assets folder.

4. Select the image, then use the Property inspector to apply the **img_float** rule, as shown in Figure 3.

5. Repeat Step 3 for the second broken image link, linking it to two_dolphins_small.jpg.

6. Create a new global selector in CSS Designer in the su_styles.css file named **.img_float_right** with the following properties and values:

   All margins: **10px**;

   Float: **none**;

   Border-width: **thin**;

   Border-style: **solid**;

   Border-color: **#312E2E**;

7. Repeat step 6 to create a selector in the su_styles.css file for tablet size devices named **.img_float_right** with the float property set to **right**.

(continued)

Figure 3 *Saving an image file in the assets folder*

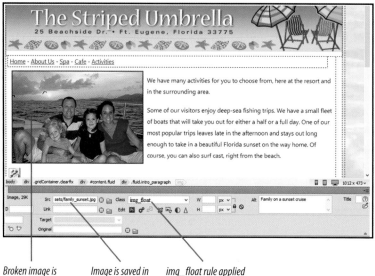

Broken image is replaced when file is saved in the assets folder

Image is saved in assets folder

img_float rule applied

Figure 4 *Assets panel with two new images added*

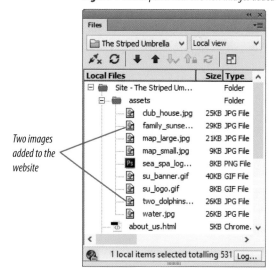

Two images added to the website

Figure 5 *Creating an external link to the Blue Angels website*

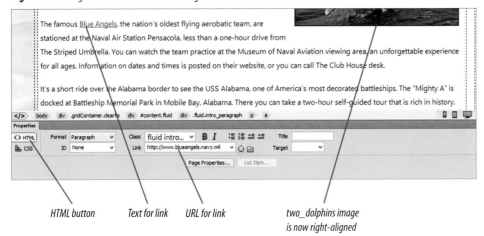

HTML button Text for link URL for link   two_dolphins image
                           is now right-aligned

Typing URLs

Typing URLs in the Link text box in the Property inspector can be tedious. When you need to type a long and complex URL, it is easy to make mistakes and create a broken link. You can avoid such mistakes by copying and pasting the URL from the Address text box (Internet Explorer) or Location bar (Mozilla Firefox) to the Link text box in the Property inspector. Copying and pasting a URL ensures that the URL is entered correctly.

This selector will inherit the global .img_float_right selector, except with the float set to right for tablet and desktop sizes.

8. Apply the .img_float_right selector to the two_dolphins_small.jpg, then refresh the files panel if necessary.

   The two new files are copied into the assets folder, as shown in Figure 4.

9. Scroll down, then select the text "Blue Angels" in the first line of the third to last paragraph.

10. Select the **HTML button** `<> HTML` in the Property inspector to switch to the HTML Property inspector if necessary, place the insertion point in the Link text box, type **http://www.blueangels.navy.mil**, press **[Enter]** (Win) or **[return]** (Mac), click on or tap the link to deselect it, then compare your screen to Figure 5.

11. Repeat Steps 9 and 10 to create a link for the USS Alabama text in the next paragraph: **http://www.ussalabama.com**.

12. Save your work, preview the page in your browser, test all the links to make sure they work, then close your browser.

TIP You must have an active Internet connection to test the external links. If selecting a link does not open a page, make sure you typed the URL correctly in the Link text box.

You opened The Striped Umbrella website, replaced the existing activities page, then imported images into the site. You created a new selector similar to the img_float selector but with a right alignment rather than a left alignment. You applied a different selector to each image. You added two external links to other sites, then tested each link in your browser.

Create an internal link

1. Select the text "fishing excursions" in the third paragraph.

2. Select the **Browse for File button** 📁 next to the Link text box in the HTML Property inspector, navigate to the site root folder, then double-click **fishing.html** in the Select File dialog box to set the relative path to the fishing page.

   The filename fishing.html appears in the Link text box in the Property inspector, as shown in Figure 6. (The link is deselected in the figure for readability.)

   TIP Pressing [F4] will hide or redisplay all panels, including the Property inspector and the panels on the right side of the screen.

3. Select the text "dolphin cruises" in the same sentence.

4. Select the **Browse for File button** 📁 next to the Link text box in the HTML Property inspector, then double-click **cruises.html** in the Select File dialog box to specify the relative path to the cruises page.

   The words "dolphin cruises" are now a link to the cruises page.

5. Save your work, preview the page in your browser, verify that the internal links work correctly, then close your browser.

   The fishing and cruises pages do not have page content yet, but serve as placeholders until they do.

You created two internal links on the activities page, then tested the links in your browser.

Figure 6 *Creating an internal link on the activities page*

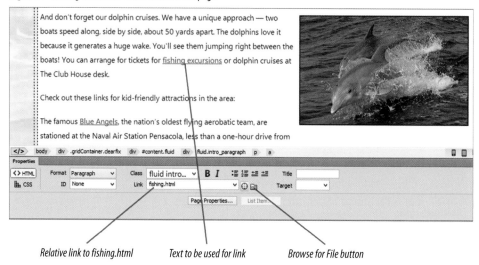

Relative link to fishing.html   Text to be used for link   Browse for File button

---

Using Case-Sensitive Links

When you hear that text is "case sensitive," it means that the text will be treated differently when it is typed using uppercase letters rather than lowercase letters, or vice-versa. With some operating systems, such as Windows, it doesn't matter which case you use when you enter URLs. However, with other systems, such as UNIX, it does matter. To be sure that your links will work with all systems, use lowercase letters for all URLs. This is another good reason to select and copy a URL from the browser address bar, and then paste it in the Link text box or Dreamweaver code when creating an external link. You won't have to worry about missing a case change.

Figure 7 *Assets panel with four external links*

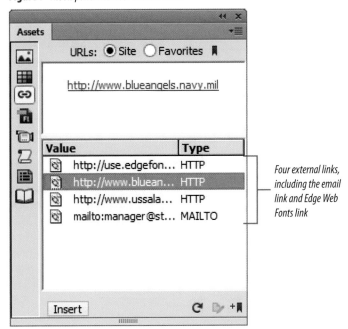

Four external links, including the email link and Edge Web Fonts link

View links in the Assets panel

1. Open the Assets panel.
2. Select the **URLs button** in the Assets panel.
3. Select the **Refresh Site List button** if necessary to see the links listed.

   Four links appear in the Assets panel: one external link for the email link on the home page; one external link to the Adobe Edge Web Fonts site; and two external links, to the Blue Angels and USS Alabama websites on the activities page, as shown in Figure 7. Notice that the internal links do not appear in the Assets panel. The Assets panel shows the links for the entire site, not just for the open page.
4. Close the Assets panel.
5. Close the activities page.

You viewed the external links on the activities page in the Assets panel.

Use IDs to Navigate
TO SPECIFIC PAGE LOCATIONS

What You'll Do

In this lesson, you will assign four IDs to page elements on the spa page: one for the top of the page and three for each of the spa services lists. You will then create internal links to each ID.

Inserting Page Markers with IDs

Some web pages have so much content that users must scroll repeatedly to get to the bottom of the page and then back up to the top of the page. To make it easier for users to navigate to specific areas of a page without scrolling, you can use a combination of internal links and targets to designated locations on a page. A **target** is the location on a web page that a browser displays when users select an internal link. For example, you can assign an ID called "top" to a page element such as an image or div, at the top of a web page, and then create a link to it from the bottom of the page.

You can also assign IDs to page elements in strategic places on a web page, such as at the beginning of paragraph headings. The Neighbor's Mill website shown in Figure 8 uses a div with the ID "wrap" at the top of each page and a text link at the bottom of each page that links to it. This gives users a way to

quickly return to the top of a page after they have scrolled down through the page content.

To assign an ID to a page element, select a tag you intend to use for a link. For instance, if you want to link to the top of a page, select a tag such as an image or div that is at the top of the page, then assign an ID to it if it does not have one. If it does have one, use the assigned ID for your target. You should choose short names that describe the named location on the page.

Creating Internal Links to IDs

Once you assign an ID to a page element, you can create an internal link to it using one of two methods. You can select the text or image on the page that you want to use to make a link, and then drag the Point to File button from the Property inspector to the location of the ID on the page. Or, you can select the text or image to which you want to use to make a link, then type # followed by the ID name (such as "#top") in the Link text box in the Property inspector.

Figure 8 *Neighbor's Mill website with a link to the top of a page*

Div with ID at the top of the page

Text link to div with ID at the top of the page

Source: Neighbor's Mill Bakery & Cafe

Assign IDs to tags

1. Open dw5_2.html, save it as **spa.html**, replacing the spa page, but not updating links, then close dw5_2.html.

2. Place the insertion point in the div containing the background banner image.

   The Class text box in the Property inspector shows that the class tag for this div is fluid header_div.

3. Type **banner** in the ID text box, replacing None, in the Property inspector, as shown in Figure 9.

TIP When typing ID names, use lowercase letters, no spaces, and no special characters. Also, avoid using a number as the first character.

4. Scroll down the spa page to the list of massages, select the **Massages** heading, type **massages** in the ID text box in the Property inspector, then press **[Enter]** (Win) or **[return]** (Mac)

(continued)

Figure 9 *Adding an ID to a div tag*

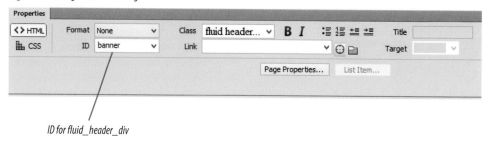

ID for fluid_header_div

Using Visual Aids

The Visual Aids submenu on the View menu gives you several choices for displaying page elements in Design View, such as Invisible Elements, which include comments, line breaks, and embedded styles. Other options in the Visual Aids submenu are CSS Layout Backgrounds, CSS Layout Box Model, CSS Layout Outlines, Table Widths, Table Borders, Image Maps, and Invisible Elements. The Hide All option hides all of these page elements. In later chapters, as you work with each page object that these refer to, you will see the advantages of displaying them. The CSS options allow you to see the formatting properties for CSS layout blocks such as the outline, background color, and margins.

Figure 10 *The Massages heading in Split view*

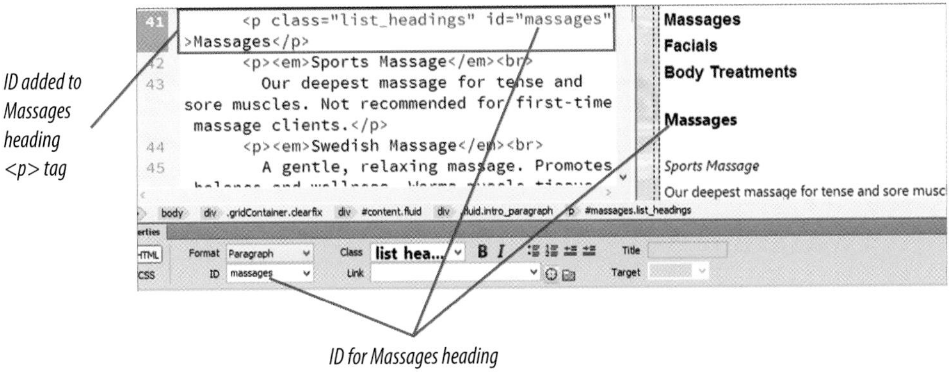

ID added to Massages heading <p> tag

ID for Massages heading

5. Deselect the Massages heading, place the insertion point inside the heading, switch to Show Code and Design views, then locate the id="massages" tag that you added to the Massages heading, as shown in Figure 10.

6. Return to Design view, scroll down to the Facials heading, select the **Facials heading**, type **facials** in the ID text box in the Property inspector, then press **[Enter]** (Win) or **[return]** (Mac).

7. Scroll down to the Body Treatments heading, select the **Body Treatments** heading, type **body_treatments** in the ID text box in the Property inspector, then press **[Enter]** (Win) or **[return]** (Mac).

8. Save your work.

You assigned four IDs to four spa page tags: one to the banner in the div at the top of the page and one to each of the three spa treatment headings.

Create an internal link to an ID

1. Select the word **Massages** just under The Sea Spa Services heading and type **#massages** in the Link text box in the Property inspector, as shown in Figure 11.

   The word "Massages" is now linked to the massages ID for the Massages heading. When users select the word "Massages" at the top of the page, the browser will display the Massages heading at the top of the browser window. The Link text box on the Property inspector now reads #massages.

   TIP An ID name is always preceded by a pound (#) sign in the Link text box in the Property inspector.

2. Repeat Step 1 to create internal links for the Facials and Body Treatments headings to **#facials** and **#body_treatments**.

   (continued)

Figure 11 *Linking the Massages heading to the massages ID*

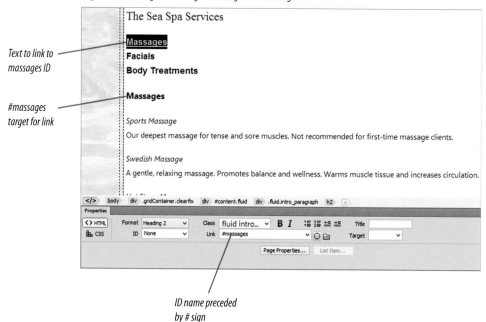

Text to link to massages ID

#massages target for link

ID name preceded by # sign

Figure 12 *Spa page with internal links to IDs*

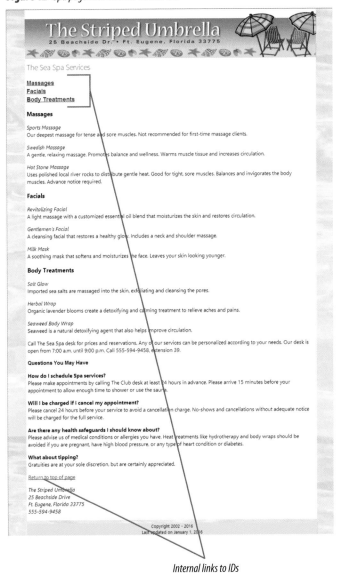

Internal links to IDs

3. Scroll down to the bottom of the page, then place the insertion point at the end of the last sentence on the page, after the word "appreciated."

4. Press **[Enter]** (Win) or **[return]** (Mac) to insert a paragraph break, then type **Return to top of page**.

5. Select the text "Return to top of page", then enter **#banner** in the Link text box in the Property inspector.

6. Save your work, preview the page in your browser, as shown in Figure 12, then test the links to each ID, using the Back button to return to the links.

   When you select the Body Treatments link in the browser, the associated target ID may appear in the middle of the page instead of at the top. This happens because the spa page is not long enough to position this ID at the top of the page.

7. Close your browser.

You created internal links to the ID names for the Spa Services headings and to the top of the spa page. You then previewed the page in your browser and tested each link.

Create, Modify, and
COPY A MENU BAR

What You'll Do

 In this lesson, you will create a menu bar on the spa page that can be used to link to each main page in the website. The menu bar will have five elements: Home, About Us, Cafe, Spa, and Activities. You will also copy the new menu bar to other pages in the website. On each page you will modify the appropriate element state to reflect the current page.

Creating a Menu Bar

To make your website more visually appealing, you can add special effects. For example, you can create a menu bar with rollover images rather than with plain text links. One way to do this is to use HTML5 <nav> tags to create navigation buttons that link to the pages in your website. To do this, you first insert a navigation tag using the Insert panel. Next, you select the placeholder text for each button and type replacement names to use for each of your links, called **items**, using list items in an unordered list. Once your navigation elements are in place, use CSS styles to modify both the navigation bar code and the unordered list items code. With a little patience and creativity, you can create an attractive, interactive menu bar.

You can add special effects for menu bar items by changing the characteristics for each item's state. A **state** is the condition of the item relative to the pointer. You can create a rollover effect for each menu item by using different background and text colors for each

state to represent how the menu item appears when the users move their pointer over it or away from it. You can also create special effects for web page links. The United States Botanic Garden website shown in Figure 13 uses several different types of links: plain text links, links created as list items, and links created with images. They also use a CSS3 mega drop-down menu. A **mega menu** is a type of menu that uses sub-menus to group related pages under a main menu item. When you select a main menu item, a second menu drops down with additional menu items to choose from. When the pointer moves away from the main menu item, the sub-menu closes. This is a way to provide a hierarchy of links, yet conserve space on the page by not making them all visible all of the time.

You insert a menu bar on a web page using the Insert Navigation command in the Structure category on the Insert panel. Dreamweaver adds the menu bar links to the page and adds JavaScript code and CSS styles to the code to make the links respond to user input. In the code, the links are placed within <nav> tags, which clearly indicate to screen readers that this is a navigational element, a semantic markup that helps provide accessibility.

There are other methods that you can use to create a menu bar with images, such as an image map. You will learn about image maps in Lesson 4.

Copying and Modifying a Menu Bar

After you create a menu bar, you can save time by copying and pasting it to the other main pages in your site. Make sure you place the menu bar in the same position on each page. This practice ensures that the menu bar will look the same on each page, making it easier for users to navigate to all the pages in your website. If you are even one line or one pixel off, the menu bar will appear to "jump" as it changes position from page to page. When you learn to use templates, you can create a main page template with a menu bar, then base the rest of your pages on the template. This makes it easy to provide continuity across the site and is easier to update when changes are needed.

Figure 13 *United States Botanic Garden website*

Links created as list items

Images used for links

Source: United States Botanic Garden

Create a menu bar

1. Change to Code view, place the insertion point in front of the opening `<h1>` tag before the page heading "The Sea Spa Services", then return to Design view.

2. With the insertion point in front of The Sea Spa Services, press **[Enter]** (Win) or **[return]** (Mac), select the **Structure category** on the Insert panel, then select **Navigation**.

3. In the Insert Navigation dialog box, type **menu_bar** in the Class text box, verify that **Insert as Fluid Element** is checked, as shown in Figure 14, then select **OK** to close the dialog box.

   The placeholder text for the menu bar appears inside a layout box outline under the banner on the page, as shown in Figure 15.

You created a navigation bar element on the spa page.

Figure 14 *The Insert Navigation dialog box*

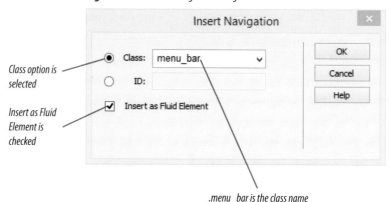

Class option is selected

Insert as Fluid Element is checked

.menu_bar is the class name

Figure 15 *The default placeholder text for the new menu bar*

Default placeholder text for the menu bar

Understanding the Web Accessibility Initiative - Accessible Rich Internet Applications Suite

The Web Accessibility Initiative Accessible Rich Internet Applications Suite (WAI-ARIA) is a resource for applying best practices when adding advanced user interface controls to a website. Functions such as drag-and-drop or browsing through a menu can be difficult for users who rely on assistive devices to navigate a site. WAI-ARIA, at w3.org/TR/wai-aria/, provides guidelines and techniques for planning and implementing accessible content. It also provides presentations, handouts, and tutorials for developers who are interested in learning how to provide content that all users can easily navigate, such as providing alternative keyboard navigation for web objects primarily designed to function using mouse clicks or screen taps. The information offered through WAI-ARIA is developed by the Protocols and Formats Working Group (PFWG), a part of the World Wide Web Consortium (W3C).

Figure 16 *The default placeholder text for the menu bar selected*

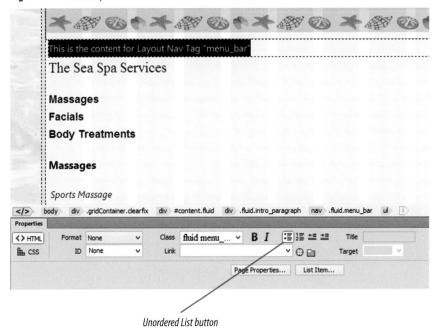

Unordered List button

Figure 17 *The unordered list item in Code view*

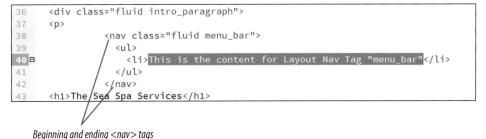

Beginning and ending <nav> tags

Add items to a menu bar

1. Click in the default menu bar text, select the text, then select the **Unordered list button** :≡ on the Property inspector, as shown in Figure 16.

2. Switch to Code view, then verify that the selected placeholder text is between the beginning and ending unordered list tag. If it is not, cut and paste it as shown in Figure 17. If you don't see a <p> tag before the opening <nav> tag, place the insertion point in front of the opening <nav> tag, and type **<p>**.

3. Return to Design view, reselect the placeholder text if necessary, type **Home**, press **[Enter]** (Win) or **[return]** [Mac], then continue by adding About Us, Sand Crab Cafe, Sea Spa, and Activities to serve as the five links in the menu bar.

   The default placeholder text for the menu bar is replaced with text to use for the links to the five main pages in the website.

(continued)

4. Use the Property inspector to link each item as follows: Home: **index.html**; About Us: **about_us.html**; Sand Crab Café: **café.html**; The Sea Spa: **spa.html**; and Activities: **activities.html**.

5. Compare your page to Figure 18, then save your work.

You created an unordered list from the five menu items, then linked each item to its page.

Figure 18 *The menu bar items linked to their pages*

Unordered list items with links added

Inserting a Fireworks Menu Bar

Another option for adding a menu bar to your page is to create a menu bar in Adobe Fireworks and import it onto an open page in Dreamweaver. Adobe Fireworks is a bitmap and vector graphics editor used for creating website images and designs. To do this you first create a menu bar in Fireworks and export the file to a Dreamweaver local site folder. This file contains the HTML code that defines the menu bar properties. Next, open the page you want to insert it on in Dreamweaver, then use the Insert, Image, Fireworks HTML command to place the HTML code on the page. You can also use Dreamweaver to import rollover images and buttons created in Fireworks.

Figure 19 *The ul li a properties*

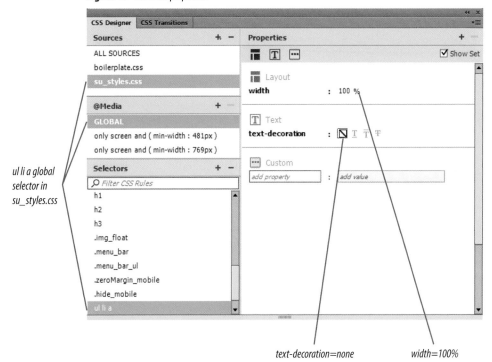

ul li a global selector in su_styles.css

text-decoration=none   width=100%

1. If necessary, place the insertion point in the menu bar, select **su_styles.css** in the Sources pane in CSS Designer, select **GLOBAL** in the @Media pane, select the **Add Selector button** ➕ , then verify that ul li a is the selected name in the selectors pane, and then press **[Enter]** (Win) or **[return]** [Mac].

   The suggested name is based on the location of the insertion point. In this case, ul li a indicates that the insertion point was in an unordered list, it's in a list item, and is a link. This is a standard HTML tag, and these tags do not have to begin with a period, as do the custom tags that you create.

2. Add the following properties and values in the Properties pane:

   width = **100%;**

   text-decoration = **none;**

   Setting the width to 100% tells the selector to occupy 100% of its space, and setting the text decoration to none removes the underline from the links.

3. With the ul li a selector still highlighted, select the **Show Set check box** in the Properties pane and compare your screen to Figure 5-19.

   (continued)

4. Create a new global tag selector in the su_styles.css file named **li**, and then set the list item Display property to **inline**.

Even though you see the word "inline" in light gray text in the Display property value text box, it is serving as a property value placeholder. To make sure it is actually assigned as a property value, it must be selected. This insures that the inline display value will be added to the li tag selector and will be listed as a li property value when the Show Set checkbox is selected in the Properties pane.

5. Select the su_styles.css GLOBAL **menu_bar selector**, then set the following property and value:

   text-align = **center**;

   The menu bar is now horizontal instead of vertical on the page, as shown in Figure 21.

6. Save your work, then preview the page in a browser.

7. Close the browser.

You used CSS to assign properties to menu bar elements.

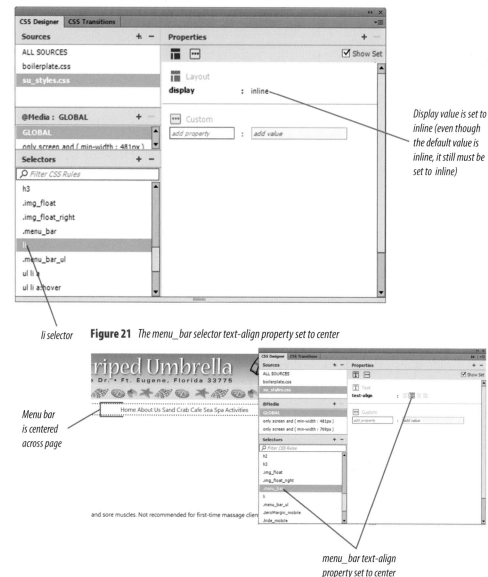

Figure 20 *The li selector display property set to inline*

Display value is set to inline (even though the default value is inline, it still must be set to inline)

li selector

Figure 21 *The menu_bar selector text-align property set to center*

Menu bar is centered across page

menu_bar text-align property set to center

Figure 22 *Choosing a background color for the menu bar*

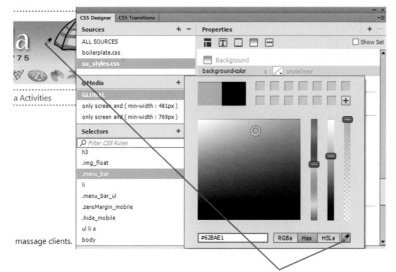

Eye dropper selects a blue from the banner

Figure 23 *Adding left and right padding properties to the ul li a selector*

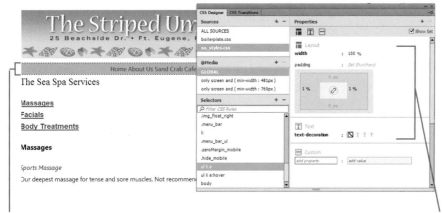

Settings add some space between the links

Properties added to the ul li a global selector

Edit CSS menu bar selectors

1. Select the GLOBAL selector **menu_bar** in CSS Designer if necessary, then select the **background-color box** to open the color picker.

2. Select the **Eyedropper tool**, select a shade of blue from the banner background, as shown in Figure 22, then move the pointer over the page and click to close the color picker.

   The menu bar now has a blue background that blends with the banner.

3. Select the GLOBAL selector **ul li a** in CSS Designer then add the following properties and values:

   left padding =**1%**

   right padding = **1%**

4. Show the ul li a set properties, compare your screen to Figure 23, save your work, preview the page in the browser, then close the browser.

   These settings put some space between the links. However, the navigation bar is not the same width as the banner because the container it is in, the .intro_paragraph selector, needs an adjustment.

   (continued)

5. Select the **GLOBAL .intro_paragraph selector** in the su_styles.css file, then change the width to **100%** and the padding to **0px** on all sides.

Changing the container width spreads the banner across the container so its edges line up with the banner edges, as shown in Figure 24.

6. Select the **su_styles.css file** on the Related Files toolbar, then scroll to locate the ul li a selector, which is toward the end of the Mobile Layout section, around line 160.

This selector is inherited by the other device sizes, but the rule is not duplicated in the other sections of the code. Therefore, if you want to change a property or value, you must duplicate the code for the other two device sizes, then modify the property values that you want to change for those devices.

7. Copy all of the code for this selector, including its brackets, then paste it into the Tablet Layout: 481px to 768px section of the code (which begins around line 180), before the closing bracket for that section, and then paste it into the Desktop Layout: 769 px to a max of 1232 px section (which begins around line 233).

8. Modify the desktop size ul li a selector to set the padding to **4%** for the left side and **4%** for the right side.

Adjusting the padding percentages increases the space between the menu bar items to better fit the display size.

9. Save your work, select **Source Code** on the Related files toolbar to return to the spa page, change to Design view, then view the menu bar using Live view in all three screen sizes.

(continued)

Figure 24 *Adjusted menu bar width*

The menu bar width is now equal to the width of the banner

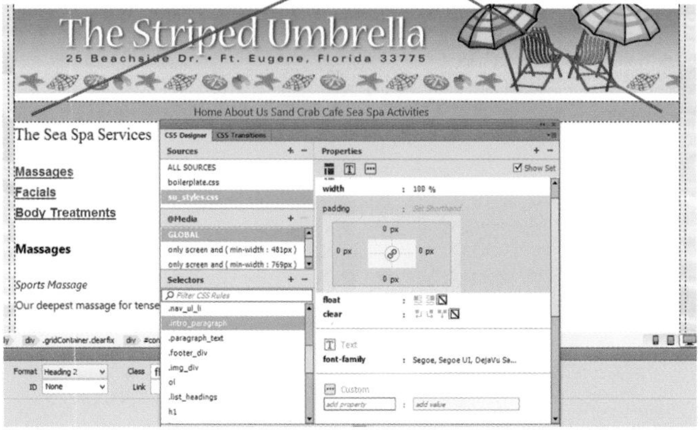

Figure 25 *A menu element with the pointer over it changes color*

Menu item changes colors when the pointer is placed over it

Figure 26 *Copying the code for the new menu bar*

```
37      <div class="fluid intro_paragraph">
38        <p>
39          <nav class="fluid menu_bar">
40          <ul>
41          <li><a href="index.html">Home</a></li>
42          <li><a href="about_us.html">About Us</a></li>
43          <li><a href="cafe.html">Sand Crab Cafe</a></li>
44          <li><a href="spa.html">Sea Spa</a></li>
45          <li><a href="activities.html">Activities</a></li>
46        </ul></nav>
47          <h1>The Sea Spa Services</h1>
```

Copy the selected code for the menu bar, including the <p> tag on the line above it

Figure 27 *Selecting the original menu bar before replacing it*

```
36        <div class="fluid intro_paragraph">
37        <nav class="fluid intro_paragraph">
38          <a href="index.html">Home</a> - <a href="about_us.html">About Us</a> - <a href=
          "spa.html">Spa</a> - <a href="cafe.html">Cafe</a> - <a href="activities.html">
          Activities</a></nav>
39          <a href="assets/family_sunset.jpg"><img src="assets/family_sunset.jpg" alt="Family
          on a sunset cruise" class="img_float"/></a>
```

Select the original menu bar, then replace it with the new code

Figure 28 *The activities page with the completed menu bar*

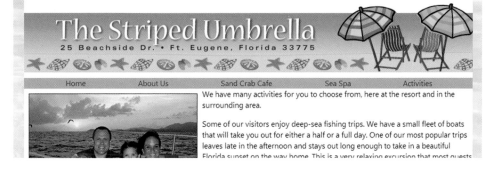

Now all of the menu items fit on the screen, regardless of the display size. Finally, you will adjust the menu bar appearance when a user points to an item in a browser.

10. Add one more global selector in the su_styles.css file named **ul li a:hover** with the following properties: Set the text color value to the **brown starfish color**, using the Color picker and the Eye Dropper; then set the background-color value to the **sand color**.

11. Save all files, then go to Live view and hover the pointer over a menu bar item as shown in Figure 25.

You used global selectors to format menu bar spacing and colors.

Copy and paste a menu bar

1. Change to Code view, then select the code for the menu bar, as shown in Figure 26.

2. Select **Edit** on the Menu bar, then select **Copy**.

3. Double-click **activities.html** on the Files panel to open the activities page.

4. Switch to Code view if necessary, select the code for the five links on the Activities page as shown in Figure 27, select **Edit** on the Menu bar, select **Paste**, return to Design view, compare your screen to Figure 28, save the page, then test the links in Live view.

5. Repeat Step 4 to replace the original menu bar on the index page and add the new menu bar to the about_us page, then save your work.

6. Preview the activities page in your browser, test the menu bar on the home, about_us, spa, and activities pages, then close your browser. Close all open pages.

You copied the menu bar on the spa page to three additional pages in The Striped Umbrella website.

Create an
IMAGE MAP

What You'll Do

In this lesson, you will create an image map by placing a hotspot on The Striped Umbrella banner on the about_us page that will link to the home page.

Understanding Image Maps

Another way to create links for web pages is to combine them with images by creating an image map. An **image map** is an image that has one or more hotspots placed on top of it. A **hotspot** is a selectable area on an image that, when the user selects it, links to a different location on the page or to another web page. For example, see the National Park Service website shown in Figure 29. When you select a state, you link to information about national parks in that state.

You can create hotspots by first selecting the image on which you want to place a hotspot, and then using one of the hotspot tools in the Property inspector to define its shape.

There are several ways to create image maps to make them user-friendly and accessible. One way is to be sure to include alternate text for each hotspot. Another is to draw the hotspot boundaries a little larger than they need to be to cover the area you want to set as a link. This allows users a little leeway when they place their mouse over the hotspot by creating a larger target area for them. Always assign a unique name for each image map.

Dreamweaver hotspot tools make creating image maps a snap. In addition to the Rectangle Hotspot tool, you can create any shape you need using the Circle Hotspot tool and the Polygon Hotspot tool. For instance, on a map of the United States, you can draw an outline around each state with the Polygon Hotspot tool and then make each state "selectable." You can easily change and rearrange hotspots on the image. Use the Pointer Hotspot tool to select the hotspot you would like to edit. You can drag one of the hotspot selector handles to change its size or shape. You can also move the hotspot by dragging it to a new position on the image. It is a good idea to limit the number of complex hotspots in an image because the code can become too lengthy for the page to download in a reasonable length of time.

Figure 29 *Viewing an image map on the National Park Service website*

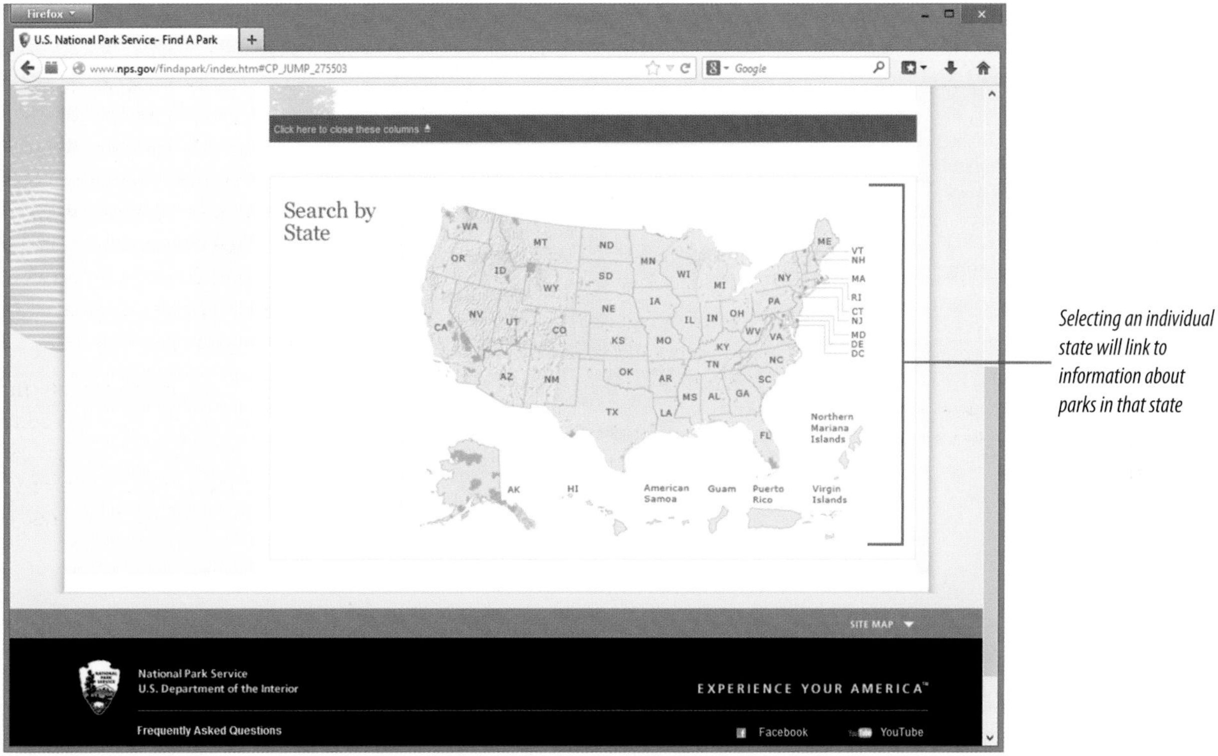

Selecting an individual state will link to information about parks in that state

Source: National Park Service

Create an image map

1. Open the about us page, place the insertion point in the banner div, change to Code view to verify that the insertion point is between the div tags, then insert the file **transparent_gif** from the assets folder in the drive and folder where you store your Chapter 5 Data Files. To make an image map, you have to select an image. Since the banner is a background image, it cannot be selected. You insert a transparent image on top of the banner background so you can create an image map over the banner.

2. Select the transparent_image on the about_us page, then select the **Rectangle Hotspot tool** in the Property inspector.

3. Drag the **pointer** to create a rectangle over the transparent image over the banner, as shown in Figure 30.

TIP To adjust the shape of a hotspot, select the Pointer Hotspot tool in the Property inspector, then drag a sizing handle on the hotspot.

4. Drag the **Point to File button** next to the Link text box in the Property inspector to the index.html file on the Files panel to link the hotspot to the index page.

5. Replace the default text "Map" with **Home** in the Map text box in the Property inspector to give the image map a unique name.

6. Select the **Target list arrow** in the Property inspector, then select **_top**.

   When the hotspot is selected, the _top option opens the home page in the same window. See Table 2 for an explanation of the four target options.
   (continued)

Figure 30 *A hotspot drawn on the transparent image over the banner background*

Transparent image

Hotspot

Rectangle Hotspot tool

TABLE 2: OPTIONS IN THE TARGET LIST	
Target	**Result**
_blank	Displays the destination page in a separate browser window
new	Displays the destination page in a new tab (CSS3)
_parent	Displays the destination page in the parent frameset (replaces the frameset)
_self	Displays the destination page in the same frame or window
_top	Displays the destination page in the whole browser window

© 2015 Cengage Learning®

Working with Links and Navigation

Figure 31 *Hotspot properties*

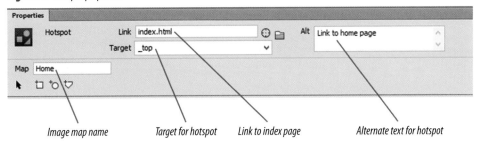

Image map name — *Target for hotspot* — *Link to index page* — *Alternate text for hotspot*

Figure 32 *Preview of the image map on the activities page in the browser*

When pointer is over the hotspot, the link appears in the bottom-left corner of the screen in some browsers

Pointing finger indicates pointer is over the link hotspot

7. Type **Link to home page** in the Alt text box in the Property inspector, as shown in Figure 31.

8. Save your work, preview the page in your browser, then place the pointer over the image map.

   As you place the pointer over the hotspot, the pointer turns to a pointing finger, indicating that it is a link, as shown in Figure 32.

9. Select the link to test it, close the browser, then close all open pages.

You created an image map on the banner of the about_us page using the Rectangle Hotspot tool. You then linked the hotspot to the home page.

Manage WEBSITE LINKS

What You'll Do

 In this lesson, you will use some Dreamweaver reporting features to check The Striped Umbrella website for broken links and orphaned files.

Managing Website Links

Because the World Wide Web changes constantly, websites might be up one day and down the next. If a website changes server locations or goes down due to technical difficulties or a power failure, the links to it become broken. Broken links, like misspelled words on a web page, indicate that a website is not being maintained diligently.

Checking links to make sure they work is an ongoing and crucial task you need to perform on a regular basis. You must check external links manually by reviewing your website in a browser and selecting each link to make sure it works correctly. The Check Links Sitewide feature is a helpful tool for managing internal links. You can use it to check your entire website for the total number of links and the number of links that are broken, external, or orphaned, and then view the results in the Link Checker panel. **Orphaned files** are files that are not linked to any pages in the website.

DESIGNTIP

Using Good Navigation Design

As you work on the navigation structure for a website, you should try to limit the number of links on each page to no more than is necessary. Too many links may confuse users of your website. You should also design links so that users can reach the information they want within a few clicks or taps. If finding information takes more than three or four clicks or taps, the user may become discouraged or "lost" in the site. It's a good idea to provide visual clues on each page to let users know where they are, much like a "You are here" marker on a store directory at the mall, or a breadcrumbs trail. A **breadcrumbs trail** is a list of links that provides a path from the initial page you opened in a website to the page that you are currently viewing. Many websites provide a list of all the site's pages, called a **site map**. A site map is similar to an index. It lets users see how the information is divided between the pages and helps them locate the information they need quickly.

Figure 33 *Link Checker panel displaying external links*

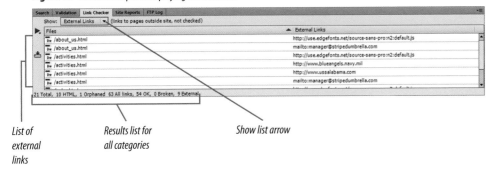

List of external links

Results list for all categories

Show list arrow

Figure 34 *Link Checker panel displaying one orphaned file*

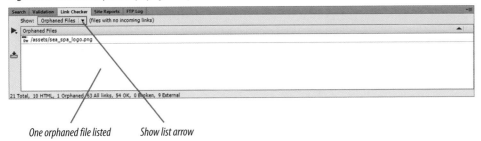

One orphaned file listed

Show list arrow

Figure 35 *Assets panel displaying links*

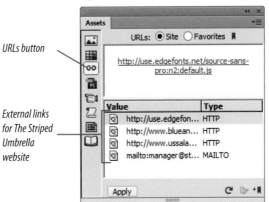

URLs button

External links for The Striped Umbrella website

Manage website links

1. Select **Site** on the Menu bar, point to **Advanced**, then select **Recreate Site Cache**.

2. Select **Site** on the Menu bar, then select **Check Links Sitewide**.

   The Results tab group opens, with the Link Checker panel in front. By default, the Link Checker panel initially lists any broken internal links found in the website. The Striped Umbrella website has no broken links.

3. Select the **Show list arrow** in the Link Checker panel, select **External Links**, then compare your screen to Figure 33.

4. Select the **Show list arrow**, then select **Orphaned Files** to view the orphaned files in the Link Checker panel, as shown in Figure 34.

   The Striped Umbrella website has one orphaned file, sea_spa_logo.png. You may use this file later, so you leave it in the assets folder. (*Hint*: if you see more orphaned files listed, recreate your site cache and try again.)

5. Right-click (Win) or Control-click (Mac) in an empty area of the Results tab group title bar, then select **Close Tab Group**.

6. Display the Assets panel if necessary, then select the **URLs button** ⌘ in the Assets panel if necessary to display the list of links in the website.

   The Assets panel displays the external links used in the website, as shown in Figure 35.

You used the Link Checker panel to check for broken links, external links, and orphaned files in The Striped Umbrella website. You also viewed the external links in the Assets panel.

Update a page

1. Open dw5_3.html from the drive and folder where you store your Data Files, then save it as **fishing.html** in the striped_umbrella local site root folder, overwriting the existing fishing page, but not updating the links.

   The page elements are updated with the website style sheets.

2. Select the broken link image placeholder, select the **Browse for File button** 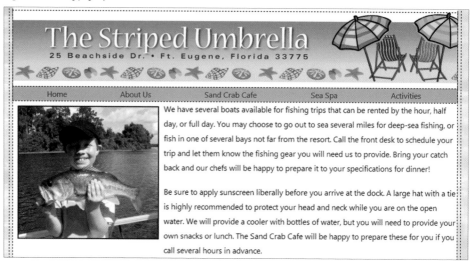 next to the Src text box in the Property inspector, browse to the drive and folder where you store your Data Files, open the assets folder, then select the file **fisherman.jpg** to copy the file to the striped_umbrella assets folder.

3. Deselect the image placeholder and the image appears, as shown in Figure 36.

4. Save and close the fishing page, then close the dw5_3.html page.

5. Open dw5_4.html from the drive and folder where you store your Data Files, then save it as **cruises.html** in the striped_umbrella local site folder, overwriting the existing cruises page, but not updating the links.

   The links to the website CSS files are in place and format the page elements. Since you haven't yet corrected the path for the image, you can't see the styles applied to the image yet.

   (continued)

Figure 36 *Fishing page updated*

The Striped Umbrella
25 Beachside Dr. • Ft. Eugene, Florida 33775

| Home | About Us | Sand Crab Cafe | Sea Spa | Activities |

We have several boats available for fishing trips that can be rented by the hour, half day, or full day. You may choose to go out to sea several miles for deep-sea fishing, or fish in one of several bays not far from the resort. Call the front desk to schedule your trip and let them know the fishing gear you will need us to provide. Bring your catch back and our chefs will be happy to prepare it to your specifications for dinner!

Be sure to apply sunscreen liberally before you arrive at the dock. A large hat with a tie is highly recommended to protect your head and neck while you are on the open water. We will provide a cooler with bottles of water, but you will need to provide your own snacks or lunch. The Sand Crab Cafe will be happy to prepare these for you if you call several hours in advance.

Testing Your Website Against the Wireframe

Another test you should run regularly is a comparison of how your developing website pages are meeting the specifications of your wireframe prototype. Compare each completed page against its corresponding wireframe to make sure that all page elements have been placed in their proper locations on the page. Verify that all specified links have been included and test them to make sure that they work correctly. You might also consider hiring site-usability testers to test your site navigation. A site usability test provides impartial feedback on how intuitive and user-friendly your site is to use.

Figure 37 *Cruises page updated*

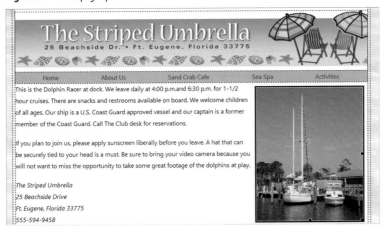

6. Select the broken link image placeholder, select the **Browse for File button** 📁 next to the Src text box in the Property inspector, then browse to the drive and folder where you store your Data Files, open the assets folder, then select the file **boats.jpg** to copy the file to the striped_umbrella assets folder.

   TIP If you have trouble selecting the placeholder, click or tap the middle of the placeholder to select it.

7. Deselect the image placeholder and the image will appear as shown in Figure 37.

8. Add the following properties and values to the **GLOBAL.gridContainer** selector:

   border-width: **thin**;

   border-style: **solid**;

   border-color: **#272525**;

   background-color: **#FFFFFF**.

9. Save your work.

   The border properties add a thin border to set off the page area in a browser. The white background adds a little space around the page area so the text doesn't come so close to the edge of the page.

10. Preview each page in the browser, close the browser, test them in Live view in three different sizes, then close all open pages.

You added content to two previously blank pages in the website and previewed each page to check for consistent layout. You also added some properties to the GLOBAL .grid_container selector to add some white space and a border around each page.

Incorporate Web 2.0
TECHNOLOGY

What You'll Do

In this lesson, you will explore some of the Web 2.0 applications that can be used to engage website users.

What Exactly Is Web 2.0?

The term **Web 2.0** describes the evolution of web applications that facilitate and promote information sharing among Internet users. These applications not only reside on computers, but on cell phones, in cars, on portable GPS devices, and in game devices. **GPS (Global Positioning System)** devices are used to track your position through a global satellite navigation system, and are popular to use for driving directions, hiking, and map making. Web 2.0 applications do not simply display information for users to read passively; they allow users to actively contribute to the content.

RSS feeds are another easy way to share information with users. **RSS** stands for **Really Simple Syndication**. Websites use **RSS feeds** to distribute news stories, information about upcoming events, and announcements. Web users can subscribe to RSS feeds to receive regular releases of information from a site. Users can download and play these digitally broadcasted files called **podcasts (Programming On Demand)** using devices such as computers or MP3 players. Many news organizations and educational institutions publish both audio and video podcasts. Video podcasts are referred to as **vodcasts** or **vidcasts**.

Web 2.0 also includes social networking. **Social networking** refers to any web-based service that facilitates social interaction among users. Examples of social networking sites include **Facebook**, **Pinterest**, and **Match. com**. These sites allow users to set up profile pages and post information on them for others to view. Facebook pages often contain lots of text, images, and videos. Pinterest is an online pinboard for sharing crafts, recipes, and other items of interest.

A wiki is another example of a Web 2.0 application. The term **wiki** (named for the Hawaiian word for "quick") refers to a site where a user can use simple editing tools to contribute and edit the page content in a site. A good example is **Wikipedia**, an online encyclopedia. Wikipedia allows users to post new information and edit existing information on any topic. Although people have different opinions about the academic integrity of the information on Wikipedia, Wikipedia is a rich source of information. Proponents argue that its many active and vigilant users maintain its information integrity.

Blogs (web logs) are another example of a Web 2.0 application. **Blogs** are websites where the website owner regularly posts commentaries and opinions on various topics. Content can consist of text, video, or images. Users can respond to the postings and read postings by other users. **Twitter** is a website where users can post short messages, called **tweets**. Twitter is considered a blog or a micro blog, because you cannot enter more than 140 characters in each post. To use Twitter, you must first join by creating a free account. Then you can post messages about yourself, "follow" other people's tweets, and invite others to "follow" you. **Tumblr** is another popular blog where you can post and share text, photos, music, and videos.

There are many video sharing applications such as Skype, Google Video Chat, and YouTube. **Skype** and **Google Video Chat** are free applications that you use to communicate live with other people through video conferencing, using a high-speed Internet connection and a web camera, called a **web cam**. **YouTube** is a website where you can upload and share videos. To upload videos, you need to register with the site.

So how do these various Web 2.0 components relate to the process of creating websites? Most websites today engage their users in one or more of these applications. The Peace Corps website, shown in Figure 38, has links to Facebook, Twitter, YouTube, and others. When you are designing a site, one of the decisions you must make is not if, but how you

will incorporate Web 2.0 technology to fully engage your users. To incorporate one of these applications into your website, first register to set up an account on the social networking site, then place a link on one of your site's web pages (usually the home page) that links to each social networking site and opens your page. For example, if your Twitter account is located at twitter.com/your_name, add this link to your home page using the Twitter logo as a graphic link. You can download social networking sites' logos from their websites. Some applications specify how you should refer to and link to their site.

Using the applications that are a part of Web 2.0 with your website can bring your site from simply presenting information

on pages for users to read to facilitating a compelling dialog between the users and the site. They will no longer be just "users," but active participants.

Web 3.0 will be the next generation of the Web. With Web 3.0, browsers will be able to handle multiple searches simultaneously. For instance, you could search for a recent Oscar best picture nominee and sushi restaurant in the vicinity of the theater where it is playing. iPhones and Google Androids come with a personal assistant you can "talk" with, rather than typing in searches. Browsers may soon be able to do this, too. The more information that is stored from your past searches, the more they will get to "know" you and be able to give responses that fit your profile.

Figure 38 *Viewing social networking links on the Peace Corps website*

Links to Facebook, Twitter, YouTube, Tumblr, LinkedIn, Pinterest, Instagram

Source: The Peace Corps

Create external and internal links.

1. Open the Blooms & Bulbs website.
2. Open dw5_5.html from the drive and folder where you store your Data Files, then save it as **newsletter.html** in the Blooms & Bulbs website, overwriting the existing file without updating the links. Close dw5_5.html.
3. Select each broken image and browse to the assets folder in the drive and folder where you store your Chapter 5 Data Files and copy the ruby_grass, trees, and plants broken images to the local site assets folder.
4. Create a new global selector to the bb_styles.css file to modify the <h2> tag as follows:

    font-color: **#003300**
    font-family: Segoe, Segoe UI, DejaVu Sans; Trebuchet MS; Verdana, sans-serif
    font-weight: bold
    font-size: large

5. Modify the <h1> rule (which you created in Chapter 3) as follows:

    font-size: x-large
    font-color: #003300

6. Add a new global selector to the blooms_styles.css file that modifies the <h3> tag as follows:

    font-color: #003300
    font-family: Segoe, Segoe UI, DejaVu Sans; Trebuchet MS; Verdana, sans-serif
    font-weight: bold
    font-size: medium

7. Apply the img_float rule to the ruby_grass and plants images.

8. Apply the img_float_right rule to the trees image.
9. Scroll to the bottom of the page, then link the National Gardening Association text to **http://www.garden.org**.
10. Link the Organic Gardening text to **http://www.organicgardening.com**.
11. Link the Southern Living text to **http://www.southernliving.com/southern**.
12. Save all files, then preview the page in your browser, verifying that each link works correctly.
13. Close your browser, returning to the newsletter page in Dreamweaver.
14. Scroll to the paragraph about gardening issues, select the gardening tips text in the last sentence, then link the selected text to the tips.html file in the blooms local site folder.
15. Change the page title on the Document toolbar to read **Blooms & Bulbs Gardening Matters**, then save your work.
16. Open the plants page and add this new paragraph to the bottom of the page: **In addition to these marvelous roses, we have many annuals, perennials, and water plants that have just arrived.**
17. Link the "annuals" text to the annuals.html file, link the "perennials" text to the perennials.html file, and the "water plants" text to the water_plants.html file.
18. Save your work, test the links in your browser, then close your browser. (*Hint*: These pages do not have content yet, but are serving as placeholders.)

Use IDs to navigate to specific page locations.

1. Switch to the newsletter page, then select the Grass heading and add the ID **grass**.
2. Select the Trees heading, then add the ID **trees**.
3. Select the Plants heading, then add the ID **plants**.
4. Select the word "grass" in the Gardening Issues paragraph and type **#grass** in the Link text box in the Property inspector.
5. Select the word "trees" in the Gardening Issues paragraph and type **#trees** in the Link text box in the Property inspector.
6. Select the word "plants" in the Gardening Issues paragraph and type **#plants** in the Link text box in the Property inspector.
7. Save your work, view the page in your browser, test all the links to make sure they work, then close your browser.

Create, modify, and copy a menu bar.

1. Change to Code view for the plants page, then place the insertion point in front of the opening <h1> tag before the page heading "Featured Spring Plant: Roses!", enter a paragraph break, then return to Design view.
2. With the insertion point in front of "Featured Spring Plant: Roses!", enter a paragraph break, select the Structure category on the Insert panel, then select Navigation.
3. Type **menu_bar** in the Class text box, verify that Insert as Fluid Element is checked, then select OK to close the Insert Navigation dialog box.

4. Select the default placeholder text in the menu_bar container, then select the Unordered List button in the Property inspector.

5. Verify in Code view that the placeholder text is between the beginning and ending unordered list item tag. If it is not, cut and paste it to that position in the code.

6. Return to Design view, select the default placeholder text, if necessary, type **Home**, press [Enter] (Win) [return] [Mac], then continue by adding **Newsletter**, **Plants**, **Tips**, and **Workshops** to serve as the five links in the menu bar.

7. Use the Property inspector to link each item as follows: Home: index.html; Newsletter: newsletter.html; Plants: plants.html; Tips: tips.html; and Workshops: workshops.html.

8. Place the insertion point in the menu bar, select bb_styles.css in the Sources pane in CSS Designer, select GLOBAL in the @Media pane, select the Add Selector button then select the ul li a default GLOBAL selector name in the Selectors pane.

9. Add the following properties and values in the Properties pane:
width = **100%**;
text-decoration = none;

10. Select the bb_styles.css GLOBAL menu_bar selector, then set the following property and value:
text-align = center;

11. Save your work, preview the page in a browser, then close the browser.

12. Select the bb_styles.css GLOBAL menu_bar selector again, then select the background-color box to open the Color picker.

13. Select the Eyedropper tool, then select a shade of light gold from the text in the banner background.

14. Create a new GLOBAL selector in the bb_styles.css file named **li**, then add the following property and value:
display = inline;

15. Select the GLOBAL selector ul li a in CSS Designer then add the following properties and values:
left padding = **4%**;
right padding = **4%**;

16. Save your work, then preview the page in your browser.

17. Select the GLOBAL .intro_paragraph selector in the bb_styles.css file, then change the padding to **0px** on all sides and the width to **100%**.

18. Switch to the bb_styles.css file, then scroll to locate the ul li a selector in the code.

19. Copy all of the code for this selector, then paste it into the tablet (only screen and (min-width: 481px), and desktop (min-width: 769px), sections of the code.

20. Modify the tablet size ul li a selector code to set the padding to **1%** for the left side and **1%** for the right side.

21. Modify the global size ul li a selector to set the padding to **1%** for the left side and **1%** for the right side.

22. Modify the Tablet .header_div selector to add a height value of **110px**; then modify the .header_div background-repeat value in the Desktop selector to repeat-x.

23. Add the following properties and values to the GLOBAL .gridContainer selector:
border-width = thin;
border-style = solid;
border-color = **#272525**;
background-color= **#FFFFFF**.

Figure 39 *Completed Skills Review*

24. Add one more GLOBAL selector in the bb_styles.css file named ul li a:hover with the following properties: set the text color using the Color picker eye dropper to pick up a dark purple in a flower on the banner; then for the background color, use the Eye Dropper to pick up the a light purple from a flower.

25. Save your work, then preview the page in a browser to see if you are satisfied with your menu bar color scheme. If you are not, try different colors for your ul li a:hover selector.

26. Copy the new menu bar to the index, newsletter, and tips pages.

27. Save all files, then go to Live view and point to (hover over) a menu bar item to see the rollover effect.

Create an image map.

1. On the newsletter page, place the insertion point in the banner div then insert the file transparent_gif from the assets folder in the drive and folder where you store your Chapter 5 Data Files.

2. Use the Rectangle Hotspot tool to draw an image map across the transparent image on the banner, then link it to the home page.

3. Name the image map **home** and set the target to _top.

4. Add the alternate text **Link to home page**, save the page, then preview it in the browser to test the link.

5. Close the browser.

Manage website links.

1. Use the Link Checker panel to view and fix broken links and orphaned files in the Blooms & Bulbs website. (*Hint*: Remember to recreate your site cache if you see any. That usually fixes them.)

2. Open dw5_6.html from the drive and folder where you store your Data Files, then save it as **annuals. html**, replacing the original file. Do not update links, but save the file coleus.jpg from the Chapter 5 Data Files assets folder to the assets folder of the website.

3. Close dw5_6.html.

4. Apply the img_float rule to the coleus image.

5. Repeat Steps 2 and 3 using dw5_7.html to replace perennials.html, saving the fiber_optic_grass.jpg file in the local site assets folder and using dw5_8.html to replace water_plants.html, saving the water_lily.jpg file in the local site assets folder.

6. Save your work, then preview each page in the browser, testing each link to make sure they all work correctly. As you preview each page, compare the different page sizes to the sample pages shown in Figures 40a, b, and c.

7. Close all open pages.

Figure 40a *Completed Skills Review*

Figure 40b & c *Completed Skills Review*

Home   Newsletter   Plants   Tips   Workshops

Welcome to Blooms & Bulbs. We carry a variety of plants and shrubs along with a large inventory of gardening supplies. Our four greenhouses are full of healthy young plants just waiting to be planted in your yard. We grow an amazing selection of annuals and perennials. We also stock a diverse selection of trees, shrubs, tropicals, water plants, and ground covers. Check out our garden ware for your garden accents or as gifts for your gardening friends. We are happy to deliver or ship your purchases.

Our staff includes a certified landscape architect, three landscape designers, and six master gardeners. We offer detailed landscape plans tailored to your location as well as planting and regular maintenance services. We have enjoyed serving Alvin and the surrounding area for twelve years now. Stop by and see us soon!

Blooms & Bulbs
Highway 43 South
Alvin, TX 77501
555-248-0806
Customer Service

Copyright 2002 - 2016
Last updated on May 2, 2014

Home   Newsletter   Plants   Tips   Workshops

Featured Spring Plant: Roses!

Who can resist the romance of roses? Poets have waxed poetically over them throughout the years. Many persons consider the beauty and fragrance of roses to be unmatched in nature. The varieties are endless, ranging from floribunda to hybrid teas to shrub roses to climbing roses. Each variety has its own personality and preference in the garden setting. The Candy Cane Floribunda is a beautiful rose with cream, pink, and red stripes and swirls. They have a heavy scent that will remind you of the roses you received on your most special occasions. These blooms are approximately four inches in diameter. They bloom continuously from early summer to early fall. The plants grow up to four feet tall and three feet wide. They are shipped bare root in February.

For ease of growing, Knock Out® roses are some of our all-time favorites. Even beginners will not fail with these garden delights. They are shrub roses and prefer full sun, but can take partial shade. They are disease resistant and drought tolerant. You do not have to be concerned with either black spot or dead-heading with roses such as the Knock out®, making them an extremely low-maintenance plant. They are also repeat bloomers, blooming into late fall. The shrub can grow quite large, but can be pruned to any size. Pictured here is Southern Belle. Check out all our varieties as you will not fail to have great color with these plants. You must see a close-up of these beauties! Select the image to enlarge it.

In addition to these marvelous roses, we have many annuals, perennials, and water plants that have just arrived.

Use Figures 41, 42, 43, and 44 as guides to continue your work on the TripSmart website, which you began in Project Builder 1 in Chapter 1 and developed in the previous chapters. You have been asked to create a new page for the website that lists helpful links for customers. You will add content to the destinations, eqypt, and argentina pages.

1. Open the TripSmart website.
2. Open dw5_9.html from the drive and folder where you store your Data Files, then save it as **services.html** in the TripSmart local site folder, replacing the existing file, but not updating links.
3. Close dw5_9.html.
4. Assign the **IDs reservations**, **outfitters**, **tours**, and **links** to the respective headings on the page, then link each ID to "Reservations," "Travel Outfitters," "Escorted Tours," and "Helpful Links in Travel Planning" in the first paragraph, as shown in Figure 43.
5. Link the text "on-line catalog" in the Travel Outfitters paragraph to the catalog.html page.
6. Link the text "CNN Travel Channel" under the heading Helpful Links in Travel Planning to **http://www.cnn.com/TRAVEL**.
7. Repeat Step 7 to create links for the rest of the websites listed:
   U.S. Department of State: **http://travel.state.gov**
   Yahoo Currency Converter:
   http://finance.yahoo.com/currency-converter
   The Weather Channel: **http://www.weather.com**
8. Save the services page, preview the page in the browser and test each link, then close the browser.

Figure 41 *Completed Project Builder 1*

TripSmart has several divisions of customer service to assist you in planning and making reservations for your trip, shopping for your trip wardrobe and providing expert guide services. Give us a call and we will be happy to connect you with one of the following departments: Reservations, Travel Outfitters, or Escorted Tours. If you are not quite ready to talk with one of our departments and would prefer doing some of your own research first, may we suggest beginning with our Helpful Links in Travel Planning.

Reservations

Our Reservations Department is staffed with five Certified Travel Agents, each of whom is eager to assist you in making your travel plans. They have specialty areas in Africa, the Caribbean, South America, Western Europe, Eastern Europe, Asia, Antarctica, and Hawaii and the South Pacific. They also specialize in Senior Travel, Family Travel, Student Travel, and Special Needs Travel. Call us at *(555) 848-0807* extension 75 or e-mail us at Reservations to begin making your travel plans now. We will be happy to send you brochures and listings of Internet addresses to help you get started. We are open from 8:00 a.m. until 6:00 p.m. CST.

Travel Outfitters

Our travel outfitters are seasoned travelers that have accumulated a vast amount of knowledge in appropriate travel clothing and accessories for specific destinations. Climate and seasons, of course, are important factors in planning your wardrobe for a trip. Area customs should also be taken in consideration so as not to offend the local residents with inappropriate dress. When traveling abroad, we always hope that our customers will represent our country well as good ambassadors. If they can be comfortable and stylish at the same time, we have succeeded! Our clothing is all affordable and packs well on long trips. Most can be washed easily in a hotel sink and hung to drip-dry overnight. Browse through our on-line catalog, then give us a call at *(555) 433-7844* extension 85. We will also be happy to mail you a catalog of our extensive collection of travel clothing and accessories.

Escorted Tours

Our Escorted Tours department is always hard at work planning the next exciting destination to offer our TripSmart customers. We have seven professional tour guides that accompany our guests from the United States point of departure to their point of return.

Our current feature package tour is to Peru. Our local escort is Don Eugene. Don has traveled Peru extensively and enjoys sharing his love for this exciting country with others. He will be assisted after arrival in Peru with the services of archeologist JoAnne Rife, anthropologist Christina Elizabeth, and naturalist Iris Albert. Call us at *(555) 848-0807* extension 95 for information on the Peru trip or to learn about other destinations being currently scheduled.

Helpful Links in Travel Planning

The following links may be helpful in your travel research. Happy surfing!

CNN Travel Channel - News affecting travel plans to various destinations

US Department of State - Travel warnings, passport information, and more

Yahoo! Currency Converter - Calculate the exchange rate between two currencies

The Weather Channel - Weather, flight delays, and driving conditions

TripSmart
1106 Beechwood
Fayetteville, AR 72704
555-848-0807
Contact Us

Copyright 2002 - 2016
Last updated on May 2, 2014

9. Enter a paragraph break before the first paragraph on the services page, change to Code view, delete the   code after the opening <p> tag, then insert a navigation bar with the class name **menu_bar**.

10. Use the Property inspector to create an unordered list from the default placeholder menu bar text, then type text for the links: **Home**, **Catalog**, **Services**, **Tours**, and **Newsletter**. (Remember to add paragraph returns after all but the last menu item.)

11. Link each item as follows: Home: index.html; Catalog: catalog.html; Services: services.html; Tours: tours.html; and Newsletter: newsletter.html.

12. Place the insertion point in the menu bar, then add a global selector in the tripsmart_styles.css source in CSS Designer, with the default selector name (ul li a).

13. Add the following properties and values in the Properties pane:
width = 100%;
text-decoration = none;

14. Select the tripsmart_styles.css GLOBAL menu_bar selector, then set the following properties and values:
text-color = (a color of your choice using the eye dropper tool)
text-align = center;
background-color = (a color of your choice using the eye dropper)

15. Save your work.

16. Create a new GLOBAL selector in the tripsmart_styles.css file named **li**, then add the following property and value: display = inline;

17. Modify the GLOBAL selector named ul li a to add the following properties and values:
left padding = **1%**;
right padding = **1%**.

18. Save your work, then preview the page in the browser and test the links.

19. Switch to the tripsmart_styles.css file, then scroll to locate the ul li a selector in the code.

20. Copy the ul li a selector to the tablet and desktop section of the tripsmart_styles.css code, then select padding sizes for the ul li a selector for the mobile and tablet size sections of the code.

Figure 42 *Completed Project Builder 1*

Destinations: Egypt and Argentina

We are featuring two new trips for the coming year. The first is to Egypt. After arriving, we will check into our hotel and enjoy the sights for two days in Cairo, including the famous Egyptian Museum of Antiquities. Next, we will fly to Luxor to visit the Temple of Karnak and then boad our luxury Nile cruise boat, the Sun Queen VII. As we slowly cruise down the Nile, our stops will include Qena, the Ptolemaic Temple of Goddess Hathor in Denderah, the Edfu Temple, the Kom Ombo Temple, and the Philae Temple. We will enjoy a felucca ride around Elephantine Island, and then attend a formal farewell dinner the last night onboard our boat. We return to Cairo and enjoy a day in the market and a walking tour of the old walled city of Cairo.

Argentina is our next destination. We begin our tour in Buenos Aires on our first day with an orientation to this lovely city, including the gardens of Palermo, San Telmo, the business center, La Boca, and Recoleta Cemetery. That evening we will attend a Tango class to learn basic tango steps before having a chance to show off our talents at a dinner and tango show. The two main features for most people on this trip are the magnificient Iguassu Falls and Perito Moreno Glacier. The most adventurous can strap on trampons and trek across the glacier. A trek across a glacier with the beautiful blue Patagonia skys overhead is not to be forgotten. With luck, you will witness a calving, when ice breaks off the glacier with a crash of thunder and falls to the water.

21. Add one more selector in the tripsmart_styles.css file named **ul li a:hover** with text and background colors of your choice. Then make any other modifications to your selectors using properties and values of your choice.

22. Preview the page in a browser to text the links and evaluate your color choices.

23. When you are satisfied, copy the new menu bar to the index, newsletter, and tours pages.

24. Save all files, then go to Live view and hover over a menu bar item to see the rollover effect.

25. Place the insertion point in the banner div on the newsletter page, then insert the file transparent_gif from the assets folder in the drive and folder where you store your Chapter 5 Data Files.

26. Use the Rectangle Hotspot tool to draw an image map across the transparent image on the banner, then link it to the home page.

27. Name the image map **home** and set the target to _top.

28. Add the alternate text **Link to home page**, save the page, then preview it in the browser to test the link.

29. Close the browser.

Figure 43 *Completed Project Builder 1*

Destination: Egypt

We have a really special trip planned for next November. Egypt - the land of kings and pharaohs! This ten-day adventure will begin in Cairo as we visit the Giza Plateau to see the pyramids of Cheops, Chepheren, and Mycerinus. We will also visit the Great Sphinx and the Egyptian Museum of Antiquities before we leave Cairo for our cruise along the Nile. We board the Egyptian Queen at Luxury and enjoy stops along the way to the Valley of the Kings, the Valley of the Queens, the Ptolemaic temple, the Temple of Horus, and the Temple of Philae on the island of Agilika. When we return to Cairo, you will have the opportunity to do some shopping in the famous Khan El-Khalili Bazaar and enjoy an unforgettable performance of the El-Tannoura Egyptian Heritage Dance Troup.

To provide the finest in personal attention, this tour will be limited to no more than twenty people. The price schedule is as follows: Land Tour and Supplemental Group Air, $5,500.00; International Air, $1,350.00; and Single Supplement, $1,000.00. Entrance fees, hotel taxes, and services are included in the Land Tour price. Ship gratuities are also included for the Egyptian Queen crew and guides. A deposit of $500.00 is required at the time the booking is made. Trip insurance and luggage insurance are optional and are also offered for an extra charge. A passport and visa will be required for entry into Egypt. Call us at 555-555-0807 for further information and the complete itinerary from 8:00 a.m. to 6:00 p.m. (Central Standard Time).

30. Open the tours page, save it as the **egypt** page, overwriting the original eqypt page, then close both the tours and egypt pages.

31. Open dw5_10.html from the drive and folder where you store your Data Files, then save it as **argentina. html**, replacing the original file. Do not update links, but save the files iguazu_falls.jpg and glacier.jpg from the Chapter 5 Data Files assets folder to the assets folder of the website, then format them with an image class selector.

32. Close dw5_10.html, then open dw5_11.html, and save it as the **tours** page. Correct the links to the two images, then format them with an image class selector.

33. In the first paragraph of the tours page, add a link to the egypt page using the word "egypt" in the first paragraph, then add a link to the argentina page using "argentina" in the second paragraph.

34. Save your work, then preview each page in the browser, testing each link to make sure they all work correctly.

35. Use the Link Checker panel to view and fix broken links and orphaned files. (*Hint*: Remember to recreate your site cache if you see any. That usually fixes them.)

36. Close all open pages.

Figure 44 *Completed Project Builder 1*

Destination: Argentina

We have Argentina from north to south and exciting locations in between. We start in Buenos Aires for our arrival in country. Visit the many landmarks of Buenos Aires, including the Plaza de Mayo, Casa Rosada (Presidential Palace) and the Cabildo. Known as the "Paris of South America," the city's European influences are on display in the architecture, cuisine and other facets of daily life. Stroll the lovely parks of Palermo; the charming quarters of San Telmo, birthplace of the tango; the bustling banking and business center; the barrio of La Boca; and Recoleta Cemetery where Eva Peron is interred.

Our next stop is Iguassu Falls, a breath taking natural wonder of the world with its 275 cascades that spread across a gulf of nearly two miles. We will go on a catwalk extending 3,600 feet over Devil's Throat , a rolling cataract marking the border of Brazil and Argentina and view the many distinct falls from balconies in both countries. You will be talking about the magnificience of these massive works of nature for many years.

Barlioche, Argentina's "Little Switzerland" in Pantagonia is our next stop. This snow peaked wonderland allows viewing some of the most attractive scenery in Argentina, a panoply of lush hills, snow-topped peaks and lakes reflecting a crisp blue sky,

You are continuing your work on the Carolyne's Creations website, which you started in Project Builder 2 in Chapter 1 and developed in the previous chapters. Chef Carolyne has asked you to create a page describing her cooking classes offered every month. You will create the content for that page and individual pages describing the children's classes and the adult classes. Refer to Figures 45, 46, and 47 for possible solutions.

1. Open the Carolyne's Creations website.
2. Open dw5_12.html from the drive and folder where you store your Data Files, save it as **classes.html** in the local site folder of the Carolyne's Creations website, overwriting the existing file and not updating the links. Close dw5_12.html.
3. Select the text "adults' class" in the last paragraph, then link it to the adults.html page. (*Hint*: This page has not been developed yet.)

4. Select the text "children's class" in the last paragraph and link it to the children.html page. (*Hint*: This page has not been developed yet.)
5. Create an e-mail link from the text "Sign me up!" that links to **carolyne@carolynescreations.com**.
6. Insert the egyptian_traditional_dessert.jpg from the assets folder where you store your Data Files at the beginning of the second paragraph, add appropriate alternate text, then choose your own alignment and formatting settings.
7. Check any other pages with images and adjust your image rules if necessary to improve the appearance of each page.

Figure 45 *Completed Project Builder 2*

Cooking Classes are fun!

Chef Carolyne loves to offer a fun and relaxing cooking school each month in her newly refurbished kitchen. She teaches an adults' class on the fourth Saturday of each month from 6:00 to 8:00 pm. Each class will learn to cook a complete dinner and then enjoy the meal at the end of the class with a wonderful wine pairing. This is a great chance to get together with friends for a fun evening.

Chef Carolyne also teaches a children's class on the second Tuesday of each month from 4:00 to 5:30 pm. Our young chefs will learn to cook two dishes that will accompany a full meal served at 5:30 pm. Children aged 5–8 years accompanied by an adult are welcome. We also host small birthday parties where we put the guests to work baking and decorating the cake! Call for times and prices.

We offer several special adults' classes throughout the year. The Valentine Chocolate Extravaganza is a particular favorite. You will learn to dip strawberries, make truffles, and bake a sinful Triple Chocolate Dare You Torte. We also host the Not So Traditional Thanksgiving class and the Super Bowl Snacks class each year with rave reviews. Watch the website for details! Prices are $40.00 for each adults' class and $15.00 for each children's class. Sign up for classes by calling 555-963-8271 or by emailing us: Sign me up! See what's cooking this month for the adults' class and children's class.

8. Create a new menu bar using selectors of your choice. Refer to Figure 45 as you work. (*Hint*: The menu bar on Figure 45 was styled with 3% padding on the left and right sides of each menu bar item.)

9. Make any other adjustment to your selectors if you like, then save your work and close the classes page. (*Hint*: If you used an Edge Webfont, use the Command, Cleanup Webfonts Script Tag (Current Page) on each page on which you used a Webfont.)

10. Open dw5_13.html from the drive and folder where you store your Data Files, then save it as **children.html,** overwriting the existing file and not updating links. Save the image children_cooking.jpg from the assets folder where you store your Data Files to the website assets folder, then make any adjustments to your selectors to enhance the design if you like.

11. Copy the menu bar from the classes page to the children page, save your work, compare your screen to Figure 46, then close the children page.

12. Repeat Steps 10 and 11 to open the dw5_14.html file and save it as **adults.html**, overwriting the existing file and saving the file egyptian_lunch from the assets folder where you save your Data Files, then use alignment settings of your choice. Compare your work to Figure 47 for a possible solution, then save and close the files.

Figure 46 *Completed Project Builder 2*

FOR ALL OCCASIONS
555-963-8271

CAROLYNE'S CREATIONS

Home   Shop   Classes   Catering   Recipes

Children's Cooking Class for March:
Oven Chicken Fingers, Chocolate Chip Cookies

This month we will be baking oven chicken fingers that are dipped in a milk and egg mixture, then coated with breadcrumbs. The chocolate chip cookies are based on a famous recipe that includes chocolate chips, M&Ms, oatmeal, and pecans. Yummy! We will be learning some of the basics like how to cream butter and crack eggs without dropping shells into the batter.

We will provide French fries, green beans, fruit salad, and a beverage to accompany the chicken fingers.

Carolyne's Creations
496 Maple Avenue
Seven Falls, Virginia 52404
555-963-8271
Email Carolyne Kate

13. Open the index page and replace the old menu bar with the new one.

14. Repeat Step 13 to replace all old menu bars on the rest of the completed pages in the site.

15. Save all the pages, then check for broken links and orphaned files. You will see one orphaned file, cc_logo.gif. Since this is only used for a background image, it shows up as an orphaned file. Since you are using it, do not delete it.

16. Make any selector edits of your choice to improve the design of the pages.

17. Preview all the pages in your browser, check to make sure the links work correctly, close your browser, then close all open pages.

Figure 47 *Completed Project Builder 2*

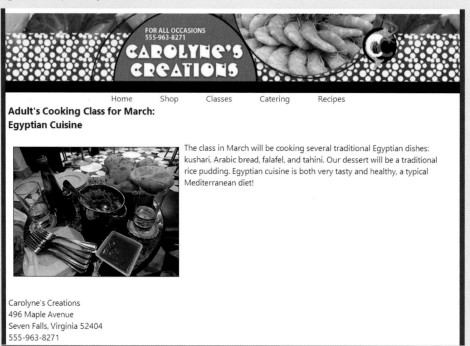

Sherrill Simmons is a university English instructor. She would like to find new ways to engage her students through her university website. She decided to explore incorporating podcasts, FaceBook, and Twitter. She spends several hours looking at other websites to help her get started.

1. Connect to the Internet, then navigate to the Federal Bureau of Investigation website at fbi.gov, as shown in Figure 48.
2. Browse through the site and locate the link to "Podcasts & Radio." What are the options they have provided for their users to download and listen to them?

Figure 48 *Design Project*

Source: The Federal Bureau of Investigation

3. Navigate to the U.S. Navy website at navy.mil, as shown in Figure 49.
4. Describe how the Navy is using Web 2.0 technology. What do you think their purpose might be for incorporating each application?
5. Which Web 2.0 applications would you include on your website if you were Sherrill?
6. Describe how you would use each one of them to engage her students.

Figure 49 *Design Project*

Source: The United States Navy

In this assignment, you will continue to work on the website that you started in Chapter 1 and developed in the previous chapters.

You will continue building your website by designing and completing a page with a menu bar. After creating the menu bar, you will copy it to each completed page in the website. In addition to the menu bar, you will add several external links and several internal links to other pages as well as to IDs on a page. You will also link text to a named anchor. After you complete this work, you will check for broken links and orphaned files.

1. Consult your wireframe to decide which page or pages you would like to develop in this chapter. Decide how to design and where to place the menu bar, IDs, and any additional page elements you decide to use. Decide which reports should be run on the website to check for accuracy.
2. Research websites that could be included on one or more of your pages as external links of interest to your users. Create a list of the external links you want to use. Using your wireframe as a guide, decide where each external link should be placed in the site.
3. Add the external links to existing pages or create any additional pages that contain external links.
4. Create IDs to use to link to key locations on the page, such as the top of the page, then link appropriate text on the page to them.
5. Decide on a design for a menu bar that will be used on all pages of the website.
6. Create the menu bar and copy it to all finished pages on the website.
7. Think of a good place to incorporate an image map, then add it to a page. Remember if you want to create an image map over a background image, you will need to place a transparent image on top of the background image first.
8. Decide on at least one Web 2.0 application that you might like to incorporate and determine how and on what page they would be included.
9. Use the Link Checker panel to check for broken links and orphaned files.
10. Use the checklist in Figure 50 to make sure your website is complete, save your work, then close all open pages.

Figure 50 *Portfolio Project checklist*

Website Checklist

1. Do all pages have a page title?
2. Does the home page have a description and keywords?
3. Does the home page contain contact information?
4. Does every page in the website have consistent navigation links?
5. Does the home page have a last updated statement that will automatically update when the page is saved?
6. Do all paths for links and images work correctly?
7. Do all images have alternate text?
8. Do the colors work together to create a pleasing design for each page?
9. Are there any unnecessary files that you can delete from the assets folder?
10. Is there a style sheet with at least two styles?
11. Did you apply the style sheet to all page content?
12. Does at least one page contain links to one or more IDs?
13. Does at least one page contain either an ID used for a link or an internal link?
14. Do all pages look good using at least two different browsers and three different screen sizes?
15. Did you incorporate at least one Web 2.0 technology?

CHAPTER **6**   **POSITIONING OBJECTS WITH CSS AND TABLES**

1. Create a page using a Fluid Grid layout
2. Add and position divs
3. Add content to divs
4. Create a table
5. Resize, split, and merge cells
6. Insert and align images in table cells
7. Insert text and format cell content

CHAPTER 6 POSITIONING OBJECTS WITH CSS AND TABLES

Introduction

To create an organized, attractive web page, you need precise control of the position of page elements. CSS page layouts can provide this control. **CSS page layouts** consist of containers formatted with CSS rules into which you place page content. These containers can accommodate images, blocks of text, videos, or any other page element. The appearance and position of the containers are set through the use of HTML tags known as **div tags**. Using div tags, you can position elements next to each other as well as on top of each other.

Another option for controlling the placement of page elements is through the use of tables. **Tables** are placeholders made up of small boxes called **cells**, into which you can insert text and graphics. Cells in a table are arranged horizontally in **rows** and vertically in **columns**. Using tables on a web page gives you control over the placement of each object on the page, similar to the way CSS layout blocks control placement. In this chapter, you use a predesigned CSS Fluid Grid page layout with one default div tag to position text and graphics. You then add a table to one of the CSS blocks.

Using Div Tags Versus Tables for Page Layout

Div tags and tables both enable you to control the appearance of content in your web pages. Unlike tables, div tags let you stack your information, allowing for one piece of information to be visible at a time. Tables are static, which makes it difficult to change them quickly as need arises. Div tags can be dynamic, changing in response to variables such as a mouse click. You can create dynamic div tags using JavaScript **behaviors**, simple action scripts that let you incorporate interactivity by modifying content based on variables like user actions. For example, you could add a JavaScript behavior to text in a div tag to make it become larger or smaller when the pointer hovers over it.

Designers previously used tables to position content on web pages. Since the inception of CSS, designers have moved to positioning most page content with CSS layouts. However, tables are still used for some layout purposes, such as arranging tabular data on a page. As a designer, you should become familiar with the tools that are available to you, including CSS and tables, then decide which tool meets current standards and is best suited for the current design challenge.

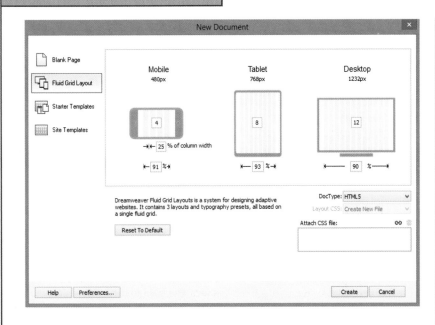

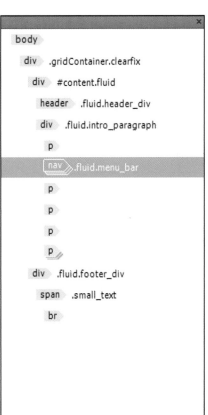

Create a Page
USING A FLUID GRID LAYOUT

What You'll Do

In this lesson, you will create a new page based on a predesigned CSS layout to become the new cafe page for the website.

Understanding Div Tags

Div tags are HTML tags that define how areas of content are formatted or positioned on a web page. For example, when you center an image on a page or inside a table cell, Dreamweaver automatically inserts a div tag in the HTML code. In addition to using div tags to align page elements, designers also use them to assign background colors or borders to content blocks, CSS styles to text, and many other properties to page elements. One type of div tag is an AP div tag. AP stands for absolutely positioned, so an **AP div tag** creates a container that has a specified, fixed position on a web page. The resulting container that an AP div tag creates on a page is called an **AP element**.

Using CSS Fluid Grid Layouts

Because building a web page using div tags can be tedious for beginning designers, Dreamweaver CC provides a default Fluid Grid layout in the New Document dialog box, as shown in Figure 1.

Fluid Grid layouts are layouts based on three device sizes: Mobile, Tablet, and Desktop.

Each device size is based on a grid system similar to column guides. CSS style sheets control the way the page content is displayed across the grids, with each grid using slightly different selector properties and values tailored to the device being used to display the page. The theory is that a designer can design a single page, but modify the way the content is displayed by changing the style sheet properties so the content will be attractive and readable regardless of the screen size used to display it.

A Fluid Grid layout contains div tags that control the placement of page content using placeholders. Each div tag container has placeholder text that appears until you replace it with your own content. Because div tags use CSS for formatting and positioning, designers prefer them for building web page content. When you use a Dreamweaver Fluid Grid layout you can be sure that your pages will appear with a consistent design when viewed in all browsers and all device sizes. Once you become more comfortable using a Fluid Grid layout, you will be able to modify the code to customize your own designs.

Viewing CSS Layout Blocks

As you design your page layouts using div tags, use Design view to see and adjust CSS content blocks. In Design view, text or images that have been aligned or positioned using div tags have a dotted border, as shown in Figure 2. In the Visual Aids list on the View menu, you can display selected features of div tag elements, such as CSS Layout Backgrounds, CSS Layout Box Model, and CSS Layout Outlines. The CSS Layout Box Model displays the padding and margins of a block element.

Figure 1 *New Document dialog box*

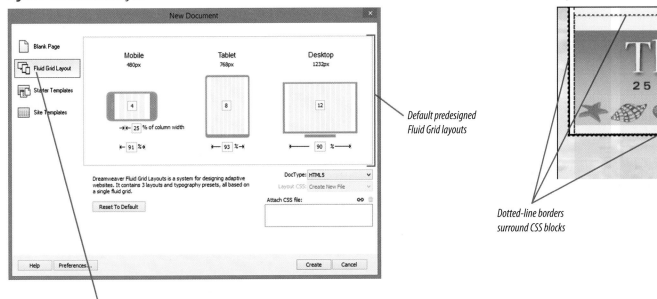

Fluid Grid Layout option

Default predesigned Fluid Grid layouts

Figure 2 *CSS blocks defined by dotted borders*

Dotted-line borders surround CSS blocks

Using Tracing Images for Page Design

Another design option for creating a page layout is to use a tracing image. A **tracing image** is an image that is placed in the background of a document. By adjusting the transparency (opacity) of the image, you can then use it to create page elements on top of it, similar to the way you would place a piece of tracing paper on top of a drawing and trace over it. The tracing image serves as a guide or pattern. You can delete it after you complete your design. To insert a tracing image, Use the Modify, Page Properties, Tracing Image dialog box or the View, Tracing Image, Load command. Browse to select the image you want to use for the tracing image, then adjust the transparency as desired.

Create a page with a Fluid Grid layout

1. Open The Striped Umbrella website.
2. Select **File** on the Menu bar, select **New**, then select **Fluid Grid Layout**, as shown in Figure 3. Fluid Grid layouts are used to create **adaptive websites**, meaning that the website appearance adapts to match the device size on which it is displayed. The dialog box shows diagrams of the three preset device sizes: Mobile, Tablet, and Desktop, and how the fluid column grid appears at each size. The three preset sizes for Mobile, Tablet, and Desktop devices are shown with a diagram of the columns that make up each grid.
3. Select the **Attach Style Sheet button** 🔗 in the bottom-right corner of the dialog box, select the **Browse** button, navigate to the local site folder if necessary, select **boilerplate.css**, select **OK**, verify that the **Link** option is selected, then select **OK** to attach the boilerplate.css style sheet.
4. Select the **Attach Style Sheet button** again, then select **Browse**.
5. Select **su_styles.css**, select **OK**, verify that the **Link** option is selected, then select **OK** to close the Select Style Sheet File dialog box.

   Both style sheets that are used to style the pages in the website will be attached to the new page, as shown in Figure 4.
6. Select **Create** in the New Document dialog box, and in the File name text box in the Save As dialog box, type **su_styles_default**, then select **Save**.

   Each time you create a new Fluid Grid Layout page, Dreamweaver generates a style sheet file that defines the styles for the layout sizes for each device. When the first page was created for The Striped Umbrella website, I named this style sheet

   (continued)

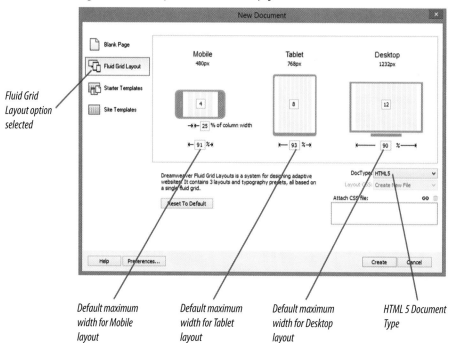

Figure 3 *Fluid Grid Layout selected for the new page*

Fluid Grid Layout option selected

Default maximum width for Mobile layout

Default maximum width for Tablet layout

Default maximum width for Desktop layout

HTML 5 Document Type

Using XML and XSL to Create and Format Web Page Content

You can also create information containers on your web pages using XML, Extensible Markup Language, and XSL, Extensible Stylesheet Language. **XML** is a language that you use to structure blocks of information, similar to HTML. It uses similar opening and closing tags and the nested tag structure that HTML documents use. However, XML tags do not determine how the information is formatted, which is handled using XSL. **XSL** is similar to CSS; the XSL stylesheet information formats the containers created by XML. Once the XML structure and XSL styles are in place, **XSLT**, **Extensible Stylesheet Language Transformations**, interprets the code in the XSL file to transform an XML document, much like style sheet files transform HTML files from an unformatted file to a formatted file. XSL transformations can be written as client-side or server-side transformations. To create XML documents, use the XML page type in the Blank page category in the New Document dialog box.

Figure 4 *Boilerplate.css and su_styles.css files will be attached to the new page*

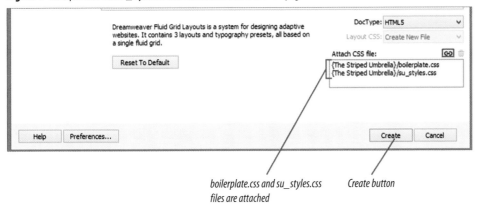

boilerplate.css and su_styles.css
files are attached

Create button

Figure 5 *New page based on a Fluid Grid layout*

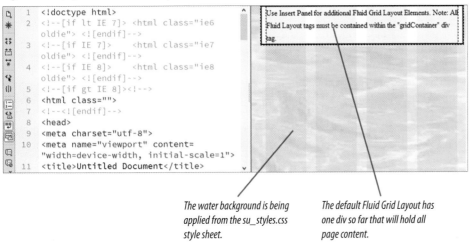

The water background is being
applied from the su_styles.css
style sheet.

The default Fluid Grid Layout has
one div so far that will hold all
page content.

su_styles.css file. You have since added styles to it and modified its styles as you've added pages and page elements. If you save over this file now, you will lose these changes. Therefore, you saved the new style sheet file as su_styles_default.css so it will not overwrite the modified file, preserving the styles you have been using. You can compare the two files if you want to see the differences between the styles that were in place when you started and the styles that you added and/or modified. We will remove the link to this new style sheet file on the new page to avoid any potential style conflicts.

The new blank page opens in Split view, as shown in Figure 5. You can tell that the page is reading the style sheet you have been using because you see the water background in Design view.

7. Save the open file as **cafe.html**, overwriting the existing blank cafe page.

8. Select **OK** to close the error message about the Edge Web Fonts, if one opens.

   The error message tells you that a selector in the su_styles.css code refers to an Adobe Edge Web font and an external link to the Typekit site.

9. Switch to Code view, select the link to the su_styles_default.css file, then delete it and return to Design view. If you see two links to the boilerplate.css file, delete one of them.

   You did not delete these files from the website; you just removed the links to them on the cafe page.

You created a new page based on a Fluid Grid layout with the two attached style sheets for The Striped Umbrella website. You renamed the new, default style sheet that was automatically generated, and saved the new document as cafe.html, overwriting the existing blank cafe page. Last, you deleted the link to the new style sheet file on the cafe page to prevent any style conflicts.

Add and Position
DIVS

What You'll Do

  In this lesson, you will add three divs to the cafe page: one for a header, one for the menu bar, and one for a photo of the cafe.

Understanding How to Create a New Page with Fluid Grid Layouts

You gained understanding of the power of divs combined with style sheets as you worked through Chapters 1 through 5. You also examined how the Fluid Grid layouts and Media queries features customize web pages for specific device sizes. You created a new page based on a Fluid Grid layout in Lesson 1. Now you will learn how to add new divs to a page.

When you use Fluid Grid layouts and style sheets to design new website pages, you move from long, complicated page code to much shorter page code, because the bulk of the code moves from the pages to the style sheets.

Once you have style sheets in place to format your pages, most of the work is done. Then to add a new page, you can:

- Save an existing page with a new file name and replace the content with new content;
- Create a site template from an existing page and use it to create new pages; or
- Use the New Document dialog box to create a blank page. When you use the New Document dialog box, as you did in Lesson 1, attaching the existing style sheet files to it ensures that the new page will have a similar design as the existing pages.

Every new blank page, by default, has one div called .gridContainer.clearfix, as shown in Figure 6. This div acts as a "wrapper" inside

Using Dreamweaver New Page Options

You can use either the Welcome Screen or the New command on the File menu to create several different types of pages. The predesigned CSS page layouts make it easy to design accessible web pages based on Cascading Style Sheets, without an advanced level of expertise in writing HTML code. Predesigned templates are another time-saving feature that promotes consistency across a website. Fluid Grid layouts, Starter Templates, and Site Templates are a few of the other options. It is worth the time to explore each category to understand what is available to you as a designer. Once you have selected a page layout, you can customize it to suit your client's content and design needs.

which all other divs are placed. All Fluid Grid tags must be placed inside this div, between its opening and closing <div> tags. A new page also contains an additional div on the page, located inside the .gridContainer.clearfix div. This div has the default name "div1". You should give this div a more meaningful name, such as "header_div" or "main_content_div". Dreamweaver automatically adds the word "fluid" to the div name for each div you create in a Fluid Grid layout to help identify divs that are based on a Fluid Grid layout.

Controlling Div Placement on a Page

After you have used div tags to create divs, you can rearrange and/or resize the divs on the page. There are several tools available to help you: your style sheets, the Fluid Grid Layout guides, the Element Quick View tool, and the HUD Options mini-toolbar. Figure 7 shows the Fluid Grid Layout guides, the Element Quick View tool, and the HUD Options mini-toolbar.

Fluid Grid Layout guides are visual aids that show you the number of columns used for each view: Mobile, Tablet, and Desktop. You can turn Fluid Grid Layout guides on and off with the Hide Fluid Grid Layout Guides/Show Fluid Grid Layout Guides button on the Document toolbar, as shown in Figure 7.

Selecting the **Element Quick View button**, as shown in Figure 7, shows a visual representation of the HTML DOM structure for the page. **DOM** stands for Document Object Model, a convention that represents

Figure 6 *Code for a new blank page*

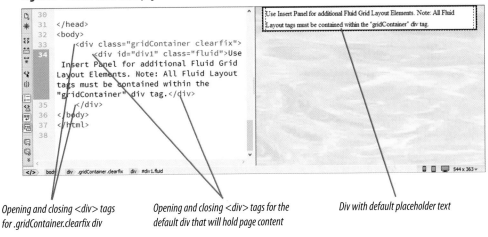

Opening and closing <div> tags for .gridContainer.clearfix div

Opening and closing <div> tags for the default div that will hold page content

Div with default placeholder text

Figure 7 *Viewing tools for managing divs*

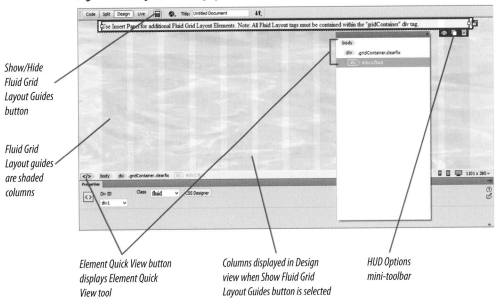

Show/Hide Fluid Grid Layout Guides button

Fluid Grid Layout guides are shaded columns

Element Quick View button displays Element Quick View tool

Columns displayed in Design view when Show Fluid Grid Layout Guides button is selected

HUD Options mini-toolbar

the order and type of elements used in a web page. The Element Quick View button lets you view each defined page element in a tree diagram so you can quickly see the order and position of each element relative to the other page elements. A folder icon represents every element. When you see multiple folder icons stacked, as shown in Figure 8, select a folder to see other elements nested inside the element. This is similar to expanding and collapsing folders in File Explorer by selecting the plus or minus sign.

When you display Fluid Grid layout guides and select a div, a mini-toolbar, sometimes referred to as a HUD and shown in Figure 7, appears next to a div border. **HUD** is an acronym for Heads Up Display. You can use the HUD to hide, duplicate, move, or delete a div. The name comes from the idea that you don't have to open panels to perform basic editing using divs; you can keep your "head up" or focused on the div itself while making changes.

These tools help you understand the relative position of each div on a page so you can easily position or change the order of the div elements.

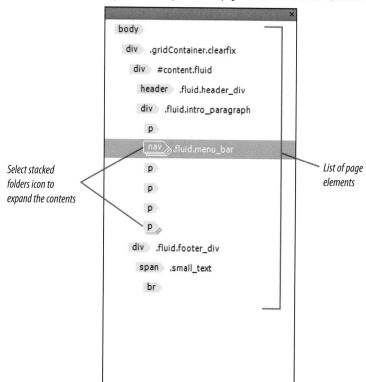

Figure 8 *Viewing the order of page elements with Element Quick View*

Select stacked folders icon to expand the contents

List of page elements

The Evolution of HTML5

HTML has been in existence since the early 1990s, but it wasn't until 1997 that the then current version, HTML4, became a W3C recommendation. Many HTML4 attributes such as body background, align, cell padding, and hspace are now added using CSS3. HTML5 introduced new ways to add interactivity and tags that support semantic markup, such as the <nav> tag used for navigation links. In Chapter 3 you learned about using semantic markup to incorporate meaning with your HTML markup. Other semantic HTML5 tags include <header>, <footer>, <article>, <audio>, <section>, and <video>. HTML5 is still a work in progress, but most modern browsers support it. HTML5 also introduces markup for Web applications (apps), an exploding sector of Web development.

Figure 9 *Renaming the default div id "div_1" to "content"*

```
32   <body>
33       <div class="gridContainer clearfix">
34           <div id="content" class="fluid">
         Use Insert Panel for additional Fluid Grid
          Layout Elements. Note: All Fluid Layout
         tags must be contained within the
         "gridContainer" div tag.</div>
35           </div>
```

div id is changed to "content"

Figure 10 *Selecting the placeholder text for the content div*

```
32   <body>
33       <div class="gridContainer clearfix">
34           <div id="content" class="fluid">
         Use Insert Panel for additional Fluid Grid
          Layout Elements. Note: All Fluid Layout
         tags must be contained within the
         "gridContainer" div ta * </div>
35           </div>
```

Figure 11 *Adding a class style for the header selector*

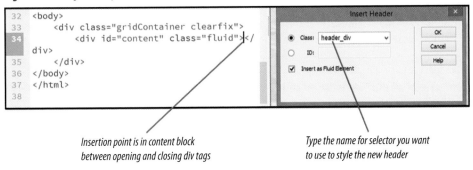

Insertion point is in content block between opening and closing div tags

Type the name for selector you want to use to style the new header

Add divs to a page and view them using Element Quick View

1. With the new blank cafe page open in Design view, change to Split view, then scroll to find the code for the div id="div1".

2. Select the default name **div_1**, then type **content**, as shown in Figure 6-9.

   The default name div_1 is replaced with the name content. This will match the rest of the pages in the site and allow the content div selector to apply the properties and values previously defined in the su_styles.css file.

3. In the Code view window, select the **placeholder text** in the content div, as shown in Figure 6-10, then delete it.

4. With the insertion point between the opening and closing <div> tags, select **Header** in the Structure category of the Insert panel.

5. Type **header_div** in the Insert Header dialog box, as shown in Figure 11, select **OK**, then delete the header placeholder text.

(continued)

6. Select **Refresh** on the Property inspector.

The header div is now filled with the banner background from the existing selector property in the su_styles.css file, as shown in Figure 12.

TIP You may need to select the Desktop size button on the status bar to see the banner shown.

7. Change to Design view, then select the **Element Quick View button** </> on the status bar.

8. Select each **stacked folder icon** to expand them, if necessary, then look at the page structure, as shown in Figure 13.

Recall that Dreamweaver adds the word "fluid" to each fluid grid selector name.

You renamed the default placeholder div on the cafe page, added a new header div inside it, then viewed the page structure with Element Quick View.

Figure 12 *Assigning the header selector to the header*

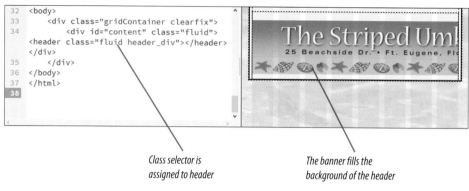

Class selector is
assigned to header

The banner fills the
background of the header

Figure 13 *Viewing the page DOM structure with Element Quick View*

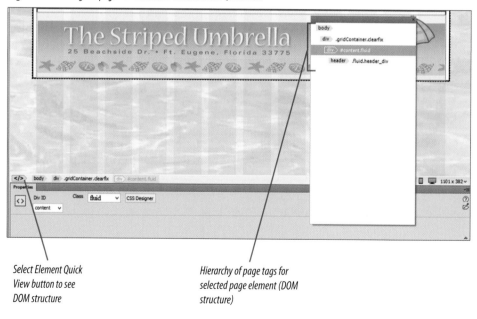

Select Element Quick
View button to see
DOM structure

Hierarchy of page tags for
selected page element (DOM
structure)

Figure 14 *Assigning a class name to a new div*

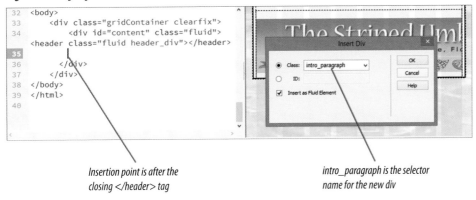

Insertion point is after the
closing </header> tag

intro_paragraph is the selector
name for the new div

Figure 15 *Viewing the new intro_paragraph div added under the header*

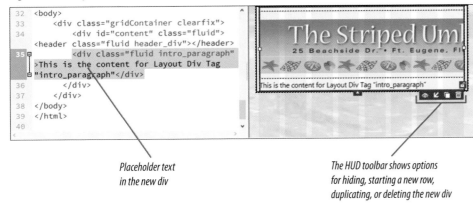

Placeholder text
in the new div

The HUD toolbar shows options
for hiding, starting a new row,
duplicating, or deleting the new div

Figure 16 *Selecting and copying the navigation code from the index page*

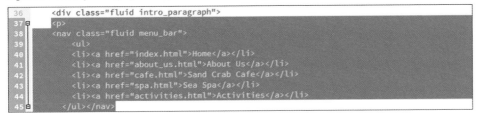

Add a new div and paste the menu bar into it

1. Change to Split view, then place the insertion point after the closing </header> tag as shown in Figure 14.

   If you find it is easier to read through your code with spaces separating each div, add a paragraph break in Code view, as shown in Figure 14. Paragraph breaks entered in Code view do not affect the page design; they just make it easier to read the code.

2. Select **Div** in the Structure category of the Insert panel, type **intro_paragraph** in the Class text box in the Insert Div dialog box, as shown in Figure 14, then select **OK**.

   The new header is placed on the page with default placeholder text, as shown in Figure 15. You are now ready to insert the website menu bar, but it will be faster to copy the menu bar code from another page.

3. Verify that the fluid grid layout guides are showing, then select the border of the new div in the Design view pane.

   The HUD toolbar appears with buttons to control the div appearance and position on the page.

4. Open the index page, switch to Code view if you prefer the full Code window, then copy the code for the menu bar beginning with the <p> tag immediately above it, as shown in Figure 16.

(continued)

5. Switch to the cafe page in Code or Split view, place the insertion point after the closing header tag if necessary, paste the copied code, open the Property inspector if necessary, select **Refresh** in the Property inspector, then compare your screen to Figure 17.

   The menu bar is placed on the cafe page.

6. Place the insertion point before the last two ending </div> tags near the bottom of the page, select **Footer** in the Structure category of the Insert panel, type **footer_div** in the class text box in the Insert Div dialog box, then select **OK**.

   The new footer is placed on the page with default placeholder text, as shown in Design view in Figure 18.

   TIP To quickly determine which ending </div> tag goes with which beginning <div> tag, select either the beginning or ending tag to highlight it, then scroll to find the highlighted tag that it begins or ends.

7. Close the index page, then save your work.

   (continued)

Figure 17 *Pasting the menu bar from the index page to the cafe page*

```
35          <header class="fluid
header_div"></header>
36          <p>
37          <nav class="fluid menu_bar">
38          <ul>
39          <li><a href="index.html"
>Home</a></li>
40          <li><a href=
"about_us.html">About Us</a></li>
41          <li><a href="cafe.html">
Sand Crab Cafe</a></li>
42          <li><a href="spa.html">
Sea Spa</a></li>
43          <li><a href=
"activities.html">Activities</a></li>
44          </ul>
45          </nav>
```

Figure 18 *The footer with placeholder text on the cafe page*

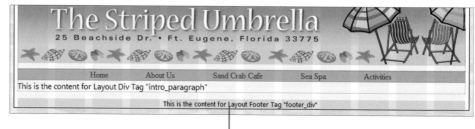

Placeholder text for the footer
is added automatically

Figure 19 *Setting the position for the new image_div*

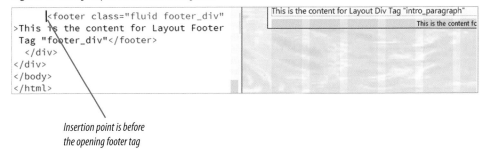

```
        <footer class="fluid footer_div"
>This is the content for Layout Footer
 Tag "footer_div"</footer>
    </div>
</div>
</body>
</html>
```

This is the content for Layout Div Tag "intro_paragraph"

This is the content fc

Insertion point is before
the opening footer tag

Figure 20 *Placeholder text in new div for image placement*

Figure 21 *The menu bar with updated font-family property*

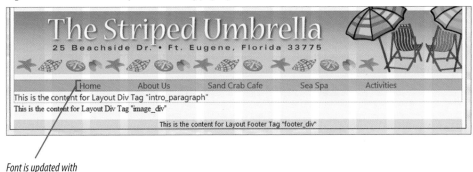

Font is updated with
added property

8. In Split view, place the insertion point in front of the opening <footer> tag, as shown in Figure 19.

9. Select **Div** in the Structure category of the Insert panel, type **image_div** in the Insert Div dialog box, then select **OK**.

   This is a div that will hold a large image of the cafe.

10. Save your work, return to Design view, then compare your screen to Figure 20.

    You notice the menu bar is no longer formatted with the correct font. This is because when you created this page, the tags for the .menu_bar selector were above the div for the .intro_paragraph selector, so the .menu_bar selector does not have a font-family property assigned.

11. Select **su_styles.css** in the Sources pane in CSS Designer, select **GLOBAL** in the @Media pane, then select **.menu_bar** in the Selectors pane.

12. Select the default **font-family value**, then select **Segoe, Segoe UI, DejaVu Sans, Trebuchet MS, Verdana, sans-serif.**

TIP You may need to deselect the Show Only Set Properties checkbox to access the text properties.

Now the menu bar elements appear in the correct font, as shown in Figure 21.

13. Save your work.

You added a new div for paragraph text to the cafe page, added navigation and footer tags, then added an additional div to use to place a large image. Last, you added a font-family property to the .menu_bar selector.

Add Content to
DIVS

What You'll Do

In this lesson, you will add text to the intro paragraph div and add an image to the image div on the cafe page. Then you will exchange the position of the two divs on the page and return them to their original positions.

Understanding Div Tag Content

As you remember, a div tag is a container that formats blocks of information on a web page, such as background colors, images, links, tables, and text. Once you have created a layout using div tags, you are ready to insert and format text. As with formatting text on a web page, you should use CSS styles to format text in div tags. You can also add all other properties such as text indents, padding, margins, and background color using CSS styles.

In this lesson, you continue to use your Fluid Grid layout to add content to the new cafe page. You have added several CSS layout blocks to the page and are ready to fill them with the cafe page content.

Writing for the Web

It doesn't matter how attractive or informative your text is if it isn't readable. Readability is determined by the complexity of your sentences, the average number of sentences per paragraph, and the average length of your words. Unless you are writing for a technical or scientific website, you should keep your reading level between the seventh and eighth grade levels to reach the largest audience. To evaluate the reading level of text on a page, copy and paste the text into Microsoft Word. Open the Word Options dialog box, select Proofing, then select the Show readability statistics check box. Next, use the Check Spelling and Grammar command and the Readability Statistics dialog box will open to show the results for your text. The grade level for the text on the index page is 7.9.

Understanding CSS Code

CSS rules can reside in the Head section of a page or in an external style sheet. The code for a CSS container begins with the class, or name of the rule, and is followed by rule properties. In Figure 22, the styles shown are from a section of the boilerplate.css file that is created by default when you create a Fluid Grid Layout page. These styles are tag selectors (meaning that they are used to modify standard HTML tags, rather than class styles you create), so they do not begin with a period in front of the name. The tag selector name is the tag itself. For instance, a selector to modify the horizontal rule tag (<hr>) is named hr. Unless otherwise specified, these tag selectors will apply to all page elements to which you apply these tags. For instance, any text surrounded by a <b> or <strong> tag will appear in bold.

In Lesson 1, you attached the boilerplate.css file to the Striped Umbrella cafe page. This CSS file contains global styles to help format page content based on Fluid Grid layouts. The selectors in this file are grouped by function with the category noted in comments. **Comments** are gray, non-executable tags proceeded by "/*". This notation tells the browser to skip over the lines of code that follow it until it comes to an ending comment tag, "*/". Comments can help you learn more about HTML code, so it is worth the time to stop and read them. Figure 22 shows selectors grouped as Link selectors and Typography selectors.

Figure 22 *Viewing the boilerplate.css code*

```
54  /* ===============================================================
55      Links
56      =========================================================== */
57
58  a { color: #00e; }
59  a:visited { color: #551a8b; }
60  a:hover { color: #06e; }
61  a:focus { outline: thin dotted; }
62
63  /* Improve readability when focused and hovered in all browsers: h5bp.com/h */
64  a:hover, a:active { outline: 0; }
65
66
67  /* ===============================================================
68      Typography
69      =========================================================== */
70
71  abbr[title] { border-bottom: 1px dotted; }
72
73  b, strong { font-weight: bold; }
74
75  blockquote { margin: 1em 40px; }
```

Link selectors

Typography selectors

Add text to a CSS container

1. With the cafe page open in Design view, delete the **placeholder** text in the intro_paragraph div, being careful not to delete a beginning or ending <div> tag.

TIP Remember that it's easier to leave at least one character in the placeholder text, then delete it after you have placed new content.

2. Open your file manager program, open the file **cafe.txt** from the drive and folder where you store your Data Files, then copy and paste the contents into the intro_paragraph div, as shown in Figure 23.

3. Close the cafe.txt file, then switch to Code view to verify that there is a <p> tag in front of the pasted text and insert one if one was not automatically added.

4. Open the index page, copy the two lines of text in the footer, then paste them in the footer on the cafe page, replacing the footer placeholder text, as shown in Figure 24.

5. Close the index page.

You replaced the placeholder text in the content div with text from the cafe.txt file, copied the footer text from the index page, then used it to replace the footer placeholder text on the cafe page.

Figure 23 *Pasting text into the content div*

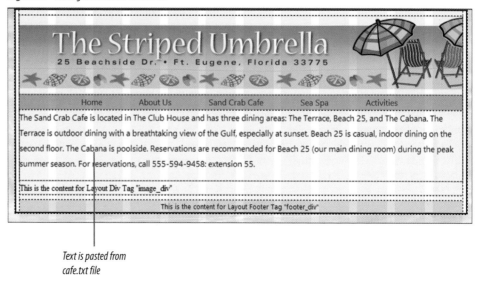

Text is pasted from
cafe.txt file

Figure 24 *The footer placeholder text replaced with website footer text*

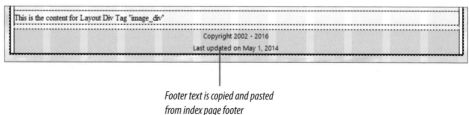

Footer text is copied and pasted
from index page footer

Positioning Objects with CSS and Tables

Figure 25 *The cafe page with the cafe photo added*

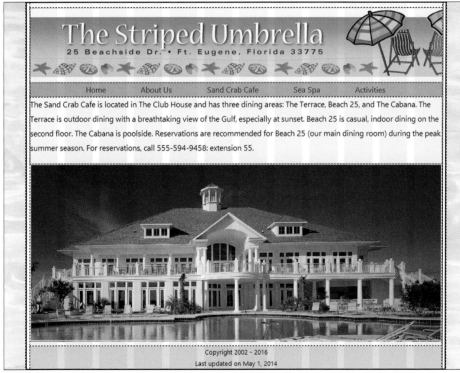

The Sand Crab Cafe is located in The Club House and has three dining areas: The Terrace, Beach 25, and The Cabana. The Terrace is outdoor dining with a breathtaking view of the Gulf, especially at sunset. Beach 25 is casual, indoor dining on the second floor. The Cabana is poolside. Reservations are recommended for Beach 25 (our main dining room) during the peak summer season. For reservations, call 555-594-9458: extension 55.

Club house photo provided by Spectrum Resorts of The Beach Club in Gulf Shores, Alabama

Viewing Options for CSS Layout Blocks

You can view your layout blocks in Design view in several ways. You can choose to show or hide outlines, temporarily assign different background colors to each individual layout block, or view the **CSS Layout Box Model** (padding, margins, borders, etc.) of a selected layout. To change these options, use the View > Visual Aids menu, and then select or deselect the CSS Layout Backgrounds, CSS Layout Box Model, or CSS Layout Outlines menu choice.

Add an image to a CSS container

1. Place the insertion point in the img_div, then carefully delete the placeholder text (not a div tag).
2. Select the **Insert** menu, point to **Image**, then select **Image** to open the Select Image Source dialog box.
3. Navigate to the assets folder where you store your Data Files, and select the image club_house_oceanside.jpg, as shown in Figure 25.
4. Save your work, then view the Desktop, Tablet, and Mobile sizes.
5. Preview the page in your browser, then close the browser.

You added an image to the cafe page.

Reorder page elements

1. With the fluid grid layout guides displayed, place the pointer in the introductory paragraph.

   The div is selected and you see a small black triangle, called a handle, pointing downward on the bottom border of the div.

   If you don't see the black handles after you select the paragraph, check to see if your Fluid Grid Layouts are displayed.

2. Place the pointer over the handle to see the tool tip **Swap DIV.intro_paragraph with DIV. image_div**, as shown in Figure 26.

   Selecting this handle will change the position of the two divs. The image div will move above the intro_paragraph div.

3. Select the handle.

   The image div moves above the intro_paragraph div. Notice there are two handles now, as shown in Figure 27. The first one can be used to swap the image div back under the intro_paragraph div. The second one can be used to swap the image div with the footer div. The tool tips tell you where the div will go if selected.

TIP Your handles will appear side by side when there is not enough room in the Document window to show the entire div. They will appear one beneath the other if there is enough room to see the entire div.

(continued)

Figure 26 *Preparing to move the intro paragraph div*

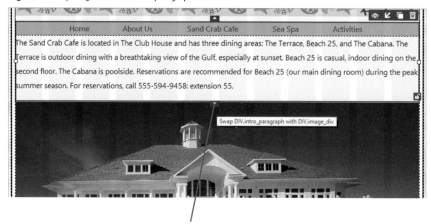

Selecting handle will swap the div according to tool tip

Figure 27 *The image div changed positions with the intro paragraph div*

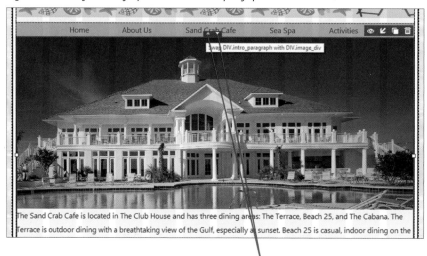

Select handles to move div up or down

Positioning Objects with CSS and Tables

Figure 28 *The intro paragraph div moved under the footer div*

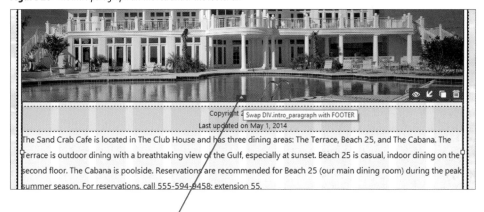

Select handle to swap intro
paragraph div with footer

Figure 29 *All divs are back in their original position*

Positioning Divs Side by Side

To position two divs side by side on a page, use CSS Designer to set a width expressed in percent for each div so the two widths together are less than or equal to 100%. Next, set the float for the first div to left and the float for the second div to right.

Content for Div 1   Content for Div 2

4. Select the handle pointing downward, **Swap DIV.intro_paragraph with FOOTER**.

   Now the intro_paragraph is below the footer, as shown in Figure 28.

5. Select the handle pointing up, **Swap DIV. intro_paragraph with FOOTER**.

   The image div is back above the intro_paragraph div.

6. Select the handle pointing up, **Swap DIV.intro_paragraph with DIV.image_div**.

   Figure 29 shows the introductory paragraph above the image once again. The footer is also back at the bottom of the page.

You moved the divs on the page into different positions, then moved them back to their original positions.

Create
A TABLE

What You'll Do

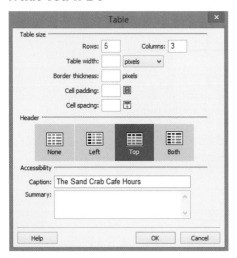

 In this lesson, you will create a table for the cafe page in The Striped Umbrella website to provide a grid for the cafe hours.

Understanding Table Modes

Now that you have learned how CSS can act as containers to hold information in place on web pages, let's look at tables as another layout tool. Tables are great when you need a grid layout on a page for a list of data.

Creating a Table

To create a table, select the Table button in the Common category on the Insert panel to open the Table dialog box. You can enter values for the number of rows and columns in the Table dialog box, but the rest of the table properties should be assigned using CSS. If you only plan to use one table design in a site, you can create a rule to modify the <table> tag and save it in your website style sheet.

You then use this rule to add formatting options to the table such as adding a border or table width. The **border** is the outline or frame around the table and is measured in pixels. The table width can be specified in units of measure such as pixels, or as a percentage. When the table width is specified as a percentage, the table width expands to fill up its container (the browser window, a CSS container, or another table). Setting table widths as percentages works best with Fluid Grid layouts. Table width is set using the Width property in the Box category of the relevant CSS style.

To align a table on a page or within a CSS layout block, use the Float property in the Box category. A table placed inside another table is called a **nested table**. **Cell padding** is the distance between the cell content and the **cell walls**, the lines inside the cell borders. **Cell spacing** is the distance between cells. Neither cell padding or cell spacing is supported by HTML5, however, so it's better to address spacing issues by assigning styles.

Before you create a table, you should include in your wireframe a plan for it that shows its location on the page and the placement of text and graphics in its cells. You should also decide whether to include borders around the tables. Setting the border value to 0 causes the table borders to be invisible. Users will not realize that you used a table unless they look at the code.

Setting Table Accessibility Preferences

You can make a table more accessible to visually impaired users by adding a table caption and a table header that screen readers can read. A **table caption** appears at the top of a table and describes the table contents. **Table headers** are another way to provide information about table content. Table headers can be placed at the top of columns. They are automatically centered and bold and are used by screen readers to help users identify the table content. Table captions and headers are created with the Table dialog box.

Formatting Tables with HTML5 and CSS3

Many of the HTML codes used to format tables in HTML4 are now considered to be **deprecated**, or no longer within the current standard and in danger of becoming obsolete. As you design web pages, it is best to avoid using deprecated tags because eventually they will cause problems when they are no longer supported by newer browsers. Deprecated HTML4 table tags include summary, cellpadding, cellspacing, align, width, and bgcolor.

Rather than format tables using the Table dialog box or the Property inspector, use CSS to create rules that modify table properties and content. You can either add properties to the <table> tag itself or create new class rules that you can then assign to specific tables. Use the HTML5 tags <th> and <caption>. The table header <th> tag is a type of cell that contains header information, such as column headings, that identify the content of the data cells below them. The <caption> tag is the caption, or title, of a table and describes the table content. These tags provide greater accessibility, because they are used by screen readers. They also add value as semantic markup because they help to label and describe table content.

Create a table

1. Place the insertion point in the intro_paragraph div, switch to Code view, then place the insertion point after the ending div tag for the intro_paragraph div.

2. Return to Design view, then use the Insert panel to insert a new div named **table_div**.

   Placeholder text appears in table_div, as shown in Figure 30.

3. Carefully delete the placeholder text, then select **Table** in the Common category on the Insert panel.

   The Table dialog box opens.

4. Type **5** in the Rows text box, type **3** in the Columns text box, if necessary, delete any value previously left in the Table width, Border thickness, Cell padding, or Cell spacing text boxes, then select the **Top** Header.

   TIP It is better to add more rows than you think you need when you create your table. After they are filled with content, it is easier to delete rows than to add rows if you decide later to split or merge cells in the table.

5. In the Caption text box, type **The Sand Crab Cafe Hours**, compare your screen to Figure 31, then select **OK**.

   The table appears very small because the width for the table has not yet been set. You will define a new table CSS rule to use to format the table.

You created a table in a new div on the cafe page that will display the cafe hours with five rows and three columns. You used a top header and added a table caption that will be read by screen readers.

Figure 30 *New div inserted for a table*

New div with
placeholder text

Figure 31 *Table dialog box*

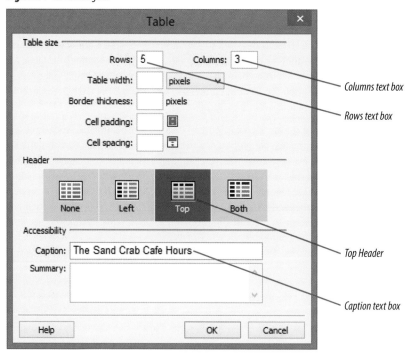

Columns text box

Rows text box

Top Header

Caption text box

Figure 32 *Setting table selector properties*

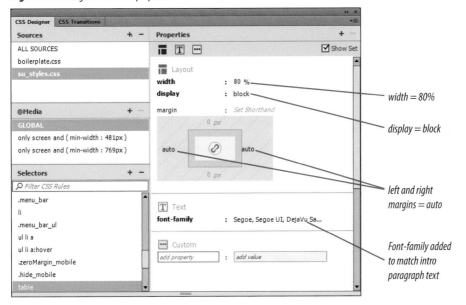

width = 80%

display = block

left and right margins = auto

Font-family added to match intro paragraph text

Figure 33 *Viewing the new table in the table div*

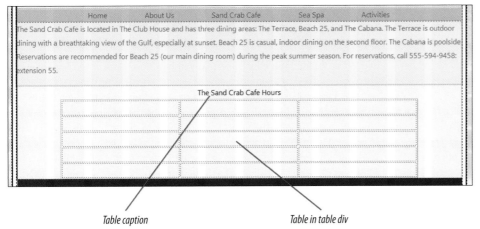

Table caption

Table in table div

Set table properties

1. Use CSS Designer to add a new global tag selector in the su_styles.css file named **table**.

   This rule will format the only table in the website.

2. Select the **Layout category** in the Properties pane, then add the following properties and values as shown in Figure 32:

   width: **80%;**

   display: **block;**

   margin-left: **auto;**

   margin-right: **auto;**

   font-family: **Segoe, Segoe UI, DejaVu Sans, Trebuchet MS, Verdana, Sans-serif;**

   These settings will set the table to 80% width and centered on the page with a specified font family to match the intro paragraph text.

   The <table> selector modified the table by setting the width and alignment on the page, as shown in Figure 33.

3. Save your work.

You modified the table rule by adding table width and margin properties.

Resize, Split,
AND MERGE CELLS

What You'll Do

In this lesson, you will set the width of the table cells to be split across the table in predetermined widths. You will then split one cell. You will also merge some cells to provide space for the table header.

Modifying Table Structure

To create HTML5-compliant table coding, you should resize tables, rows, and cells using Cascading Style Sheets. If you only have one table in your site, you can modify the <table> tag by assigning properties and values to set the table width. If you have multiple tables, you can create a new class rule for each table and format each individually using class rule properties. This will allow you to use multiple tables with differing widths. When you first create a table, the columns have equal widths. To widen a column and meet HTML5 standards, use the column group tag <colgroup> to set properties for an entire column or the column tag <col> to set properties for an individual cell.

Sometimes you want to adjust the cells in a table by splitting or merging them. To **split** a cell means to divide it into multiple rows or columns. To **merge** cells means to combine multiple cells into one cell. Using split and merged cells gives you more flexibility and control in placing page elements in a table and can help you create a more visually exciting layout. When you merge cells, the

Adding or Deleting a Row

As you add new content to your table, you might find that you have too many or too few rows or columns. You can add or delete one row or column at a time or several at once using commands on the Modify menu. When you add a new column or row, you must first select the existing column or row to which the new column or row will be adjacent. Because of this, it can be challenging to add or delete rows after you have split and merged cells. The Insert Rows or Columns dialog box lets you choose how many rows or columns you want to insert or delete, and where you want them placed in relation to the selected row or column. The new column or row will have the same formatting and number of cells as the selected column or row. You can also use the shortcut menu or keyboard shortcuts to add or delete rows.

HTML tag used to describe the merged cell changes from a width size tag to a column span or row span tag. For example, <td colspan="2"> is the code for two cells that have been merged into one cell that spans two columns.

QUICK TIP

You can split merged cells and merge split cells.

Understanding Table Tags

When formatting a table, it is important to understand the basic HTML table tags. The tags for creating a table are <table> </table>. The tags to create table rows are <tr></tr>. The tags used to create table data cells are <td></td>. The tags used to create table header cells are <th> </th>. Dreamweaver places the < > code into each empty table cell at the time you create it. The < > code represents a nonbreaking space, or a space that a browser will display on the page. Some browsers collapse an empty cell, which can ruin the look of a table. The nonbreaking space holds the cell until you place content in it, when at that time it is automatically removed.

DESIGNTIP

Using Nested Tables

A nested table is a table inside a table. Place the insertion point in the cell where you want to insert the nested table, then select the Table button on the Insert panel. A nested table is a separate table that can be formatted differently from the table in which it is placed. Nested tables are useful when you want part of your table data to have visible borders and part to have invisible borders. For example, you can nest a table with red borders inside a table with invisible borders. You need to plan carefully when you insert nested tables. It is easy to get carried away and insert too many nested tables, which makes it more difficult to apply formatting and rearrange table elements. Before you insert a nested table, consider whether you could achieve the same result by adding rows and columns or by splitting cells.

Split cells

1. Place the insertion point inside the first cell in the last row, then select **<td>** in the tag selector.

TIP You can select the cell tag <td> (the HTML tag for that cell) on the tag selector to select the corresponding cell in the table. When a tag is selected, the tag color on the tag selector changes from a black to a turquoise font. You can also just place the insertion point inside the cell before you begin Step 2.

2. Select the **Splits cell into rows or columns button** ⫴ in the Property inspector.

3. Select the **Split cell into Rows option button** (if necessary), type **2** in the Number of rows text box (if necessary), as shown in Figure 34, select **OK**, then deselect the cell.

   The cell is split, as shown in Figure 35.

TIP To create a new row at the end of a table, place the insertion point in the last cell, then press [Tab].

You split a cell into two rows.

Figure 34 *Splitting a cell into two rows*

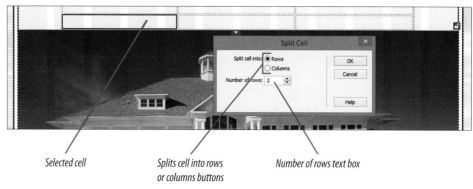

Selected cell   Splits cell into rows   Number of rows text box
                       or columns buttons

Figure 35 *Splitting one cell into two rows*

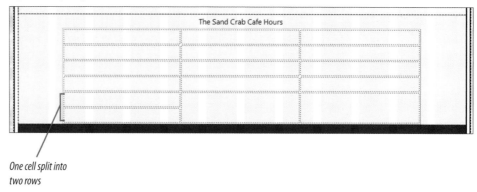

One cell split into
two rows

Figure 36 *Merging selected cells into one cell*

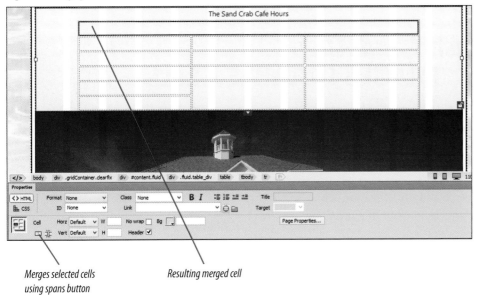

Merges selected cells
using spans button

Resulting merged cell

Figure 37 *Code for merged cells*

```
<div class="fluid table_div">
    <table>
        <caption>
            The Sand Crab Cafe Hours
        </caption>
        <tbody>
            <tr>
                <th colspan="3" scope="col"> </th>
            </tr>
```

colspan tag

Nonbreaking space

Merge cells

1. Place the insertion point in the first cell in the top row, then drag to the right to select the three cells in the top row.

2. Select the **Merges selected cells using spans button** ▭ in the Property inspector.

   The three cells are merged into one cell, as shown in Figure 36. This merged cell will act as a table header. Descriptive text in this cell will spread across the table width.

TIP You can only merge cells that are adjacent to each other.

3. Select the **Show Code view button** ` Code `, then view the code for the merged cells, as shown in Figure 37.

   Notice the table tags denoting the column span (th colspan="3") and the nonbreaking space ( ) inserted in the empty cell.

4. Select the **Show Design view button** ` Design `, select and merge the first cells in rows 2, 3, 4, and 5 in the left column, then save your work.

You merged three cells in the first row to make room for the table header. You then merged four cells in the left column to make room for an image.

Insert and Align
IMAGES IN TABLE CELLS

What You'll Do

In this lesson, you will insert an image of a bowl of soup in the left column of the table. After placing the image, you will align it within the cell.

Inserting Images in Table Cells

You can insert images in the cells of a table using the Image command in the Images menu on the Insert panel. If you already have images saved in your website that you would like to insert in a table, you can drag them from the Assets panel into the table cells. When you add a large image to a cell, the cell expands to accommodate the inserted image. Figure 38 shows the USHorse.biz website, which uses several tables for page layout and contains images in some of the table cells. Notice that some images appear in cells by themselves, and some appear in cells containing text or other graphics. Some cells have a light background, and some have a darker background.

Aligning Images in Table Cells

You can align images both horizontally and vertically within a cell. With HTML5, it's best to align an image by creating a rule with alignment settings, then apply the rule to the image content. For example, if you

Positioning Objects with CSS and Tables

have inserted an image in a table cell, you can create a Class rule in your style sheet called something like img_table_cell, then assign a center-align property to the rule. After saving the rule, select the image, then apply the img_table_cell rule to it. It will then center-align within the table cell.

Another way to align content in table cells is to add a style to the individual cell tag that sets the cell alignment. For example, add the code "style=text-align:center" to the cell tag for the cell you want to modify to center the cell's contents.

Figure 38 *USHorse.biz website*

Source: USHorse.biz

Insert images in table cells

1. Place the insertion point in the merged cells in the left column of the table (under the merged cell in the top row).

2. Insert **shrimp_bisque.jpg** from assets folder in the drive and folder where you store your Data Files, then type **Gulf Shrimp Bisque** for the alternate text.

3. Compare your screen to Figure 39.

   TIP Don't be concerned if your table spacing does not match the figure at this time. You will fix this shortly when you set the cell widths.

4. Refresh the Files panel and verify that the new image was copied to The Striped Umbrella website assets folder.

5. Save your work.

You inserted an image into a table cell on the cafe page.

Figure 39 *Image inserted into table cell*

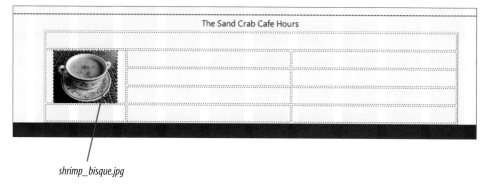

shrimp_bisque.jpg

Using Rulers, Grids, and Guides for Positioning Page Content

To help you position your page content, the View menu offers Grid and Guides choices. **Grids** provide a graph paper-like view of a page. Horizontal and vertical lines fill the page when this option is turned on. You can edit the line colors, the distance between them, whether they are composed of lines or dots, and whether or not objects "snap" to them. **Guides** are horizontal or vertical lines that you drag onto the page from the rulers. You can edit both the colors of the guides and the color of the distance, a feature that shows you the distance between two guides. You can lock the guides so you don't accidentally move them and you can set them either to snap to page elements or have page elements snap to them. To display grids or guides, select View on the Menu bar, point to Grid, then select Show Grid or point to Guides and then select Show Guides.

Figure 40 *Setting the display and margin properties for the tr td img*

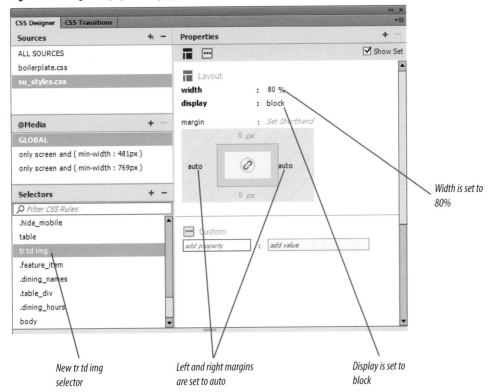

New tr td img
selector

Left and right margins
are set to auto

Display is set to
block

Width is set to
80%

Align graphics in table cells

1. Select the **shrimp bisque image**.

2. Use CSS Designer to add a global tag selector in su_styles.css, with the name that appears as the default name after you select the Add Selector button, **tr td img**.

   You'll add properties and values to this selector to center the image in the table cell.

3. Deselect the Show Set check box if necessary, then add the following properties and values to the tr td img selector as shown in Figure 40:

   width: **80%;**

   display: **block;**

   margin-left: **auto;**

   margin-right: **auto**.

4. Save your work.

You center-aligned cell content by editing the tr td img selector.

Insert Text and Format
CELL CONTENT

What You'll Do

The
Striped
Umbrella

Home   About Us   Sand Crab Cafe   Sea Spa   Activities

The Sand Crab Cafe is located in The Club House and has
three dining areas: The Terrace, Beach 25, and The Cabana.
The Terrace is outdoor dining with a breathtaking view of
the Gulf, especially at sunset. Beach 25 is casual, indoor
dining on the second floor. The Cabana is poolside.
Reservations are recommended for Beach 25 (our main
dining room) during the peak summer season. For
reservations, call 555-594-9458: extension 55.

The Sand Crab Cafe Hours

Our dining hours are listed below.

The Terrace	11:00 a.m. - 9:00 p.m.
Beach 25	7:00 a.m. - 11:00 p.m.
The Cabana	10:00 a.m. - 7:00 p.m.

Gulf Shrimp Room service is available from 6:00 a.m.
to 12:00 a.m.
Bisque Please call extension 54 to place an order.

 *In this lesson, you will type the cafe hours in the table. You
will also format the text to enhance its appearance on the
page. Last, you will add formatting to some of the cells
and cell content.*

Inserting Text in a Table

You can enter text in a table either by typing
it in a cell, copying it from another source
and pasting it into a cell, or importing it from
another program. Once you place text in a
table cell, you can format it to make it more
readable and more visually appealing on the
page.

Formatting Cell Content

To format the contents of a cell, select the
cell contents, then apply formatting to it. For
example, you can select an image in a cell and
add properties such as a font, font size, or
background color by using a class rule. Or, you
can select text in a cell and use the Blockquote
or Remove Blockquote buttons in the HTML
Property inspector to move the text farther
away from or closer to the cell walls.

If a cell contains multiple objects of the same
type, such as text, you can format each item
individually by applying different CSS rules
to each one.

Formatting Cells

Formatting a cell is different from formatting
a cell's contents. Formatting a cell can include
setting properties that visually enhance the
cell's appearance, such as setting a cell width
and assigning a background color. To format
a cell with code that is HTML5 compliant,
use tags to define a column group style
<colgroup>, which will format all cells in
a particular column. You can also use the
column tag <col> to apply formatting styles
to individual cells. Once you have created
your styles, you add them to the code for
the appropriate columns or cells you wish to
format.

QUICK TIP

Although you can set some table and cell properties using the
Property inspector, strive to use CSS Styles for all formatting tasks.

Figure 41 *Typing text into cells*

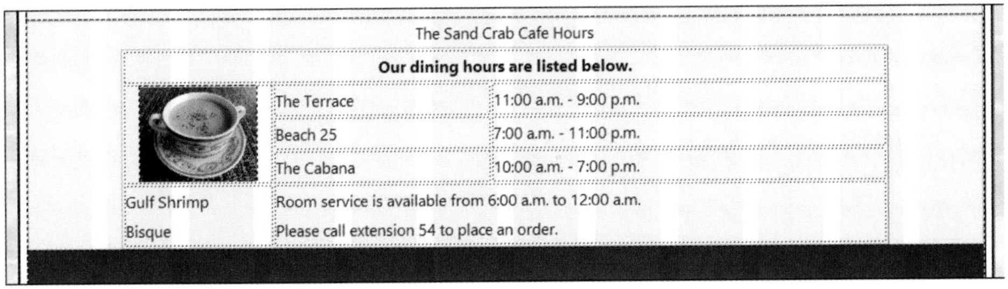

The Sand Crab Cafe Hours		
Our dining hours are listed below.		
(cup image)	The Terrace	11:00 a.m. - 9:00 p.m.
	Beach 25	7:00 a.m. - 11:00 p.m.
	The Cabana	10:00 a.m. - 7:00 p.m.
Gulf Shrimp	Room service is available from 6:00 a.m. to 12:00 a.m.	
Bisque	Please call extension 54 to place an order.	

Insert text

1. Place the insertion point in the cell below the bisque image type **Gulf Shrimp**, press **[Shift] [Enter]** (Win) or **[shift][return]** (Mac), then type **Bisque**.

   TIP If you can't see the last lines you typed, toggle Live view, or resize your screen to refresh it.

2. Place the insertion point in the top row of the table, then type **Our dining hours are listed below**.

   The text is automatically bolded because you selected the top row header when you created the table. A table's header row is bold by default.

3. Merge the two bottom-right cells in the last row, then enter the cafe dining area names, hours, and room service information in the cell rows, as shown in Figure 41. Use a line break after the first line of text in the last cell.

   TIP Don't be concerned about the table appearance yet. Deselect the table as you work to refresh it to display properly.

You entered text in the table to provide information about the dining room hours.

Importing and Exporting Data from Tables

You can import and export tabular data into and out of Dreamweaver. **Importing** means to bring data created in another software program into Dreamweaver, and **exporting** means to save data created in Dreamweaver in a special file format that can be opened by other programs. Files that are imported into Dreamweaver must be saved as delimited files. Tabular data is data that is arranged in columns and rows and separated by a **delimiter**: a comma, tab, colon, semicolon, or similar character. **Delimited files** are database, word processing, or spreadsheet files that have been saved as text files with delimiters such as tabs or commas separating the data. Programs such as Microsoft Access and Microsoft Excel offer many file formats for saving files. To import a delimited file, select File on the Menu bar, point to Import, then select Tabular Data. The Import Tabular Data dialog box opens, offering you formatting options for the imported table. To export a table that you created in Dreamweaver, select File on the Menu bar, point to Export, then select Table. The Export Table dialog box opens, letting you choose the type of delimiter you want for the delimited file.

Format cell content

1. Use CSS Designer to create a new global selector in the su_styles.css file named **.feature_item**.

2. Add the following properties and values to the Text category for the .feature_item selector, as shown in Figure 42:

   color: **#000033**;

   font-family: **lobster-two**;

   font-style: **italic**;

   font-weight: **400**;

   font-size: **large**.

   If you don't have the lobster-two font listed, use the Manage Fonts dialog box to open the Adobe Edge Web Fonts list and add it. You'll use this rule to format the name of the featured dessert.

3. Select **Gulf Shrimp Bisque** under the bisque image, select the **CSS button** on the Property inspector, then apply the **.feature_item rule** to the text.

4. Save your work, select **Update** in the Update Web Fonts dialog box, then select **Close** to close the Update Pages dialog box.

   Updating the script tags on the rest of the pages in the website will make the lobster-two font available for those pages, also.

You created a new rule in the su_styles.css style sheet and used it to format text in a table cell.

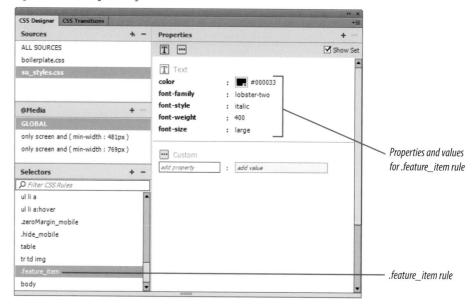

Figure 42 *Formatting text using a Class rule*

Properties and values for .feature_item rule

.feature_item rule

POWER USER SHORTCUTS	
To do this:	**Use this shortcut:**
Insert table	[Ctrl][Alt][T] (Win) or ⌘ [option][T] (Mac)
Select a cell	[Ctrl][A] (Win) or ⌘ [A] (Mac)
Merge cells	[Ctrl][Alt][M] (Win) or ⌘ [option][M] (Mac)
Split cell	[Ctrl][Alt][S] (Win) or ⌘ [option][S] (Mac)
Insert row	[Ctrl][M] (Win) or ⌘ [M] (Mac)
Insert column	[Ctrl][Shift][A] (Win) or ⌘ [Shift][A] (Mac)
Delete row	[Ctrl][Shift][M] (Win) or ⌘ [Shift][M] (Mac)
Delete column	[Ctrl][Shift][-] (Win) or ⌘ [Shift][-] (Mac)
Increase column span	[Ctrl][Shift][]] (Win) or ⌘ [Shift][]] (Mac)
Decrease column span	[Ctrl][Shift][[] (Win) or ⌘ [Shift][[] (Mac)

© 2015 Cengage Learning®

Figure 43 *Adding a text-align property to a class selector*

The Sand Crab Cafe Hours		
Our dining hours are listed below.		
	The Terrace	11:00 a.m. - 9:00 p.m.
	Beach 25	7:00 a.m. - 11:00 p.m.
	The Cabana	10:00 a.m. - 7:00 p.m.
	Room service is available from 6:00 a.m. to 12:00 a.m.	
Gulf Shrimp *Bisque*	Please call extension 54 to place an order.	

Bisque text is centered in cell

Format cells

1. Place the insertion point in the cell with the bisque text.

   Notice that the .feature_item rule is applied to the text. You will modify the .feature_item rule to add an alignment value.

2. Select the **.feature_item global selector** if necessary, then add the **text-align: center** property and set the width in the Layout category to **25%**.

   The text is now centered in the cell, as shown in Figure 43.

You modified the .feature_item class global selector.

Modify table text for different device sizes

1. Switch to the su_styles.css file, then scroll to locate the global table selector code.
2. Copy the table selector code, then paste it into both the tablet and desktop sections of code.
3. Use CSS Designer to edit the global table selector font-size to small, as shown in Figure 44.
4. Edit the tablet table selector font-size to small, as shown in Figure 45.
5. Edit the desktop table selector to change the font-size to **medium**, then save your work.

You copied the global table selector to the tablet and desktop sections of the su_styles.css code, then modified the global and tablet text size.

Figure 44 *The global table selector settings*

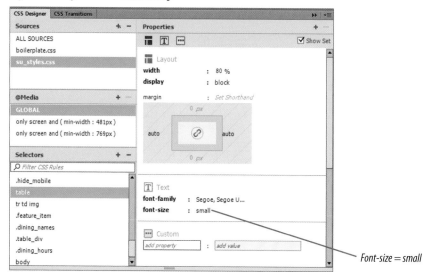

Font-size = small

Figure 45 *The tablet table selector settings*

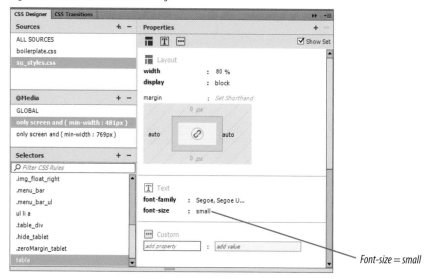

Font-size = small

Figure 46 *Placing horizontal rules in the table*

season. For reservations, call 555-594-9458: extension 55.

The Sand Crab Cafe Hours

Our dining hours are listed below.

The Terrace	11:00 a.m. - 9:00 p.m.
Beach 25	7:00 a.m. - 11:00 p.m.
The Cabana	10:00 a.m. - 7:00 p.m.

Room service is available from 6:00 a.m. to 12:00 a.m.
Please call extension 54 to place an order.

Gulf Shrimp Bisque

Horizontal rules added

Modify cell content

1. Place the insertion point after the word "bisque" in the bottom left cell, then press **[Tab]**.

   Pressing the Tab key while the insertion point is in the last cell of the table creates a new row. Even though it looks like the cell with the room service information is the last cell, it is not because of the merged cells.

2. Merge the cells in the new row, place the insertion point in the merged cells, select **Insert** on the Menu bar, then select **Horizontal Rule**.

3. Place the insertion point in front of the table header, insert another horizontal rule, then save your work.

4. Switch to Live view, then compare your table to Figure 46.

You added two horizontal rules to the table to set the table off from the rest of the page.

Check layout in all device sizes

1. Still in Live view, select the Desktop size button ![desktop icon], then compare your screen to Figure 47a.

   All figures shown on this page are without Fluid Grid Layout Guides shown.

2. Select the Tablet size button ![tablet icon], then compare your screen to Figure 47b.

3. Select the Mobile size button ![mobile icon], then compare your screen to Figure 47c.

4. Return to Desktop view, then turn off Live view.

5. Add the page title **The Striped Umbrella Sand Crab Cafe** in the Title text box, then save your work.

You viewed the new table using Desktop, Tablet, and Mobile size views.

Figure 47a *Cafe table in Desktop view*

Figure 47b *Cafe table in Tablet view*

Figure 47c *Cafe table in Mobile view*

Figure 48 *Validating HTML5 markup*

W3C validation
button

Validate HTML5 markup

1. Verify that the Source Code button is selected on the Related Files toolbar.

2. Select **File** on the Menu bar, point to **Validate**, then select **Validate Current Document (W3C)**.

   Before you validate a page, be sure that the HTML file is selected on the Related Files toolbar.

3. Select **OK** to close the W3C Validator Notification dialog box.

   The Results panel shows no errors or warnings found, as shown in Figure 48.

4. Select the **panel options button**, then select **Close Tab Group**.

   The Results panel closes.

5. Close all open files.

TIP If you see any errors or warnings listed, refer to the line number that corresponds to each error, then check your code to locate and correct the error.

You validated the cafe page and the Results panel showed that no errors were found.

Validating Your Pages Against HTML5 Standards

One of the tests you should run on your web pages is to validate your page code against current HTML5 standards. Dreamweaver provides a quick way to test each page with the Validation panel in the Results panel group. When you select the W3C Validation button , Dreamweaver connects to the W3C server, submits the page code, and records the results in the Validation panel. If you want to test your pages against other versions of HTML, select the Validate Current Document (W3C) button, select Settings, then choose the additional version or versions of HTML you would like to use for validation.

Create a page using a Fluid Grid layout

1. Open the Blooms & Bulbs website.
2. Open the New Document dialog box to create a new Fluid Grid Layout page, and browse to attach the boilerplate.css and bb_styles.css style sheets.
3. Select Create in the New Document dialog box, type **bb_styles_default** in the File name text box in the Save As dialog box, then save the new file as workshops.html, overwriting the existing workshops page. Close the Web Fonts dialog box if it opens.
4. In Code view, delete the link to the bb_styles_default.css file, and if you have two links to the boilerplate.css file, you can delete one of them.

Add and position divs

1. In Design view, place the insertion point in the placeholder text on the page or select the #div1.fluid tag in the Tag Selector, select the default name div_1 on the HTML Property inspector, then type **content** to rename the div.
2. In Code view, select the placeholder text in the content div, then delete it.
3. With the insertion point between the opening and closing content <div> tags, use the Insert panel Structure category to insert a Header.
4. Type **header_div** in the Insert Header dialog box, change to Design view, delete the placeholder text, then select the Element Quick View button on the status bar.
5. Select any stacked folder icons to expand them, if necessary, then look at the page structure, noting each tag that has been added to the page.

6. Close Element Quick View, change to Split view, then place the insertion point after the closing </header> tag.
7. Insert a new div from the Structure category of the Insert panel, then type **intro_paragraph** in the class text box in the Insert Div dialog box and select OK.
8. Open the index page, switch to Code view if necessary, then copy the code for the menu bar beginning with the <p> tag immediately to the left of it.
9. Switch to the workshops page in Code view, place the insertion point after the closing header tag if necessary, then paste the copied code.
10. Place the insertion point before the last two ending </div> tags at the bottom of the page, insert a Footer from the Structure category on the Insert panel, type **footer_div** in the class text box in the Insert Div dialog box, then select OK.
11. Close the index page, then save your work.
12. In Split view, place your insertion point in front of the opening <footer> tag.
13. Select Div in the Structure category of the Insert panel, type **image_div** in the Insert Div dialog box, then select OK.
14. Save your work, then return to Design view.
15. In CSS Designer, select bb_styles.css in the Sources pane, select GLOBAL in the @Media pane, then select .menu_bar in the Selectors pane.
16. Select the default font-family value, then select Segoe, Segoe UI, DejaVu Sans, Trebuchet MS, Verdana, sans-serif.
17. Save your work.

Add content to divs

1. With the workshops page open, delete the placeholder text in the Intro_paragraph div, being careful not to delete a beginning or ending <div> tag.
2. Open your file manager program, open the file composting.txt from the drive and folder where you store your Data Files, then copy and paste the contents into the Intro_paragraph div.
3. Close the composting.txt file.
4. Add a paragraph break after the sentence "New Composting Workshop!" and the following paragraph if necessary.
5. Apply the H2 format to the "New Composting Workshop!" heading.
6. Open the index page, copy the two lines of text in the footer, then paste them in the footer on the workshops page, replacing the footer placeholder text. Close the index page.
7. Place the insertion point in the img_div, then carefully delete the placeholder text (being careful not to delete a div tag).
8. Use the Insert panel to insert the image shade_garden.jpg from the Chapter 6 assets folder in the location where you store your Data Files, in the image div, and add **Shade garden with water feature** as the alternate text.
9. Save your work, then view the Desktop, Tablet, and Mobile sizes.
10. Preview the page in your browser, then close the browser.
11. Place the pointer in the introductory paragraph, then verify that you have your Fluid Grid Layout guides displayed. Display them if you do not.

12. Switch to Live view, place the pointer over the triangle (handle) at the bottom of the intro_paragraph div to see the tool tip Swap DIV.intro_paragraph with DIV.image_div, then select the handle.
13. Select the handle pointing up, swap DIV.intro_paragraph with DIV.image_div, then return to Design view and turn off Live view.

Create a table

1. Place the insertion point in the intro paragraph div, switch to Code view, then place the insertion point after the ending div tag for the intro paragraph div.
2. Return to Design view, then use the Insert panel to insert a new div named **table_div**.
3. Carefully delete the div placeholder text, then insert a table from the Common category on the Insert panel.
4. In the Table dialog box, select **5** rows, **3** columns, and a **Top** header. All other values should be empty.
5. In the Caption text box, type **Blooms & Bulbs Spring Workshops**.
6. Use CSS Designer to add a new global tag selector in the bb_styles.css file named **table**.
7. Using the Layout and Text categories in the Properties pane, then add the following properties and values:
   display: **block**
   width: **80%**
   margin-left: **auto**
   margin-right: **auto**
   font-family: **Segoe, Segoe UI, DejaVu Sans, Trebuchet MS, Verdana, Sans-serif**
8. Save your work.

Resize, split, and merge cells

1. Click or tap the last cell in the last row, then split the cell into 2 rows.
2. Merge the three cells in the top row of the table.
3. Merge the second, third, fourth, and fifth cells in the first column.
4. View the cells in Code view, then return to Design view.
5. Save your work.

Insert and align images in table cells

1. In the merged cells in the first column, insert the image pink_rose.jpg from the drive and folder where your Chapter 6 Data Files are stored.
2. Use CSS Designer to add a global tag selector in the bb_styles.css file with the name **tr td img**.
3. Add the following properties to the tr td img tag:
   width: **85%**
   display: **block**
   margin-left: **auto**
   margin-right: **auto**
4. Use the Property inspector to add the alternate text **Pink Rose**.
5. Create a new global class selector in the bb_styles.css file named **.feature_flower** with the following property and value:
   width: **25%**
6. Place the insertion point in the cell with the pink rose image.
7. Select the <td> tag on the Status bar, select the Class list arrow, then select **feature_flower**.
8. Add a global class selector named **.workshop_date** with the following property:
   width: 50%

9. Place the insertion point in the first cell that will contain a workshop date, then use the Property inspector to apply the .workshop_date rule, as shown in Figure 49 on the next page.
10. Save your work.

Insert text and format cell content

1. Type **Currently Scheduled Spring Workshops - Call for Availability** in the merged cells in the top row.
2. Type the names and dates of the workshops from Figure 49 in the table cells.
3. In the last cell in the last row, type **Classes are limited to 25 members. Bring work gloves!** (Don't be concerned if your text wraps differently than the text shown in the figure. It display correctly after you adjust the font size.)
4. Place the insertion point in the last cell of the last row, press the Tab key to insert a new row, merge the three cells, then insert a horizontal rule from the Insert menu.
5. Place the insertion point in front of the table header, then insert another horizontal rule.
6. Switch to the bb_styles.css file, then scroll to locate the table selector code.
7. Copy the table selector code, then paste it into both the tablet and desktop sections of code.
8. Add a property to change the global table selector font-size to small.
9. Edit the desktop table selector font-size to medium, then save your work
10. Preview the workshops page in mobile, tablet, and desktop sizes.
11. Preview the workshops page in a browser.
12. Close all open files.

Figure 49 *Completed Skills Review*

In this exercise, you continue your work on the TripSmart website that you began in Project Builder 1 in Chapter 1 and developed in the previous chapters. You are ready to begin work on a page featuring a catalog item. You plan to use a CSS Fluid Grid layout with a table to place the information on the page.

1. Open the TripSmart website.
2. Create a new Fluid Grid Layout page, and browse to attach the boilerplate.css and tripsmart_styles.css style sheets.
3. Use **tripsmart_styles_default** in the File name text box in the Save As dialog box, then save the new file as **catalog.html**, overwriting the existing catalog page.
4. Delete the link to the tripsmart_styles_default.css file in the catalog page code.
5. Place the insertion point in the placeholder text on the page, select the default name div_1 on the Property inspector, type **content** to rename the div, then delete the placeholder text in the content div.
6. With the insertion point between the opening and closing content <div> tags, insert a Header with the name **header_div**, then delete the placeholder text in the header_div.
7. Insert a new div after the closing header tag named **intro_paragraph**.
8. Open the index page, switch to Code view, copy the code for the menu bar beginning with the <p> tag immediately above it, then close the index page.

9. Switch to the catalog page, then paste the copied code after the closing header div.
10. Insert a footer before the last two ending </div> tags at the bottom of the page with the class name **footer_div**, then save your work.
11. In CSS Designer, select the global selector .menu_bar in tripsmart_styles.css, then add the default font-family value Segoe, Segoe UI, DejaVu Sans, Trebuchet MS, Verdana, sans-serif.
12. With the catalog page open, open your file manager program, open the file hiking.txt from the drive and folder where you store your Data Files, then copy and paste the contents into the intro_paragraph div.
13. Close the hiking.txt file.
14. Add a paragraph break after the sentence "Take a hike!"
15. Apply the H2 format to the "Take a hike!" heading.
16. Open the index file, copy the two lines of text in the footer, then paste them in the footer on the catalog page, replacing the footer placeholder text.
17. Save your work, close the index page, then view the Desktop, Tablet, Mobile sizes, and a browser.
18. In Code view, place the insertion point after the ending intro_paragraph div, then use the Insert panel to insert a new div named **table_div**.
19. Carefully delete the table div placeholder text, then insert a table from the Common category on the Insert panel.
20. In the Table dialog box, select **8** rows, **3** columns, and a Top header. All other values should be empty.

21. In the Caption text box, type **Hiking Clothing and Accessories**
22. Use CSS Designer to add a new global tag selector in the bb_styles.css file named **table**.
23. Using the Layout and Text categories in the Properties pane, add the following properties and values:
    display: block
    width: **80%**
    margin-left: auto
    margin-right: auto
    font-family: Segoe, Segoe UI, DejaVu Sans, Trebuchet MS, Verdana, Sans-serif
24. Save your work.
25. Merge the three cells in the top row, then add the header **Come See Our New Spring Hiking Gear!** to the top row.
26. Merge the remaining cells in the middle column, then save your work.
27. Insert the image three_hikers.jpg from the Chapter 6 assets folder in the location where you store your Data Files, in the merged cells in the second column.
28. Use CSS Designer to add a global tag selector in the tripsmart_styles.css file with the name tr td img.
29. Add the following properties to the tr td img tag:
    width: **85%**
    display: block
    margin-left: auto
    margin-right: auto
30. Use the Property inspector to add the alternate text **Three hikers in Patagonia** to the three hikers image.

31. Create a new global class selector in the tripsmart_styles.css file named .featured_items with the following property and value: width: **40%**

32. Place the insertion point in the cell with the three hikers image.

33. Select the <td> tag on the Property inspector, select the Class list arrow, then select featured_items.

34. Add a global class selector named .catalog_items with the following property: width: **30%**

35. Select the empty cells in the first column, use the Property inspector to apply the .catalog_items class, then save your work.

36. Create a global class selector named .catalog_prices, set its Width property to 30%, then apply .catalog_prices to the empty cells in the third column.

37. Type the names of the featured catalog items and prices from Figure 50 in the first six cells in the first and third columns.

38. Add selectors of your own or edit any of the selector properties used for the table to customize the page.

39. Insert a new row at the end of the table, merge the cells in the new row, then insert a horizontal rule.

40. Place the insertion point in front of the table header, then insert another horizontal rule.

41. Switch to the tripsmart_styles.css file, then scroll to locate the table selector code.

42. Copy the table selector code, then paste it into both the tablet and desktop sections of code.

43. Add a property to change the global table selector font-size to small.

44. Edit the desktop table selector font-size to medium.

45. Save your work, preview the catalog page in the browser, mobile, tablet, and desktop sizes, then compare your screen to Figure 45.

46. Close all open files.

Figure 50 *Sample Project Builder 1*

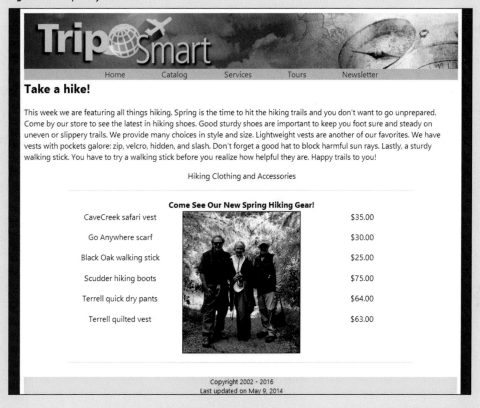

PROJECT BUILDER 2

Use Figure 51 as a guide to continue your work on the Carolyne's Creations website that you started in Chapter 1 and developed in the previous chapters. You are now ready to begin work on a page showcasing the company's catering services. You decide to use a Fluid Grid layout and add a small table.

1. Open the Carolyne's Creations website, create a new Fluid Grid Layout page, and browse to attach the boilerplate.css and cc_styles.css style sheets.
2. Use **cc_styles_default** in the File name text box in the Save As dialog box, then save the new file as catering.html, overwriting the existing catering page. Close the Web Fonts dialog box if it opens.
3. Delete the link to the cc_styles_default.css file in the catering page code.
4. Place the insertion point in the placeholder text on the page, select the default ID div1 on the Property inspector, then type **content** to rename the div ID, then delete the placeholder text in the content div.
5. With the insertion point between the opening and closing content <div> tags, insert a Header with the name **header_div**, then delete the placeholder text in the header_div.
6. Insert a new div after the closing header tag named **intro_paragraph**, then save your work.
7. Open the index page, switch to Code view, copy the code for the menu bar beginning with the <p> tag immediately above it, then close the index page.
8. Switch to the catering page, then paste the copied code after the closing header div.

9. Insert a footer before the last two ending </div> tags at the bottom of the page with the class name **footer_div**, then save your work.
10. Verify that the font used in the menu bar is the same as on the index page menu bar.
11. Place the insertion point between the intro_ paragraph div tags, open your file manager program, open the file marshmallows.txt from the drive and folder where you store your Data Files, then copy and paste the contents into the intro_paragraph div.
12. Close the marshmallows.txt file.
13. Add a paragraph break after the sentence "Special Treats for Valentine's Day".
14. Apply the H3 format to the "Special Treats for Valentine's Day" heading.
15. Open the index file, copy the two lines of text in the footer, then paste them in the footer on the catering page, replacing the footer placeholder text.
16. Save your work, then view the Desktop, Tablet, Mobile sizes, and a browser.
17. In Code view, place the insertion point after the ending intro_paragraph div, then use the Insert panel to insert a new div named **table_div**.
18. Carefully delete the div placeholder text, then insert a table from the Common category on the Insert panel.
19. In the Table dialog box, select **6** rows, **3** columns, and a Top Header. All other values should be empty.
20. Use CSS Designer to add a new global tag selector in the cc_styles.css file named **table**.

21. Using the Layout and Text categories in the Properties pane, then add the following properties and values:
    display: block
    width: **80%**
    margin-left: auto
    margin-right: auto
    font-family: Segoe, Segoe UI, DejaVu Sans, Trebuchet MS, Verdana, Sans-serif
22. Save your work.
23. Merge the three cells in the top row, then add the header **Marshmallow Flavors and Prices** to the top row.
24. Merge the cells in the first column, then insert the image marshmallows.jpg from the assets folder in the location where you store your Data Files in the merged cells in the first column, then add appropriate alternate text.
25. Use CSS Designer to add a global tag selector in the cc_styles.css file with the name tr td img.
26. Add the following properties to the tr td img tag:
    width: **85%**
    display: block
    margin-left: auto
    margin-right: auto
27. Create a new global class selector in the cc_styles.css file named **.marshmallow_image** with the following property and value:
    width: **40%**
28. Place the insertion point in the cell with the marshmallow image.

29. Select the <td> tag on the Property inspector, select the Class list arrow, then select marshmallow_image.
30. Add two new global class selectors named **.marshmallow_flavors** and **.marshmallow_prices** with the following property: width: **30%**
31. Type the marshmallow flavors in the second column and the marshmallow prices in the third column, as shown in Figure 51.
32. Merge the two cells in the last row, then enter the text shown in Figure 51.
33. Customize the table with new or modified properties or page elements. (*Hint*: In Figure 51 an Adobe Edge Web Font was used for the marshmallow flavors and the table tag was modified to add a border around it.)
34. Save your work, then preview the catering page in mobile, tablet, and desktop sizes.
35. Preview the catering page in the browser.

Figure 51 *Completed Project Builder 2*

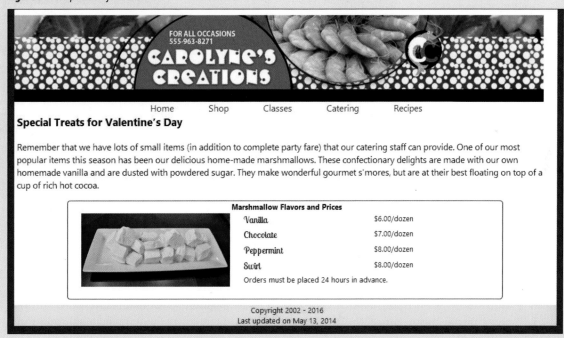

Jon Bishop is opening a new restaurant and wants to launch his restaurant website two weeks before his opening. He has hired you to create the site and has asked for several design proposals. You begin by looking at some restaurant sites with pleasing designs.

1. Connect to the Internet, then go to jamesatthemill.com, as shown in Figure 52.
2. How are CSS styles used in this site?
3. How are CSS styles used to prevent an overload of information in one area of the screen?
4. View the source code for the page and locate the HTML tags that control the CSS layout on the page.
5. Use the Reference panel in Dreamweaver to look up the code used in this site to place the content on the page. (*Hint*: To do this, make note of a tag that you don't understand, then open the Reference panel and find that tag in the Tag list in the Reference panel. Select it from the list and read the description in the Reference panel.)
6. Do you see any tables on the page? If so, how are they used?

Figure 52 *Design Project*

Source: James at the Mill

For this assignment, you continue to work on the portfolio project that you have been developing since Chapter 1. No Data Files are supplied. You are building this website from chapter to chapter, so you must do each Portfolio Project assignment in each chapter to complete your website.

You continue building your website by designing and completing a page that uses a CSS layout for page design.

1. Consult your wireframe to decide which page to create and develop for this chapter. Draw a sketch of the page to show how you plan to use CSS to lay out the content.
2. Create the new page for the site using a Fluid Grid layout.
3. Add text, background images, and background colors to each container.
4. Create the navigation links that will allow you to add this page to your site.
5. Update the other pages of your site so that each page includes a link to this new page.
6. Add images in the containers (where appropriate), making sure to align them attractively.
7. Review the checklist in Figure 53 and make any necessary changes.
8. Save your work, preview the page in your browser, make any necessary modifications to improve the page appearance, close your browser, then close all open pages.

Figure 53 *Portfolio Project checklist*

> ### Website Checklist
> 1. Do all pages have a page title?
> 2. Do all navigation links work correctly?
> 3. Did you validate your code for at least one level of HTML?
> 4. Did you use a fluid grid page layout for at least one page?
> 5. Do your pages look the same in at least two current browsers and three screen sizes?
> 6. Does all content in your CSS containers appear correctly?

CHAPTER **7** **MANAGING A WEB SERVER AND FILES**

1. Perform website maintenance
2. Publish a website and transfer files
3. Check files out and in
4. Cloak files
5. Import and export a site definition
6. Evaluate web content for legal use
7. Present a website to a client

MANAGING A WEB
SERVER AND FILES

Introduction

Once you have created all the pages of your website, finalized all the content, and performed site maintenance, you are ready to publish your site to a remote server so the rest of the world can access it. In this chapter, you start by running some reports to make sure the links in your site work properly and that any orphaned files are removed. You remember from Chapter 5 that orphaned files are files that are not linked to any pages in a website. Next, you set up a connection to the remote site for The Striped Umbrella website. You then transfer files to the remote site and learn how to keep them up to date. You also check out a file so that it is not available to other team members while you are editing it and you learn how to cloak files. When a file is **cloaked**, it is excluded from certain processes, such as being transferred to the remote site. Next, you export the site definition file from The Striped Umbrella website so that other designers can import the site. Finally, you research important copyright issues that affect all websites, and learn how to present your work to a client.

Preparing to Publish a Site

Before you publish a site, it is extremely important that you test it to make sure the content is accurate and up to date and that everything is functioning properly. When viewing pages over the Internet, users find it frustrating to select a link that doesn't work or to wait for pages that load slowly because of large graphics and animations. Remember that the typical user has a short attention span and limited patience.

Before you publish your site, be sure to use the Link Checker panel to check for broken links and orphaned files. Make sure that all image paths are correct and that all images load quickly and have alternate text. Verify that all pages have titles. View the pages in at least two different browsers and different versions of the same browser to ensure that everything works correctly. View the pages on a mobile, tablet, and desktop device. The more frequently you test, the better the chance that your users will have a positive experience at your site and want to return. Finally, before you publish your pages, verify that all content is original to the website, or has been obtained legally and is used properly without violating the copyright of someone else's work.

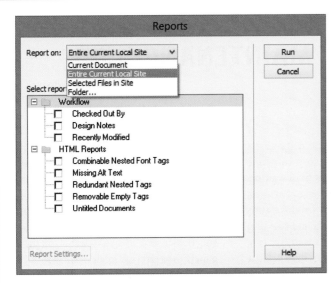

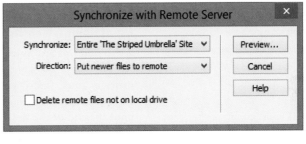

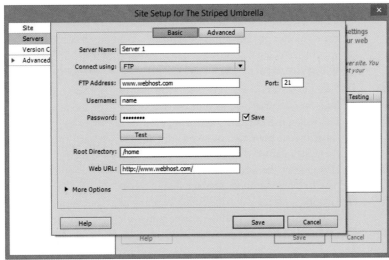

Perform
WEBSITE MAINTENANCE

What You'll Do

 In this lesson, you will use Dreamweaver site management tools to check for broken links, orphaned files, and missing alternate text. You will also validate your markup to locate CSS3 and HTML5 errors. You will then evaluate and correct any problems that you find.

Maintaining a Website

As you add pages, links, and content to a website, it can quickly become difficult to manage. You'll find it easier to locate and correct errors as you go, rather than waiting until the end of the design phase. Perform maintenance tasks frequently to make sure your website operates smoothly and remains "clean." After publishing your website, run maintenance checks at regular intervals to make sure it is always error-free. You have already been introduced to some of the tools described in the following paragraphs. Now you can put them into practice.

Using the Assets Panel

Use the Assets panel to check the list of images and colors used in your website. If you see images listed that are not being used, you should move them to a storage folder outside the website until you need them. You should also look at your colors listed in the Assets panel. Do they complement each other, creating a pleasing color palette? Will any of them cause contrast problems, especially with mobile devices?

Checking Links Sitewide

Before and after you publish your website, you should use the Link Checker panel to make sure all internal links are working. If the Link Checker panel displays any broken links, repair them. If it displays any orphaned files, evaluate whether to delete them or link them to existing pages. To delete a file that you decide not to use, select it in the Files panel, then press [Delete] or right-click the file, select Edit, then select Delete. You should also check all external links by testing them in a browser to make sure that all links find the intended website.

Using Site Reports

You can use the Reports command in the Site menu to generate five different HTML reports to help you maintain your website. Choose the type of report you want to run in the Reports dialog box, shown in Figure 1. You can specify whether to generate the report for the current document, the entire current local site, selected files in the site, or a selected folder. You can also generate workflow reports to see files that have been checked out by others or recently modified or you can view the Design Notes attached to files.

Design Notes are separate files in a website that contain additional information about a page file or a graphic file. If several designers are working collaboratively to design a site, they can record notes to exchange information with other design team members about the status of ongoing work on a file. Design Notes are also a good place to store information about the source files for graphics, such as Photoshop or Fireworks files.

Validating Markup

Because you can choose the language you use to create web pages, such as PHP or HTML, it's important to ensure that the various language versions are compatible. To address this need, Dreamweaver can validate markup. To **validate markup**, Dreamweaver submits the files to the W3C Validation Service to search through the code to look for errors that could occur with different language versions, such as XHTML or HTML5. To validate code for a page, select the File, Validate, Validate Current Document (W3C) command. Dreamweaver then sends the page code to the live W3C site to be validated. The Results tab group displaying the Validation panel opens and lists any pages with errors, the line numbers where the errors occur, and an explanation of the errors. You should also submit your CSS files for CSS validation to the W3C Validation Service at jigsaw.w3.org/css-validator.

Testing Pages

Finally, you should test your website using many different types and versions of browsers, platforms, and screen resolutions. Test every link to make sure it connects to a valid, active website.

If, in your testing, you find any pages that download slowly, reduce their size to improve performance. Consider optimizing graphics by cropping or resizing images, reducing the number of media files, or streamlining the page code.

As part of your ongoing site testing, you should present the web pages at strategic times in the development process to your team members and to your clients for feedback and evaluation. Analyze all feedback on the website objectively, incorporating both the positive and the negative comments to help you make improvements to the site and meet the clients' expectations and goals.

Figure 1 *Reports dialog box*

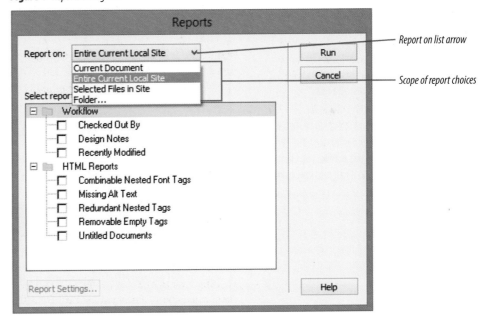

Check for broken links

1. Open The Striped Umbrella website.
2. Open the Files panel, if necessary.
3. Select **Site** on the Menu bar, point to **Advanced**, then select **Recreate Site Cache**.

   It is a good idea to recreate the site cache to force Dreamweaver to refresh the file listing before running reports.
4. Select **Site** on the Menu bar, then select **Check Links Sitewide**.

   No broken links are listed in the Link Checker panel of the Results Tab Group, as shown in Figure 2.

You verified that there are no broken links in the website.

Check for orphaned files

1. On the Link Checker panel, select the **Show list arrow**, then select **Orphaned Files**.

   There are two orphaned files, as shown in Figure 3. You may use the logo file later, so you leave it in the local site folder for now. The second file is the su_styles_default.css file. You want to keep it for reference, so it can also stay in the local site folder for now.
2. Close the Results Tab Group.

You found two orphaned files in the website, but decided to leave them there for now.

Figure 2 *Link Checker panel displaying no broken links*

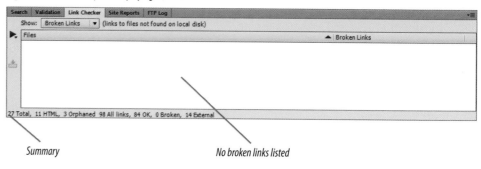

Summary — No broken links listed

Figure 3 *Link Checker panel displaying two orphaned files*

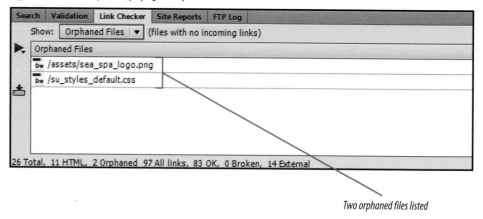

Two orphaned files listed

Validating Accessibility Standards

HTML Reports can help ensure that your website conforms to current accessibility standards. HTML Reports provide an easy way to check for missing alternate text, missing page titles, and improper markup. You can run HTML Reports on the current document, selected files, or the entire local site.

Figure 4 *Reports dialog box with Untitled Documents option selected*

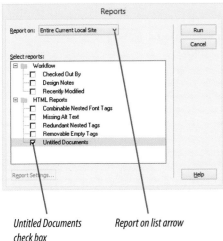

Untitled Documents
check box

Report on list arrow

Figure 5 *No pages listed without a title*

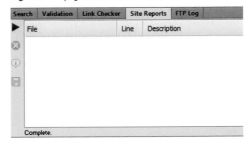

Figure 6 *Reports dialog box with Missing Alt Text option selected*

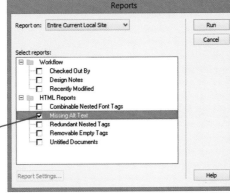

Missing Alt Text
check box

Figure 7 *Site Reports panel displaying no missing alt text*

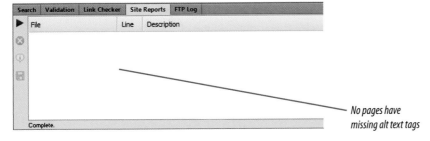

No pages have
missing alt text tags

Check for untitled documents

1. Select **Site** on the Menu bar, then select **Reports** to open the Reports dialog box.

2. Select the **Report on list arrow**, select **Entire Current Local Site**, select the **Untitled Documents check box**, as shown in Figure 4, then select **Run**.

   The Site Reports panel opens in the Results Tab Group, and does not list any pages with unassigned titles, as shown in Figure 5.

You ran a report for untitled documents, and did not find any files listed without assigned page titles.

Check for missing alternate text

1. Using Figure 6 as a guide, run another report that checks the entire current local site for missing alternate text.

   There are no images with missing alternate text, as shown in Figure 7.

2. Close the Results Tab Group.

You ran a report to check for missing alternate text in the entire site.

Validate for HTML5 standards

1. Select **File** on the Menu bar, select **Validate**, select **Validate Current Document (W3C)**, then select **OK** to close the W3C Validator Notification dialog box.

   The Validation panel shows no errors or warnings for HTML5, as shown in Figure 8.

2. Open each page in the website, then repeat Step 1 to validate each page.

3. Close the Results Tab Group, then close any open pages.

You validated each page against HTML5 markup standards and no errors or warnings were found.

Figure 8 *Validation panel with no errors or warnings found*

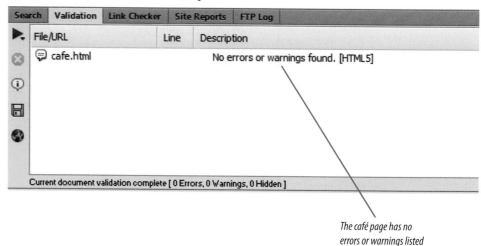

The café page has no errors or warnings listed

Figure 9 *Submitting a style sheet for validation*

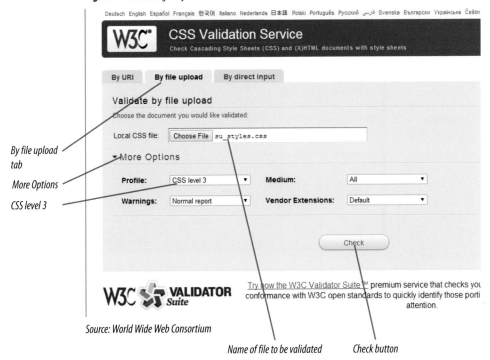

By file upload tab

More Options

CSS level 3

Source: World Wide Web Consortium

Name of file to be validated   *Check button*

Figure 10 *W3C validation results for su_styles.css file*

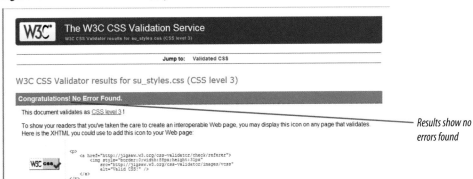

Results show no errors found

Source: World Wide Web Consortium

Validate CSS

1. Open your browser and go to **jigsaw.w3.org/css-validator**.

    The CSS Validation Service provides a fast way to validate the code in your style sheets to be sure they are compliant with the most current published CSS standards.

2. Select the **By file upload tab**, select **Choose File (or Browse) button** next to the Local CSS file text box, navigate to your website's local site folder, double-click to select **su_styles.css**, select **More Options**, then select **CSS level 3**, as shown in Figure 9.

3. Select **Check**, then view the validation results, as shown in Figure 10.

    There are no errors listed in the su_styles.css file.

4. Close the browser and return to Dreamweaver.

You submitted the main style sheet for validation and found that it met CSS3 standards.

Enable Design Notes

1. Select **Site** on the Menu bar, select **Manage Sites**, verify that The Striped Umbrella site is selected, select the **Edit the currently selected site button** ✎, select **Advanced Settings**, then select **Design Notes**.

2. Select the **Maintain Design Notes check box**, if necessary, as shown in Figure 11.

   When this option is selected, designers can record notes about a page in a separate file linked to the page. For instance, a Design Note for the index.html file would be saved in a file named index.html.mno. Dreamweaver creates a folder named _notes and saves all Design Notes in that folder. This folder does not appear in the Files panel, but it is visible in the local site folder in File Explorer (Win) or Finder (Mac).

3. Select **File View Columns**, then select **Notes** in the Name column.

4. Select the **Edit existing Column button** ✎, select the **Options**: **Show check box**, if necessary, then select **Save**.

   The Notes row now displays the word "Show" in the Show column, as shown in Figure 12, indicating that the Notes column will be visible in the Files panel.

5. Select **Save** to close the Site Setup for The Striped Umbrella dialog box, then select **Done** in the Manage Sites dialog box.

You set the preference to use Design Notes in the website. You also set the option to display the Notes column in the Files panel.

Figure 11 *Design Notes setting in the Site Setup for The Striped Umbrella*

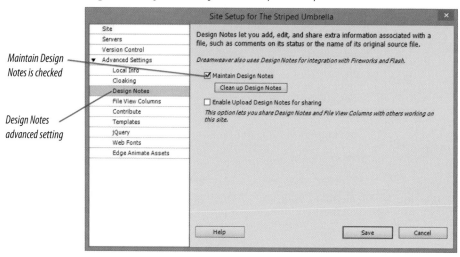

Maintain Design Notes is checked

Design Notes advanced setting

Figure 12 *Showing the Notes column in the Site Setup for The Striped Umbrella*

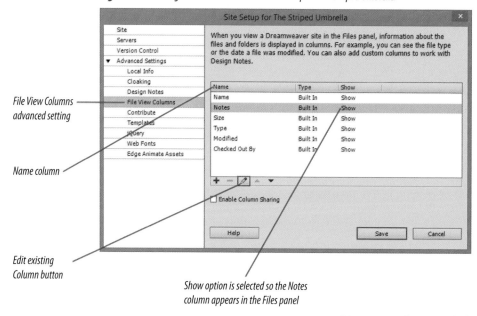

File View Columns advanced setting

Name column

Edit existing Column button

Show option is selected so the Notes column appears in the Files panel

Figure 13 *Design Notes dialog box*

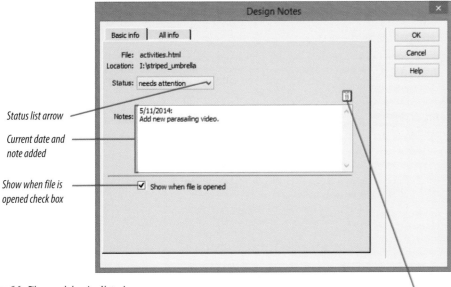

Status list arrow

Current date and note added

Show when file is opened check box

Insert date button

Figure 14 *Files panel showing Notes icon*

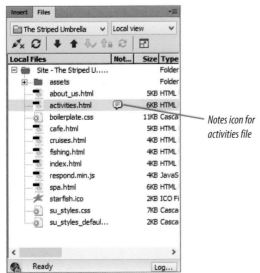

Notes icon for activities file

Associate a Design Note with a file

1. Open the activities page, select **File** on the Menu bar, select **Design Notes**, then select the **Basic info tab**, if necessary.

   The Design Notes dialog box opens. You can enter a note related to the open file in the text box. You can also assign the note a status, insert today's date, and indicate if the note appears whenever the file is opened.

2. Select the **Insert date button** 🗓 above the Notes text box on the right.

   The current date is added to the Notes text box.

3. Place the insertion point under the date, then type **Add new parasailing video.** in the Notes text box.

4. Select the **Status list arrow**, then select **needs attention**.

5. Select the **Show when file is opened** check box, as shown in Figure 13, then select **OK**.

6. Select the **Refresh button** 🔁 on the Files panel.

   An icon 💬 appears next to the activities page in the Notes column in the Files panel as shown in Figure 14, indicating that there is a Design Note attached to the file.

You added a Design Note to the activities page with the current date and a status indicator. The note opens each time the file is opened.

Edit a Design Note

1. Select **File** on the Menu bar, then select **Design Notes** to open the Design Note associated with the activities page.

TIP You can also right-click (Win) or [control]-click (Mac) the filename in the Files panel, then select Design Notes to open the Design Note. You can also double-click or double-tap the Note icon to open a Design Note.

2. Edit the note by adding the sentence **Ask Sue Geren to send the file**. after the existing text in the Notes section, as shown in Figure 15, then select **OK** to close it.

   Dreamweaver created a file named activities.html.mno in a new folder called _notes in the local site folder. This folder and file do not appear in the Files panel unless you have selected the option to show hidden files and folders. To show hidden files, select the Files Panel options button, then select View, Show Hidden Files. However, you can switch to File Explorer (Win) or Finder (Mac) to see them without selecting this option. When you select the option to Enable Upload Design Notes for sharing, you can share the notes with team members working with you on the site.

3. Right-click (Win) or [control]-click (Mac) **activities.html** in the Files panel, then select **Explore** (Win) or **Reveal in Finder** (Mac).

   (continued)

Figure 15 *Adding to the note for the activities page*

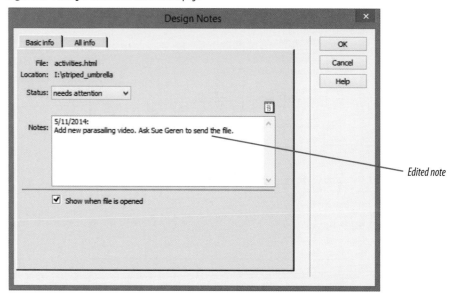

Edited note

Deleting a Design Note

There are two steps to deleting a Design Note that you don't need anymore. The first step is to delete the Design Note file. To delete a Design Note, right-click the filename in the Files panel that is associated with the Design Note you want to delete, and then select Explore (Win) or Reveal in Finder (Mac) to open your file management system. Open the _notes folder, delete the .mno file in the files list, and then close Explorer (Win) or Finder (Mac). You perform the second step in Dreamweaver: Select Site on the Menu bar, select Manage Sites, select Edit the currently selected site button, select Advanced Settings, then select the Design Notes category. Confirm that Maintain Design Notes is still selected, then select the Clean up Design Notes button. (*Note:* Don't do this if you deselect Maintain Design Notes first or it will delete all of your Design Notes!) The Design Notes icon will be removed from the Notes column in the Files panel. After you delete the .mno file, you can select the Refresh button in the Files panel, and it will be removed.

Figure 16 *File Explorer displaying the _notes folder and file*

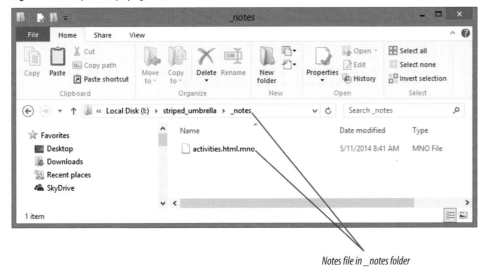

Notes file in _notes folder

4. Double-click the **_notes** folder to open it, then double-click the file **activities.html.mno**, shown in Figure 16, to open the file in Dreamweaver.

The notes file opens in Code view in Dreamweaver, as shown in Figure 17.

TIP If you see a message asking what program you want to use to open the file, select Dreamweaver.

5. Read the file, close it, close Explorer (Win) or Finder (Mac), then close the activities page.

You opened the Design Notes dialog box and edited the note in the Notes text box. Next, you viewed the .mno file that Dreamweaver created when you added the Design Note.

Figure 17 *Code for the activities.html.mno file*

```
1  <?xml version="1.0" encoding="utf-8" ?>
2  <info>
3      <infoitem key="notes" value="5/11/2014: &#xD;Add new parasailing
   video. Ask Sue Geren to send the file." />
4      <infoitem key="status" value="needs attention" />
5      <infoitem key="showOnOpen" value="true" />
6  </info>
7
```

Publish a Website
AND TRANSFER FILES

What You'll Do

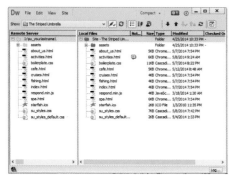

 In this lesson, you will set up remote access to either an FTP folder or a local/network folder for The Striped Umbrella website. You will also view a website on a remote server, upload files to it, and synchronize the files.

Defining a Remote Site

As you learned in Chapter 1, publishing a site means transferring a copy of all the site's files to a web server. A **web server** is a computer with software that enables it to host websites and is connected to the Internet with an IP (Internet Protocol) address so that it is available on the Internet. Before you can publish a site to a web server, you must first define the remote site by specifying the Servers settings in the Site Setup dialog box as shown in Figure 18. You can specify remote settings when you first create a new site and define the local site folder (as you did in Chapter 1 when you defined the remote access settings for The Striped Umbrella website). Or you can do it after you have completed all of your pages and are confident that your site is ready for public viewing. To specify the remote settings for a site, select the Add new Server button in the Site Setup

Figure 18 *Accessing the server settings in the Site Setup dialog box*

Servers tab

Add new Server button

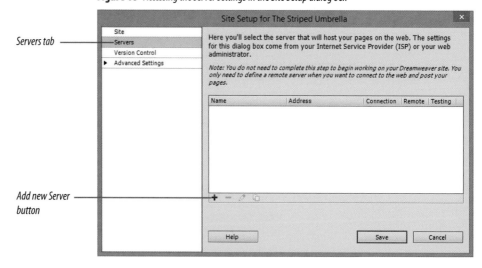

dialog box, then add your server name, and choose a connection setting, which specifies the type of server you will use. You can set up multiple servers with Dreamweaver. You can set up a server for testing purposes only and a server for the live website. The most common connection setting is FTP (File Transfer Protocol). If you choose FTP, you need to specify a server address and folder name on the FTP site where you want to store your remote site root folder. You can also use **Secure FTP (SFTP)**, which lets you encrypt file transfers to protect your files, user names, and passwords. To use SFTP, select SFTP on the Connect using list in the site setup dialog box. You also need to enter login and password information. Figure 19

shows an example of FTP settings in the Add new server dialog box.

QUICK TIP

If you do not have access to an FTP site, you can publish a site to a local/network folder. This is referred to as a **LAN**, or a Local Area Network. Use the alternate steps provided in this lesson to publish your site to a local/network folder.

Viewing a Remote Site

Once you have set up a remote server, you can then view the remote folder in the Files panel by choosing Remote server from the View list. If your remote site is located on an FTP server, Dreamweaver will connect to it. You will see the File Activity dialog box showing the progress of the connection. You can also use the

Connect to Remote Server button on the Files panel toolbar to connect to the remote site. If you defined your site on a local/network folder, then you don't need to use the Connect Remote Server button; the local site folder and any files and folders it contains appear in the Files panel when you switch to Remote server view.

Transferring Files to and from a Remote Site

After you set up a remote site, you **upload**, or copy, your files from the local version of your site to the remote host. To do this, view the site in Local view, select the files you want to upload, and then select the Put File(s) button on the Files panel toolbar. The Put File(s) button includes the name of the server in the tooltip.

Figure 19 *Viewing remote server settings*

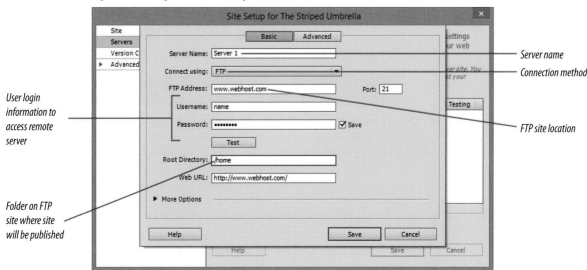

Once you select this button, a copy of the files is transferred to the remote site. To view the uploaded files, switch to Remote server in the Files panel. Or, you can expand the Files panel to view both the Remote Site and the Local Site panes by selecting the Expand to show local and remote sites button in the Files panel.

If a file you select for uploading requires additional files, such as graphics or a style sheet file, a dialog box opens after you select the Put File(s) button and asks if you want those files (known as **dependent files**) to be uploaded. By selecting Yes, all dependent files for the selected page will be uploaded to the appropriate folder in the remote site. If a file that you want to upload is located in a folder in the local site, the folder will automatically be transferred to the remote site.

QUICK TIP

To upload an entire site to a remote host, select the local site folder, then select the Put File(s) button.

If you are developing or maintaining a website in a group environment, there might be times when you want to transfer or **download** files that other team members have created from the remote site to your local site. To do this, switch to Remote Server in the Files panel, select the files you want to download, then select the Get File(s) button on the Files panel toolbar. The Get File(s) button includes the name of the server in the tooltip.

Synchronizing Files

To keep a website up to date—especially one that contains several pages and involves several team members—you need to update and replace files. Team members might make changes to pages on the local version of the site or make additions to the remote site. If many people are involved in maintaining a site, or if you are constantly making changes to the pages, ensuring that both the local and remote sites have the most up-to-date files

could get confusing. Luckily, you can use the Synchronize command to keep things straight. The **Synchronize command** instructs Dreamweaver to compare the dates of the saved files in both versions of the site, then transfers only copies of files that have changed. To synchronize files, use the Synchronize Files dialog box, shown in Figure 20. You can synchronize an entire site or only selected files. You can also specify whether to upload newer files to the remote site, download newer files from the remote site, or both.

Figure 20 *Synchronize Files dialog box*

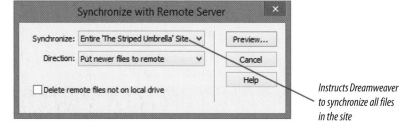

Instructs Dreamweaver to synchronize all files in the site

Understanding Dreamweaver Connection Options for Transferring Files

The connection types with which you are probably the most familiar are FTP and Local/Network. Other connection types that you can use with Dreamweaver include Microsoft Visual SafeSource (VSS), and WebDav. **WebDav** stands for Web-based Distributed Authoring and Versioning. This type of connection is used with the WebDav protocol. An example would be a website residing on an Apache web server. The **Apache web server** is a public domain, open source web server that is available using several different operating systems including UNIX and Windows. **RDS** stands for Remote Development Services, and is used with web servers using Cold Fusion.

Figure 21 *FTP settings specified in the Site Setup for The Striped Umbrella dialog box*

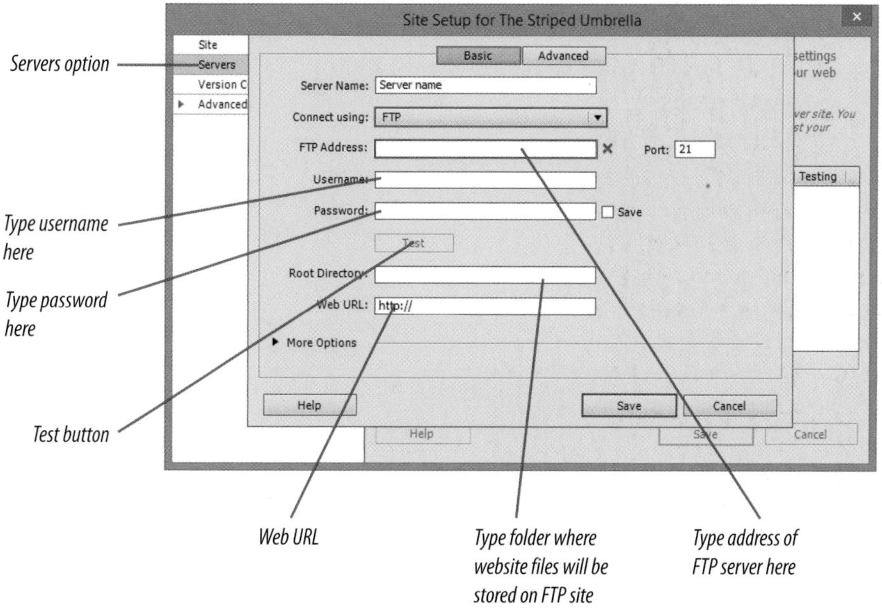

Servers option

Type username here

Type password here

Test button

Web URL — Type folder where website files will be stored on FTP site — Type address of FTP server here

Site Setup for The Striped Umbrella

- Site
- Servers
- Version C
- Advanced

Basic | Advanced

Server Name: Server name

Connect using: FTP

FTP Address: ___ ✕ Port: 21

Username: ___

Password: ___ ☐ Save

Test

Root Directory: ___

Web URL: http://

▶ More Options

Help | Save | Cancel

Testing

Comparing Two Files for Differences in Content

There are situations where it would be helpful to be able to compare the contents of two files, such as a local file and the remote version of the same file; or an original file and the same file that has been saved with a different name. Once the two files are compared and differences are detected, you can merge the information in the files. A good time to compare files is before you upload them to a remote server to prevent accidentally writing over a file with more recent information. To compare files, you must first locate and install a third-party file comparison utility, or "dif" tool, such as FileMerge or Beyond Compare. (Dreamweaver does not have a file comparison tool included as part of the software, so you need to download one.) If you are not familiar with these tools, find one using your favorite search engine.

After installing the file comparison utility, use the Preferences command on the Edit menu to open the Preferences dialog box, then select the File Compare category. Next, browse to select the application you want to use to compare files. After you have set your Preferences, select the Compare with Remote Server command on the File menu to compare an open file with the remote version.

Set up a web server connection on an FTP site

NOTE: Complete these steps only if you know you can store The Striped Umbrella files on an FTP site and you know the login and password information. If you do not have access to an FTP site, complete the exercise called Set up a web server connection to a local or network folder on Page 7-18.

1. Select **Site** on the Menu bar, then select **Manage Sites**.

2. Select **The Striped Umbrella** in the Manage Sites dialog box, if necessary, then select the **Edit currently selected site button** ✐.

3. Select **Servers** in the Site Setup dialog box, select the **Add new Server** button ➕, type your server name, select the **Connect using list arrow**, select **FTP** if necessary, then compare your screen to Figure 21.

4. Enter the FTP Address, Username, Password, Root Directory, and Web URL information in the dialog box.

TIP You must have file and folder permissions to use FTP. The server administrator can give you this and also tell you the folder name and location you should use to publish your files.

5. Select the **Test button** to test the connection to the remote site.

6. If the connection is successful, select **Save** to close the dialog box; if it is not successful, verify that you have the correct settings, then repeat Step 5.

7. Select **Save** to close the open dialog box, select **Save** to close the Site Setup dialog box, then select **Done** to close the Manage Sites dialog box.

You set up remote access information for The Striped Umbrella website using FTP settings.

Set up a web server connection to a local or network folder

NOTE: Complete these steps if you do not have the ability to post files to an FTP site and could not complete the previous set of steps.

1. Using File Explorer (Win) or Finder (Mac), create a new folder on your hard drive or on a shared drive named **su_yourlastname** (e.g., if your last name is Jones, name the folder **su_jones**).

2. Switch back to Dreamweaver, open The Striped Umbrella website, then open the Manage Sites dialog box.

3. Select **The Striped Umbrella**, if necessary, then select the **Edit the currently selected site button** to open the Site Setup for The Striped Umbrella dialog box.

TIP You can also double-click the site name in the Site Name box in the Files panel to open the Site Setup dialog box.

4. Select **Servers**, then select the **Add new Server button** .

5. Type **SU Remote** for the Server Name, select the **Connect using list arrow**, then select **Local/Network**.

6. Select the **Browse button** next to the Server Folder text box to open the Choose Folder dialog box, navigate to and double-click the folder you created in Step 1, then select **Select Folder** (Win) or **Choose** (Mac).

7. Compare your screen to Figure 22, select **Save**, select **Save** to close the Site Setup dialog box, then select **Done**.

You created a new folder and specified it as the remote location for The Striped Umbrella website, then set up remote access to a local or network folder.

Figure 22 *Local/Network settings in the Site Setup for The Striped Umbrella dialog box*

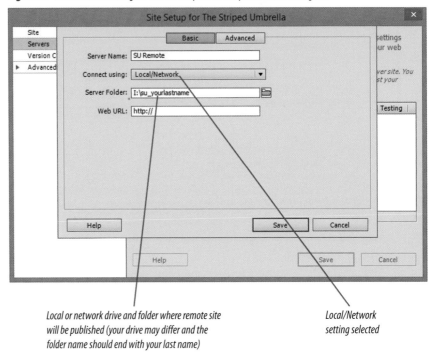

Local or network drive and folder where remote site will be published (your drive may differ and the folder name should end with your last name)

Local/Network setting selected

Testing Your Site's Usability

Once you have at least a prototype of the website ready to evaluate, it is a good idea to conduct a site usability test. This is a process that involves asking unbiased people, who are not connected to the design process, to use and evaluate the site. A comprehensive usability test includes pre-test questions, participant tasks, a post-test interview, and a post-test survey. This provides much-needed information as to how usable the site is to those unfamiliar with it. Typical questions include: "What are your overall impressions?"; "What do you like the best and the least about the site?"; and "How easy is it to navigate inside the site?" For more information, go to w3.org and search for "site usability test."

Figure 23 *Connecting to the remote server*

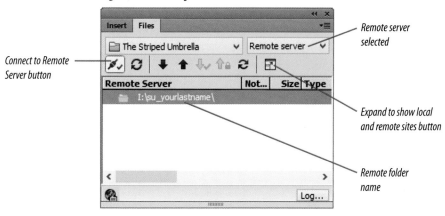

Connect to Remote
Server button

Remote server
selected

Expand to show local
and remote sites button

Remote folder
name

Figure 24 *Viewing the local and remote site folders*

Remote folder

Disconnect from
Remote Server button

Local site folder

Collapse to show only local
or remote site button

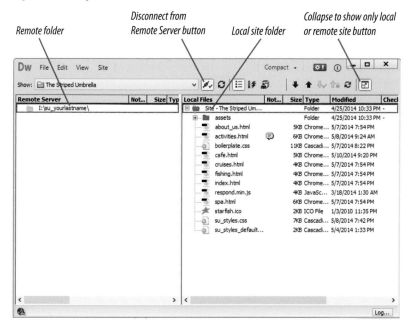

View a website on a remote server

1. Select the **View list arrow** in the Files panel, select **Remote server**, then compare your screen to Figure 23.

   If you set your remote access to be a local or network folder, then the su_yourlastname folder appears in the Files panel. If your remote access is set to an FTP site, Dreamweaver connects to the host server and displays the remote folders and file.

2. Select the **Expand to show local and remote sites button** on the Files panel to view both the Remote Server and Local Files panes. The su_yourlastname folder appears in the Remote Server portion of the expanded Files panel, as shown in Figure 24.

TIP If you don't see your remote site files, select the Connect to Remote Server butt0on or the Refresh button . If you don't see two panes, one with the remote site files and one with the local files, drag the panel border to enlarge the panel.

When the Files panel is expanded to show both the local and remote sites, the Expand to show local and remote sites button becomes the Collapse to show only local or remote site button. and the Connect to Remote Server button becomes the Disconnect from Remote Server button .

You used the Files panel to set the view for The Striped Umbrella site to Remote view. You then connected to the remote server to view the remote folder you created earlier.

Upload files to a remote server

1. Select the **about_us.html file**, then select the **Put file(s) to "Remote Server" button** 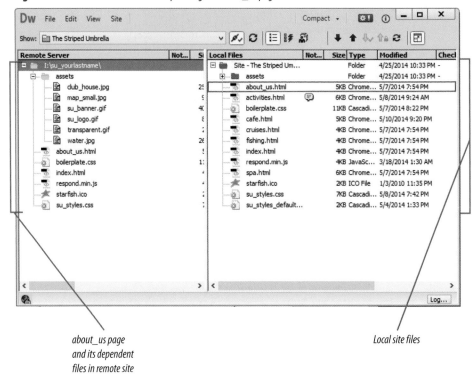 on the Files panel toolbar.

   Notice that the Put File(s) to "Remote Server" button screentip includes the name of the remote server you are using. The Dependent Files dialog box opens, asking if you want to include dependent files.

2. Select **Yes**.

   The about_us file, the style sheet files, and the image files used in the about_us page are copied to the remote server. The Background File Activity dialog box appears and flashes the names of each file as they are uploaded.

3. Expand the assets folder in the remote site if necessary, then compare your screen to Figure 25.

   The remote site now lists the additional files: the about_us page, the image files, and the external style sheet files, all of which are needed by the about_us page.

TIP You might need to expand the su_yourlastname folder in order to view the uploaded files and folders.

You used the Put File(s) button to upload the about_us file and all files that are dependent files of the about_us page.

Figure 25 *Remote view of the site after uploading the about_us page*

about_us page
and its dependent
files in remote site

Local site files

Continuing to Work While Transferring Files to a Remote Server

During the process of uploading files to a remote server, there are many Dreamweaver functions that you can continue to use while you wait. For example, you can create a new site, create a new page, edit a page, add files and folders, and run reports. However, there are some functions that you cannot use while transferring files, many of which involve accessing files on the remote server or using Check In/ Check Out.

Figure 26 *Synchronize with Remote Server dialog box*

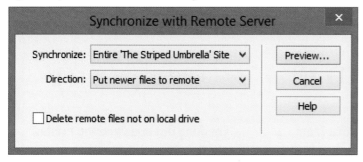

Figure 27 *Files that need to be uploaded to the remote site*

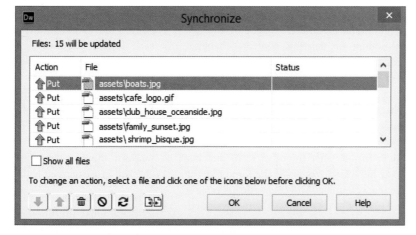

Uploading Files to the Creative Cloud

Another way to store your website files is to upload them to your Adobe Creative Cloud account. Recall from the Creative Cloud Guide at the beginning of this book that you are given 20GB of storage with your Creative Cloud account. Use this space to store archive copies of older versions of your website files and backup copies of your current website files. To upload files, open the Actions menu and create a new folder. Next, select the folder, select Actions, then select Upload. You will be prompted to browse to the files you want to upload. After locating your files, select them and the upload will begin.

Synchronize files

1. Select the **Collapse to show only local or remote site button** ⬚, change to Local view, then open each page in the website in Code view and locate any that are missing the link to the website favicon in the line above the code for the page title.

2. Open the index page, if necessary, then copy the code in the head content that links the favicon to the page.

3. Paste the favicon link to any pages you identified in Step 1, then save and close any open pages.

4. Select the **Synchronize button** ⟳ on the Files panel toolbar to open the Synchronize with Remote Server dialog box.

5. Select the **Synchronize list arrow**, then select **Entire 'The Striped Umbrella' Site**.

6. Select the **Direction list arrow**, select **Put newer files to remote** if necessary, then compare your screen to Figure 26.

7. Select **Preview**.

   The Background File Activity dialog box might appear and flash the names of all the files from the local version of the site that need to be uploaded to the remote site. The Synchronize dialog box, shown in Figure 27, opens and lists all the files that need to be uploaded to the remote site.

8. Select **OK**.

   All the files from the local The Striped Umbrella site are copied to the remote version of the site. If you expand the Files panel, you will notice that the remote folders are yellow (Win) or blue (Mac) and the local folders are gray.

You synchronized The Striped Umbrella website files to copy all remaining files from the local site folder to the remote site folder.

Check Files
OUT AND IN

What You'll Do

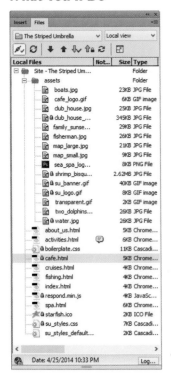

 In this lesson, you will use the Site Setup dialog box to enable the Check Out feature. You will then check out the cafe page, make a change to it, and then check it back in.

Managing a Website with a Team

When you work on a large website, chances are that many people will be involved in keeping the site up to date. Different individuals will need to make changes or additions to different pages of the site by adding or deleting content, changing graphics, updating information, and so on. If everyone had access to the pages at the same time, problems could arise. For instance, what if you and another team member both made edits to the same page at the same time? If you post your edited version of the file to the site after the other team member posts his edited version of the same file, the file that you upload will overwrite his version and none of his changes will be incorporated. Fortunately, you can avoid this scenario by using Dreamweaver's collaboration tools.

Checking Out and Checking In Files

Checking files in and out is similar to checking library books in and out. No one else can access the same copy that you have checked out. Using Dreamweaver's Check Out feature ensures that team members cannot overwrite each other's pages. When this feature is enabled, only one person can work on a file at a time. To check out a file, select the file you want to work on in the Files panel, and then select the Check Out File(s) button on the Files panel toolbar. Files that you have checked out are marked with green check marks in the Files panel. Files that have been checked in are marked with padlock icons.

After you finish editing a checked-out file, save and close the file, and then select the Check In button to check the file back in and make it available to other users. When a file is checked in, you cannot make edits to it unless you check it out again. Figure 28 shows the Check Out File(s) and Check In buttons on the Files panel toolbar. The two buttons appear grayed out because the Check Out feature was not enabled.

Enabling the Check Out Feature

To use the Check Out feature with a team of people, you must first enable it. To turn on this feature, check the Enable file check-out check box in the Remote Server section of the Servers Advanced tab in the Site Setup dialog box. If you do not want to use this feature, you should turn it off so you won't have to check files out every time you open them.

Using Subversion Control

Another file management tool is Subversion control. A remote SVN (Apache Subversion) repository is used to maintain current and historical versions of your website files. It is used in a team environment to move, copy, and delete shared files. You can protect files from being accessed using the svn:ignore property to create a list of files that are to be ignored in a directory.

Figure 28 *Check Out File(s) and Check In buttons on the Files Panel toolbar*

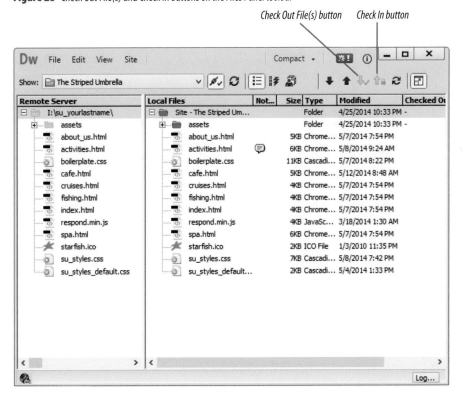

Check Out File(s) button   Check In button

Activate the Enable file check-out feature

1. Change to expanded view in the Files panel, select **Site** on the Menu bar, select **Manage Sites** to open the Manage Sites dialog box, select **The Striped Umbrella** in the list if necessary, then select the **Edit the currently selected site button** to open the Site Setup for The Striped Umbrella dialog box.

2. Select **Servers**, select your remote server, select the **Edit existing Server button**, select the **Advanced tab**, then select the **Enable file check-out check box**.

3. Check the **Check out files when opening check box**, if necessary.

4. Type your name in the Check-out Name text box.

5. Type your email address in the Email Address text box.

6. Compare your screen to Figure 29, select **Save** to close the open dialog box, select **Save** to close the Site Setup for The Striped Umbrella dialog box, then select **Done** to close the Manage Sites dialog box.

You used the Site Definition for The Striped Umbrella dialog box to enable the Check Out feature, which tells team members when you are working with a site file.

Figure 29 *Enabling the Check Out feature*

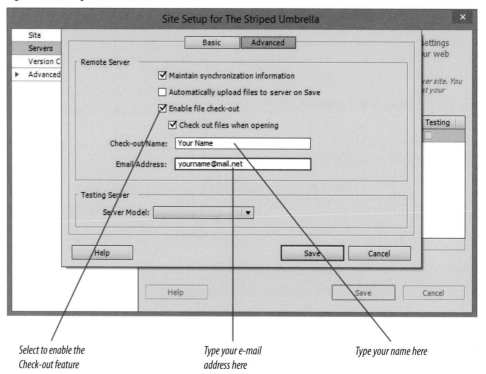

Select to enable the Check-out feature

Type your e-mail address here

Type your name here

Figure 30 *Files panel in Local view after checking out cafe page*

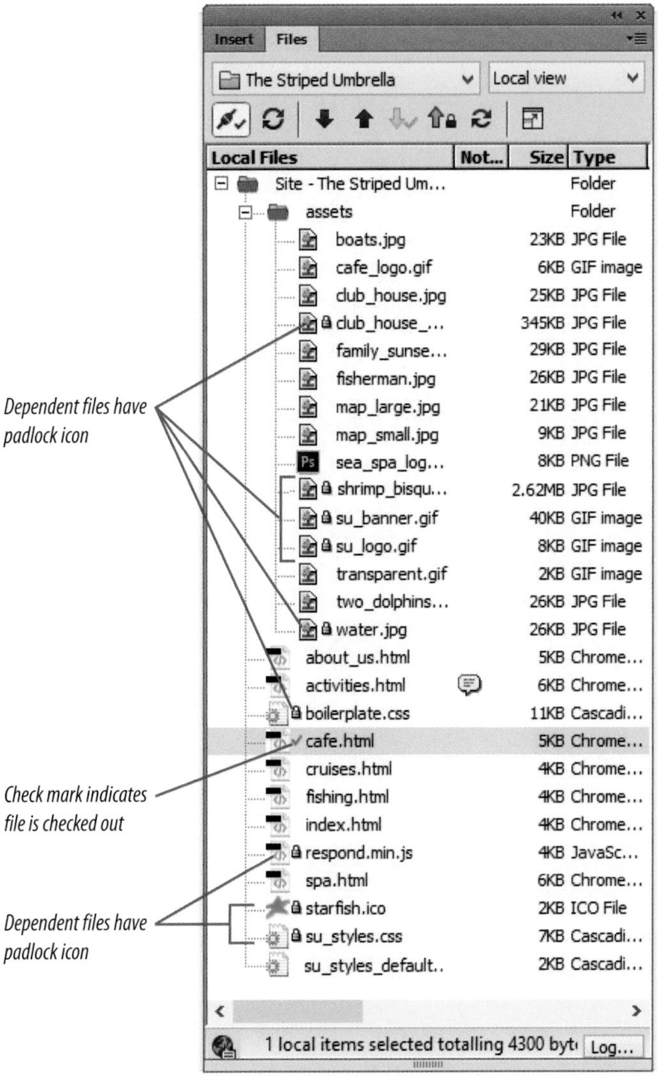

Dependent files have padlock icon

Check mark indicates file is checked out

Dependent files have padlock icon

Check out a file

1. Select the **cafe page** in the Local Files list in the Files panel.

2. Select the **Check Out File(s) button** on the Files panel toolbar.

   The Dependent Files dialog box appears, asking if you want to include all files that are needed for the cafe page.

3. Select **Yes**, expand the assets folder if necessary in the local site files, select the **Collapse to show only local or remote site button**, select the **View list arrow**, select **Local view** if necessary, then compare your screen to Figure 30.

   The cafe file has a check mark next to it indicating you have checked it out. The dependent files have a padlock icon, indicating that they cannot be changed as long as the cafe file is checked out.

You checked out the cafe page so that no one else can use it while you work on it.

Check in a file

1. Open the cafe page, change the closing hour for The Cabana in the table to **8:00 p.m.**, then save your changes.

2. Close the cafe page, then select the **cafe page** in the Files panel.

3. Select the **Check In button** 🔒 on the Files panel toolbar.

   The Dependent Files dialog box opens, asking if you want to include dependent files.

4. Select **Yes**, select another file in the Files panel to deselect the cafe page, then compare your screen to Figure 31.

   A padlock icon appears instead of a green check mark next to the cafe page on the Files panel. The padlock icon indicated that the file is read-only now and cannot be edited unless it is checked out.

You made a content change on the cafe page, then checked in the cafe page, making it available for others to check it out.

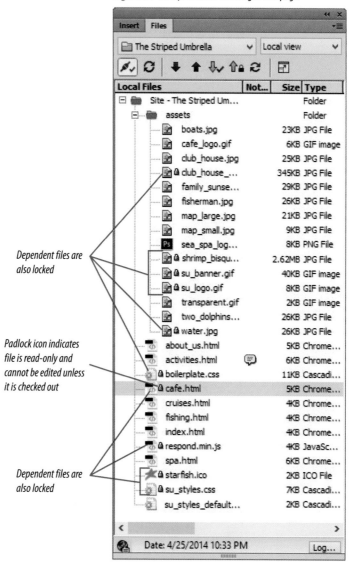

Figure 31 *Files panel after checking in cafe page*

Dependent files are also locked

Padlock icon indicates file is read-only and cannot be edited unless it is checked out

Dependent files are also locked

Figure 32 *Files panel after turning off the read-only feature*

Files panel showing:

Local Files	Not...	Size	Type
Site - The Striped Um...			Folder
assets			Folder
boats.jpg		23KB	JPG File
cafe_logo.gif		6KB	GIF image
club_house.jpg		25KB	JPG File
club_house_...		345KB	JPG File
family_sunse...		29KB	JPG File
fisherman.jpg		26KB	JPG File
map_large.jpg		21KB	JPG File
map_small.jpg		9KB	JPG File
sea_spa_log...		8KB	PNG File
shrimp_bisqu...		2.62MB	JPG File
su_banner.gif		40KB	GIF image
su_logo.gif		8KB	GIF image
transparent.gif		2KB	GIF image
two_dolphins...		26KB	JPG File
water.jpg		26KB	JPG File
about_us.html		5KB	Chrome...
activities.html		6KB	Chrome...
boilerplate.css		11KB	Cascadi...
cafe.html		5KB	Chrome...
cruises.html		4KB	Chrome...
fishing.html		4KB	Chrome...
index.html		4KB	Chrome...
respond.min.js		4KB	JavaSc...
spa.html		6KB	Chrome...
starfish.ico		2KB	ICO File
su_styles.css		7KB	Cascadi...
su_styles_default...		2KB	Cascadi...

All files are now unlocked

Edit site preferences

1. Select **Site** on the Menu bar, select **Manage Sites** to open the Manage Sites dialog box, select **The Striped Umbrella** in the list, then select the **Edit the currently selected site button** ✐ to open the Site Setup for The Striped Umbrella dialog box.

2. Select **Servers**, select your remote server, select the **Edit existing Server button** ✐ , select the **Advanced tab**, then deselect the **Enable file check-out check box**.

   Now that you understand how to use this feature, it will be easier to have this option turned off so that each time you open a page you will not have to check it out the next time you use it.

3. Select **Save** to close the open dialog box, select **Save** to close the Site Setup dialog box, then select **Done** to close the Manage Sites dialog box.

4. Right-click the **local site folder** in the Files panel, then select **Turn off Read Only** (Win) or **Unlock** (Mac).

   All files are writeable now and the padlock icons have disappeared, as shown in Figure 32.

You disabled the Enable file check-out feature and then turned off the Read-only feature for all site files.

Cloak
FILES

What You'll Do

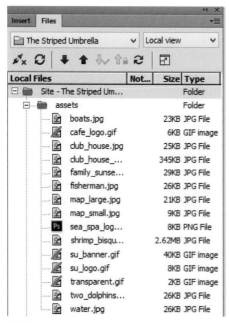

 In this lesson, you will cloak the assets folder so that it is excluded from various operations, such as the Put, Get, Check In, and Check Out commands. You will also use the Site Setup dialog box to cloak all .gif files in the site.

Understanding Cloaking Files

There may be times when you want to exclude a particular file or files from being uploaded to a server. For instance, suppose you have a page that is not quite finished and needs more work before it is ready to be viewed by others. You can exclude such files by **cloaking** them, which marks them for exclusion from several commands, including Put, Get, Synchronize, Check In, and Check Out. Cloaked files are also excluded from site-wide operations, such as checking for links or updating a template or library item. You can cloak a folder or specify a type of file to cloak throughout the site.

QUICK TIP

By default, the cloaking feature is enabled. However, if for some reason it is not turned on, open the Site Setup dialog box, select Advanced Settings, select Cloaking, then select the Enable Cloaking check box.

Cloaking a Folder

In addition to cloaking a file or group of files, you might also want to cloak an entire folder. For example, if you are not concerned with replacing outdated image files, you might want to cloak the assets folder of a website to save time when synchronizing files. To cloak a folder, select the folder, select the Files panel Options button, point to Site, point to Cloaking, and then select Cloak. The folder you cloaked and all the files it contains appear with red slashes across them, as shown in Figure 33. To uncloak a folder, select the Panel options button on the Files panel, point to Site, point to Cloaking, and then select Uncloak.

QUICK TIP

To uncloak all files in a site, select the Files Panel options button, point to Site, point to Cloaking, then select Uncloak All.

Cloaking Selected File Types

There may be times when you want to cloak a particular type of file, such as a JPG file.

To cloak a particular file type, open the Site Setup dialog box, select Advanced Settings, select Cloaking, select the Cloak files ending with check box, and then type a file extension in the text box below the check box. All files throughout the site that have the specified file extension will be cloaked.

Figure 33 *Cloaked assets folder in the Files panel*

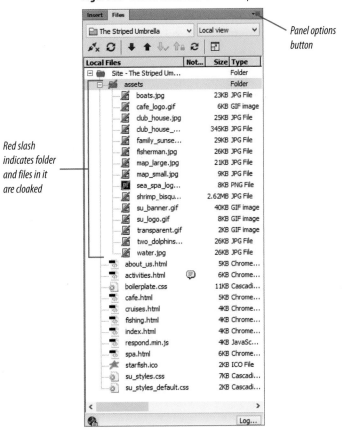

Panel options button

Red slash indicates folder and files in it are cloaked

Cloak and uncloak a folder

1. Verify that Local view is displayed in the Files panel, then open the Manage Sites dialog box.

2. Select **The Striped Umbrella** if necessary, select the **Edit the currently selected site button** 🖉 to open the Site Setup for The Striped Umbrella dialog box, select **Advanced Settings**, select **Cloaking**, verify that the Enable Cloaking check box is checked, select **Save**, then select **Done**.

3. Expand and select the **assets folder** in the Files panel, select the **Files Panel options button** 📝, point to **Site**, point to **Cloaking**, select **Cloak**, then compare your screen to Figure 34.

   A red slash now appears on top of the assets folder in the Files panel, indicating that all files in the assets folder are cloaked and will be excluded from putting, getting, checking in, checking out, and many other operations.

   TIP You can also cloak a folder by right-clicking (Win) or [control]-clicking (Mac) the folder, pointing to Cloaking, then selecting Cloak.

4. Right-click (Win) or [control]-click (Mac) the **assets folder**, point to **Cloaking**, then select **Uncloak**.

   The assets folder and all the files it contains no longer appear with red slashes across them, indicating they are no longer cloaked.

   You cloaked the assets folder so that this folder and all the files it contains would be excluded from many operations, including uploading and downloading files. You then uncloaked the assets folder.

Figure 34 *Assets folder after cloaking*

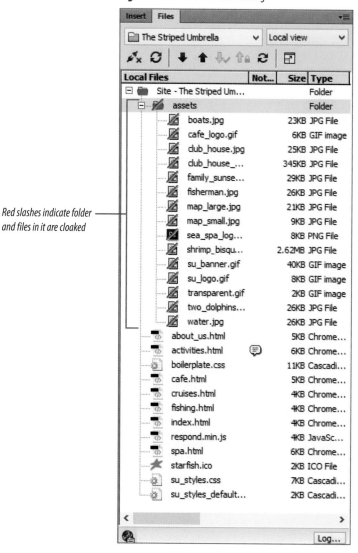

Red slashes indicate folder and files in it are cloaked

Managing a Web Server and Files

Figure 35 *Specifying a file type to cloak*

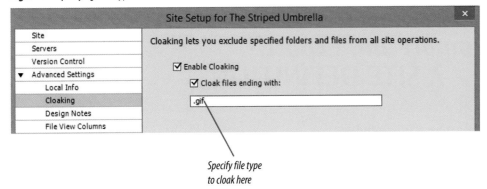

Specify file type
to cloak here

Figure 36 *assets folder in Files panel after cloaking .gif files*

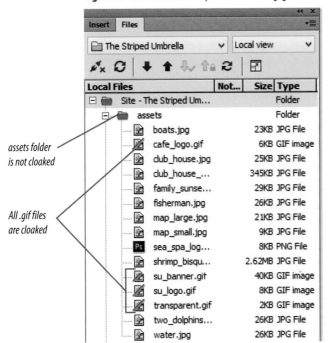

assets folder
is not cloaked

All .gif files
are cloaked

Cloak selected file types

1. Right-click (Win) or [control]-click (Mac) the **assets folder** in the Files panel, point to **Cloaking**, then select **Settings** to open the Site Setup for The Striped Umbrella dialog box with the Cloaking category selected.

2. Select the **Cloak files ending with check box**, select the text in the text box that appears, type **.gif** in the text box, then compare your screen to Figure 35.

3. Select **Save**.

   A dialog box opens, indicating that the site cache will be recreated.

4. Select **OK**, expand the assets folder if necessary, then compare your screen to Figure 36.

   All of the .gif files in the assets folder appear with red slashes across them, indicating that they are cloaked. Notice that the assets folder is not cloaked.

5. Select the **local site folder** in the Files panel, right-click, point to **Cloaking**, select **Uncloak All**, then select **Yes** to close the warning message.

   All files are uncloaked now and will not be excluded from any site commands.

You cloaked all the .gif files in The Striped Umbrella website. You then uncloaked all files.

Import and Export
A SITE DEFINITION

What You'll Do

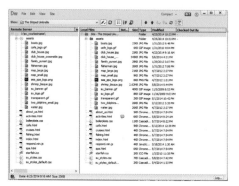

In this lesson, you will export the site definition file for The Striped Umbrella website. You will then import The Striped Umbrella website.

Exporting a Site Definition

When you work on a website for a long time, it's likely that at some point you will want to move it to another machine or share it with other collaborators who will help you maintain it. When you move a site, you need to move its site definition. The **site definition** for a website contains important information about the site, including its URL, preferences that you've specified, and other secure information, such as login and password information. You can use the Export command to export the site definition file to another location. The Export command creates a file with an .ste file extension. To do this, open the Manage Sites dialog box, select the site you want to export, and then select Export currently selected site. Because the site definition file contains password information that you will want to keep secret from other site users, you should never save the site definition file in the website. Instead, save it in an external folder.

Importing a Site Definition

If you want to be able to access the site settings in a website that someone else has created, you can import the site definition file once you have the necessary .ste file. To do this, select Import Site in the Manage Sites dialog box to open the Import Site dialog box, navigate to the .ste file you want to import, then select Open.

Figure 37 *Saving The Striped Umbrella.ste file in the su_site_definition folder*

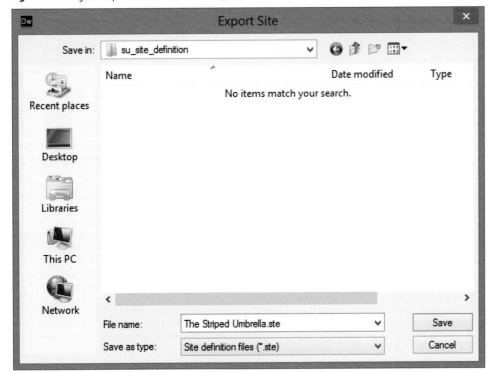

Export a site definition

1. Use File Explorer (Win) or Finder (Mac) to create a new folder on your hard drive or external drive named **su_site_definition**.

2. Switch back to Dreamweaver, open the Manage Sites dialog box, select **The Striped Umbrella**, then select the **Export the currently selected site(s) button** ⬏ to open the Export Site dialog box.

   TIP If you see a message asking if you are exporting the site to back up your settings or to share your settings with other users, choose the Back up my settings option, then select OK.

3. Navigate to and double-click to open the **su_site_definition folder** that you created in Step 1, as shown in Figure 37, select **Save**, then select **Done**.

You used the Export command to create the site definition file and saved it in the su_site_definition folder.

Import a site definition

1. Open the Manage Sites dialog box, select **The Striped Umbrella**, then select **Import Site** to open the Import Site dialog box.

2. Navigate to the su_site_definition folder, compare your screen to Figure 38, select **The Striped Umbrella.ste**, then select **Open**.

   A dialog box opens and says that a site named The Striped Umbrella already exists. It will name the imported site The Striped Umbrella 2 so that it has a different name.

3. Select **OK**.

4. Select **The Striped Umbrella 2** if necessary, select the **Edit the currently selected site(s) button** 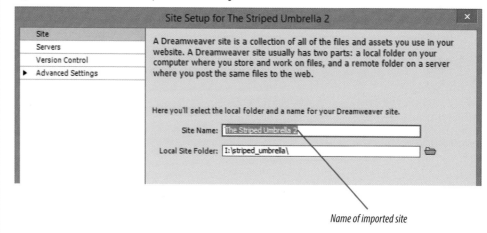, then compare your screen to Figure 39.

   The settings show that The Striped Umbrella 2 site has the same local site folder and default images folder as The Striped Umbrella site. Both of these settings are specified in The Striped Umbrella.ste file that you imported. Importing a site in this way makes it possible for multiple users with different computers to work on the same site.

   TIP Make sure you know who is responsible for which files to keep from overwriting the wrong files when they are published. The Synchronize Files and Check In/Check Out features are good procedures to use with multiple designers.

5. Select **Save**, select **OK** to close the warning message, then select **Done**.

   TIP If a dialog box opens warning that the local site folder chosen is the same as the folder for the site "The Striped Umbrella," select OK. Remember that you only import the site settings when you import a site definition. You are not importing any of the website files.

You imported The Striped Umbrella.ste file and created a new site, The Striped Umbrella 2.

Figure 38 *Import Site dialog box*

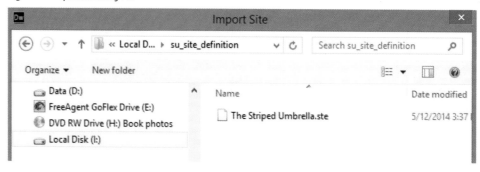

Figure 39 *Site Definition for The Striped Umbrella 2 dialog box*

Name of imported site

Figure 40 *Viewing The Striped Umbrella 2 website files*

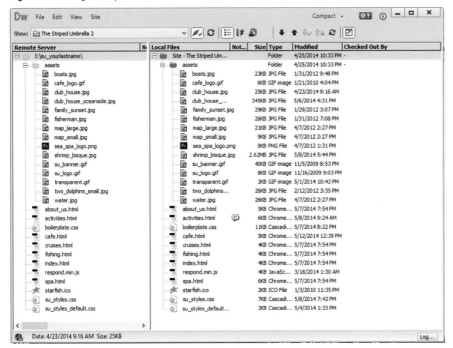

POWER USER SHORTCUTS	
To do this:	**Use this shortcut:**
Get	[Ctrl][Shift][D] (Win) or ⌘ [Shift][D] (Mac)
Check Out	[Ctrl][Alt][Shift][D] (Win) or ⌘ [opt] [Shift][D] (Mac)
Put	[Ctrl][Shift][U] (Win) or ⌘ [Shift][U] (Mac)
Check In	[Ctrl][Alt][Shift][U] (Win) or ⌘ [opt][Shift][U] (Mac)
Check Links Sitewide	[Ctrl][F8] (Win) or [fn] ⌘ [F8] (Mac)

View the imported site

1. Select the **Expand to show local and remote sites button** on the Files panel toolbar to expand the Files panel.

2. Select the **Refresh button** to view the files in the Remote Site pane.

   As shown in Figure 40, the site is identical to the original The Striped Umbrella site, except the name has been changed to The Striped Umbrella 2.

3. Expand the local site folder in the Local Files pane to view the contents, if necessary.

   TIP If you don't see your remote site files, select the Connect to Remote Server button.

4. Select the **Collapse to show only local or remote site button** to collapse the Files panel.

5. Open the Manage Sites dialog box, verify that The Striped Umbrella 2 site is selected, select the **Delete the currently selected site(s) button** ﹘, select **Yes** in the warning dialog box, then select **Done** to close the dialog box.

   This does not delete all of the files that were created; it only removes the site from Dreamweaver's site management list.

6. Close all open pages, then close Dreamweaver.

You viewed the expanded Files panel for The Striped Umbrella 2 website, then deleted The Striped Umbrella 2 website.

Evaluate Web Content FOR LEGAL USE

What You'll Do

Source: Library of Congress

In this lesson, you will examine copyright issues in the context of using content gathered from sources such as the Internet.

Can I Use Downloaded Media?

The Internet has made it possible to locate compelling and media-rich content to use in websites. A person who has learned to craft searches can locate a multitude of interesting objects, such as graphics, animations, sounds, and text. But just because you can find it easily does not mean that you can use it however you want or under any circumstance. Learning about copyright law can help you decide whether or how to use content created and published by someone other than yourself.

Understanding Intellectual Property

Intellectual property is a product resulting from human creativity. It can include inventions, movies, songs, designs, clothing, and so on.

The purpose of copyright law is to promote progress in society, not expressly to protect the rights of copyright owners. However, the vast majority of work you might want to download and use in a project is protected by either copyright or trademark law.

Copyright protects the particular and tangible *expression* of an idea, not the idea itself.

If you wrote a story using the idea of aliens crashing in Roswell, New Mexico, no one could copy or use your story without permission. However, anyone could write a story using a similar plot or characters— the *idea* of aliens crashing in Roswell is not copyright-protected. Generally, copyright lasts for the life of the author plus 70 years.

Trademark protects an image, word, slogan, symbol, or design used to identify goods or services. For example, the Nike swoosh, Disney characters, or the shape of a classic Coca-Cola bottle are works protected by trademark. Trademark protection lasts for 10 years with 10-year renewal terms, lasting indefinitely provided the trademark is in active use.

What Exactly Does the Copyright Owner Own?

Copyright attaches to a work as soon as you create it; you do not have to register it with the U.S. Copyright Office. A copyright owner has a "bundle" of six rights, consisting of:

1) reproduction (including downloading)
2) creation of **derivative works** (for example, a movie version of a book)
3) distribution to the public

4) public performance
5) public display
6) public performance by digital audio transmission of sound recordings

By default, only a copyright holder can create a derivative work of his or her original by transforming or adapting it.

Understanding Fair Use

The law builds in limitations to copyright protection. One limitation to copyright is **fair use**. Fair use allows limited use of copyright-protected work. For example, you could excerpt short passages of a film or song for a class project or parody a television show. Determining if fair use applies to a work depends on the *purpose* of its use, the *nature* of the copyrighted work, *how much* you want to copy, and the *effect* on the market or value of the work. However, there is no clear formula on what constitutes fair use. It is always decided on a case-by-case basis.

How Do I Use Work Properly?

Being a student doesn't mean you can use any amount of any work for class. On the other hand, the very nature of education means you need to be able to use or reference different work in your studies. There are many situations that allow you to use protected work.

In addition to applying a fair use argument, you can obtain permission, pay a fee, use work that does not have copyright protection, or use work that has a flexible copyright

license, where the owner has given the public permission to use the work in certain ways. For more information about open-access licensing, visit creativecommons.org. Work that is no longer protected by copyright is in the **public domain**; anyone can use it however they wish for any purpose. In general, the photos and other media on Federal government websites are in the public domain.

Understanding Licensing Agreements

Before you decide whether to use media you find on a website, you must decide whether you can comply with its licensing agreement. A **licensing agreement** is the permission given by a copyright holder that conveys the right to use the copyright holder's work under certain conditions.

Websites have rules that govern how a user may use its text and media, known as **terms of use**. Figures 41, 42, and 43 are great examples of clear terms of use for the Library of Congress website.

A site's terms of use do not override your right to apply fair use. Also, someone cannot compile public domain images in a website and then claim they own them or dictate how

Figure 41 *Library of Congress home page*

Link to legal information regarding the use of content on the website

Source: Library of Congress

the images can be used. Conversely, someone can erroneously state in their terms of use that you can use work on the site freely, but they may not know the work's copyright status. The burden is on you to research the veracity of anyone claiming you can use work.

Obtaining Permission or a License

The **permissions process** is specific to what you want to use (text, photographs, music, trademarks, merchandise, and so on) and how you want to use it (school term paper, personal website, fabric pattern). How you want to use the work determines the level and scope of permissions you need to secure. The fundamentals, however, are the same. Your request should contain the following:

- Your full name, address, and complete contact information.
- A specific description of your intended use. Sometimes including a sketch, storyboard, wireframe, or link to a website is helpful.
- A signature line for the copyright holder.
- A target date when you would like the copyright holder to respond. This can be important if you're working under deadline.

Posting a Copyright Notice

The familiar © symbol or "Copyright" is no longer required to indicate copyright, nor does it automatically register your work, but it does serve a useful purpose. When you post or publish it, you are stating clearly to those who may not know anything about copyright law that this work is claimed by you and is not in the public domain. Your case is made even stronger if someone violates your copyright

Figure 42 *Library of Congress website legal page*

Source: Library of Congress

and your notice is clearly visible. That way, a violator can never claim ignorance of the law as an excuse for infringing. Common notification styles include:

Copyright 2015
Cengage Learning
or
© 2015 Cengage Learning®

Giving proper attribution for text excerpts is a must; giving attribution for media is excellent practice, but is never a substitute for applying a fair use argument, buying a license, or simply getting permission.

You must provide proper citation for materials you incorporate into your own work, such as the following:

References

Waxer, Barbara M., and Baum, Marsha L. 2006. *Internet Surf and Turf—The Essential Guide to Copyright, Fair Use, and Finding Media.* Boston: Thomson Course Technology.

This expectation applies even to unsigned material and material that does not display the copyright symbol (©). Moreover, the expectation applies just as certainly to ideas you summarize or paraphrase as to words you quote verbatim.

Guidelines have been written by the American Psychological Association (APA) to establish an editorial style to be used to present written material. These guidelines include the way citations are referenced. Here's a list of the elements that make up an APA-style citation of web-based resources:

- Author's name (if known)
- Date of publication or last revision (if known), in parentheses
- Title of document
- Title of complete work or website (if applicable), underlined
- URL

Following is an example of how you would reference the APA Style Home page on the Reference page of your paper:

APA Style.org., from APA Online website, Retrieved from http://www.apastyle.org/index.aspx.

There are APA styles that are used for other sources of text such as magazines, journals, newspaper articles, blogs, and email messages. Here's a list of the elements that make up an APA-style citation of images, sounds, or video:

- Name of the researching organization
- Date of publication
- Caption or description
- Brief explanation of what type of data is there and in what form it appears (shown in brackets)
- Project name and retrieval information.

Another set of guidelines used by many schools and university and commercial presses is the Modern Language Association (MLA) style. For more information, go to mla.org.

Figure 43 *Library of Congress website copyright information*

About Copyright and the Collections

Whenever possible, the Library of Congress provides factual information about copyright owners and related matters in the catalog records, finding aids and other texts that accompany collections. As a publicly supported institution, the Library generally does not own rights in its collections. Therefore, it does not charge permission fees for use of such material and generally does not grant or deny permission to publish or otherwise distribute material in its collections. Permission and possible fees may be required from the copyright owner independently of the Library. It is the researcher's obligation to determine and satisfy copyright or other use restrictions when publishing or otherwise distributing materials found in the Library's collections. Transmission or reproduction of protected items beyond that allowed by fair use requires the written permission of the copyright owners. Researchers must make their own assessments of rights in light of their intended use.

If you have any more information about an item you've seen on our website or if you are the copyright owner and believe our website has not properly attributed your work to you or has used it without permission, we want to hear from you. Please contact OGC@loc.gov with your contact information and a link to the relevant content.

View more information about copyright law from the U.S. Copyright Office

Source: Library of Congress

Present a
WEBSITE TO A CLIENT

What You'll Do

Source: WireframeSketcher

In this lesson, you will explore options for presenting a website to a client at the completion of a project.

Are You Ready to Present Your Work?

Before you present a website to a client as a finished project, you should do a final check on some important items. First, do all your final design and development decisions reflect your client's goals and requirements? Does the website not only fulfill your client's goals and requirements, but those of the intended audience as well? Second, did you follow good web development practices? Did you check your pages against your wireframes as you developed them? Did you check each page against current accessibility standards? Did you run all necessary technical tests, such as validating the code, and searching for missing alternate text or missing page titles? Did you verify that all external and internal links work correctly? Third, did your final delivery date and budget meet the timeframe and budget you originally promised the client?

If you find that you did spend more time on the site than you expected to, determine if it was because you underestimated the amount of work it would take, ran into unforeseen technical problems, or because the client changed the requirements or increased the scope of the project as it went

along. If you underestimated the project or ran into unexpected difficulties from causes other than the client, you usually cannot expect the client to make up the difference without a prior agreement. No client wants surprises at the end of a project, so it's best to communicate frequently and let the client know the status of all site elements as you go.

If the client changes the project scope, make sure you discuss the implication of this with the client. Ideally, you have made the client aware of any schedule or budget changes at the time they began to occur, and the client expects that your estimate will grow by a predictable, agreed-upon amount.

Client communication, both at the beginning of a project and throughout a project, is critical to a successful web design and a solid customer relationship. In building a house, a good architect makes an effort to get to know and understand a new client before beginning a house design. The design must be functional and meet the client's checklist of requirements, but it must also fit the client's personality and taste. The final structure must continue to meet those needs; the same is true of a website.

Some clients have a difficult time looking at architectural drawings and visualizing what the home will look like, so architects use different methods to communicate their design. Some use scale mockups, 3-D renderings, or photos of similarly styled homes to help the client visualize what their home will look like when completed. Web designers use similar strategies. You may be capable of building a great website, but you must communicate with the client from the beginning of the project to set and satisfy client expectations. Without this mutual understanding, the project's successful completion will be at risk. It is much less expensive to make changes and adjustments at the beginning of a project, and as changes occur, rather than close to completion. Communication is key.

What Is the Best Way to Present Your Work?

Ideally, you presented some form of prototype of the website at the beginning of the development process. You may have chosen to use low-fidelity wireframes such as one created in Microsoft PowerPoint or Adobe Photoshop. Or you may have used a high-fidelity wireframe that is interactive and multidimensional such as OverSight, ProtoShare, or WireframeSketcher, as shown in Figure 44. To communicate with your client and ensure a mutual understanding of the project, you could also use **BaseCamp**, a web-based project collaboration tool that many companies use. There is a monthly fee

for using it, based on the number of projects you are running and your storage needs. You can use BaseCamp throughout the project cycle, not just at the end. To present the final project, consider publishing the site to a server and sending the client a link to view the completed website. Creating PDFs of the site and sending them to the client for approval is another possible method.

Another communication option is to invite the client to your office and do a full walkthrough of the site with them, which offers them a chance to ask questions. This is probably one of the best options if it is feasible. If you have taken the time to build a relationship of trust over the project, neither side should expect unpleasant surprises at the end.

Figure 44 *WireframeSketcher website*

Source: WireframeSketcher

Perform website maintenance.

1. Open the Blooms & Bulbs website, then re-create the site cache.
2. Use the Link Checker panel to check for broken links, then fix any broken links that appear.
3. Use the Link Checker to check for orphaned files. If any orphaned files appear in the report, take steps to link them to appropriate pages or decide if you need to remove them.
4. Run an Untitled Documents report for the entire local site. If the report lists any pages that have no titles, add page titles to the untitled pages, and edit any titles if they seem incomplete. Run the report again to verify that all pages have page titles.
5. Run a report to look for missing alternate text. Add alternate text to any graphics that need it, then run the report again to verify that all images contain alternate text.
6. Submit the bb_styles.css file for CSS3 validation and correct any errors that are found.
7. Validate the workshops page for HTML5 markup and correct any errors that are found.
8. Verify that the Design Notes preference is enabled and add a Design Note to the workshops page as follows: **Shoot a video of the hanging baskets class to add to the page**. Add the status **needs attention**, add the current date, and check the Show when file is opened option.

Publish a website and transfer files.

1. Set up web server access for the Blooms & Bulbs website on an FTP server or a local/network server (whichever is available to you) using **blooms_yourlastname** as the remote folder name.
2. View the Blooms & Bulbs remote site in the Files panel.
3. Upload the water_lily.jpg file to the remote site, then view the remote site.
4. Add the code that links the favicon to the head content of any pages in the site that do not have it.
5. Synchronize all files in the Blooms & Bulbs website, so that all files from the local site are uploaded to the remote site.

Check files out and in.

1. Enable the Enable file check-out feature.
2. Check out the plants page and all dependent pages.
3. Open the plants page, change the heading to **"Featured Spring Plants: Roses, Roses, Roses!"**, then save the file.
4. Check in the plants page and all dependent files.
5. Disable the Enable file check-out feature.
6. Turn off Read Only (Win) or Unlock (Mac) for the entire site.

Cloak files.

1. Verify that cloaking is enabled in the Blooms & Bulbs website.
2. Cloak the assets folder, then uncloak it.
3. Cloak all the JPG files in the Blooms & Bulbs website, then expand the assets folder if necessary to view the cloaked files in the Files panel.
4. Uncloak the JPG files.

Import and export a site definition.

1. Create a new folder named **blooms_site_definition** on your hard drive or external drive.
2. Export the Blooms & Bulbs site definition to the blooms_site_definition folder.
3. Import the Blooms & Bulbs site definition to create a new site called **Blooms & Bulbs 2**.
4. Make sure that all files from the Blooms & Bulbs website appear in the Files panel for the imported site, then compare your screen to Figure 45.
5. Remove the Blooms & Bulbs 2 site.
6. Close all open files.

Figure 45 *Completed Skills Review*

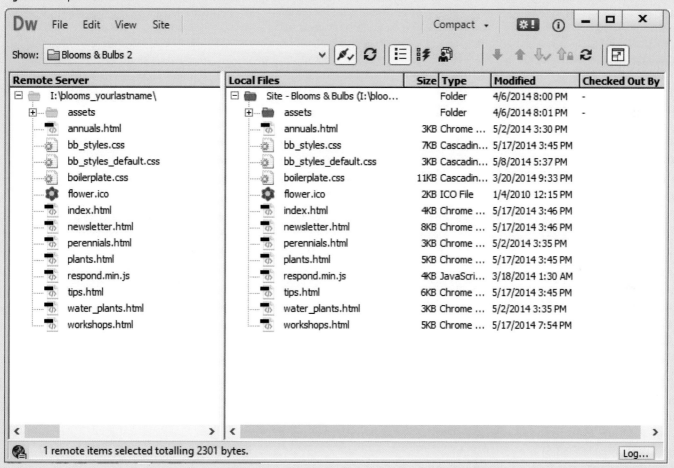

In this Project Builder, you publish the TripSmart website that you have developed throughout this book to a local/network folder. Thomas Howard, the owner, has asked that you publish the site to a local folder as a backup location. You first run several reports on the site, specify the remote settings for the site, upload files to the remote site, check files out and in, and cloak files. Finally, you export and import the site definition.

1. Use the TripSmart website that you began in Project Builder 1 in Chapter 1 and developed in previous chapters.
2. Use the Link Checker panel to check for broken links, then fix any broken links that appear.
3. Use the Link Checker to check for orphaned files. If any orphaned files appear in the report, take steps to link them to appropriate pages or remove them.
4. Evaluate your colors in your site. Do they work together to create an attractive design?
5. Run an Untitled Documents report for the entire local site. If the report lists any pages that lack titles, add page titles to the untitled pages. Run the report again to verify that all pages have page titles.
6. Run a report to look for missing alternate text. Add alternate text to any graphics that need it, then run the report again to verify that all images contain alternate text.
7. Submit the tripsmart_styles.css file for CSS3 validation and correct any errors that are found.
8. Validate the catalog page for HTML5 markup and correct any errors that are found.

9. Enable the Design Notes preference, if necessary, and add a design note to the Argentina page as follows: **Add a video of the glacier in Patagonia.** Add the current date, the status **needs attention** and check the Show when file is opened option. Turn on the Show Notes feature in the Files View Columns dialog box.
10. If you did not do so in Project Builder 1 in Chapter 1, use the Site Definition dialog box to set up web server access for a remote site using a local or network folder.
11. Upload the index page and all dependent files to the remote site.
12. View the remote site to make sure that all files uploaded correctly.
13. Add the code that links the favicon to the head content of any pages in the site that do not have it.
14. Synchronize the files so that all other files on the local TripSmart site are uploaded to the remote site.

15. Enable the Enable file check-out feature.
16. Check out the index page in the local site and all dependent files.
17. Open the index page, close the index page, then check in the index page and all dependent pages.
18. Disable the Enable file check-out feature, then turn off the read-only status (Win) or unlock (Mac) for the entire site.
19. Cloak all JPG files in the website.
20. Export the site definition to a new folder named **tripsmart_site_definition**.
21. Import the TripSmart.ste file to create a new site named TripSmart 2.
22. Expand the assets folder in the Files panel if necessary, then compare your screen to Figure 46.
23. Remove the TripSmart 2 site.
24. Uncloak all files in the TripSmart site, then close any open files.

Figure 46 *Sample completed Project Builder 1*

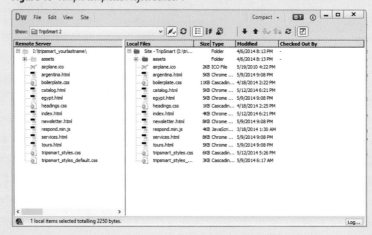

In this Project Builder, you finish your work on the Carolyne's Creations website. You are ready to publish the website to a remote server and transfer all the files from the local site to the remote site. First, you run several reports to make sure the website is in good shape. Next, you enable the Enable file check-out feature so that other staff members may collaborate on the site. Finally, you export and import the site definition file.

1. Use the Carolyne's Creations website that you began in Project Builder 1 in Chapter 1 and developed in previous chapters.
2. If you did not do so in Project Builder 2 in Chapter 1, use the Site Definition dialog box to set up web server access for a remote site using either an FTP site or a local or network folder.
3. Run reports for broken links and orphaned files, correcting any errors that you find.
4. Run reports for untitled documents and missing alt text, correcting any errors that you find.
5. Submit the cc_styles.css file for CSS3 validation and correct any errors that are found.
6. Validate the catering page for HTML5 markup and correct any errors that are found.
7. Upload the classes.html page and all dependent files to the remote site.
8. View the remote site to make sure that all files uploaded correctly.

9. Synchronize the files so that all other files on the local Carolyne's Creations site are uploaded to the remote site.
10. Enable the Enable file check-out feature.
11. Check out the classes page and all its dependent files.
12. Open the classes page, then change the price of the adult class to **$45.00**.
13. Save your changes, close the page, then check in the classes page and all dependent pages.

14. Disable the Enable file check-out feature, then turn off read only for the entire site.
15. Export the site definition to a new folder named **cc_site_definition**.
16. Import the Carolyne's Creations.ste file to create a new site named Carolyne's Creations 2.
17. Expand the local site folder in the Files panel if necessary, compare your screen to Figure 47, then remove the Carolyne's Creations2 site.

Figure 47 *Sample completed Project Builder 2*

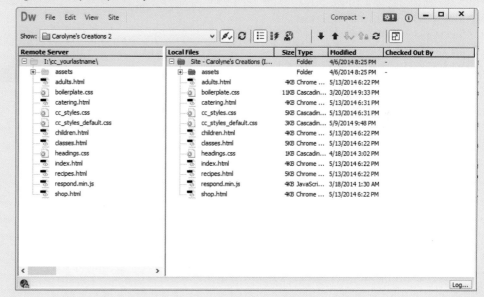

Throughout this book you have used Dreamweaver to create and develop several websites that contain different elements, many of which are found in popular commercial websites. For instance, Figure 48 shows the National Science Foundation website. This website contains many types of interactive elements, such as image maps and rollovers—all of which you learned to create in this book.

1. Connect to the Internet, then go to the National Science Foundation at www.nsf.gov.
2. Spend some time exploring the pages of this site to familiarize yourself with its elements.
3. Type a list of all the elements in this site that you have learned how to create in this book. After each item, write a short description of where and how the element is used in the site.
4. Select the link for the Site Map in the menu bar at the bottom of the page. Describe the information provided with the site map.
5. Select the Text Only Version and View Mobile Site links at the very bottom of the page. Describe what happens when you select each link.
6. Print the home page and one or two other pages that contain some of the elements you described and attach it to your list.

Figure 48 *Design Project*

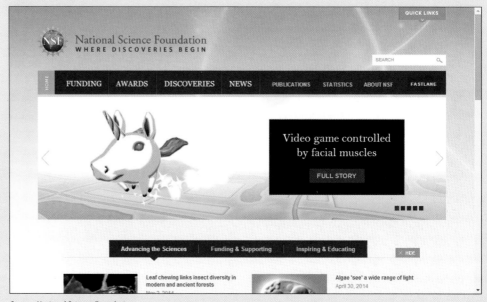

Source: National Science Foundation

In this project, you will finish your work on the website that you created and developed throughout this book. You publish your site to a remote server or local or network folder.

1. Before you begin the process of publishing your website to a remote server, make sure that it is ready for public viewing. Use Figure 49 to assist you in making sure your website is complete. If you find problems, make the necessary changes to finalize the site.

2. Decide where to publish your site. The folder where you will publish your site can be either an FTP site or a local/network folder. If you are publishing to an FTP site, be sure to write down all the information you will need to publish to the site, including the URL of the FTP host, the directory on the FTP server where you will publish your local site folder, and the login and password information.

3. Use the Site Setup dialog box to specify the remote settings for the site using the information that was decided upon in Step 2.

4. Transfer one of the pages and its dependent files to the remote site, then view the remote site to make sure the appropriate files were transferred.

5. Synchronize the files so that all the remaining local pages and dependent files are uploaded to the remote site.

6. Enable the Enable file check-out feature.

7. Check out one of the pages. Open the checked-out page, make a change to it, save the change, close the page, then check the page back in.

8. Cloak a particular file type.

9. Export the site definition for the site to a new folder on your hard drive or on an external drive.

10. Close any open pages, then exit Dreamweaver.

Figure 49 *Portfolio Project*

Website Checklist

1. Are you satisfied with the content and appearance of every page?
2. Are all paths for all links and images correct?
3. Does each page have a title?
4. Does the stylesheet pass CSS3 validation?
5. Do all images have appropriate alternate text?
6. Have you eliminated any orphaned files?
7. Have you deleted any unnecessary files?
8. Have you viewed all pages using at least two different browsers and three different screen sizes?
9. Does the home page have keywords and a description?
10. Is all text based on a CSS style?

© 2015 Cengage Learning®

CHAPTER **1**

GETTING STARTED WITH
FLASH

1. Understand the Flash workspace
2. Open a document and play a Flash movie
3. Create and save a Flash movie
4. Work with the Timeline
5. Import graphics and work with libraries
6. Plan an application and use Help

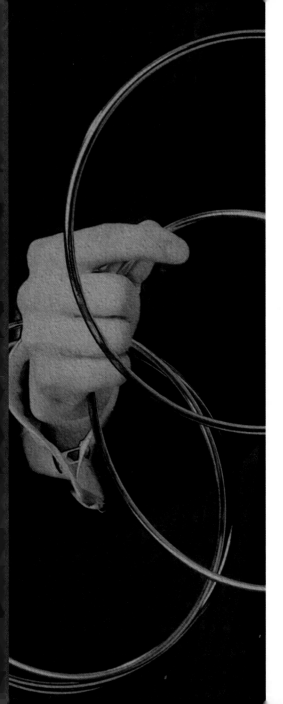

GETTING STARTED
WITH FLASH

Introduction

Adobe has created an integrated set of tools and technologies used to develop and deliver compelling applications running on computers, websites, and mobile devices. These include Flash Player, which is used to display Flash content on the Web, and Adobe AIR, which is used to deploy Flash applications on desktops, mobile devices, and televisions. At the heart of these tools and technologies is Adobe Flash Professional CC.

Adobe Flash Professional CC is a development tool that allows you to create compelling interactive applications, which often include animation. Flash is an excellent program for creating applications that are used for the following: **entertainment** (such as standalone games running on computers and mobile devices, and multiplayer social games running on Facebook); **business** (such as banner ads and stock market analytic tools); **education** (such as interactive simulations and museum exhibits); **government** (such as interactive national park tours); and **personal use** (such as GPS-based interactive street maps).

Flash is popular with developers because they can create these applications and deliver them in multiple ways: on desktop computers,

smartphones, tablets, and even TVs. An example is Sesame Street. Using Flash technologies Sesame Street developers were able to repurpose their television content to create games and other applications that run on computers, smartphones (iPhone, Windows, and Android models), and tablets such as the iPad. Flash is helping them leverage resources, both personnel and content, because the ability to create one application and use it on several devices saves development time and money.

Flash has become the standard for both professional and casual application developers, as well as for web developers. There are more than three million Flash designers and developers. 24 of the top 25 Facebook games and more than 20,000 mobile apps were built using Flash technologies. Flash is the leading program for creating animations, such as product demonstrations and banner ads, used in websites. It has exceptional drawing tools and tools for creating interactive controls, such as navigation buttons and menus. Furthermore, it provides the ability to incorporate sounds and video easily into an application. This chapter provides an overview of Flash and presents concepts that are covered in more detail in later chapters.

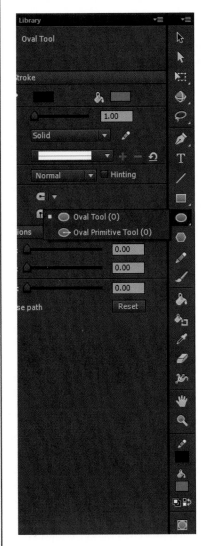

Understand the
FLASH WORKSPACE

What You'll Do

 In this lesson, you will learn about the development workspace in Adobe Flash and how to change Flash settings to customize your workspace.

Organizing the Flash Workspace

As a designer, one of the most important things for you to do is to organize your workspace— that is, to decide what to have displayed on the screen and how to arrange the various tools and panels. Because **Flash** is a powerful program with many tools, your workspace may become cluttered. Fortunately, it is easy to customize the workspace to display only the tools needed at any particular time.

The development process in Flash operates according to a movie metaphor: objects placed on the Stage also are incorporated in frames on a Timeline. As you work in Flash, you create a movie by arranging objects (such as graphics and text) on the Stage, and then animating the objects using the Timeline. You can play the movie on the Stage as you are working on it by using the movie controls (start, stop, rewind, and so on). Once completed, the movie can become part of an application, such as a game, or used in a website. Unless otherwise noted, the term *movie* refers to Flash-created movies.

When you start a new Flash movie (also called a document), three basic parts of the workspace are displayed: a menu bar that organizes commands within menus, a Stage

where objects are placed, and a Timeline used to organize and control the objects on the Stage. In addition, one or more panels may be displayed. Panels, such as the Tools panel, are used when working with objects and features of the movie. Figure 1 shows a typical Flash workspace.

Stage

The **Stage** contains all of the objects (such as drawings, photos, animations, text, and videos) that are part of the movie that will be seen by your viewers. It shows how the objects behave within the movie and how they interact with each other. You can resize the Stage and change the background color applied to it. You can draw objects directly on the Stage or drag them from the Library panel to the Stage. You can also import objects developed in another program directly to the Stage. You can specify the size of the Stage (in pixels), which will be the size of the display area for the application on your smartphone or within your browser window. The gray area surrounding the Stage is the **Pasteboard**. You can place objects on the Pasteboard as you are creating a movie. However, neither the Pasteboard nor the objects on it will appear when the movie is played.

Timeline (Frames and Layers)

The **Timeline** is used to organize and control the movie's contents by specifying when each object appears on the Stage. The Timeline is critical to the creation of movies because a movie is merely a series of still images that appear over time. The images are contained within **frames**, which are segments of the Timeline. Frames in a Flash movie are similar to frames in a motion picture. When a Flash movie is played, a playhead moves from frame to frame on the Timeline, causing the content of each frame to appear on the Stage in a linear sequence.

The Timeline indicates where you are at any time within the movie and allows you to insert, delete, select, copy, and move frames. The Timeline contains **layers** that help to organize the objects on the Stage. You can draw and edit objects on one layer without affecting objects on other layers. Layers are a way to stack objects so they can overlap and give a 3D appearance on the Stage.

Panels

Panels are used to view, organize, and modify objects and features in a movie. The most commonly used panels are the Tools panel, the Properties panel (also called the Property inspector), and the Library panel. The **Tools panel** contains a set of tools, such as the rectangle, oval and text tools, used to draw and edit graphics and text. The **Properties panel** is used to display and change the properties of an object, such as the size and transparency of a circle. The **Library panel** is used to store and organize the various assets in your movie such as graphics, buttons, sounds, and video.

You can control which panels are displayed individually or you can choose to display

Figure 1 *A typical Flash workspace*

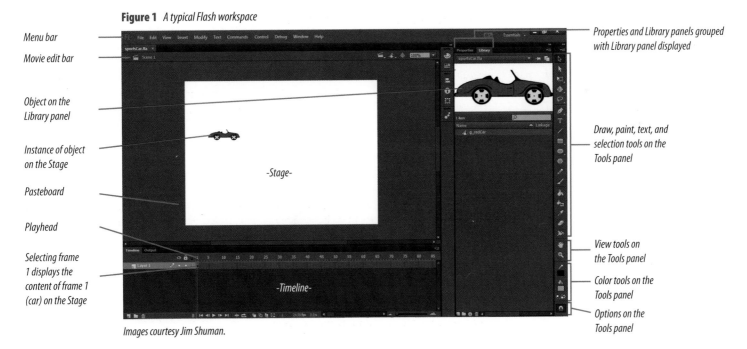

Menu bar

Movie edit bar

Object on the Library panel

Instance of object on the Stage

Pasteboard

Playhead

Selecting frame 1 displays the content of frame 1 (car) on the Stage

Properties and Library panels grouped with Library panel displayed

Draw, paint, text, and selection tools on the Tools panel

View tools on the Tools panel

Color tools on the Tools panel

Options on the Tools panel

Images courtesy Jim Shuman.

panel sets. **Panel sets** are groups of the most commonly used panels. For example, the Properties and the Library panels are often grouped together to make a panel set.

Although several panels open automatically when you start Flash, you may choose to close them and then display them only when they are needed. This keeps your workspace from becoming too cluttered. Panels are floating windows, meaning that you can move them around the workspace. This allows you to group (dock) panels together as a way to organize them in the workspace. In addition, you can control how a panel is displayed. That is, you can expand a panel to show all of its features or collapse it to show only the title bar. Collapsing panels reduces the clutter on your workspace, provides a larger area for the Stage, and still provides easy access to often used panels.

If you choose to rearrange panels, first decide if you want a panel to be grouped (docked) with another panel, stacked above or below another panel, placed as a floating panel, or simply positioned as a stand-alone panel. An example of each of these is shown in Figure 2. When panels are grouped and expanded, clicking on a panel's tab makes it the active panel so that the panel features are displayed.

The key to rearranging panels is the blue drop zone that appears when a panel is being moved. The drop zone is the area to which the panel can move and is indicated by either a blue line or a rectangle with a blue border. A single blue line indicates the position for stacking a panel above or below another panel. A rectangle with a blue border indicates the position for grouping panels. If you move a panel without using a drop zone, the panel becomes a floating panel and is neither grouped nor stacked with other panels. To move a panel, you drag the panel by its tab until the desired blue drop zone appears, then you release the mouse button. Figure 3 shows the Library panel being grouped with the Properties panel. The process is to drag the Library

Figure 2 *Arranging panels*

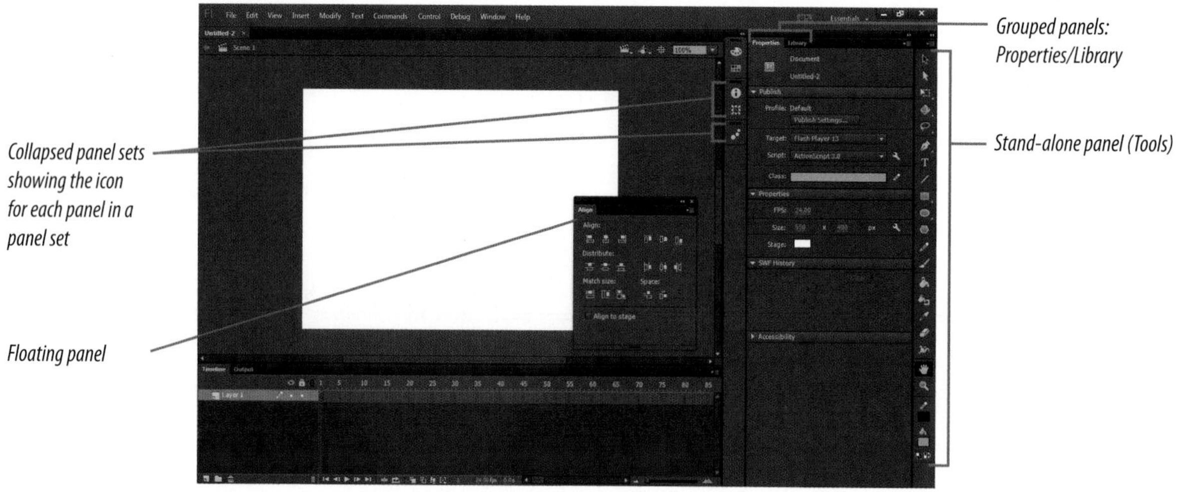

Collapsed panel sets showing the icon for each panel in a panel set

Floating panel

Grouped panels: Properties/Library

Stand-alone panel (Tools)

panel tab adjacent to the Properties panel tab. Notice the rectangle with the blue border that surrounds the Properties panel. This indicates the drop zone for the Library panel. (*Note*: Dragging a panel by its tab moves only that panel. To move a panel set you must drag the group by its title bar.)

Floating panels can be resized by dragging the left side, right side, or bottom of the panel. Also, you can resize a panel by dragging one of the bottom corners. In addition to resizing panels, you can collapse a panel so that only its title bar appears, and then you can expand it to display the entire panel. The Collapse to Icons button is located in the upper-right corner of each panel's title bar, as shown in Figure 3. The

Collapse to Icons button is a toggle button, which means it changes or toggles between two states. When clicked, the Collapse to Icons button changes to the Expand Panels button.

If you want to close a panel, you can click the Panel options button (shown in Figure 3) to display a drop down menu and then click the Close option. Alternately, you can right-click (Win) or [control]-click (Mac) the panel tab and choose Close. If the panel is a floating panel you can click the Close button on the title bar. Finally, if the panel is expanded, you can display the Window menu and deselect the panel (or panel group).

Arranging panels can be a bit tricky. It's easy to start moving panels around and find

that the workspace is cluttered with panels arranged in unintended ways. To clean up your workspace, you can close a panel(s) or simply display the default Essentials workspace described below.

Flash provides several preset workspace configurations that provide panels and panel sets most often used by designers, developers, and animators. The default workspace, shown in Figure 4, is named Essentials and can be displayed by clicking the Essentials button on the far right side of menu bar and choosing Reset "Essentials". (*Note*: Your Essentials button may be below your menu bar.) Alternately, you can choose Reset "Essentials" from the Workspaces command on the Window

Figure 3 *Grouping the Library panel with the Properties panel*

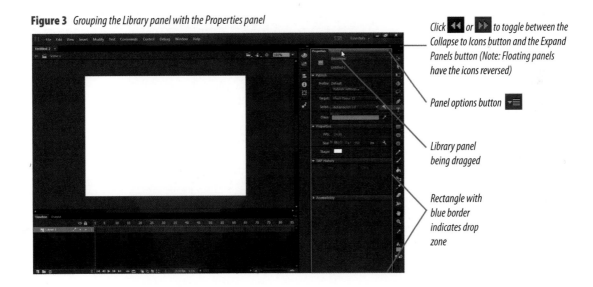

Click ◀◀ or ▶▶ to toggle between the Collapse to Icons button and the Expand Panels button (Note: Floating panels have the icons reversed)

Panel options button ▼≡

Library panel being dragged

Rectangle with blue border indicates drop zone

menu. This workspace includes the Timeline panel (grouped with the Output panel, which displays feedback such as error messages when a movie is tested.); the Tools panel which is expanded; the Properties and Library panels grouped and expanded; and several other panel sets that are stacked and collapsed. Your Essentials workspace may open with additional panel sets that are grouped depending on user settings and previous use. You can expand and collapse these grouped panels sets by clicking the Expand Panels button or the Collapse to Icons button. To open a single panel set, you click an icon in the set. The Essentials workspace is a good development environment when learning Flash.

Regardless of how you decide to customize your development workspace, the Stage and the menu bar are always displayed. Usually, you display the Timeline, Tools panel, Library panel, Properties panel, and one or more other panels.

Other changes that you can make to the workspace are to change the size of the Stage, move the Stage around the Pasteboard, and change the size of the Timeline panel. To increase the size of the Stage so that the objects on the Stage can be edited more easily, you can change the magnification setting using commands on the View menu or by using the Zoom tool on the Tools panel. The Hand tool on the Tools panel and the scroll bars at

the bottom and right of the Stage can be used to reposition the Stage. The Timeline can be resized by dragging the top border. As your Flash movie gets more complex, you will use more layers on the Timeline. Increasing the size of the Timeline allows you to view more layers at one time.

QUICK TIP

When working with panels, you can collapse, move, and close them to best meet your working style. Settings for an object, such as the fill color of a circle, are not lost if you close or collapse a panel. If, at any time the panels have become confusing, simply return to the Essentials workspace, and then open and close panels as needed.

Essentials button

Figure 4 *The Essentials workspace*

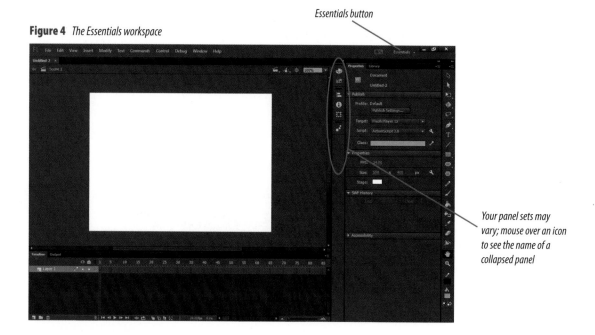

Your panel sets may vary; mouse over an icon to see the name of a collapsed panel

Getting Started with Flash

Figure 5 *The Flash Welcome screen*

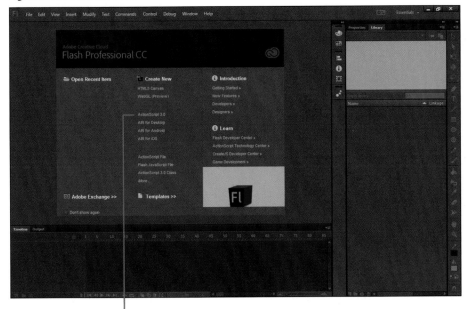

Click to create a
new Flash document

Start Adobe Flash and work with panels

1. Start the Adobe Flash Professional CC program .

   The Adobe Flash Professional CC welcome screen appears, as shown in Figure 5. This screen allows you to open a recent document or create a new Flash document.

2. Click **ActionScript 3.0** under Create New.

3. Click the **Essentials button** on the menu bar, click **Reset "Essentials"**, then click **Yes**.

   Note: The Essentials button may be under the menu bar.

   TIP When you open a new file or as you are rearranging your workspace, use the Reset "Essentials" option to display the default workspace.

4. Click **Window** on the menu bar, then note the panels with check marks.

   The check marks identify which panels and panel sets are open.

   TIP The Properties and Library panels may be grouped. Also, the Color, Swatches, Align, Info, Transform, and Motion Presets panels may be grouped, stacked, and/ or collapsed, depending upon the configuration of your Essentials workspace. If so, only the panel that is active will have a check mark.

5. With the Window menu still open, click **Hide Panels**.

6. Click **Window** on the menu bar, then click **Timeline**.

7. Click **Window** on the menu bar, then click **Tools**.

8. Click **Window** on the menu bar, then click **Library**.

   Because the Library and Properties panels are grouped, they are both displayed, with the Library panel as the active panel.

(continued)

9. Click the **Properties panel tab**.

   The Properties panel is the active tab and the panel's features are displayed.

10. Click the **Library panel tab**, then drag the **Library panel** to the left side of the Stage as a floating panel.

11. Click the **Collapse to Icons button** ◄◄ on the Library panel title bar.

12. Click the **Expand Panels button** ►► on the Library panel title bar.

13. Click the **Library panel tab**, drag the **Library panel tab** to the right of the Properties panel tab, then when a rectangle with a blue border appears, as shown in Figure 6, release the mouse button to group the panels.

    Note: If the panels do not appear grouped, repeat the step making sure there is a rectangle with a blue border before releasing the mouse button.

14. Click the **Collapse to Icons button** ►► in the upper-right corner of the grouped panels, as shown in Figure 6.

15. Click the **Expand Panels button** ◄◄ to display the grouped panels.

16. Click **Essentials** on the menu bar, click **Reset "Essentials"**, then click **Yes**.

17. Click the **Color panel button** 🎨 .

    The Color panel is expanded and shown grouped with the Swatches panel.

18. Click the **Collapse to Icons button** ►► for the Color panel set.

19. Click **Essentials** on the menu bar, click **Reset "Essentials"**, then click **Yes**.

You started Flash and configured the workspace by hiding, moving, and displaying panels.

Figure 6 *Library panel grouped with the Properties panel*

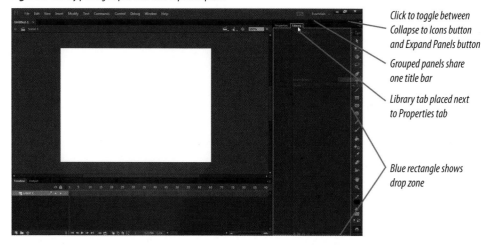

Click to toggle between Collapse to Icons button and Expand Panels button

Grouped panels share one title bar

Library tab placed next to Properties tab

Blue rectangle shows drop zone

Understanding Your Workspace

Organizing the Flash workspace is like organizing your desktop. You may work more efficiently if you have many of the most commonly used items in view and ready to use. Alternately, you may work better if your workspace is relatively uncluttered, giving you more free "desk space." Fortunately, Flash makes it easy for you to decide which items to display and how they are arranged while you work. You should become familiar with quickly opening, collapsing, expanding, and closing the various windows, toolbars, and panels in Flash, and experimenting with different layouts and screen resolutions to find the workspace that works best for you. Be sure to use screentips, such as those associated with the Collapse to Icons button, the Expand Panels button, and panel sets, to help you identify components of your workspace.

Getting Started with Flash

Figure 7 *Changing the size of the Timeline panel*

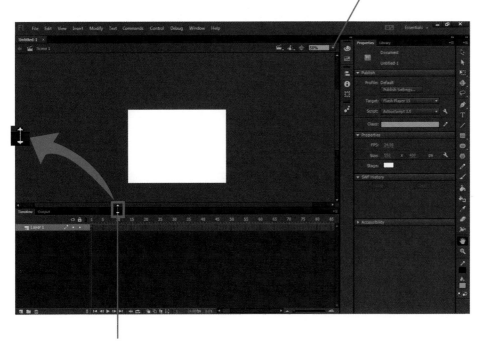

View list arrow

Double-headed pointer

Alternate Ways to Complete a Task

Flash often provides alternative ways to complete the same task. For instance, if you want to change the view (zoom in and out) of the Stage you could use the following methods:

- the Magnification command on the View menu
- the View list options on the Movie edit bar
- the Zoom tool on the Tools panel
- the Zoom In and Zoom Out commands on the View menu
- the [Ctrl][=] and the [Ctrl][-] shortcut key combinations (Windows)
- the [command][=] and [command][-] shortcut key combinations (Mac)

Change the Stage view and display of the Timeline

1. Click the **Hand tool** 🖑 on the Tools panel, click the middle of the Stage, then drag the **Stage** around the Pasteboard.
2. Click **View** on the menu bar, point to **Magnification**, then click **Center the Stage**.
3. Click **View** on the menu bar, point to **Magnification**, then click **50%**.
4. Move the pointer to the top of the Timeline title bar then, when the pointer changes to a double-headed pointer ⇕, click and drag the **title bar** up to increase the height of the Timeline, as shown in Figure 7.
   Increasing the height of the Timeline panel allows you to view more layers as you add them to the Timeline.
5. Move the pointer to the top of the Timeline title bar then, when the pointer changes to a double-headed pointer ⇕, click and drag the **title bar** down to decrease the height of the Timeline.
6. Double-click the word **Timeline** to collapse the Timeline.
7. Click the word **Timeline** again to expand the Timeline.
8. Click the **View list arrow** on the movie edit bar as shown in Figure 7, then click **100%**.
9. Click the **Essentials button** on the menu bar, click **Reset "Essentials"**, then click **Yes**.
10. Click **File** on the menu bar, then click **Close**.

You used a View command to change the magnification of the Stage; you used the Hand tool to move the Stage around the workspace; you resized, collapsed, and expanded the Timeline panel; then you closed the document.

Open a Document and
PLAY A FLASH MOVIE

What You'll Do

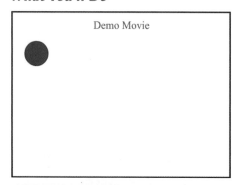

Demo Movie

Demo Movie

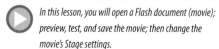

In this lesson, you will open a Flash document (movie); preview, test, and save the movie; then change the movie's Stage settings.

Opening a Movie in Flash

Flash files are called documents (or movies, interchangeably) and have an .fla file extension. If you have created a movie in Flash and saved it with the name myMovie, the complete filename will be myMovie.fla. Files with the .fla file extension can only be opened and edited using Flash. After they are opened, you can edit and resave them.

In order for Flash movies to be viewed on computers that do not have the Flash program installed, the movies must be saved in a different file format. The three most common file formats for distributing Flash movies are Flash Player (.swf), Adobe AIR (.air), and HTML5 Canvas (.js). Flash Player and HTML5 files are used on websites for everything from interactive product demonstrations to banner ads. Adobe AIR files are used for a much broader range of applications such as interactive games, tutorials, product demonstrations, and productivity software. An important feature of AIR applications, also called apps, is that they can be played on any device (computer, mobile, TV) without the Flash Player and without a browser. The Publish command is used to convert a Flash

FLA movie to a SWF or an AIR format. HTML5 file formats are specified when you start a new Flash document. Depending on the target you specify (Flash Player, Air, or HTML5) the filename extension will be changed to either Flash Player (.fla), Air (.air), or HTML5 (.js). For example, when a Flash file named myMovie.fla is published using the Publish command and the target is Flash Player (the default target), a new file named myMovie.swf is created. Flash SWF movies can be played in a browser without the Flash program, but the Flash Player must be installed on the computer. Flash Players are pre-installed on almost all computers. For those that do not have the player, it can be downloaded free from the Adobe website, *www.adobe.com.* Because .swf files cannot be edited in the Flash program, you should preview the Flash .fla files on the Stage and test them before you publish them. Be sure to keep the original .fla file so that you can make changes, if needed, at a later date. HTML5 Canvas files are specified when you first start a new Flash document. Alternately, the contents of the timeline can be copied from a Flash .fla movie to an HTML Canvas document.

Previewing a Movie

After creating a new Flash movie or opening a previously saved movie, you can preview it within the workspace in several ways. When you preview a movie, you play the frames by directing the playhead to move through the Timeline as you watch the movement on the Stage.

Control Menu Commands (and Keyboard Shortcuts)

Figure 8 shows the Control menu commands, which resemble common video player options:

- Play begins playing the movie frame by frame, from the location of the playhead to the end of the movie. For example, if the playhead is on frame 5 and the last frame is frame 40, choosing the Play command will play frames 5–40 of the movie.

QUICK TIP

When a movie starts, the Play command changes to a Stop command. You can also stop the movie by pressing [Enter] (Win) or [return] (Mac).

- Rewind moves the playhead to frame 1.
- Go To End moves the playhead to the last frame of the movie.
- Step Forward One Frame moves the playhead forward one frame at a time.
- Step Backward One Frame moves the playhead backward one frame at a time.

You can turn on the Loop Playback setting to allow the movie to continue playing repeatedly. A check mark next to the Loop Playback command on the Control menu indicates that the feature is active. To turn off this feature, click the Loop Playback command.

Control Buttons

You can also preview a movie using the Control buttons located on the status bar at the bottom of the Timeline. Figure 8 shows these buttons.

Figure 8 *Control menu commands and control buttons*

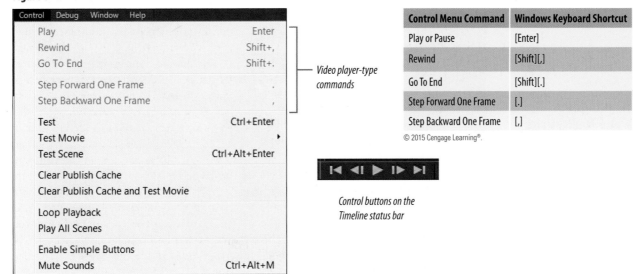

Control Menu Command	Windows Keyboard Shortcut	Mac Keyboard Shortcut
Play or Pause	[Enter]	[return]
Rewind	[Shift][,]	⌘ [R]
Go To End	[Shift][.]	
Step Forward One Frame	[.]	[.]
Step Backward One Frame	[,]	[,]

© 2015 Cengage Learning®.

Control buttons on the Timeline status bar

Control menu

Testing a Movie

When you play a movie within the Flash workspace, some interactive functions (such as navigation buttons that are used to jump from one part of the movie to another) do not work. You can use the Test Movie command on the Control menu to play the movie with full functionality in a Flash Player window or in a browser on a computer using the SWF format. In addition, the Test Movie command can be used to play a movie on a mobile device that is attached to your computer using a USB cable.

Documents, Movies, and Applications

As you work in Flash, you are creating a document. When you save your work as an .fla file, you are saving the document. This is consistent with other Adobe products, such as Photoshop, that use the word *document* to refer to work created in that program. In addition, because Flash uses a movie metaphor with a Stage, Timeline, frames, animations, and so on, the work done in Flash is often referred to as a movie. So, the phrase *Flash document* and the phrase *Flash movie* are synonymous. Movies can be as small and simple as a ball bouncing across the screen or as complex as a full-length interactive adventure game. Products such as games and educational software, as well as online advertisements and product demonstrations, are referred to as applications (see Figure 9). Applications usually contain multiple Flash documents or movies that are linked.

Using the Flash Player

To view a Flash SWF movie on the web, your computer needs to have the Flash Player installed. An important feature of multimedia players, such as the Flash Player, is the ability to decompress a file that has been compressed. Compressing a file gives it a small file size, which means it can be delivered more quickly over the Internet than its uncompressed counterpart. In addition to Adobe, companies such as Apple (QuickTime) and Microsoft (Windows Media Player) create players that allow applications to be viewed on the web. These applications can be created by Apple, Microsoft, or other companies. The multimedia players are distributed free and can be downloaded from the company's website. The Flash Player is created by Adobe and the latest version is available at *www.adobe.com*. Flash movies that are created for the HTML5 format and AIR format do not need the Flash Player to be displayed.

Figure 9 *Example of an application*

Source: New York Philharmonic Kidzone.

Figure 10 *Playhead moving across Timeline*

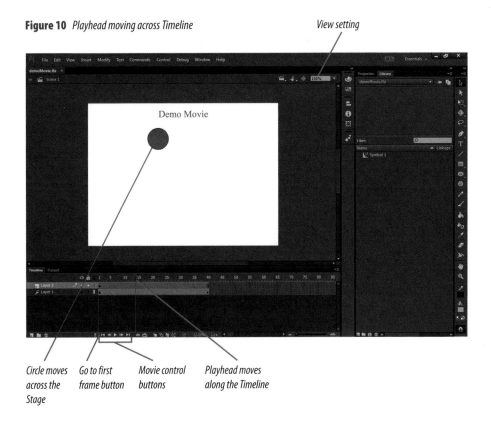

View setting

Circle moves across the Stage *Go to first frame button* *Movie control buttons* *Playhead moves along the Timeline*

Using Options and Shortcuts

As you know, there is often more than one way to complete a particular command when using Flash. For example, if you want to rewind a movie you can use the control on the Control menu, use the control on the Timeline status bar, press [Shift][,], or drag the playhead to frame 1. In addition, Flash provides context menus that are relevant to the current selection. For example, if you point to a graphic and right-click (Win) or [control]-click (Mac), a menu opens with graphic-related commands, such as Cut and Copy. Shortcut keys are also available for many of the most common commands, such as [Ctrl][Z] (Win) or [command][Z] (Mac) for Undo.

Open and play a movie using the Control menu and movie control buttons

1. Open fl1_1.fla from the drive and folder where your Data Files are stored, then save it as **demoMovie.fla**.

2. Verify the view is set to 100%.

   The view setting is displayed on the movie menu bar, which is above and to the right of the Stage.

3. Click **Control** on the menu bar, then click **Play**.

   Notice how the playhead moves across the Timeline as the blue circle moves from the left of the Stage to the right, as shown in Figure 10.

4. Click **Control** on the menu bar, then click **Rewind**.

5. Press [**Enter**] (Win) or [**return**] (Mac) to play the movie, then press [**Enter**] (Win) or [**return**] (Mac) again to stop the movie before it ends.

6. Click the **Go to first frame button** at the bottom of the Timeline status bar, as shown in Figure 10.

7. Use all the movie control buttons on the Timeline status bar to preview the movie.

8. Click and drag the **playhead** back and forth to view the contents of the movie frame by frame.

9. Click number **1** on the Timeline to select the frame.

10. Press the **period key** several times, then press the **comma key** several times to move the playhead one frame at a time forward and backward.

You opened a Flash movie and previewed it, using various controls.

Test a movie

1. Click **Control** on the menu bar, point to **Test Movie**, then click **In Flash Professional**.

   The Flash Player window opens, as shown in Figure 11, and the movie starts playing and replaying automatically.

2. Right-click (Win) or [control]-click (Mac) the Flash Player window, review the available commands, then click **Play** to stop the movie.

3. Right-click (Win) or [control]-click (Mac) the Flash Player window, then click **Play** to start the movie.

4. Click the **Close button** 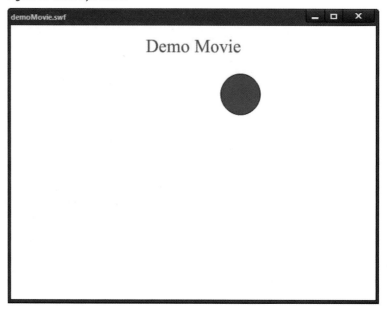 on the Flash Player window to close the window.

5. Use your file management program to navigate to the drive and folder where you saved the demoMovie.fla file and notice the demoMovie.swf file.

   TIP When you test a movie, Flash automatically creates a file that has an .swf extension in the folder where your movie is stored and then plays the movie in the Flash Player.

6. Return to the Flash program.

7. Click **1** on the Timeline.

You tested a movie in the Flash Player window and viewed the .swf file created as a result of testing the movie, and then displayed the contents of frame 1.

Figure 11 *Flash Player window*

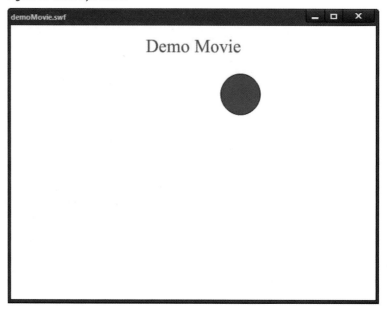

Getting Started with Flash

Figure 12 *Document Settings dialog box*

Width box

Height box

Stage color swatch

Figure 13 *Completed changes to the document properties*

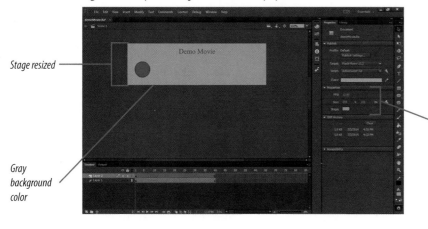

Stage resized

Gray background color

Document properties displayed on the Properties panel when you click the Stage.

Change the document properties

1. Click **Modify** on the menu bar, then click **Document**.

   The Document Settings dialog box opens.

2. Click in the **height text box** to select the number 400, then type **160**.

3. Click the **Stage color swatch**, then, in the far-left column of the Color Swatch palette, click the fourth color from the top, which is the **gray (#999999) color swatch**.

   Note: The color code for a color appears next to the sample color swatch above the palette as you point to a color. The Color Swatch palette allows you to click a color to choose it or to enter a number that represents the color.

4. Review the remaining default values shown in Figure 12, then click **OK**.

   The dialog box closes.

5. Click the **Stage**.

   TIP   You can use the Properties Panel instead of the Document Settings dialog box to change the Document properties as shown in Figure 13. You must click the Stage to display the settings.

6. Press **[Enter]** (Win) or **[return]** (Mac) to play the movie.

7. Click **File** on the menu bar, then click **Save As**.

8. Navigate to the drive and folder where your Data Files are stored, type **demoMovieBanner** for the filename, then click **Save**.

9. Click **File** on the menu bar, then click **Close**.

You set the document properties including the size of the Stage and the background color, then you saved the document.

Create and
SAVE A FLASH MOVIE

What You'll Do

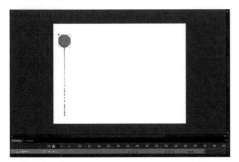

In this lesson, you will create a Flash movie that will include a simple animation, add animation effects, and then save the movie.

Creating a Flash Movie

Flash movies are created by placing objects (graphics, text, sounds, photos, and so on) on the Stage, editing these objects (for example, changing their brightness), animating the objects, and adding interactivity with buttons and menus. You can create graphic objects in Flash using the drawing tools, or you can create them in another program, such as Adobe Illustrator or Adobe Photoshop, and then import them into a Flash movie. In addition, you can acquire clip art and stock photographs and import them into a movie. When objects are placed on the Stage, they are automatically placed on a layer and in the selected frame on the Timeline.

Figure 14 shows a movie that has a circle object created in Flash. Notice that the playhead is on frame 1 of the movie. The object placed on the Stage appears in frame 1 and appears on the Stage when the playhead is on frame 1. The dot in frame 1 on the Timeline indicates that this frame is a keyframe. The concept of keyframes is critical to understanding how Flash works. A **keyframe** indicates that there is a change in the movie, such as the start of an animation, or the resizing of an object on the Stage.

A keyframe is automatically designated in frame 1 of every layer. In addition, you can designate any frame to be a keyframe.

The circle object in Figure 14 was created using the Oval tool. To create an oval or a rectangle, you select the desired tool and then drag the pointer over an area on the Stage. *Note:* Flash uses one button on the Tools panel to group the Rectangle Primitive and Rectangle tools, and another button to group the Oval and Oval Primitive tools. To display a menu of these tools, click and hold the rectangle (or oval) button on the Tools panel to display the menu and then click the tool you want to use. If you want to draw a perfect circle or square, press and hold [Shift] after the tool is selected, and then drag the pointer. If you make a mistake, you can click Edit on the menu bar, and then click Undo. To make changes to an object, such as resizing or changing its color, or to animate an object, you must first select it. You can use the Selection tool to select an entire object or group of objects. You drag the Selection tool pointer around the entire object to make a **marquee**. An object that has been selected displays a dot pattern or a blue border. In order for an object to be animated it must be converted into a symbol. When a symbol is selected it displays a blue bounding box, not a dot pattern.

Creating an Animation

Figure 15 shows a movie that has 24 frames. When you are working with an object to create an animation, the background color on the Timeline will appear yellow. After the animation has been created and the object is deselected the background color changes to blue. For example, in Figure 15, the yellow background color on the Timeline indicates a motion animation that starts in frame 1 and ends in frame 24. The yellow color will change to blue after the object is deselected. The dotted line on the Stage indicates the path the object will follow during the animation. In this case, the object will move from left to right across the Stage. The movement of the object is caused by having the object in different places on the Stage in different frames of the movie. In this case, frame 12 displays the object midway through the animation and frame 24 displays the object at the end of the animation. A basic motion animation requires two keyframes. The first keyframe sets the starting position of the object, and the second keyframe sets the ending position of the object. The number of frames from keyframe to keyframe determines the length of the animation. If the starting keyframe is frame 1 and the ending keyframe is frame 24, the object will be animated for 24 frames. As an object is being animated, Flash automatically fills in the frames between these keyframes, with a process called **motion tweening**.

The Motion Tween Animation Process

Having an object move around the screen is one of the most common types of animations. Flash provides a process called motion tweening that makes it relatively simple to move objects. In order to animate an object it must be converted into a symbol. Practically any object, including a drawing, photo, or button, can be converted into a symbol. Creating a symbol allows you to reuse the object for this and other movies, as well as apply a motion tween.

The process to animate an object is to select the object on the Stage, then select the Motion Tween command from the Insert menu. If the object is not a symbol, a dialog box opens asking if you want to convert the object to a symbol. The final step in the animation

Figure 14 *Circle object in frame 1*

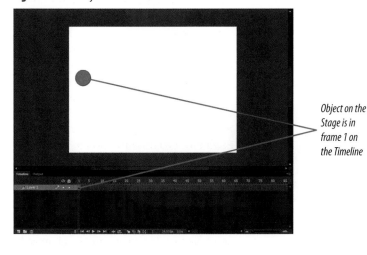

Object on the Stage is in frame 1 on the Timeline

Figure 15 *Motion animation*

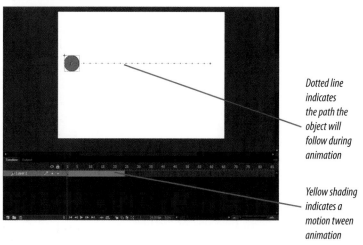

Dotted line indicates the path the object will follow during animation

Yellow shading indicates a motion tween animation

process is to select the ending frame for the animation and drag the object to another location on the Stage.

Two important things happen during the animation process. First, the Timeline shows the **tween span** (also called **motion span**), which is the number of frames in the motion tween. The tween span in this example extends for 24 frames. The default tween span when starting from frame 1 of a new movie is determined by the number of frames per second setting. In this example, we used the default setting of 24 frames per second, so the initial number of frames in a tween for this movie is 24 frames.

The length of the motion tween is determined by the last frame in the movie automatically or by you manually if you designate a frame other than the last frame of the movie as the end of the animation. If a movie has an ending frame beyond frame 1, the tween span will extend to the end of the movie. For example, if a movie has 50 frames and you insert a motion tween starting at frame 1, the tween span will extend from frames 1 through 50. Likewise, if a movie has an ending frame in frame 10 and you insert a motion tween in frame 1, the motion tween will extend from frame 1 to frame 10. Finally, a motion tween does not have to start in frame 1. You can start a motion tween in a frame other than frame 1 by clicking the frame on the layer you want to contain the motion tween, inserting a keyframe in that frame, and then continuing with the steps to insert a motion tween (selecting or creating

the object to be tweened, inserting the tween and moving the object).

You can increase or decrease the length of the animation by pointing to either end of the **tween** span and dragging it to a new frame. The tween span will have more or fewer frames based on this action. The duration of the tween will still be based on the number of frames per second setting. For example, if we drag the tween span from frame 24 to frame 48, there are now 48 frames in the tween span. The tween span will still play at 24 frames

per second because we did not change that setting. It will take two seconds to play the new tween span.

Second, a dotted line, called the **motion path**, represents the path the object takes from the beginning frame to the ending frame. This path can be reshaped to cause the object to travel in a non-linear way, as shown in Figure 16. Reshaping a path can be done by using the Selection tool on the Tools panel. You see the tween span on the Timeline and the motion path on the Stage.

Figure 16 *A reshaped motion path*

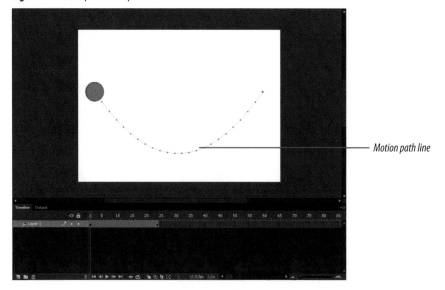

Motion path line

Getting Started with Flash

Motion Presets

Flash provides several preconfigured motion tweens that you can apply to an object on the Stage. These allow you to bounce an object across the Stage, fly-in an object from off the Stage, cause an object to pulsate and to spiral in place, as well as many other types of object animations. Figure 17 shows the Motion Presets panel where you choose a preset and apply it to an object. You can preview each preset before applying it and you can easily change to a different preset, if desired.

Adding Effects to an Object

In addition to animating the location of an object (or objects), you can also animate an object's appearance. Objects have properties such as color, brightness, and size. You can alter an object's properties as it is being animated using the motion tween process. For example, you could give the appearance of the object fading in by changing its transparency (alpha setting) or having it grow larger by altering its size over the course of the animation. Another useful effect is applying filters, such as drop shadows or bevels. All of these changes can be made by selecting the object, and then using commands on the Properties panel.

Figure 17 *Motion Presets panel*

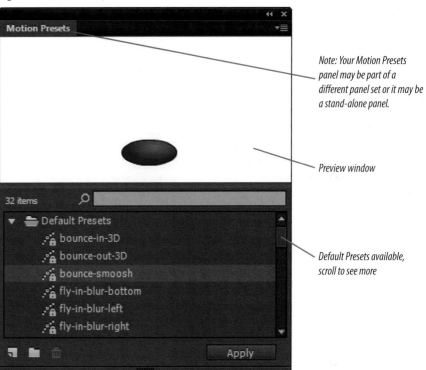

Note: Your Motion Presets panel may be part of a different panel set or it may be a stand-alone panel.

Preview window

Default Presets available, scroll to see more

Create objects using drawing tools

1. Click **ActionScript 3.0** to open a new Flash document.

2. Save the movie as **tween.fla**.

3. Verify the view is set to 100%.

4. Click and hold the **Oval tool** ⬭ on the Tools panel to display the list of tools, as shown in Figure 18, then click the **Oval tool** ⬭.

5. Verify that the Object Drawing option ◉ in the Options area of the Tools panel is not active, as shown in Figure 18.

6. Click the **Fill Color tool color swatch** 🎨 on the Tools panel, then, if necessary, click the **red color swatch** in the left column of the color palette.

7. Set the **Stroke Color tool color** swatch on the Tools panel to **black**, as seen in Figure 18.

8. Press and hold **[Shift]**, drag the **pointer** on the left side of the Stage to draw the circle, as shown in Figure 19, then release the mouse button.

   Pressing and holding [Shift] creates a circle.

   TIP Use the Undo command on the Edit menu to undo an action.

9. Click the **Selection tool** 🖈 on the Tools panel, drag a **marquee** around the object to select it, as shown in Figure 20, then release the mouse button.

   The object appears covered with a dot pattern.

   You created an object using the Oval tool, and then selected the object using the Selection tool.

Figure 18 *Drawing tools menu*

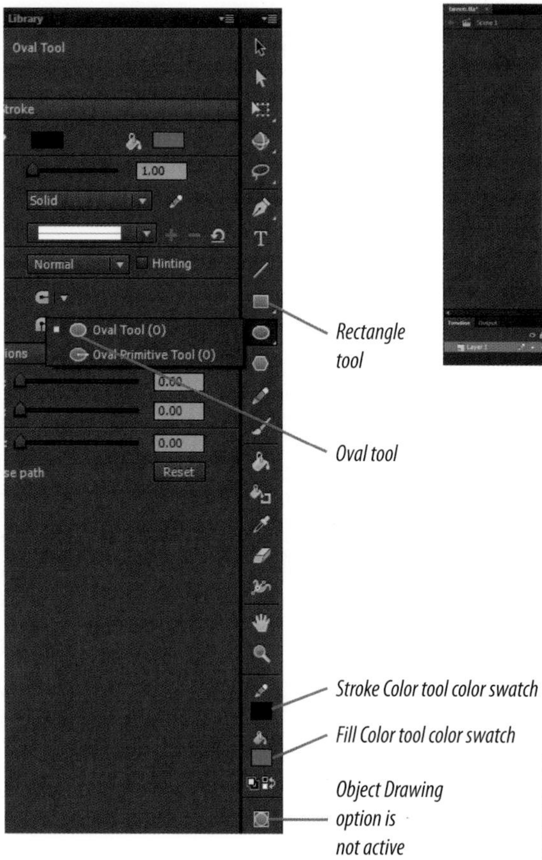

Rectangle tool

Oval tool

Stroke Color tool color swatch

Fill Color tool color swatch

Object Drawing option is not active

Figure 19 *Drawing a circle*

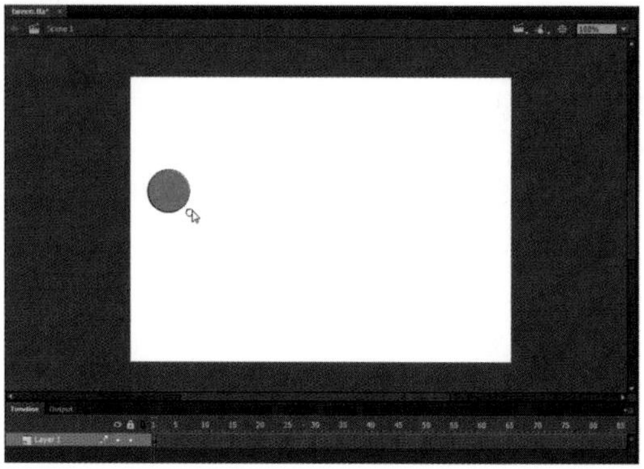

Figure 20 *Creating a marquee selection*

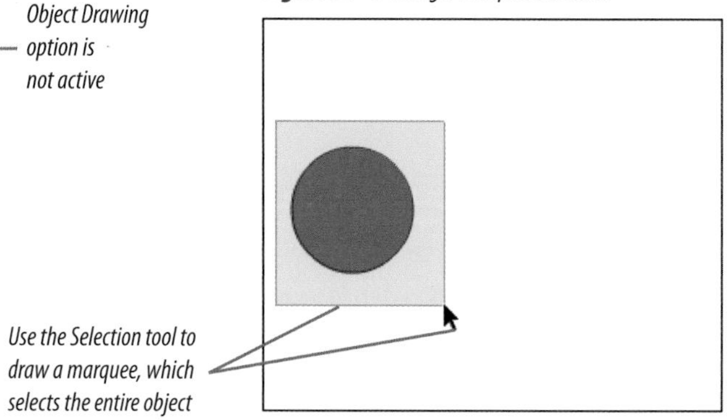

Use the Selection tool to draw a marquee, which selects the entire object

Figure 21 *The circle on the right side of the Stage*

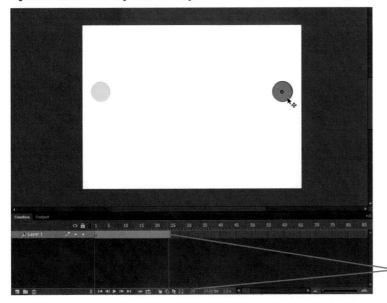

Indicates the active
frame, which is frame 24

Create a motion tween animation

1. Click **Insert** on the menu bar, then click **Motion Tween**.

   The Convert selection to symbol for tween dialog box opens.

2. Click **OK**.

   A blue border surrounds the object, indicating that the object is a symbol. Notice that, in this example, the playhead automatically moved to frame 24, the last frame in the tween span. When you move the object to a new location on the Stage, the object's new location will be reflected in frame 24.

3. Click and then drag the **circle** to the right side of the Stage, as shown in Figure 21, then release the mouse button.

4. Press **[Enter]**(Win) or **[return]**(Mac) to play the movie.

   The playhead moves through frames 1–24 on the Timeline, and the circle moves across the Stage.

5. Click **frame 12** on Layer 1 on the Timeline.

   Verify the frame number on the status bar of the Timeline is 12. If the playhead is not at frame 12, use the period and comma keys to move the playhead to frame 12. Notice that the object is halfway across the screen. This is the result of the tweening process in which the frames between 1 and 24 are filled in with the object in the correct location for each frame.

   (continued)

6. Verify the Selection tool 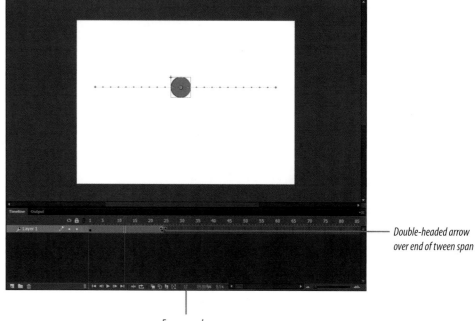 is active, then point to the end of the tween span on the Timeline until the pointer changes to a double-headed arrow ↔, as shown in Figure 22.

7. Click and drag the **tween span** to frame 48, then verify the frame number on the status bar is 48, or adjust as needed.

8. Press **[Enter]**(Win) or **[return]**(Mac) to play the movie.

   Notice it now takes longer (2 seconds, not 1 second) to play the movie. Also notice that a diamond character appears in frame 48, indicating that it is now a Property keyframe. A Property keyframe indicates a change in the property of an object. In this case, it indicates the location of the object on the Stage has changed from frame 24 to frame 48.

9. Click **frame 24** and notice that the object is now halfway across the screen.

10. Click **File** on the menu bar, then click **Save**.

You created a motion tween animation and changed the length of the tween span.

Figure 22 *Pointing to the end of the tween span*

Double-headed arrow over end of tween span

Frame number

Getting Started with Flash

Figure 23 *Using the Selection tool to reshape a motion path*

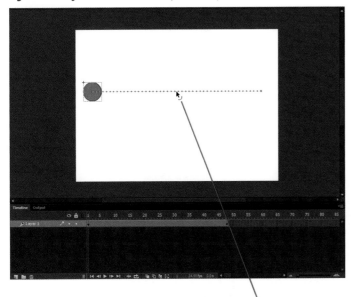

The pointer changed to
an arrow with an arc

Reshape the motion path

1. Click **File** on the menu bar, click **Save As**, then save the document with the filename **tweenEffects.fla**.

2. Verify the Selection tool ▨ is active.

3. Click **frame 1** to select it.

   Note: When a step in this book tells you to click a frame, click the frame on the layer, not the number on the Timeline.

4. Point to just below the middle of the path until the pointer changes to an arrow with an arc ▨, as shown in Figure 23.

(continued)

5. Click and drag the **path** to reshape the path, as shown in Figure 24.

6. Play the movie.

   Note: When a step in this book tells you to play the movie, press [Enter] (Win) or [return] (Mac).

7. Test the movie.

   Note: When a step in this book tells you to test the movie, click Control on the menu bar, point to Test Movie, then click In Flash Professional. Alternately, you can press [Ctrl][Enter] (Win) or [command][return](Mac).

8. View the movie, then close the Flash Player window.

9. Click **Edit** on the menu bar, then click **Undo Reshape**.

   Note: The Undo command starts with the most recent action and moves back through the actions. As a result, you may have to click Undo more than one time before you are able to click Undo Reshape.

You used the Selection tool to reshape a motion path and the Undo command to undo the reshape.

Figure 24 *Reshaping the motion path*

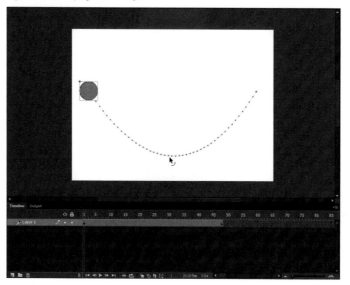

Figure 25 *The Properties panel displayed*

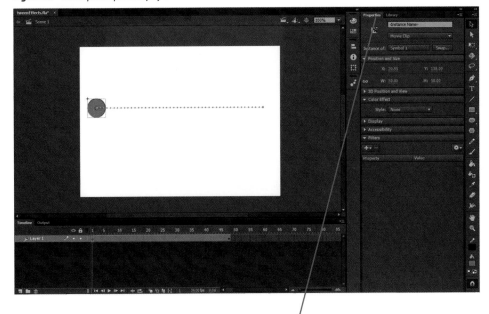

Properties panel and
its features

Change the transparency of an object

1. Click **frame 1** to select it, then click the **circle object** on the Stage to select it.

2. Click the **Properties panel tab** to display the Properties panel, as shown in Figure 25.

   Note: If the Properties panel is not open, click Window on the menu bar, then click Properties.

   Note: To verify the object is active, review the available settings on the Properties panel. Make sure Position and Size is one of the options.

3. Click **Color Effect** on the Properties panel to display the Color Effect area if it is not already displayed, click the **Style list arrow**, then click **Alpha**.

4. Drag the **Alpha slider** ▢ to **0**.

   The object becomes transparent. The bounding box indicates the location of the object and displays the Stage color, white.

5. Click **frame 48** on the layer to select it.

6. Click the bounding box on the Stage to select the object and check that the object's properties are displayed on the Properties panel.

   Note: To verify the object is active, review the available settings on the Properties panel. Make sure Position and Size is one of the options.

7. Drag the **Alpha slider** ▢ to **100**.

8. Play the movie.

9. Test the movie, then close the Flash Player window.

You used the Color Effect option on the Properties panel to change the transparency of an object.

Resize an object

1. Click **frame 1** to select it, then click inside the bounding box on the Stage to select the **circle object**.

2. Click **Position and Size** on the Properties panel if this area is not already open.

3. Write down the W (width) and H (height) settings of the object.

   The width and height are the dimensions of the bounding box around the circle object.

4. Click **frame 48** to select it, then click the **circle object** to select it.

5. Verify the Lock icon 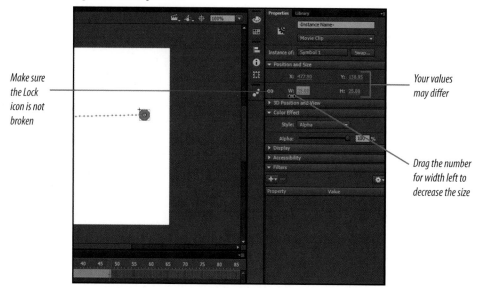 on the Properties panel is not broken.

   Note: If the lock is broken, click the broken lock to lock it, as shown in Figure 26, to ensure the width and height change proportionally.

6. Point to the number next to W: and when the pointer changes to a double-headed arrow ⟨🖐⟩, drag the 🖐 **pointer** left to decrease the width so that the circle shrinks to about half its size, as shown in Figure 26.

   Hint: You can also click a value on the Properties panel and type a new value.

   Note: Resizing the object will reposition it. In this case it causes the object to move up and the motion path to angle up.

7. Test the movie, then close the Flash Player window.

8. Click **frame 48** to select it, then click the **circle object** to select it.

9. Change the **width** to its original size.

   (continued)

Figure 26 *Resizing the circle*

Make sure the Lock icon is not broken

Your values may differ

Drag the number for width left to decrease the size

Figure 27 *Displaying the list of filters*

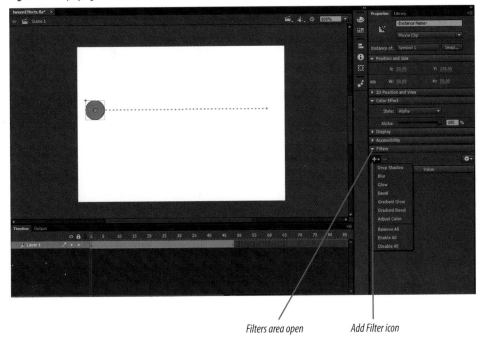

Filters area open   Add Filter icon

10. Click **frame 1**, click the **circle object** to select it, then drag the **Alpha slider** to **100**.

You used the Position and Size option on the Properties panel to change the size of an object and the Color Effect option to change the alpha.

Add a filter to an object

1. Verify the object is selected by viewing the Properties panel and verifying the object's properties are displayed.
2. Click **Filters** on the Properties panel to display the Filters area if it is not already displayed.
3. Click the **Add Filter icon** in the Filters area to display the list of filters, as shown in Figure 27.
4. Click **Drop Shadow**, point to the number for the angle, then when the pointer changes to a double-headed arrow, drag the **pointer** right to change the number of degrees to **100**.
5. Click **frame 1** to select it, then play the movie.
6. Click **frame 1** to select it, then click the **circle object** to select it.
7. Click **Drop Shadow** in the Filters area, then click the **Delete Filter icon** in the Filters area.

   The drop shadow filter is removed from the circle object.
8. Click the **Add Filter icon** to display the list of filters.
9. Click **Bevel**, test the movie, then close the Flash Player window.

You used the Filters option on the Properties panel to add and delete filters.

Add a motion preset

1. Verify the playhead is on frame 1, then click the object to select it.

2. Click **Window** on the menu bar, then click **Motion Presets**.

   The Motion Presets panel opens. It may open as a stand-alone panel or it may be grouped with other panels.

3. Drag the **Motion Presets panel or the panel set** by its title bar (not one of the tabs) to the right so that it does not obscure the Stage.

4. Click the **expand icon** ▶ for the Default Presets, then click **bounce-smoosh** and watch the animation in the preview widow, as shown in Figure 28.

5. Click **Apply**.

   A dialog box opens asking if you want to replace the current motion object with the new selection. You can only apply one motion tween or motion preset to an object at any one time.

6. Click **Yes**.

   The bevel filter is deleted and a new, vertical path is displayed.

7. Play the movie, then test the movie.

   Notice the circle object disappears from the Stage.

8. Close the Flash Player window.

9. Click **View** on the menu bar, point to **Magnification**, then click **50%**.

10. Click **frame 1**, click the **Selection tool** ▷ , draw a **marquee** around the circle object and the path to select both of them.

(continued)

Figure 28 *The Motion Presets panel*

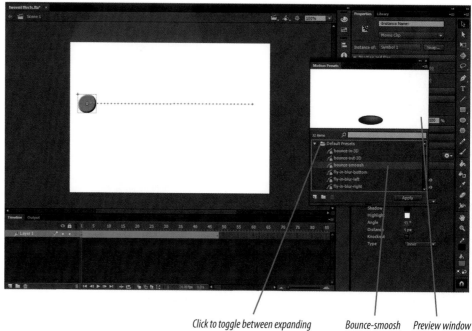

Click to toggle between expanding and collapsing the list

Bounce-smoosh option selected

Preview window

Getting Started with Flash

Figure 29 *Diamond characters indicating Property keyframes*

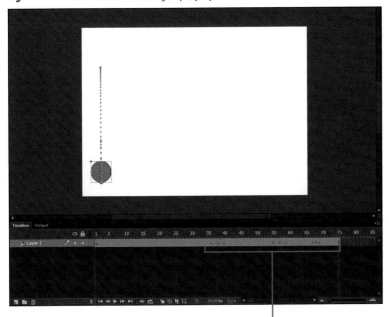

*Diamond characters
appear where the ball
is resized*

11. Press and hold the **up arrow key [↑]** on the keyboard to move the circle object and the path toward the top of the Stage.

12. Click **View** on the menu bar, point to **Magnification**, then click **100%**.

13. Click **View** on the menu bar, point to **Magnification**, then click **Center the Stage**.

14. Test the movie, then close the Flash Player window.

    Notice the Timeline has several diamond characters, as shown in Figure 29. Each one is a Property keyframe and indicates a change in the object during the motion tween, such as when the ball is resized.

15. Click **frame 1** to select it, then drag the **playhead** from frame 1 to the last frame and notice the change that occurs at each keyframe.

16. Click **frame 1** to select it, then display the Motion Presets panel.

17. Scroll the list of motion presets, click **pulse**, click **Apply**, then click **Yes**.

18. Test the movie, then close the Flash Player window.

19. Close the Motion Presets panel, if necessary.

20. Save and close the movie.

You applied motion presets to an object and viewed how keyframes identify changes in the motion tween.

Work with
THE TIMELINE

What You'll Do

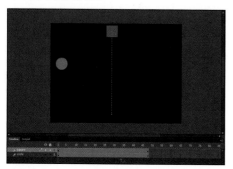

 In this lesson, you will add another layer, allowing you to create an additional animation, and you will use the Timeline to help organize the contents of your movie.

Understanding the Timeline

The Timeline organizes and controls a movie's contents over time. By learning how to read the information provided on the Timeline, you can identify what will be happening in a movie, frame by frame. You can identify which objects are animated, what types of animations are being used, when the various objects will appear in a movie, when changes are made to the properties of an object, which objects will appear on top of others, and how fast the movie will play. Features of the Timeline are shown in Figure 30 and explained in this lesson.

Learning About Layers

Flash uses two types of spatial organization. First, there is the position of objects on the Stage, and then there is the stacking order of objects that overlap. An example of overlapping objects is text placed on a banner. In this case, the banner background might be placed on one layer and the banner text might be placed on a different layer. Layers are used on the Timeline as a way of organizing objects. Placing objects on their own layer makes them easier to work with, especially when reshaping them, repositioning them on the Stage, or rearranging their order in relation to other objects. In addition, layers are useful for organizing other elements such as sounds, animations, and video.

Each new Flash movie contains one layer, named Layer 1. **Layers** are like transparent sheets of plastic that are stacked on top of each other, as shown in Figure 31, which also

Figure 30 *Elements of the Timeline*

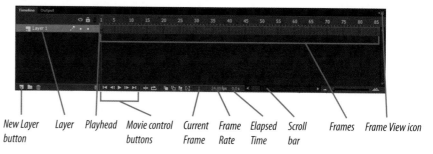

New Layer button | Layer | Playhead | Movie control buttons | Current Frame | Frame Rate | Elapsed Time | Scroll bar | Frames | Frame View icon

shows how the stacked objects appear on the Stage. Each layer can contain one or more objects. In Figure 31, the tree is on one layer, the heading "Solitude" is on another layer, and the colored backdrop is on a third layer. You can add layers using the Timeline command on the Insert menu or by clicking the New Layer icon on the Timeline status bar. Placing objects on different layers and locking the layers helps avoid accidental changes to one object when you are editing another.

When you add a new layer, Flash stacks it on top of the other layer(s) on the Timeline. The stacking order of the layers on the Timeline is important because objects on the Stage appear in the same stacking order. For example, if you have two overlapping objects, and the top layer has a drawing of a tree and the bottom layer has a drawing of a house, the tree appears as though it is in front of the house. You can change the stacking order of layers simply by dragging them up or down in the list of layers. You can name layers, hide them so their

contents do not appear on the Stage, and lock them so that they cannot be edited. Naming a layer provides a clue to the objects on that layer. For example, naming a layer "Logo" might indicate that the object on the layer is the company's logo. Hiding layers can reduce the clutter on the Stage and make it easier to work with selected objects on the layer(s) that are not hidden. Locking layers prevents the objects from being accidentally edited.

Using Frames and Keyframes

The Timeline is made up of individual segments called **frames**. The contents of each layer appear as the playhead moves over the frames, so any object in frame 1, no matter which layer it is on, appears on the Stage whenever frame 1 is played. Frames are numbered in increments of five for easy reference. The upper-right corner of the Timeline contains the Frame View icon. Clicking this icon displays a menu that provides different views of the Timeline, for example, showing more frames or showing a

preview (thumbnails) of the objects on a layer. The status bar at the bottom of the Timeline indicates the current frame (the frame that the playhead is currently on), the frame rate (frames per second, also called fps), and the elapsed time from frame 1 to the current frame. Frames per second is the unit of measure for movies. If the frame rate is set to 24 frames per second and the movie has 48 frames, the movie will take 2 seconds to play.

Keyframes are locations on the Timeline where a new occurrence of an object appears or a change is made in the object. So, if you draw an object on the Stage, the current frame will need to be changed to a keyframe. In addition, if you create a motion tween, the first frame of the tween span will be a keyframe. One type of keyframe is a Property keyframe, which is used to specify locations on the Timeline where you want an animation or object to change. For example, you might have an animation of an object that moves across the Stage in frames 1 through 20. If you decide to resize the object in frame 5, a Property keyframe will appear on the Timeline in frame 5 when you make the change to that object. Another type of keyframe is a blank keyframe, which is used to indicate that no content (objects) appears in that frame.

Interpreting the Timeline

The Timeline provides many clues to what is happening on the Stage. Interpreting these clues is essential to learning Flash. These clues are in the form of characters and colors that appear on the Timeline. Figure 32 shows the most common characters and colors. These

Figure 31 *The concept of layers*

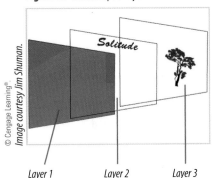

© Cengage Learning®.
Image courtesy Jim Shuman.

Layer 1   Layer 2   Layer 3

The Stage

are explained next. Others will be discussed in subsequent chapters. The top layer on the Timeline in Figure 32 shows that frame 1 is a blank keyframe as indicated by the unfilled circle. No content will appear in frame 1 of this layer. In addition, the gray background which extends to frame 24 indicates a span of blank frames. An unfilled rectangle appears at the end of the span and indicates the end of the blank frames. The next layer shows a keyframe with content as indicated by the filled circle. The content in this frame also appears in frames 2-24 as indicated by the gray background. Again, an unfilled rectangle appears at the end of the span and indicates the end of the frames with the same content. The next layer shows a keyframe in frame 1 and a motion tween using the contents of frame 1 as indicated by the blue background in frames 2-24. A property keyframe (indicated by a diamond) appears at the end of this span because a change has been made to the object being animated, such as moving it to a different location on the Stage. The bottom layer shows a keyframe in frame 1 and property keyframes (indicated by diamonds) in frames 5, 10, 15, 20 and 24.

Figure 33 shows the Timeline of the movie created in Lesson 3 but with the addition of a second object, a square at the top of the Stage. By studying the Timeline, you can learn several things about the square object and this movie. First, the yellow color highlighting in Layer 2 indicates that this layer is active. Second, the square object is placed on its own layer, Layer 2 (indicated by the yellow color that highlights the layer name and the motion animation). Third, the layer has a motion animation (indicated by the highlighted frames and the motion path on the Stage). Fourth, the animation runs from frame 1 to frame 48. Fifth, if the objects intersect during the animation, the square will be on top of the circle, because the layer it is placed on (Layer 2) is above the layer that the circle is placed on (Layer 1). Sixth, the frame rate is set to 24, which means that the movie will play 24 frames per second. Seventh, the playhead is at frame 1, which causes the contents of frame 1 for both layers to appear on the Stage.

Figure 32 *Common characters and colors on the Timeline*

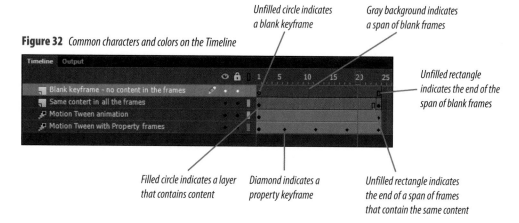

Unfilled circle indicates a blank keyframe

Gray background indicates a span of blank frames

Unfilled rectangle indicates the end of the span of blank frames

Filled circle indicates a layer that contains content

Diamond indicates a property keyframe

Unfilled rectangle indicates the end of a span of frames that contain the same content

Figure 33 *The Timeline of a movie with a second object*

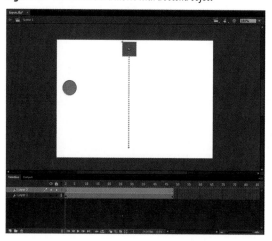

Getting Started with Flash

Figure 34 *Drawing a square*

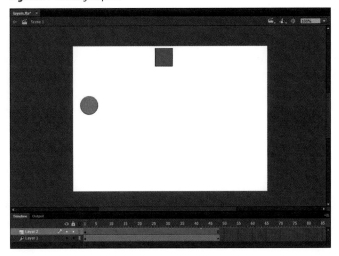

Figure 35 *Positioning the square at the bottom of the Stage*

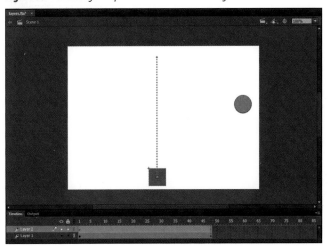

Add a layer

1. Open tween.fla, then save it as **layers.fla**.
2. Click **frame 1** on Layer 1.
3. Click **Insert** on the menu bar, point to **Timeline**, then click **Layer**.

   A new layer—Layer 2—appears at the top of the Timeline.

You added a layer to the Timeline.

Create a second animation

1. Click **frame 1** on Layer 2.
2. Click and hold the **Rectangle tool** on the Tools panel, then click the **Rectangle tool** on the menu that opens.
3. Click the **Fill Color tool color swatch** on the Tools panel, then click the **blue color swatch** in the left column of the color palette.
4. Press and hold [**Shift**], then draw a **square** resembling the dimensions and position of the square shown in Figure 34.
5. Click the **Selection tool** on the Tools panel, then drag a **marquee** around the square to select the object.
6. Click **Insert** on the menu bar, click **Motion Tween**, then click **OK** in the Convert selection to symbol for tween dialog box.
7. Click **frame 48** on Layer 2, then drag the **square** to the bottom of the Stage, as shown in Figure 35.

   When you click frame 48, the circle object moves to the right side of the Stage. Remember, when a frame is selected, all objects in that frame on every layer appear on the Stage.
8. Play the movie.

   The square appears on top if the two objects intersect.

You drew an object and used it to create a second animation.

Work with layers and view Timeline features

1. Click **Layer 2** on the Timeline, then drag **Layer 2** below Layer 1.

   Layer 2 is now the bottom layer, as shown in Figure 36.

2. Play the movie and notice how the square appears beneath the circle if the objects intersect.

3. Click **Layer 2** on the Timeline, then drag **Layer 2** above Layer 1.

4. Play the movie and notice how the square now appears on top of the circle if they intersect.

5. Click the **Show or Hide This Layer icon** next to **Layer 1** to hide the layer, then compare your image to Figure 37.

   After you click the Show or Hide This Layer icon, it changes from a black dot to an X, as shown in Figure 37.

6. Click the **Show or Hide This Layer icon** next to **Layer 1** to show the layer.

7. Click the **Lock or Unlock All Layers icon** to lock all layers, then try to select and edit an object.

8. Click the **Lock or Unlock All Layers icon** again to unlock the layers.

9. Click the **Frame View icon** ![icon] on the upper-right corner of the Timeline title bar, as shown in Figure 37, to display the menu.

10. Click **Small** to display more frames.

11. Click the **Frame View icon** ![icon], then click **Normal**.

You changed the order of the layers, the display of frames, and the way the Timeline is viewed.

Figure 36 *Changing the stacking order of layers*

Figure 37 *Hiding Layer 1*

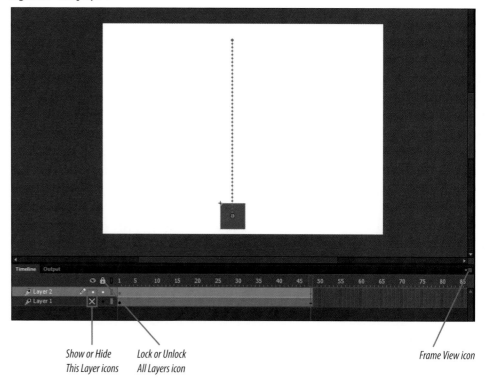

Show or Hide This Layer icons   Lock or Unlock All Layers icon   Frame View icon

Figure 38 *Changing the frame rate*

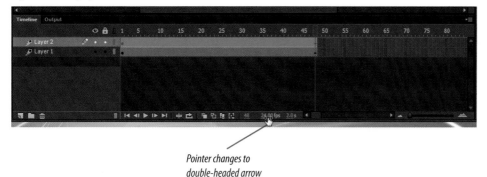

Pointer changes to
double-headed arrow

Figure 39 *Displaying the Properties option*

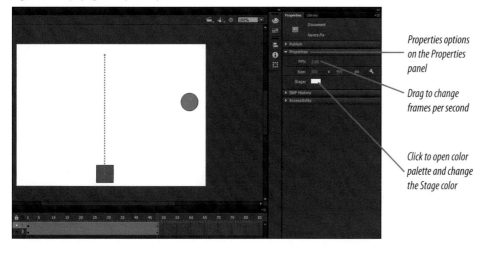

Properties options
on the Properties
panel

Drag to change
frames per second

Click to open color
palette and change
the Stage color

Modify the frame rate and change the layer names

1. Point to the **Frame Rate (fps)** on the Timeline status bar so the pointer changes to the double-headed arrow, as shown in Figure 38.

2. Drag the **pointer** left to change the frame rate to **3**.

TIP Alternately, you can click the frame rate number, then type a new number.

3. Play the movie and notice that the speed of the movie changed.

4. Click a blank area of the Stage, then verify the Properties panel is the active panel. If not, click **Window**, then click **Properties**.

5. If the Properties options are not displayed, as shown in Figure 39, click **Properties** on the Properties panel.

   When the Stage is clicked, the Properties panel provides information about the Stage, including size and background color.

6. Use the Properties panel to change the frame rate (fps) to **18** and the Stage color to **black**.

7. Click the **tick mark** for **24** on the Timeline and notice the position of the objects on the Stage.

8. Drag (Scrub) the **playhead** left and right to display frames one by one.

9. Double-click **Layer 1** on the Timeline, type **circle**, then press **[Enter]**(Win) or **[return]**(Mac).

10. Change the name of Layer 2 to **square**.

11. Test the movie, save your work, then close the document.

You changed the frame rate of the movie and named layers.

Import Graphics and WORK WITH LIBRARIES

What You'll Do

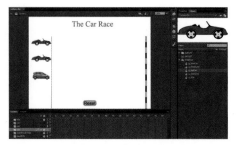

Images courtesy Jim Shuman. ©iStock.com/AtomA.

 In this lesson, you will use the Library panel to organize the symbols in a movie.

Understanding Graphic Types

Flash provides excellent drawing tools, which allow you to create various objects that can be changed into symbols. In addition, you can import graphics and other assets, such as photographs and sounds. There are two types of graphic files, bitmap graphics and vector graphics. They are distinguished by the way in which the image is represented.

Bitmap images are made up of a group of tiny dots of color called **pixels** (picture elements). Bitmap graphics are often used with photographic images because they can represent subtle gradients in color. However, one disadvantage of bitmap graphics is the inability to enlarge the graphic without distorting the image. This is because both the computer screen's resolution (pixels per inch) and the number of pixels making up the image are a fixed number. So, when you enlarge an image each pixel must increase in size to fill the larger image dimensions. This causes the pixels to display jagged edges, as shown in Figure 40.

Vector graphics represent an image as lines and arcs that are combined to create various geometric shapes, such as circles and rectangles. Flash drawing tools create vector graphics. One advantage of vector graphics is that they can be resized without distorting the image. The reason is that the geometric shapes are based on mathematical models that are recalculated when the image is resized. Figure 41 shows an example of a vector graphic before and after resizing. Vector graphics are best used for drawings rather than for images requiring photographic quality.

There are several programs that allow you to create and edit graphics including Adobe Illustrator, Fireworks, and Photoshop. There are also clip art and stock photograph collections that are available online. Filename extensions identify the file type. For example, .jpg, .tif, .png, and .gif are file formats for bitmap graphics and .ai is a vector file format.

Getting Started with Flash

Importing and Editing Graphics

Once you have identified the graphic you would like to include in a Flash document, you can use the Import feature to bring the graphic into Flash. The process for importing is to select the Import command from the File menu and specify where to import (Stage or Library). Then you navigate to the location where the file is stored and select it. After importing a vector graphic you can work with it as you would any graphic. Because bitmap graphics are not easy to edit in Flash, you may want to use another program, such as Photoshop, to obtain the desired size, color, and other enhancements before importing the graphic.

Figure 40 *Bitmap graphic enlarged*

Photo courtesy Jim Shuman.

Figure 41 *Vector graphic enlarged*

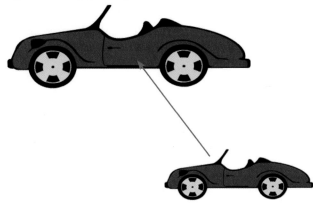

Image courtesy Jim Shuman.

Understanding the Library

The library in a Flash document contains the symbols and other items such as imported graphics, videos, and sounds. The Library panel provides a way to view and organize these items, and allows you to change the item name, display item properties, and add and delete items. Figure 42 shows the Library panel for a document. Refer to this figure as you read the following descriptions of the parts of the library.

Tab title—Identifies the panel title, in this case, the Library panel.

Panel options list arrow—Opens the Panel options menu, shown in Figure 43, which provides access to several features used to edit symbols (such as renaming symbols) and organize symbols (such as creating a new folder).

Figure 42 *The Library panel*

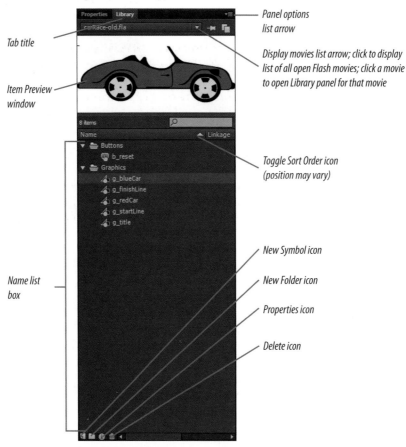

Tab title

Item Preview window

Name list box

Panel options list arrow

Display movies list arrow; click to display list of all open Flash movies; click a movie to open Library panel for that movie

Toggle Sort Order icon (position may vary)

New Symbol icon

New Folder icon

Properties icon

Delete icon

Image courtesy Jim Shuman.

Display movies list arrow—Opens a menu showing all open movies. You use this menu to select an open document (movie) and display the Library panel associated with that open document. This allows you to use the items from one movie in another movie. For example, you may have

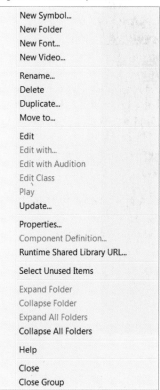

Figure 43 *The Panel options menu*

developed a drawing in one Flash movie that you converted to a symbol and now you want to use that symbol in the movie you are working on. With both documents open, you simply use the Display movies list arrow to display the library with the desired symbol, and then drag the symbol to the Stage of the current movie. This will automatically place the symbol in the library for the current movie. In addition to the movie libraries, you can create permanent libraries that are available whenever you start Flash. Flash also has sample libraries that contain buttons and other objects. The permanent and sample libraries are accessed through the Common Libraries command on the Window menu. All assets in all of these libraries are available for use in any movie.

Item Preview window—Displays the selected item. If the item is animated or if it is a sound file, a control button appears, allowing you to preview the animation or play the sound.

Name list box—Lists the folder and item names. Each item type has a different icon associated with it. Clicking an item name or icon displays the item in the Item Preview window.

Toggle Sort Order icon—Allows you to reorder the list of folders and items within folders.

New Symbol icon—Displays the Create New Symbol dialog box, allowing you to create a new symbol.

New Folder icon—Allows you to create a new folder.

Properties icon—Displays the Properties dialog box for the selected item.

Delete icon—Deletes the selected item or folder.

To make changes to an item, you can double-click either the item icon on the Library panel, the item in the Item Preview window, or the item on the Stage to display the edit window.

Create folders on the Library panel

1. Open fl1_2.fla, then save it as **carRace.fla**.

2. Verify the Properties panel, the Library panel, and the Tools panel are displayed.

3. Click **View** on the menu bar, point to **Magnification**, and then click **Fit in Window**.

   This movie has five layers containing various graphic objects such as text, lines, and cars. There is also a button object.

4. Click the **Show or Hide All Layers icon** 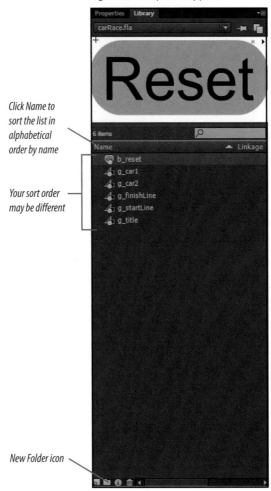 on the Timeline to hide all of the layers.

5. Click each **X** in the Show or Hide All Layers column to show the contents of each layer, click the **Show or Hide This Layer icon** to hide the contents of that layer, then after viewing the contents of each layer, click the **Show or Hide All Layers icon** on the Timeline to show all of the layers.

6. Display the Library panel.

7. Click each item on the Library panel to display it in the Item Preview window.

   Notice that there is one button symbol (b_reset) and five graphic symbols.

8. Click **Name** on the Name list box title bar, as shown in Figure 44, and notice how the items are sorted.

9. Repeat Step 8 and notice how the items are sorted.

You opened a Flash movie and sorted items on the Library panel.

Figure 44 *The open Library panel*

Click Name to sort the list in alphabetical order by name

Your sort order may be different

New Folder icon

Figure 45 *The Library panel with the folders added*

Buttons folder

Graphics folder

Figure 46 *The Library panel after moving the symbols to the folders*

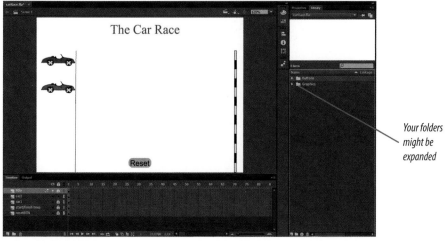

The Car Race

Reset

Your folders might be expanded

Images courtesy Jim Shuman.

Organize items within Library panel folders

1. Click the **New Folder icon** on the Library panel, as shown in Figure 44.
2. Type **Graphics** in the Name text box for the new folder, then press [**Enter**] (Win) or [**return**] (Mac).
3. Click the **New Folder icon** on the Library panel.
4. Type **Buttons** in the Name text box for the new folder, then press [**Enter**] (Win) or [**return**] (Mac).

   Your Library panel should resemble Figure 45.
5. Drag the **g_title symbol** from the Library panel to the Graphics folder.
6. Drag the other graphic symbols to the Graphics folder.
7. Drag the **b_reset symbol** to the Buttons folder, then compare your Library panel to Figure 46.
8. Click the **Graphics folder expand icon** to open it and display the graphic symbols.
9. Click the **Buttons folder expand icon** to open it and display the button symbol.
10. Click the **Graphics folder collapse icon** to close the folder.
11. Click the **Buttons folder collapse icon** to close the folder.

   Note: To remove an item from a folder, drag the item down to a blank area of the Library panel.

You created new folders, organized the symbols within the folders, and then opened and closed the folders.

Rename symbols and delete a symbol

1. Click the **expand icon** ▶ for the Graphics folder to display the symbols.

2. Right-click (Win) or [control]-click (Mac) the **g_car1 symbol**, then click **Rename**.

3. Type **g_redCar** in the Name text box, then press **[Enter]** (Win) or **[return]** (Mac).

4. Repeat Steps 2 and 3 to rename the g_car2 symbol as **g_blueCar**.

5. Study the Stage and notice the finish line at the right side of the Stage.

6. Click **g_finishLine** on the Library panel to select it.

7. Click the **Delete icon** 🗑 at the bottom of the Library panel.

8. Study the Stage and notice the finish line is deleted.

   Your Library panel should resemble Figure 47.

   TIP You can also select an item and press [Delete], or you can use the Panel options menu on the Library panel to remove an item from the library. The Undo command in the Edit menu can be used to undelete an item.

9. Click **Edit** on the menu bar, then click **Undo Delete Library Item**.

You used the Library panel to rename symbols, delete a symbol, and undo the delete.

Figure 47 *Updated Library panel*

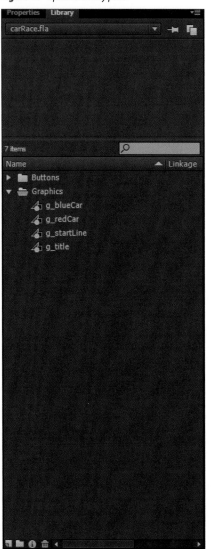

Figure 48 *Positioning car3 on the Stage*

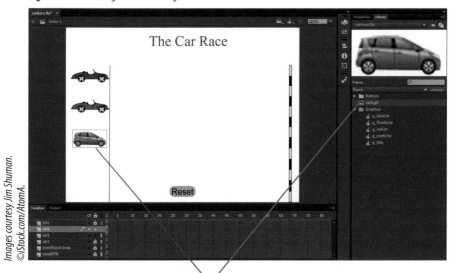

Drag car3 icon from the
Library panel to the Stage

Images courtesy Jim Shuman.
©iStock.com/AtomA.

Import graphics

1. Click **File** on the menu bar, point to **Import**, then click **Import to Library**.

   The process of preparing to import may take a few moments. Eventually, the Import to Library dialog box will open.

2. Navigate to the folder where your Data files are stored, click **car3.gif**, then click **Open**.

   The file car3.gif is a digital illustration that was edited in Photoshop and saved as a .gif file.

3. Display the Library panel and notice the icon used for bitmap graphics.

4. Insert a new layer above the car2 layer and name it **car3**.

5. Click **frame 1** of the car3 layer.

6. Drag the **car3 icon** from the Library panel to the Stage below the blue car as shown in Figure 48.

7. With car3 selected, click the **Properties tab** to display the Properties panel.

8. Verify the **Lock width and height values together** icon ⊖ is unbroken.

9. Change the width to **300**.

10. Change the width of the blue car to **300**.

    Notice when the images are enlarged car3, the bitmap image, is distorted. The blue car, a vector image, is not distorted.

11. Undo the size changes, save your work, then close the document.

You imported a bitmap graphic to the Library panel and enlarged the image.

Plan an
APPLICATION AND USE HELP

What You'll Do

Purpose	"What do we want to accomplish?"
Audience	"Who will use our application or website?"
Treatment	"What is the look and feel?"
Specifications	"What does the application include and how does it work?"

© Cengage Learning®.

In this lesson, you will learn how to plan a Flash application. You will also learn about the guidelines for screen design and the interactive design of applications.

Planning an Application

Flash can be used to develop entire products, such as games that run on smartphones, or animations that are part of a product, such as an educational tutorial, and delivered via the Internet, a webinar, or a DVD. You can use Flash to create enhancements to web pages, such as animated logos, interactive navigation buttons, and banner ads. No matter what the application, the first step is planning. Often, the temptation is to jump right into the program and start developing movies. The problem is that this invariably results in a more time-consuming process at best, and wasted effort, resources, and money at worst. The larger and more complex the project is, the more critical the planning process becomes. Planning an application should involve the following steps:

Step 1: Stating the Purpose (Goals). "What, specifically, do we want to accomplish?"

Determining the goals is a critical step in planning because goals guide the development process, keep the team members on track, and provide a way to evaluate the application, both during and after its development.

Step 2: Identifying the Target Audience. "Who will use our application?"

Understanding the potential viewers helps in developing an application that can address their needs. For example, children respond to exploration and surprise, so having a dog wag its tail when the mouse pointer rolls over it might appeal to this audience.

Step 3: Determining the Treatment. "What is the look and feel?"

The treatment is how the application will be presented to the user, including the tone, approach, and emphasis.

Tone—Will the application be humorous, serious, light, heavy, formal, or informal? The tone of an application can often be used to make a statement, for instance, projecting a progressive, high-tech, well-funded corporate image.

Approach—How much direction will be provided to the user? An interactive game might focus on exploration such as when the user points to an object on the screen and the object becomes animated; while an informational application might provide lots of direction and include lists of options in the form of drop-down menus.

Emphasis—How much emphasis will be placed on the various multimedia elements? For example, a company may want to develop a business application that shows the features of its new product line, including video demonstrations and sound narrations of how each product works. The budget might not allow for the expense of creating the videos, so the emphasis would shift to still pictures with text descriptions.

Step 4: Developing the Specifications and Storyboard. "What precisely does the application include and how does it work?"

The **specifications** state what will be included in each screen, including the arrangement of each element and the functionality of each object (for example, what happens when you click the button labeled Skip Intro). Specifications should include the following:

Playback System—The choice of what configuration to target for playback is critical, especially Internet connection speed, browser versions, screen resolution, screen size (especially when targeting mobile devices), and plug-ins.

Elements to Include—The specifications should include details about the various elements that are to be included in the application. What are the dimensions for the animations, and what is the frame rate? What are the sizes of the various objects such as photos, buttons, and so on? What fonts, font sizes, and font formatting will be used? Should video or sound be included?

Functionality—The specifications should include the way the program reacts to an action by the user, such as a mouse click. For example, clicking a door (object) might cause a doorbell to ring (sound), the door to open (an animation), an "exit the program" message to appear (text), or an entirely new screen to be displayed.

Using Screen Design Guidelines

The following screen design guidelines are used by application developers. The implementation of these guidelines is affected by the goals of the application, the intended audience, and the content.

Balance in screen design refers to the distribution of optical weight in the layout. Optical weight is the ability of an object to attract the viewer's eye, as determined by the object's size, shape, color, and so on. The screen in Figure 49 shows a somewhat balanced design with the bright buttons at the bottom balanced against the heading near the top; and the icons on the left balanced against the satellite image on the right. However, the overall feel is less formal than a precisely balanced layout would project. In general, a balanced design is more appealing to a viewer. However, for a game application a balanced layout may not be desired.

Figure 49 *Sample screen design*

nasa.gov http://spaceplace.nasa.gov/satellite-insight/en/#/review/satelliteinsight/SatelliteInsight.swf

Unity helps the screen objects reinforce each other. **Intra-screen unity** has to do with how the various screen objects relate and how they all fit in. For example, a children's game might only use cartoon characterizations of animals for all the objects—including navigation buttons and sound control buttons, as well as the on-screen characters. **Inter-screen unity** refers to the design that viewers encounter as they navigate from one screen to another, and it provides consistency throughout the application. For example, all navigation buttons are located in the same place on each screen.

Movement refers to the way the viewer's eyes move through the objects on the screen. Different types of objects and various animation techniques can be used to draw the viewer to a location on the screen.

For example, a photo of a waterfall may cause the viewer's eyes to follow the flow of the water down, especially if the waterfall is animated. The designer could then place an object, such as a logo or a sales message, below the waterfall.

Using Interactive Design Guidelines

In addition to screen design guidelines, interactive guidelines determine the interactivity of the application. The following guidelines are not absolute rules since they are affected by the goals of the application, the intended audience, and the content:

- Make it simple, easy to understand, and easy to use so that viewers do not have to spend time learning what the application is about and what they need to do.
- Build in consistency in the navigation scheme. Help the users know where they are in the application and help them avoid getting lost.
- Provide feedback. Users need to know when an action, such as clicking a button, has been completed. Changing its color or shape, or adding a sound can indicate this.
- Give the user control. Allow the user to skip long introductions; provide controls for starting, stopping, and rewinding animations, video, and audio; and provide controls for adjusting audio.

Using Storyboards

Simple applications, such as a banner ad on a website, may consist of a single Flash animation, but complex applications, such as games, often include several animations within one or more Flash movies. No matter how extensive the application, storyboards can be invaluable in the development process. A storyboard is a series of pictures that illustrate the sequence of events in an animation. See Figure 50. A storyboard can be extremely elaborate and include color images, scripts,

Figure 50 *Sample storyboard*

Image courtesy Jim Shuman.

Getting Started with Flash

and notations for dialog, sound effects, transitions, and movement. Or, it can be as simple as black and white stick figures. Storyboards can be created using templates and even computer programs or simply sketched out. As part of the pre-production process, storyboards are an easy way to test out an idea by helping you visualize the progression of events. This allows you to make adjustments before development begins. Then the storyboard becomes a basic blueprint for the creation of the animation and a guide for those involved in the development process such as Flash designers, developers, and artists.

Rich Media Content and Accessibility

Flash provides the tools that allow you to create compelling applications and websites by incorporating rich media content, such as animations, sound, and video. Generally, incorporating rich media enhances the user's experience. However, accessibility becomes an issue for those persons who have visual, hearing, or mobility impairments, or have a cognitive disability. Designers need to utilize techniques that help ensure accessibility, such as providing consistency in navigation and layout, labeling graphics, captioning audio content throughout the applications and website, and providing keyboard access.

The Flash Workflow Process

After the planning process, you are ready to start work on the Flash documents. The following steps can be used as guidelines in a general workflow process suggested by Adobe.

Step 1: Create and/or acquire the elements to be used in the application. The elements include text, photos, drawings, video, and audio. The elements become the raw material for the graphics, animations, menus, buttons, and content that populate the application and provide the interactivity. You can use the various Flash drawing and text tools to create your own images and text content; or, you can use another program, such as Adobe Photoshop, to develop the elements, and then import them into Flash. Alternately, you can acquire stock clip art and photographs. You can produce video and audio content in-house and import it into Flash or you can acquire these elements from a third party.

Step 2: Arrange the elements and create the animations. Arrange the elements (objects) on the Stage and on the Timeline to define when and how they appear in your application. Once the elements are available, you can create the various animations called for in the specifications.

Step 3: Apply special effects. Flash provides innumerable special effects that can be applied to the various media elements and animations. These include graphic and text filters, such as drop shadows, blurs, glows, and bevels. In addition, there are effects for sounds and animations such as fade-ins and fade-outs, acceleration and deceleration, morphing, and even 3D effects.

Step 4: Create the interactivity. Flash provides a scripting feature, ActionScript, which allows you to develop programming code to control how the media elements behave, including how various objects respond to user interactions, such as clicking buttons and rolling over images.

Step 5: Test and publish the application. Testing can begin before the actual development process with usability testing, which involves potential users being observed as they navigate through thumbnail sketches of the storyboard. Testing should continue throughout the development process, including using the Test Movie feature in the Control menu to test the movie using the Flash Player and to publish the movie in order to test it in a browser.

Project Management

Developing any extensive application, such as a game, involves project management. A project plan needs to be developed that provides the project scope and identifies the milestones, including analyzing, designing, building, testing, and launching. Personnel and resource needs are identified, budgets built, tasks assigned, and schedules developed. Successful projects are a team effort relying on the close collaboration of designers, developers, project managers, graphic artists, programmers, testers, and others. Adobe provides various product suites, such as the Creative Suite 6 Design and Web Premium, that include programs such as Flash, Dreamweaver, Photoshop, Illustrator, and Edge Animate. These are the primary tools needed to develop interactive applications. These programs are designed for easy integration. So, a graphic artist can use Photoshop to develop an image that can easily be imported into Flash and used by an animator. In addition, other tools in the suites, such as Adobe Bridge, help ensure efficient workflow when working in a team environment. Adobe Flash Builder and Flex are tools that are used by Flash developers who focus on creating sophisticated Flash applications by writing ActionScript code.

Using the Flash Help Feature

As you are planning the application and while you are developing it, you may have specific questions about how to incorporate what you are planning using Flash. Fortunately, Flash provides a comprehensive Help feature that can be very useful when first learning the program. You access the Help feature from the Help menu. The Help feature is organized by categories, including Learn & Support/ Flash Professional Help, which have several topics such as Workspace and workflow documents. In addition, the Help feature has a Search feature. You use the Search feature to search for topics using keywords, such as Timeline. Searching by keywords accesses the Flash Community Help feature, which displays links to content relevant to the search terms. Another option in the Help menu is Adobe Online Forums. This is a link to Flash Professional forums sponsored by Adobe. You can ask questions and join groups discussing various Flash-related topics. Other resources not affiliated with Adobe are available through the web. You may find some by searching the web for Flash resources.

Figure 51 *The Flash Help categories*

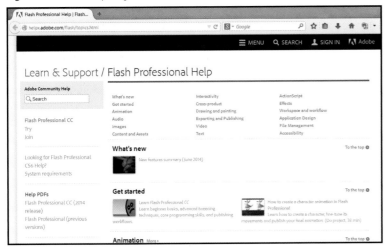

Figure 52 *The Flash Support & Community Help site*

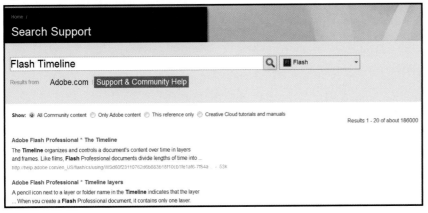

Use Flash Help

1. Start a new Flash document.

2. Click **Help** on the menu bar, then click **Flash Help**.

   Note: If you see a page not found message, be sure you are connected to the Internet.

3. Maximize the Help window to view the Help screen, as shown in Figure 51.

4. Scroll down, display the **Workspace and workflow** section, then click **Flash workflow and workspace**.

5. Scroll down the page to **General Flash workflow** and read the list of basic steps.

6. Scroll to display the top of the Help window.

7. Click in the **Search text box**, then type **Flash Timeline**.

8. Press **[Enter]** (Win) or **[return]** (Mac) to access the Community Help site, as seen in Figure 52.

9. Scroll down the page and study the various links provided on the site.

10. Close the Flash Help site, then exit the Flash program.

You used the Flash Help feature to access information on the Timeline and the community help feature.

Open a document and understand the Flash workspace.

1. Start Flash, open fl1_3.fla, then save it as **skillsDemo1.fla**. This movie has two layers. Layer 1 contains the heading and the rectangle at the top of the Stage. Layer 2 contains an animation that runs for 75 frames.

2. Change the magnification to 50% using the View menu. (*Hint*: Click View, point to Magnification, then click 50%.)

3. Change the magnification to Fit in Window.

4. Change the Timeline view to Small, then change it back to Normal. (*Hint*: Click the Frame View icon in the upper-right corner of the Timeline title bar.)

5. Hide all panels.

6. Display the Tools panel, Timeline panel, Properties panel, and the Library panel if it did not open with the Properties panel.

7. Group the Library and Properties panels if they are not already grouped.

8. Drag the Library panel from the Properties panel, then position it on the Stage.

9. Collapse the Library panel.

10. Close the Library panel to remove it from the screen.

11. Reset the Essentials workspace.

Play and test a Flash movie.

1. Drag the playhead to view the contents of each frame. Use the commands on the Timeline status bar to play and rewind the movie.

2. Press [Enter] (Win) or [return] (Mac) to play and stop the movie.

3. Test the movie in the Flash Player window, then close the Flash Player window.

Change the document size and Stage color.

1. Use the Properties settings on the Properties panel to change the Stage height to 380. (*Hint*: Click a blank area of the Stage to select it.)

2. Change the Stage color to a medium gray color (#999999).

3. Change the magnification to 100%.

4. Play the movie.

Create and save a Flash movie.

1. Insert a new layer above Layer 2, then select frame 1 on the new layer, Layer 3.

2. Draw a green ball in the middle of the left side of the Stage, approximately the same size as the red ball. (*Hint*: The green gradient color can be used to draw the ball. Several gradient colors are found in the bottom row of the color palette when you click the Fill Color tool on the Tools panel.)

3. Use the Selection tool to draw a marquee around the green ball to select it, then create a motion tween to animate the green ball so that it moves across the screen from left to right. (*Hint*: After inserting the motion tween, select frame 75 on Layer 3 before repositioning the green ball.)

4. Use the Selection tool to reshape the motion path to an arc by dragging the middle of the path downward.

5. Play the movie.

6. Use the Undo command to undo the reshape. (*Note*: You may need to use the Undo feature twice.)

7. Use the Selection tool to select frame 75 of the Layer 3, click the green ball to select it, then use the Properties panel to change the transparency (alpha) from 100% to 20%. (*Hint*: If the Properties panel Color Effect option is not displayed, make sure the Properties panel is open and click the green ball to make sure it is selected.)

8. Play the movie.

9. Click frame 75 on Layer 3 and click the green ball to select it.

10. Use the Properties panel to decrease the width of the ball to approximately half its size. (*Hint*: Make sure the lock width and height value icon on the Properties panel is unbroken. You may need to click the Stage to have the new value take effect.)

11. Play the movie.

12. Select frame 1 on Layer 3, then click the green ball to select it.

13. Use the Filters option on the Properties panel to add a drop shadow.

14. Play the movie.

15. Select frame 1 on Layer 2, then click the red ball to select it.

16. Open the Motion Presets panel, then add a bounce-smoosh preset.

17. Move Layer 3 below Layer 2.

18. Play the movie.

19. Save the movie.

Work with the Timeline.

1. Change the frame rate to 8 frames per second, play the movie, change the frame rate to 24, then play the movie again.
2. Change the view of the Timeline to display more frames.
3. Change the view of the Timeline to display Normal view.
4. Click frame 1 on Layer 1, use the playhead to display each frame, then compare your screens to Figure 53.
5. Save the movie.

Import a graphic and resize it.

1. Use the Document Settings dialog box to change the Stage color to white.
2. Insert a new layer, then rename the layer **gray backdrop**.
3. Drag the new layer beneath the other layers.
4. Import the grayBkDrop.bmp graphic to the Library.
5. Select frame 1 of the gray backdrop layer.
6. Drag the GrayBkDrop.bmp symbol from the Library to the stage.
7. Change the dimensions of the object to a width of 550 and a height of 380.
8. Center the image on the Stage.
9. Lock the gray backdrop layer.
10. Hide and show each layer to determine the contents on the layer.

11. Rename the layers using these names: **heading**, **green ball**, and **red ball**. Use clues on the Timeline to help you know what to name each layer.

12. Test the movie then close the Flash Player window.
13. Save and close the Flash document.

Figure 53 *Completed Skills Review*

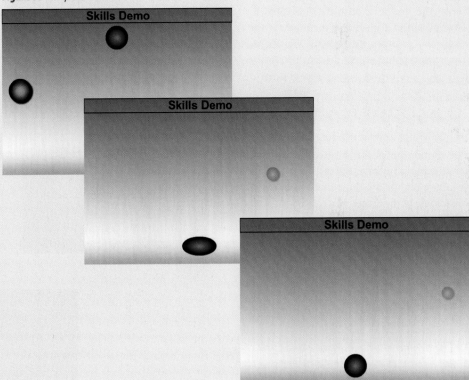

A friend cannot decide whether or not to sign up for a class in Flash. You help her decide by showing her what you already know about Flash. You want to show her how easy it is to create a simple animation because you think she'd enjoy a class in Flash. You decide to animate three objects. The first object is placed on the center of the Stage and pulsates throughout the movie. The second object enters the Stage from the left side and moves across the middle of the Stage and off the right side of the Stage. The third object enters the Stage from the right side and moves across the middle of the Stage and off the left side of the Stage. The motion paths for the two objects that move across the Stage are reshaped so they go above and below the pulsating object in the middle of the Stage.

1. Open a Flash document, then save it as **demonstration.fla**.
2. Verify the view is set to 100%.
3. Use the tools on the Tools panel to create a circle (or object of your choice) and color of your choice on the middle of the Stage.
4. Draw a marquee around the object to select it and apply a pulse motion preset.
5. Insert a new layer, then select frame 1 on the layer.
6. Create a simple shape or design using a color of your choice, and place it off the left side of the Stage and halfway down the Stage.

7. Select the object and insert a motion tween that moves the object directly across the screen and off the right side of the Stage. (*Hint*: After inserting the motion tween, select the last frame in the motion span and drag the object off the right side of the Stage.)
8. Reshape the motion path so that the object goes in an arc below the center pulsating object.
9. Insert a new layer, then select frame 1 on the new layer.
10. Create an object using the color of your choice and place it off the right side of the Stage and halfway down the Stage.

11. Draw a marquee to select the object and insert a motion tween that moves the object directly across the screen and off the left side of the Stage.
12. Reshape the motion path so that the object goes in an arc above the center pulsating object.
13. Play the movie.
14. Add a Stage color.
15. Rename the layers with descriptive names.
16. Play the movie, test it, then close the Flash Player window.
17. Save the movie, then compare your movie to the sample provided in Figure 54.

Figure 54 *Sample completed Project Builder 1*

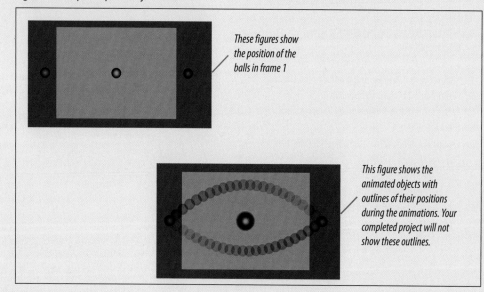

These figures show the position of the balls in frame 1

This figure shows the animated objects with outlines of their positions during the animations. Your completed project will not show these outlines.

You've been asked to develop a simple movie about recycling for a day care center. For this project, you will add two animations to an existing movie. You will show three objects that appear on the screen at different times, and then move each object to a recycle bin at different times. You can create the objects using any of the Tools on the Tools panel.

1. Open fl1_4.fla, then save it as **recycle.fla**.
2. Play the movie and study the Timeline to familiarize yourself with the movie's current settings. Currently, there are no animations.
3. Insert a new layer above Layer 2, click frame 1 on the new layer, then draw a small object in the upper-left corner of the Stage.
4. Create a motion tween that moves the object to the recycle bin. (*Hint*: After inserting the motion tween, be sure to select frame 40 on the new layer before moving the object to the recycle bin. *Note*: At this time, the object will appear on top of the recycle bin when it is placed in the bin.)
5. Reshape the path so that the object moves in an arc to the recycle bin.
6. Insert a new layer above the top layer, click frame 1 on the new layer, draw a small object in the upper-center of the Stage, then create a motion tween that moves the object to the recycle bin.
7. Insert a new layer above the top layer, click frame 1 on the new layer, draw a small object in the upper-right corner of the Stage, then create a motion tween that moves the object to the recycle bin.
8. Reshape the path so that the object moves in an arc to the recycle bin.
9. Move Layer 1 to the top of all the layers. (*Note:* Layer 1 contains the front of the box. Moving Layer 1 above the other layers causes the objects on those layers to be hidden behind the front of the box.)
10. Play the movie and compare your movie to the sample provided in Figure 55.
11. Save the movie.

Figure 55 *Sample completed Project Builder 2*

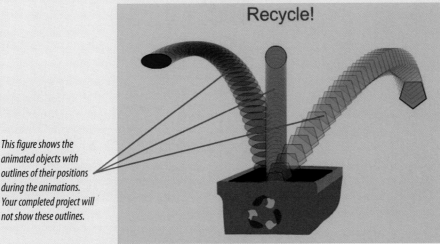

This figure shows the animated objects with outlines of their positions during the animations. Your completed project will not show these outlines.

Figure 56 shows screens from a mobile app that is described on the National Park Service website. Study the figure and answer the following questions. For each question, indicate how you determined your answer.

1. Connect to the Internet, then go to *www.nps.gov/ nama/photosmultimedia/app-page.htm (Note:* The screens displayed on the website may be different than those in Figure 56.)

2. Open a document in a word processor or open a new Flash document, save the file as **dpc1**, then answer the following questions. (*Hint:* Use the Flash Text tool if you open a Flash document.)

   - Whose application is this?
   - What is the goal(s) of the application?
   - Who is the target audience?
   - What treatment (look and feel) is used?

   - What are the design layout guidelines being used (balance, movement, etc.)?
   - How can animation enhance this app?
   - Do you think this is an effective design for the organization, its products, and its target audience? Why, or why not?
   - What suggestions would you make to improve the design, and why?

Figure 56 *Design Project*

Courtesy of National Park Service website – www.nps.gov; © Google 2012. www.nps.gov/nama/photosmultimedia/app-page.htm

rous companies in the business ...websites and applications for ...these companies use Flash as ...ary development tools. These ...note themselves through their ...and usually provide online ...samples of their work. Log ...et, then use your favorite ...nd keywords such as Flash ...Flash animators to locate three of these companies, and generate the following information for each one. A sample website is shown in Figure 57.

1. Company name:
2. Contact information (address, phone, and so on):
3. Website URL:
4. Company mission:
5. Services provided:
6. Sample list of clients:
7. Describe three ways the company seems to have used Flash in its website. Were these effective? Why, or why not?
8. Describe three applications of Flash that the company includes in its portfolio (or showcases or samples). Were these effective? Why, or why not?
9. Would you want to work for this company? Why, or why not?
10. Would you recommend this company to another company that was looking to create an application or enhance its website? Why, or why not?

Figure 57 *Sample website for Portfolio Project*

Source: Flash Developer.

CHAPTER 2

DRAWING OBJECTS AND WORKING WITH SYMBOLS AND INTERACTIVITY

1. Use the Flash drawing tools and work with drawn objects

2. Align objects to the Stage

3. Work with text and text objects

4. Create symbols and instances

5. Create buttons

6. Assign actions to frames and buttons using code snippets

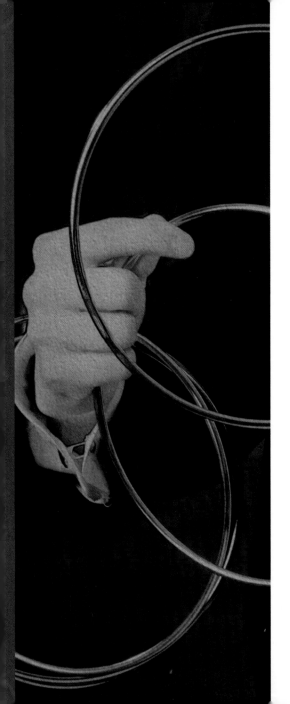

CHAPTER 2

DRAWING OBJECTS AND WORKING WITH SYMBOLS AND INTERACTIVITY

Introduction

Computers can display graphics in either a bitmap or a vector format. The difference between these formats is in how they describe an image. A bitmap graphic represents an image as an array of dots, called **pixels**, which are arranged within a grid. Each pixel in an image has an exact position on the screen and a precise color. To make a change in a bitmap graphic, you modify the pixels. When you enlarge a bitmap graphic, the number of pixels remains the same, resulting in jagged edges that decrease the quality of the image. A vector graphic represents an image using lines and curves, which you can resize without losing image quality. Also, the file size of a vector image is generally smaller than the file size of a bitmap image, which makes vector images particularly useful for an application. However, vector graphics are not as effective as bitmap graphics for representing photo-realistic images. Even so, one of the most compelling features of Flash is the ability to create and manipulate vector graphics.

Images (objects) created using Flash drawing tools are vector graphics, and have a stroke (border line), a fill, or both. In addition, the stroke of an object can be segmented into smaller lines. You can modify the size, shape, rotation, and color of each stroke, fill, and segment.

Once a graphic has been created using the Flash drawing tools it can be converted into a symbol. Symbols are important because they can be used to keep the file size of a movie as low as possible. There are three types of symbols: graphic, movie clip, and button. Graphic symbols are basic images, such as drawings and photos, used in a movie. Movie clip symbols are Flash movies that are nested within another movie. For example, you could have a movie clip of a car wheel rotating that becomes part of another movie of the car moving across the stage. Button symbols are images that allow the user to interact with the movie. For example, the user might have to click a button symbol labeled "Start" to begin a movie. In order for this interactivity to occur, you must assign ActionScript code to the button symbol. When images are converted to symbols, the distinction between the fill and the stroke no longer applies. You can't edit them as separate parts of the image.

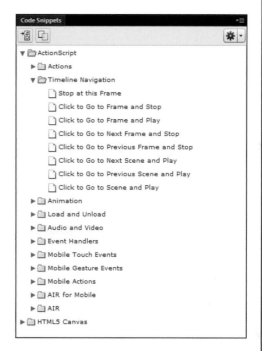

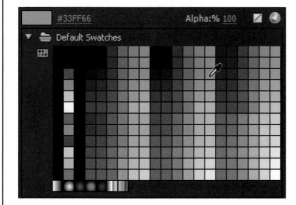

Use the Flash Drawing Tools and
WORK WITH DRAWN OBJECTS

What You'll Do

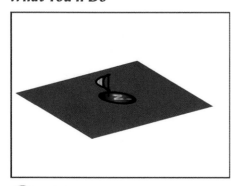

 In this lesson, you will use several drawing tools to create various vector graphics.

Using Flash Drawing and Editing Tools

When you point to a tool on the Tools panel, its name appears next to the tool. Figure 1 identifies the tools described in the following paragraphs. Several of the tools have options that modify their use. For example, the Brush tool has options for changing the size and shape of the brush head. These options are available in the Options area of the Tools panel when the tool is selected.

Selection—Used to select an object or parts of an object, such as the stroke or fill, and to reshape and reposition objects. The options for the Selection tool are Snap to Objects (aligns objects), Smooth (smooths lines), and Straighten (straightens lines).

Subselection—Used to select, drag, and reshape an object. Vector graphics are composed of lines and curves (each of which is a segment) connected by **anchor points**. Selecting an object with this tool displays the anchor points and allows you to use them to edit the object.

Free Transform—Used to rotate, scale, skew, and distort objects.

Gradient Transform—Used to transform a gradient fill by adjusting the size, direction, or center of the fill.

The Free and Gradient Transform tools are grouped within one icon on the Tools panel. To see the menu containing grouped tools, click and hold the tool icon until the menu opens.

3D Rotation—Used to create 3D effects by rotating movie clips in 3D space on the Stage.

3D Translation—Used to create 3D effects by moving movie clips in 3D space on the Stage.

The 3D Rotation and the 3D Translation tools are grouped on the Tools panel.

Lasso—Used to select objects or parts of objects by drawing a line around them.

Magic Wand—Used to select areas of a bitmap graphic that contain similar colors. The Magic Wand tool is grouped with the Lasso tool.

Pen—Used to draw lines and curves by creating a series of dots, known as anchor points, that are automatically connected. Other tools used to add, delete, and convert the anchor points created by the Pen tool are grouped with the Pen tool.

Text—Used to create and edit text.

Line—Used to draw straight lines. You can draw vertical, horizontal, and 45° diagonal lines by pressing and holding [Shift] while drawing the line.

Rectangle—Used to draw rectangular shapes. Press and hold [Shift] to draw a perfect square.

Rectangle Primitive—Used to draw objects with properties, such as corner radius that can be changed using the Properties panel. The Rectangle and Rectangle Primitive tools are grouped.

Oval—Used to draw oval shapes. Press and hold [Shift] to draw a perfect circle.

Oval Primitive—Used to draw objects with properties, such as inner radius, that can be changed using the Properties panel. The Oval and Oval Primitive tools are grouped.

PolyStar—Used to draw polygons and stars.

Pencil—Used to draw freehand lines and shapes. The Pencil Mode option displays a menu with the following commands: Straighten (draws straight lines), Smooth (draws smooth curved lines), and Ink (draws freehand with no modification).

Brush—Used to draw (paint) with brush-like strokes. Options allow you to set the size and shape of the brush, and to determine the area to be painted, such as inside or behind an object.

Paint Bucket—Used to fill enclosed areas of a drawing with color. Options allow you to fill areas that have gaps and to make adjustments in a gradient fill.

Ink Bottle—Used to apply line colors and thickness to the stroke of an object.

Eyedropper—Used to select stroke, fill, and text attributes so they can be copied from one object to another.

Eraser—Used to erase lines and fills. Options allow you to choose what part of the object to erase, as well as the size and shape of the eraser.

Width—Used to add widths of varying forms and thickness to drawings on the Stage.

Hand—Used to move the Stage around the Pasteboard by dragging the Stage.

Zoom—Used to change the magnification of an area of the Stage. Clicking an area of the Stage zooms in and holding down [Alt] (Win) or [option] (Mac) and clicking zooms out.

Stroke Color—Used to set the stroke color of drawn objects.

Fill Color—Used to set the fill color of drawn objects.

Black and White—Used to set the stroke color to black and the fill color to white.

Swap colors—Used to swap the stroke and fill colors.

Options—Used to select an option for a tool, such as the type of rectangle (object drawing mode) or size of the brush when using the Brush tool.

Figure 1 *Flash tools*

- Selection
- Subselection
- Free Transform (Gradient)
- 3D Rotation (3D Translation)
- Lasso (Magic Wand)
- Pen (Add Anchor Point, etc.)
- Text
- Line
- Rectangle (Rectangle Primitive)
- Oval (Oval Primitive)
- PolyStar
- Pencil
- Brush
- Paint Bucket
- Ink Bottle
- Eye dropper
- Eraser
- Width
- Hand
- Zoom
- Stroke Color
- Fill Color
- Swap colors
- Black and White
- Options area showing Object Drawing icon

Working with Grouped Tools

To display a list of grouped tools, you click the tool and hold the mouse button until the menu opens. For example, if you want to select the Gradient Transform tool and the Free Transform tool is displayed, you click and hold the Free Transform tool. Then, when the menu opens, you click the Gradient Transform tool. You know a tool is a grouped tool if you see an arrow in the lower-right corner of the tool icon.

Working with Tool Options

Some tools have additional options that allow you to modify their use. For example, the brush tool has options to set the brush size and to set where the brush fill will be applied. If additional options for a tool are available, they appear at the bottom of the Tools panel in the Options area when the tool is selected. Figure 1 shows the Rectangle tool selected, and the options area shows the the object drawing mode which can be turned off or on. If the option has a menu associated with it, such as a list of brush sizes for the brush tool, then the option icon will have an arrow in the lower-right corner. Click and hold the option until the menu opens.

Tools for Creating Vector Graphics

The Oval, Rectangle, Pencil, Brush, Line, and Pen tools are used to create vector objects.

Selecting Objects

Before you can edit a drawing, you must first select the object, or the part of the object, on which you want to work. Drawn objects are made up of a stroke and a fill. A stroke can have several segments. For example, a rectangle has four stroke segments, one for each side of the object. These can be selected separately or as a whole. Flash highlights objects that have been selected, as shown in Figure 2. When the stroke of an object is selected, a dotted colored line appears. When the fill of an object is selected, a dot pattern appears. When the stroke and fill of an object are selected, both the stroke and the fill appear dotted. When a group of objects is selected, a bounding box appears.

Using the Selection Tool

You can use the Selection tool to select part or all of an object, and to select multiple objects. To select only the fill, click just the fill; to select only the stroke, click just the stroke. To select both the fill and the stroke of one object, double-click the object, hold [Shift] and click the fill and stroke or draw a marquee around it. To select part of an object, drag a marquee that defines the area you want to select, as shown in Figure 2. To select multiple objects or combinations of strokes and fills, press and hold [Shift], then click each stroke or fill you want to select. To deselect an object(s), click a blank area of the Stage.

Using the Lasso Tool

The Lasso tool provides more flexibility than the Selection tool when selecting an object(s) or parts of an object on the Stage. You can use the tool in a freehand manner to draw any shape that then selects the object(s) within the shape. Alternately, you can use the Polygon Mode option to draw straight lines and connect them to form a shape that will select any object(s) within the shape.

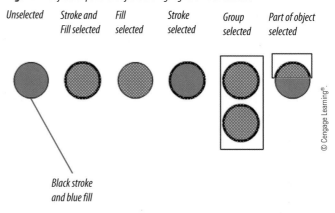

Figure 2 *Objects or parts of objects are highlighted when selected*

Unselected   *Stroke and Fill selected*   *Fill selected*   *Stroke selected*   *Group selected*   *Part of object selected*

© Cengage Learning®

Black stroke and blue fill

Drawing Objects and Working with Symbols and Interactivity

Drawing Models

Flash provides two drawing models. In the Merge Drawing Model, the stroke and fill of an object are separate. Thus, as you draw an object such as a circle, the stroke and fill can be selected individually as described earlier. When using the Object Drawing Model, the stroke and fill are combined and cannot be selected individually. However, you can use the Break Apart option from the Modify menu to separate the stroke and fill so that they can be selected individually. You can toggle between the two modes by clicking the Object Drawing option icons in the Options area of the Tools panel as shown in Figure 3.

Working with Colors

Flash allows you to change the color of the stroke and fill of an object. Figure 4 shows the colors area of the Properties panel. To change a color, you click the color swatch of the Stroke color or the color swatch of the Fill color, and then select a color swatch on the Color palette. The Color palette, as shown in Figure 5, allows you to select a color from the palette or type in a six-character code that represents the values of three colors (red, green, blue), referred to as RGB. When these characters are combined in various ways, they can represent virtually any color. The values are in a hexadecimal format (base 16), so they include letters and digits (A–F + 0–9 = 16 options), and they are preceded by a pound sign (#). The first two characters represent the value for red, the next two for green, and the last two for blue. For example, #000000

represents black (lack of color); #FFFFFF represents white; and #33FF66 represents a shade of green. You do not have to memorize the codes. There are reference manuals with the codes, and many programs allow you to set the values visually by selecting a color from a palette. You can also use the Properties panel to change the stroke and fill colors.

You can set the desired colors before drawing an object, or you can change a color of a previously drawn object. You can use the Ink Bottle tool to change the stroke color, and you can use the Paint Bucket tool to change the fill color. You can turn off either the stroke or the fill by selecting the No Stroke icon or the No Fill icon in the color palette.

Working with Gradients

A gradient is a color fill that makes a gradual transition from one color to another. Gradients can be very useful for creating a 3D effect, drawing attention to an object, and

Figure 3 *Drawing Model icons*

Object Drawing Model

Merge Drawing Model

Figure 4 *The colors area of the Properties panel*

Stroke color   Fill color

Figure 5 *Color palette showing the hexadecimal number*

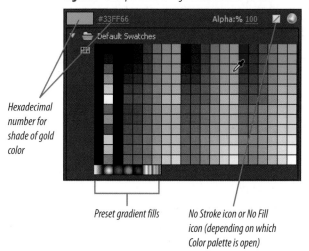

Hexadecimal number for shade of gold color

Preset gradient fills

No Stroke icon or No Fill icon (depending on which Color palette is open)

generally enhancing the appearance of an object. You can apply a gradient fill by using the Paint Bucket tool. The position of the Paint Bucket tool over the object is important because it determines the direction of the gradient fill. The Color palette can be used to create and alter custom gradients.

Copying and Moving Objects

To copy an object, select it, and then click the Copy command on the Edit menu. To paste the object, click one of the Paste commands on the Edit menu. You can copy an object to another layer by selecting the frame on the layer you want to copy the object to, and then pasting the object. You can copy and paste more than one object by selecting all the objects before using the Copy or Paste commands.

You move an object by selecting it and dragging it to a new location. You can position an object more precisely by selecting it and then pressing the arrow keys, which move the selection up, down, left, and right in small increments. On addition, you can change the X and Y coordinates on the Properties panel to position an object exactly on the Stage.

Transforming Objects

You use the Free Transform tool and the Transform panel to resize, rotate, skew, and reshape objects. After selecting an object, you click the Free Transform tool to display eight square-shaped handles used to transform the object, and a circle-shaped transformation point located at the center of the object. The transformation point is the point around which the object can be rotated. You can also change its location.

Resizing an Object

You enlarge or reduce the size of an object using the Scale option, which is available when the Free Transform tool is active. The process is to select the object and click the Free Transform tool, and then click the Scale option in the Options area of the Tools panel. Eight handles appear around the selected object. You drag the corner handles to resize the object without changing its proportions. That is, if the object starts out as a square, dragging a corner handle will change the size of the object, but it will still be a square. On the other hand, if you drag one of the middle handles, the object will be reshaped as taller, shorter, wider, or narrower. In addition, you can change the Width and Height settings on the Properties panel to resize an object in increments of one-tenth of one pixel.

Rotating and Skewing an Object

You use the Rotate and Skew option of the Free Transform tool to rotate an object and to skew it. The process is to select the object, click the Free Transform tool, and then click the Rotate and Skew option in the Options area of the Tools panel. Eight handles appear around the object. You drag the corner handles to rotate the object, or you drag the middle handles to skew the object, as shown in Figure 6. The Transform panel can be used to rotate and skew an object in a more precise way; select the object, display the Transform panel (available via the Window menu), enter the desired rotation or skew in degrees, and then press [Enter] (Win) or [return] (Mac).

Figure 6 *Using handles to manipulate an object*

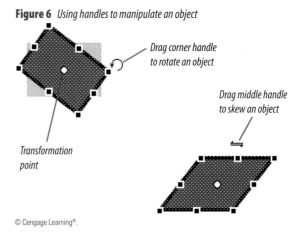

Drag corner handle to rotate an object

Drag middle handle to skew an object

Transformation point

© Cengage Learning®.

Distorting an Object

You can use the Distort and Envelope options to reshape an object by dragging its handles. The Distort option allows you to reshape an object by dragging one corner without affecting the other corners of the object. The Envelope option provides more than eight handles to allow more precise distortions. These options are accessed through the Transform command on the Modify menu.

Flipping an Object

You use a Flip option on the Transform menu to flip an object either horizontally or vertically. You select the object, click the Transform command on the Modify menu, and then choose Flip Vertical or Flip Horizontal. Other Transform options allow you to rotate and scale the selected object.

The Remove Transform command allows you to restore an object to its original state.

Reshaping a Segment of an Object

You use the Subselection tool to reshape a segment of an object. You click an edge of the object to display handles that can be dragged to reshape the object.

You use the Selection tool to reshape objects. When you point to the edge of an object, the pointer displays an arc symbol. Using the Arc pointer, you drag the edge of the object you want to reshape, as shown in Figure 7. If the Selection tool points to a corner of an object, the pointer changes to an L-shape. You drag the pointer to reshape the corner of the object.

Figure 7 *Using the Selection tool to distort an object*

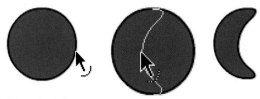

© Cengage Learning®.

Use the Rectangle tool and Properties panel

1. Open fl2_1.fla from the drive and folder where your Data Files are stored, then save it as **tools.fla**.

2. Click **Essentials** on the menu bar, click **Reset "Essentials"**, then click **Yes**.

3. Point to each tool on the tools panel, then read its name.

4. Click the **Rectangle tool** 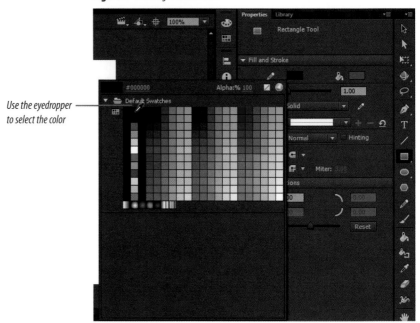, then verify the Fill and Stroke area is displayed on the Properties panel.

   Hint: If after clicking the Rectangle tool the Fill and Stroke area is not displayed, click the Selection tool, then click the Rectangle tool.

5. Click the **Stroke color swatch** in the Fill and Stroke area to display the color palette, then click the **black** color at the top left of the palette, as shown in Figure 8.

6. Click the **Fill color swatch** in the Fill and Stroke area to display the color palette, then click the **blue** color at the left side of the palette.

7. Use the **Stroke** option in the Fill and Stroke area of the Properties panel to change the stroke size to **4** as shown in Figure 9.

8. Verify the Object Drawing option in the Options area of the Tools panel is not active (depressed).

(continued)

Figure 8 *Selecting the black color*

Use the eyedropper to select the color

Figure 9 *Changing the stroke size*

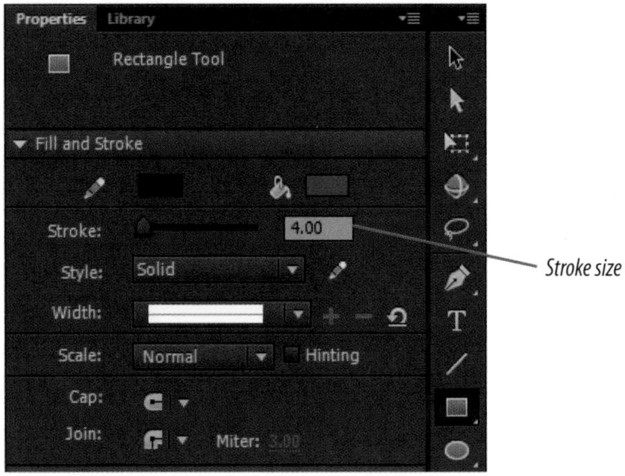

Stroke size

Drawing Objects and Working with Symbols and Interactivity

Figure 10 *Drawing a square*

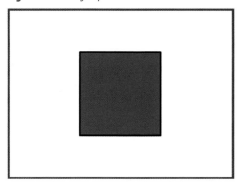

Figure 11 *Separating the fill from the stroke*

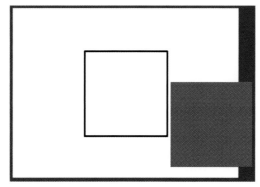

Figure 12 *Selecting a stroke segment*

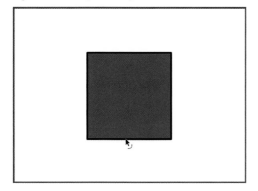

9. Hold down **Shift**, then draw a square near middle of screen, as shown in Figure 10.

10. Click the **Selection tool** , then drag a **marquee** around the object to select the entire object.

11. Click and drag the object around stage, then click on a blank area of the stage to deselect the object.

12. Click on the **fill area** of the object, then use the Properties panel to change the fill color to red.

13. Use the **Undo** command on the Edit menu to undo the color change.

    Note: You may need to use the Undo command twice.

14. Verify the fill area is selected, then click and drag the fill to separate it from the stroke, as shown in Figure 11.

15. Use the **Undo** command in the File menu to undo the move.

16. Click a blank area of the Stage to deselect the fill area.

17. Point to the bottom edge of the object, then when the pointer changes to an arrow with an arc , as shown in Figure 12, click to select the bottom stroke segment.

18. Use the Properties panel to change the Stroke color to **red**, then undo the color change.

19. Use the **Selection tool** to select the object including the stroke and fill.

(continued)

20. Click the **Stroke color swatch** 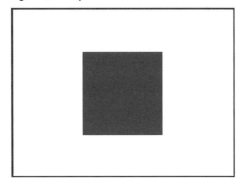 on the Properties panel, then select the **No Stroke icon** in the upper right of the Color Palette to remove the square's black outline.

21. Click a blank area of the Stage to deselect the object.

    Your screen should resemble Figure 13.

You set properties for an object, drew an object, and changed its properties.

Resize and reshape an object

1. Click the **Free Transform tool** on the Tools panel, then drag a **marquee** around the object to display handles on the square's sides, and one in the middle.

2. Point to the upper-middle handle, then when the pointer changes to a double-headed pointer ↕, click and slowly drag the pointer down and then back up.

   Hint: Hold down Shift to maintain a square shape.

3. Repeat Step 2 using a corner handle.

4. Use the **Undo** command as many time as necessary to return the object to its original shape.

5. Verify that the Free Transform tool is still selected, and then draw a **marquee** to select the object.

6. Point slightly above and to the right of the upper-middle handle, until the pointer changes to **two pointed lines**, then click and slowly drag the cursor to the right as shown in Figure 14.

7. Point slightly to the right of the upper-right corner of the object, until the point changes to an arrow with an arc below it, then click and rotate the object as shown in Figure 15.

(continued)

Figure 13 *The object without a stroke*

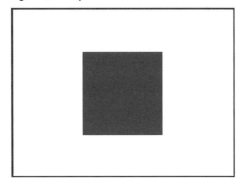

Figure 14 *Using the Free Transform tool to skew an object*

Drag the pointer above a middle handle to skew the object

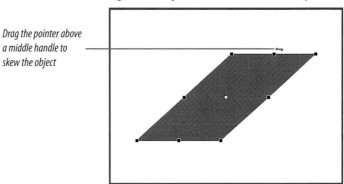

Figure 15 *Using the Free Transform tool to rotate an object*

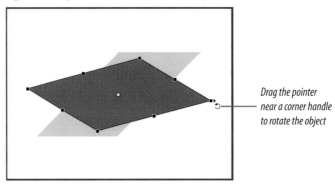

Drag the pointer near a corner handle to rotate the object

Drawing Objects and Working with Symbols and Interactivity

Figure 16 *Drawing an oval*

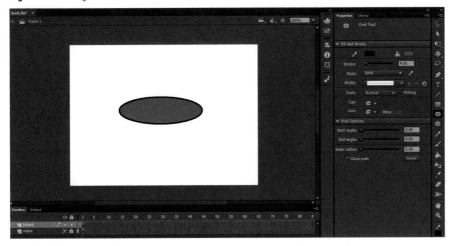

Figure 17 *Reshaping an object*

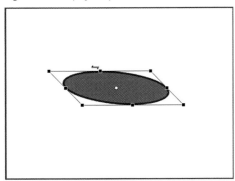

Figure 18 *A new oval object*

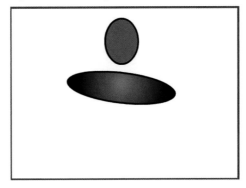

8. Rename Layer 1 as **water**, lock the layer, then hide the layer.

9. Insert a new layer, name it **board**, then click **frame 1** of the board layer.

10. Click the **Oval tool** 🔘 on the Tools panel, set the stroke color to **black** and the fill color to **blue**, then draw an oval as shown in Figure 16.

11. Click the **Free Transform tool** 🔲 on the Tools panel, then drag a **marquee** around the object to select it.

12. Point slightly above to the right of the upper-middle handle, until the cursor changes to two pointed lines ▬▬, then click and slowly drag the cursor to the left as shown in Figure 17.

13. Verify the object is selected, click the **Fill color swatch** 🪣 ▬ on the Properties panel, click the **red gradient** color in the bottom-left of the color palette.

    Notice how the gradient fills the object.

14. Click the **Paint Bucket tool** 🪣 on the Tools panel, then click inside the object in several locations and notice the changes to the gradient fill.

15. Click the **Selection tool** ▸ on the Tools panel, click a **blank area** of the Stage to deselect the object, then **lock** the layer.

16. Insert a new layer, name it **sail**, then click **frame 1** of the sail layer.

17. Click the **Oval tool**, then use the Properties panel to change the fill color to **blue**.

18. Draw another **oval** above the first one similar to Figure 18.

(continued)

19. Click the **Selection tool** on the Tools panel, then point to the right edge of the oval.

20. When the normal black arrow pointer changes to an arrow pointer with an arc, click on the right edge of the object and drag the right side of the oval to the left as shown in Figure 19, then release the mouse.

21. Click on a blank area of the Stage to deselect the object.

22. Click the **Paint Bucket tool** on the Tools panel, click the **Fill color swatch** on the Properties panel, then click the **rainbow swatch** at the bottom of the color palette.

23. Click inside the blank area of the object, as shown in Figure 20, to fill it with the rainbow colors.

24. Use the **Selection tool** to drag a **marquee** around the sail to select it, then click and drag it to position it as shown in Figure 21.

25. Click a blank area of the Stage, then lock the **board** layer.

You used the Free Transform tool to reshape and rotate objects.

Use the Line and Brush tools

1. Insert a new layer, name it **pole**, then click **frame 1** of the pole layer.

2. Click the **Line tool** on the Tools panel, then draw the line shown in Figure 22.

(continued)

Figure 19 *Reshaping the oval*

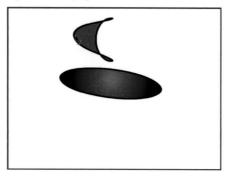

Figure 20 *Adding a fill color*

Figure 21 *Repositioning the sail*

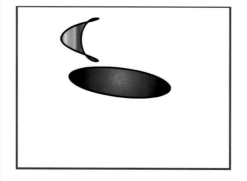

Figure 22 *Drawing a line*

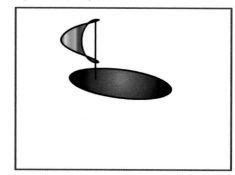

Drawing Objects and Working with Symbols and Interactivity

Figure 23 *Selecting a brush shape*

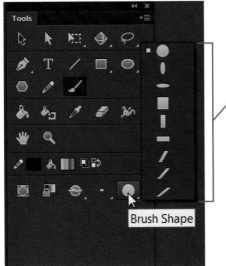

Brush shape options

Figure 24 *Selecting the objects*

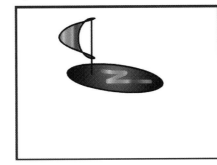

Figure 25 *The completed drawing*

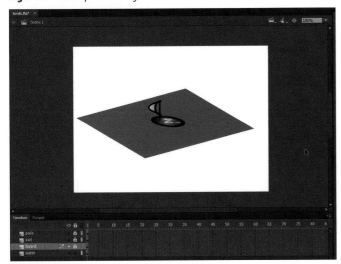

3. Click the **Brush tool** on the Tools panel, then display the Option area of the Tools panel.

   Hint: The Options area is at the bottom of the Tools panel. If the Options area is not visible, you may need to drag the Tools panel by its title bar to display it as a floating panel.

4. Click the **Brush Shape option** to display the shapes, as shown in Figure 23, then click the **circle** shape.

5. Click the **Brush Size option** to display the sizes, then click the **middle** size.

6. Draw a design of your choice on the board.

   Notice the Brush tool uses the fill color. The pen, pencil, and line tools use the stroke color.

7. **Unlock** the board and sail layers, then use the **Selection tool icon** to drag a **marquee** around all the displayed objects, as shown in Figure 24.

8. Verify the Lock width and height values together icon is locked, then change the width to **100**.

9. Drag the objects to the middle of the Stage.

10. Click a blank area of the Stage to deselect the objects, then **lock** the pole, sail, and board layers.

11. **Unhide** and **unlock** the water layer.

12. Click the water object to select it, then change the width to **500**.

13. Drag the water object to the **center** of the Stage.

14. Your screen should resemble Figure 25.

15. Test the movie, then close the Flash Player window.

16. Save your work, then close the document.

You used the Line and Brush tools and set options for the Brush tool.

Lesson 1   Use the Flash Drawing Tools and Work with Drawn Objects

Align Objects
TO THE STAGE

What You'll Do

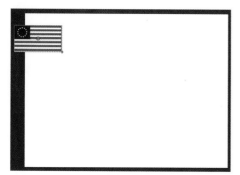

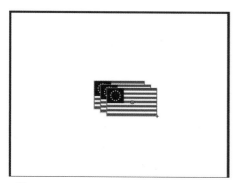

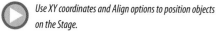
Use XY coordinates and Align options to position objects on the Stage.

Positioning Objects on the Stage

Movies often have several objects that appear on the Stage at any given time. Flash designers pay special attention to the layout of the objects on the Stage and to their relationship to each other. In addition, because animation is usually involved in a movie, the movement of objects around the Stage needs to be precisely planned. Effective positioning of objects begins with an understanding of the Stage dimensions and how they are determined.

The Stage dimensions are made up of pixels (dots) matching the Stage size. So, a Stage size of 550 × 400 would be 550 pixels wide and 400 pixels high. Each pixel has a location on the Stage designated as the X (across) and Y (down) coordinates. The location of any object on the Stage is determined by its position from the upper-left corner of the Stage, which is 0,0 and the object's registration point. The registration point of an object is used to align it with the coordinates. The registration point, which is shown as a crosshair, is initially set at the upper-left corner of an object, as shown in Figure 26. So, an object having coordinates of 100,100 would be positioned at 100 pixels across and 100 pixels down the Stage, as shown in Figure 26. The Properties panel

displays the X,Y values of any selected object. The most precise way to position an object on the Stage is to use the Properties panel to enter X and Y values for the object. Other ways to position objects on the Stage include using rulers, gridlines, and guides, as well as the align options. The Rulers, Grid, and Guides commands, which are found on the View menu, are used to turn on and off these features. Figure 26 shows the rulers and the ruler lines, which are used to indicate the position of an object. (*Note*: Normally ruler lines display on top of objects on the Stage. In Figure 26, the registration point is displayed above the ruler lines to show its exact placement.)

After displaying the rulers, you can drag the lines from the top ruler or the left side ruler to the Stage. To remove a ruler line, you drag the ruler line up to the top ruler or across to the left ruler.

Figure 27 shows the Stage with gridlines displayed. The gridlines can be used to position an object. You can modify the grid size and color. In addition to using rulers and guides to help place objects, you can create a new layer as a Guide layer that you use to position objects on the Stage. When you turn gridlines and guides on, they appear on the

Drawing Objects and Working with Symbols and Interactivity

Stage. However, they do not appear in the Flash movie when you test or publish it.

Using the Align Panel

Figure 28 shows the Align panel, which allows you to position objects on the Stage either relative to the Stage or to other objects. The Align panel has four areas (Align, Distribute, Match size, Space) each with options. The Align options are used to align the edge or center of an object with the edge or center of the Stage—or, if multiple objects are selected, to align their edges and centers. The Distribute options are used to position objects across or down the Stage. The Match size options are used to resize selected objects to match the height and/or width of the largest object or to match the Stage if the Align to stage option is selected. The Space options are used to space out objects evenly across and down the Stage.

Figure 26 *Using rulers to position an object*

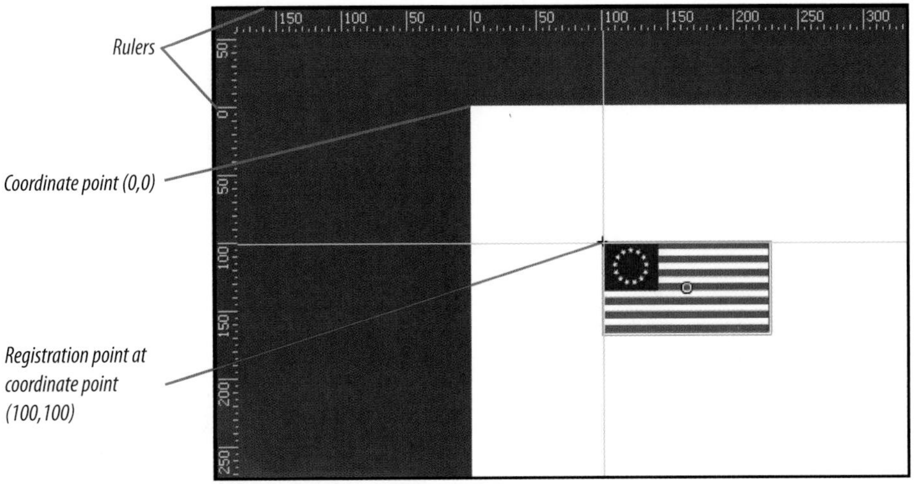

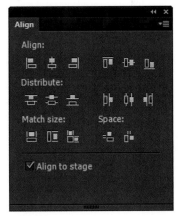

Rulers
Coordinate point (0,0)
Registration point at coordinate point (100,100)

Figure 27 *Using gridlines to position an object*

Scene 1
100%

Figure 28 *The Align panel*

Align
Align:
Distribute:
Match size:
Space:
Align to stage

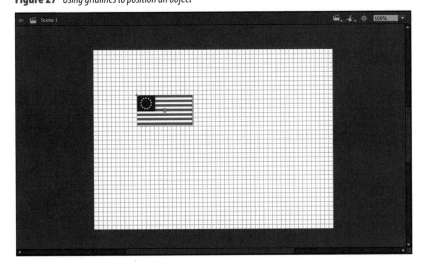

Use XY coordinates to position objects on the Stage

1. Open fl2_2.fla, then save it as **alignObjects.fla**.

   This movie has one object that has been converted into a symbol. Therefore, there are no separate fill and stroke segments.

2. Click the **Selection tool** 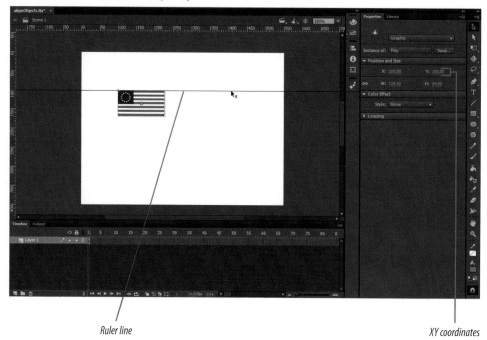 on the Tools panel, click the **flag** on the Stage, then display the Properties panel, if it is not displayed.

   Notice the X and Y coordinates are set to 100.

3. Click **View** on the menu bar, then click **Rulers**.

4. Click and hold anywhere on the **horizontal ruler** at the top of the Stage, then drag the mouse pointer down to position the blue horizontal line at 100 on the vertical ruler, as shown in Figure 29.

5. Click and hold anywhere on the **vertical ruler** at the left of the Stage, then drag the mouse pointer right to position the blue vertical line at 100 on the horizontal ruler.

   The blue lines are called ruler lines. The point where the two ruler lines cross identifies the X,Y coordinates 100,100. The ruler lines meet at the registration point of the object.

6. Click the **flag**, click **100** next to X: on the Properties panel, type **0**, then press **[Enter]** (Win) or **[return]** (Mac).

   This aligns the registration point of the object to the left edge of the Stage.

7. Repeat Step 6 to change the Y value to **0**.

8. Type **550** for the X value and **400** for the Y value.

   Notice the flag is positioned off the Stage because the registration point is in the upper-left corner of the object.

   (continued)

Figure 29 *Position an object on the Stage using XY coordinates*

Ruler line

XY coordinates

Drawing Objects and Working with Symbols and Interactivity

Figure 30 *Setting the Registration point*

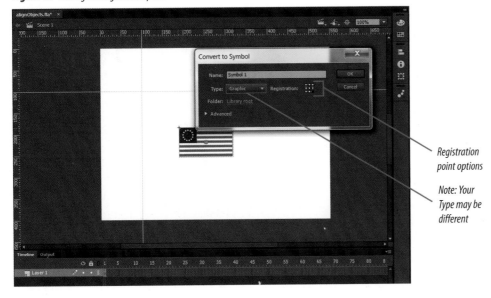

Registration point options

Note: Your Type may be different

9. Change the view to **50%.**

10. Point to the **flag,** then click and drag the **flag** around the Stage noticing how the values for X and Y on the Properties panel change.

11. Change the view to **100%.**

12. Click the flag, then use the **arrow keys** on the keyboard to move the flag one pixel at a time in all four directions.

13. Click **Modify** on the menu bar, then click **Convert to Symbol.**

    The Convert to Symbol dialog box opens allowing you to change the registration point.

14. Click the **lower-right icon** as shown in Figure 30, then click **OK.**

    Notice the registration point is now located on the lower-right corner of the flag.

15. Change the **X** and **Y** values on the Properties panel to **100** and **100.**

    Notice the flag is now positioned using the new location of the registration point.

16. Click **View** on the menu bar, point to **Grid**, then click **Show Grid**.

17. Drag each **ruler line** to its respective ruler to remove it from the Stage.

18. Click **View** on the menu bar, then click **Rulers** to remove them from view.

19. Click **View** on then menu bar, point to **Grid**, then click **Show Grid**.

20. Save, then close the Flash document.

You used the X and Y values of an object to position it on the Stage. You used the Convert to Symbol dialog box to change the registration point of an object.

Use the Align options

1. Open fl2_3.fla, then save it as **alignOptions.fla**.
   This document has three objects (flags) of different sizes randomly placed on the Stage.

2. Click **Essentials** on the menu bar, click **Reset "Essentials"**, then click **Yes**.

3. Click **Window** on the menu bar, then click **Align** to open the Align panel set.

   TIP Alternately, you can click the Align icon ▣ that is part of a collapsed panel set on your workspace.

4. Drag the **Align panel set** by its title bar, not its tab, and position it adjacent to the right side of the Stage, as shown in Figure 31.

5. Verify the Align to stage check box on the Align panel is active (checked).

6. Click the **largest flag** to select it, then click the **Align left edge icon** ▣.

7. Point to the next **Align icon** ▣, read the name that appears, then click the **Align horizontal center icon** ▣ and notice the new position of the object on the Stage.

8. Click the other **Align options** on the top row of the Align panel.

9. Click the **Align horizontal center icon** ▣, then click the **Align vertical center icon** ▣.

   When you use these two align options together, they position the center of the object at the center of the Stage.

   (continued)

Figure 31 *Positioning the Align panel set*

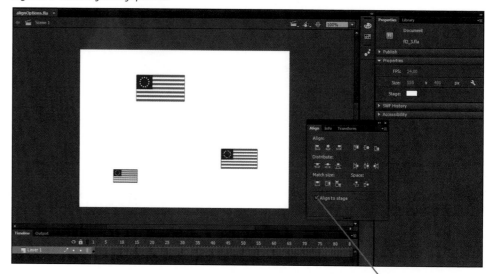

Be sure Align to stage
is active (checked)

Drawing Objects and Working with Symbols and Interactivity

Figure 32 *All three objects selected*

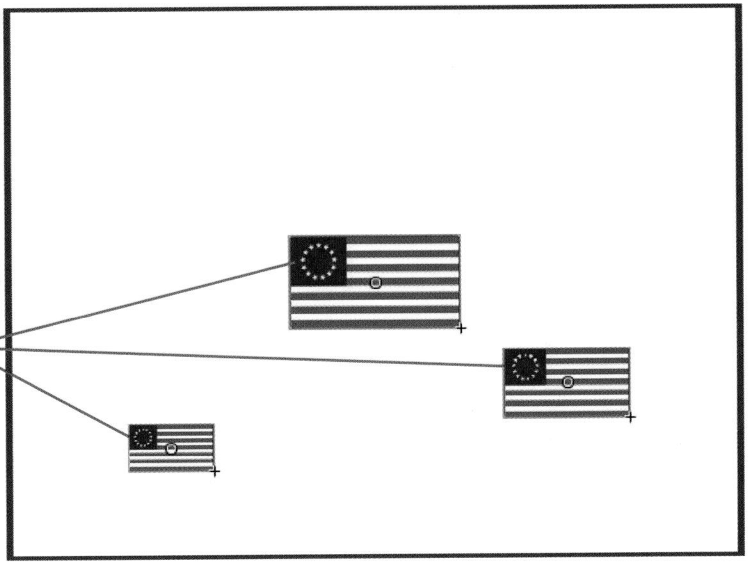

The flags have a blue border, indicating all three objects are selected.

10. Click the **Match width icon** , then click the **Match height icon** .

    This image is a bitmap so it becomes distorted as it is resized.

11. Click **Edit** on the menu bar, then click **Undo Match Size**.
12. Click **Edit** on the menu bar, then click **Undo Match Size**.
13. Use the **Selection tool**  to draw a marquee around all three flags to select them, as shown in Figure 32.
14. Click the **Align left edge icon** , then click the **Align horizontal center icon** .
15. Click the **Space evenly vertically icon** , then click the **Align vertical center icon** .
16. Click the **Align to stage check box** to make this feature not active.
17. With all three objects selected, click each of the **Align options** on the top row of the Align panel.

    Notice that the objects align to each other instead of the Stage.

18. Click the **Match width and height icon** 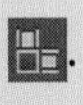.

    This changes the dimension of each object to match the size of the largest object.

19. Close the Align panel set, then save and close the Flash document.

You used the Align panel to position objects on the Stage relative to the Stage and to each other.

Work with Text
AND TEXT OBJECTS

What You'll Do

Use XY coordinates and align options to position objects on the Stage.

Learning About Text

Flash provides a great deal of flexibility when using text. Among other settings for text, you can specify the typeface (font), size, style (bold, italic), and color (including gradients). You can transform the text by rotating, scaling, skewing, and flipping it. You can even break apart a letter and reshape its segments.

Entering Text and Changing the Text Block for Classic Text

It is important to understand that text is entered into a text block, as shown in Figure 33. You use the Text tool to place a text block on the Stage and to enter and edit text. A text block expands as more text is entered and may even extend beyond the edge of the Stage. You can adjust the size of the text block so that it is a fixed width by dragging the handle in the upper-right corner of the block. Figure 34 shows the process of using the Text tool to enter text and resize the text block. Once you select the Text tool, you click the

Stage where you want the text to appear. An insertion point indicates where the next character will appear in the text block when it is typed. You can resize the text block to a fixed width by dragging the circle handle. After resizing the text block, the circle handle changes to a square, indicating that the text block now has a fixed width. Then, when you enter more text, it automatically wraps within the text block. You can resize the width of a text block at any time by selecting it with the Selection tool (either clicking on the text or drawing a marquee around it) and dragging any handle.

Changing Text Attributes

You can use the Properties panel to change the font, size, and style of a single character or an entire text block. Figure 35 shows the Properties panel when a text object is selected. You select text, display the Properties panel, and make the changes. You use the Selection tool to select the entire text block by drawing a marquee around it. You use the Text tool to select a single character or string of characters by dragging the I-beam pointer over the text you want to select, as shown in Figure 36.

Working with Paragraphs

To make it easier to work with large bodies of text, such as paragraphs, Flash provides many of the features found in a word processor. You can align paragraphs (left, right, center, justified) within a text block, set margins (space between the border of a text block and the paragraph text), set indents for the first line of a paragraph, and set line spacing (distance between paragraphs) using the Properties panel.

Transforming Text

It is important to understand that a text block is an object. Therefore, you can apply filters, such as drop shadows, and you can transform (reshape, rotate, skew, and so on) a text block in the same way you transform other objects. If you want to transform individual characters within a text block, you must first break apart the text block. To do this, you use the Selection tool to select the text block, then you click the Break Apart command on the Modify menu. Each character (or a group of characters) in the text block can now be selected and transformed.

Figure 35 *The Properties panel when a text object is selected*

Click to expand and see available options

Figure 33 *A text block*

This is a text block used to enter text.

Figure 34 *Using the Text tool*

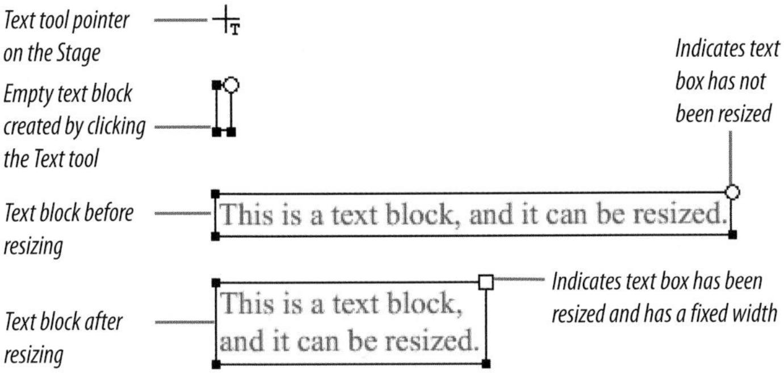

Text tool pointer on the Stage

Empty text block created by clicking the Text tool

Indicates text box has not been resized

Text block before resizing — This is a text block, and it can be resized.

Indicates text box has been resized and has a fixed width

Text block after resizing — This is a text block, and it can be resized.

© Cengage Learning®.

Figure 36 *Dragging the I-beam pointer to select text*

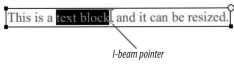

I-beam pointer

Enter text and change text attributes

1. Open a new Flash ActionScript 3.0 document, then save it as **textObjects.fla**.

2. Click the **Text tool** T and study the Properties panel.

3. Click the left-center of the Stage, then type **We have great events each year including a Rally!**

4. Click the **I-Beam pointer** ⊺ before the word "Rally" to insert the cursor there, as shown in Figure 37, then type **Car** followed by a space.

5. Drag the **I-Beam pointer** ⊺ across the text to select all the text.

6. Make the following changes in the Character area of the Properties panel: Family: **Arial**; Style: **Bold**; Size: **16**; Color: **#990000**, then click the **text box**.

   Your Properties panel should resemble Figure 38.

7. Verify the text block is selected, position the **text pointer** ⊥ᴛ over the circle handle until the pointer changes to a double arrow ←→, then drag the **handle** left until the text box resembles Figure 39.

8. Select the text using the I-Beam pointer ⊺, then click the **Align center icon** ▤ in the Paragraph area of the Properties panel.

9. Click the **Selection tool** ▷ on the Tools panel, click the **text object**, then drag the **object** to the lower-middle of the Stage.

   TIP The Selection tool is used to select the text block. The Text tool is used to create the text box, and to select and edit the text within the text block.

   You entered text and changed the font, type size, and text color; you also resized the text block and changed the text alignment.

Figure 37 *Using the Text tool to enter text*

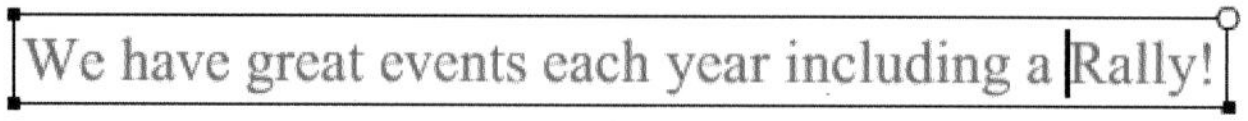

We have great events each year including a |Rally!

Figure 38 *Changes to the Character area of the Properties panel*

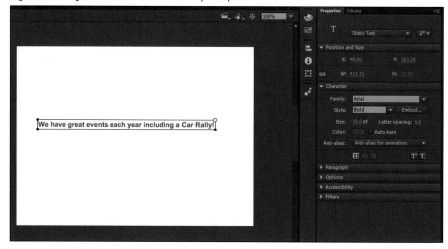

Figure 39 *Resizing the text block*

Drag the handle
to this position

Figure 40 *The Filters options on the Properties panel*

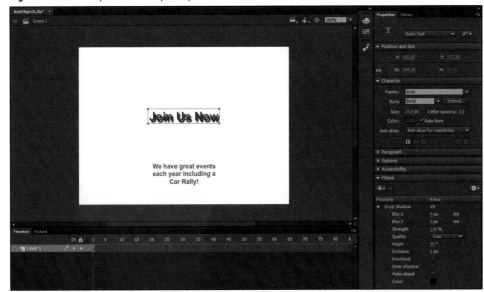

Add a Filter effect to text

1. Click the **Text tool** T on the Tools panel, click the center of the Stage, then type **Join Us Now**. *Hint*: If the text box does not appear, double-click the Stage.

2. Drag the **I-Beam pointer** I across the text to select it, then use the Properties panel to change the Font size to **30** and the Text (fill) color to **#003399**.

3. Click **Character** on the Properties panel to close the Character area, then close all areas on the Properties panel except for the Filters area.

4. Click the **Selection tool** on the Tools panel, then verify the text block is selected.

5. Click the **Add filter icon** at the bottom of the Filters area, then click **Drop Shadow**.

6. Point to the **Angle value** in the Filters area of the Properties panel, then, when the pointer changes to a double-headed arrow, drag the **pointer** to the right to view the effect on the shadow, then set the Angle to **50**.

7. Point to the **Distance value** until the pointer changes to a double-headed arrow, then drag the **pointer** to the right and notice the changes in the drop shadow.

8. Set the Distance to **6**.

9. Verify the text box is selected, drag the **text box** as needed to match the placement shown in Figure 40, then save your work.

You used the Filter panel to create a drop shadow, then made changes to it.

Skew text and align objects

1. Click the **Text tool** to select it, click the pointer near the top left of the Stage, then type **Classic Car Club**.

2. Click **Character** on the Properties panel to display the Character area.

   The attributes of the new text reflect the most recent settings entered on the Properties panel.

3. Drag the **I-Beam pointer** to select the text, then use the Character area of the Properties panel to change the font size to **40** and the fill color to **#990000**.

4. Click the **Selection tool** on the Tools panel, click the **text box** to select it, then click the **Free Transform tool** on the Tools panel.

5. Click the **Rotate and Skew option** in the Options area of the Tools panel.

6. Drag the **top middle handle** to the right, as shown in Figure 41, to skew the text.

7. Click the **Selection tool** on the Tools panel.

8. Drag a **marquee** around all of the objects on the Stage to select them.

9. Click **Modify** on the menu bar, point to **Align**, click **Align to stage** to make it active.

10. Click **Modify** on the menu bar, point to **Align**, then click **Horizontal Center**.

11. Click a blank area of the Stage to deselect the objects.

You entered a heading, changed the font size and color, and skewed text using the Free Transform tool, then you aligned the objects on the Stage.

Figure 41 *Skewing the text*

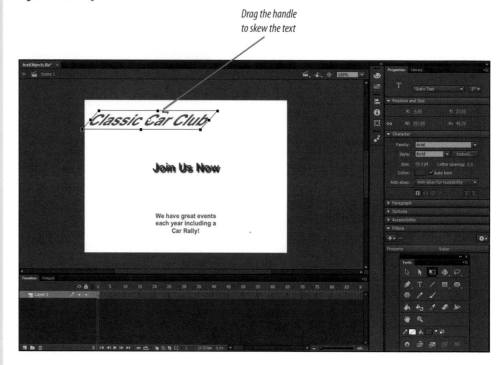

Drag the handle to skew the text

Drawing Objects and Working with Symbols and Interactivity

Figure 42 *Reshaping a letter*

Drag this anchor point; notice the lines are
drawn from the anchor points on either side of
the anchor point being dragged

Figure 43 *Applying a gradient fill to each letter*

Reshape and apply a gradient to text

1. Click the **Selection tool** , click the **Classic Car Club text block** to select it, click **Modify** on the menu bar, then click **Break Apart**.

   The letters are now individual text blocks.

2. Click **Modify** on the menu bar, then click **Break Apart**.

   The letters are filled with a dot pattern, indicating that they can now be edited.

3. Click the **Zoom tool** on the Tools panel, then click the first **"C"** in Classic.

4. Click the **Subselection tool** on the Tools panel, then click the **edge** of the letter **"C"** to display the object's segment handles.

5. Drag a **lower anchor point** on the "C" in Classic, as shown in Figure 42.

6. Click the **Selection tool** , then click a blank area of the Stage to deselect the objects.

7. Click the **View list arrow** on the movie menu bar, then click **Fit in Window**.

8. Click the **Fill Color tool color swatch** on the Tools panel, then click the **red gradient color swatch** in the bottom row of the Color palette.

9. Click the **Paint Bucket tool** on the Tools panel, then click the **top** of each letter to change the fill to a red gradient, as shown in Figure 43.

10. Save your work, then close the document.

You broke apart a text block, reshaped text, and added a gradient to the text.

Create Symbols
AND INSTANCES

What You'll Do

Image courtesy Jim Shuman.

 In this lesson, you will create a graphic symbol, turn it into an instance, and then edit it.

Working with Symbols

An important benefit of Flash is its ability to create movies with small file sizes. This allows the movies to be delivered from the web or displayed on a mobile device more quickly. One way to keep the file size small is to create reusable graphics, buttons, and movie clips. Flash allows you to create a graphic (drawing) and then make unlimited copies, which you can use throughout the current movie and in other movies. Flash calls the original drawing a **symbol** and the copied drawings **instances**. Flash stores symbols on the Library panel—each time you need a copy of the symbol, you can open the Library panel and drag the symbol to the Stage, which creates an instance (copy) of the symbol. Using instances reduces the movie file size because Flash stores only the information about the symbol's properties (size, shape, color), and a link is established between the symbol and an instance so that the instance has the same properties (such as color and shape) as the symbol. There are two especially valuable editing features of this process. First, if you have created several instances of a symbol and decide to change the same property for every instance, all that is needed is to edit the symbol. For example, if a logo appears in several places in an application and you need to change the color of each instance of the logo, you simply change the color of the symbol. Because the instances are linked to the symbol they are automatically updated. Second, you can change the properties of an individual instance of a symbol in one of two ways. You can change properties associated with the whole instance, such as size or transparency, and you can skew or rotate the instance. So if you have a symbol that is a tree, you can make the tree bigger or smaller, or you can make the tree lean to the left as if it is blowing in the wind. However, if you want to change individual parts of the instance, then you must break the link between the instance and the symbol. When you break the link between an instance and a symbol, the instance becomes an object that can be edited. For example, thinking about our tree now as an object, you can make the leaves on the tree different colors. You can only do this if you break the link between the instance and the symbol. When you break the link, changes you make to the object are not reflected in the symbol or any instances of the symbol. Likewise, if subsequently you make changes to the symbol, the changes will not be reflected in the unlinked object. The process for unlinking an instance is to select the instance on the Stage and choose the Break Apart command from the Modify menu.

Understanding Symbol Types

There are three categories of symbols: graphic, button, and movie clip. A graphic symbol is useful because you can reuse a single image and make changes in each instance of the image. A button symbol is useful because you can create buttons for interactivity, such as starting or stopping a movie. A movie clip symbol is useful for creating complex animations because you can create a movie within a movie. For example, you could have a movie with a car moving across the screen and its wheels rotating. The wheel animation would be created as one movie clip symbol and

attached to each wheel of the animated car. Symbols can be created from objects you draw using the Flash drawing tools. In addition, you can import graphics into a Flash document that can then be converted to symbols.

Creating a Graphic Symbol

You can use the New Symbol command on the Insert menu to create and then draw a symbol. You can also draw an object and then use the Convert to Symbol command on the Modify menu to convert the object

to a symbol. The Convert to Symbol dialog box, shown in Figure 44, allows you to name the symbol and specify the type of symbol you want to create (Movie Clip, Button, or Graphic). When naming a symbol, it's a good idea to use a naming convention that allows you to quickly identify the type of symbol and to group like symbols together. For example, you could identify all graphic symbols by naming them g_*name* and all buttons as b_*name*. In Figure 44, the drawing on the Stage is being converted to a graphic symbol.

Figure 44 *Using the Convert to Symbol dialog box to convert an object to a symbol*

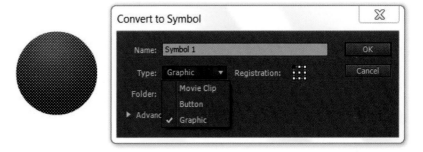

After you complete the Convert to Symbol dialog box, Flash places the symbol on the Library panel, as shown in Figure 45. In Figure 45, an icon identifying the symbol as a graphic symbol and the symbol name are listed on the Library panel, along with a preview of the selected symbol. To create an instance of the symbol, you simply drag a symbol from the Library panel to the Stage. To edit a symbol, you can double-click it on the Library panel or you can use the Edit Symbols command on the Edit menu. Either way displays the symbol in an edit window, where changes can be made to it. When you edit a symbol, the changes are reflected in all instances of that symbol in your movie. For example, you can draw a car, convert the car to a symbol, and then create several instances of the car. You can uniformly change the size of all the cars by double-clicking the car symbol on the Library panel to open the edit window, and then rescaling it to the desired size.

Working with Instances

You can have as many instances as needed in your movie, and you can edit each one to make it somewhat different from the others. You can rotate, skew (slant), and resize graphic and button instances. In addition, you can change the color, brightness, and transparency. However, there are some limitations. An instance is a single object with no segments or parts, such as a stroke and a fill. You cannot select a part of an instance. Therefore, any changes to the color of the instance are made to the entire object. Of course, you can use layers to stack other objects on top of an instance to

change its appearance. In addition, you can use the Break Apart command on the Modify menu to break the link between an instance and a symbol. Once the link is broken, you can make any changes to the object, such as changing its stroke and fill color. However, because the link is broken, the object is no longer an instance of the original symbol. So, if you make any changes to the original symbol, then the unlinked object is not affected.

The process for creating an instance is to open the Library panel and drag the desired symbol to the Stage. Once the symbol is on the Stage, you select the instance by using the Selection tool to drag a marquee around it. A blue bounding box indicates that the object is selected. Then, you can use the Free Transform tool options (such as Rotate and Skew, or Scale) to modify the entire image, or you can use the Break Apart command to break apart the instance and edit individual strokes and fills.

Figure 45 *A graphic symbol on the Library panel*

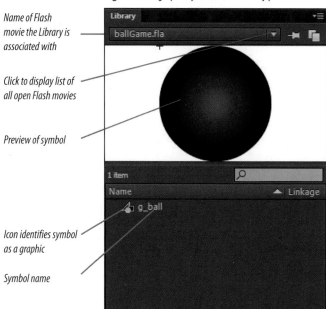

Name of Flash movie the Library is associated with

Click to display list of all open Flash movies

Preview of symbol

Icon identifies symbol as a graphic

Symbol name

Drawing Objects and Working with Symbols and Interactivity

Figure 46 *Options in the Convert to Symbol dialog box*

Click to set
Registration to
upper-left corner

Figure 47 *Newly created symbol on the Library panel*

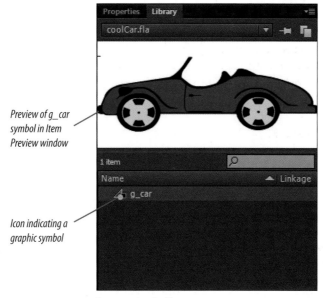

Preview of g_car
symbol in Item
Preview window

Icon indicating a
graphic symbol

Image courtesy Jim Shuman.

Create a symbol

1. Open fl2_4.fla from the drive and folder where your Data Files are stored, then save it as **coolCar.fla**.

   This document has one object, a car, that was created using the Flash drawing tools.

2. Verify the Properties panel, the Library panel, and the Tools panel are displayed.

3. Set the magnification to **Fit in Window**.

4. Click the **Selection tool** on the Tools panel, then drag a **marquee** around the car to select it.

5. Click **Modify** on the menu bar, then click **Convert to Symbol**.

6. Type **g_car** in the Name text box.

7. Click the **Type list arrow** to display the symbol types, then click **Graphic**, as shown in Figure 46.

8. Set the **registration** to the upper-left corner as shown in Figure 46 if necessary, then click **OK**.

9. Click the **Library panel tab**, study the Library panel as shown in Figure 47, then save your work.

   The Library panel displays the symbol (red car) in the Item Preview window, an icon indicating that this is a graphic symbol, and the name of the symbol (g_car). The symbol is contained in the library, and the car on the Stage is now an instance of the symbol.

You opened a file with an object, converted the object to a symbol, and displayed the symbol on the Library panel.

Create and edit an instance

1. Point to the **car image** in the Item Preview window of the Library panel, then drag the **image** to the Stage beneath the first car, as shown in Figure 48.

   Both cars on the Stage are instances of the graphic symbol on the Library panel.

   TIP You can also drag the name of the symbol or its icon from the Library panel to the Stage.

2. Verify the bottom car is selected, click **Modify** on the menu bar, point to **Transform**, then click **Flip Horizontal**.

3. Display the Properties panel, then display the Color Effect area if it is not already showing.

4. Click the **Style list arrow**, then click **Alpha**.

5. Drag the **Alpha slider** left then right, then set the transparency to **50%**.

   Notice how the transparency changes. Figure 49 shows the transparency set to 50%.

6. Click a blank area of the Stage to deselect the object, then save your work.

   Changing the alpha setting gives the car a more transparent look.

You created an instance of a symbol and edited the instance on the Stage.

Figure 48 *Creating an instance of a symbol*

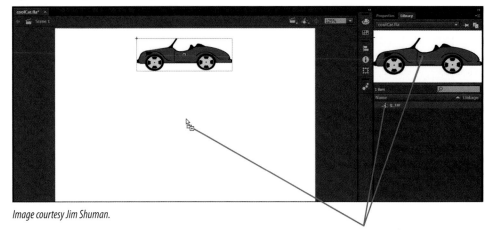

Image courtesy Jim Shuman.

Drag the car image, the name of the symbol, or its icon from the Library panel to below the original instance to create a second instance of the symbol

Figure 49 *The alpha set to 50%*

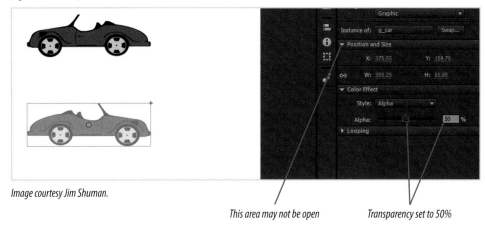

Image courtesy Jim Shuman.

This area may not be open   *Transparency set to 50%*

Figure 50 *Edit window*

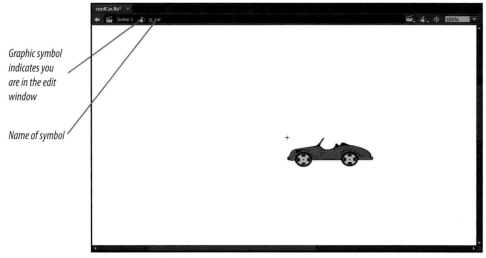

Graphic symbol indicates you are in the edit window

Name of symbol

Image courtesy Jim Shuman.

Edit a symbol in the edit window

1. Display the Library panel, double-click the **g_car symbol icon** on the Library panel to display the edit window, then compare your screen to Figure 50.

   The g_car symbol appears in the edit window, indicating that you are editing the g_car symbol.

   TIP You can also edit a symbol by selecting it on the Stage, clicking Edit on the menu bar, then clicking Edit Symbols.

2. Click a blank area of the edit window to deselect the car.

3. Verify the Selection tool is selected, then click the **light gray hubcap** inside the front wheel to select it.

4. Press and hold **[Shift]**, then click the **hubcap** inside the back wheel so both hubcap fills are selected.

   (continued)

5. On the Properties panel, set the **Fill Color** to the **blue gradient color swatch** in the bottom row of the color palette.

6. Deselect the image, display the Library panel, and then compare your screen to Figure 51.

   Changes you make to the symbol affect every instance of the symbol on the stage. The hubcap fill becomes a blue gradient on the Library panel and on the Stage.

7. Click **Scene 1** at the top left of the edit window to exit the edit window and return to the main Timeline and main Stage, then save your work.

You edited a symbol in the edit window that affected all instances of the symbol.

Figure 51 *Edited symbol*

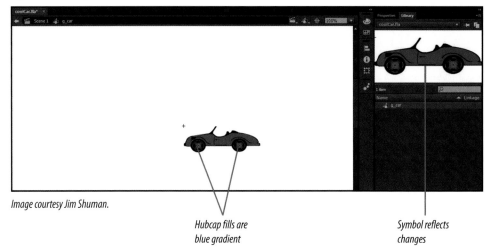

Image courtesy Jim Shuman.

Hubcap fills are blue gradient

Symbol reflects changes

Drawing Objects and Working with Symbols and Interactivity

Figure 52 *The car with the maroon body selected*

Image courtesy Jim Shuman.

Figure 53 *Changing the symbol affects only the one instance of the symbol*

Instance of the symbol —

Object that is no
longer an instance
of the symbol —

Image courtesy Jim Shuman.

Break apart an instance

1. Drag a **marquee** around the bottom car to select it if it is not selected.

2. Click **Modify** on the menu bar, then click **Break Apart**.

    The object is no longer linked to the symbol, and its parts (strokes and fills) can now be edited.

3. Click a blank area of the Stage to deselect the object.

4. Click the blue **front hubcap**, press and hold **[Shift]**, then click the **blue back hubcap** so both hubcaps are selected.

5. Set the **Fill Color** to the **light gray color swatch (#999999)** in the left column of the color palette.

6. Double-click the **g_car symbol icon** on the Library panel to display the symbol, which has blue hubcaps, in the edit window.

7. Click the **maroon front body** of the car to select it, press and hold **[Shift]**, then click the **maroon back body** of the car, as shown in Figure 52.

8. Set the **Fill Color** to the **red gradient color swatch** in the bottom row of the color palette.

9. Click **Scene 1** at the top left of the edit window, then compare your images to Figure 53.

    The body color of the car in the original instance is a different color, but the body color of the car to which you applied the Break Apart command remains unchanged.

10. Save your work, then close the document.

You used the Break Apart command to break the link between one instance and its symbol, you edited the object created using the Break Apart command, and then you edited the symbol, which only affected the instance still linked to the symbol.

Create
BUTTONS

What You'll Do

© Cengage Learning®.

Image courtesy Jim Shuman.

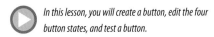 *In this lesson, you will create a button, edit the four button states, and test a button.*

Understanding Buttons

Button symbols are used to provide interactivity. When you click a button, an action occurs, such as starting an animation or jumping to another frame on the Timeline. Any object, including Flash drawings, text blocks, and imported graphic images, can be made into buttons. Unlike graphic symbols, buttons have four states: Up, Over, Down, and Hit. These states correspond to the use of the mouse and recognize that the user requires feedback when the mouse is pointing to a button and when the button has been clicked. This is often shown by a change in the button (such as a different color or different shape). An example of a button with different colors for the four different states is shown in Figure 54. These four states are explained in the following paragraphs.

Up—Represents how the button appears when the mouse pointer is not over it.

Over—Represents how the button appears when the mouse pointer is over it.

Down—Represents how the button appears after the user clicks the mouse.

Hit—Defines the area of the screen that will respond to the pointer. In most cases, you will want the Hit state to be the same or similar to the Up state in location and size.

When you create a button symbol, Flash automatically creates a new Timeline. The Timeline has only four frames, one for each button state. The Timeline does not play; it merely reacts to the mouse pointer by displaying the appropriate button state.

The process for creating and previewing buttons is as follows:

Create a button symbol—Draw an object or select an object that has already been created and placed on the Stage. Use the Convert to

Figure 54 *The four button states*

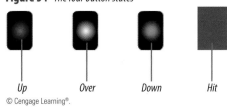

© Cengage Learning®.

Image courtesy Jim Shuman.

Symbol command on the Modify menu to convert the object to a button symbol and to enter a name for the button.

Edit the button symbol—Select the button and choose the Edit Symbols command on the Edit menu or double-click the button symbol on the Library panel. This displays the edit window, which includes the button Timeline, shown in Figure 55. You use the button Timeline to work with the four button states. The Up state is the original button symbol. Flash automatically places it in frame 1. You need to determine how the original object will change for the other states. To change the button for the Over state, click frame 2 and insert a keyframe. This automatically places a copy of the button that is in frame 1 into frame 2. Then, alter the button's appearance for the Over state, for instance, by changing the fill color. Use the same process for the Down state. For the Hit state, you insert a keyframe in frame 4 and then specify the area on the screen that will respond to the pointer. If you do not specify a hit area, the image for the Down state is used for the hit area. You add a keyframe to the Hit frame only if you are going to specify the hit area.

Return to the main Timeline—Once you've finished editing a button, you choose the Edit Document command on the Edit menu or click Scene 1 above the edit window to return to the main Timeline.

Preview the button—By default, Flash disables buttons so that you can manipulate them on the Stage. You can preview a button by choosing the Enable Simple Buttons command on the Control menu. You can also choose the Test Movie command on the Control menu to play the movie and test the buttons.

Figure 55 *The edit window showing the button symbol and the button Timeline*

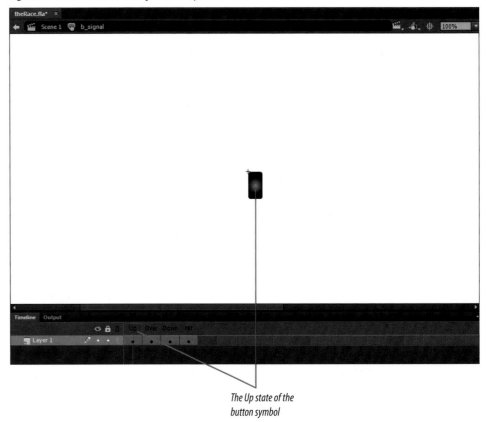

The Up state of the button symbol

Create a button

1. Open fl2_5.fla, then save it as **theRace.fla**. This movie is similar to the car race movie in Chapter 1.

2. Insert a new layer above the top layer on the Timeline, then name the layer **signal.**

3. Click and hold the **Rectangle tool**, then click the **Rectangle Primitive tool** 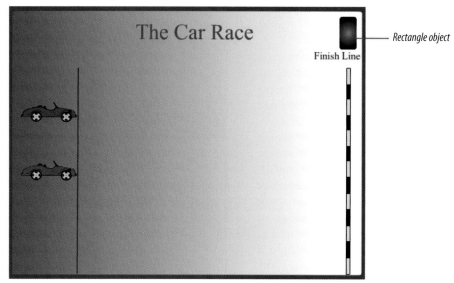.

4. Use the Properties panel to set the **Stroke Color** to **No Stroke** and the **Fill Color** to a **red gradient**.

5. Click the **Reset button** in the Rectangle Options area of the Properties panel, then set the Rectangle corner radius to **5**.

   Note: the Reset button clears any previous corner radius setting.

6. Draw the **rectangle** shown in Figure 56.

7. Click the **Zoom tool** on the Tools panel, then click the **rectangle** to enlarge it.

8. Click and hold the **Free Transform tool** on the Tools panel, then click the **Gradient Transform tool**.

9. Click the **rectangle**, then drag the **diagonal arrow** toward the center of the rectangle as shown in Figure 57 to make the red area more round.

10. Use the **Selection tool** to drag a **marquee** around the rectangle.

11. Click **Modify** on the menu bar, then click **Convert to Symbol**.

12. Type **b_signal** in the Name text box, click the **Type list arrow**, click **Button**, then click **OK**.

13. Display the Library panel.

You created a button symbol on the Stage.

Figure 56 *The rectangle object*

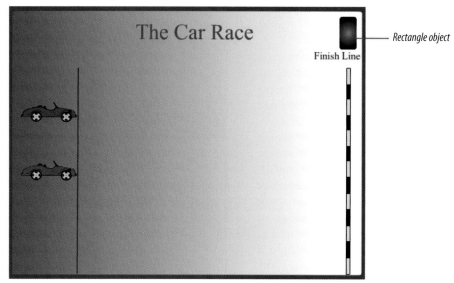

— Rectangle object

Image courtesy Jim Shuman.

Figure 57 *Adjusting the gradient*

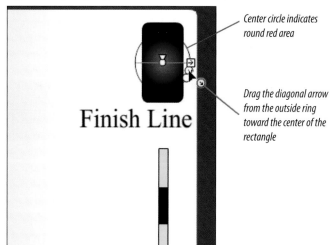

Center circle indicates round red area

Drag the diagonal arrow from the outside ring toward the center of the rectangle

Drawing Objects and Working with Symbols and Interactivity

Figure 58 *Specifying the hit area*

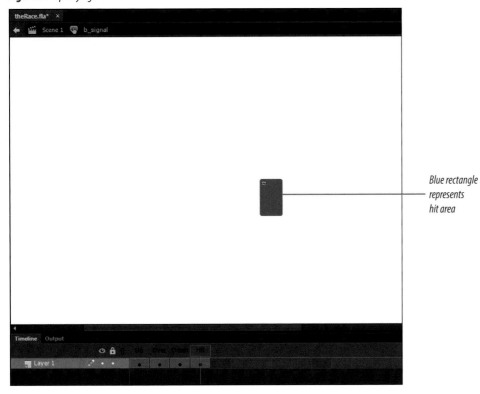

Blue rectangle
represents
hit area

Edit a button and specify a hit area

1. Right-click (Win) or control-click (Mac) **b_signal** on the Library panel, then click **Edit**.

   Flash displays the edit window showing the Timeline with four button states.

2. Click the blank **Over frame** on Layer 1, then insert a **keyframe**.

TIP The [F6] key inserts a keyframe in the selected frame. The [fn] key may need to be used with some Mac keyboards.

3. Display the Properties panel, click the button, then set the **Fill Color** to the **gray gradient color swatch** on the bottom of the color palette.

TIP If the gradient is not selected, try clicking the edge of the gradient swatch rather than the middle.

4. Insert a **keyframe** in the Down frame on Layer 1.

5. Set the **Fill Color** to the **green gradient color swatch** on the bottom of the color palette.

6. Insert a **keyframe** in the Hit frame on Layer 1.

7. Select the **Rectangle tool** on the Tools panel then set the **Fill Color** to the **blue color swatch** in the left column of the color palette.

8. Draw a **rectangle** slightly larger than the button as shown in Figure 58, then release the mouse button.

TIP The Hit area will not be visible on the Stage when you return to the main Timeline.

9. Click **Scene 1** above the edit window to return to the main Timeline.

You edited a button by changing the color of its Over and Down states, and you specified the Hit area.

Test a button

1. Click the **Selection tool** 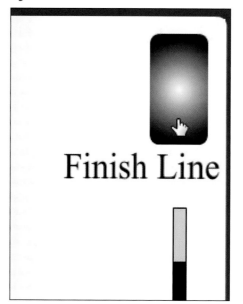, then click a blank area of the Stage.

2. Click **Control** on the menu bar to display the Control menu, then click **Enable Simple Buttons** if it is not already checked.

   This command allows you to test buttons on the Stage without viewing the movie in the Flash Player window.

3. Point to the **signal button** on the Stage, then compare your image to Figure 59.

   The pointer changes to a hand, indicating that the object is clickable, and the button changes to a gray gradient, the color you selected for the Over state.

4. Press and hold the **mouse button**, then notice that the button changes to a green gradient, the color you selected for the Down state, as shown in Figure 60.

5. Release the mouse and notice that the button changes to a gray gradient, the color you selected for the Over state.

(continued)

Figure 59 *The button's Over state*

Finish Line

Figure 60 *The button's Down state*

Finish Line

The Button Hit Area

All buttons have an area that responds to the mouse pointer, including rolling over the button and clicking it. This hit area is usually the same size and shape as the button itself. However, you can specify any area of the button to be the hit area. For example, you could have a button symbol that looks like a target with just the bulls-eye center being the hit area.

Drawing Objects and Working with Symbols and Interactivity

Figure 61 *The button's Up state*

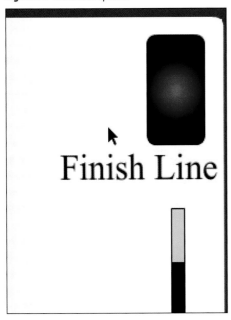

Figure 62 *Typing an instance name*

Instance name

6. Move the mouse away from the signal button, and notice that the button returns to a red gradient, the Up state color, as shown in Figure 61.

7. Click **Control** on the menu bar, then click **Enable Simple Buttons** to turn off the command.

8. Click the **View list arrow** above the Stage, then click **Fit in Window**.

    This shortcut allows you to change the magnification view without using the Magnification command on the View menu or the Zoom tool on the Tools panel.

You used the mouse to test a button and view the button states.

Give the symbol an instance name

1. Use the **Selection tool** on the Tools panel to draw a **marquee** around the button to select it.

2. Click in the **Instance name box** at the top of the Properties panel, then type **signal** as shown in Figure 62.

3. Press **[Enter]** (Win) or **[return]** (Mac).

    Giving the symbol an instance name allows the symbol to be referenced in ActionScript code as you assign an action to the button.

4. Save your work.

You assigned an instance name to a symbol.

LESSON 6

Assign Actions to Frames and
BUTTONS USING CODE SNIPPETS

What You'll Do

Image courtesy Jim Shuman.

In this lesson, you will use ActionScript code snippets to assign actions to frames and buttons.

Understanding Actions

In a basic movie, Flash plays the frames sequentially without stopping for user input. However, you often want to provide users with the ability to interact with the movie by allowing them to perform actions, such as starting and stopping the movie or jumping to a specific frame in the movie. One way to provide user interaction is to assign an action to the Down state of a button. Then, whenever the user clicks the button, the action occurs. Flash provides a scripting language, called ActionScript, that allows you to add actions to buttons and other objects within a movie. For example, you can place a stop action in a frame that pauses the movie, and then you can assign a gotoAndPlay action to a button that starts the movie when the user clicks the button.

Analyzing ActionScript

ActionScript, which is a powerful scripting language, allows those with even limited programming experience to create complex actions. For example, you can create order forms that capture user input or volume controls that display when sounds are played.

ActionScript 3.0 and Code Snippets

Adobe has identified two types of Flash CC users, designers and developers. Designers focus more on the visual features of a Flash movie, including the user interface design, drawing objects, and acquiring and editing additional assets (such as graphic images). By contrast, developers focus more on the programming aspects of a Flash movie, including creation of complex animations and writing the code that specifies how the movie responds to user interactions. In many cases, designers and developers work together to create sophisticated Flash applications. In other cases, designers work without the benefit of a developer's programming expertise. In order to accommodate the varying needs of these two types of users, Flash CC provides **code snippets**, predefined blocks of ActionScript 3.0 code.

Drawing Objects and Working with Symbols and Interactivity

Code snippets are provided for a number of features that can be added to an application including navigation, animation, audio, and video. Figure 63 shows the Code Snippets panel with the list of categories and the Timeline Navigation category expanded to show the code snippets available in that category. Figure 64 shows the "Click to Go to Frame and Play" code snippet after it has been inserted in the Script pane. The Script pane is a window that displays ActionScript code and allows you to edit the code. The code begins with several comment lines that are grayed out. These are instructions that guide you through the use of the code. The code starts in line 19 with an add mouse click event listener for a button instance named signal followed by a function named fl_ClickToGoToAndPlayFromFrame. This line of code essentially "listens" for a mouse click on the button with an instance name of signal and then calls the function. A function has code that is executed when the function is called. Line 21 identifies the start of the function and line 23 has the code that is executed when the user clicks the signal button. In this case the code causes the playhead to jump to Frame 2. The actual default frame number to go to is 5. The number 5 was changed to 2 by the movie Developer. The instructions indicate that you replace the number 5 with the frame number you would like the playhead to move to when the symbol instance (signal)

Figure 63 *The Code Snippets panel*

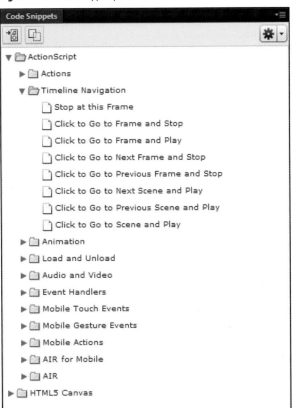

is clicked. The process for using this code snippet follows.

- Create a button symbol and give it an instance name. The instance name will be used in the code.
- Select the button instance on the Stage. (*Note*: Even though you select the button on the Stage, the AS3 code will be placed in a frame on a layer named actions (or Actions), not in a frame containing the button. If there is no layer named actions or Actions, Flash will create one and name it Actions.)
- Open the Code Snippets panel and double-click the desired snippet to enter that code in the Script pane.
- Edit the code as needed, such as editing the actions you want executed. For instance, you can change the frame number that the function should go to and play when the code is executed.

Think of code snippets as templates that allow you to make changes to customize the code. These could be changes in function names, frame numbers, or properties such as ease values.

Figure 64 *The Actions panel after adding a code snippet*

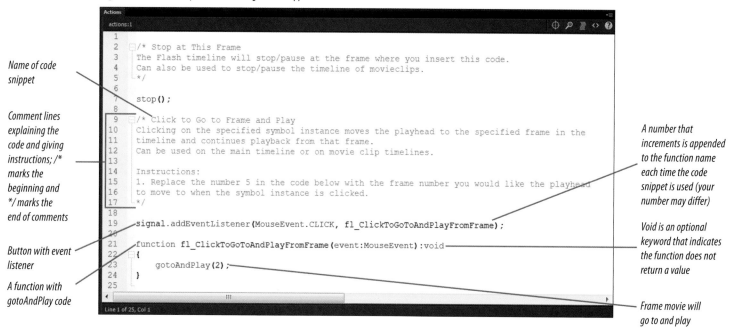

Name of code snippet

Comment lines explaining the code and giving instructions; /* marks the beginning and */ marks the end of comments

Button with event listener

A function with gotoAndPlay code

A number that increments is appended to the function name each time the code snippet is used (your number may differ)

Void is an optional keyword that indicates the function does not return a value

Frame movie will go to and play

Figure 65 *The Actions panel showing the code that stops the movie at the current frame (frame 1)*

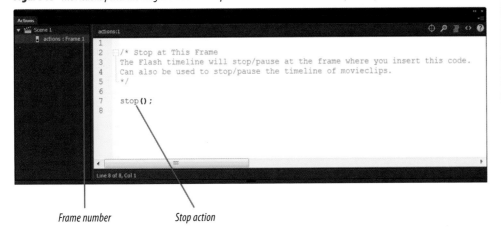

Frame number   Stop action

Assign a stop action to frames

1. Click **Control** on the menu bar, point to **Test Movie**, then click **in Flash Professional**.

   The movie plays and continues to loop.

2. Close the Flash Player window.

3. Insert a new layer, name it **actions**, then click **frame 1** on the layer.

4. Click **Window** on the menu bar, then click **Code Snippets** to open the Code Snippets panel.

5. Open the **ActionScript folder**, open the **Timeline Navigation subfolder**, then double-click **Stop at this Frame**.

6. Click a blank area of the Actions panel.

   The Actions panel is displayed as shown in Figure 65. The code that has been inserted into the Actions panel that will cause the playhead to stop at the current frame—that is, frame 1.

   Note: The Actions panel has been resized to show the code.

7. Minimize the Actions panel.

8. Click frame **65** on the actions layer.

9. Click **Insert** on the menu bar, point to **Timeline**, then click **Keyframe**.

10. Verify Frame 65 on the actions layer is selected, then double-click **Stop at this Frame** on the Code Snippets panel.

11. Close the Actions panel.

12. Test the movie.

    The movie does not play because a stop action is assigned to frame 1.

13. Close the Flash Player window.

You inserted a layer and assigned a stop action to the first and last frames of the layer.

Assign a play action to a button

1. **Minimize** the Code Snippets panel.

2. Click **frame 1** on the signal layer, then use the Selection tool to select the signal button on the Stage.

3. Display the **Code Snippets panel**, then double-click **Click to Go to Frame and Play**.

4. Study the code on the **Actions panel**, which causes the playhead to jump to a specified frame is inserted into the Actions panel.

   Notice that the next-to-last line of code reads "gotoAndPlay(5);". The 5 indicates the frame number the playhead will jump to when the button is clicked. This is the default frame number that is automatically inserted into the code. You need to change 5 to 2.

5. Edit the code to change 5 to **2**, as shown in Figure 66, just as if you were editing text in a word processor, then close the Actions panel and the Code Snippets panel.

6. Test the movie, then **click the signal button** to play the animation.

7. Close the Flash Player window.

You assigned an instance name to an object and used Code Snippets to assign a "go to and play" action to a button.

Assign a goto frame action to a button

1. Click **Control** on the menu bar, point to **Test Movie,** then click **in Flash Professional**.

2. Click the **signal button**.

   The movie plays and stops, and the word Reset, which is actually a button, appears.

   (continued)

```
Actions
actions:1

 8
 9   □/* Click to Go to Frame and Play
10    Clicking on the specified symbol instance moves the playhead to the specified frame in the timeline
11    Can be used on the main timeline or on movie clip timelines.
12
13    Instructions:
14    1. Replace the number 5 in the code below with the frame number you would like the playhead to move
15   └*/
16
17    signal.addEventListener(MouseEvent.CLICK, fl_ClickToGoToAndPlayFromFrame);
18
19    function fl_ClickToGoToAndPlayFromFrame(event:MouseEvent):void
20   □{
21        gotoAndPlay(2);
22    }
23
```

Change the frame number to 2

Drawing Objects and Working with Symbols and Interactivity

Figure 67 *Changing the frame number to cause the playhead to jump to frame 1*

```
Actions
actions:65
 8
 9    /* Click to Go to Frame and Stop
10    Clicking on the specified symbol instance moves the playhead to the specified frame in the timeline
11    Can be used on the main timeline or on movie clip timelines.
12
13    Instructions:
14    1. Replace the number 5 in the code below with the frame number you would like the playhead to move
15    */
16
17    resetBtn.addEventListener(MouseEvent.CLICK, fl_ClickToGoToAndStopAtFrame);
18
19    function fl_ClickToGoToAndStopAtFrame(event:MouseEvent):void
20    {
21        gotoAndStop(1);
22    }
23
```

*Change the frame
number to 1*

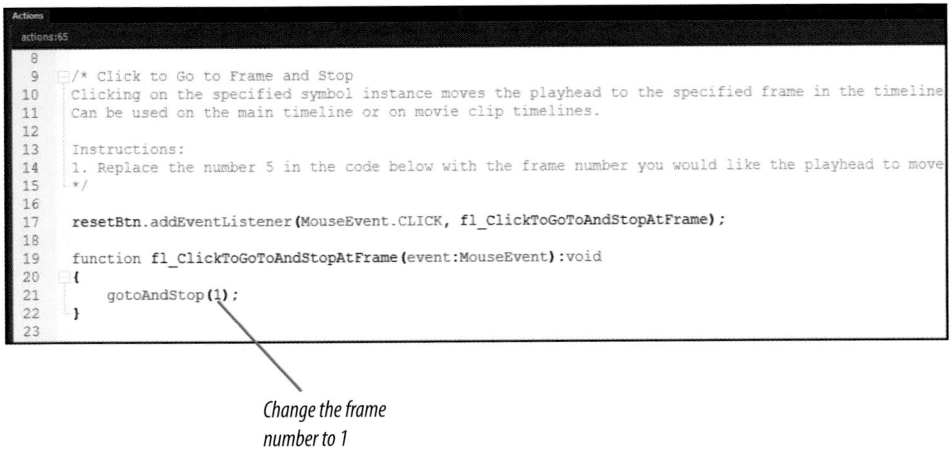

3. Click the **Reset button** and notice nothing happens because it does not have an action assigned to it.

4. Close the Flash Player window.

5. Click **frame 65** on the resetBTN layer to display the Reset button on the Stage.

   Note: You many need to close and/or move the Actions panel to view the Reset button on the Stage.

6. Click the **Reset button** on the Stage to select it, then give it an instance name of **resetBTN**.

7. Display the **Code Snippets panel**, open the **ActionScript** folder, open the **Timeline Navigation** folder, then double-click **Click to Go to Frame and Stop**.

8. On the Actions panel, change the frame number from 5 to **1** at the bottom of the code as shown in Figure 67.

   Note: The Actions panel has been resized to show the code.

9. Test the movie, click the **signal button** to start the movie, then when the movie stops, click the **Reset button.**

   The goto action you assigned to the Reset button causes the playhead to jump to frame 1, the beginning of the movie.

10. Close the Flash Player window, close the Actions and Code Snippets panels, then save and close the movie.

You used the Actions panel to assign an action to a button.

Use drawing tools and alignment options.

1. Open fl2_6.fla and rename it as **skillsDemo2.fla**. This document consists of a single image that has been imported to the Library, placed on the Stage and converted to a graphic symbol named g_beachScene. The layer for the graphic is named beachScene and has been locked.
2. Add a layer and name it **umbrellaTop**.
3. Select frame 1 of the umbrellaTop layer.
4. Use the drawing tools to create the top part of the umbrella similar to the one shown in Figure 68. The graphic should include a rainbow gradient. (*Hint:* you can use the Oval tool to draw an oval and the eraser tool to delete part of it. You can also use the Selection and Subselection tools to reshape the object. Alternately, you could use the Brush tool or other tools of your choice to create the object. Then you can use the Free Transform tool to rotate the object.)
5. Convert the drawing into a graphic symbol named **g_umbrellaTop**.
6. Add a layer and name it **umbrellaHandle**.
7. Select frame 1 of the umbrellaStand layer and create an umbrella handle similar to the one shown in Figure 68.

(*Hint:* The handle in Figure 68 was created using the line tool and the variable width option of the Fill and Stroke area of the Properties panel.)
8. Convert the drawing into a graphic symbol named **g_umbrellaHandle**.
9. Drag the umbrellaHandle layer below the umbrellaTop layer.
10. Use the Free Transform tool to draw a marquee around both objects to select them.
11. Rotate the selected objects as shown in Figure 68.
12. Use the Properties panel to set the position of the objects to X:**180** and Y:**217**.
13. Lock the umbrellaTop and umbrellaHandle layers.

Use text tools and work with text objects.

1. Insert a new layer and name it **title**.
2. Click frame 1 on the title layer, create a text block at the top middle of the Stage with the words BeachBall Spin using Arial as the font, blue as the color, and 20-pt as the font size.
3. Use the Align panel to center the text block horizontally on the Stage.
4. Insert a new layer above the title layer and name it **titleBkgnd**.

5. Draw a primitive rectangle with a corner radius of 10, a medium gray fill (#999999) and no stroke that covers the BeachBall Spin title text.
6. Verify the rectangle is selected, then convert it to a graphic symbol with the name **g_titleBkgnd**.
7. Use the Align panel to center the text block horizontally on the Stage.
8. Move the title layer so it is above the titleBkgnd layer.
9. Lock the title and titleBkgnd layers.

Create a symbol.

1. Insert a new layer and name it **beachBall spin** to the Library.
2. Import the beachBall.png image to the Library.
3. Select frame 1 on the beachBall spin layer and drag the beachBall image from Library to the Stage.
4. With the image selected display the Properties panel and verify the Lock width and height values together icon is locked.
5. Change the width to **60**.
6. Change the position of the image to X:**40** and Y:**300**.
7. Convert the ball to a graphic symbol with the name **g_beachBall**. (*Note:* Be sure to select Graphic as the symbol type.)

Drawing Objects and Working with Symbols and Interactivity

Figure 68 *Completed Skills Review*

Images courtesy Jim Shuman.

8. Double-click the g_beachBall symbol on the Library panel to open the edit window, add a text block that sits on top of the ball with the words Play Ball, formated with black, Times New Roman, 12-pt, bold. When you are finished, the text should look like the text on the multi-colored beachball in Figure 68. *Hint:* After you change the font size, you may need to resize the text box and then reposition it (by dragging it or using the arrow keys on the keyboard).

9. Click Scene 1 to return to the main Timeline, then with the ball selected, create a motion tween animation that moves the ball from the left edge of the Stage to the right edge of the Stage. Be sure to click frame 24 on the beachBall spin layer before moving the ball.

10. Insert keyframes in frame 24 of each of the other layers.

11. Click frame 1 on the beachBall spin layer, the use the Selection tool to drag the middle of the motion path up to near the middle of the Stage to create an arc.

12. Select the last frame of the animation on the Timeline and set Rotate to 1 time in the Rotation area of the Properties panel.

13. Play the movie.
    The ball should move across the Stage in an arc and spin at the same time.

14. Lock the beachBall spin layer.

Create and edit an instance.

1. Insert a new layer and name it **blueBall**.
2. Click frame 1 on the blueBall layer, then draw a circle with a width of 55 pixels, no stroke and a blue gradient fill.
3. Drag the blueBall so that it is centered over the beachBall image.
4. Select the ball and convert it to a graphic symbol with the name g_blueBall.
5. Insert a new layer, click frame 12 on the layer and insert a keyframe.
6. Rename the layer greenBall.
7. Drag the g_blueBall symbol from the Library panel so it is on top of the multi-colored ball, which, at frame 12, is near the middle of the Stage.
8. With the ball selected, click Modify on the menu bar, click Break Apart and change the fill color of the ball to a green gradient.

9. Select the greenBall object and convert it to a graphic symbol with the name **g_greenBall**.
10. Move the beachBall spin layer to above the other layers, then lock all layers.
11. Play the movie, then save your work.

Create a button.

1. Insert a new layer above the title layer.
2. Click frame 24 of the new layer and insert a keyframe.
3. Create a text block with the word **Reset** formatted with blue, bold, 20-pt Arial, then center the text block horizontally near the bottom of the Stage.
4. Select the text. (*Hint:* Use the Selection tool to drag a marquee around the object.)
5. Convert the selected object to a button symbol and name it **b_reset**.
6. Verify the Reset button is selected on the Stage, then use the Properties panel to give it an instance name of **resetBtn**.
7. Display the Library panel, then double-click the b_reset symbol to display it in the edit window.
8. Insert a keyframe in the Over frame.

9. Use the Text tool to select the text and change the color to a light shade of gray.
10. Insert a keyframe in the Down frame.
11. Select the text and change the color to a darker shade of gray.
12. Insert a keyframe in the Hit frame.
13. Draw a rectangular object that covers the button area for the Hit state.
14. Click Scene 1 to exit the edit window and return to the main Timeline.
15. Change the layer name to resetButton.
16. Save your work.

Test a button.

1. Click Control on the menu bar, then click Enable Simple Buttons to turn on Enable Simple Buttons.
2. Point to the button and notice the color change.
3. Click the button and notice the other color change.
4. Turn off Enable Simple Buttons.

Stop a movie by assigning an action to a frame.

1. Insert a new layer and name it **Actions**.
2. Scroll the Timeline to display frame 1.
3. Use the Selection tool to click on a blank area of the Stage, click 1 on the Timeline to remove the yellow highlighting, click frame 24 on the Actions layer, then insert a keyframe in frame 24 on the new layer.
4. With frame 24 selected, display the Code Snippets panel.
5. Assign a stop action to the frame.
6. Click frame 1 on the Actions layer.
7. Assign a stop action to frame 1.
8. Save your work.

Assign a goto action to a button.

1. Lock all layers except for beachBall spin layer.
2. Click frame 1 of the beachBall spin layer and verify the beachBall object is selected.
3. Convert the beachBall graphic to a Button symbol with the name **b_beachBall**.
4. Give the button an instance name of **beachBallBtn**.
5. Display the Library panel and display the edit window for the beachBall button.
6. Insert a keyframe in the Over frame and verify the object is selected.
7. Click Modify in the menu bar and click Break Apart.
8. Use the Text tool to highlight the text and change the fill to white.

9. Insert a keyframe in the Down frame and verify the object is selected.
10. Use the Text tool to highlight the text and change the fill to a dark shade of gray.
11. Click Scene 1 to return to the main Timeline.
12. Click frame 1 on the beachBall spin layer and verify the object on the Stage is selected.
13. With the beachBall button selected, use the Code Snippets panel to create the code that causes the playhead to go to and play frame 2 when the button is clicked.
14. Unlock the resetButton layer, then click frame 24 of the resetButton layer and verify the Reset button is selected.
15. With the Reset button selected, use the Code Snippets panel to create the code that cause the playhead to go to and play frame 1 when the button is clicked.
16. Lock all layers.
17. Test the movie, then compare your image to Figure 68.
18. Close the Flash Player window, then save your work.
19. Exit Flash.

A local travel company, Odyssey Adventure Tours, has asked you to design sample opening screens for its new application. The goal of the application is to inform potential customers of its services. The company specializes in exotic treks, tours, and cruises. Thus, while its target audience spans a wide age range, they are all looking for something out of the ordinary. The initial opening screen is the company's home screen and allows the user to click on the company logo to go to an introduction. The home screen also allows the user to click on a button to skip the introduction and display a screen that will eventually have menu options. The home screen may become part of a website, a mobile app, and/or a link on a Facebook site.

1. Open a new Flash document using ActionScript 3.0 and save it as **odysseyTours2.fla**. Create the Flash movie shown in Figure 69.

2. Set the document properties, including the Stage color.

3. Create the following on separate layers and name the layers:
   - A text heading; select a font size and font color. Skew the heading.
   - A subheading with a different font size and color.
   - Text that appears below the logo. (You will insert the logo in Step 5.)
   - A CONTINUE button with text that has a different color for the Up, Over and Down states. Select the CONTINUE button and give it an instance name of **continueBtn**.

4. Use one or more of the align features (gridlines, rulers, Align command on the Modify menu, arrow keys) to align the objects on the Stage.

5. Import the OAT logo to the Library. Add a layer and name it **logo**. Drag the logo by its symbol from the Library panel to the Stage and center it across the Stage.

6. Insert keyframes in frame 5 of all of the layers except the logo, the CONTINUE button, and the layer with the text below the logo.

7. Add a new layer, name it **actions**, and select frame 1 on the actions layer.

8. Use the Code Snippets panel to:
   - Add a stop action to frame 1.
   - Add a goto and play action to the CONTINUE button that jumps to frame 5.
   Note: do not add an action to the logo at this time.

9. Add a new layer and name it **home btn**. Select frame 5 of the layer and:
   - Add a keyframe.
   - Add a stop action.
   - Create a HOME button.
   - Have the movie jump to frame 1 when the HOME button is clicked.

10. Compare your image to the example shown in Figure 69.

11. Save your work.

12. Test the movie, close the Flash Player window, then close the movie.

Figure 69 *Sample completed Project Builder 1*

©iStock.com/sbayram

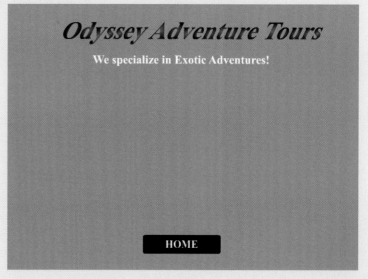

You have been asked to create several sample designs for the opening screen of an application of a new organization called The Jazz Club. The club is being organized to bring together music enthusiasts for social events and charitable fundraising activities. The club members plan to sponsor weekly jam sessions and a show once a month. Because the club is just getting started, the organizers are looking to you for help in developing an application. This screen may become part of a website, a mobile app, and/or a link on a Facebook site.

1. Plan the application by specifying the goal, target audience, treatment ("look and feel"), and elements you want to include (text, graphics, sound, and so on). Figure 70 shows a sample project that you can use as a guide or you can create your own design.
2. Sketch out a screen design that shows the layout of the objects. Be creative in your design.
3. Open a new Flash ActionScript 3.0 document and save it as **theJazzClub2.fla**.
4. Set the document properties, including the Stage size and Stage color, if desired.

5. Display the gridlines and rulers and use them to help align objects on the Stage.
6. Create a heading, text objects, and drawings (such as the lines) to be used as links to the categories of information provided on the application. (*Note*: If you decide to use the design in Figure 70, some of the characters are individual text blocks [e.g. the S in Sessions] allowing you to move the text block

without moving the other characters. *Hint*: Use the Oval, Line, and Brush tools to create the notes. After selecting the Brush tool, experiment with the different Brush tool shapes found in the Options area at the bottom of the Tools panel.)
7. Hide the gridlines and rulers.
8. Save your work.

Figure 70   *Sample completed Project Builder 2*

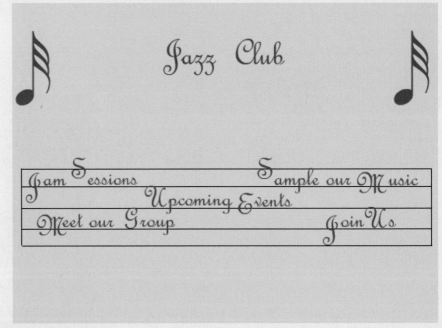

Image courtesy Jim Shuman.

Figure 71 shows the home page of a website. Study the figure and complete the following. For each question indicate how you determined your answer.

1. Connect to the Internet, go to *www.nps.gov*, then select Explore Nature.
2. Open a document in a word processor or open a new Flash document, save the file as **dpc2**, then answer the following questions. (*Hint*: Use the Text tool in Flash.)
   - Whose website is this?
   - What is the goal(s) of the site?
   - Who is the target audience?
   - What treatment ("look and feel") is used?
   - What are the design layout guidelines being used (balance, movement, and so on)?
   - If you wanted to add animation to this screen, what element might you animate?
   - Do you think this is an effective design for the organization, its goals, and its target audience? Why or why not?
   - What suggestions would you make to improve the design and why?

Figure 71 *Design Project*

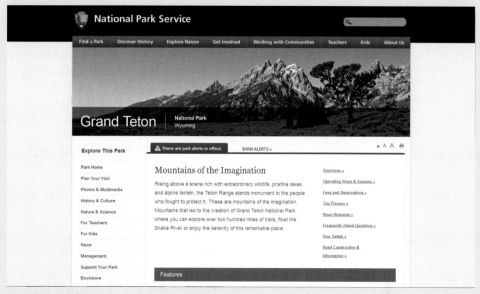

Source: *National Park Service*

PORTFOLIO PROJECT

You have decided to create a personal portfolio of your work that you can use when you begin your job search. The portfolio will be part of a website with a link on your Facebook page.

1. Research what should be included in a portfolio.
2. Plan the site by specifying the goal, target audience, treatment ("look and feel"), and elements you want to include (text, graphics, sound, and so on).
3. Sketch an opening screen that shows the layout of the objects. Be creative in your design.
4. Design the opening screen to include personal data (such as a Biography object that will link to your personal data, work history, and education), contact information (such as a Contact me object that will link to your contact information), and samples of your work (such as Animations, Graphics, and Screen Designs objects that will link to samples of your work). The categories and titles are up to you.
5. Open a new Flash document using ActionScript 3.0 and save it as **portfolio2.fla**.
6. Set the document properties, including the Stage size and Stage color, if desired.
7. Display the gridlines and rulers and use them to help align objects on the Stage. (*Note:* The sample completed Portfolio Project shown in Figure 72 uses seven layers. As you complete the following steps include layers for:
   - the blue border that surrounds the entire screen
   - the title (My Portfolio) with a blue background
   - the placeholder for the content
   - the text for the menu categories
   - the home button on the second screen
   - the category title (Biography) on the second screen
   - actions (Code Snippets)
8. Add a border the size of the Stage. (*Hint:* Use the Rectangle tool, then set the Stroke color to a color of your choice and the Fill color to no color ☑ .
9. Create a title with its own background.
10. Create the placeholder for the content.
11. Create the text buttons that will be used as links to the categories of information provided on the website. Be sure to give the button instance names. (*Hint:* In the example shown in Figure 72, the Brush Script Std font is used. You can replace this font with Impact or any other appropriate font on your computer.)
12. Insert keyframes in frame 5 for all layers.
13. Select frame 5 and create a second screen that:
    - Includes a Home button (with an instance name).
    - Includes a category title (Biography).
    - Removes the Biography menu item.
14. Use code snippets to:
    - Stop the movie in frames 1 and 5.
    - Creates a goto action for the Biography and Home buttons.
15. Hide the gridlines and rulers.
16. Lock all the layers.
17. Save your work, then compare your image to the example shown in Figure 72.

Drawing Objects and Working with Symbols and Interactivity

Figure 72 *Sample Completed Portfolio Project*

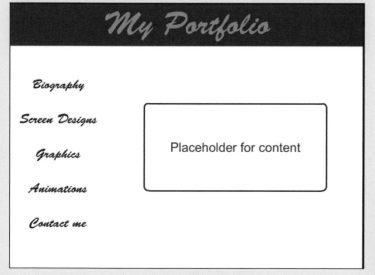

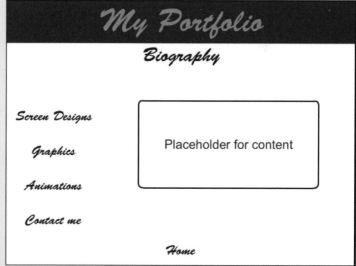

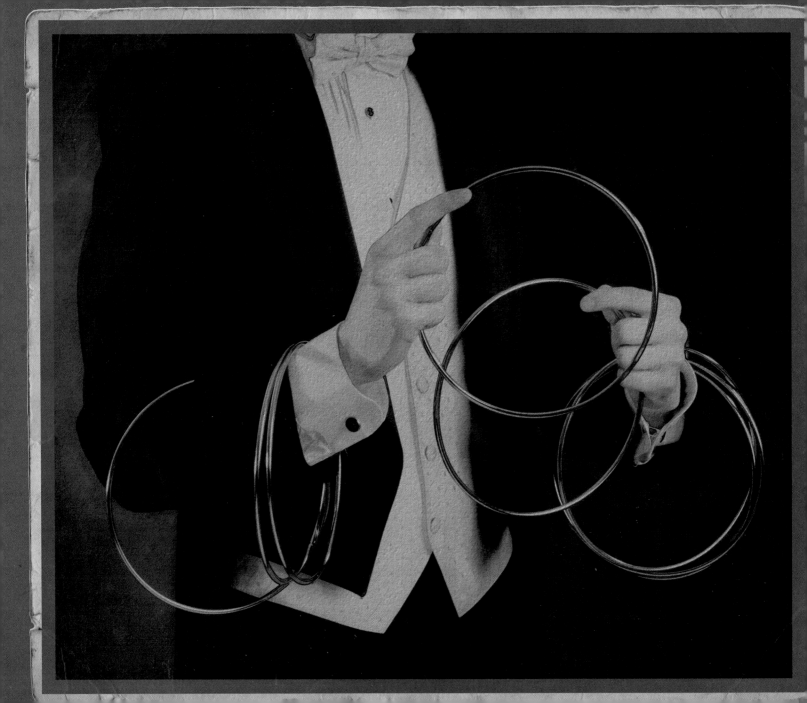

ADOBE FLASH CC

CHAPTER **3** **CREATING**
ANIMATIONS

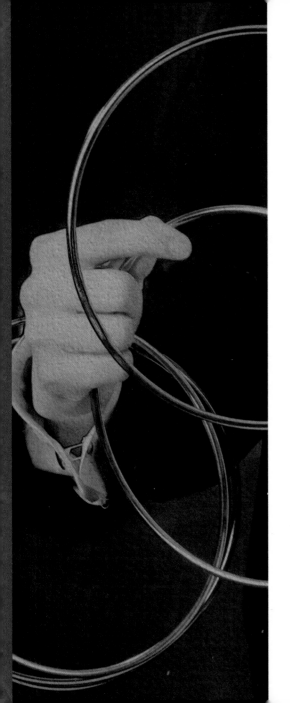

CHAPTER 3 CREATING ANIMATIONS

Introduction

Animation can be an important part of your application or website, whether the focus is on entertainment (provides interactive games), e-commerce (attracts attention and provides product demonstrations), or education (simulates complex processes such as DNA replication).

How Does Animation Work?

The perception of motion in an animation is actually an illusion. Animation is like a motion picture in that it is made up of a series of still images. Research has found that our eye captures and holds an image for one-tenth of a second before processing another image. By retaining each impression for one-tenth of a second, we perceive a series of rapidly displayed still images as a single, moving image. This phenomenon is known as **persistence of vision** and it provides the basis for the frame rate in animations. Frame rates of 10–12 frames-per-second (fps) generally provide an acceptably smooth computer-based animation. Lower frame rates result in a jerky image, while frame rates over 30 fps may result in a blurred image. In addition, higher frame rates may increase file size because more frames are needed for a 5 second animation running at 30 fps than at 10 fps. After creating an animation you can experiment with various frame rates to obtain the desired effect. Flash uses a default frame rate of 24 fps.

Flash Animation

Creating animation is one of the most powerful features of Flash, yet developing basic animations is a simple process. Flash allows you to create animations that can move and rotate an object around the Stage, as well as change its size, shape, or color. You can also use the animation features in Flash to create special effects, such as an object zooming or fading in and out. You can combine animation effects so that an object changes shape and color as it moves across the Stage. Animations are created by changing the content of successive frames. Flash provides two animation methods: frame-by-frame animation and tweened animation. Tweened animations can be motion, classic, or shape tweens.

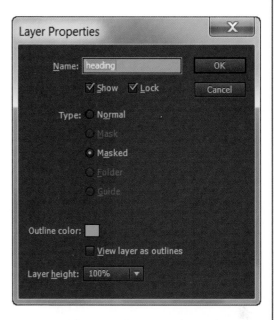

Create Motion Tween ANIMATIONS

What You'll Do

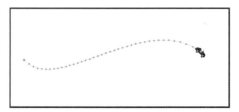

Image courtesy Jim Shuman.

In this lesson, you will create and edit motion tween animations.

Understanding Motion Tween Animations

An animation implies some sort of movement in an object. However, the concept of animation is much broader. Objects have specific properties such as position, size, color, and shape. Any change in a property of an object over time (i.e., across frames on the Timeline) can be considered an animation. So, having an object start at the left of the screen in frame 1 and then having it move across the screen and end up at the right side in frame 10 would be a change in the position property of the object. Each of the in-between frames (2-9) would show the position of the object as it moves across the screen. In a motion tween animation, you specify the position of the object in the beginning and ending frames and Flash fills in the in-between frames, a process known as **tweening**. Fortunately, you can change several properties with one motion tween. For example, you could have

a car move across the screen and, at the same time, you could have the size of the car change to give the impression of the car moving away from the viewer.

The process for creating a motion tween animation is to select the frame and layer where the animation will start. If necessary, insert a keyframe (by default, frame 1 of each layer has a keyframe). Select the object on the Stage, then select the Motion Tween command from the Insert menu. If the object is not already a symbol, you will be asked if you want to convert it to a symbol. You must convert the object to a symbol if prompted because only symbols and text fields can have a motion tween applied. Then you select the ending frame and make any changes to the object, such as moving it to another location or resizing it. After you make the change, a keyframe automatically appears in the ending frame you selected. When you create a motion tween, a tween span appears on the Timeline.

Creating Animations

Tween Spans

Figure 1 shows a motion tween animation of a car that starts in frame 1 and ends in frame 24. The **Onion Skin** feature is enabled so that outlines of the car are displayed for each frame of the animation in the figure. The Onion Skin feature is useful when developing an animation, but it is not how the completed animation will appear. Figure 1 shows the button that turns the Onion Skin feature on and off.

After turning the feature on, the numbers of the frames that will be affected are highlighted on the Timeline. You can change which frames display as outlines by dragging either end of the highlight. Notice a blue highlight appears on the Timeline for the frames of the animation. The blue highlighted area is called the tween or motion span. The length of the motion tween is determined by the last frame in the movie or by other keyframes on the layer. (*Note*:

The default tween span when starting from frame 1 of a new movie is determined by the number of frames in one second of the movie. So, if the frame rate is 24 frames per second, then the span is 24 frames.) You can increase or decrease the number of frames in the span by dragging the end of the span. In addition, you can move the span to a different location on the Timeline, and you can copy the span to have it apply to another object.

Figure 1 *Sample motion tween animation*

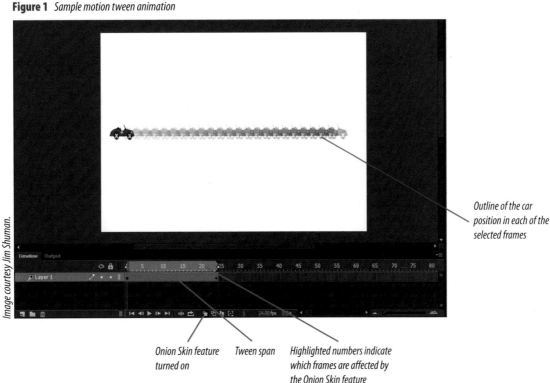

Outline of the car
position in each of the
selected frames

Onion Skin feature
turned on

Tween span

Highlighted numbers indicate
which frames are affected by
the Onion Skin feature

Motion Path

The animation shown in Figure 2 includes a position change (from frame 1 to frame 24); a motion path showing the position change is displayed on the Stage. Each dot on the path corresponds to a frame on the Timeline and indicates the location of the object (in this example, the car) when the frame is played. A motion path can be altered by dragging a point on the path using the Selection tool or by using the Subselection tool to manipulate Bezier handles as shown in Figure 3. Bezier curves employ a mathematical method for drawing curves. The shape of a Bezier curve can be altered by moving the handles attached to the end points of the curve.

In addition, an entire path can be moved around the Stage and reshaped using the Free Transform tool.

Property Keyframes

A keyframe indicates a change in a Flash movie, such as the start or ending of an animation. Motion tween animations use property keyframes that are specific to each property such as a position keyframe, color keyframe, or rotation keyframe. In most cases these are automatically placed on the Timeline as the motion tween animation is created.

Keep in mind:

- Only one object on the Stage can be animated in each tween span.

- You can have multiple motion tween animations playing at the same time if they are on different layers.
- A motion tween is, in essence, an object animation because, while several changes can be made to an object's properties, only one object is animated for each motion tween.
- The types of objects that can be tweened include graphic, button, and movie clip symbols, as well as text fields.
- You can remove a motion tween animation by clicking the tween span on the Timeline and choosing Remove Tween from the Insert menu.

Figure 2 *The motion path*

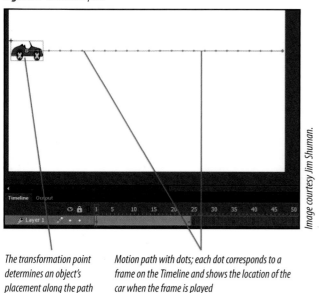

Image courtesy Jim Shuman.

The transformation point determines an object's placement along the path

Motion path with dots; each dot corresponds to a frame on the Timeline and shows the location of the car when the frame is played

Figure 3 *Bezier handles used to alter the path*

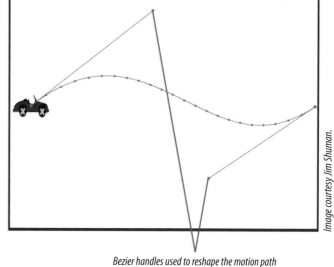

Image courtesy Jim Shuman.

Bezier handles used to reshape the motion path

Creating Animations

Figure 4 *Positioning the car object*

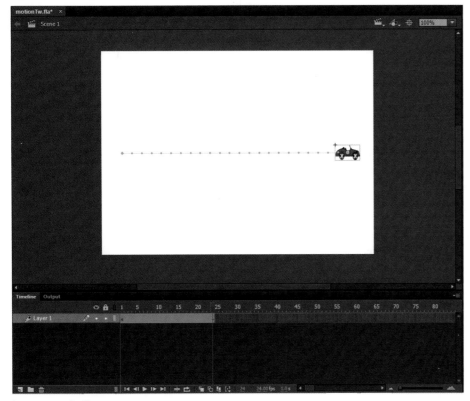

Image courtesy Jim Shuman.

Figure 5 *Changing the end of the tween span*

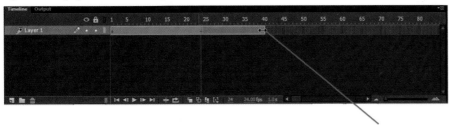

Drag pointer to here

Create a motion tween animation

1. Open fl3_1.fla from the drive and folder where your Data Files are stored, then save it as **motionTw.fla**.

   This document has one drawn object—a car that has been converted to a symbol.

2. Click the **Selection tool** on the Tools panel, if necessary, then click the **car** to select it.

3. Click **Insert** on the menu bar, then click **Motion Tween**.

   Notice the tween span appears on the Timeline. Because you started in frame 1, the number of frames in the span equals the frames per second for the movie.

4. Verify the playhead is on the last frame of the tween span, then drag the **car** to the right side of the Stage, as shown in Figure 4.

   A motion path appears on the Stage with dots indicating the position of the object for each frame. A diamond symbol appears in frame 24, which is the end of the tween span. The diamond symbol is a position keyframe and it is automatically inserted at the end of the tween path.

   Note: The end of this tween span is determined by the document frame rate, which is 24 fps. To see the diamond symbol more clearly, move the playhead.

5. Point to the end of the tween span, then, when the pointer changes to a double arrow ↔, drag the **tween span** to frame 40, as shown in Figure 5.

(continued)

6. Click 1 on the Timeline, then press the **period key** to move the playhead one frame at a time and notice the position of the car for each frame.

7. Press **[Enter]** (Win) or **[return]** (Mac) to play the movie.

8. Click **Control** in the menu bar, point to **Test Movie**, then click **In Flash Professional**.

9. View the movie, then close the Flash Player window.

10. Double-click **Layer 1** on the **Timeline**, then change the layer name to **red car**.

11. Save your work.

You created a motion tween animation, extended the length of the animation, and viewed the position of the animated object in each frame of the animation.

Edit a motion path

1. Click the **Selection tool** ▶ on the Tools panel, if necessary, then click a blank area of the Stage to deselect the object.

2. Click **frame 1** on the red car layer.

3. Point to the middle of the motion path, as shown in Figure 6.

4. When the pointer changes to a pointer with an arc ▶, drag the ▶ **pointer** down, as shown in Figure 7.

(continued)

Figure 6 *Pointing to the middle of the path*

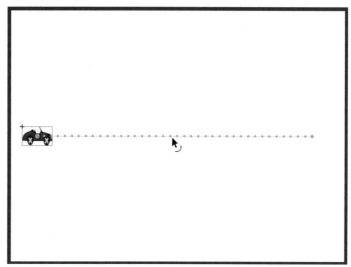

Image courtesy Jim Shuman.

Figure 7 *Dragging the motion path down*

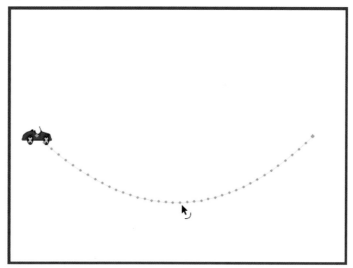

Image courtesy Jim Shuman.

Creating Animations

Figure 8 *Displaying the Bezier handles*

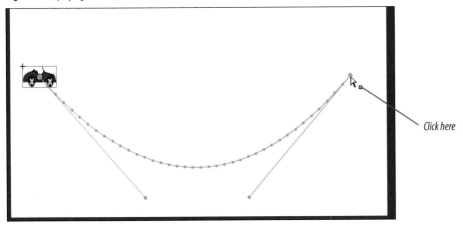

Click here

Image courtesy Jim Shuman.

Figure 9 *Using the handles to alter the shape of the path*

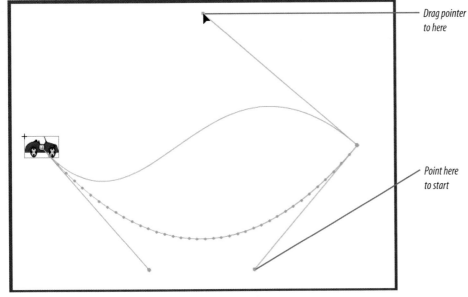

Drag pointer
to here

Point here
to start

Image courtesy Jim Shuman.

5. Play the movie.

   Notice the car is not oriented to the path. That is, the front of the car does not align with the path. Later in this lesson you will learn to orient an object to a curved path.

6. Click **frame 1** on Layer 1.

7. Click the **Subselection tool** ▶ on the Tools panel, point to the end of the motion path, then, when the pointer changes into an arrow with a small square ▶ □, click the end of path to display Bezier handles, as shown in Figure 8.

8. Point to the **lower-right handle**, then when the pointer changes to a delta symbol ▶, drag the **handle** up and toward the center of the Stage to form a horizontal S shape, as shown in Figure 9.

9. Click the **Selection tool** ▶ on the Tools panel, then click a blank area of the Stage.

10. Play the movie.

11. Test the movie, then close the Flash Player window.

12. Save the movie.

You edited a motion path by using the Selection tool to drag the path and by using the Subselection tool to display and reposition Bezier handles.

Change the Ease value of an animation

1. Play the movie and notice that the car moves at a constant speed.

2. Click **frame 1** on the red car layer, then display the Properties panel.

3. Point to the **Ease value**, then when the pointer changes to a hand with a double arrow ⇄, drag the ⇄ **pointer** to the right to set the value at **100**, as shown in Figure 10.

4. Play the movie.

   The car starts out moving fast and slows down near the end of the animation. Notice the word "out" is displayed next to the ease value on the Properties panel indicating that the object will ease out, that is slow down, at the end of the animation.

5. Click **frame 1** on the red car layer.

6. Point to the Ease value on the Properties panel, then drag the ⇄ **pointer** to the left to set the value to **−100**.

7. Play the movie.

   The car starts out moving slowly and speeds up near the end of the animation. Notice the word "in" is displayed next to the ease value on the Properties panel. Also, notice the dots are grouped closer together at the beginning of the motion path indicating that the object does not move very far in that section of the path.

8. Click **frame 1** on the red car layer, then set the Ease value to **0**.

9. Save your work.

You changed the ease out and ease in values of the animation.

Figure 10 *Changing the ease value*

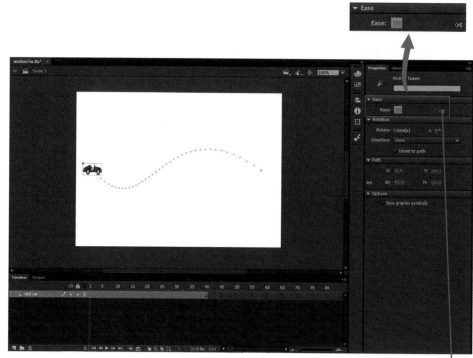

Image courtesy Jim Shuman.

Drag the pointer to the right

Figure 11 *Changing the width of the object*

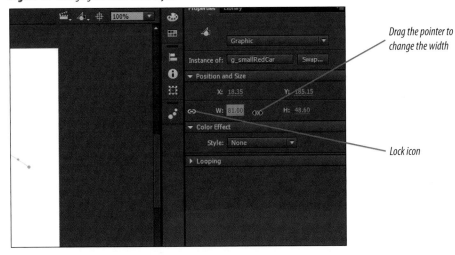

Drag the pointer to change the width

Lock icon

Figure 12 *Using the Free Transform tool to skew the object*

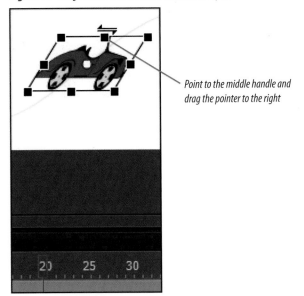

Point to the middle handle and drag the pointer to the right

Image courtesy Jim Shuman.

Resize and reshape an object

1. Verify frame 1 is selected, click the **Selection tool** , then click the **car**.
2. Display the Properties panel, verify the lock icon is not broken, point to the **W: value**, then, when the pointer changes to a hand with a double arrow , drag the **pointer** to the right to set the value to **81**, as shown in Figure 11.

   The car in frame 1 is now wider and taller.
3. Play the movie.
4. Click **frame 40** on the red car layer, then click the **car**.
5. Point to the **W: value** on the Properties panel, then drag the **pointer** to the left to set the value to **30**.

   The car in frame 40 is now less wide and tall.
6. Play the movie.

   The car starts out large and ends up small.
7. Click **frame 20** on the red car layer.
8. Click the **Free Transform tool** on the Tools panel, then click the **Rotate and Skew option** if it is not active.
9. Point to the **top middle handle**, then, when the pointer changes to a double line , drag the **pointer** to the right to skew the object, as shown in Figure 12.

   A keyframe indicating a change in the property (skew) of the object appears in frame 20.
10. Play the movie, use the Undo command on the Edit menu to undo the skew, then save the movie.

    Note: You may have to click the Undo command more than one time to undo the skew.

    The skew keyframe is removed from frame 20.

You resized and skewed a motion tween object.

Orient an object to a path

1. Play the movie.

   Notice the car follows the path but it is not oriented to the path.

2. Click **frame 1** on the red car layer.

3. Click the **Orient to path check box** in the Rotation area of the Properties panel.

4. Click the **Free Transform tool** on the Tools panel, then click the **Rotate and Skew option** in the Options area of the Tools panel if it is not active.

5. Point to the upper-right corner of the car, then, when the pointer changes into a circular arrow, rotate the front of the car so that it aligns with the path, as shown in Figure 13.

6. Click **frame 40** on the red car layer, then rotate the back end of the car so that its back end aligns with the path, as shown in Figure 14.

7. Play the movie.

   The car is oriented to the path.

   Notice the diamond symbols in the frames on the red car layer. These are rotation keyframes that indicate the object will change in each frame as it rotates to stay oriented to the path.

8. Test the movie, then close the Flash Player window.

9. Save your work, then close the document.

You oriented an object to a motion path and aligned the object with the path in the first and last frames of the motion tween.

Figure 13 *Aligning the car to the path*

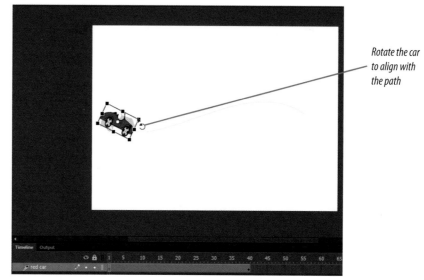

Rotate the car to align with the path

Image courtesy Jim Shuman.

Figure 14 *Aligning the car to the end of the motion path*

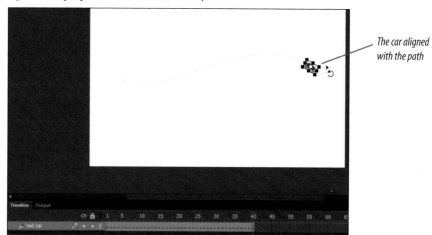

The car aligned with the path

Image courtesy Jim Shuman.

Figure 15 *Dragging the biker symbol to the Stage*

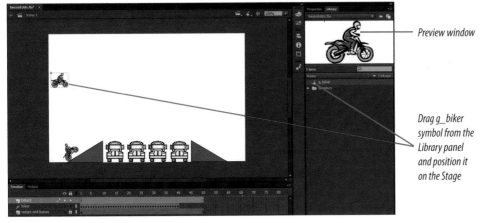

Preview window

Drag g_biker
symbol from the
Library panel
and position it
on the Stage

Image courtesy Jim Shuman.

Figure 16 *Selecting the path with the Free Transform tool*

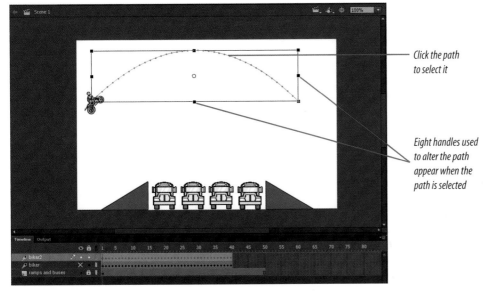

Click the path
to select it

Eight handles used
to alter the path
appear when the
path is selected

Image courtesy Jim Shuman.

Lesson 1   Create Motion Tween Animations

Copy a motion path

1. Open fl3_2.fla, save it as **tweenEdits.fla**, then play the movie.

   This movie has a motion tween that animates from frame 1 to frame 40. Notice the rotation keyframes on the biker layer.

2. Insert a **new layer** at the top of the Timeline, then name it **biker2**.

   Notice the last frame of the new layer is the same (50) as the last frame of the movie.

3. Click **frame 1** on the biker2 layer.

4. Click the **Selection tool** on the Tools panel, then display the Library panel.

5. Click the **g_biker symbol** on the Library panel to display the image in the Preview window.

6. Drag the **g_biker symbol** from the Library panel to the Stage, as shown in Figure 15.

   This creates a new instance of the g_biker symbol.

7. Click any frame on the tween span on the biker layer, then click the **original biker** on the Stage.

   The motion tween is selected as indicated by the yellow highlight on the biker layer.

8. Click **Edit** on the menu bar, point to **Timeline**, then click **Copy Motion**.

9. Click the **new instance** of the biker, click **Edit** on the menu bar, point to **Timeline**, then click **Paste Motion**.

10. Play the movie, then hide the biker layer.

11. Click **frame 1** on the biker2 layer, click the **Free Transform tool** on the Tools panel, then click the path to select it, as shown in Figure 16.

(continued)

12. Click **Modify** on the menu bar, point to **Transform**, then click **Flip Horizontal**.

13. Click a blank area of the Stage, then click the bike object.

14. Click **Modify** on the menu bar, point to **Transform**, then click **Flip Horizontal**.

15. Click **frame 1** on the biker2 layer, then click the **path** to select it.

16. Use the arrow keys on the keyboard to position the path, as shown on Figure 17.

17. Click a blank area of the Stage to deselect the path, click the biker with the Free Transform tool , then rotate the biker to align it with the path.

18. Use the arrow keys to align the biker, as shown in Figure 18.

19. Unhide the biker layer, then play the movie.

You copied a motion path to another object, adjusted the position of the path and oriented the object to the path.

Remove a motion tween

1. Click any frame on the biker2 layer to select the tween span on the Timeline.

2. Click **Insert** on the menu bar, then click **Remove Tween**.

3. Click **biker2** on the Timeline to select the layer.

4. Click the **Delete icon** 🗑 on the Timeline status bar to delete the biker2 layer. Your screen should resemble Figure 19.

5. Test the movie, then close the Flash Player window.

6. Save your work.

You removed an object's motion tween, then deleted a layer containing a motion tween.

Creating Animations

Figure 17 *Positioning the path*

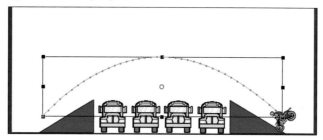

Image courtesy Jim Shuman.

Figure 18 *Aligning the biker to the path*

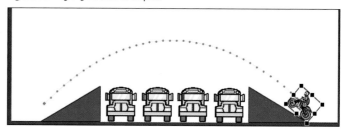

Image courtesy Jim Shuman.

Figure 19 *Timeline showing the motion tween removed*

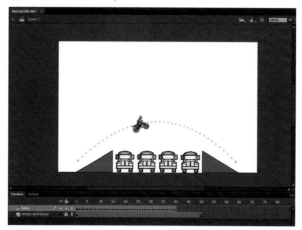

Image courtesy Jim Shuman.

Figure 20 *Changing the rotate value*

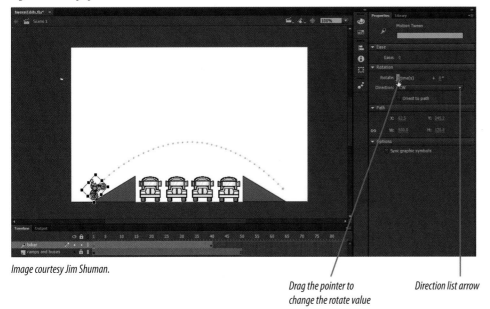

Image courtesy Jim Shuman.

Drag the pointer to
change the rotate value

Direction list arrow

Figure 21 *The Properties panel showing that the rotate value is set to 0 times*

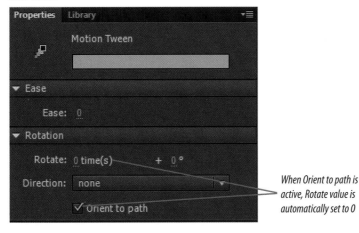

When Orient to path is
active, Rotate value is
automatically set to 0

Rotate an object

1. Click **frame 1** on the biker layer, then display the Properties panel.

2. Point to the **Rotate times value** in the Rotation area of the Properties panel, then, when the pointer changes to a hand with a double arrow, drag the **pointer** to the right to set the count to **1**, as shown in Figure 20.

3. Click the **Direction list arrow**, click **CW** (Clockwise) if necessary, click **frame 1** on the biker layer, then play the movie.

   The biker object rotates one time in a clockwise direction. Look at the Timeline. Notice the rotation keyframes have been removed from the motion tween span. This is because, as the biker rotates, he is no longer oriented to the path. Motion tweens do not allow an object to be rotated and oriented to a path simultaneously because orienting an object to a path rotates the object in each frame along the path. You can use a classic tween to rotate and orient an object to a path at the same time. The remaining keyframes at the beginning and ending of the tween span are used to align the biker to the ramp.

4. Click **frame 1** on the biker layer, set the rotation count to **2**, set the Direction to **CCW** (Counter Clockwise), then play the movie.

5. Click **Orient to path** to select it.

   The rotate value is automatically set to no times (indicated by a 0), as shown in Figure 21.

6. Play the movie, then save your work.

You caused an object to rotate by setting the rotate value and specifying a rotation direction.

Work with multiple motion tweens

1. Click frame **40** on the biker layer, then click the **biker** on the Stage.

2. Lock the **biker layer**, then insert a **new layer** above the biker layer and name it **bikeOffStage**.

3. Click frame **40** on the bikeOffStage layer.

4. Click **Insert** on the menu bar, point to **Timeline**, then click **Keyframe**.

5. Display the Library panel.

6. Drag an instance of the **g_biker symbol** from the Library panel so it is on top of the biker on the Stage, as shown in Figure 22.

7. Verify the Free Transform tool ▦ is selected, then click the **Rotate and Skew option** ⬜ in the Options area of the Tools panel.

8. Rotate the object to orient it to the other biker, then use the arrow keys on the keyboard to align the two biker objects.

9. Click frame **41** on the **bikeOffStage** layer, then insert a **keyframe**.

10. Use the **arrow keys** on the keyboard and the **Free Transform tool** ▦ to align the biker with the bottom of the ramp, as shown in Figure 23.

(continued)

Figure 22 *Placing an instance of the g_biker symbol on top of the object on the Stage*

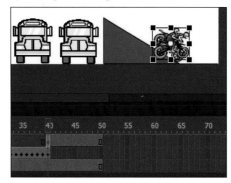

Image courtesy Jim Shuman.

Figure 23 *Aligning the biker with the ramp*

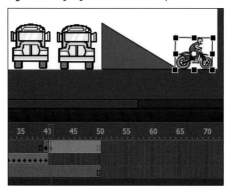

Image courtesy Jim Shuman.

Creating Animations

Figure 24 *Dragging the biker object off the Stage*

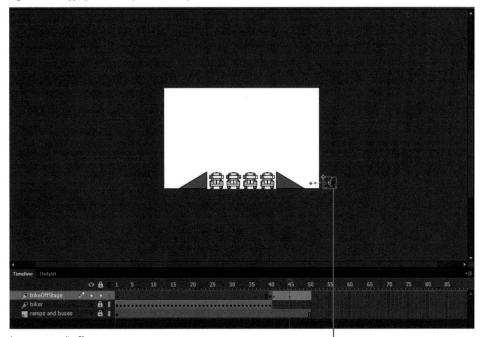

Image courtesy Jim Shuman.

Drag the object off the Stage

11. Click the **Selection tool** , then click the **biker**.

12. Use the Magnification options on the View menu to display the entire Stage and part of the Pasteboard.

13. Click **Insert** on the menu bar, then click **Motion Tween**.

14. Click **frame 45** on the bikeOffStage layer, then drag the **biker** off the Stage, as shown in Figure 24.

15. Use the Magnification options to change the view to Fit in Window.

16. Test the movie, then close the Flash Player window.

17. Save your work, then close the document.

You created a second motion tween for the movie.

Create Classic Tween
ANIMATIONS

What You'll Do

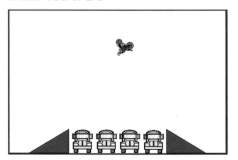

Image courtesy Jim Shuman.

 In this lesson, you will create a motion guide and attach an animation to it.

Understanding Classic Tweens

Classic tweens are similar to motion tweens in that you can create animations that change the properties of an object over time. Motion tweens are easier to use and allow the greatest degree of control over tweened animations. Classic tweens are a bit more complex to create, however, they provide certain capabilities that some developers desire. For example, with a motion tween (which consists of one object over the tween span), you can alter the Ease value so that an object starts out fast and ends slow. But, with a classic tween, you can alter the Ease value so that an object starts out fast, slows down, and then speeds up again. The process for creating a classic tween animation that moves an object is to select the starting frame and, if necessary, insert a keyframe. Next, insert a keyframe at the ending frame. The two keyframes and all the frames between them will be used for the animation. Next, click any frame on the layer between the keyframes. Then select Classic Tween from the Insert menu, select the ending frame, and move the object to the position you want it to be in the ending frame.

Understanding Motion Guides

When you use motion tweening to generate an animation that moves an object, a motion path that shows the movement is automatically created on the Stage. When you use classic tweening, the object moves in a straight line from the beginning location to the ending location on the Stage. There is no path displayed. You can draw a path, called a **motion guide**, that can be used to alter the path of a classic tween animation, as shown in Figure 25. A motion guide is drawn on the motion guide layer with the classic tween animation placed on its own layer beneath a motion guide layer, as shown in Figure 26. The process for creating a motion guide and attaching a classic tween animation to it is:

- Create a classic tween animation.
- Insert a new layer above the classic tween animation layer and change the layer properties to a Guide layer. Drag the classic tween animation layer to the guide layer so that it indents, as shown in Figure 26. This indicates that the classic tween animation layer is associated with the motion guide layer.

- Click the Guide layer and draw a path using the Pen, Pencil, Line, Circle, Rectangle, or Brush tools.
- Attach the object to the path by clicking the first keyframe of the layer that contains the animation, and then dragging the object by its transformation point to the beginning of the path. Click the end keyframe and then repeat the steps to attach the object to the end of the path.

Depending on the type of object you are animating and the path, you may need to orient the object to the path.

The advantages of using a motion guide are that you can have an object move along any path, including a path that intersects itself, and you can easily change the shape of the path, allowing you to experiment with different motions. A consideration when using a motion guide is that, in some instances, orienting the object along the path may result in an unnatural-looking animation. You can fix this by stepping through the animation one frame at a time until you reach the frame where the object is positioned poorly. You can then insert a keyframe and adjust the object as desired.

Transformation Point and Registration Point

Each symbol has a transformation point in the form of a circle (O) that is used to orient the object when it is being animated. For example, when you rotate a symbol, the transformation point is the pivot point around which the object rotates. The transformation point is also the point that snaps to a motion guide, as shown in Figure 25. When attaching an object to a path, you can drag the transformation point to the path. The default position for a transformation point is the center of the object. You can reposition the transformation point while in the symbol edit mode by dragging the transformation point to a different location on the object. Objects also have a registration point (+) that determines the X and Y coordinates of an object on the Stage. The transformation and registration points can overlap—this is displayed as a plus sign within a circle ⊕.

Figure 25 *A motion guide with an object (biker) attached*

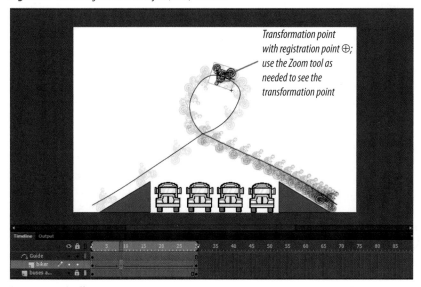

Transformation point with registration point ⊕; use the Zoom tool as needed to see the transformation point

Image courtesy Jim Shuman.

Figure 26 *A motion guide layer with a classic tween on the layer beneath it*

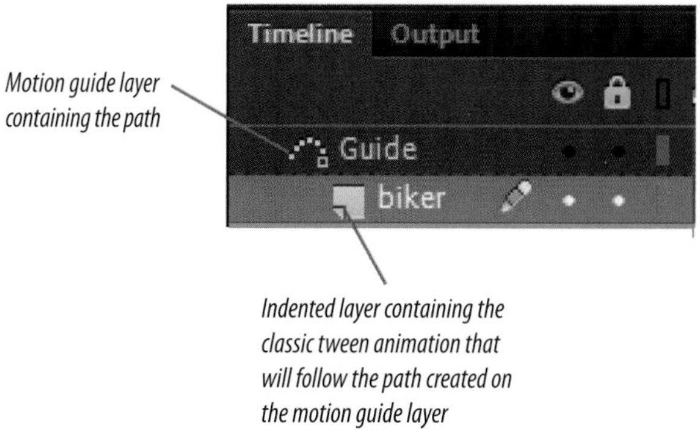

Motion guide layer containing the path

Indented layer containing the classic tween animation that will follow the path created on the motion guide layer

Create a classic tween animation

1. Open fl3_3.fla, then save it as **cTween.fla**.
2. Insert a **new layer**, then name it **biker**.
3. Click **frame 1** on the biker layer, then drag the **g_biker symbol** from the Library panel to the Stage, as shown in Figure 27.
4. Click a blank area of the Stage, click **frame 30** on the biker layer, then Insert a **Keyframe**.
5. Drag the **biker** to the position shown in Figure 28.
6. Click **frame 2** on the biker layer, click **Insert** on the menu bar, then click **Classic Tween**.

   An arrow appears on the Timeline indicating that this is a classic tween.
7. Play the movie.

You created an animation using a classic tween.

Add a motion guide and orient the object to the guide

1. Insert a **new layer**, then name it **Guide**.
2. Click **Modify** on the menu bar, point to **Timeline**, then click **Layer Properties**.
3. Click the **Guide option button**, click **OK**, then drag the **biker layer** up to the Guide layer, as shown in Figure 29.

   The biker layer indents below the Guide layer.
4. Click **frame 1** on the Guide layer, click the **Pencil tool** 🖉 on the Tools panel, click the **Pencil Mode tool** ⑤ in the Options area at the bottom of the Tools panel, click **Smooth**, then set the Stroke Color to **black**.
5. Point to the middle of the biker, then draw a **line** with a loop similar to the one shown in Figure 30.

(continued)

Figure 27 *Positioning the biker symbol on the Stage*

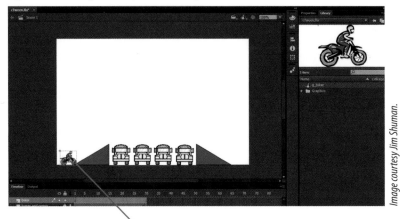

Image courtesy Jim Shuman.

Drag g_biker symbol from the Library panel and position it on the Stage

Figure 28 *Repositioning the biker*

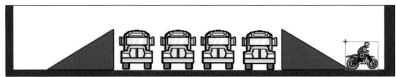

Image courtesy Jim Shuman.

Figure 29 *Dragging the biker layer up to the Guide layer*

Drag biker layer up to but not above the Guide layer

Figure 30 *Drawing a guide path on a Guide layer*

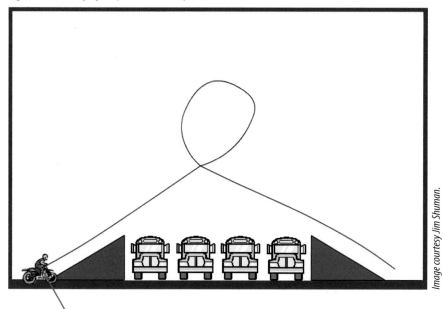

Image courtesy Jim Shuman.

Point to the middle of the biker object

Figure 31 *Aligning the object with the guide path*

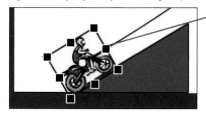

Align this handle to the path

Image courtesy Jim Shuman.

Figure 32 *Aligning the object with the end of the guide path*

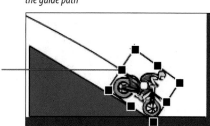

Align this handle to the path

Image courtesy Jim Shuman.

6. Click **frame 30** on the biker layer, click the **Selection tool** , then drag the **biker** so that the **transformation point** touches the end of the path.

   Hint: Use the Zoom tool to zoom in on the biker to make it easier to see you have placed the transformation point on the path.

7. Play the movie.

   The biker should follow the path. If not, make sure the biker is attached to the beginning and end of the path.

8. Click **frame 1** on the biker layer, then click the **biker** to select the object.

9. Click the **Free Transform tool** on the Tools panel, then rotate the **biker,** as shown in Figure 31.

10. Click **frame 30** on the biker layer, then rotate the **biker**, as shown in Figure 32.

11. Click the **Selection tool** , then click **frame 1** on the biker layer.

12. Display the Properties panel, then click the **Orient to path check box**.

13. Play the movie.

14. Click **frame 1** on the biker layer, set the Ease value on the Properties panel to **100**, then click **frame 1** on the biker layer to accept the value.

15. Click each frame on the **biker layer** until you locate the highest point on the motion path, insert a **keyframe** on that frame, set the Ease value to **100**, then click **frame 1** on the biker layer to accept the value. Setting the Ease values in steps 14 and 15 will cause the biker to start out fast, slow down at the top of the loop and speed up again.

16. Test the movie, save your work, then close the document.

You added a motion guide, oriented the animated object to the guide, and set Ease values.

Create Frame-by-Frame
ANIMATIONS

What You'll Do

© Cengage Learning®.

 In this lesson, you will create frame-by-frame animations.

Understanding Frame-by-Frame Animations

A frame-by-frame animation (also called a frame animation) is created by specifying the object that is to appear in each frame of a sequence of frames. Figure 33 shows three images that are variations of a cartoon character. In this example, the head and body remain the same, but the arms and legs change to represent a walking motion. If these individual images are placed into succeeding frames (with keyframes), an animation is created.

Frame-by-frame animations are useful when you want to change individual parts of an image. The images in Figure 33 are simple—only three images are needed for the animation. However, depending on the complexity of the image and the desired movements, the time needed to display each change can be substantial. When creating a frame-by-frame animation, you need to consider the following points:

■ *The number of different images.* The more images there are, the more effort is needed to create them. However, the greater the number of images, the less change you need to make in each image and the more

realistic the movement in the animation may seem.

■ *The number of frames in which each image will appear.* Changing the number of frames in which the object appears may change the effect of the animation. If each image appears in only one frame, the animation may appear rather jerky, since the frames change very rapidly. However, in some cases, you may want to give the impression of a rapid change in an object, such as rapidly blinking colors. If so, you could make changes in the color of an object from one frame to another.

■ *The movie frame rate.* Frame rates below 10 may appear jerky, while those above 30 may appear blurred. The frame rate is easy to change, and you should experiment with different rates until you get the desired effect.

Keyframes are critical to the development of frame animations because they signify a change in the object. Because frame animations are created by changing the object, each frame in a frame animation may need to be a keyframe. The exception is when you want an object displayed in several frames before it changes.

Creating a Frame-by-Frame Animation

To create a frame animation, select the frame on the layer where you want the animation to begin, insert a keyframe, and then place the object on the Stage. Next, select the frame where you want the change to occur, insert a keyframe, and then change the object. You can also add a new object in place of the original one. Figure 34 shows the first three frames of an animation in which three different objects are placed one on top of the other in succeeding frames. In the figure, the movement is shown as shadows. These shadows are visible because the Onion Skin feature is turned on. In this movie, the objects stay in place during the animation. However, a frame animation can also involve movement of the object around the Stage.

Using the Onion Skin Feature

Normally, Flash displays one frame of an animation sequence at a time on the Stage. Turning on the Onion Skin feature allows you to view an outline of the object(s) in any number of frames. This can help in positioning animated objects on the Stage.

Figure 33 *Three images used in an animation*

Image courtesy Jim Shuman.

Figure 34 *A frame-by-frame animation of 3 figures appearing to walk in place*

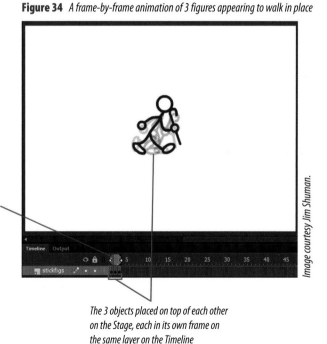

Onion Skin feature is turned on so that all of the objects in frames 1-3 are viewable even though the playhead is on frame 1

The 3 objects placed on top of each other on the Stage, each in its own frame on the same layer on the Timeline

Image courtesy Jim Shuman.

Create an in-place frame-by-frame animation

1. Open fl3_4.fla, then save it as **frameAn.fla**.

2. Set the view to **Fit in Window**.

3. Insert a **new layer**, name it **stickfigs**, click **frame 1** of the stickfigs layer, then drag **stickfig1** from the Library panel to the center of the Stage so it touches the white walkway.

   Note: You can use the Align panel to center the object horizontally across the Stage.

4. Click a blank area of the Stage, click **frame 2** of the stickfigs layer to select it, then insert a **Keyframe**.

5. Drag **stickfig2** so it is on top of stickfig1, as shown in Figure 35, use the arrow keys on the keyboard to align the heads, then click a blank area of the Stage to deselect stickfig2.

6. Select **stickfig1** by clicking the foot that points up as shown in Figure 36, then press **[Delete]**.

7. Click **frame 3** on the stickfigs layer to select it, insert a **keyframe,** drag **stickfig3** so it is on top of stickfig2, then use the **arrow keys** on the keyboard to align the heads.

8. Click a blank area of the Stage to deselect stickfig3.

9. Select stickfig2 by clicking the foot that points down as shown in Figure 37, then press **[Delete]**.

10. Change the frame rate to **6**.

11. Play the movie.

You created a frame-by-frame animation.

Figure 35 *Dragging stickfig2 on top of stickfig1*

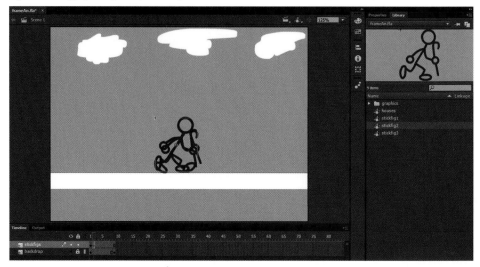

Image courtesy Jim Shuman.

Figure 36 *Selecting stickfig1*

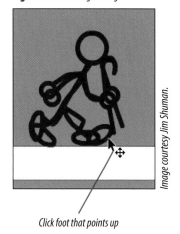

Click foot that points up

Image courtesy Jim Shuman.

Figure 37 *Selecting stickfig2*

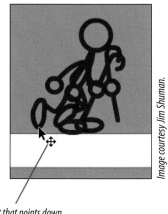

Click foot that points down

Image courtesy Jim Shuman.

Figure 38 *Moving the houses layer to below the stickfigs layer*

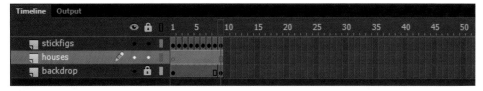

Figure 39 *Positioning the houses symbol on the Stage*

© 2015 Cengage Learning®.

Figure 40 *Repositioning the houses object*

© 2015 Cengage Learning®.

Copy frames and add a moving background

1. Click **frame 1** of the stickfigs layer, press and hold **[Shift]**, then click **frame 3**.

2. Click **Edit** on the menu bar, point to **Timeline**, click **Copy Frames**, then click **frame 4** of the stickfigs layer.

3. Click **Edit** on the menu bar, point to **Timeline**, then click **Paste Frames**.

4. Click **frame 7**, then repeat step 3.

5. Click **frame 10** of the stickfigs layer, press and hold **[Shift]**, then click **frame 13**.

6. Click **Edit** on the menu bar, point to **Timeline**, then click **Remove Frames**.

7. Play the movie.

8. Insert a **new layer**, name the layer **houses**, then drag the **houses layer** below the stickfigs layer, as shown in Figure 38.

9. Click a blank area of the Stage, click **frame 1** of the houses layer, drag the **houses symbol** from the Library panel to the Stage, position the houses as shown in Figure 39, then play the movie.

10. Click **frame 1** of the houses layer, click **Insert** on the menu bar, then click **Motion Tween**.

11. Click **frame 9** on the houses layer, then drag the **houses object** to the left, as shown in Figure 40.

12. Test the movie, close the Flash Player window.

13. Save your work, then close the document.

You copied frames and added a motion tween to a movie with an in-place frame-by-frame animation.

Create a frame-by-frame animation of a moving object

1. Open fl3_5.fla, then save it as **frameM.fla**.

   This document has a backdrop layer that contains a row of houses and clouds.

2. Insert a **new layer**, then name it **stickFigs**.

3. Use the Magnification options on the View menu to display the entire Stage and part of the Pasteboard.

4. Click **frame 5** on the stickFigs layer, then insert a **keyframe**.

5. Drag **stickfig1** from the Library panel to the left edge of the Stage, as shown in Figure 41.

6. Click **frame 6** on the stickFigs layer, click **Insert** on the menu bar, point to **Timeline**, then click **Blank Keyframe**.

   A blank keyframe keeps the object in the previous frame from appearing in the current frame.

7. Click the **Edit Multiple Frames button** on the Timeline status bar to turn it on.

   This allows you to view the contents of more than one frame at a time.

8. Drag **stickfig2** from the Library panel to the right of stickfig1, as shown in Figure 42.

9. Click **frame 7** on the stickFigs layer, then insert a **Blank Keyframe**.

10. Drag **stickfig3** to the right of stickfig2, as shown in Figure 43.

   (continued)

Figure 41 *Positioning stickfig1 on the Stage*

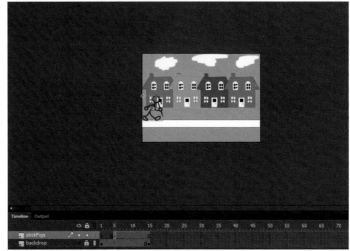

© 2015 Cengage Learning®.

Figure 42 *Positioning stickfig2 on the Stage*

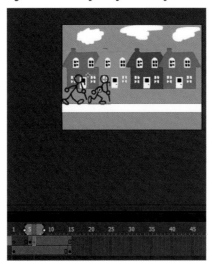

© 2015 Cengage Learning®.

Figure 43 *Positioning stickfig3 on the Stage*

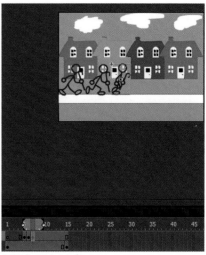

© 2015 Cengage Learning®.

Figure 44 *Adding stickfig1 as the final object*

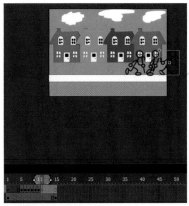

Working with Frames

Selecting frames
To select one frame: click the frame.
To select a range of contiguous frames: Shift-click additional frames.
To select non-contiguous frames: Control-click (Win) or ⌘-click (Mac).
To select all frames on the Timeline: click Edit on the menu bar, point to Timeline, then click Select All Frames.

Removing frames
Select the frame(s), click Edit on the menu bar, point to Timeline, then click Remove Frames.
This removes frames from the timeline and moves the contents of succeeding frames left based on the number of frames removed.

Copy and paste
Select the frame(s), click Edit on the menu bar, point to Timeline, click Copy Frames, select the frame to copy to, click Edit on the menu bar, point to Timeline, then click Paste Frames.

Clear contents
Select the frame(s), click Edit on the menu bar, point to Timeline, then click Clear Frames.
This leaves the frame(s) on the Timeline but the content is cleared and not available for pasting. (*Note*: If you select a frame within a motion tween and choose the Clear Frames option, all of the frames of the motion tween will cleared.)

---

11. Click **frame 8** on the stickFigs layer, insert a **Blank Keyframe**, then drag **stickfig1** from the Library panel to the right of stickfig3.

    Note: In this frame-by-frame animation each object must be placed individually rather than using a copy and paste process.

12. Click **frame 9** on the stickFigs layer, insert a **Blank Keyframe**, then drag **stickfig2** to the right of stickfig1.

13. Click **frame 10** on the stickFigs layer, insert a **Blank Keyframe**, then drag **stickfig3** to the right of stickfig2.

14. Click **frame 11** on the stickFigs layer, insert a **Blank Keyframe**, then drag **stickfig1** to the right of stickfig2 and partially off the Stage.

    Your screen should resemble Figure 44.

15. Test the movie.

    Notice how the figure seems to hesitate at the end of the movie before looping to the start of the movie. This is because there are still frames in the movie that have no content.

16. Close the Flash Player window, click **frame 12** on the stickFigs layer, then insert a **Blank Keyframe**.

17. Click the **Edit Multiple Frames button** 🔲 on the Timeline status bar to turn it off.

18. Test the movie, then close the Flash Player window.

19. Change the frame rate to **6 fps**.

20. Test the movie, then close the Flash Player window.

21. Save the movie, then close the document.

You created a frame-by-frame animation that causes objects to appear to move across the screen.

Create Shape Tween
ANIMATIONS

What You'll Do

Image courtesy Jim Shuman.

In this lesson, you will create a shape tween animation and specify shape hints.

Understanding Shape Tweening

In previous lessons, you learned that you can use motion tweening to change the shape of an object. You accomplish this by selecting the Free Transform tool and then dragging the handles to resize and skew the object. While this is easy and allows you to include motion along with the change in shape, there are two drawbacks. First, you are limited in the type of changes (resizing and skewing) that can be made to the shape of an object. Second, you must work with the same object throughout the animation. When you use **shape tweening**, however, you can have an animation change the shape of an object to any form you desire, and you can include two objects in the animation with two different shapes. As with motion tweening, you can use shape tweening to change other properties of an object, such as its color, location, and size.

Using Shape Tweening to Create a Morphing Effect

Morphing involves changing one object into another, sometimes unrelated, object. For example, you could turn a robot into a

human, or turn a football into a basketball. The viewer sees the transformation as a series of incremental changes. In Flash, the first object appears on the Stage and changes into the second object as the movie plays. The number of frames included from the beginning to the end of this shape tween animation determines how quickly the morphing effect takes place. The first frame in the animation displays the first object and the last frame displays the second object. The in-between frames display the different shapes that are created as the first object changes into the second object.

When working with shape tweening, you need to keep the following points in mind:

- Shape tweening can be applied only to editable graphics. To apply shape tweening to instances, groups, symbols, text blocks, or bitmaps, you must break apart the object to make it editable. To do this, you use the Break Apart command on the Modify menu. When you break apart an instance of a symbol, it is no longer linked to the original symbol.

- You can shape tween more than one object at a time as long as all the objects are on the same layer. However, if the shapes are complex and/or if they involve movement in which the objects cross paths, the results may be unpredictable.

- You can use shape tweening to move an object in a straight line, but other options, such as rotating an object, are not available.
- You can use the settings on the Properties panel to set options (such as the Ease value, which causes acceleration or deceleration) for a shape tween.
- Shape hints can be used to control more complex shape changes.

Properties Panel Options

Figure 45 shows the Properties panel options for a shape tween. The options allow you to adjust several aspects of the animation, as described in the following:

- Adjust the rate of change between frames to create a more natural appearance during the transition by setting an Ease value. Setting the value between −1 and −100 will begin the shape tween gradually and accelerate it toward the end of the animation. Setting the value between 1 and 100 will begin the shape tween rapidly and decelerate it toward the end of the animation. By default, the rate of change is set to 0, which causes a constant rate of change between frames.
- Choose a Blend option. The Distributive option creates an animation in which the in-between shapes are smoother and more irregular. The Angular option preserves the corners and straight lines and works only with objects that have these features. If the objects do not have corners, Flash defaults to the Distributive option.

Shape Hints

You can use shape hints to control the shape's transition appearance during animation. Shape hints allow you to specify a location on the beginning object that corresponds to a location on the ending object. Figure 46 shows two shape animations of the same objects, one using shape hints and the other not using shape hints. The figure also shows how the object being reshaped appears in one of the in-between frames. Notice that with the shape hints, the object in the in-between frame is more recognizable.

Figure 45 *The Properties panel options for a shape tween*

Figure 46 *Two shape animations with and without shape hints*

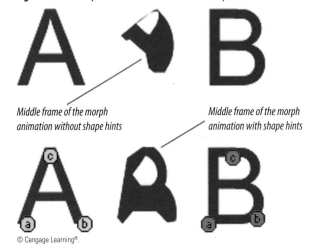

Middle frame of the morph animation without shape hints

Middle frame of the morph animation with shape hints

© Cengage Learning®.

Create a shape tween animation

1. Open fl3_6.fla, then save it as **antiqueCar.fla**.
2. Set the view to **Fit in Window**.
3. Click **frame 30** on the shape layer, then insert a **keyframe**.
4. Click the **Selection tool** ⟍ on the Tools panel. Notice the graphic is editable as indicated by the dot pattern.
5. Click a blank area of the pasteboard to deselect the car.
6. Move the pointer towards the top of the car near the right side until it changes to an arc pointer ⟍⟓, then use the arc pointer ⟍⟓ to drag the **car top** to above the steering wheel, as shown in Figure 47.

    Note: Be sure you are using the arc pointer and not the corner pointer.
7. Click anywhere on the shape layer between frames 1 and 30.
8. Click **Insert** on the menu bar, then click **Shape Tween**.
9. Click **frame 1** on the shape layer, then play the movie.
10. Click **frame 30** on the shape layer.
11. Click the **Selection tool** ⟍ on the Tools panel, then drag a **marquee** around the car to select it if it is not already selected.
12. Drag the **car** to the right side of the Stage, then change the fps to **12**.
13. Test the movie, then close the Flash Player window.
14. Change the fps to **24**, save the movie and close it.

You created a shape tween animation, causing an object to change shape as it moves over several frames.

Figure 47 *Reshaping an object*

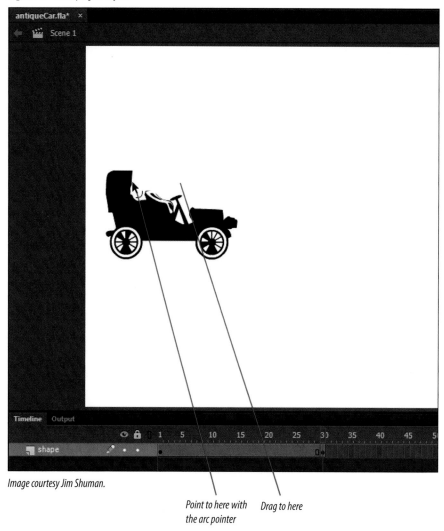

Image courtesy Jim Shuman.

Point to here with the arc pointer

Drag to here

Figure 48 *Editing multiple frames*

Drag to frame 1

Start here

Figure 49 *Positioning the car instance on the Stage*

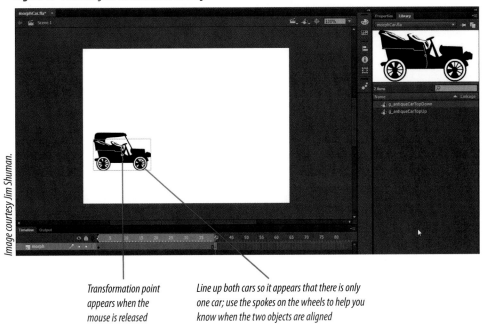

Image courtesy Jim Shuman.

Transformation point appears when the mouse is released

Line up both cars so it appears that there is only one car; use the spokes on the wheels to help you know when the two objects are aligned

Create a morphing effect

1. Open fl3_7.fla, then save it as **morphCar.fla**.

2. Click **frame 40** on the morph layer.

3. Click **Insert** on the menu bar, point to **Timeline**, then click **Blank Keyframe**.

TIP Inserting a blank keyframe prevents the object in the preceding keyframe from automatically being inserted into the frame with the blank keyframe. This is necessary when morphing two objects.

4. Click the **Edit Multiple Frames button** on the Timeline status bar, then drag the left side of the **Multiple Frames highlight** to frame 1 as shown in Figure 48.

   Turning on the Edit Multiple Frames feature allows you to align the two objects to be morphed.

5. Drag the **g_antiqueCarTopDown graphic** symbol from the Library panel directly on top of the car on the Stage, as shown in Figure 49.

TIP Use the arrow keys to move the object as needed.

6. Make sure the g_antiqueCarTopDown object is selected, click **Modify** on the menu bar, then click **Break Apart**.

   This allows the object to be reshaped.

7. Click the **Edit Multiple Frames button** to turn off the feature.

8. Click anywhere between frames 1 and 40 on the morph layer, click **Insert** on the menu bar, then click **Shape Tween**.

9. Click **frame 1** on the Timeline, then play the movie.

   The first car morphs into the second car.

You created a morphing effect, causing one object to change into another.

Adjust the rate of change in a shape tween animation

1. Click **frame 40** on the morph layer.

2. Click the **Selection tool**  on the Tools panel, then drag a **marquee** around the car to select it, if it is not already selected.

3. Drag the **car** to the right side of the Stage.

4. Click **frame 1** on the morph layer.

5. Set the Ease value on the Properties panel to **−100**, as shown in Figure 50.

6. Click the **Stage** to deselect the car.

7. Play the movie.

   The car starts out slow and speeds up as the morphing process is completed.

8. Repeat Steps 4 and 5, but change the Ease value to **100**.

9. Click **frame 1** on the Timeline, then play the movie.

   The car starts out fast and slows down as the morphing process is completed.

10. Test the movie, then close the Flash Player window.

11. Save your work, then close the movie.

You added motion to a shape tween animation and changed the Ease value.

Figure 50 *Setting the ease value of the morph*

Image courtesy Jim Shuman.

Creating Animations

Figure 51 *Positioning a shape hint*

Figure 52 *Adding shape hints*

Figure 53 *Matching shape hints*

Use shape hints

1. Open fl3_8.fla, then save it as **shapeHints.fla**.

2. Play the movie and notice how the L morphs into a Z.

3. Change the view to 200%, then click **frame 15** on the Timeline, the midpoint of the animation.

   Notice the shape is unrecognizable.

4. Click **frame 1** on the hints layer to display the first object.

5. Make sure the object is selected, click **Modify** on the menu bar, point to **Shape**, then click **Add Shape Hint**.

6. Drag the **Shape Hint icon** to the location shown in Figure 51.

7. Repeat Steps 5 and 6 to set a second and third Shape Hint icon, as shown in Figure 52.

   Notice the shape hints are placed at the major points of the image. For more complex objects you can use more shape hints and experiment with their placement.

8. Click **frame 30** on the hints layer.

   The shape hints are stacked on top of each other.

9. Drag the **Shape Hint icons** to match Figure 53.

10. Click **frame 15** on the hints layer, then notice how the object is more recognizable now that the shape hints have been added.

11. Click **frame 1** on the Timeline, then play the movie.

12. Save your work, then close the movie.

You added shape hints to a morph animation.

Create Movie CLIPS

What You'll Do

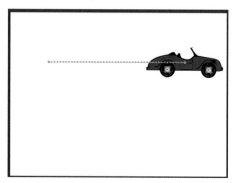

Image courtesy Jim Shuman.

In this lesson, you will create, edit, and animate a movie clip.

Understanding Movie Clip Symbols

Until now you have been working with two kinds of symbols, graphic and button. A third type is a **movie clip symbol**, which provides a way to create more complex types of animations. A movie clip is essentially a movie within a movie. Each movie clip has its own Timeline, which is independent of the main Timeline. This allows you to nest a movie clip that is running one animation within another animation or in a scene on the main Timeline. Because a movie clip retains its own Timeline, when you insert an instance of the movie clip symbol into a Flash document, the movie clip continues in an endless loop even if the main Timeline stops.

The wheels on a car rotating while the car is moving across the screen is an example of a movie (the moving car) with a nested animation (the rotating wheels). The nested animation is a movie clip. To create the animated movie clip, a drawing of a wheel separate from the car is converted into a movie clip symbol. Then the movie clip symbol is opened in the edit window, which includes a Timeline that is unique to the movie clip. In the edit window, an animation is created that causes the wheel to rotate. After exiting the edit window and returning to the main Timeline, an instance of the movie clip symbol is placed on each wheel of the car. Finally, the car, including the wheels, is animated on the main Timeline. As the car is moving across the screen, each wheel is rotating according to the movie clip Timeline. This process is shown in Figure 54.

In addition to allowing you to create more complex animations, movie clips help to organize the different reusable pieces of a movie and provide for smaller movie file sizes. This is because only one movie clip symbol needs to be stored on the Library panel while an unlimited number of instances of the symbol can be used in the Flash document.

An animated movie clip can be viewed in the edit window that is displayed when you double-click the movie clip symbol on the Library panel; and it can be viewed when you test or publish the movie that contains the movie clip. It is important to note that an animated movie clip cannot be viewed simply by playing the movie on the main Timeline.

In this lesson, you will learn how to create a movie clip symbol from a drawn object, edit the movie clip to create an animation, and nest the movie clip in another animation.

Figure 54 *The process of nesting a movie clip within an animation*

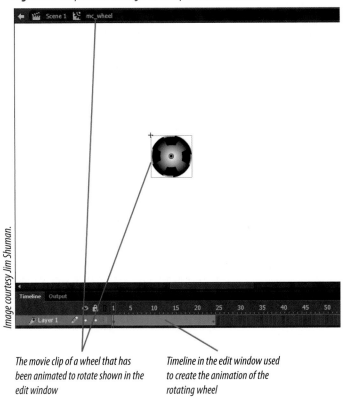

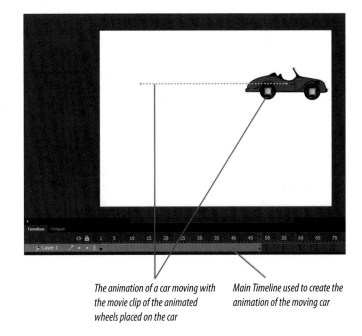

Image courtesy Jim Shuman.

The movie clip of a wheel that has been animated to rotate shown in the edit window

Timeline in the edit window used to create the animation of the rotating wheel

The animation of a car moving with the movie clip of the animated wheels placed on the car

Main Timeline used to create the animation of the moving car

Break apart a graphic symbol and select parts of the object to separate from the graphic

1. Open fl3_9.fla, then save it as **mClip.fla**.

   This document has one graphic symbol—a car that has been placed on the Stage.

2. Click the **Selection tool** on the Tools panel, then click the **car** to select it.

3. Click **Modify** on the menu bar, then click **Break Apart**.

4. Click a blank area of the Stage to deselect the object.

5. Click the **Zoom tool** on the Tools panel, then click the **front wheel** two times to zoom in on the wheel.

6. Click the **Selection tool** on the Tools panel.

7. Click the **gray hubcap**, press and hold **[Shift]**, then click the black and dark gray parts of the wheel, as shown in Figure 55.

   Hint: There are several small parts to the wheel, so click until a dot pattern covers the entire wheel, but do not select the tire. Use the Undo command if you select the tire.

8. Drag the **selected area** down below the car, as shown in Figure 56.

9. Compare your selected wheel to Figure 56, if your wheel does not match the figure, use the Undo command to move the wheel back to its original position, and repeat step 7.

You broke apart a graphic symbol and selected parts of the object to separate from the graphic.

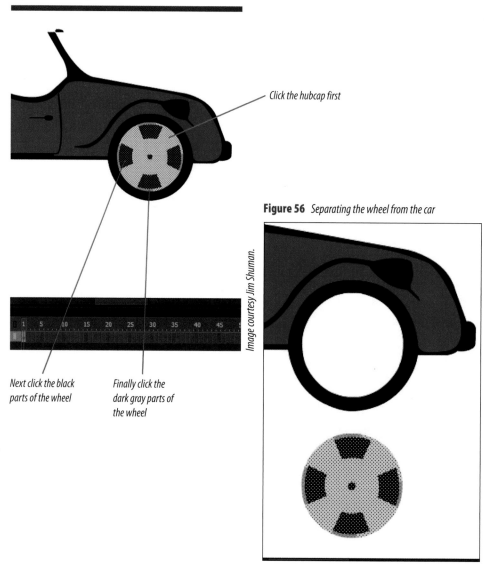

Figure 55 *Selecting the wheel*

Click the hubcap first

Next click the black parts of the wheel

Finally click the dark gray parts of the wheel

Figure 56 *Separating the wheel from the car*

Image courtesy Jim Shuman.

Image courtesy Jim Shuman.

Creating Animations

Figure 57 *Selecting the gray area of the wheel*

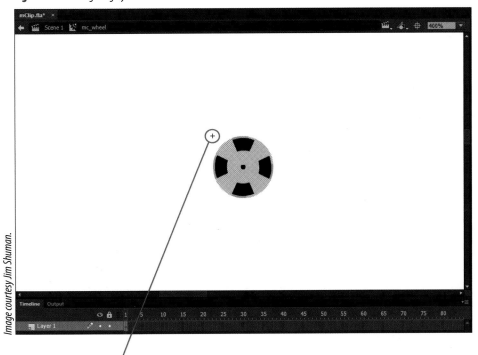

Image courtesy Jim Shuman.

The location of your registration point may differ.

Create and edit a movie clip

1. Verify the wheel is selected, click **Modify** on the menu bar, then click **Convert to Symbol**.

2. Type **mc_wheel** for the Name, select **Movie Clip** for the Type, then click **OK**.

3. Display the Library panel.

   Notice the mc_wheel movie clip and the movie clip icon appear on the Library panel.

4. Double-click the **mc_wheel icon** on the Library panel to display the edit window.

5. Click the **Zoom tool** on the Tools panel, then click the **wheel** twice to zoom in on the wheel.

   The movie clip has been broken apart as indicated by the dot pattern.

6. Click the **Selection tool**, click a blank area of the Stage to deselect the object, then click the **gray area** of the wheel to select it, as shown in Figure 57.

7. Display the Properties panel.

8. Click the **Fill Color swatch**, then click the **gray gradient color swatch** in the bottom row of the palette.

You created a movie clip symbol and edited it to change the color of the object.

Animate a movie clip

1. Click the **Selection tool** 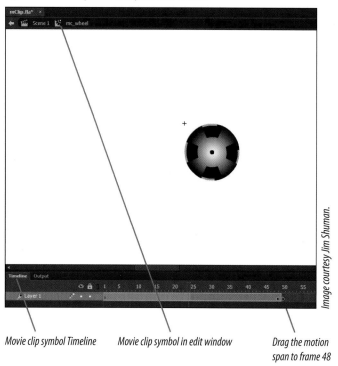, then drag a **marquee** around the entire wheel to select it.

2. Click **Insert** on the menu bar, click **Motion Tween**, then click **OK** for the Convert selection to symbol for tween dialog box.

3. Point to the end of the tween span on Layer 1 of the Timeline, then, when the pointer changes to a double-headed arrow ↔, drag the **span** to frame 48, as shown in Figure 58.

4. Click **frame 1** on Layer 1.

5. Display the Properties panel.

6. Change the Rotate value to **4** times and verify the Direction is CW (Clockwise), as shown in Figure 59.

   Hint: If you don't see the Rotate option, click the Selection tool, then drag a marquee around the object.

7. Set the frame rate on the Timeline status bar to **12**.

8. Press **[Enter]** (Win) or **[return]** (Mac) to play the Timeline for the mc_wheel movie clip symbol.

9. Click **Scene 1** near the top left side of the edit widow to exit the edit window.

10. Drag the **wheel** on the Stage up and position it so it is back inside the front tire of the car.

(continued)

Figure 58 *Increasing the motion span on the Timeline*

Movie clip symbol Timeline   Movie clip symbol in edit window   Drag the motion span to frame 48

Image courtesy Jim Shuman.

Figure 59 *Changing the Rotate value*

Properties   Library

Motion Tween

▼ Ease

Ease: 0

▼ Rotation

Rotate: 4 time(s)   +   0 °

Direction: CW

☐ Orient to path

Creating Animations

Figure 60 *Repositioning the car*

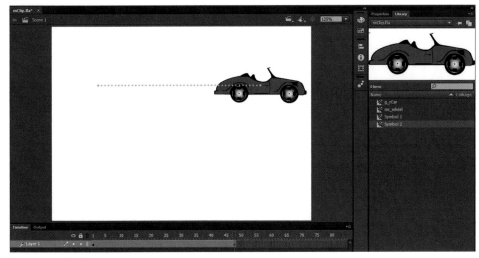

Image courtesy Jim Shuman.

11. Display the Library panel, then drag the **mc_wheel movie clip** from the Library panel and position it using the arrow keys as needed so it is on the back wheel.

12. Click **View** on the menu bar, point to **Magnification**, then click **Fit in Window**.

13. Test the movie and notice how the wheels turn, then close the Flash Player window.

14. Click the **Selection tool** , then drag a **marquee** around the car to select it and the wheels.

15. Click **Insert** on the menu bar, click **Motion Tween**.

16. Click **OK** to convert the selection to a symbol for tweening.

17. Drag the **tween span** on Layer 1 to frame 48.

    This will match the number of frames in the mc_wheel movie clip.

18. Click **frame 48** on Layer 1, then drag the **car** to the right side of the Stage, as shown in Figure 60.

19. Test the movie, then close the Flash Player window.

    Note: You may receive a message alerting you to a missing font, indicating that the file's fonts are not available on your computer. Flash automatically substitutes fonts that will work. If you play the movie by pressing [Enter] (Win) or [return] (Mac), the car will move across the Stage but the wheel animation will not be visible. This is because nested movie clips only appear when the movie is played using the Flash Player.

20. Save your work, then close the document.

You edited a movie clip to create an animation, then nested the movie clip in an animation on the main Timeline.

Animate Text and
ADD A MASK EFFECT

What You'll Do

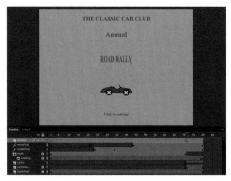

Image courtesy Jim Shuman.

 In this lesson, you will add a mask effect and animate text by rotating, zooming, and resizing it.

Animating Text

You can motion tween text block objects just as you do graphic objects. You can resize, rotate, reposition, and change the colors of text blocks. Figure 61 shows three examples of animated text with the Onion Skin feature turned on. When the movie starts, each of the following occurs one after the other:

- The Classic Car Club text block scrolls in from the left side to the top center of the Stage. This is done by creating the text block, positioning it off the Stage, and creating a motion-tweened animation that moves it to the Stage.
- The Annual text block appears and rotates five times. This occurs after you create the Annual text block, position it in the middle of the Stage under the heading, and use the Properties panel to specify a clockwise rotation that repeats five times.
- The ROAD RALLY text block slowly zooms out and appears in the middle of the Stage. This occurs after you create the text block and use the Free Transform tool handles to resize it to a small block at the beginning of the animation. Then, you resize the text block to a larger size at the end of the animation.

Once you create a motion animation using a text block, the text block becomes a symbol and you are unable to edit individual characters within the text block unless you use the Break Apart command. You can, however, edit the symbol as a whole.

Understanding Mask Layers

A **mask layer** allows you to cover up the objects on one or more layers and, at the same time, create a window through which you can view objects on those layer(s). You can determine the size and shape of the window and specify whether it moves around the Stage. Moving the window around the Stage can create effects such as a spotlight that highlights certain content on the Stage, drawing the viewer's attention to a specific location. Because the window can move around the Stage, you can use a mask layer to reveal only the area of the Stage and the objects you want the viewer to see.

You need at least two layers on the Timeline when you are working with a mask layer. One layer, called the mask layer, contains the window object through which you view the objects, which are on a second layer below the mask layer. The second layer, called the masked layer, contains the object(s) that are viewed through the window. Figure 62 shows how a mask layer works: The top part of the figure shows the mask layer with the window in the shape of a circle. The next part of the figure shows the layer to be masked. The last part of the figure shows the result of applying the mask. Figure 62 illustrates the simplest use of a mask layer. In most cases, you want to have other objects appear on the Stage and have the mask layer affect only a certain portion of the Stage.

The process for using a mask layer follows:

■ Insert a new layer that will become the masked layer—add the objects that you want to display through the mask layer window. Alternately, you can use an

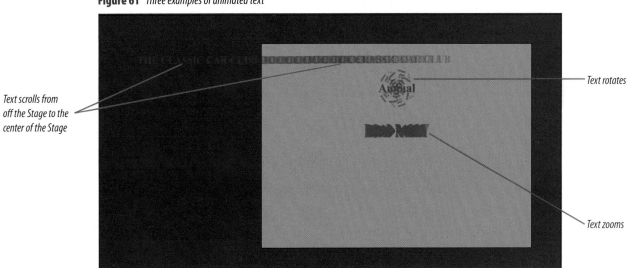

Figure 61 *Three examples of animated text*

Text scrolls from off the Stage to the center of the Stage

Text rotates

Text zooms

existing layer that already contains the objects you want to mask.

- Insert a new layer above the masked layer that will become the mask layer. A mask layer always masks the layer(s) immediately below it.

- Draw a filled shape, such as a circle, or create an instance of a symbol that will become the window on the mask layer. Flash ignores bitmaps, gradients, transparency colors, and line styles on a mask layer. On a mask layer, filled areas become transparent and non-filled areas become opaque when viewed over a masked layer.

- Select the layer you want to be the mask layer and open the Layer Properties dialog box. To open the Layer Properties dialog box, click Modify on the menu bar, point to the Timeline, then click Layer Properties. In the Layer Properties dialog box, select Mask as the layer type. Flash converts the layer to the mask layer.

- Select the layer you want to apply the mask to and open the Layer Properties dialog box, then select Masked as the layer type. Flash converts the layer to the masked layer.

- Lock both the mask and masked layers.

- To mask additional layers: Drag an existing layer beneath the mask layer, or create a new layer beneath the mask layer and use the Layer Properties dialog box to convert it to a masked layer. Adding additional masked layers allows you to reveal more than one object with the same mask layer. For example, you could have a mask layer that reveals constellations on one masked layer and animated shooting stars on another masked layer.

- To unlink a masked layer: Drag it above the mask layer, or select it and select Normal from the Layer Properties dialog box.

Figure 62 *A mask layer with a window*

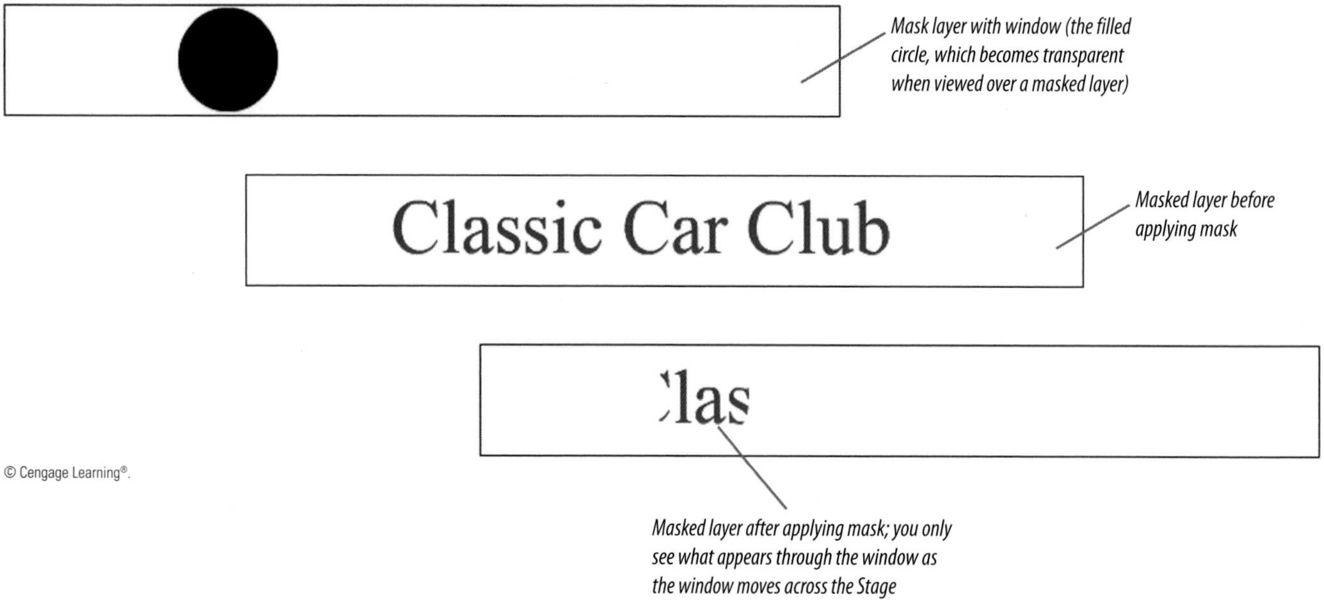

Mask layer with window (the filled circle, which becomes transparent when viewed over a masked layer)

Masked layer before applying mask

Masked layer after applying mask; you only see what appears through the window as the window moves across the Stage

© Cengage Learning®.

Creating Animations

Figure 63 *Rotating the front of the car up*

Image courtesy Jim Shuman.

Figure 64 *Drawing two lines*

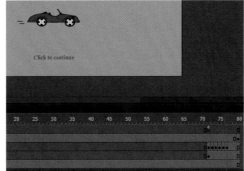

Image courtesy Jim Shuman.

Figure 65 *The car positions frame by frame*

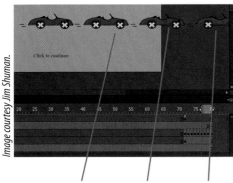

Car in frame 78   Car in frame 79   Car in frame 80

Image courtesy Jim Shuman.

1. Open fl3_10.fla, then save it as **textAn.fla**.
2. Test the movie, click the **continue** button, then close the Flash Player window.

   This document has a heading and a continue button.
3. Click frame 72 of the carGo layer, then insert a **Keyframe**.
4. Drag the **g_car symbol** from the Library to above the continue button, then **center** it across the screen.
5. Click a blank area of the Stage, then insert a **Keyframe** in frame 73 of the carGo layer.
6. Select the **Free Transform tool** from the Tools panel, then click the **car**.
7. Rotate the front of the car **up one position** as shown in Figure 63.
8. Insert a **Keyframe** in frame 74 of the carGo layer, then rotate the front of the car **up one more position**.
9. Insert a **Keyframe** in frame 75 of the carGo layer, then rotate the front of the **car down one position**.
10. Insert a **Keyframe** in frame 76 of the carGo layer, then rotate the front of the **car down to a level position**.
11. Insert a **Keyframe** in frame 77 of the carGo layer, then use the **Pencil tool** to draw the **two lines** shown in Figure 64.
12. Insert a **Keyframes** in frames 78, 79 and 80 of the carGo layer, and **move the car** to the positions shown in Figure 65.
13. Test the movie, close the Flash Player window, then save your work.

You created a frame-by-frame animation.

Create a mask layer

1. Insert a **new layer** above the Actions layer, then click **frame 1** on the new layer.

2. Select the **Oval tool** on the Tools panel, set the Stroke Color to **No Stroke** , then set the Fill Color to **black**.

3. Draw the circle shown in Figure 66, click the **Selection tool** on the Tools panel, then drag a **marquee** around the circle to select it.

4. Click **Insert** on the menu bar, click **Motion Tween**, then click **OK** to convert the drawing into a symbol so that it can be tweened.

   Note: Flash converts the object to a movie symbol as the default symbol type. To convert the object to a different symbol type, you must convert the symbol manually.

5. Click **frame 71** on Layer 1, then drag the **circle** to the position shown in Figure 67.

6. Verify the layer is selected, then click **Modify** on the menu bar, point to **Timeline**, then click **Layer Properties**.

7. Verify that the Show check box is selected in the Name area, change the Name to **mask**, click the **Mask option button** in the Type area, then click **OK**.

   The mask layer has a mask icon next to it on the Timeline.

   Hint: Alternately, you can lock the layer using the Lock This Layer icon on the Timeline.

8. Play the movie from frame 1 and notice how the circle object covers the text on the heading layer as it moves across the Stage.

   Note: The circle object will not become transparent until a masked layer is created beneath it.

(continued)

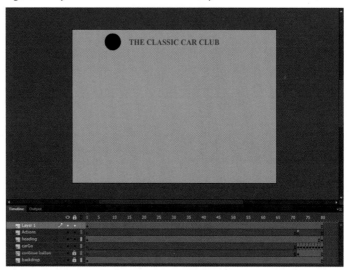

Figure 66 *Object to be used as a window on a mask layer*

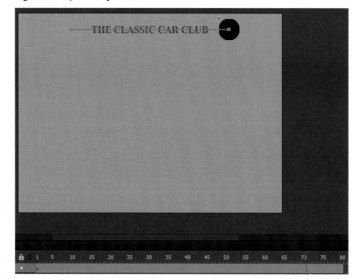

Figure 67 *Repositioning the circle*

Creating Animations

Figure 68 *The completed Layer Properties dialog box*

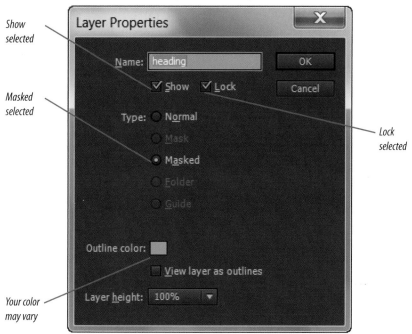

Show selected

Masked selected

Your color may vary

Lock selected

9. **Click and hold** on frame 72 on the mask layer, then drag to frame 80 to select the frames.

10. Click **Edit** on the menu bar, point to **Timeline**, then click **Remove Frames**.

11. Lock the mask layer.

You created a mask layer containing a circle object that moves across the Stage.

Create a masked layer

1. Click **heading** on the Timeline to select the heading layer, click **Modify** on the menu bar, point to **Timeline,** then click **Layer Properties** to open the Layer Properties dialog box.

2. Verify that the Show check box is selected in the Name area, click the **Lock check box** to select it, click the **Masked option button** in the Type area, compare your dialog box to Figure 68, then click **OK**.

   Classic Car Club on the Stage seems to disappear. The heading layer is indented and has a shaded masked icon next to it on the Timeline.

3. Play the movie and notice how the circle object acts as a window to display the text on the heading layer.

4. Click **Control** on the menu bar, point to **Test Movie,** then click **in Flash Professional**.

5. View the movie, then close the Flash Player window.

6. Save your work, then close the movie.

You used the Layer Properties dialog box to create a masked layer.

Create rotating text

1. Insert a **new layer** above the mask layer, then name it **rotateText**.
2. Click a blank area of the Stage, insert a **keyframe** in frame 24 on the layer, then hide the **mask layer**.
3. Click the **Text tool** 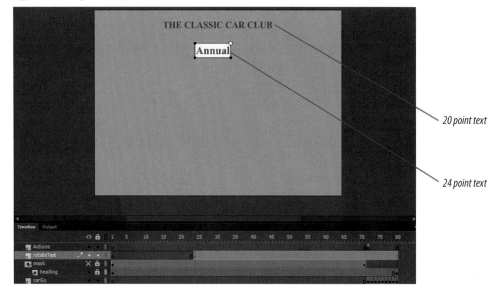 on the Tools panel, then change the Character properties on the Properties panel to **Times New Roman**, size **24**, style **bold** and color **blue** (#0000FF).
4. Position the pointer under the "A" in "CLASSIC," then click.
5. Type **Annual**, then compare your image to Figure 69.
6. Click the **Selection tool** on the Tools panel, then use the Align panel to center the text block horizontally across the Stage.
7. Verify the text box is selected, click **Insert** on the menu bar, then click **Motion Tween**.
8. Click **frame 24** on the rotateText layer, then set the Rotate value on the Properties panel to **2** times with a **CW** (clockwise) direction.
9. Point to the end of the tween span (frame 80), then drag the ⟷ **pointer** to frame 34, as shown in Figure 70.
10. Click **frame 80** on the rotateText layer, then insert a **keyframe**.

    The keyframe is needed to display the word Annual in frames 34 to 80.
11. Unhide the mask layer, click **1** on the Timeline, then play the movie.

    The Annual text rotates clockwise two times.

You created a text block, applied a motion tween, and used the Properties panel to rotate the text block.

Figure 69 *Adding the Annual text block*

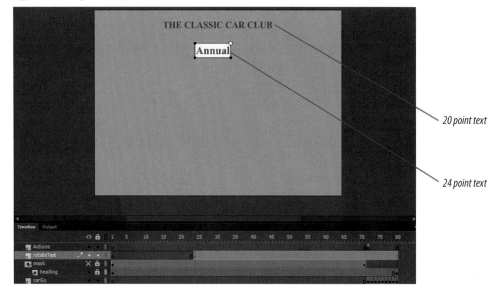

20 point text

24 point text

Figure 70 *Resizing the motion span from frame 80 to frame 34*

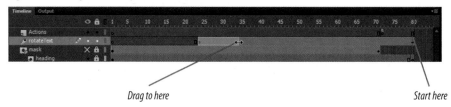

Drag to here

Start here

Figure 71 *Using the Text tool to type ROAD RALLY*

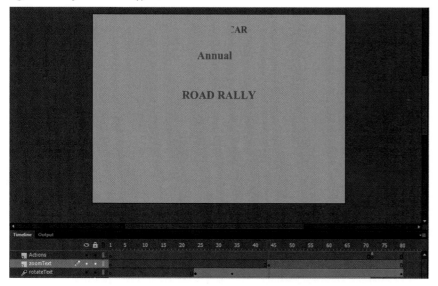

Figure 72 *Resizing the Text block*

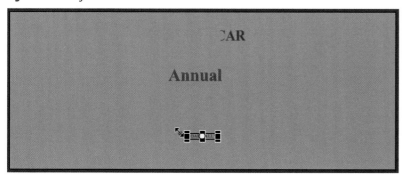

Create an animation that resizes a text box

1. Insert a **new layer**, name it **zoomText**, click a blank area of the Stage, then insert a **keyframe** in frame 44 on the layer.

2. Click the **Text tool** ⊤, position the pointer beneath the Annual text block, then type **ROAD RALLY**, as shown in Figure 71.

3. Click the **Selection tool** ↖, then use the Align panel to center the text block horizontally across the Stage.

4. Click **frame 44** on the zoomText layer, click **Insert** on the menu bar, then click **Motion Tween**.

5. Click **frame 44** on the zoomText layer, click the **Free Transform tool** ⊞, then click the **Scale option** ⊞ in the Options area of the Tools panel.

6. Drag the **upper-left corner handle** inward to resize the text block, as shown in Figure 72.

7. Click **frame 80** on the zoomText layer, verify the Scale option ⊞ in the Options area of the Tools panel is selected, then drag the **upper-left corner handle** outward to resize the text block to approximately its original size.

TIP   If the text appears upside down or backwards, you can use the Undo feature several times to return the text to its original size before you resized the text in step 6. Then repeat step 6, being careful not to resize the text too small.

8. Test the movie, then close the Flash Player window.

You created a motion animation that caused text to zoom in and appear larger.

LESSON 7

Add SOUND

What You'll Do

Image courtesy Jim Shuman.

 In this lesson, you will add sound to an animation and to a button click event.

Incorporating Animation and Sound

Sound can be extremely useful in a Flash movie. Sounds are often the only effective way to convey an idea, elicit an emotion, dramatize a point, and provide feedback to a user's action, such as clicking a button. How would you describe in words or show in an animation the sound a whale makes? Think about how chilling it is to hear the footsteps on the stairway of a haunted house. Consider how useful it is to hear the pronunciation of "buenos dias" as you are studying Spanish. All types of sounds can be incorporated into a Flash movie: for example, CD-quality music that might be used as background for a movie; narrations that help explain what the user is seeing; various sound effects, such as a car horn beeping; and recordings of special events, such as a presidential speech or a rock concert.

The process for adding a sound to a movie follows:

- Import a sound file into a Flash movie; Flash places the sound file in the movie's Library.

- Create a new layer.
- Select the desired frame on the new layer where you want the sound to play and drag the sound symbol to the Stage.

Instead of dragging the sound symbol to the Stage, you can use the Properties panel, as shown in Figure 73, to select the desired sound file. You can also use options on the Properties panel to specify special effects (such as Fade in and Fade out).

In addition to adding a sound to a layer, you can sync a sound with a button. For example, you might want to have a sound play when a button is clicked. The process for synchronizing a sound to a button follows:

- Display the Edit window for the button.
- Add a layer. The sound should be on its own layer.
- Select the frame for the desired button event (such as down).
- Use the Properties panel to select the sound file.
- Select Event as the Sync option.
- Exit the Edit window and return to the Stage.

You can place more than one sound file on a layer, and you can place sounds on layers that have other objects. However, it is recommended that you place each sound on a separate layer so that it is easier to identify and edit. In Figure 74, the sound layer shows a wave pattern that extends from frame 1 to frame 24. The wave pattern gives some indication of the volume of the sound at any particular frame. The higher spikes in the pattern indicate a louder sound. The wave pattern also gives some indication of the pitch.

The denser the wave pattern, the lower the pitch. You can alter the sound by adding or removing frames. However, removing frames may create undesired effects. It is best to make changes to a sound file using a sound-editing program.

You can import the following sound file formats into Flash:

- ASND (Windows or Macintosh)
- WAV (Windows only)
- AIFF (Macintosh only)

- MP3 (Windows or Macintosh)

If you have QuickTime 4 or later installed on your computer, you can import these additional sound file formats:

- AIFF (Windows)
- SD 2 (Sound Designer II; Macintosh only)
- MOV or QT (Sound Only QuickTime Movies; Windows or Macintosh)
- AU (Sun AU; Windows or Macintosh)
- SND (System 7 Sounds; Macintosh only)
- WAV (Macintosh)

Figure 73 *Properties panel sound options*

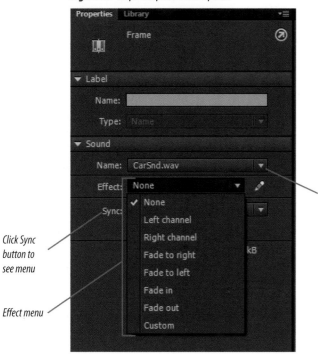

Name list arrow; click to see list of available sounds

Click Sync button to see menu

Effect menu

Figure 74 *A wave pattern displayed on a sound layer*

Add sound to a movie

1. Open textAn.fla, then save it as **rallySnd.fla**.

2. Play the movie and notice that there is no sound.

3. Click the Selection tool, click the **Actions layer**, insert a **new layer**, then name it **carSnd**.

4. Click a blank area of the Stage, then insert a **keyframe** in frame 73 on the carSnd layer.

5. Click **File** on the menu bar, point to **Import**, then click **Import to Library**.

6. Use the Import to Library dialog box to navigate to the drive and folder where your Data Files are stored, click the **CarSnd.wav file**, then click **Open**.

7. Display the Library panel, click **CarSnd.wav**, then click the **Play button ▶** in the upper-right corner of the Preview window.

8. Click **frame 73** on the carSnd layer.

9. Drag the **CarSnd sound symbol** 🔊 to the Stage, as shown in Figure 75.

   After you release the mouse button, the wave pattern appears on the carSnd layer starting in frame 73.

10. Change the frame rate to **12 fps**.

11. Test the movie.

12. Click the **Click to continue button** to move the playhead to the frame that starts the sound.

13. Close the Flash Player window.

You imported a sound and added it to a movie.

Figure 75 *Dragging the CarSnd symbol to the Stage*

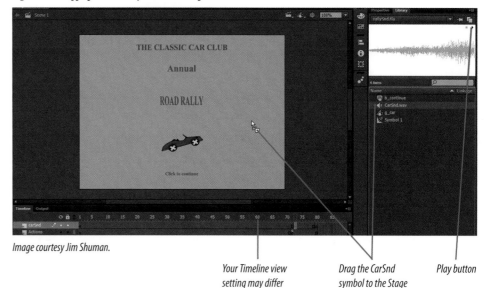

Image courtesy Jim Shuman.

Your Timeline view setting may differ   Drag the CarSnd symbol to the Stage   Play button

Figure 76 *Sound added to a button*

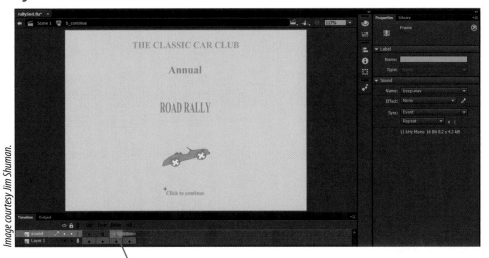

Image courtesy Jim Shuman.

Sound wave pattern
appears in the
selected frame

Adding Sounds to a Movie's Timeline and to a Button's Timeline

When adding a sound to a movie's Timeline, the sound will play when the playhead reaches the frame containing the sound wave. In some instances, the user may need to click a button to cause the playhead to move to the frame containing the sound wave. However, in these instances, the sound is not associated with the button because the sound is part of the movie's Timeline and not part of the button's Timeline. To associate a sound with a button, you place the sound wave on the Timeline for the button. Then, whenever the button is pressed, the sound plays.

Add sound to a button

1. Unlock the continue button layer, then click **frame 72** on the Timeline.

2. Click the **Selection tool** ▸ on the Tools panel, drag a **marquee** around "Click to continue" to select the button, then double-click the **button** to display the button's Timeline.

3. Insert a **new layer** name it **sound**, then click a blank area of the Stage.

4. Click the **Down frame** on the sound layer, click **Insert** on the menu bar, point to **Timeline**, then click **Blank Keyframe**.

5. Import the **beep.wav** file to the Library.

6. Display the Properties panel, click the **Name list arrow** in the Sound area, then click **beep.wav**.

7. Click the **Sync list arrow** on the Properties panel, click **Event**, then compare your screen to Figure 76.

8. Click **Scene 1** on the upper left of the edit window title bar to display the main Timeline.

9. Test the movie, click the **Click to continue button** and listen to the sounds, then close the Flash Player window.

10. Save your work, then close the movie.

You added a sound layer to a button, imported a sound, then attached the sound to the button.

Plan for complex movies and animations.

1. Start Flash, open fl3_11.fla from the drive and folder where your Data Files are stored, then save it as **skillsDemo3a.fla**.

2. Set the view to Fit in Window.

   In this Flash document, you will create a movie that will display a clock (a movie clip) with a minute hand (a movie clip) and an hour hand (a movie clip) that are rapidly spinning. The clock will be a button so that when the user clicks the clock it displays wings (two movie clips) and flies around the screen. All of the necessary graphic objects are available on the Library panel. A folder named "Graphics archive" contains graphics, such as a background image, that are used in the movie. You don't need to use these files and can simply ignore the folder that contains them. The movie currently has a background graphic (water and clouds) and a text title (Time Flies).

Create a mask effect.

1. Add a layer above the clock layer, then click a blank area of the Stage.

2. Click frame 12 on the new layer, then insert a keyframe.

3. Click frame 1 on the new layer, then use the oval tool to draw a circle anywhere on the stage that is slightly larger than the clock with no stroke and a blue fill.

4. Position the circle to the left of the clock.

5. Select the circle and create a motion tween.

6. Click frame 11 on the new layer, then move the circle to the right of the clock.

7. Click frame 12 on the new layer, then hold down [Shift] and click frame 70.

8. Remove the selected frames.

9. Select frame 1 of the new layer.

10. Change the properties of the new layer so that it is a locked mask layer with the name **mask**.

11. Slowly drag the clock layer up to the mask layer to turn it into a masked layer.
    The clock layer should be indented beneath the mask layer.

12. Lock the clock layer.

13. Play the movie.

Create a movie clip symbol.

1. Create a new movie clip symbol named **mc_clock**.

2. Verify you are in the edit window for the mc_clock movie clip, rename Layer 1 **clockFace**, then drag the g_clock face graphic symbol to the Stage.

3. Use the Properties panel to set the X and Y position values to 0 and 0.

4. Add a new layer, name it **hourHand**, zoom to 400, scroll to see the clock, drag the mc_hourHand movie clip so the colored circle on the hand aligns with the clock's registration symbol.

5. Change the view to 800%, click the Free Transform tool then drag the transformation point (the white circle) of the hour hand object to the middle of the colored circle at the left of the object. This will set the pivot point for the object as it spins around.

6. Add a new layer, name it **minuteHand**, drag the mc_minuteHand movie clip to the middle of the clock so that the circles of the objects overlap, then use the arrow keys to align the two hands.

7. Drag the transformation point (white circle) of the minute hand object to the middle of the colored circle at the bottom of the object.

8. Change the view to Fit in Window.

9. Add a new layer named **wings**, move it below the clockFace layer, then click frame 1 on the wings layer.

10. Drag the mc_left wings to the upper-left side of the clock, then drag the mc_right wings to the upper-right side of the clock.

11. Use the Free Transform tool and the arrow keys to rotate the wings as needed to place the wings so they appear to be connected to the clock.

12. Insert keyframes in frame 60 on all the layers, then return to the main Timeline and change the zoom back to Fit in Window.

13. Add a layer at the top of the Timeline, name it **clockAn**, click a blank area of the Stage, then insert a keyframe in frame 12 on the layer.

14. Drag the mc_clock movie clip symbol to the lower middle of the Stage and set the position to X:**275** and Y:**308**.
    This is the same location as the clock on the clock layer.

Animate the movie clip symbol.

1. Verify frame 12 on the clockAn layer is selected, then create a motion tween.
2. Select frame 60 on the clockAn layer, then drag the clock to the upper-left corner of the Stage.
3. Use the Properties panel to resize the clock to approximately one-fourth of its original size, then adjust the position of the clock so it is in the upper-left corner of the Stage, as shown in Figure 77.
4. Use the Selection tool to reshape the motion path to an arc.
5. Use the Subselection tool to display the Bezier handles and reshape the motion path to an S curve, then compare your screen to Figure 77.

Create an invisible button.

1. Insert a new layer, name it **button**, then click a blank area of the Stage.
2. Insert a keyframe in frame 12 of the button layer.
3. Remove all the frames after frame 12.
4. Select frame 12 on the button layer.
5. Draw a circle with no stroke and a black color the same size as the clockface, and place the object over the clockface.
6. Convert the object to a button symbol with the name **b_clockBtn**.
7. Give the object an instance name of **clockBtn**.
8. Double-click the object to view it in the edit window.
9. Insert a keyframe in the Hit frame.
   This will define the hit area for the button.
10. Display the main Timeline.
11. Verify the clockBtn object is selected.

12. Open the Code Snippets panel, open the ActionScript folder, then open the Timeline Navigation folder.
13. Double-click "Click to Go to Frame and Play" to add the code to the Actions panel.
14. Display the Actions panel and change "gotoAndPlay(5)" to "gotoAndPlay(13)" to have the playhead jump to frame 13 when the button is clicked.
15. Verify the object is selected, display the Properties panel, then set the Alpha option in the Styles list of the Color Effect area to 0.
16. Select frame 12 on the Actions layer.
17. Open the Code Snippets panel, open the ActionScript folder, then open the Timeline Navigation folder.
18. Double-click "Stop at this Frame".
19. Select frame 70 on the Actions layer, then insert a keyframe.
20. Close the Actions and the Code Snippets panels.
21. Test the movie.

Figure 77 *Motion path for clock movie clip symbol*

Image courtesy Jim Shuman.

Animate text.

1. Insert a keyframe in frame 12 of the text layer, then select frame 1 of that layer.
2. Create a motion tween that rotates the text 3 times in a clockwise direction.
3. Add a new layer and insert a keyframe in frame 13 of that layer.
4. Drag the g_text symbol from the Library to the Stage and set the position to X:**380** and Y:**20**.
5. Insert a keyframe in frame 24 of the new layer, then drag to text to a new position on the screen.
6. Insert keyframes in frames 35, 46, and 57 of the new layer and drag the text to a new position for each keyframe.
7. Change the layer name to **textAn**.
8. Test the movie, then compare your screens with Figures 77 and 78.
9. Lock all the layers.
10. Save your work.

Figure 78 *Completed Skills Review 3a*

Image courtesy Jim Shuman.

Plan for complex movies and animations, continued.

1. Open fl3_12.fla from the drive and folder where your Data Files are stored, then save it as **skillsDemo3b**.
2. Set the view to 100%.

   This movie has an Actions layer with stop actions in frames 1 and 156. When the start button in frame 1 is clicked, the playhead jumps to frame 2 to start the movie. A cloud image appears, starting in frame 38, and a background image spans the entire movie from frame 1 through frame 156. The completed movie will have a guide layer for a plane that is animated, a morph effect, and sound.

Animate an object using a guide layer.

1. Insert a layer above the cloud-image layer, name it **plane**, then click on a blank area of the Stage.
2. Insert a keyframe in frame 2 of the plane layer.
3. Drag the g_plane-sm symbol from the Library panel to the Stage.
4. Resize the object to a width of 90 and set the position at X:**500** and Y:**240**.
5. Insert a keyframe in frame 20 of the plane layer.
6. Change the position of the plane to X:**230** and Y:**260**.
7. Select any frame from frames 2 to 19 on the plane layer, then insert a classic tween.
8. Insert a new layer and name it **guide**, then click a blank area of the Stage.
9. Change the layer to a guide layer.
10. Click a blank area of the Stage, then insert keyframes in frames 2 and 20 of the guide layer.
11. Drag the plane layer up to the guide layer to have it become a guided layer.
12. Select frame 2 of the guide layer.
13. Use the Edit Multiple Frames feature to display both planes.
14. Use the pencil tool to draw a path with a loop that connects both planes.

    Note: you can select the path by double-clicking it with the Selection tool and then use the Smooth option at the bottom of the tools panel to smooth out the path.
15. Click each plane with the Free Transform tool and verify the transformation points on the planes touch each end of the path.

    Hint: Use the Zoom tool to enlarge the view of a plane; the Free Transform tool to view the transformation point; and the Free Transform tool to drag the planes so that their transformation point is at each end of the path line. Drag the planes and not their transformation points.
16. Use the Free Transform tool to rotate the planes to orient them to the path.
17. Deselect the Multiple Frames feature.
18. Use the Selection tool to select frame 2 on the plane layer, then click the Orient to path check box on the Properties panel.
19. Remove frames 21 through 156 on the guide and plane layers.
20. Test the movie.

    If the plane does not loop, verify that the path is connected to the transformation points of each plane.

Create a morph effect.

1. Insert a layer above the cloud-image layer, name the layer **morph**, then click a blank area of the Stage.
2. Insert a keyframe in frame 21 of the morph layer.
3. Click frame 20 of the plane layer, then select the plane.
4. Select Copy from the Edit menu to copy the plane.
5. Select frame 21 of the morph layer, then select Paste in Place from the Edit menu to put a copy of the plane in the morph layer at the same location as the plane on the plane layer.
6. Break apart the plane object.
7. Click a blank area of the Stage, then insert a blank keyframe in frame 60 on the morph layer.
8. Turn on the Edit Multiple Frames feature to view the plane, then drag the g_hotair-sm symbol to position it over the plane, near the center of the Stage.
9. Turn off the Edit Multiple frames feature, verify the hotair balloon is selected and break it apart.
10. Click any frame in the morph layer between frames 21 and 60, then insert a shape tween.
11. Remove frames 61 through 156 on the morph layer.
12. Test the movie.

Create a motion tween animation.

1. Insert a new layer above the morph layer, name it **hotair-An**, then click a blank area of the Stage.
2. Insert a keyframe in frame 60 of the hotair-An layer.
3. Drag the g_hotair-sm symbol from the Library and place it directly on top of the hotair balloon on the Stage.
4. With the object selected, insert a motion tween.
5. Select frame 156 of the hotair-An layer.
6. Change the view to 50%, then drag the balloon at an angle off the top right side of the stage.
7. Change the view to 100%.

Add sound to a movie.

1. Add a new layer above the hotair-An layer, and name the layer **sound-plane**.
2. Click a blank area of the Stage, then insert a keyframe in frame 2 of the sound-plane layer.
3. Select frame 2, then drag the plane-snd symbol from the Library to the Stage.
4. Notice the sound wave pattern on the Timeline.
5. Add a new layer and name it **sound-balloon**.
6. Click a blank area of the Stage, then insert a keyframe in frame 57 of the sound-balloon layer.
7. Select frame 57, then drag the hotair-snd symbol from the Library to the Stage.

Add sound to a button.

1. Display the b_start button in the Edit window.
2. Add a layer and name it **sound**.
3. Click a blank area of the Stage, then insert a keyframe in the Down frame of the sound layer.
4. Drag the buttonClick.wav sound from the Library to the Stage.
5. Display the main Timeline.
6. Lock all of the layers.
7. Test the movie, then compare your work to Figures 79 and 80.
8. Close the Flash Player window.
9. Save your work and exit Flash.

Figure 79 *The plane looping*

Image courtesy Jim Shuman.

Figure 80 *The plane morphing into the hot air balloon*

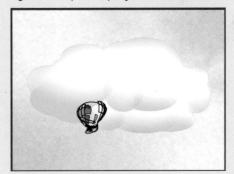

Image courtesy Jim Shuman.

PROJECT BUILDER 1

Odyssey Tours would like you to build a banner for its website that, when a button is clicked, will display a series of animations.

1. Open a new Flash ActionScript 3.0 document, then save it as **odysseyTours3**. *Note:* You may receive a message alerting you to a missing font, indicating that the file's fonts are not available on your computer. Flash automatically substitutes fonts that will work.
2. Change the Stage dimensions to 550 × 70. For the following, place each item on its own layer and name the layer appropriately.
3. Create a background image that has no stroke and a red gradient fill.
4. Create a button that says "see specials".
5. When the movie starts, have the "Traveling? Check out our Specials" text pulse in the center of the banner.
6. When the button is clicked, have the "Travel Specials" text fly in from above and the "New York to London" text scroll in from the bottom.
7. Have the price appear one character at a time.
8. Add stop actions to the appropriate frames.
9. Test the movie, click the see specials button, then compare your screens to Figures 81 and 82.
10. Close the Flash Player window, save your work, and close the document.

Figure 81 *The banner's opening screen*

Figure 82 *The completed Project Builder 1*

Creating Animations

You have been asked to demonstrate some of the animation features of Flash. You have decided to create a movie clip that includes a frame-by-frame animation and then use the movie clip in a motion tween animation. Figure 83 shows the stick figure that will walk across the screen and jump up as it moves along. The movement across the screen is created using a motion tween. The jumping up is created using a movie clip, as shown in Figure 84.

To complete this project, do the following:

1. Open fl3_13.fla, then save the movie as **jumper3.fla**.
2. Display the Library panel, then click on each of the graphic symbols and view them in the Preview window.

3. Add a color for the Stage, then add the sidewalk, the lines for the sidewalk, and the houses, adding layers as needed and naming them appropriately.
4. Create a new movie clip. (*Note*: You can create a new movie clip by selecting New Symbol from the Insert menu, then you can drag objects from the Library panel to the movie clip edit window.)
5. In the edit window, edit the clip to create a frame-by-frame animation of the stick figures walking in place. In the edit window, place a keyframe in the first six frames of the movie clip Timeline. Click frame 1, then drag stickfig1 to the Stage. Use the transformation point to place the figure. Click frame 2, then drag stickfig2 to the Stage. Click frame 3, then drag stickfig3 to the Stage. Continue until each of the six frames has one stick figure.

6. Click frame 1, then use the period key to click through the movie. Click one frame and move the stick figure in that frame so it is above its original location. This placement creates the jumping effect.
7. Exit the edit window and place the movie clip on the Stage on its own layer, then create a motion tween that moves the movie clip from the left side to the right side of the Stage.
8. Add keyframes to the other layers to be sure objects on those layers appear on the Stage for the full length of the movie.
9. Test the movie. Change the fps setting as needed to create a more realistic effect, then retest the movie. (*Note*: Movie clips do not play from the Stage, you must use the Test Movie command.)
10. Close the Flash Player movie, then save the movie.

Figure 83 *Sample completed Project Builder 2*

Jumper3 movie

© 2015 Cengage Learning®.

Figure 84 *Movie clip edit screen*

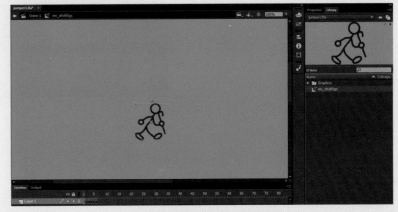

mc_stickfigs symbol in edit window

Figure 85 shows a website for kids. Study the figure and complete the following. For each question, indicate how you determined your answer.

1. Connect to the Internet, then go to *www.smokeybear.com/kids*.

2. Open a document in a word processor or open a new Flash document, save the file as **dpc3**, then answer the following questions. (*Hint*: Use the Text tool in Flash.)

   - What seems to be the purpose of this site?
   - Who is the target audience?
   - How would you use a frame animation in this site?
   - How would you use a motion tween animation?
   - How would you use a motion guide?
   - How would you use motion animation effects?
   - How would you animate the text?
   - How would you use a mask effect?
   - How would you use sound?

Figure 85 *Design Project*

Source: USDA Forest Service.

Creating Animations

This is a continuation of the Portfolio Project in Chapter 2, which is the development of a personal portfolio. In this project, you will create several buttons for the sample animations screen and link them to the animations that appear on separate screens.

1. Open portfolio2.fla (the file you created in Portfolio Project, Chapter 2) and save it as **portfolio3.fla**. *Note*: You may receive a font missing message. This is because the font(s) are not available on your computer. Flash automatically substitutes fonts that will work.

2. Create, on its own layer, an Animations screen (similar to the Biography screen) as shown in Figure 86. *Note*: Each of the options is a button that will jump to a screen and play the appropriate animation. As you complete the following steps to create the animations, be sure to place the animations on their own layer and use keyframes to stagger them down the Timeline. There are several objects in the Data files folder that can be used for the animations. If desired, you can create or acquire your own objects.

3. Create a motion tween animation on a separate screen or use the passing cars animation from Chapter 2, and link it to the appropriate button on the Sample Animations screen by assigning a goto action to the button.

4. Create a frame-by-frame animation, and link it to the appropriate button on the Sample Animations screen.

5. Create a motion path animation, and link it to the appropriate button on the Sample Animations screen.

6. Create several text animations, using scrolling, rotating, and zooming; then link them to the appropriate button on the Sample Animations screen.

7. Create a shape tween animation, and link it to the appropriate button on the Sample Animations screen.

8. Create a shape tween animation that produces a morphing effect using shape hints, and link it to the appropriate button on the Sample Animations screen.

9. Add a sound that plays during one of the animations.

10. Extend the Home button that links all screens to the Home screen.

11. Create frame actions that cause the movie to stop after each animation has been played.

12. Test the movie.

13. Save your work, then compare sample pages from your movie to the example shown for one of the screens in Figure 87.

Figure 86 *Sample completed Portfolio Project*

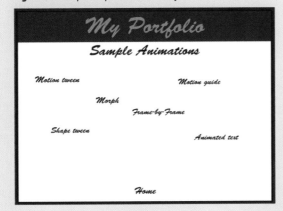

Sample Animations page

Figure 87 *Sample animation*

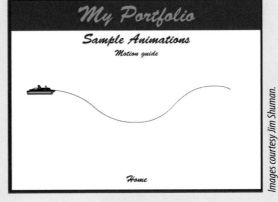

A sample animation

Images courtesy Jim Shuman.

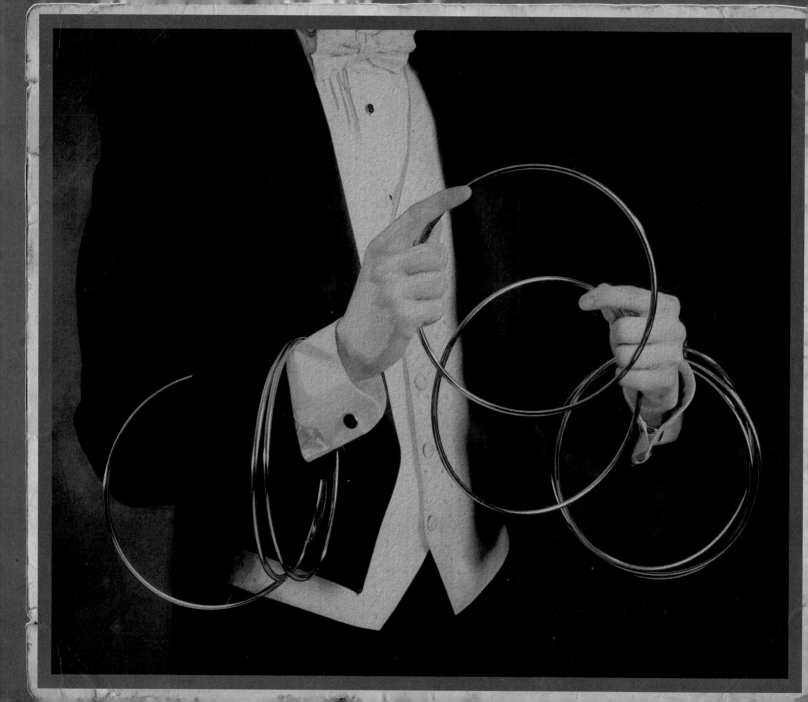

CHAPTER **4** DEVELOPING MOBILE
APPLICATIONS

1. Create and publish applications for
   mobile devices
2. Use the Mobile Content Simulator
3. Repurpose mobile applications
4. Use the Accelerometer
5. Use touch and gesture events

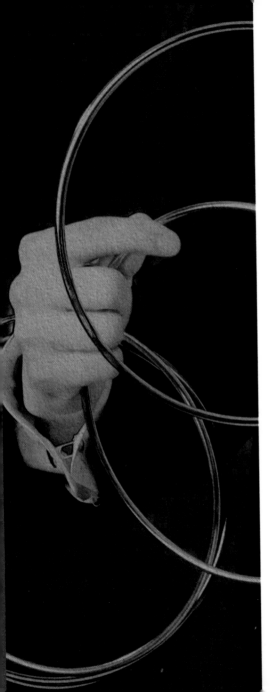

CHAPTER 4

DEVELOPING MOBILE
APPLICATIONS

Introduction

The enormous popularity of mobile devices (smartphones and tablets) has driven a need for the development of applications that run on these devices. These applications include games (such as the popular Angry Birds); educational applications (such as Curious George); informational applications (such as the National Park Service); and business applications (such as Photoshop Touch). Adobe has responded to this need by incorporating new features in its latest version of Flash that allow easy development and deployment of mobile applications. These features include Code Snippets for Touch and Gesture events, such as tap, zoom, and rotate; Apple iOS and Android publish settings; and templates for Android applications. In addition, Flash allows you to test a mobile application using the on-screen **Mobile Content Simulator**. The Simulator displays the application as it would appear on a mobile phone, and allows you to use events and gestures such as touch, zoom, and swipe

to see how the application reacts. *Note:* If you have access to an Android device you can use it to test the applications you develop in this chapter.

The actual development process for mobile applications is not significantly different from stand-alone and web applications. Both require identifying the purpose, target audience, treatment and specification, as covered in Chapter 1. However, there are considerations that need to be addressed when developing for mobile devices as opposed to desktop displays. These include screen size (smaller), processor speed (slower), and user interactivity (touch, swipe, pinch, and so on).

Until now you have been creating Flash applications and publishing them as SWF files to be viewed in a web browser using the Flash Player. Flash provides another technology, AIR (Adobe Integrated Runtime), that creates applications that can be played without a browser. An AIR app can be displayed on stand-alone computers as well as mobile devices.

```
31              {
32                  textb.text = "a Hit";
33              }
34          }
35      /* Simple Timer
36      Displays a countdown timer in the Output panel until 30 seconds elapse.
37      This code is a good place to start for creating timers for your own purposes.
38
39      Instructions:
40      1. To change the number of seconds in the timer, change the value 30 in the f
41      */
42
43      var fl_TimerInstance:Timer = new Timer(1000, 30);
44      fl_TimerInstance.addEventListener(TimerEvent.TIMER, fl_TimerHandler);
45      fl_TimerInstance.start();
46
47      var fl_SecondsElapsed:Number = 1;
48
49      function fl_TimerHandler(event:TimerEvent):void
50      {
51          trace("Seconds elapsed: " + fl_SecondsElapsed);
52          fl_SecondsElapsed++;
53          textb.text = String(fl_SecondsElapsed);
54      }
55
```

Create and Publish Applications for
MOBILE DEVICES

What You'll Do

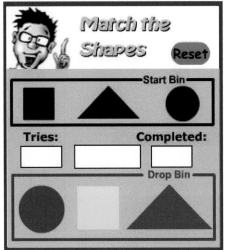

© 2015 Cengage Learning®.

 In this lesson, you will publish a Flash application for a mobile device.

Understanding the Development Process for Mobile Apps

Flash CC allows you to quickly and easily develop applications for mobile devices, such as smartphones and tablets. Flash CC specifically targets Android and iOS (Apple) devices because of their large markets. You can start a new AIR for Android or AIR for iOS application or you can repurpose an existing Flash document. In either case, you create the application in Flash and publish it as an AIR file. The publishing process requires specifying various settings by completing several dialog boxes. Figure 1 shows the Publish Settings dialog box for an AIR for Android app.

The AIR for Android Settings dialog box has five tabs: General, Deployment, Icons, Permissions, and Languages, which are explained here briefly.

Settings on the General Tab

Output file: Displays the name and location of the AIR file. The .apk file extension indicates an AIR for Android package file.

App name: Displays the name that appears on the mobile device when the app is downloaded. Also, this is the name used when searching for the app in the Android market.

App ID: Displays a string of characters that uniquely identifies the application; the characters you type are preceded by "air" when the ID is displayed.

Version: Displays a version number for the application, which can be changed as new versions of the application are published.

Version label: Used to describe the version (optional).

Aspect Ratio: Determines how the application is displayed. There are several options available: Portrait maintains the portrait orientation of the application no matter how the mobile device is turned. Landscape maintains the landscape orientation of the application no matter how the mobile device is turned. Auto, when selected along with Auto orientation, launches the application on the device in either portrait or landscape mode, depending on the current orientation of the device.

Full screen: Sets the application to run in full screen mode.

Auto orientation: Allows the application to switch from portrait to landscape mode and vice versa, depending on the current orientation of the device; must be used in conjunction with Aspect Ratio Auto mode.

Render mode: Allows you to specify which method the AIR runtime uses to render graphic content.

Included Files: Displays the files and folders to include in your application package. Allows you to add files, such as video, audio, or SWF files. By default, the main SWF file and the application descriptor XML file are included. The descriptor XML file contains all the general settings such as the Output file, App name, Version, and so on.

While you can make changes in the General settings, the default settings are often acceptable.

Settings on the Deployment Tab

Figure 2 shows the AIR for Android Settings dialog box with the Deployment tab active. These settings allow you to create a certificate that identifies who you are to the user.

Certificate: The digital certificate for the application. Digital certificates are used to verify the identity of the developer.

Password: The password for the selected digital certificate.

Android deployment type: Android applications can be deployed in three different ways. Device release allows creation of applications

Figure 1 *The AIR for Android Settings dialog box*

Figure 2 *The Deployment tab settings*

for the marketplace or any other distribution medium, such as a website. Emulator release is used to test the application when an emulator program is available. Debug allows on-device debugging.

AIR runtime: The AIR app uses an AIR runtime plug-in. There are two choices for making sure the user has the runtime plug-in: Embed AIR runtime with the application or Get AIR runtime from. (A message will appear on a device that does not have the runtime plug-in, allowing the user to choose to go to the specified location, Google Android Market or Amazon Appstore.)

After publishing: Two choices are available: Install application on the connected Android device or Launch application on the connected Android device. You can select either choice or both choices, whichever best meets your needs.

When you click the Create button on the Deployment tab, the Create Self-Signed Digital Certificate dialog box appears as shown in Figure 3. This dialog box allows you to identify the app developer, including the Publisher name, Organization unit, and Organization name. In addition, you can create a password, then specify the type of encryption and the certificate validity period (25 years minimum). The Save as

Figure 3 *The Create Self-Signed Digital Certificate dialog box*

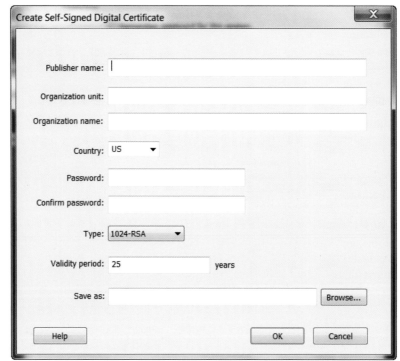

option allows you to specify the filename and storage location for the certificate.

Settings on the Icons Tab

An icon is the graphic associated with the application. For mobile devices, the icon displays on the user's mobile device when the application is downloaded. The user simply taps the icon to launch the app. The Icons tab in the AIR for Android Settings dialog box, shown in Figure 4, allows you to specify four graphic files of varying sizes (36×36, 48×48, 72×72 and 96×96). These sizes are in pixels and the graphics must be a PNG file type. If no icons are provided by the developer, a generic Android icon displays.

Settings on the Permissions Tab

Figure 5 shows the AIR for Android Settings dialog box with the Permissions tab active. You use settings on this tab to specify which services and data the application has access to on the device. Clicking on a Permission Name displays a description of the selection.

Figure 4 *The Icons tab*

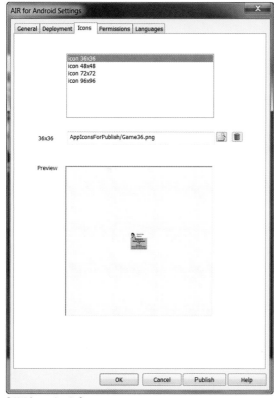

© 2015 Cengage Learning®.

Figure 5 *The Permissions tab settings*

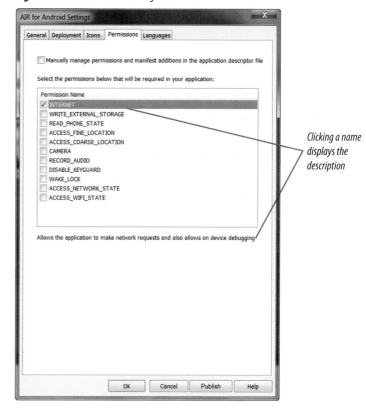

Clicking a name displays the description

Settings on the Languages Tab

The Languages tab in the AIR for Android Settings dialog box allows you to specify the languages that will be supported by your application.

Mobile App Gestures and Events

While you can take an already developed Flash file and repurpose it for mobile devices by completing the AIR publishing process, it will not have any of the features users are accustomed to, such as pinch to zoom or swipe, unless you have specifically added these features to your Flash file. These features, called gestures and events, can easily be incorporated into a Flash file that you want to publish as a mobile app by using Code Snippets. These are small blocks of code that you apply to an object in your app or the app in general. For example, if you would like your users to be able to zoom in and out on an object, such as a map, you can select the map on the Stage and apply the Pinch to Zoom Event from the Code Snippets panel. Code Snippets are written in ActionScript 3, so the Publish Settings for your app must specify this version of ActionScript. Figure 6 shows the Code Snippets panel with the Pinch to Zoom Event highlighted under the Mobile Gesture Events category. Notice the other events including Pan, Rotate, and Swipe. *Note:* The process for creating an AIR for iOS app is similar to an AIR for Android app. This book focuses on Air for Android.

Figure 6 *Code Snippets panel with the Pinch to Zoom Event highlighted*

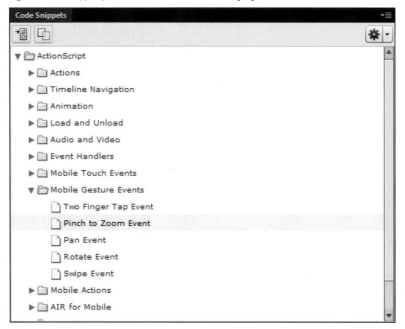

Figure 7 *Changing the publish target to AIR for Android*

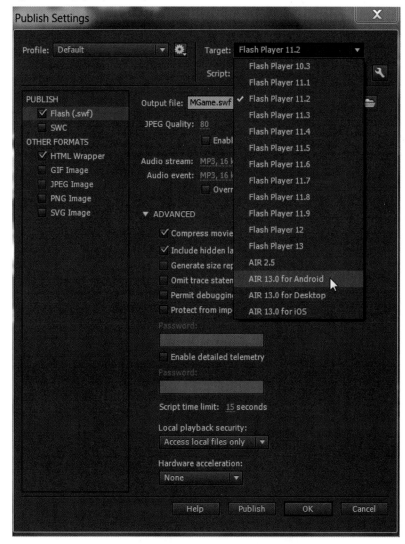

Adapt a Flash app for use on mobile devices

1. Open fl4_1.fla, then save it as **MGame.fla**.

2. Click **Control** on the menu bar, point to **Test Movie**, then click **In Browser**.

3. Play the game by dragging the black shapes onto the matching colored shapes, then close the browser.

4. Click **File** on the menu bar, then click **Publish Settings**.

5. Click the **Target list arrow**, then click **AIR 13.0 for Android** (or the latest version) as shown in Figure 7.

6. Click the **Player Settings icon** to the right of the Target list box in order to display the AIR for Android Settings dialog box.

   The General tab settings are displayed. Study these settings and notice that the first part of the filename, MGame, is used for the Output file, App name, App ID, and the included files. You will use the default settings.

7. Click the **Icons tab**.

8. Verify icon 36×36 is highlighted, then click the **Search icon**.

9. Navigate to the location where your data files are stored, click **Game36.png**, then click **Open**.

   A message may appear indicating that the icon must be copied to a folder relative to the root content folder, that is where you have saved the MGame.fla file. If so, click OK.

10. Click **icon 48×48** to highlight it, click the **Search icon**, click **Game48.png**, click **Open**, then click **OK**, if necessary.

(continued)

11. Click **icon 72×72** to highlight it, click the **Search icon**, click **Game72.png**, click **Open**, then click **OK**, if necessary.

    Note: No icon is needed for the 96×96 option.

12. Click the **Permissions tab**.

13. Click **CAMERA**, then read the description.

14. Click **INTERNET**, then read the description.

15. Click the **INTERNET check box** to select it, then click the **Languages tab**.

16. Click the **English check box** to select it, then click the **Deployment tab**.

17. Click the **Create button** to begin the process for creating a Self-Signed Certificate.

18. Type your name, organization unit (your program or department), and organization name (such as your school).

19. Type a password of your choice, making sure to remember it, then type the password again in the Confirm text box to confirm it.

    Your dialog box should resemble Figure 8.

20. Click the **Browse button**, then navigate to the folder where your solution files are stored.

    The Select File Destination dialog box is displayed. Notice the filename is entered and the file type is p12, designating this as a Certificate File.

21. Verify your solution file folder is the active destination folder, then click **Save**.

22. Click **OK** in the Create Self-Signed Digital Certificate dialog box.

    After a few moments the following message appears: Self-signed certificate has been created.

    (continued)

Figure 8 *The completed certificate*

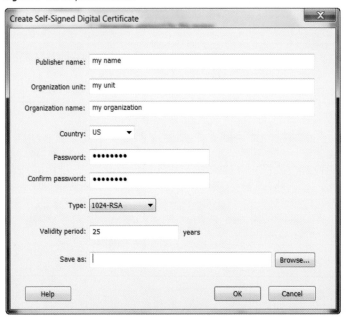

Testing an App on a Mobile Device

Flash CC allows you to test your application on a mobile device that is connected to your computer. You must configure your device to accept the app as explained in the steps below. *Note:* Depending on the model of your mobile device, these steps may vary. Also, you may need to update the device driver on your device.

To prepare your Android (2.2 or above) device for testing a mobile app:

1. Go to Settings for your device (such as on your smartphone).
2. Scroll to and select Applications, then verify "Unknown Sources" is checked.
3. Scroll to and select Development, then verify "USB debugging" is checked.
4. Connect your USB cable from the computer to your phone (the same cable used to charge your device).

Even if you do not have an Android device, you can still learn the mobile app publishing process by completing this lesson.

Figure 9 *The completed Deployment settings*

23. Click **OK** to close the message box and the Create Self-Signed digital Certificate dialog box.

24. In the Deployment tab, type your password.

25. Verify Device release and Embed AIR runtime with application are selected, as shown in Figure 9.

    Note: If you have an Android (2.2+) phone or tablet and you want to test this app, click the "Install application on the connected Android device checkbox" to select it. Make sure that the settings on your smartphone "Unknown Sources" and "USB debugging" have been turned on and that your Android 2.2+ mobile device is connected to the computer with a USB cable. If you do not have a phone to test this app you can continue with the following steps.

26. Click the **Publish button**.

    The publish process may take several moments.

27. Click **OK** to close the AIR for Android Settings dialog box when the publishing process is complete.

28. Click **OK** to close the Publish Settings dialog box.

29. **Save** the application, then close the application.

    Note: If you connected an Android (2.2+) phone or tablet to your computer using the steps on the previous page, the app icon will appear on the connected Android device as an app. You can tap the icon and play the game.

You repurposed and published a Flash application for delivery on a mobile device.

Use the Mobile Content
SIMULATOR

What You'll Do

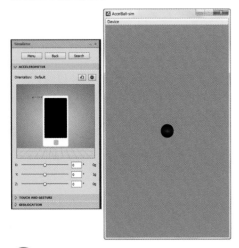

 In this lesson, you will use the Mobile Content Simulator to test a mobile application

Understanding the Simulator

Throughout the development process it is important to test the application to determine if it is performing as planned. Ideally, developers would test their mobile application on all of the targeted devices. However, given the number of mobile devices available today this is not feasible. Flash provides a feature in CC called the Mobile Content Simulator. As the name implies, this feature allows you to simulate the use of an application on a mobile device, such as a smartphone. When you are developing an application and are ready to test a feature such as a pinch and zoom event, you select the Test movie option from the Control menu, and then select In AIR Debug Launcher (Mobile). All mobile applications developed in Flash are AIR files, which means they do not need the Flash Player to run.

After you select In AIR Debug Launcher (Mobile), two windows appear as shown in Figure 10. The Simulator window is used to simulate the movement of the phone and the actions of the user. The figure shows the Simulator window with the ACCELEROMETER area open. The AIR preview window, which is labeled "Device", displays the application as it will be seen on a user's phone. This simulation of the application is manipulated in the Simulator window. The ACCELEROMETER area in the Simulator window is used to simulate the user's movement of the phone. For example, if you have a ball on the screen and you tilt the phone graphic in the Simulator window, the ball in the AIR preview window will respond by moving around the screen.

Figure 11 shows two other groups of settings in Simulator window: the TOUCH AND GESTURE group and the GEOLOCATION group. The TOUCH AND GESTURE settings are used to simulate user actions such as drag, zoom, and swipe. The GEOLOCATION settings are used to test an application that utilizes location data.

Other features available via the Simulator window are listed below:

- Menu, Back, Search buttons—used to simulate the operation of buttons found on Android phones; you must use ActionScript to simulate the operation of these buttons.
- Accelerometer Settings button—used to change the view of the phone

- Accelerometer X, Y, and Z settings—used to tilt and rotate the phone
- Touch and Gesture Touch layer check box—used to make the application respond to touch and gesture events
- Touch and Gesture Alpha setting—used to simulate various lighting conditions, such as the glare from the sun
- Touch and Gesture radio buttons—used to select the desired event to simulate

- Geolocation options—used to enter location data for the application

Figure 10 *Mobile Content Simulator window and the AIR preview window*

Simulator window with Accelerometer feature expanded

AIR preview window

Figure 11 *The Touch and Gesture and the Geolocation screens*

Simulator window with Touch and Gesture feature expanded

Simulator window with Geolocation feature expanded

The Output Panel

When you test an application using the Mobile Content Simulator, information about the file will be displayed on the Output panel at the bottom of the Flash workspace. At a minimum, the size of the SWF file after it has been decompressed is displayed, as shown in Figure 12. Initially, when a Flash FLA file is published, it is compressed to reduce the file size. In order to be viewed it needs to be decompressed,

a process that is transparent to the user. A common use for the Output panel is debugging an application; the programmer can use information on the Output panel to determine where in the ActionScript code a problem occurs. One technique is to use a trace statement to display information as the application is running, for example:

trace("Seconds elapsed: " +
    fl_SecondsElapsed);

This line of code sends the number of seconds that have elapsed since the start of the application to the Output panel as shown in Figure 12.

The Output panel is grouped with the Timeline panel. *Note:* In this and following chapter, you will be using the Code Snippets and Actions panels. At times these panels may obscure the Stage. It's up to you to minimize or close the panels as necessary.

Figure 12 *The Output panel*

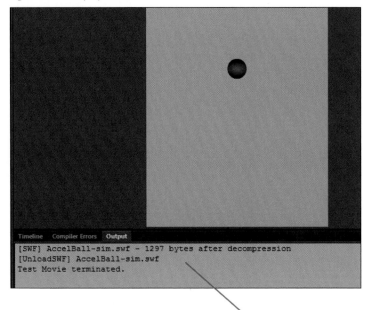

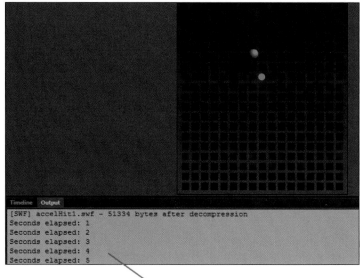

Information about the file appears on the Output panel

Trace statement in the ActionScript code causes information to be displayed on the Output panel as the application is running

Figure 13 *Inserting code using a Code Snippet*

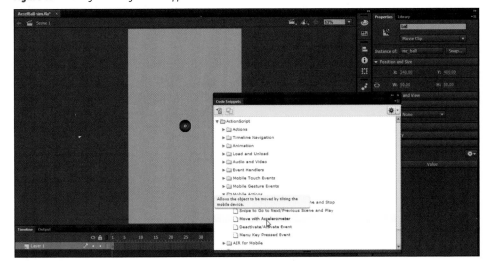

Use the Mobile Content Simulator

1. Click **File** on the menu bar, then click **New**.

2. Verify the General tab is displayed in the New Document dialog box, then double-click **AIR for Android**.

3. Save the document as **AccelBall-sim**, then change the view to **Fit in Window**.

4. Click **Modify** in the menu bar, then click **Document**.

5. Change the Stage color to #999999 (a shade of gray), then click **OK**.

6. Use the oval tool to draw a **circle** with a **blue gradient** color and a width and height of **50** pixels, then center the object on the stage.

7. Verify the object is selected, then convert it to a movie clip symbol with the name **mc_ball**.

8. Verify the object is selected, then use the Properties panel to give it an instance name of **ball**.

9. Verify the object is selected, click **Window** in the menu bar, then click **Code Snippets**.

10. Open the **ActionScript** folder, then open the **Mobile Actions** folder.

11. Point to **Move with Accelerometer** as shown in Figure 13, read the screentip, then double click **Move with Accelerometer** to display the code in the Actions panel.

    Notice that an Actions layer has been added to the Timeline. Frame 1 of the Actions layer contains the code for the Move with Accelerometer event.

    (continued)

12. Close the **Actions** and **Code Snippets** panels.

13. Click **Control** on the menu bar, point to **Test Movie**, then click **In AIR Debug Launcher (Mobile)**.

    The Mobile Content Simulator window appears along with the AIR preview window, which is labeled Device.

14. Click the **Settings button** ⚙ in the Simulator window, then click **Flat**.

    Now you only see the end of the device in the Simulator window, as if the user is looking at the top of the device.

15. Change the **X** setting to −90 as shown in Figure 14, then press **[Enter]** (Win) or **[return]** (Mac).

    This changes the orientation of the simulated device to show it as though the user is holding it face up.

    (continued)

Figure 14 *Changing the Simulator settings for the Accelerometer*

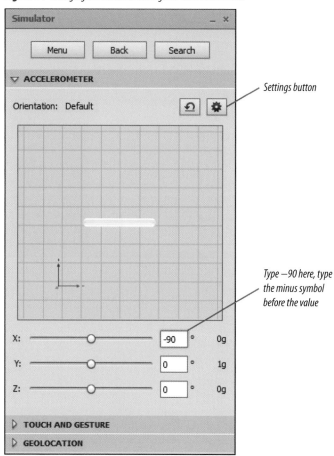

Settings button

Type −90 here, type the minus symbol before the value

Figure 15 *Positioning the pointer on the device*

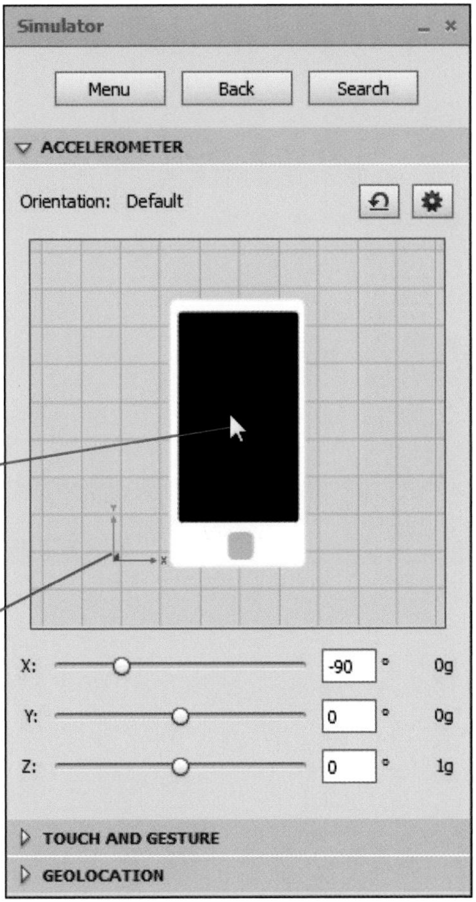

Point here

These lines represent the x, y, and z axes orientation for the device

16. Point to the center of the device as shown in Figure 15, hold down the mouse button, then rotate the mouse in a small circular motion to simulate moving the device.

    Notice how the ball in the AIR preview window moves as the device in the Simulator window moves. Notice also how the x, y, and z axes in the Simulator window also move as the device is rotated.

    Note: If the ball moves off the screen, close the AIR preview window and repeat, Steps 13–16.

17. Close the Device window to return to the Flash workspace.

18. Save your work, then close the application.

You developed an Android app and used the AIR preview window to simulate the movement of an object on a mobile device.

Use Code Snippets to add touch gesture events

1. Open fl4_2.fla, then save it as **MGame-sim.fla**.

   This is a modified version of the application adapted in Lesson 1. You will use Code Snippets to add touch gesture events and then use the Mobile Content Simulator to test the app.

2. Display the Timeline (if necessary), click **frame 2** on the shapes layer, then click a blank area of the screen.

3. Click the **black square** to select it.

4. Click **Window** in the menu bar, then click **Code Snippets**.

5. Open the **ActionScript** folder, then open the **Mobile Touch Events** folder.

6. Point to **Touch and Drag Event** to read the description in the screentip, as shown in Figure 16, and then double-click **Touch and Drag Event**.

   The Actions panel displays the code for the Touch and Drag event.

7. If necessary, drag the Actions panel out of the way so you can see the app interface, then click the **black triangle** to select it.

8. Display the Code Snippets panel, then double-click **Touch and Drag Event**.

9. Click the **black circle** to select it.

10. Display the Code Snippets panel, then double-click **Touch and Drag Event**.

(continued)

Figure 16 *Selecting the Touch and Drag Event*

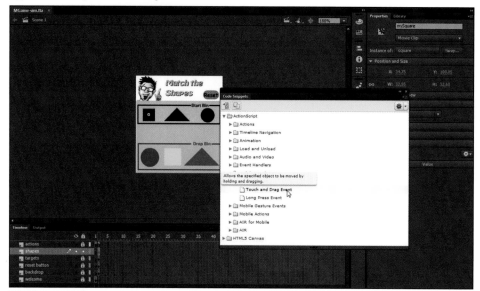

© 2015 Cengage Learning®.

Developing Mobile Applications

Figure 17 *Dragging the square in the preview window*

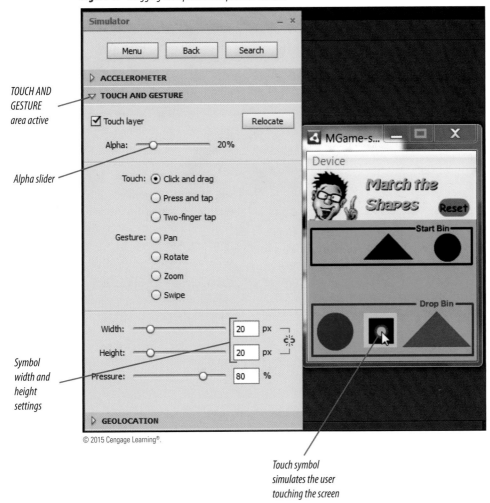

TOUCH AND
GESTURE
area active

Alpha slider

Symbol
width and
height
settings

Touch symbol
simulates the user
touching the screen

© 2015 Cengage Learning®.

11. Close the Code Snippets and Action panels, click **Control** on the menu bar, point to **Test Movie**, then click **In AIR Debug Launcher (Mobile)**.

12. Click **TOUCH AND GESTURE** in the Simulator window, then click the **Touch layer check box** to select it.

13. Verify the Click and drag radio button is selected, then click and drag the **black square** in the AIR preview window to position it over the yellow square as shown in Figure 17.

    Note: The touch symbol ⬤ simulates the user touching the screen.

14. In the TOUCH AND GESTURE area of the Simulator window, change the Width and Height settings for the touch symbol to **40**, then click and drag the **black triangle** in the AIR preview window.

15. Close the AIR preview window to return to the Flash workspace.

16. Close the Actions and Code Snippets panels.

17. Save your work, then close the application.

You used the Code Snippets panel to add mobile events to an application and tested the application using the Mobile Content Simulator.

Repurpose Mobile
APPLICATIONS

What You'll Do

In this lesson, you will repurpose an application for a mobile phone and a tablet

Repurposing Mobile Applications

A goal of mobile developers is to be able to create one application and use it for a variety of phones and tablets. This reduces development time and allows assets, such as photos, graphics and text to be reused. Ultimately, this lowers overall development costs. Mobile devices have significant variation in screen resolutions as shown in Table 1. Therefore, repurposing an application often requires resizing the objects on the Stage. To make this easier, Flash allows objects to be resized as the dimensions of the Stage are changed. When you select the Scale content check box in the Document Settings dialog box, as shown in Figure 18, the size of the objects on the Stage will be changed automatically to correspond with any change in the Stage dimensions. Figure 19 shows an application in two different stage sizes. Notice how the objects have been resized to fit the smaller stage.

Changing the size of the objects may not be enough to optimize the application for playback on a specific device. Selected objects may need

TABLE 1: SCREEN RESOLUTIONS OF VARIOUS PHONE AND TABLET MOBILE DEVICES		
Phone	**Screen H × W (pixels)**	**Operating System**
Apple iPhone	1920 × 1080 1334 × 750	iOS
Samsung Galaxy	1920 × 1080	Android
Blackberry	1280 × 768	Android
Tablet		
Samsung Galaxy	2560 × 1600	Android
Apple iPad	2048 × 1536	iOS
Surface Pro	2160 × 1440	Android

additional resizing as well as repositioning. For example, an application that is designed to be displayed in portrait orientation on a smartphone may not appear as intended on a tablet device without rearranging the objects for display in landscape orientation. In addition, buttons that are a part of a phone application may need to have their hit area enlarged to make it easier for users to tap them.

When creating a scalable application, the developer needs to set an initial target including the device type and operating system. The most popular smartphones run the Android operating system or, in the case of iPhones, the Apple iOS operating system. Fortunately, the development and deployment processes for these two types of devices are similar.

Figure 18 *The Scale content with stage option*

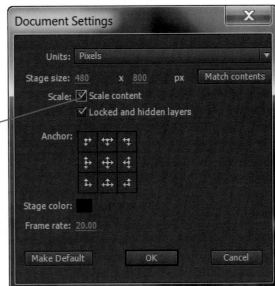

Select this option to have objects on the Stage resize as the Stage dimensions are changed

Figure 19 *Stage objects scaled as the Stage size is changed*

 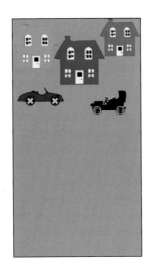

© Cengage Learning®.

Resize an application for a smartphone

1. Open fl4_3.fla, then save it as **phoneF.fla**.

   The Stage dimensions are width: 230 px and height: 250 px.

2. Test the movie, then close the Flash Player window.

3. Click **Modify** on the menu bar, then click **Document**.

4. Change the stage dimensions to width: **480** and height: **800**, a common size for smartphones.

5. Click the **Scale content check box** to select the option, then click **OK**.

6. Change the view to **Fit in Window**, then test the movie.

7. Click each button to view the resized objects, then close the Flash Player window.

8. Click **File** on the menu bar, then click **Publish Settings** to display the Publish Settings dialog box.

9. Click the **Target list arrow** ▼ as shown in Figure 20, click **AIR 13.0 for Android**, then click **OK**.

10. Click **Control** on the menu bar, point to **Test Movie**, click **In AIR Debug Launcher (Mobile)**, then click the buttons to play the application.

    Notice the blank space that appears at the bottom of the smartphone screen. This area is reserved for the phone's menu buttons

11. Close the AIR preview window, then save your work.

You resized an application by scaling the content.

Figure 20 *Publish Target options*

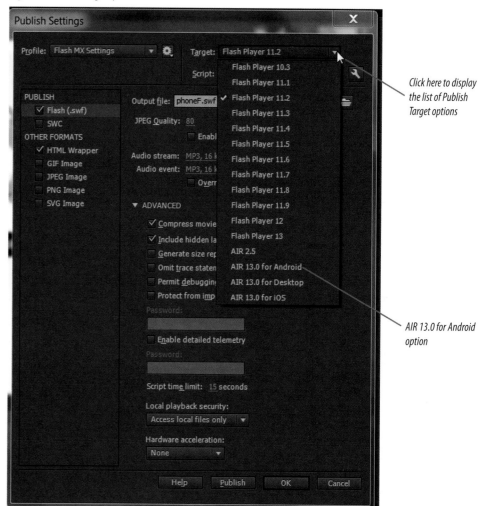

Click here to display the list of Publish Target options

AIR 13.0 for Android option

Figure 21 *Repositioning the buttons*

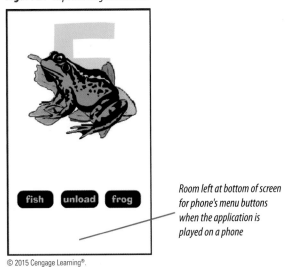

Room left at bottom of screen
for phone's menu buttons
when the application is
played on a phone

© 2015 Cengage Learning®.

Figure 22 *Changing the hit area*

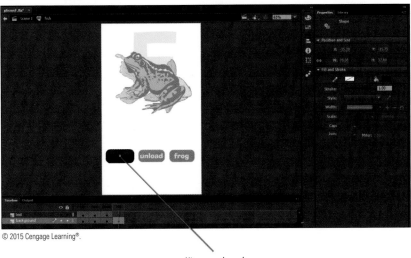

© 2015 Cengage Learning®.

Hit area enlarged
and repositioned

Alter objects and reposition them

1. Display the Timeline, then unlock all layers.

2. Click a blank area of the Stage to deselect all the objects.

3. Click the **Selection tool** ➤ on the tool panel, click the **fish button**, press **[Shift]**, then click the **unload** and **frog buttons** to select all three buttons.

4. Reposition the buttons near the bottom of the Stage (while still leaving space for the phone's menu buttons), as shown in Figure 21.

5. Double-click the **fish button** to display it in the edit window.

6. Click the **Hit frame** of the background layer, then click the **black oval** that covers the button.

7. Display the Properties panel, verify the lock icon 🔗 is locked, then resize the oval to a width of **70**.

8. Click a blank area of the stage, click the **black oval**, then use the arrow keys to position the black oval over the button, as shown in Figure 22.

9. Click **Scene 1** to return to the main Timeline.

10. Repeat Steps 5 through 9 to enlarge the hit area for the unload and frog buttons.

(continued)

11. Click the **F** on the Stage.

12. Display the Properties panel, then verify the lock icon  in the Position and Size area is locked.

13. Change the width to **400**.

14. Verify F is selected, click the **Style list arrow** in the Color Effect area of the Properties panel, then click **Alpha**.

15. Change the Alpha setting to **50%**, then click a blank area of the stage.

16. Reposition the letter F, the fish, and the frog to resemble Figure 23.

17. Click **Control** on the menu bar, point to **Test Movie**, then click **In AIR Debug Launcher (Mobile)**.

18. Click each button to play the application.

19. Close the AIR preview window.

20. Save your work.

You resized and repositioned selected objects to make the application more appropriate for a smartphone.

Figure 23 *Repositioning the objects on the Stage*

Figure 24 *Repositioning the objects*

Resize an application for a tablet device

1. Save the application as **tabletF.fla**.
2. Click **Modify** on the menu bar, then click **Document**.
3. Change the width to **1280**, click the **Scale content check box** to select it, then click **OK**.
4. Change the view to **Fit in Window**.
5. Change the Stage color to **#009900**.
6. Click the letter **F**, then display the Properties panel.

   Notice the width of the letter F has increased from 400.
7. Reposition the three buttons, the fish, and frog to the approximate location shown in Figure 24.

   Hint: Use the Rulers feature from the View menu.
8. Click **Control** on the menu bar, point to **Test Movie**, then click **In AIR Debug Launcher (Desktop)**.

   Note: Because you are testing for a tablet and not a phone, you use the Desktop setting and not the Simulator window.
9. Click the buttons, then close the AIR preview window.
10. Save your work.
11. Close the application.

You changed the dimensions of an application to accommodate a tablet device and resized and repositioned selected objects.

Use the
ACCELEROMETER

What You'll Do

 In this lesson, you will use the accelerometer feature of a mobile device

Understanding the Accelerometer

In Lesson 2 you learned how the Accelerometer is used to simulate the movement of a mobile device. In this lesson you will learn additional features of the Accelerometer. When playing games on a mobile device, one of the most often used features is having objects move in response to the movement of the device. That is, the user tilts or rotates the device and an object moves. This could be as simple as a ball rolling around the screen or as complex as an avatar moving through a virtual environment. The device's built-in accelerometer controls this movement and ActionScript code in Flash controls the accelerometer. That is, ActionScript code is used to access the device's accelerometer and determine such things as the sensitivity of the object to the movement of the device and whether or not the object remains on the screen. Figure 25 shows the code to access the accelerometer and move the object (in this case a ball) based on the movement of the mobile device. *Note:* ActionScript is an

Object Oriented programming language. It is somewhat intuitive, meaning that the code is often easy to follow even though a person may have no programming experience. The following explanations are meant to give you an idea of how ActionScript is used to enhance an application. Detailed instructions are provided in the steps used in this lesson.

The following lines of code move the ball as the mobile device is moved.

ball.x −= event.accelerationX;

ball.y += event.accelerationY;

The first line of this code adjusts the x position of the object with the instance name ball according to the movement of the device along its x axis. The second line of code adjusts the y position of the object with the instance name ball according to the movement of the device along its y axis.

You can increase the sensitivity of the object by increasing the amount of movement of the object in relation to the movement of

Developing Mobile Applications

the device. This is done by multiplying the event.accelerationX and event.accelerationY by some number. For example, the lines of code listed next increase the x and y movement of the ball by a factor of 30 in relation to the movement of the device.

ball.y −= event.accelerationX*30;

ball.y += event.accelerationY*30;

Keeping the Object on the Screen

In most cases you want the object to remain on the Stage. If an object moves off the screen it may be difficult to have it reappear. The code that keeps the ball from moving off the Stage is shown in Figure 26 and discussed next. The screen size for this sample discussion is 480 wide and 800 high.

if (ball.x > (480 - ball.width / 2))

This line of code checks to see if the x position of the ball is greater than the width of the screen (480) minus the width of the ball divided by 2. This assumes the registration point (the point that is used to align the x and y coordinates) is in the middle of the ball. Thus, if the ball reaches the right edge of the screen the following code is executed:

{

ball.x = 480 - ball.width / 2;

}

Figure 25 *Code to access the device's accelerometer*

```
35
36    /* Move with Accelerometer
37    Allows the object to be moved by tilting the mobile device.
38
39    Instructions:
40    1. To increase or decrease the amount of movement, replace the
41    number 30 below with the number of pixels you want the symbol
42    instance to move when tilting the mobile device.
43    Note the number 30 appears twice in the code below.
44    */
45
46    var fl_Accelerometer:Accelerometer = new Accelerometer();
47    fl_Accelerometer.addEventListener(AccelerometerEvent.UPDATE, fl_AccelerometerUpdateHandler);
48
49    function fl_AccelerometerUpdateHandler(event:AccelerometerEvent):void
50    {
51        ball.x -= event.accelerationX*30;
52        ball.y += event.accelerationY*30;
53    }
54
```

Line 35 of 54, Col 1

Figure 26 *Code to keep the object on the screen*

```
23
24    if (ball.x > (480 - ball.width / 2)) {
25        ball.x = 480 - ball.width / 2;
26    }
27    if (ball.x < (0 + ball.width / 2)) {
28        ball.x = 0 + ball.width / 2;
29    }
30    if (ball.y > (800 - ball.width / 2)) {
31        ball.y = 800 - ball.width / 2;
32    }
33    if (ball.y < (0 + ball.width / 2)) {
34        ball.y = 0 + ball.width / 2;
35    }
36
```

Line 23 of 81, Col 1

This line of code sets the x position of the ball to 480 minus the width of the ball divided by 2. That is, it sets the right edge of the ball to the right edge of the screen.

```
if (ball.x < (0 + ball.width / 2)) {

    ball.x = 0 + ball.width / 2;

}

if (ball.y > (800 - ball.width / 2)) {

    ball.y = 800 - ball.width / 2;

}

if (ball.y < (0 + ball.width / 2)) {

    ball.y = 0 + ball.width / 2;

}
```

These twelve lines of the code keep the ball within the boundary of the screen. Each of the *if* statements checks the location of the ball based on its x or y coordinate and adjusts the location of the ball if necessary.

Using Templates

Flash provides several templates for developing mobile applications for Android and iOS devices. Figure 27 shows the New from Template dialog box with AIR for Android on the Templates tab selected. Selecting a template displays a preview screen and a description. In this case the Accelerometer template is selected, displaying a green ball on a black grid background and the description: "Android document with ball object reacting to accelerometer." Templates are useful for a number of reasons. First, they help in learning what a specific feature does, e.g., "What does the Accelerometer do?" Second, they help in learning how to incorporate a specific feature into an application by using the ActionScript code that is provided. Third, they can be used in prototyping to quickly explore an idea without costly in-depth development time. Fourth, they can be used as a starting place in creating an application by swapping and rearranging objects and enhancing the ActionScript code.

Using a Timer

A timer is a useful feature that is often used in games as the user competes to get the fastest time while completing an activity. Flash provides a code snippet that can be used to keep track of elapsed time. Because the elapsed time is tracked in a variable, the time

Figure 27 *The New from Template dialog box*

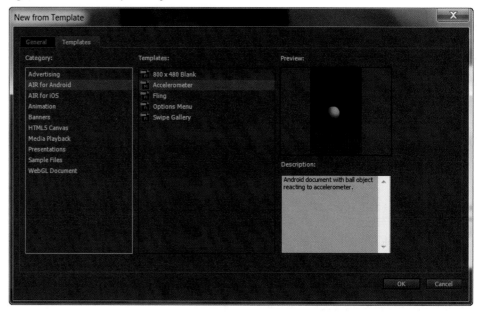

Developing Mobile Applications

is available to be used in other code such as displaying it in a text box on the screen. The code for creating a timer is shown in Figure 28 and selected lines of code are explained next.

var fl_TimerInstance:Timer = new Timer(1000, 30);

This line of code creates a variable named fl_TimerInstance and gives it a Timer data type (Variables are assigned data types to indicate what can be contained in the variable. For example, if a variable is assigned the Number data type it can contain only numeric characters.). The 1000 specifies 1000 milliseconds (1 second) as the time interval at which the timer is triggered. The 30 specifies the number of times the timer is triggered. Thus, the timer is triggered every second for 30 seconds. Both of these numbers can be changed.

var fl_SecondsElapsed:Number = 1;

This line of code creates a variable named fl_SecondsElaspsed, gives it a Number data type, and assigns an initial value of 1 to the variable.

{

trace("Seconds elapsed: " + fl_SecondsElapsed);

fl_SecondsElapsed++;

}

These last five lines of code create a trace statement that displays the elapsed seconds on the Output panel of the Timeline/Output panel set and, if desired, on the screen. This can be used for debugging the application. Also, the variable holding the elapsed seconds, fl_SecondsElapsed, is increased by one. Because the number of seconds that have elapsed is assigned to a variable, the number can be displayed within the application by simply displaying the variable. In this case a text box (instance name textb) that was created on the screen will display the variable (fl_SecondsElasped).

Providing Feedback to a User

Mobile applications, especially games, provide feedback to a user. For example, a game might indicate when two objects collide or how long an event takes to complete. One way to provide feedback is via a dynamic text box, which is a text box whose contents are controlled by ActionScript code. You use the Text tool to create a dynamic text box on the Stage and give the box an instance name so that it can be used in ActionScript code. You specify what you want to appear in the box whenever a specific event occurs. For example, you could have the words "A Hit" appear whenever the user causes two objects to collide. In addition, using a timer, you could have the text box display the number of seconds it took for the collision to occur.

Figure 28 *Code to create a timer*

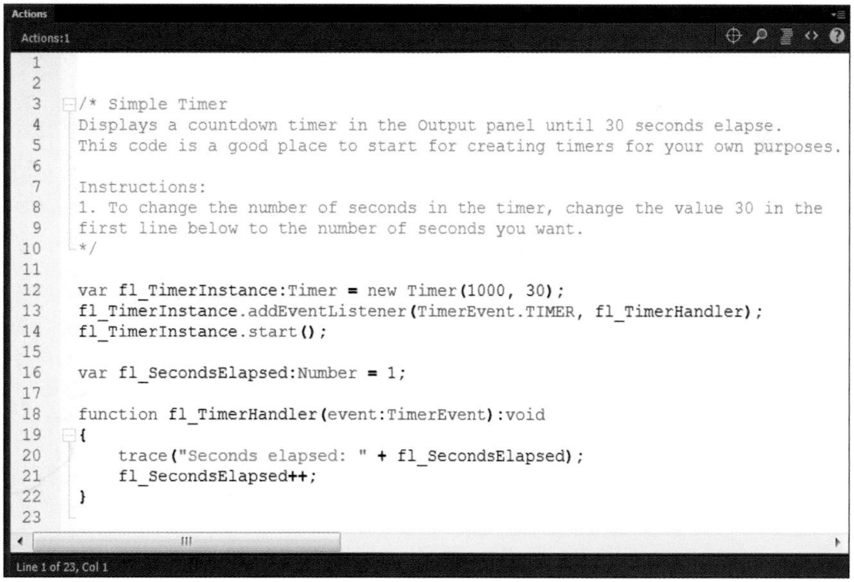

```
Actions
Actions:1                                                    ⊕ ρ ☰ ⟨⟩ ❷
 1
 2
 3    ⊟/* Simple Timer
 4     Displays a countdown timer in the Output panel until 30 seconds elapse.
 5     This code is a good place to start for creating timers for your own purposes.
 6
 7     Instructions:
 8     1. To change the number of seconds in the timer, change the value 30 in the
 9     first line below to the number of seconds you want.
10    └*/
11
12     var fl_TimerInstance:Timer = new Timer(1000, 30);
13     fl_TimerInstance.addEventListener(TimerEvent.TIMER, fl_TimerHandler);
14     fl_TimerInstance.start();
15
16     var fl_SecondsElapsed:Number = 1;
17
18     function fl_TimerHandler(event:TimerEvent):void
19    ⊟{
20         trace("Seconds elapsed: " + fl_SecondsElapsed);
21         fl_SecondsElapsed++;
22     }
23
◄              III                                                       ►
Line 1 of 23, Col 1
```

Use the Accelerometer

1. Click **File** on the menu bar, click **New**, then click the **Templates** tab.

2. Click **Air for Android** in the left pane of the New from Template dialog box, click **Accelerometer** in the right pane, then view the Preview window and read the description.

3. Click **OK**.

4. Change the view to **Fit in Window**.

5. Save the movie as **accel.fla**.

6. Click **Control** on the menu bar, point to **Test Movie**, then click **In AIR Debug Launcher (Mobile)**.

7. Click the **Settings button** ⚙ in the Simulator window, then click **Flat**.

8. Change the **X** setting to **–90** as shown in Figure 29, then press **[Enter]** (Win) or **[return]** (Mac).

9. Point to the center of the device in the Simulator window, hold down the mouse button, then rotate the **mouse** in a small circular motion to simulate moving the device.

   Notice how the ball in the AIR preview window moves as the device in the Simulator window moves and how it never leaves the screen.

TIP You can also place the pointers on other areas of the device in the Simulator window to manipulate it.

10. Close the AIR preview window.

   This closes the Simulator window and displays the Flash workspace.

You used the Mobile Content Simulator to test a Flash Accelerometer template.

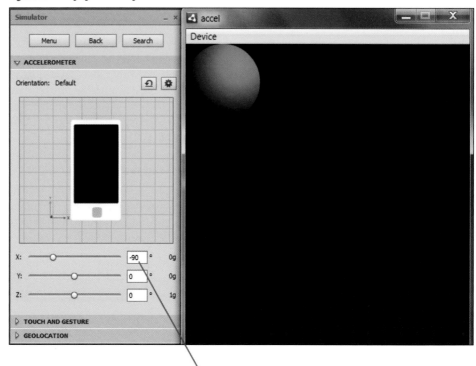

Figure 29 *Changing the X setting*

X value changed to –90

Developing Mobile Applications

Figure 30 *Displaying the open files*

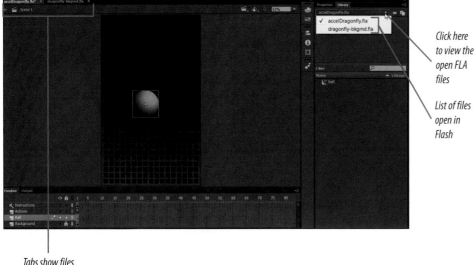

Click here to view the open FLA files

List of files open in Flash

Tabs show files open in Flash

1. Save the file as **accelDragonfly.fla**.

2. Change the frame rate to **30**.

3. Open **dragonfly-bkgrnd.fla** from the location where you store your data files.

4. Click **accelDragonFly.fla** at the top of the workspace to display the file, then click frame **1** on the Ball layer.

5. Display the Library panel, then click the **Open files list arrow** below the Library panel tab to display the files currently open in Flash, as shown in Figure 30.

6. Click **dragonfly-bkgrnd.fla** to display the Library contents for this file.

7. Drag the **animated dfly** movie clip to the Stage.

   This places the animated dfly movie clip and its associated graphics and symbols into the accelDragonfly.fla library.

8. Click the **Open files list arrow** below the Library panel tab, then click **accelDragonfly.fla** to display the contents of its library.

9. Click the **Selection tool** on the Tools panel, click the **dfly movie clip** on the Stage to select it, then press **[Delete]** to remove it from the Stage.

10. Click the **green ball** to select it, click **Modify** on the menu bar, point to **Symbol**, then click **Swap Symbol**.

    The Swap Symbol dialog box appears.

11. Click **animated dfly**, then click **OK**.

    The dfly movie clip symbol replaces the green ball movie clip symbol.

    (continued)

12. Click **Control** on the menu bar, point to **Test Movie**, then click **In AIR Debug Launcher (Mobile)**.

13. Click the **Settings button** in the Simulator window, then click **Flat**.

14. Change the **X** setting **–90**.

15. Point to the lower left of the device, hold down the mouse button, then **rotate** the mouse in a small circular motion to simulate moving the device.

16. Close the AIR preview window.

17. Display the **Timeline panel**, unlock the **Background layer**, click **frame 1** on the Background layer, click the stage, then press **[Delete]** to delete the background object.

    The Stage is a black gradient.

18. Display the Library panel, click the **Open files list arrow** below the Library panel tab to display the open files, then click **dragonfly-bkgrnd.fla** to display the Library contents for this file.

19. Verify frame 1 on the Background layer is selected, then drag the **trees movie clip** to the Stage and center it, as shown in Figure 31.

20. Test the movie using the in AIR Debug Launcher (Mobile) option, change the settings to flat and –90, then move the device to have the dragonfly circle the bottom tree and return to the top tree.

21. Close the AIR preview window.

22. Save your work, then close both applications.

You swapped symbols, changed the background of a movie, and tested it using the Mobile Content Simulator.

Figure 31 *Centering the trees movie clip on the Stage*

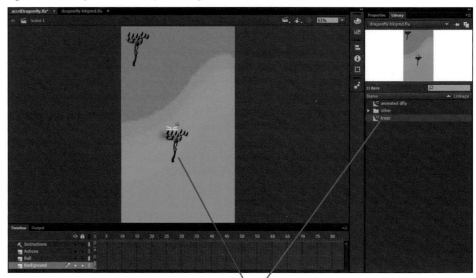

trees movie clip dragged from the Library panel and centered on the Stage

Developing Mobile Applications

Figure 32 *Positioning the circle*

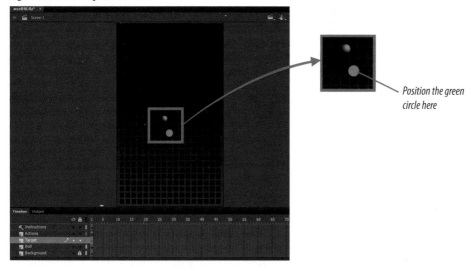

Position the green
circle here

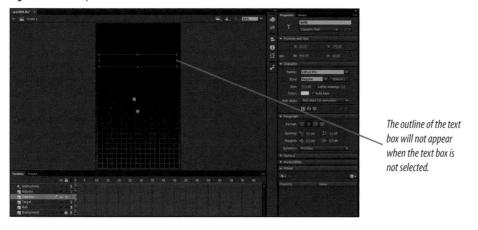

Figure 33 *The completed text box*

The outline of the text
box will not appear
when the text box is
not selected.

Add a target to an application

1. Open a new Air for Android Accelerometer template file, and save it as **accelHit.fla**.

2. Change the view to **Fit in Window**.

3. Click the **ball** on the Stage to select it, then use the Properties panel to change the ball size to **27 × 27**.

4. Insert a new layer above the Ball layer, then name it **Target**.

5. Click **frame 1** on the Target layer, then draw a circle on the Stage with size: **20 × 20**, fill color: **#00AA00**, and stroke set to **No Stroke**.

6. Position the circle as shown in Figure 32, then change the object to a movie clip symbol with the name **target_mc**.

7. Verify the circle is selected, then use the Properties panel to give it an instance name of **theTarget**.

8. Insert a layer above the Target layer, then name it **Text box**.

9. Click **frame 1** of the **Text box layer**, select the Text tool, then use the Properties panel to change the Text type to **Dynamic Text** with the following: Character Family: **Lithos Pro** (or use Arial if Lithos Pro is unavailable); Size: **40**; Color: **#CCCCCC**; Show border around text: **Deselected**; Paragraph Format: **Align center**; Behavior: **Multiline**.

10. Draw the text box near the top of the Stage, change the dimensions to Width: **440** and Height: **66**, center the text box across the Stage, then give it an instance name of **textb**.

    Your screen should resemble Figure 33.

11. Lock all layers, then save your work.

You created an object to be used as a target and added a dynamic text box.

Detect a collision and provide feedback

1. Change the frame rate to **20**.
2. Click **frame 1** on the Actions layer, then open the Actions panel.
3. Click the **Format Code icon** 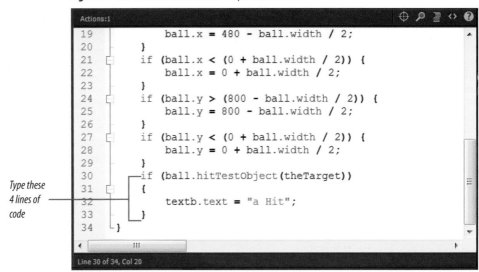 at the top of the Actions panel, then scroll to the bottom of the panel.
4. Click to the right of the second to last brace, press **[Enter]** Win or **[return]** Mac, and then type the following between the last two braces, as shown in Figure 34.

   if (ball.hitTestObject (theTarget))

   {

   textb.text = "a Hit";

   }

   This code checks to see if the ball collides with the green dot (instance name of theTarget) and, if so, the words "a Hit" are displayed in the text box named textb.

5. Click the **Format code icon** .
6. Close the Actions panel, then test the application using the Mobile Content Simulator and change the settings to flat and −90.

   TIP Change the settings to flat and −90 each time you are asked to test the application in the Mobile Content Simulator in this chapter.

7. Manipulate the Simulator in the Simulator window so that the ball in the AIR preview window collides with the green dot and notice the words "a Hit" are displayed in the dynamic text box.
8. Close the AIR preview window, then save your work.

You added ActionScript code to cause text to output when one object collides with another.

Figure 34 *The code to detect a collision and provide feedback*

```
19        ball.x = 480 - ball.width / 2;
20    }
21    if (ball.x < (0 + ball.width / 2)) {
22        ball.x = 0 + ball.width / 2;
23    }
24    if (ball.y > (800 - ball.width / 2)) {
25        ball.y = 800 - ball.width / 2;
26    }
27    if (ball.y < (0 + ball.width / 2)) {
28        ball.y = 0 + ball.width / 2;
29    }
30    if (ball.hitTestObject(theTarget))
31    {
32        textb.text = "a Hit";
33    }
34 }
```

Type these 4 lines of code

Actions:1

Line 30 of 34, Col 20

Figure 35 *Adding the code to cause the number of seconds to display in the text box*

```
31          {
32              textb.text = "a Hit";
33          }
34      }
35   /* Simple Timer
36   Displays a countdown timer in the Output panel until 30 seconds elapse.
37   This code is a good place to start for creating timers for your own purposes.
38
39   Instructions:
40   1. To change the number of seconds in the timer, change the value 30 in the f
41   */
42
43   var fl_TimerInstance:Timer = new Timer(1000, 30);
44   fl_TimerInstance.addEventListener(TimerEvent.TIMER, fl_TimerHandler);
45   fl_TimerInstance.start();
46
47   var fl_SecondsElapsed:Number = 1;
48
49   function fl_TimerHandler(event:TimerEvent):void
50   {
51       trace("Seconds elapsed: " + fl_SecondsElapsed);
52       fl_SecondsElapsed++;
53       textb.text = String(fl_SecondsElapsed);
54   }
55
```

Type this line of code

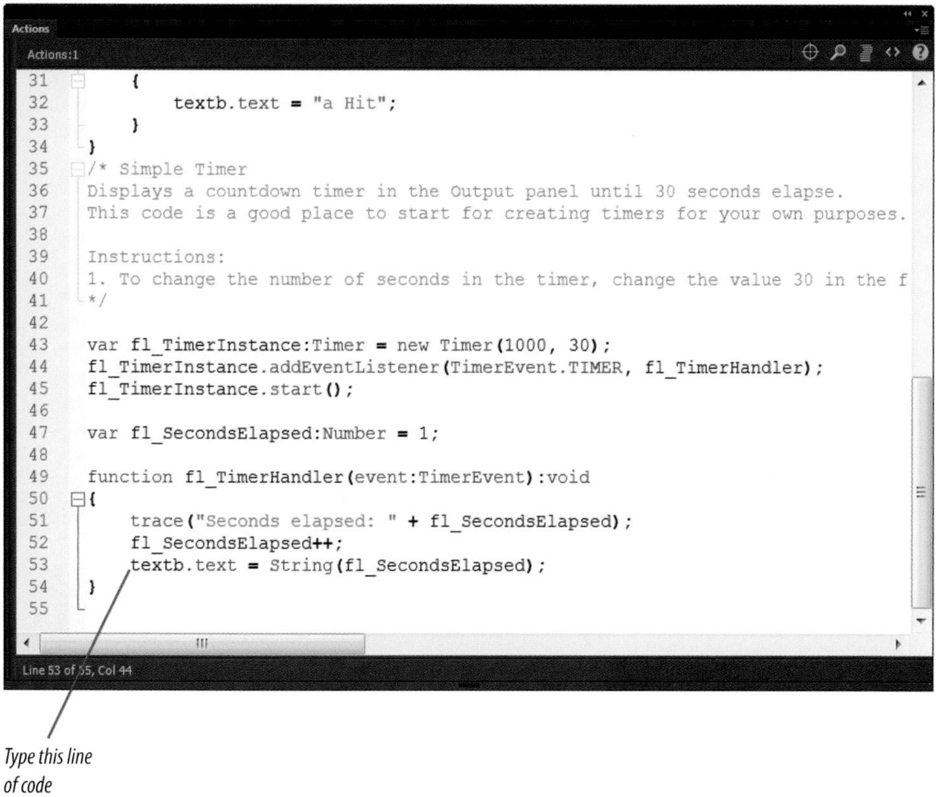

Add a timer to an application

1. Click **frame 1** on the Actions layer.

2. Click **Window** on the menu bar, then click **Code Snippets**.

3. Open the ActionScript folder, then open the Actions folder.

4. Double-click **Simple Timer**.

5. Display the Actions panel, then scroll to the bottom of the panel to view the timer code.

   Notice the variable that keeps track of the elapsed seconds is named fl_SecondsElapsed. You will use this variable to display the seconds in the dynamic text box you named textb.

6. Insert a line below fl_SecondsElapsed++; then type the following as shown in Figure 35:

   textb.text = String(fl_SecondsElapsed);

   This line of code causes the number of seconds to display in the text box.

7. Test the application using the Mobile Content Simulator and notice the timer running in the text box.

8. Manipulate the Simulator in the Simulator window so that the ball in the AIR preview window collides with the green dot and notice the words "a Hit" are again displayed in the dynamic text box.

9. Close the AIR preview window, then save your work.

You added a Code Snippet to cause the number of seconds on the timer to display in the text box.

Lesson 4   Use the Accelerometer

FLASH 4-35

Change the output in a dynamic text box

1. Display the Actions panel.

2. Change the textb.text = "a Hit"; line of code to:

   textb.text = ("a Hit at " + fl_SecondsElapsed + " seconds");

   Note that the code above breaks to two lines, but you should type it as one line on the Actions panel. This line of code causes the words "a Hit at" followed by the number of elapsed seconds followed by the word "seconds" to be displayed when the ball collides with the green dot.

3. Close the Actions panel, then test the application using the Mobile Content Simulator and notice the timer running in the text box.

4. Manipulate the Simulator in the Simulator window so that the ball in the AIR preview window collides with the green dot and notice the words "a Hit at (a number) seconds" are displayed in the dynamic text box as shown in Figure 36.

   Notice the words disappear and the timer continues to run. You can stop the timer and also have the ball disappear.

5. Close the AIR preview window.

   (continued)

Figure 36 *The text box displaying the text and the elapsed seconds*

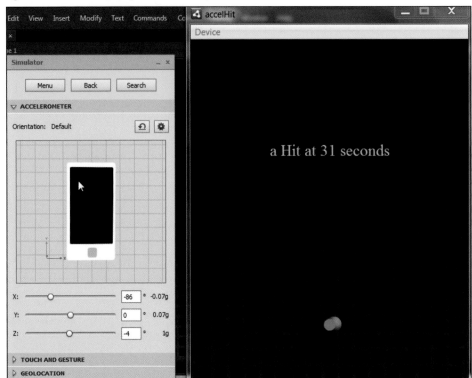

Developing Mobile Applications

Figure 37 *The code to stop the timer and remove the ball from the screen*

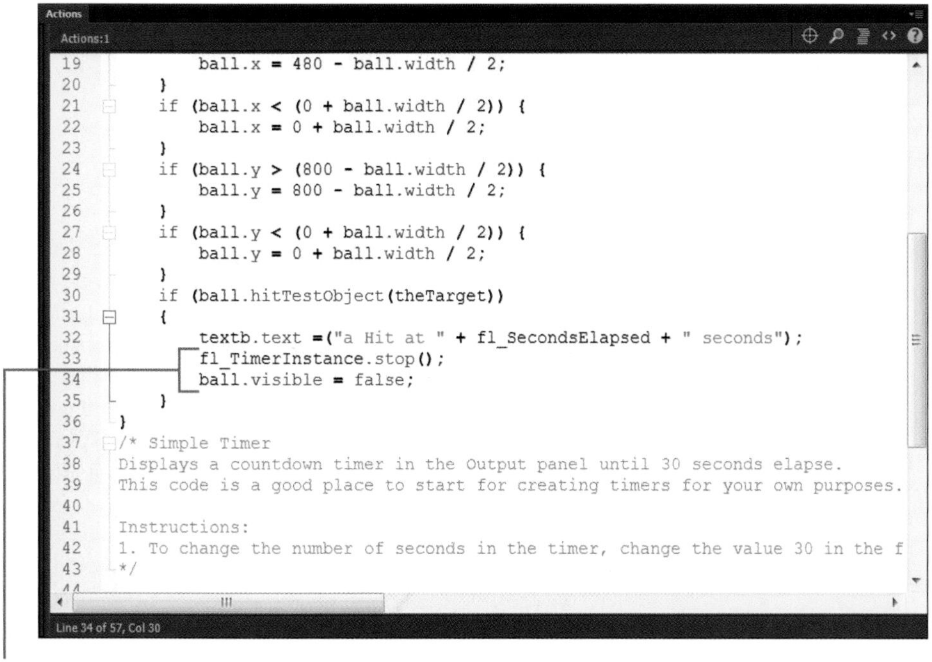

```
Actions
Actions:1                                                    ⊕ ρ ≡ <> ❼
19          ball.x = 480 - ball.width / 2;
20       }
21       if (ball.x < (0 + ball.width / 2)) {
22          ball.x = 0 + ball.width / 2;
23       }
24       if (ball.y > (800 - ball.width / 2)) {
25          ball.y = 800 - ball.width / 2;
26       }
27       if (ball.y < (0 + ball.width / 2)) {
28          ball.y = 0 + ball.width / 2;
29       }
30       if (ball.hitTestObject(theTarget))
31       {
32          textb.text =("a Hit at " + fl_SecondsElapsed + " seconds");
33          fl_TimerInstance.stop();
34          ball.visible = false;
35       }
36    }
37    /* Simple Timer
38    Displays a countdown timer in the Output panel until 30 seconds elapse.
39    This code is a good place to start for creating timers for your own purposes.
40
41    Instructions:
42    1. To change the number of seconds in the timer, change the value 30 in the f
43    */
44
Line 34 of 57, Col 30
```

Type these
2 lines of
code

6. Add the following two lines of code below the textb line as shown in Figure 37:

   fl_TimerInstance.stop();

   ball.visible = false;

   These two lines of code are placed within the opening and closing braces ({ }) of the *if* statement. The *if* statement checks to see if the ball collides with the dot, so the two lines of code are executed when the collision occurs. The first line stops the timer so that the number of seconds that has elapsed from the start of the application to the collision is displayed. The second line sets the visibility property of the ball to false which causes the ball to disappear.

7. Test the application using the Mobile Content Simulator and notice the timer running in the text box.

8. Manipulate the Simulator in the Simulator window so that the ball in the AIR preview window collides with the green dot.

   Notice that when the ball collides with the dot, the timer stops (that is, the seconds do not change) and the ball disappears.

9. Close the AIR preview window.

10. Save your work.

11. Close the application.

You added code to cause the output to specify an exact number, stop a timer, and cause an object to disappear from the screen.

LESSON 5

Use Touch and
GESTURE EVENTS

What You'll Do

Paintings courtesy B. VanDyke Shuman.

 In this lesson, you will use the Mobile Content Simulator to test touch and gesture events on a mobile device

Using Touch and Gesture Events

You can use the Mobile Content Simulator to test an application that includes Touch and Gesture events, such as drag, swipe, and zoom. You completed an example of the drag event with MGame-sim in Lesson 2. There are two ways to develop a swipe event. First, you could use the Code Snippet for the *Swipe to Go to Next/Previous Frame and Stop* mobile action. This mobile action can be used instead of clicking a button to move the playhead to the next or previous frame.

The Swipe Event code snippet is useful if you want to develop an application that allows the user to move back and forth through a series of frames. You can add this code snippet to an existing application. Second, you can use the Swipe Gallery template to add a swipe event

to a movie. Figure 38 shows the New from Template dialog box with the Swipe Gallery template selected. This template is useful if you want to develop an application that allows the user to move back and forth through a series of screens, such as a gallery of paintings. All of the screens are contained in a single frame. The Preview screen in Figure 38 shows the number 1 on a red background. This template contains four screens numbered 1–4, but only screen 1 is displayed. The other three screens, numbered 2–4, are off the right side of the Stage. The description says: "Android document with code for swipe gesture to slide a movie clip of items." Essentially, all four screens are contained in a movie clip, which in this template is called imageHolder, that can be swiped left to right or right to left to display one screen at a time. The swipe gesture event is similar to the code above except that the swipe gesture causes the movie clip to display the next or previous screen rather than the playhead moving to the next or previous frame. Because it is a movie clip you can add more screens as desired.

There is a fine distinction between the use of swiping to a frame and swiping to a screen. You use the swipe to frame when the content you have created is contained in frames. You use the swipe to screen when the content you have created is contained in a movie clip, where each frame in the movie clip is considered

a screen. Each screen contains a movie clip or other content. The content contained in the swipe movie clip (imageHolder) is stored as movie clip symbols (NobleEye_mc, WildBlue_mc, and WildGold_mc in the lesson example that follows). Generally, swiping to a screen is used when related content is displayed linearly, such as a series of photos. Swiping to a frame might be used to display distinct sections of an application, such as moving from a welcome screen to a main menu screen.

The zoom event allows the user to enlarge and reduce the size of a displayed object by pinching or spreading apart two fingers on the screen. This is especially useful with cell phones that have a small screen size. A Code Snippet (The Pinch to Zoom Event) can be used to create this event. Figure 39 shows the Code Snippets panel with the zoom options displayed within the Mobile Gesture Events folder.

Figure 38 *The New from Template dialog box with the Swipe Gallery template selected*

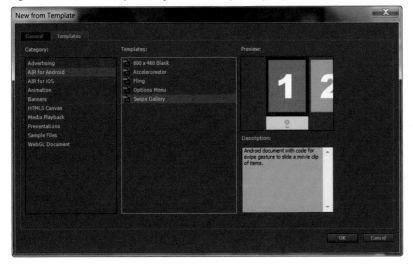

Figure 39 *The Pinch to Zoom Event option in the Code Snippets panel*

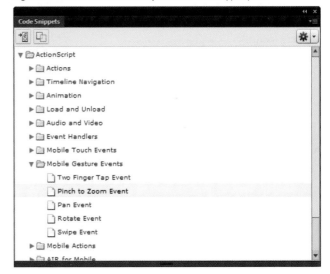

Use the swipe gesture

1. Click **File** on the menu bar, click **New**, click the **Templates tab**, click **AIR for Android**, click **Swipe Gallery**, then click **OK**.

2. Save the file as **WildHorses.fla**.

3. Change the view to **25%**.

   Notice the four objects. Each is about 425 × 575. The Stage is set to 480 × 800. The red object with the number 1 is currently on the Stage. The others are to the right of the Stage.

4. Click **Control** on the menu bar, point to **Test Movie**, then click **In AIR Debug Launcher (Mobile)**.

5. Click the **TOUCH AND GESTURE expand icon** , then click the **Touch layer check box** to select it.

6. Click the **Swipe radio button** to select it.

   The instructions on how to simulate the swipe action in the Mobile Content Simulator are listed in the Instructions area at the bottom of the Simulator window.

7. Point to the right side of the number 1, then notice the circle object that appears with the arrow cursor, as shown in Figure 40.

   This circle represents the user's touch point on their smartphone.

8. Press and slowly swipe to the **left**, then release the mouse.

9. Continue to swipe until the 4 is displayed, then swipe in the other direction until the **1** is displayed.

10. Close the AIR preview window to return to the Flash workspace.

   (continued)

Figure 40 *Pointing to the AIR preview window displays the circle object*

TOUCH AND GESTURE pane expanded

Touch layer check box

Swipe option button selected

Instruction area provides information about the selected Gesture option

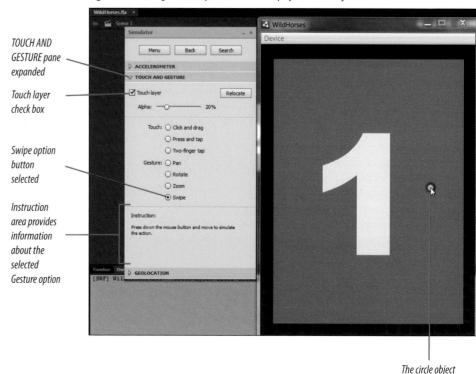

The circle object

Figure 41 *Deleting the number 2*

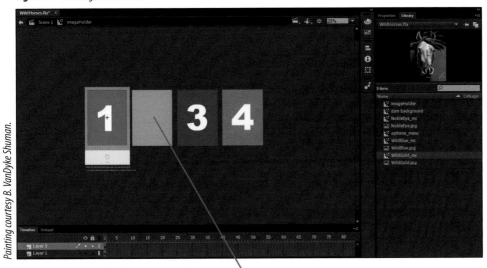

Painting courtesy B. VanDyke Shuman.

*If you delete the orange box instead of
the number 2, click Edit on the menu bar,
click Undo Delete, then repeat step 20.*

11. Change the view to **Fit in Window**.

12. Click **File** on the menu bar, click **Import**, then click **Import to Library**.

13. Navigate to your Data files, then import **NobleEye.jpg**, **WildBlue.jpg** and **WildGold.jpg** to the library.

14. Display the Library panel, then drag **NobleEye.jpg** to the Stage.

15. Verify the NobleEye.jpg object is selected, click **Modify** on the menu bar, click **Convert to Symbol**, change the symbol name to **NobleEye_mc**, select **Movie Clip** as the type, verify the registration point is set to center, then click **OK**.

    You can convert a jpg image into any symbol (movie clip, graphic or button). Converting it into a movie clip rather than a graphic symbol provides more flexibility if you decide to target the symbol in your ActionScript code.

16. Verify NobleEye_mc is selected on the Stage, then press **[Delete]** to remove it from the Stage.

17. Repeat Steps 14–16 for the other JPG files naming them **WildBlue_mc** and **WildGold_mc**.

18. Double-click **1** on the Stage to open the **imageHolder movie clip** in the edit window.

    The imageHolder movie clip is the default movie clip for the Swipe template. The movie clips you created using the jpg images will be nested in the swipe imageHolder movie clip.

19. Change the view to **25%**.

20. Click **2** in the orange box to select the number 2 only, then press **[Delete]** to remove it.

    Your screen should resemble Figure 41.

(continued)

21. Click the **orange placeholder**, click **Modify** on the menu bar, point to **Symbol**, then click **Swap Symbol**.

22. Click **NobleEye_mc** in the Swap Symbol dialog box, then click **OK**.

    Notice the horse graphic is tinted yellow. This is part of the Swipe Gallery template.

23. Display the Properties panel, then click the **Style list arrow** ▼ in the COLOR EFFECT area to display the list, as shown in Figure 42.

24. Click **None**.

25. Click 3 in the purple box to select the number 3 only, then press **[Delete]** to remove it.

26. Repeat Steps 21–24 for the **WildBlue.jpg** graphic swapping it for the purple placeholders and removing the tint.

27. Click 4 in the green box to select the number 4 only, then press **[Delete]** to remove it.

28. Repeat Steps 21–24 for the WildGold.jpg graphic swapping it for the green placeholder and removing the tint.

29. Change the view to **Fit in Window**.

30. Click **1** on the Stage to select it only the number 1, then press **[Delete]**.

(continued)

Figure 42 *The list of style options*

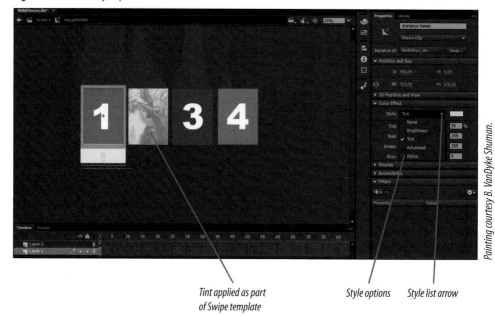

Tint applied as part of Swipe template

Style options

Style list arrow

Painting courtesy B. VanDyke Shuman.

Figure 43 *A title for screen 1*

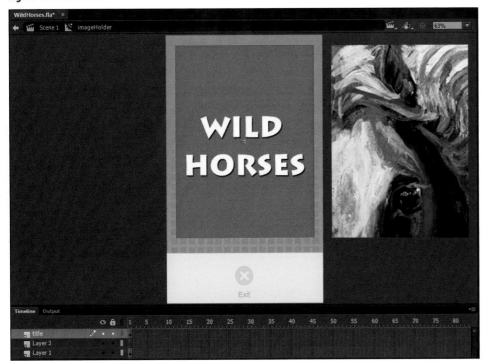

Painting courtesy B. VanDyke Shuman.

31. Insert a new layer at the top of the Timeline.

32. Name the layer **title**, then select Frame 1 on the layer.

33. Select the **Text tool** [T] on the Tools panel, then verify the Text type is set to Static Text on the Properties panel.

34. Using a font of your choice add a title to screen 1 similar to Figure 43.

35. Click **Scene 1** to return to the main timeline.

36. Click **Control** on the menu bar, point to **Test Movie**, then click **In AIR Debug Launcher (Mobile)**.

37. Click the **TOUCH AND GESTURE expand icon** [▷], then click the **Touch layer check box** to select it.

38. Click the **Swipe radio button** to select it.

39. Point to the right side of the text heading, then press and swipe until each of the 3 horses is displayed, then swipe in the other direction.

40. Close the AIR preview window.

41. Save your work.

You started a new AIR for Android Swipe Gallery template, swapped graphics, and tested the application in the Mobile Content Simulator.

Use the zoom gesture

1. Save the application as **WildHorsesZoom.fla**.

2. Click the Selection tool  on the Tools panel, then double-click the screen with the Wild Horses heading to display it in the edit window.

3. Click the **Wild Horses text** to select it.

4. Click **Modify** on the menu bar, then click **Convert to Symbol**.

5. Change the name to **WHtext_mc** and the type to **Movie Clip**, then click **OK**.

6. Verify the text is selected, then use the Properties panel to enter an instance name of **WHtext** as shown in Figure 44.

7. Click **Window** on the menu bar, then click **Code Snippets**.

8. Open the **ActionScript** folder.

9. Open the **Mobile Gesture Events** folder, then double-click **Pinch to Zoom Event**.

10. Close the Actions and Code Snippets panels.

11. Click **Scene 1** to return to the main Timeline.

12. Click **Control** on the menu bar, point to **Test Movie**, then click **In AIR Debug Launcher (Mobile)**.

(continued)

Figure 44 *Entering an instance name*

Painting courtesy B. VanDyke Shuman.

Instance name

Figure 45 *Setting the 1st touch point*

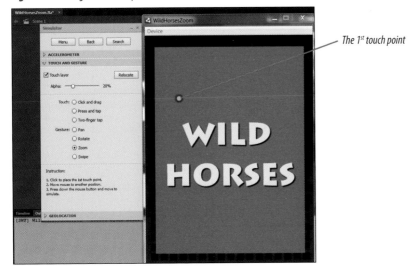

The 1st touch point

Figure 46 *Pointing to the position for the 2nd touch point*

The 2nd touch point

13. Click the **TOUCH AND GESTURE expand icon** ▷ , then click the **Touch layer check box** to select it.

14. Click the **Zoom option button** to select it.

15. Read the instructions at the bottom of the panel.

16. Click to set **touch point 1**, as shown in Figure 45.

    The touch point circle remains on the screen after you click. As you perform the next steps, keep in mind that you are simulating a pinching motion typically done with two fingers on a smartphone.

17. Point to the position shown in Figure 45, hold down but do not release the mouse button to identify touch point 2, slowly drag **touch point 2** toward touch point 1 until they touch, then drag **touch point 2** away from touch point 1.

    The text zooms in and out.

18. Click to set **touch point 1** above the text, point below the text, hold down but do not release the mouse button to identify touch point 2, slowly drag **touch point 2** toward touch point 1 until they pass each other, then drag **touch point 2** away from touch point 1.

    Notice the position of the touch points determines how the text will be shaped as the zoom occurs.

19. Close the AIR preview window.

20. Save then close the application.

You added a Code Snippet to allow for a zoom gesture and tested the feature in the mobile AIR debug launcher.

Repurpose an application and use the Mobile Content Simulator.

1. Open fl4_4.fla, then save it as **skillsDemo4-rep.fla**.

   This is a game in which the user tries to click a moving target. When the user clicks the End button, the number of hits is displayed. The stage size is 500 × 400. *Note*: A message may appear regarding fonts. If the fonts used in this file are not available on your computer, Flash will substitute another font.

2. Click Control on the menu bar, point to Test Movie, then click in Flash Professional.

3. Play the game, then close the Flash Player window.

4. Click Modify on the menu bar, then click Document.

5. Change the width to **480** and the height to **800**, a standard size for a smartphone.

6. Click the Scale content check box to select it, then click OK.

7. Change the view to Fit in Window.

8. Change the backdrop fill color and border to fit the new Stage size. (*Hint*: You can create a border by using the rectangle tool to draw a rectangle with no fill color.)

9. Change the Publish Setting target to AIR 13.0 for Android.

10. Test the movie in the Mobile Content Simulator.

11. Close the AIR preview window.

Add a mobile gesture event.

1. Click the Hit the Target Game heading on the Stage to select it.

2. Display the Code Snippets panel.

3. Select the Pinch to Zoom Event in the Mobile Gesture Events folder, then insert the code.

4. Test the application in the Mobile Content Simulator.

5. Display the Touch and Gesture settings.

6. Click the Touch layer check box to select it, then click the Zoom radio button.

7. Use the pointer to zoom the heading out.

8. Click the Touch layer check box to deselect it, then continue to play the game and compare your work to Figure 47. (*Note*: No touch gestures have been applied to the Go and End buttons and the heart, so you need to turn off the Touch layer to continue playing the game.)

9. Close the AIR preview window.

10. Save and close the application.

Use a template to create an Accelerometer application.

1. Open a new AIR for Android Accelerometer template application, then save it as **skillsDemo4-collide.fla**.

2. Select the green ball on the Stage and change the width and height to **30** pixels.

3. Draw a red ball with a height and width of **15** pixels and center the ball on the Stage. (*Hint*: Be sure the lock icon for the height and width is locked.)

4. Change the ball to a movie clip symbol with the name **rball_mc**.

5. Give the red ball an instance name of **rball**.

6. Verify the red ball is selected, then display the Code Snippets panel.

7. Expand the ActionScript folder, expand the Mobile Actions folder, then insert the Move with Accelerometer action.

8. Click frame 1 of the Actions layer, then display the Actions panel.

9. Scroll down the panel and review the code.

   Both balls will move in response to the movement of the device. However, notice the difference between the Accelerometer code for the green ball (instance name ball) and the red ball (instance name rball). The green ball, which is part of the template, contains code that keeps the ball on the Stage. The red ball, which is controlled by the code snippet does not have code to keep it on the Stage. This is intentional. The user will try to have the green ball collide with the red ball before the red ball moves off the Stage.

10. Close the Actions and Code Snippets panels, then display the Mobile Content Simulator.

11. Change the Accelerometer settings to Camera view: **Flat** and X: **−90**.

12. Slowly rotate the center of the simulator phone. Notice that both objects move.

13. Continue to move the phone until the red ball disappears.
14. Close the AIR preview window to return to the Flash workspace.

Add a timer.

1. Display the Code Snippets panel.
2. Open the ActionScript folder, open the Actions folder, then insert the Simple Timer code.
3. Display the Actions panel, then scroll to display the timer code, if necessary. (Notice the trace statement that is used to display the number of seconds that have elapsed proceeded by the words: "Seconds elapsed: ".)
4. Use the Mobile Content Simulator to test the application and notice how the Output panel displays the elapsed seconds but the seconds are not displayed in the AIR preview window. (*Note*: You may need to move the Mobile Content Simulator windows to view the Output panel.)
5. Close the AIR preview window.

Display elapsed time and add collision.

1. Add a layer and name it **text box**.
2. Select frame 1 of the text box layer, select the Text tool, then use the Properties panel to change the Text type from Static Text to Dynamic Text.
3. Change the settings for the dynamic text box to: **Arial**, **bold**, **20** pt, **white** color, **no border**, **center aligned**. (*Hint*: To create a text box with no border, you need to deselect the Show border around text option at the bottom of the Character are on the Properties panel.)

4. Draw the text box near the top of the Stage and center it across the Stage.
5. Give the text box an instance name of **textb**.
6. Click frame 1 on the actions layer, then display the Actions panel.

7. Type the following as one line of code beneath the ball.y += accelY * 30; line of code.
   textb.text = ("Elapsed time " + fl_SecondsElapsed + " seconds");
   This line of code displays a message indicating the amount of elapsed time.

Figure 47 *Completed Skills Review*

8. Use the Mobile Content Simulator to test the application, then notice the text and seconds that are displayed and compare your work to Figure 48.
9. Close the AIR preview window.
10. Click frame 1 on the Actions layer, display the Actions panel, then type the following code as the last *if* statement code, that is below the line that reads: ball.y = 0 + ball.width/2;.

    (*Note*: Be sure the code comes after the last curly brace (}) of the *if* statement for the ball.y = 0 + ball.width/2; line and before the curly brace (}) that follows the line.)

    (*Note*: The closing brace should be added automatically so you should not have to type it.)

    if (ball.hitTestObject(rball))

    {

    fl_TimerInstance.stop();

    rball.visible = false;

    }

    This code checks to see if the green ball (instance name ball) hits the red ball (instance name rball). If so, it stops the timer and has the red ball disappear. (*Note*: fl_TimerInstance may have an underscore (_) followed by a number appended to it. For example, it may display as fl_TimerInstance_2. This is caused by inserting more than one instance of the code.)
11. Use the Mobile Content Simulator to test the application.

12. Move the simulator phone until the balls collide and notice that the time stops and the red ball disappears.
13. Close the AIR preview window.
14. Save your work, then close the application.

(*Note*: You may want to change the application's frame rate and/or the size of the balls in order to change the difficulty of the application. Also, you could change the seconds for the timer so that it displays longer than 30 seconds.)

Figure 48 *Completed Skills Review*

Odyssey Adventure Tours would like you to create a prototype of a smartphone app that lets the user play a matching game involving currency symbols. To play the game, users drag and drop a currency symbol onto its name, as shown in Figure 49. If they get it correct, a message displays and if not, a different message appears. The prototype, which uses a Pound symbol for the currency, should be as simple as possible, using code snippets where appropriate.

Create the application.

1. Open a new AIR for Android application, save it as **odysseyTours4.fla**, then use Figure 49 as a guide to complete the steps that follow.
2. Change the Stage color.
3. Add a layer, name it, then create a heading.
4. Add a layer, name it, then create the four terms (Dollar, Euro, Yen, Pound).
5. Change each of the terms to a movie clip symbol with an appropriate name.
6. Give the Dollar, Euro and Yen movie clip terms appropriate instance names.
7. Give the Pound movie clip term the instance name: **pound**.
8. Add a layer, name it, then use the drawing tools to create a currency symbol.
9. Change the currency symbol to a movie clip with an appropriate name.
10. Give the currency movie clip the instance name: **pdcurrency**.
11. Add a layer, name it, then create a dynamic text box that will display the text "That's it!".
12. Give the text box the instance name: **textb**.
13. Select the currency symbol on the Stage, then display the Code Snippet panel.
14. Insert a Touch and Drag mobile touch event.
15. Click frame 1 of the Actions layer, display the Actions panel, then scroll to the bottom of the panel, if necessary.
16. Add the following 2 lines just below the event.target.stopTouchDrag(event.touchPointID); line but before the closing brace.

```
if (pdcurrency.hitTestObject(pound))
{
        textb.text = ("That's it!");
}
else
{
        textb.text = ("Sorry, try again.");
}
```

(*Note*: Watch carefully as you type the code. Remember that some closing braces are added automatically so do not type a duplicate brace. Your finished typed code should match the code in the book exactly.)

These lines test if the currency symbol (instance name pdcurrency) has hit the correct term (instance name pound). If so, the text *That's it!* displays in the text box (instance name textb). If not the text *Sorry, try again.* displays in the text box.

17. Click the Format Code button at the top of the Actions panel.
18. Save your work.

Test the application.

1. Open the Mobile Content Simulator, then expand the Touch and Gesture area.
2. Select the Touch layer check box, then drag and release the currency symbol several times to view the text that appears in the text box.
3. Close the AIR preview window.
4. Save your work, then close the application.

Figure 49 *Sample completed Project Builder 1*

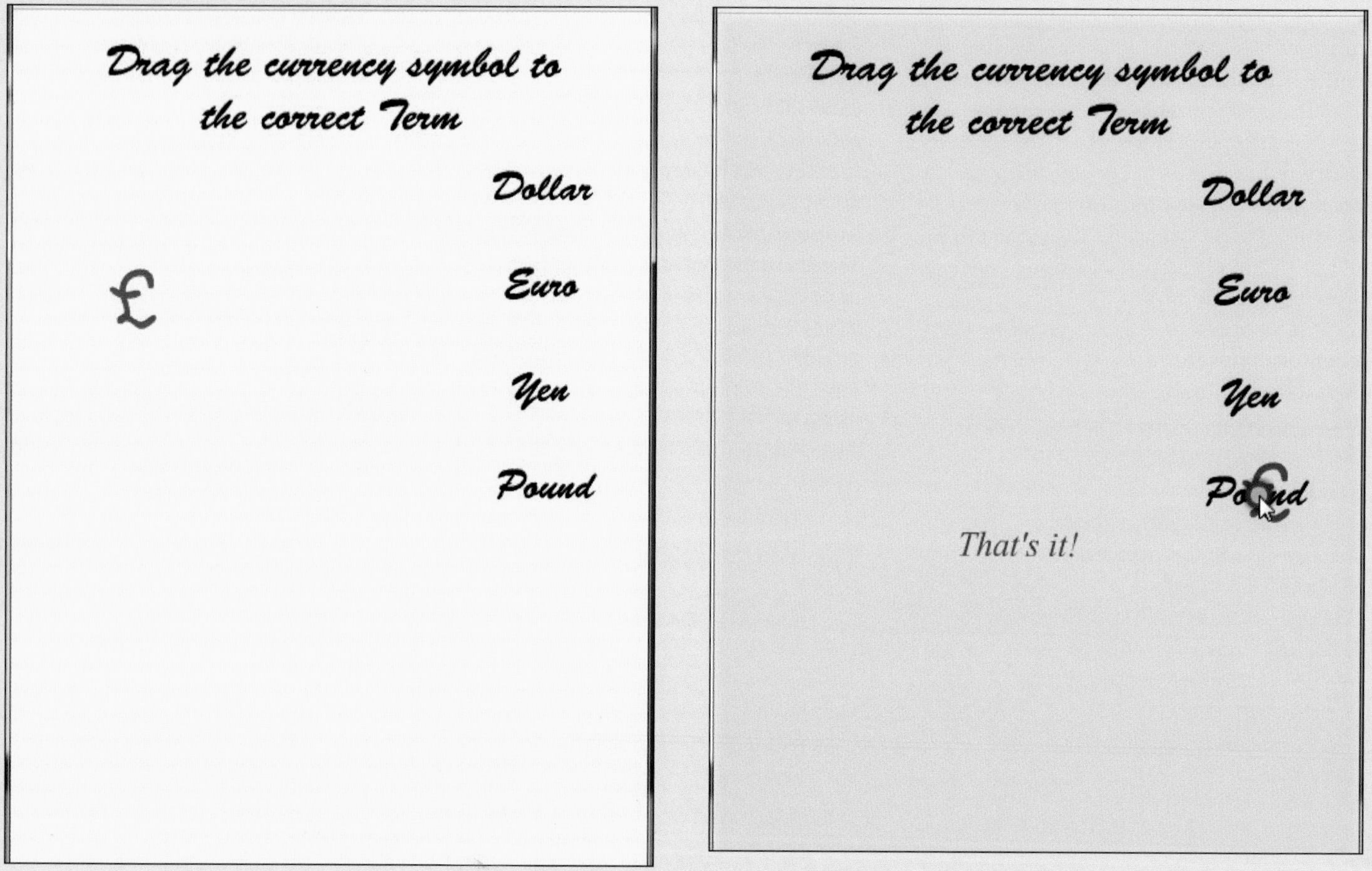

Drag the currency symbol to
the correct Term

Dollar

Euro

£

Yen

Pound

Drag the currency symbol to
the correct Term

Dollar

Euro

Yen

Pound

That's it!

You have been asked to develop a prototype application that demonstrates the use of the swipe event on a phone application. You will start with a template and repurpose it.

Use a template to create a swipe application.

1. Open a new AIR for Android Swipe Gallery template application, then save it as **swipePrototype.fla**.
2. Change the view to 50%.
3. Open the imageHolder movie clip in the edit window.
4. Click on a numbered screen and note the size of the graphic, which is smaller than the size of the Stage.
5. Return to the main Timeline.
6. Obtain three graphics, such as JPG photos, and resize them to fit the dimension of the swipe template

screen (that is, the colored area with the number). If you prefer, you can use the following three files included with your Data Files: Arc de Triomphe.jpg, Eiffel Tower.jpg, and Notre Dame.jpg.

7. Import the three graphics to the Library.
8. Drag each file to the stage, change it to a movie clip, and delete it from the Stage.
9. Open the imageHolder movie clip in the edit window and change the view to 50%.
10. Delete the number 1 on the first screen, then add a title, change it to a movie clip, and give it an instance name.
11. Delete the other numbers, swap symbols with the three new movie clips, and remove the tint from each image.
12. Return to the main Timeline.
13. Display the Mobile Content Simulator.

14. Use the Touch and Gesture Swipe gesture to display the screens.
15. Close the AIR preview window.

Add a zoom gesture.

1. Open the imageHolder in the edit window.
2. Select the movie clip on the second screen and give it an instance name.
3. Insert a Pinch to Zoom Event for the movie clip from the Mobile Gestures Events options.
4. Return to the main Timeline.
5. Display the Mobile Content Simulator.
6. Use the Touch and Gesture Swipe gesture to swipe and display the second screen.
7. Change to the Zoom gesture and zoom in and out on the screen.
8. Close the AIR preview window.
9. Save and close the application.

Figure 50 *Sample completed Project Builder 2*

Photos courtesy Jim Shuman.

Figure 51 shows a USA.gov mobile application that provides visualizations of near-real-time global climate data from NASA's fleet of Earth science satellites. Figure 51 shows the opening screen, a second screen, which contains a menu, and the two screens that show data.

1. Connect to the Internet, then go to http://www.nasa.gov/content/earth-right-now/#.VA4WtBauTFw.
2. Open a document in a word processor, save the file as **dpc4**, then answer the following questions.

   ■ Who is the audience for this app?
   ■ Could this application have been repurposed from a web site?
   ■ What mobile touch and gestures events might be used to enhance this application?
   ■ What suggestions would you make to improve the design, and why?

Figure 51 *Sample Design Project*

Source: http://www.nasa.gov/content/earth-right-now/#.VA4WtBauTFw

In this project you will repurpose an application for use on a smartphone and test it using the Mobile Content Simulator.

Resize the Stage.

1. Open fl4_5.fla, then save it as **portfolio4.fla**. (*Note*: You will need to have math.swf, shirt.swf, and shirt2.swf in the same folder as the portfolio4.fla because these files are loaded into the application when the user clicks specific buttons. The password for the clients only area is **password**.)
2. Test the application in the Flash player window by clicking the buttons, then close the Flash Player window.
3. Use the Document Settings dialog box to change the Stage dimensions to 480 width and 800 height, then choose to scale the content to the Stage.
4. Change the view to Fit in Window. Notice that the black border only encloses the top half of the stage.
5. Test the movie in the Flash player window and notice the graphics are displayed on the top half of the Stage.

Resize the Stage objects.

Note: You may want to lock and unlock layers as you work with the objects on the Stage so that you are only working with the desired objects.

1. Change the border to have it fit around the entire Stage. (*Hint*: Unlock the Border layer, select the border on the Stage and use the Properties panel to change the dimensions.)

2. Verify that the navigation buttons' white background fits the width of the Stage.
3. Move the top of the white background for the navigation buttons to the mid-point of the Stage.
4. Move the text My Portfolio above the white bar.
5. Move the navigation buttons so they are evenly spaced within the white bar.
6. Test the movie in the Flash player window, then close the window.
7. Save your work.

Change the publish settings for a mobile device.

1. Display Publish Settings dialog box.
2. Change the Target to AIR 13.0 for Android.
3. Click OK to accept the change and close the Publish setting dialog box.

Add mobile events.

1. Click the home button on the Stage to select it and notice the instance name displayed on the Properties panel.
2. Display the Code Snippets panel and insert the Pinch to Zoom Event which is located in the Mobile Gesture Events folder.
3. Test the application using the Content Simulator and use the Zoom gesture to have the button zoom in and out.
4. Close the AIR preview window.
5. Save and close the application.

Figure 52 *Sample completed Portfolio Project*

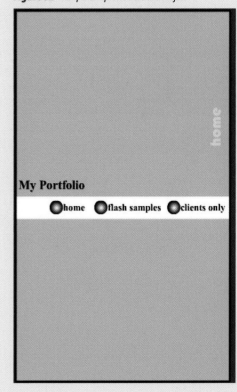

CHAPTER 5

SELECTING OPTIONS FOR
PUBLISHING
APPLICATIONS

1. Deliver Flash movies on the web using publish settings and as video files

2. Develop HTML5 Canvas documents

3. Publish AIR Applications

4. Understand Flash templates

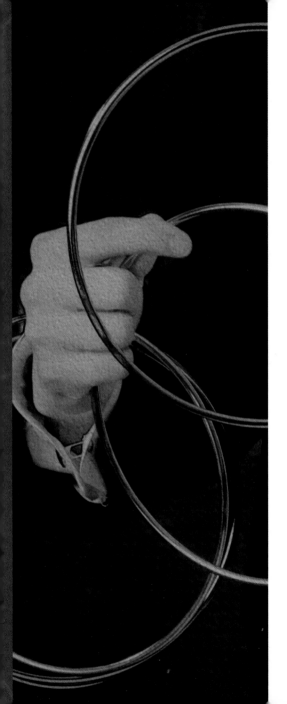

CHAPTER 5

SELECTING OPTIONS FOR PUBLISHING APPLICATIONS

Introduction

As you developed Flash applications in the preceding chapters, the focus has been on delivery through the web, using SWF files, and delivery through mobile devices using AIR for Android and AIR for iOS. Flash apps can also be delivered through stand-alone computers (AIR for desktops) and even TVs. The important thing is to determine the best delivery process to reach your target audience. In many cases, this may mean more than one delivery platform.

Adobe Flash Professional CC allows you to leverage your design and development efforts by making it easy to create an application that can be repurposed for delivery in various ways. That is, you can develop one Flash FLA file and publish it in several file formats. The three most common file formats for distributing Flash movies are Flash Player (.swf), Adobe AIR (.air), and HTML5 Canvas (.js). Flash Player and HTML5 files are used on websites for everything from interactive product demonstrations to banner ads. Adobe AIR files are used for a much broader range of applications, such as interactive games, tutorials, product demonstrations, and productivity software.

The Publish Settings feature of Flash is used to convert a Flash FLA movie to a SWF or an AIR format. You can use the Publish settings to customize an application by specifying quality, alignment, and transparency attributes. Both AIR and HTML5 file formats can be specified when you start a new Flash document or you can convert existing FLA document to AIR and HTML5 formats. Publishing a Flash FLA document for delivery in various ways does not necessarily require using the Publish Setting feature of Flash. For example, you can also export an application to video, including .mov and .mp4 formats, using the Export Video command in the File menu.

As you learned in Chapter 4, Flash provides templates that you can use as the basis for new projects. You can use all of a template, or just part of one.

In this chapter you will learn more about the Publish Settings feature of Flash, which you can use to repurpose applications for delivery on various platforms. You will also learn about exporting to a video file format. Finally, you will learn more about using Flash templates.

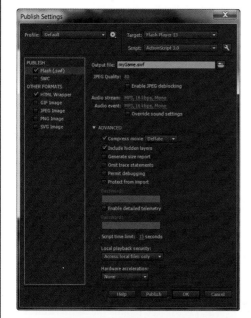

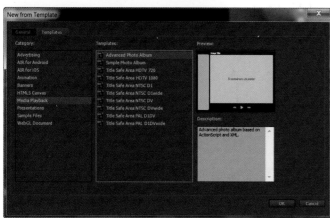

Deliver Flash Movies on the Web
USING PUBLISH SETTINGS AND AS VIDEO FILES

What You'll Do

© 2015 Cengage Learning®.

 In this lesson, you will import a video into a Flash document, change the Publish Settings, publish a Flash document for distribution on the web, insert a Flash SWF file into an HTML document, and export a Flash document as a video file.

Publishing a Movie

The Flash **Publish Settings** feature generates the files necessary to deliver Flash movies on the web. When you publish a movie using the default settings, a Flash SWF file is created that can be viewed using the Flash Player. In addition, an HTML file is created with the necessary code to instruct the browser to play the Flash file using the Flash Player. Figure 1 shows the Publish Settings dialog box with a list of the default formats for publishing a Flash movie. The Flash (.swf) and HTML Wrapper formats are selected. You can choose a combination of formats, and you can specify a different name (but not file extension) for each format. Other formats such as GIF, JPEG, and PNG are for still images that can be delivered on the web or within other applications.

When you select a format, its settings appear on the right side of the Publish Settings dialog box. Because the Flash (.swf) format is selected in Figure 1, the initial settings associated with that format are visible. To display the HTML Wrapper settings instead, you would click HTML Wrapper (the text, not the check box). The settings for the various formats allow you to specify:

- The target version of the Flash Player
- The version of ActionScript
- The desired quality for JPEG images and audio
- Other options, such as whether or not you want to compress the movie

The HTML file retains the same name as the Flash movie file, but with the file extension .html. Likewise, the SWF file has the same name as the Flash movie file, but with the .swf file extension.

So how does this work exactly? Let's consider an example. Publishing a movie named myGame.fla generates two files by default: myGame.html and myGame.swf. Figure 2 shows sample HTML code referencing a Flash Player movie in the HTML file. The movie source is set to myGame.swf; the display dimensions (determined by the size of the Stage) are set to 550 × 400; and the background color is set to black (#000000). You could use an HTML editor to change the settings rather than making changes in Flash. For example, if you wanted to change the background color to white, you could replace #000000 with #ffffff.

Inserting a SWF File into an HTML Document

Another way to deliver a Flash movie on the web is to import it into an HTML document. To accomplish this, you open the HTML document in Dreamweaver, then select the Flash SWF option from the Media command on the Insert menu. The Select SWF dialog box appears, allowing you to specify the SWF file to insert.

Figure 1 *Publish Settings dialog box*

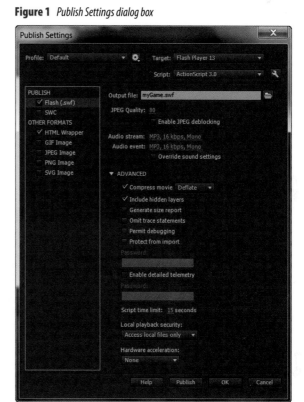

Figure 2 *Sample HTML code*

Stage width and height

```
<object type="application/x-shockwave-flash"
data="myGame.swf" width="550" height="400" id="myGame"
style="float: none; vertical-align:middle">
            <param name="movie" value="myGame.swf" />
            <param name="quality" value="high" />
            <param name="bgcolor" value="#000000" />
            <param name="play" value="true" />
            <param name="loop" value="true" />
            <param name="wmode" value="window" />
```

Movie name

Background color

Exporting to Video

A third way to deliver a Flash movie on the web is as a **video file**, such as an MP4 file. To do this, you start by creating a Flash application and saving it as a FLA file. Next, you select the Export Video command from the File menu. The Export Video dialog box appears, allowing you to specify where to save the video file. The Adobe Media Encoder dialog box appears, allowing you specify the output file format as shown in Figure 3. You click the green arrow button to complete the encoding process. The video file is saved to the drive and folder you specified in the Export Video dialog box. The video file can be inserted into a web site or played in a video player such as QuickTime.

QUICK TIP

The Flash Player is not needed to play a video file.

Figure 3 *The Adobe Media Encoder*

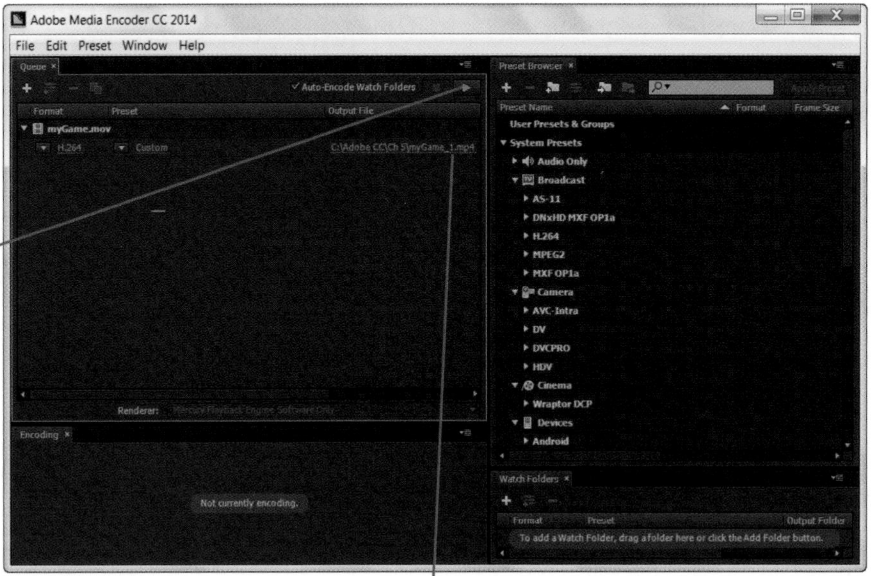

Click green arrow button to complete the encoding process

Output file

Figure 4 *The heading centered at the top of the Stage*

Static Text

Figure 5 *The completed Import Video dialog box*

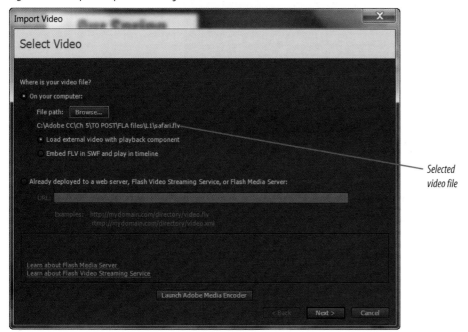

Selected video file

Import a video into a Flash document

1. Open a new ActionScript 3.0 document, then save it as **bannerAd.fla**.

2. Rename Layer 1 **heading**.

3. Change the Stage dimension to **320px** wide and **550px** high, then change the view to **Fit in Window**.

4. Click the **Text tool** on the Tools panel, display the Properties panel, then verify the Text type is set to Static Text.

5. Add the heading **Our Spring Special** with the following properties: Font: **Impact** (or a font of your choice); Size: **44pt**; Color: **#009900**.

6. Center the heading at the top of the Stage as shown in Figure 4.

7. Add a new layer and name it **video**.

8. Click **File** on the menu bar, point to **Import**, then click **Import Video**.

   The Import Video dialog box appears, allowing you to select the video to import.

9. Click the **Browse** button, then navigate to the drive and folder where your Data Files are stored.

10. Click **safari.flv**, then click **Open**.

    Your dialog box should resemble Figure 5, although your File path may differ.

    (continued)

11. Click **Next** to display the Skinning dialog box. This dialog box allows you to choose from a variety of playback controls, colors, and sizes.

12. Click the **Skin list arrow** to display the list of skins, as shown in Figure 6.

13. Click **SkinOverAllNoFullNoCaption.swf**.

14. Click **Next**.

15. Read the Finish Video Import dialog box text, then click **Finish**.

16. If necessary, position the video near the middle of the Stage.

(continued)

Figure 6 *The list of skins*

Skin list arrow

Working with Skins

When importing a video into a Flash document, you need to select a **skin**, which is a group of settings that determines the appearance and position of the play controls. Skins come in several varieties. For example, you could choose a skin that includes buttons for start, pause, rewind, audio on/off, and volume level. When selecting a skin, you can also choose the color used as a backdrop for the controls. You use the Skinning dialog box to select a skin and the background color.

Selecting Options for Publishing Applications

Figure 7 *The completed document*

17. Add a new layer, then name it **caption**.

18. Add the caption **Africa Untamed** below the video with the following properties: Font: **Trajan Pro 3** (or a font of your choice); Size: **44pt**; Style: **Bold**; Color: **#009900**. Type the word "UNTAMED" on a separate line, left-align the text, and use spaces to indent "UNTAMED."

    Your screen should resemble Figure 7.

19. Save the document.

You started a new Flash document, resized the Stage, added text, and imported a video into the document.

Publish a movie and change the Publish Settings

1. Click **Control** on the menu bar, point to **Test Movie**, then click **In Flash Professional**.

2. View the movie, then close the Flash Player window.

3. Click **File** on the menu bar, then click **Publish Settings**.

4. On the left side of the dialog box, verify that Flash (.swf) and HTML Wrapper are the only check boxes selected.

(continued)

5. On the left side of the dialog box, click **HTML Wrapper** (the text, not the check box) to view the HTML settings.

6. Click the **HTML alignment list arrow**, then click **Right** as shown in Figure 8.

   This will cause the banner to be displayed on the right side of the browser.

7. Click **Publish**, then click **OK**.

8. Use your file management program to navigate to the drive and folder where your saved documents are stored.

   Notice the files with the .swf and .html extensions. The HTML document is the wrapper that your browser uses to display the SWF movie. A second SWF file (named SkinOverAllNoFullINOCaption.swf) is used to display the skin for the video.

9. Return to Flash.

10. Click **Control** on the menu bar, point to **Test Movie**, then click **In Browser**.

    Notice the banner is on the right side of the browser widow.

11. View the movie, then close the browser window.

12. Save, then close the document.

You published a movie, changed the Publish Settings, and viewed the movie in both the Flash Player window and a browser.

Figure 8 *Changing the alignment option*

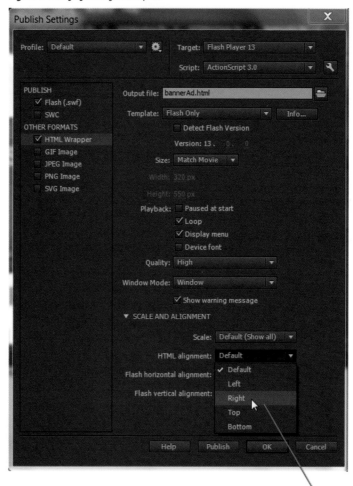

Right alignment

Selecting Options for Publishing Applications

Figure 9 *The Flash SWF placeholder*

©iStock.com/sbayram.

Flash SWF
placeholder

Insert a Flash SWF file into an HTML document

1. Start Dreamweaver.

2. Open fl5_1.html, then save it as **OATBanner**.

   Note: If a message appears asking to update links, click Yes.

3. Click the right side of the document to display an insertion line.

4. Click **Insert** on the Menu bar, point to **Media**, then click **Flash SWF**.

5. Navigate to the drive and folder where your Data Files are stored, click **bannerAd.swf**, then click **OK**.

6. Type **spring special video** in the Object Tag Accessibility Attributes dialog box, then click **OK**.

   The Flash SWF placeholder appears in the HTML document as shown in Figure 9.

7. Save the Dreamweaver document.

   Note: A Copy Dependent Files dialog box may be displayed. If so, click OK.

8. Click **File** on the menu bar, point to **Preview in Browser**, then click **Internet Explorer**.

   Note: When using Internet Explorer you may receive a message indicating that the web page is restricted from running scripts or ActiveX controls. In that case, click Allow blocked content.

9. View the web page and test the controls on the video player.

10. Close the browser window.

11. In Dreamweaver, click the **Flash SWF placeholder** to select it.

12. Click the **Wmode list button** on the Properties panel at the bottom of the screen, then click **transparent** as shown in Figure 10.

    This makes the Stage color of the SWF file transparent, revealing the web page's background color.

13. Save the document, click **File** on the menu bar, point to **Preview in Browser**, then click **Internet Explorer**.

14. Preview the web page in the browser and notice the banner ad's transparency.

15. Close the browser.

16. Close the document, then exit Dreamweaver.

You inserted a Flash SWF file into an HTML document, made changes to the file's properties, and viewed the file in a browser.

Figure 10 *Selecting the transparency setting*

©iStock.com/sbayram.

transparency setting

Selecting Options for Publishing Applications

Figure 11 *The Adobe Media Encoder dialog box*

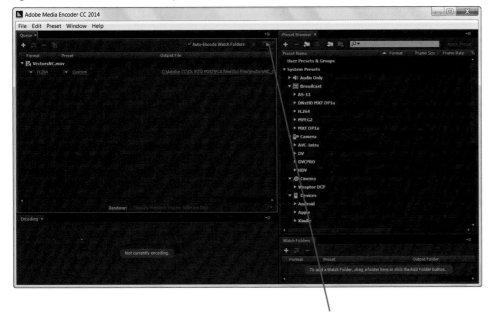

Start Queue (Return) button

Export a Flash document as a video file

1. Open fl5_2.fla and save it as **VectorsNC**.
2. Test the movie, then close the Flash Player window.
3. Click **File** on the menu bar, point to **Export**, then click **Export Video**.

   The Export Video dialog box appears.
4. Verify that the Convert video in Adobe Media Encoder check box is selected, then click the **Export** button.

   The Adobe Media Encoder window opens, as shown in Figure 11.

TIP The Adobe Media Encoder is a separate program and may take a few moments to open. Also, it may appear on the taskbar (Win) or Dock (Mac) and need to be opened from there.

5. Click the **Start Queue (Return) button** (the green arrow) to start the conversion process.
6. When the process is complete, click **File** on the Adobe Media Encoder dialog box, then click **Exit**.
7. Navigate to the drive and folder where your solution files are stored and notice the VectorsNC_1.mp4 video file.
8. Play the **VectorsNC_1.mp4** video file.
9. Close the video player.
10. Save, then close the document.

You used Adobe Media Encoder to create an MP4 video file from a Flash document.

Develop HTML5
CANVAS DOCUMENTS

What You'll Do

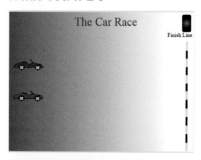

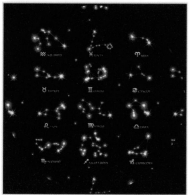

©iStock.com/Ola-Ola. Image courtesy Jim Shuman.

 In this lesson, you will convert a Flash document to an HTML5 Canvas document, and create an HTML5 Canvas document from scratch.

Using HTML5 Canvas in Flash Professional CC

The **canvas** element in HTML5 is used to turn images, photos, charts, and graphs into animated objects on a web page. You can use it to build graphics, animations, games, and interactive video. This makes it easy to transform a plain web page into a dynamic web site or mobile device application. To use the canvas element in Flash, you need to create an **HMTL5 Canvas document**. JavaScript code, rather than ActionScript code, is used in HTML5 Canvas documents. However, you do not need to write JavaScript code to create HTML5 Canvas documents. Instead, Flash provides code snippets that automatically create the necessary JavaScript code. The canvas element consists of a region of a web page defined in HTML5 code, with height and width attributes. JavaScript code then creates the content that is displayed in that region.

QUICK TIP

While you can use the HTML5 canvas element to generate graphics and animations, it offers limited options for developing applications compared to Flash. The advantage of generating HTML5 Canvas content is that the content is embedded in the web page and does not need the Flash Player plugin.

You can use the skills you've learned so far to develop HTML5 Canvas content from within Flash. In addition, you can convert applications that you previously built in Flash to HTML5 Canvas applications. There are two ways to create an HTML5 Canvas document in Flash. You can create it from scratch, or you can convert an existing Flash document to an HTML5 Canvas document. To start from scratch, you need to select the HTML5 Canvas option when creating a new document. After you save and publish the document, the word "Canvas" is appended to the name of the FLA file and two additional files are created: an HTML file with the code required to display the Canvas element content; and a JScript Script file (.js) that contains the JavaScript code used to create and manipulate the content. Figure 12 shows some JavaScript code generated by Flash for HTML5 Canvas content consisting of a white rectangle with a width of 80px and a height of 60px, that is centered on the Stage with coordinates of X:275 and Y:200. (*Note:* The file shown in Figure 12 has been edited to focus on specific code.) As you can see, JavaScript is similar in syntax to ActionScript.

When you a create HTML5 Canvas document from scratch, Flash might create an images and/or sounds folder to store images and sound, in addition to the .js and .html files. Figure 13 shows the HTML (.html) and Jscript Script (.js) files in the directory and drive where the original FLA file was saved.

To convert an existing Flash document to HTML5 Canvas content, open an existing FLA file, click the Commands menu, and then click Convert to HTML5 Canvas from AS3 document formats. When you convert a Flash document, keep in mind that Flash is a more robust content development tool than HTML5 Canvas. In other words, not all Flash features are available in the canvas element. In many cases, Flash converts unavailable features to features an HTML5 Canvas document recognizes. For example, dotted lines are not available in an HTML5 Canvas document, so they are automatically replaced with solid lines. Therefore, when repurposing an existing Flash document some tweaking may be necessary. It's important to keep an eye on the Output panel, which will display messages related to unsupported content. In addition, because HTML5 utilizes JavaScript as the scripting language, ActionScript code is grayed out on the Actions panel and must be replaced with JavaScript. To make this easier, Flash provides JavaScript code snippets that can easily be inserted into an HTML5 Canvas document.

In this lesson you will convert a Flash application to an HTML5 Canvas document. You will also create a new HTML5 Canvas document from scratch. You will be working with the Code Snippets and Actions panels.

When you select an action from the Code Snippets panel, the Actions panel appears automatically and displays the code. Your workspace may become cluttered when these panels are open. You can minimize, close or move a panel to make it easier to work. Keep in mind that you can use the [F9] key to open and close the Actions panel.

Figure 12 *JavaScript code to create a rectangle*

```
// library properties:
lib.properties = {
        width: 550,
        height: 400,
        fps: 24,
        color: "#000000",
        manifest: []   };

// stage content:
(lib.rectangle1 = function() {
        this.initialize();

// Layer 1
this.shape = new cjs.Shape();
this.shape.graphics.f("#FFFFFF").s().p

this.addChild(this.shape);
}).prototype = p = new cjs.Container();
p.nominalBounds = new cjs.Rectangle(275,200,80,60);
```

Stage and movie properties

Stage color

Rectangle position on the Stage
X: 275
Y: 200

Rectangle dimensions
80px wide
60px high

Figure 13 *The files created when developing an HTML5 Canvas document*

rectangle1	Flash Document	3 KB
rectangle1	HTML Document	1 KB
rectangle1	JScript Script File	1 KB

Convert a Flash document to an HTML5 Canvas document

1. Open fl5_3.fla, then save it as **carRace.fla**.

2. **Test** the movie in a browser, then close the browser.

   This is the Flash document completed in Chapter 2.

3. Click **Commands** on the menu bar, then click **Convert to HTML5 Canvas from AS3 document formats**.

   The Save File dialog box appears.

4. Type **carRaceCVS** for the file name, then click **Save**.

   Notice the document name near the top of the Flash window is *carRaceCVS.fla (Canvas)*, indicating that the document is formatted as an HTML5 Canvas document.

5. If necessary, click the **Output tab,** as shown in Figure 14, to display the Output panel, then read the messages.

   Five warnings are listed on the Output panel. Each issue was resolved, either through conversion or removal.

   TIP At this point in your HTML5 Canvas education, you don't need to understand all the warnings on the Output panel. But it is a good idea to check the Output panel to make sure all problems have been resolved one way or another.

6. Click **Control** on the menu bar, then point to **Test Movie**.

   Notice that the In Flash Professional option is not available. That's because you need to test HTML5 Canvas documents in a browser instead of in the Flash Player.

7. Click **In Browser**.

   The movie plays despite the warnings. However, notice the movie does not stop and the buttons

   (continued)

Figure 14 *The Output panel displaying warnings*

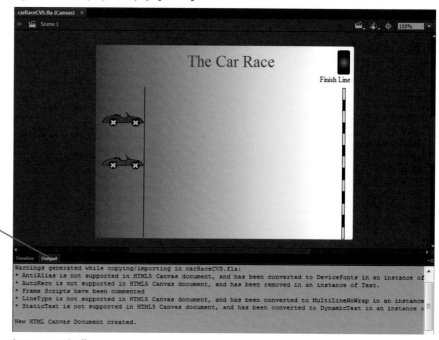

Output tab

Image courtesy Jim Shuman.

Figure 15 *Changing the frame to go to*

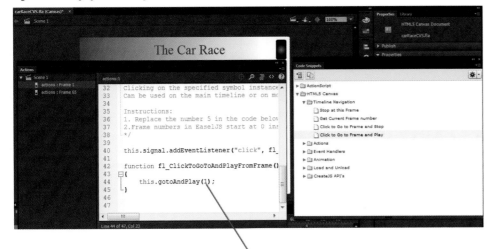

Change the 5 to 1

are not functioning. This is because HTML5 Canvas documents require JavaScript instead of ActionScript.

8. Close the browser.

9. Display the Timeline, then click Frame **1** on the actions layer.

10. Click **Window** on the menu bar, then click **Actions** to open the Actions panel.

   Notice the ActionScript code appears in light gray, indicating that it is not functional. You need to replace this code with two stop actions and two goto actions. You can insert these using code snippets.

11. Click **Window** on the menu bar, then click **Code Snippets**.

12. Open the **HTML5 Canvas folder**, then open the **Timeline Navigation folder**.

13. Double-click **Stop at this Frame**.

14. Review the newly inserted JavaScript code on the Actions panel, then scroll up to review the grayed out ActionScript code for the same action and notice the slight difference in syntax between the two types of code.

15. Minimize the Actions panel, click the **Selection tool** on the tools panel if necessary, then click the **signal button** on the Stage to select it.

16. Display the Code Snippets panel, open the **HTML5 Canvas** and **Timeline Navigation** folders, then double-click **Click to Go to Frame and Play**.

17. Display the Actions panel and change the frame number of the frame to go and play from 5 to **1** as shown in Figure 15.

TIP You need to change the frame number to 1 in this case because JavaScript frame numbers start at 0 instead of 1.

(continued)

18. Display the Timeline panel, then click frame **65** on the actions layer.

19. Display the Code Snippets panel, then double-click **Stop at this Frame**.

20. Close the Actions panel, then click the **Reset button** on the Stage to select it.

21. Display the Code Snippets panel, then double-click **Click to Go to Frame and Play**.

22. Display the Actions panel, then change the frame number of the frame to go and play from 5 to **0** as shown in Figure 16.

23. Close the Actions and Code Snippets panels.

24. Click **Control** on the menu bar, point to **Test Movie**, then click **In Browser**.

25. Click the signal and Reset buttons, then close the browser.

26. Save and close the HTML5 Canvas document.

27. Navigate to the location where your Data Files are stored and notice the JavaScript file (with the file type Jscript Script) named **carRaceCVS.js**.

    This is the file that contains the JavaScript code for the HTML5 Canvas document.

28. Close your file management program and display Flash CC.

You converted a Flash document to an HTML5 Canvas document.

Figure 16 *Changing the frame to go to*

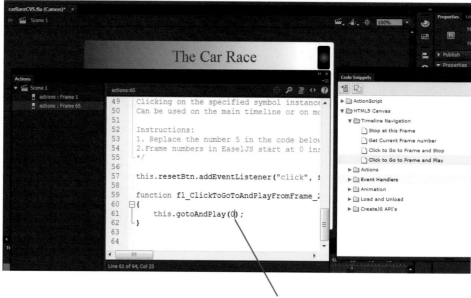

Change the 5 to 0

Selecting Options for Publishing Applications

Figure 17 *The sky-image object centered on the Stage*

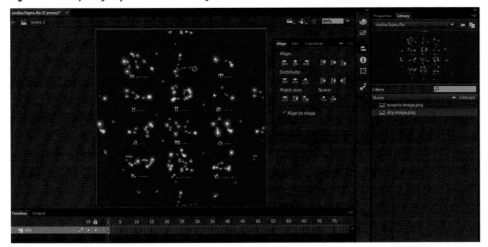

©iStock.com/Ola-Ola.

Create an HTML5 Canvas document

1. Click **File** on the menu bar, then click **New**.

2. Double-click **HTML5 Canvas** in the General tab of the New Document dialog box.

3. Save the document as **zodiacSigns.fla**.

4. Change the Stage dimensions to **540 × 540** and the Stage color to **#1C176B**.

5. Change the view to **Fit in Window.**

6. Click **File** on the menu bar, point to **Import**, then click **Import to Library**.

7. Navigate to the directory and folder where your Data Files are stored, click **sky-image.png**, then click **Open**.

8. Repeat Steps 6 and 7 and import **scorpio-image**.

9. Change the name of Layer 1 to **sky**, click a blank area of the Stage, then click Frame **1** of the sky layer.

10. Drag the **sky-image** icon from the Library to the Stage, then **center** it on the Stage as shown in Figure 17.

11. Click **Modify** on the menu bar, then click **Convert to Symbol**.

12. Change the symbol type to **Movie Clip** and the name to **sky_mc**, then click **OK**.

13. Display the Properties panel and give the object an instance name of **sky**.

14. Click **Insert** on the menu bar, then click **Motion Tween**.

15. Click Frame **1** on the sky layer, then use the Properties panel to set the rotate value to **1** and the direction to **CW**.

(continued)

16. Click Frame **1** on the sky layer, click the object to select it, click the **Style list arrow** in the Color Effect area of the Properties panel, click **Alpha**, then change the Alpha setting to **0**, if necessary.

17. Click Frame 24 on the sky layer, click within the outline of the object on the Stage, then change the alpha setting to **100**.

18. Click **Insert** on the menu bar, click **New Symbol**, change the name to **scorpio_btn** and the type to **Button**, then click **OK**.

    The edit window for the scorpio_btn object appears.

19. Draw a **120px** by **80px** rectangle with **no stroke** and a **white** fill in the center of the edit window, as shown in Figure 18.

20. In the Timeline, click the **Hit frame**, click **Insert** on the menu bar, point to **Timeline**, click **Keyframe**, then click **Scene 1** to return to the main Timeline.

21. Insert a new layer, then name it **scorpio button**.

22. Click the Selection tool [icon] on the Tools pane, click a blank area of the Stage, then insert a keyframe in frame **24** of the scorpio button layer.

23. Verify that frame 24 on the scorpio button layer is selected, then drag the **scorpio_btn** icon [icon] from the Library panel to cover the scorpio image on the Stage, as shown in Figure 19.

24. Use the Properties panel to change the Alpha setting for the button to **0**, then give the button an instance name of **scorpioBtn**.

25. Insert a new layer, name it **scorpio screen**, then insert a keyframe in frame **25** of the scorpio screen layer.

(continued)

Figure 18 *Drawing the button symbol*

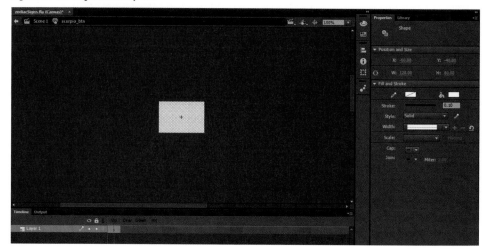

Figure 19 *Positioning the button*

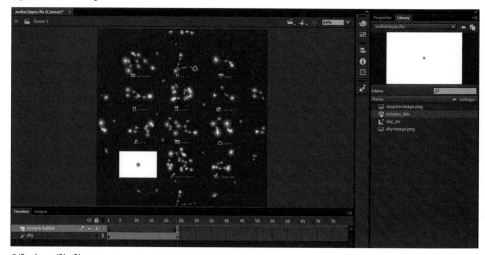

©iStock.com/Ola-Ola.

Selecting Options for Publishing Applications

Figure 20 *Typing the subheading*

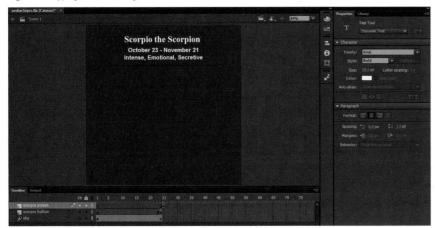

Figure 21 *Changing the go to frame number*

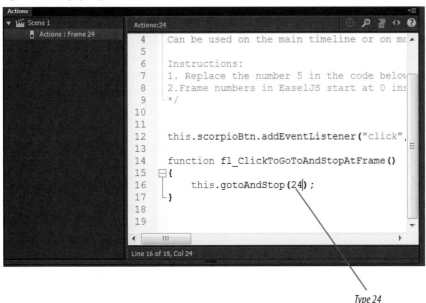

Type 24

26. Select the **Text** tool on the Tools menu, then set the text properties to: Text type: **Dynamic Text**; Font: **Charlemagne Std** (or a font of your choice); Size: **30pt**; Color: **white**.

27. Click the Stage, type the heading: **Scorpio the Scorpion** and then center the text.

28. Click a blank area of the Stage, change the font to **Arial**, the style to **Bold** and the size to **20,** then type, center, and position the subheading as shown in Figure 20.

29. Click the **Selection tool** on the Tools panel, display the Library panel, drag the **scorpio-image** icon to the Stage, then center the object on the Stage.

30. Click frame **24** on the scorpio button layer, then click inside the button object outline on the Stage.

31. Display the Code Snippets panel, open the **HTML5 Canvas folder**, open the **Timeline Navigation folder**, then double-click **Click to Go to Frame and Stop**.

32. Display the Actions panel, then change the frame number to go to from 5 to **24**, as shown in Figure 21.

33. Click frame **24** on the Actions layer, then double-click **Stop at this Frame** on the Code Snippets panel.

34. Insert a keyframe in frame 25 of the Actions layer, then use the Code Snippets panel to insert a **Stop at this Frame** action.

35. Change the frame rate to **8**.

36. Test the movie in a browser, click the scorpio image, then close the browser.

37. Save, then close the document.

You created an HTML5 Canvas document and tested it in a browser.

Publish AIR
APPLICATIONS

What You'll Do

© 2015 Cengage Learning®.

 In this lesson, you will publish a Flash AIR application for stand-alone delivery.

Understanding the Development Process for AIR Applications

Flash provides a technology, AIR (Adobe Integrated Runtime), which creates applications that can be played without a browser. An AIR app can be displayed on stand-alone computers, on the Internet, and even on television sets. AIR applications are cross-platform, which means they will play on different operating systems such as Windows and Apple computers. In addition, the AIR format allows a developer to create a single application and deliver it on multiple devices. This saves development time and money as the same content can be repurposed for different audiences. You can create an AIR application from scratch by choosing the AIR for Desktop option displayed when you choose New from the File menu. In addition you can repurpose an existing Flash application for delivery on various devices by simply changing the publish settings. However, there are always considerations that must be taken into account as content is repurposed. For example, the screen size of mobile devices requires a different design than the screen size of typical desktop computers. In this lesson you will repurpose

a Flash application so it plays as a stand-alone application on a desktop computer.

The process for creating an AIR application is similar to the process for creating mobile apps covered in Chapter 4. There are several files that are created when publishing an AIR app including the descriptor and installer files required to deploy it. Flash creates the application descriptor XML file, which contains the settings, the installer file that is used to install the application on a computer, and the SWF file when you publish the AIR application. You specify the settings for these files in the AIR Settings dialog box. Once you have created an AIR file, this dialog box can be opened from either the document Properties panel or the Publish Settings option on the File menu.

Figure 22 shows the Publish Settings dialog box with the default settings Flash (.swf), HTML Wrapper, and Flash Player 13.0. To create an AIR file you need to change the Publish Target setting from Flash Player to AIR 13.0 for Desktop, as shown in Figure 23. Then you need to open the AIR Settings dialog box and complete the settings contained within four tabs, as shown in Figure 24 and explained next. *Note*: A wrench icon appears next to the

Target option and can be used to open the AIR Settings dialog box.

Settings on the General Tab

The General tab of the AIR Settings dialog box contains the following options:

Output file: Name and location of the AIR file to be created when using the Publish command. The .air file extension indicates an AIR package file.

Output as: AIR package allows cross-platform delivery. Windows Installer provides a specific Windows installer (.exe) instead of a platform-independent AIR installer (.air).

App name: Name used by the AIR application installer to generate the application filename and the application folder. The AIR application name defaults to the name of the SWF file.

Version: Specifies a version number for the AIR application you are creating.

App ID: Identifies the AIR application with a unique ID.

Description: Used to enter a description of the AIR application, which is displayed in the installer window when the user installs the AIR application.

Copyright: Used to enter a copyright notice.

Window style: Used to specify the window style for the user interface when the user runs the AIR application on a computer.

Render mode: Used to specify whether to use the computer's CPU or graphics card when displaying images.

Profiles: Used in the programming process when targeting various devices.

Included Files: Used to add files, such as video or sound files, to the AIR application package. By default, the AIR application descriptor XML file and the main SWF file are automatically included.

Figure 22 *The Publish Settings dialog box with the default settings*

Figure 23 *Changing the Target setting*

Figure 24 *The four tabs on the AIR Settings dialog box with the General tab displayed*

Settings on the Signature Tab

Figure 25 shows the AIR Settings dialog box with the Signature tab active. You use the settings on this tab to create a certificate, or digital signature, for your application. This certificate identifies the publisher of the application and assures the user of the AIR application that the application is authentic.

Settings on the Icons Tab

Figure 26 shows the AIR Settings dialog box with the Icons tab active. An icon is the graphic that displays after you install the application and run it in the Adobe AIR runtime. It could be a logo, a drawing that represents the app, or any graphic created by the developer. You use the settings on the Icons tab to specify icons for the application. For instance, the Icons tab in the AIR Settings dialog box allows you to specify four different square sizes for an icon (16, 32, 48, and 128 pixels) to allow for the different views in which the icon appears. For example, the icon can appear in a web browser in thumbnail, detail, and tile views. It can also appear as a desktop icon and in the title of the AIR application window, as well as in other places. The icons need to be PNG file types. You can create PNG files using graphics programs such as Adobe Fireworks and Photoshop.

Settings on the Advanced Tab

Figure 27 shows the AIR Settings dialog box with the Advanced tab active. When you publish an AIR application for delivery as a stand-alone application, the user needs to install the application on a computer. You use settings on the Advanced tab to specify additional settings for the installation. For example, you can specify associated file types, size and placement of the initial window used to view the application, folder in which the application is installed, and Program menu folder in which to place the file.

Figure 25 *Signature tab settings*

Figure 26 *Icons tab settings*

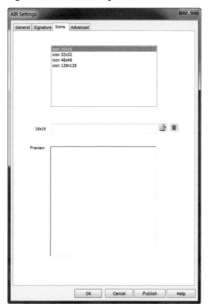

Figure 27 *Advanced tab settings*

Selecting Options for Publishing Applications

Figure 28 *Changing the General settings*

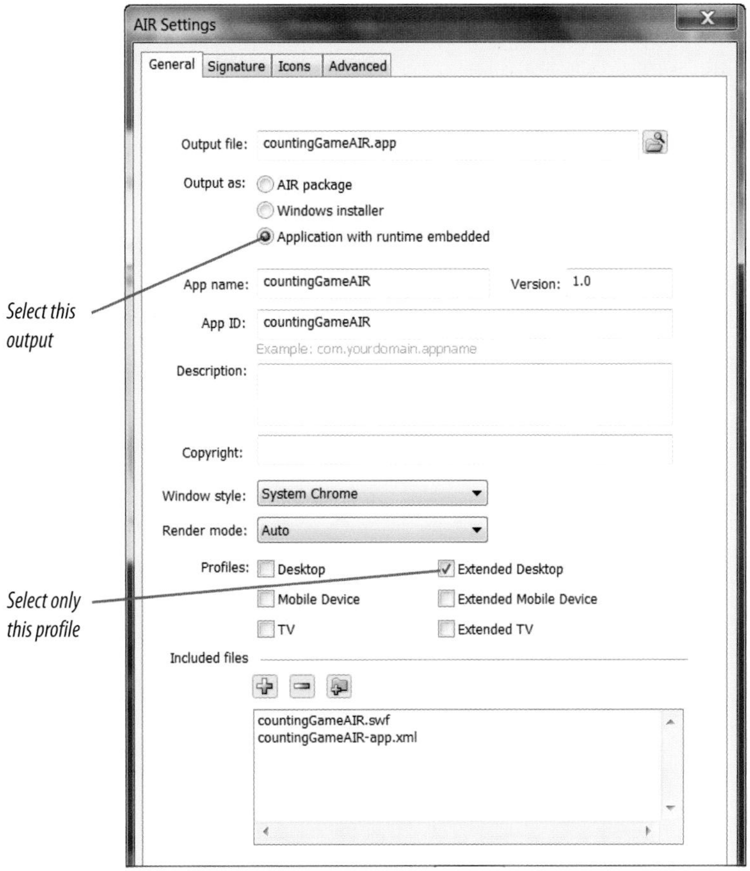

Select this output

Select only this profile

1. Open fl5_4.fla, then save it as **countingGameAIR.fla**.

2. Click **Control** on the menu bar, point to **Test Movie**, then click **In Flash Professional**.

3. Play the game, then close the Flash Player window.

4. Click **File** on the menu bar, then click **Publish Settings**.

5. Deselect HTML Wrapper, click the **Target list arrow**, then click **AIR 13.0 for Desktop** (or the latest version of AIR).

6. Click **Publish** at the bottom of the dialog box, then click the **General** tab in the AIR Settings dialog box.

7. Click **Application with runtime embedded** for the output.

8. Deselect all of the profiles except for Extended Desktop as shown in Figure 28.

9. Click the **Signature** tab, then click **Create** (Win) to display the Create Self-Designed Digital Certificate dialog box or **New** (Mac) to display the AIR Settings dialog box.

(continued)

10. Fill in the Publisher name, Organization unit, Organization name, Password, and Confirm password fields.

    Note: You can use any data you desire as you fill in the sample form, as shown in Figure 29.

11. Click **Browse** to open the Select File Destination dialog box (Win) or the Select Certificate Destination dialog box (Mac).

    By default, the file name for the certificate matches the document name.

12. Click **Save**, then click **OK** in the Certificate (Win) or AIR Settings (Mac) dialog box.

    In a moment a message appears indicating that the certificate has been created.

13. Click **OK** to close the message box.

14. Verify the Signature tab is displayed, then enter your **password**.

15. Click the Icons tab, click **icon 48x48**, then click the Search Folder icon 🔍.

16. Select **countICON48.png**, then click **Open**.

17. Click **Publish**.

    In a few moments the message "Application with runtime embedded has been created" (Win) or "The application has been successfully published" (Mac) appears.

18. Click **OK** to close the message box.

19. Click **OK** in the AIR Settings dialog box, then click **OK** in the Publish Settings dialog box.

    (continued)

Figure 29 *A sample completed Digital Certificate dialog box*

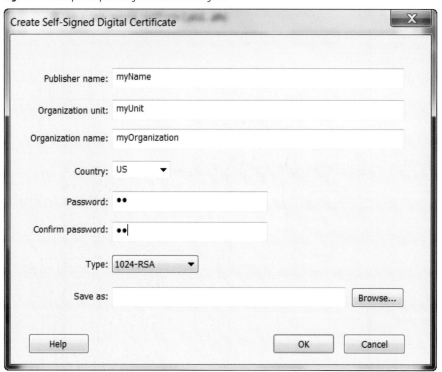

Selecting Options for Publishing Applications

Figure 30 *The AIR Preview window displaying an app*

Icon indicates the AIR
Preview window (Win)

© 2015 Cengage Learning®.

20. Click **Control** on the menu bar, point to **Test Movie**, then click **In AIR Debug Launcher (Desktop)**.

Notice the application is played in the AIR Preview window as shown in Figure 30, not the Flash Player Preview window.

21. Close the AIR Preview window.

22. Navigate to the drive and folder where you files are stored, then display the files for the countingGame.

23. Double-click the **countingGameAIR** application icon to launch the application.

Note: The countingGameAIR application icon may be stored in a folder named countingGameAIR.app.

TIP You could place this icon on the user's desktop for easy access.

24. Play the game, then close the application window.

The application plays in an application window rather than the Flash Player window.

25. Close the application window, display Flash, then save and close the application.

You repurposed a Flash document as an AIR application and played the application without a browser.

Understand FLASH TEMPLATES

What You'll Do

© 2015 Cengage Learning®.

 In this lesson, you will open and test a template, and add content to an AIR template.

Selecting the Appropriate Template

Adobe Flash Professional CC provides a number of templates that can be used as starting points for your project. For example, you could use the Load Video template to create a banner that displays a video, or the Advanced Photo Album template that displays a series of photos with user controls and captions. In addition, you can use individual elements from a template in your own Flash document. For example, you could use a button from the Animated Button Text Glow template or a cursor from the Custom Mouse Cursor Sample template. Figure 31

Figure 31 *Templates tab displaying categories and associated list of templates*

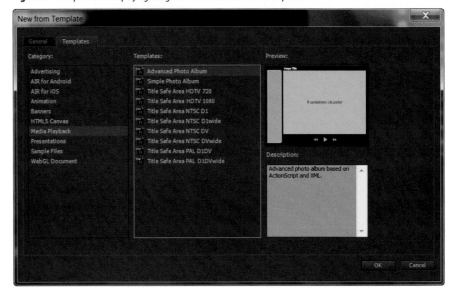

shows the Templates tab for the New From Template dialog box that is accessed from the New option on the File menu. There are ten categories of templates, with several templates in each category, each with an image and description. Figure 31 shows the Advanced Photo Album template from the Media Playback category selected with an image in the Preview window and a description. Figure 32 shows the same template on the Stage. The template categories are explained below:

- **Advertising:** Common Stage sizes used in online ads.
- **Air for Android:** Samples of popular mobile app features.
- **Air for iOS:** Common screen sizes for iOS mobile devices.
- **Animation:** Common types of animations, including animated buttons, masks and samples.
- **Banners:** Common sizes and functionality used in website interfaces.
- **HTML5 Canvas:** Sample animations and games.

- **Media Playback:** Photo albums and playback of several video dimensions and aspect ratios.
- **Presentations:** Simple and complex presentation styles.
- **Sample Files:** Examples of commonly used features in Flash Professional CC.

- **WebGL Document:** Sample animation for a WebGL document.

Figure 32 *The Advanced Photo Album template with instructions*

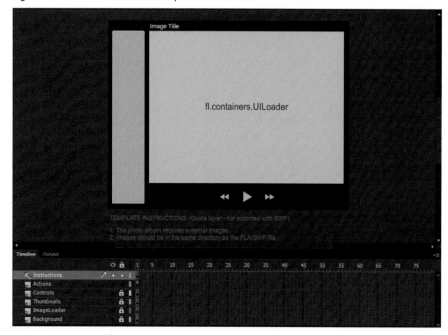

Open and test a template

1. Click **File** on the menu bar, then click **New** to display the New Document dialog box.

2. Click the **Templates** tab, click a category and a template within that category, then read the description.

3. Continue to read descriptions of other templates, then, in the Category list, click **Sample Files**.

4. In the Templates list, click **AIR Window Sample**, read the description, then click **OK**.

5. Save the document as **AIRWinSamp.fla**.

6. Change the name of Layer 1 to **layout**.

7. Click **Control** on the menu bar, point to **Test Movie**, then click **In AIR Debug Launcher (Desktop)**.

   The app appears in the AIR Preview window with orange and black minimize, maximize and close buttons as shown in Figure 33. Currently, the app has no content.

TIP Note that the AIR Preview window has its own buttons in the upper-right corner of the title. In these steps, however, you are only concerned with the orange and black buttons.

8. Click the **minimize button** and notice that the app icon appears on the taskbar (Win) or on the Dock (Mac).

9. Click the app icon to display the app, then click the **maximize button**.

10. Click the **close button** to close the app.

You opened a new template document and tested its buttons.

Figure 33 *The AIR Window Sample template*

Minimize, maximize, and close buttons

Selecting Options for Publishing Applications

Figure 34 *The combined documents*

© 2015 Cengage Learning®.

Layers pasted from the Application to the template

Add content to an AIR template

1. Open fl5_5.fla, then save it as **AIRwindow.fla**.

2. Click **Control** on the menu bar, point to **Test Movie**, then click **In AIR Debug Launcher (Desktop)**.

   This AIR app is similar to the counting game app you worked on in Lesson 3. However, the app's orientation has been changed to landscape and the objects have been moved to different positions.

3. Close the AIR preview window.

   To combine the template and game documents, you can copy and paste the layers from one to the other. Then you can copy the JavaScript code from one to the other.

4. Click **actions** in the Timeline to select the layer.

5. Press and hold [**Shift**], then click the **headings** layer to select all the layers.

6. Click **Edit** on the menu bar, point to **Timeline**, then click **Copy Layers**.

7. Click **AIRWinSamp.fla** near the top of the Flash window to display the document.

8. Click the **layout** layer on the Timeline to select it.

9. Click **Edit** on the menu bar, point to **Timeline**, then click **Paste Layers**.

   Your screen should resemble Figure 34.

   (continued)

10. Click **frame 1** on the Actions layer (not the actions layer), then press [**F9**] to display the Actions panel.

11. Click **Edit** on the menu bar, then click **Select All**.

12. Click **Edit** on the menu bar, then click **Copy**.

13. Click frame **1** on the actions layer (not the Actions layer).

14. Verify the Actions panel is displayed, click to the right of the brace (}) in line 26, then press [**Enter**] (Win) or [**return**] (Mac).

    This places the insertion point at line 27, as shown in Figure 35.

15. Click **Edit** on the menu bar, then click **Paste**.

    The JavaScript code from the template has been copied to the actions panel of the application. The Actions layer is no longer needed.

16. Click **Actions** on the Timeline to select the layer, then click the **Delete icon** to delete the layer.

17. Click **frame 3** on the layout layer, then insert a keyframe.

18. Click **Control** on the menu bar, point to **Test Movie**, then click **In AIR Debug Launcher (Desktop)**.

(continued)

Figure 35 *The insertion point at line 27*

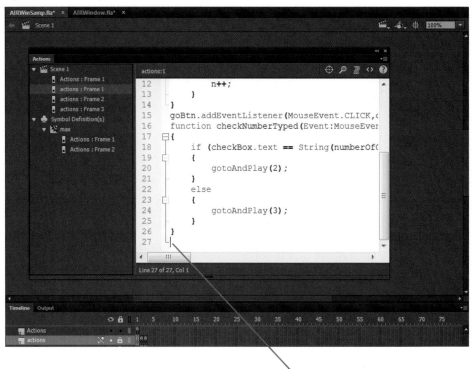

Setting the insertion point

Selecting Options for Publishing Applications

Figure 36 *The Font Embedding dialog box*

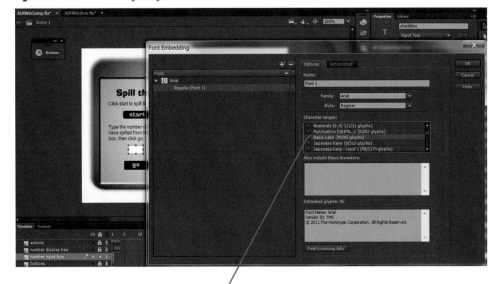

Basic Latin character
range selected

19. Play the game and notice that you are not able to type a number.

20. Close the AIR Preview window.

21. Click the **Output tab** on the Timeline and read the message about embedding fonts.

TIP Embedding fonts ensures that they will be available when the app is run.

22. Click the **Timeline tab**, then unlock the **number input box layer**, which is the third layer from the top.

23. Click **frame 1** on the number input box layer.

24. Click the **number input box** on the Stage to select it.

25. Click the **Embed** button in the Character area of the Properties panel to display the Font Embedding dialog box.

26. Scroll the **Character ranges** list to display Basic Latin, then click the **check box** to select it as shown in Figure 36.

    The Basic Latin character range will embed numeric characters.

27. Click **OK**.

28. Test the application, then close the AIR Preview window.

29. Save and close the document.

You added content to an AIR template by copying layers and JavaScript code from another AIR document.

Publish a Flash document for distribution on the web.

1. Open a new ActionScript 3.0 document, then save it as **SkillsDemo5A.fla**.
   Refer to Figure 37 as you complete this project.
2. Change the Stage dimensions to **500px** wide and **130px** high.
3. Rename layer 1 **backdrop** and draw a rectangle with a rainbow fill color (located at the right side of the gradient fills, in bottom-left corner of the color palette) that is 308px wide and 130px high, then position it on the left side of the Stage, as shown in Figure 37.
4. Add a layer, name it **border** and draw a rectangle with a black stroke and no fill, that is 130px high and 500px wide rectangle to show as a border around the Stage, as shown in Figure 37.
5. Insert a new layer, name it **heading** and add the text shown in Figure 37 using the following settings: Text type: Static Text; Font: Arial; Size: 30 pt; and Color: #003366.
6. Insert a new layer and name it **video**.
7. Import the fireworks.mp4 video with no skin. (Choose None in the Skinning dialog box.)
   Note: This video is a MP4 file format that can be displayed in a Flash application without converting to another video format.
8. Align the video placeholder as shown in Figure 37.
9. Save the document.
10. Test the movie in a browser, then close the browser window.

11. Display the Publish Settings dialog box, click HTML Wrapper (not the check box) and change the HTML alignment to right.
12. Test the movie in a browser, then close the browser window.
13. Save and close the document.

Figure 37 *Completed SkillsDemo5A*

Insert a Flash SWF file into an HTML document.

1. Start Dreamweaver, open fl5_6.html, then save it as **Celebration.html**.
   Refer to Figure 38 as you complete this project.
2. Click below the heading to set an insertion point.

Figure 38 *Completed Celebration.html*

© 2015 Cengage Learning®.

Selecting Options for Publishing Applications

3. Insert the skillsDemo5A.swf file into the Dreamweaver document with the Object tag **Celebration Fireworks Video**, then save the document.

4. Preview the document in a browser, then close the browser window.

5. Select the SWF placeholder and change the Wmode to transparent.

6. Preview the document in a browser, then close the browser window.

7. Save and close the document, then exit Dreamweaver.

Export a Flash document as a video file.

1. Open fl5_7.fla and save it as **skillsDemo5B.fla**.

2. Test the movie in the Flash Player, then close the Flash Player window.

3. Click the File menu, point to Export, then click Export Video to display the Export video dialog box.

4. Verify the Convert video in Adobe Media Encoder check box is selected.

5. Record the path for the output file shown at the bottom of the dialog box.

6. Click the Export button to open the Adobe Media Encoder window.

7. Click the green Start Queue (Return) button to start the conversion.

8. When the process is complete, close the Adobe Media Encoder window.

9. Navigate to your stored files and play the skillsDemo5B.mp4 video file, as shown in Figure 39.

10. Close the video player.

11. Save and close the Flash document.

Figure 39 *The skillsDemo5B video file displayed in a video player*

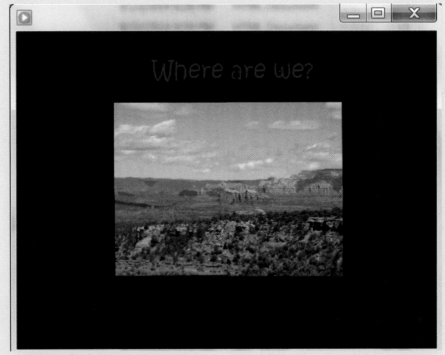

©Microsoft Incorporated. Image courtesy Jim Shuman.

Convert a Flash document to an HTML5 Canvas document.

1. Open fl5_8.fla and save it as **skillsDemo5C.fla**.
2. Test the movie in a browser, then close the browser. This movie is similar to fl5_7.fla except that some interactivity has been added.
3. Convert the document to an HTML5 Canvas document using the file name **skillsDemo5CCVS**.
4. Read the messages on the Output panel.
5. Test the movie in a browser and notice the movie does not stop.
6. Close the browser window.
7. Use codes snippets to insert stop actions in frames 24 and 25.
8. Test the movie in a browser and notice the image is not clickable.
9. Close the browser window.
10. Unlock the button layer, click frame 24 of the layer, then click the invisible button that covers the image on the Stage to select the button.
11. Display the Codes Snippets panel, then double-click Click to Go to Frame and Stop to assign a goto action to the invisible button that covers the image.
12. Use the Actions panel to change the frame to go to frame 24. (Remember, JavaScript labels the first frame 0.)
13. Test the movie in the browser, then close the browser window.
14. Lock the button layer and unlock the image layer.
15. Click frame 1 on the image layer, then click the image on the Stage.
16. Display the Code Snippets panel, open the HTML5 Canvas folder, open the Animations folder, then assign a Fade in a Movie Clip action to the image.
17. Test the movie in the browser as shown in Figure 40.
18. Close the browser window.
19. Save and close the HTML5 Canvas document.

Figure 40 *Completed skillsDemo5CCVS displayed in a browser*

Image courtesy Jim Shuman.

Create an HTML5 Canvas document.

1. Create a new HTML5 Canvas document and save it as **skillsDemo5D.fla**.
   Refer to Figure 41 as you complete this project.
2. Import the files AE-backdrop.jpg, moonB.png, star.png and ufo.png to the Library.
3. Rename Layer 1 **backdrop**, then drag the AE-backdrop image to the Stage and center it.
4. Add a layer, name it **ufo**, then drag the ufo image to just below the "A" in Abstract.
5. Verify the image is selected, then convert it to a movie clip symbol with the name **ufo_mc**.
6. Give the ufo image on the Stage an instance name of **ufo**.
7. Add a layer, name it **moon**, then drag the moonB image to the right of the heading.
8. Verify the image is selected, then convert it to a button symbol with the name **moon_btn**.
9. Give the moon object on the Stage an instance name of **moonBtn**.
10. Add a layer, name it **star**, then insert a keyframe in frame 2 of the star layer.
11. Insert a keyframe into frame 2 on the backdrop layer, then lock the backdrop layer.
12. Insert a keyframe in frame 2 of the moon layer.
13. Select frame 2 on the star layer, then drag the star image from the Library panel to beneath the heading near the center of the Stage.
14. Verify the image is selected, then convert it to a movie clip symbol with the name **star_mc**.
15. Give the star object on the Stage an instance name of **star**.
16. Click frame 1 on the Timeline and use the Code Snippets panel to assign a Stop at this Frame action to the frame.
17. Click frame 2 in the Actions layer, then assign a stop action to frame 2.
18. Select frame 1 on the ufo layer, click the ufo object on the Stage to select it, then use the Code Snippets panel to assign an Animate Horizontally animation to the image.
19. Verify the object is selected, then assign a Fade In a Movie Clip animation to the image.
20. Test the movie in a browser, verify that the UFO fades in as it crosses the screen from left to right, then close the browser window.

Figure 41 *Completed skillsDemo5D*

21. Display the Library panel, double-click moonbtn to display the Edit window, then insert a keyframe in the Hit frame.
22. Return to the main Timeline.
23. Click frame 1 on the moon layer, then select the moon object on the Stage.
24. Use code snippets to assign a go to action that jumps the playhead to frame 1. (Remember: Javascript numbers frames starting at 0.)
25. Click frame 2 on the star layer, click the star image on the Stage, then use code snippets to assign a Rotate Continuously animation to the object.
26. Test the movie in a browser and verify that the UFO fades in as it crosses the screen from left to right. Also, when you click the moon, the rotating star should appear.
27. Close the browser window.
28. Save and close the HTML5 Canvas document.

Open, test and add content to a template.

1. Open fl5_9.fla and save it as **skillsDemo5E.fla**.
2. Test the movie in the Flash Player window, then close the Flash Player window.
   This movie is similar to skillsDemo5D.fla except that it is developed as a FLA file and published as a SWF file not an HTML5 Canvas file. Refer to Figure 42 as you complete these steps.
3. Click File on the menu bar, then click New.
4. Display the Templates tab, then click the Animation category.
5. Double-click Animated Mask Shape Tween.

6. Test the movie and notice the mask used to reveal the contents.
7. Close the Flash Player window.
8. Click Mask on the Timeline to select the layer.
9. Click Edit on the menu bar, point to Timeline, then click Copy Layers.
10. Click skillsDemo5E.fla below the menu bar to display the movie.
11. Click moon on the Timeline to select the layer.
12. Click Edit on the menu bar, point to Timeline, then click Paste Layers.

Figure 42 *Completed skillsDemo5E*

13. Click moon on the Timeline to select the layer, click Modify on the menu bar, point to Timeline, then click Layer Properties.
14. Select Masked, then click OK.
15. Repeat Steps 13 and 14 for the mountain, logo, and nightsky layers.
16. Test the movie in the Flash Player window, then close the Flash Player window.
17. Save and close the document.
18. Close the template file.

Repurpose a Flash file as an AIR app.

1. Open fl5_10.fla and save it as **skillsDemo5F.fla**.
2. Test the movie in the Flash Player window, play the game, then close the Flash Player window.
3. In the Publish Settings dialog box, deselect the HTML Wrapper format, change the target to AIR 13.0 (or the latest version) for Desktop, then publish the document.
4. Click the Publish button, then continue with the publishing process as follows:
   a. General tab: Select Application with runtime embedded for the Output and deselect all of the profiles except for Extended Desktop.
   b. Signature tab: Create a Self-Designed Digital Certificate using the default name, then enter the newly created password in the Signature tab.
   c. Icons tab: Assign the mGame48.png file to the 48×48 Icon.
5. Click the Publish button in the AIR Settings dialog box, then click the OK button in the Publish Settings dialog box.
6. Test the movie using AIR Debug Launcher (Desktop).
7. Close the AIR Preview window.
8. Navigate to the drive and folder where your solution files are stored and display the skillsDemo5F file.
9. Open the skillsDemo5F.app folder.
10. Use the icon to launch the application.
11. Play the game as shown in Figure 43, then close the application widow.
12. In Flash, save and close the application.

Figure 43 *Completed skillsDemo5F*

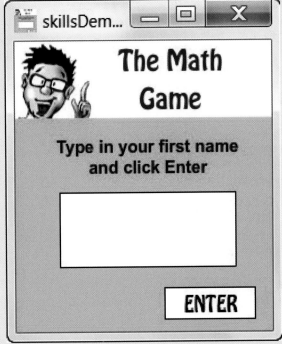

© 2015 Cengage Learning®.

Odyssey Adventure Tours (OAT) would like to have a series of games that current and potential customers can download to their desktop. You have been asked to repurpose a Flash document as an AIR document. The original Flash document is a matching game in which the user drags the names of African national parks and game reserves to match up with the countries in which they are located. The game has three screens: an opening screen that asks the user to input her name; a screen used to drag and drop the names; and a screen that displays the correct answers.

1. Open fl5_11.fla, then save it as **MatchGame.fla**.
2. Test the movie in the Flash Player window, type your name and click the Continue button.
3. Drag and drop the name of each park or game reserve to position it on top of the correct country name.
4. Click the Answers button.
5. Click the Home button to return to the opening screen.
6. Close the Flash Player window.
7. Display the Publish Settings dialog box.
8. Change the target to AIR 13.0 (or the latest version) for Desktop, then click the Publish button.
9. In the General tab of the AIR Settings dialog box, choose to output the application with runtime embedded, and only the Extended Desktop profile selected.
10. Display the Signature tab and create a Certificate, then enter the password in the Signature tab.
11. Display the Icon tab and select the matchG48icon.png image for the 48 × 48 icon.
12. Select Publish and then return to the Flash workspace.

13. Test the application using In AIR Debug Launcher (Desktop).
14. Play the game then close the AIR Preview window.
15. Navigate to your saved files and double-click the MatchGame application icon to launch the app, as shown in Figure 44.

Note: You may need to open the MatchGame.app folder to display the MatchGame application icon.

16. Close the AIR Preview window.
17. Save and close the document.

Figure 44 *Completed Project Builder 1*

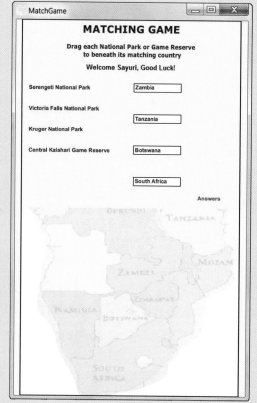

© 2015 Cengage Learning®.

In this project you will customize an interactive game based on the RPG Game Collisions Flash template. The template allows the player to use the mouse and/or keyboard controls to direct an object (a head) with the goal of collecting money and artifacts. Feedback is provided to the player as the game progresses. You start by opening and saving the template, then make changes to the various objects to customize the app.

1. Open the Templates tab in the New Document dialog box, display the Sample Files Category, then open the RPG Game Collisions template.
2. Save the document as **customGame.fla**.
3. Test the application in the Flash Player window, play the game and study how it works.
4. Close the Flash Player window.
5. Import GameBackground.png to the Library.
6. Choose New Symbol from the Insert menu, then create a movie clip with the name **GameBg**. The new symbol is displayed in the Edit window.
7. Drag the GameBackground.png image from the Library and center it on the Stage.
8. Click Scene 1 to return to the main Timeline.
9. Lock all layers except for the Worldboard layer, click frame 1 of the Worldboard layer, then click the Worldboard (green checkered background) on the Stage to select it.
10. Click Modify on the menu bar, point to Symbol, then click Swap Symbol.
11. Select the GameBg symbol and click OK.

12. Reposition the GameBg object so that it is behind the money in both the upper-left and lower-right corners of the Stage as shown in Figure 45.
    Note: The gameBackground.png image was originally created with the same dimensions as the Worldboard object.
13. Lock the Worldboard layer and unlock the WorldObjects layer.
14. Display the Library panel, then double-click the WallSquare icon to display the WallSquare image in the Edit window.
    Note: The brown WallSquare image is used to fill the vertical and horizontal bars on the Stage.
15. Click Layer 1 to select it, then click the square.
16. Use the Properties panel to change the color to a blue gradient.
17. Click Scene 1 to display the main Timeline with the Stage and notice the vertical and horizontal bars are now a blue gradient color.
18. Display the Library panel, then double-click the WaterSquare icon to display it in the Edit window.
19. Click Layer 1 to select it, then click the square.
20. Use the Properties panel to change the color to a green gradient, then display the main Timeline with the Stage.
21. Display the Gold movie clip in the Edit window.
22. Rename Layer1 **gold** and lock the layer.
23. Add a layer above the gold layer and name it **dollarSign**.
24. Click frame 1 on the dollarSign layer, then use the Text tool to type a dollar sign (**$**) with a green color and a size of 18pt.

25. Center the dollar sign over the gold object.
26. Display the main Timeline with the Stage.
27. Test the application in the Flash Player window, then close the Flash Player window.
28. Save and close the application.

Figure 45 *Completed Project Builder 2*

Figure 46 shows a page from a website created using Flash. Study the figure and complete the following.

1. Connect to the Internet, type the following URL **www.nyphilkids.org/games/main.phtml?**, click instrument Frenzy, then read and follow the directions on the screen to play the game.

2. Open a document in a word processor and save the file as **dpc5**.

   In this game, the visitor uses the arrow keys on the keyboard to move the maestro back and forth. The maestro has to catch the instrument as it drops. The visitor then moves the maestro to the correct bin for the captured instrument and presses the down arrow to drop it in the bin by category (woodwind, brass, percussion, strings). If the instrument is dropped into the correct bin, the visitor is awarded points. Missed catches are also tabulated. Assuming this game was developed in Flash Professional CC complete the following:

   - What are the steps to convert his game to an HTML5 Canvas document?
   - What are the steps to convert this game to an AIR for Desktop document?

Figure 46 *Design Project*

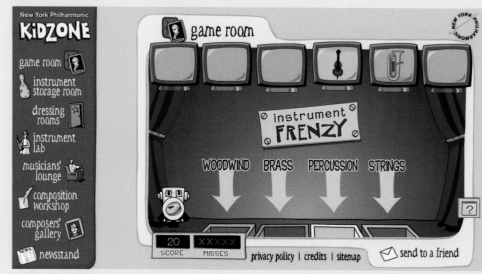

Source: New York Philharmonic Kidzone.

In this project you will repurpose a Flash document as an HTML5 Canvas document. The Flash document has two screens, My Portfolio (the home page) and My Samples. The My Portfolio screen has three buttons, as shown in Figure 47. At this point, only the Samples button works. Clicking it displays the My Samples screen. After converting the Flash document to an HTML5 Canvas document, you will need to insert the necessary JavaScript code to stop the movie from playing and to cause the Samples and Home buttons to work. You will also use code snippets to create an animation.

1. Open fl5_12,fla, then save it as **portfolio5.fla**.
2. Change the view to Fit in Window.
3. Test the movie in the Flash Player window, click the Samples button, click the Home button, then close the Flash Player window.
4. Click Commands on the menu bar, then click Convert to HTML5 Canvas from AS3 document formats.
5. Name the document **portfolio5CVS.fla**.
6. Read the messages on the Output panel.
7. Test the movie in a browser and notice the movie does not stop at each screen.
8. Close the browser, then click frame 1 on the actions layer.
9. Display the Code Snippets panel, open the HTML5 Canvas folder, then open the Timeline Navigation folder.
10. Double-click Stop at this Frame.
11. Click frame 2 on the actions layer, then insert a Stop at this Frame action.
12. Test the movie in a browser and notice that the buttons are not responsive.
13. Close the browser window.
14. Unlock the samplesBtn layer, click frame 1 on the layer, then click the Samples button on the Stage to select it.
15. Use the Code Snippets panel to assign a Click to Go to Frame and Stop action to the button.
16. Use the Actions panel to specify 1 as the frame to go to.
   Note: Remember, JavaScript starts the frame numbering as 0.
17. Repeat Steps 14 through 16 for the Home button on frame 2, specifying 0 as the frame to go to.
18. Test the movie in a browser, verify the buttons are working, then close the browser window.
19. Unlock the placeholder layer, then click frame 2 on the layer.
20. Click a blank area of the Stage to deselect the objects, then click the Placeholder for Samples text to select it.
21. Display the Code Snippets panel, open the HTML5 Canvas folder, then open the Animation folder.
22. Double-click Fade in a Movie Clip.
23. Test the movie in a browser, click the Samples button, then notice the text fading in.
24. Close the browser window, then save and close the document.

Figure 47 *Completed Portfolio Project*

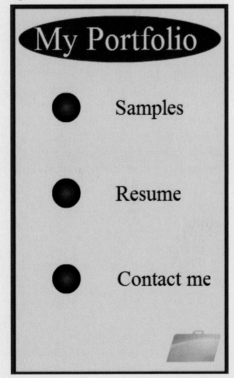

CHAPTER 1 **GETTING STARTED WITH EDGE ANIMATE**

1. Explore the Edge Animate workspace

2. Open and play an Edge Animate file and Use Help

3. Set properties and add elements

4. Animate elements with the Timeline

5. View your work in a browser

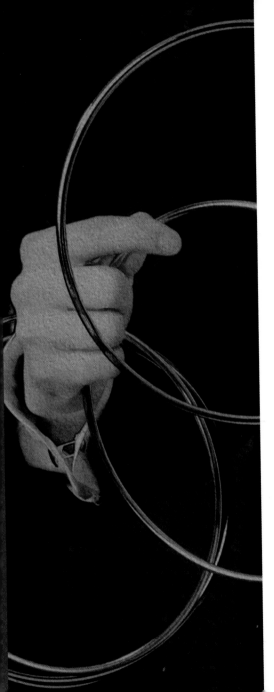

GETTING STARTED WITH
EDGE ANIMATE

Introduction

Adobe Edge is a suite of applications that includes Edge Animate, Edge Reflow, Edge Code, and Edge Inspect. These applications help designers and web developers create feature-rich web content for a variety of devices using current standards. This chapter focuses on Edge Animate, which you can use to create web-based animations. Content created in Edge Animate can be viewed using a **web browser**—also known as simply a **browser**—which is software that displays web content. Commonly used browsers include Microsoft Internet Explorer, Google Chrome, Mozilla Firefox, and Apple Safari.

Until recently, most animations on the web were created in proprietary formats such as Adobe Flash. This was necessary in part because creating animations with nonproprietary web standards like HTML and CSS was possible only at a very basic level. Although JavaScript allowed the creation of more complex animations, creating the code to do so was challenging.

In recent years, however, several factors have combined to make animations for the web easier for developers to create. As a result, animations created with HTML, CSS, and JavaScript—known as **browser-native animations**, or simply

native animations—are now preferred over Flash animations in some cases.

Native animations work by changing the values of one or more CSS properties for an HTML element over time. For example, you might change an element's vertical or horizontal position, dimensions, or color. If you had a thorough knowledge of HTML, CSS, and JavaScript programming, you could sit down and write the necessary code for a native animation from scratch. For developers who lack that knowledge—or who simply want to save time—Edge Animate is a great alternative because it enables you to create native animations using toolbars, menus, and panels that are similar to those found in many other Adobe applications, including Dreamweaver and Flash.

Edge Animate works by automating the creation of code that changes the values of CSS properties, using JavaScript when necessary. However, to use Edge Animate, you don't need any familiarity with CSS or JavaScript. Although Edge Animate provides access to the HTML and CSS code it creates for direct editing by experienced developers, you can create a web animation using modern web standards in Adobe Edge without ever interacting with the underlying code.

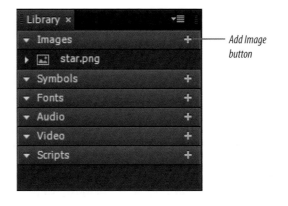

Add Image button

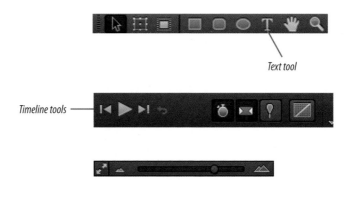

Text tool

Timeline tools

Explore the Edge ANIMATE WORKSPACE

What You'll Do

 In this lesson, you will open Edge Animate, create a new file, explore the workspace, and zoom the Stage.

Exploring the Edge Animate Workspace

When Edge Animate opens, you have three options: opening an existing file, creating a new, empty file, or creating a new file from a template that contains predetermined settings designed to expedite the process of creating a particular type of animation. After you select one of these options, you see the Edge Animate **workspace**, the screen that contains all the menus, toolbars, panels, and other items you need to create animations. As you read the following explanation of the various parts of the workspace, refer to Figure 1, which shows the workspace in its default layout, with a file open.

At the top of the workspace is the **menu bar**, which contains menus you can click to access a variety of commands related to creating animations. The **toolbar**, below the menu bar, contains buttons that let you create and select elements such as rectangles, rounded rectangles, ellipses, and text elements.

The area of the workspace that displays the animation you are working on is known as the **Stage**. You can change the properties that

Edge Animate and Flash

Adobe Flash was long the main format used for creating animations for the web. However, as mobile devices proliferated, the two major companies that maintain mobile operating systems—Apple and Google—stopped supporting Flash animations in order to extend battery life and minimize the use of system resources on devices using their operating systems. These decisions spawned new innovation in web browsers as well as in the HTML, CSS, and JavaScript languages used to create web content, resulting in a set of new features collectively known as HTML5. As a result of this innovation, web developers can create basic animations for web browsers using just HTML, CSS, and JavaScript.

Edge Animate was designed to provide a graphical interface for creating animations using HTML5 features. However, Flash is not obsolete. Edge Animate delivers only a subset of the features available in a Flash animation. In addition, Flash is still widely used in areas such as game development.

control the size and background color of the Stage. You can also add images, text, and video and audio clips to the Stage as you lay out your animation. The Stage shows the properties, such as position or color, of each element in an animation at any point in time during the animation. If you chose to start with a new, empty file, then the Stage will be blank until you actually begin creating an animation. The gray area surrounding the Stage is known as the **Overflow area**. By default, elements in the Overflow area are not visible when a user views your animation in a browser.

Below the Stage is the **Timeline**, a horizontal panel that lets you visualize the length and components of an animation. You can create an animation in Edge Animate by specifying a series of changes to the elements on the Stage, like a flipbook, and the Timeline provides an overview of the points in time in an animation when these changes happen.

The panels surrounding the Stage contain options for working with the elements of your project. Each panel's name appears in a tab at the top of the panel. These panels can be moved, resized, or closed to suit your needs. You can save a set of panels in a specific configuration to create a customized workspace. The default workspace contains the Properties, Elements, Library, and Lessons panels. Each panel contains information

Figure 1 *Edge Animate default workspace*

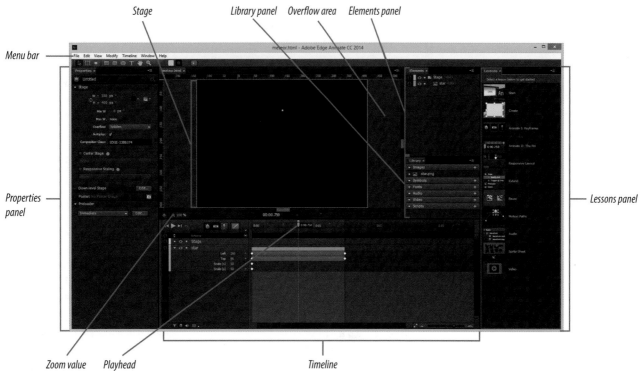

Menu bar

Stage   Library panel   Overflow area   Elements panel

Properties panel

Lessons panel

Zoom value   Playhead   Timeline

about an aspect of your project and tools for specific tasks, as follows:

- The **Properties panel** displays CSS properties and their values for the element currently selected on the Stage, or for the Stage itself if no element is selected. When you select an element, you can use the Properties panel to change the value of one or more of its properties. When creating or changing an animation, you can use the Properties panel to specify the property of an element that should be animated, and the start and end values.

- The **Elements panel** lists all the HTML elements that are part of the current file, arranged hierarchically based on their nesting in the file. You can click an element on the Elements panel to select that element on the Stage. The Elements panel also includes options that let you hide an element on the Stage without affecting its appearance in the animation, and prevent changes to an element.

- The **Library panel** lists all associated files, or **assets**, available for use with your project. The panel groups assets into the following categories: Images, Symbols, Fonts, Audio, Video, and Scripts.

- The **Lessons panel** contains links to a set of introductory tutorials that explain how to use Edge Animate.

QUICK TIP

Edge Animate also includes a Code panel that lets you view and edit the JavaScript code that is generated for your project. By default, the Code panel is not displayed.

Zooming the Stage

By default, the Stage is displayed at its actual size. However, it's sometimes useful to zoom in to make the Stage larger than the default, or zoom out to make it smaller. You can click the Zoom value at the bottom left of the Stage (see Figure 1) to edit or replace the value. You can also use shortcut keys to zoom the Stage in or out: to zoom in, you press **[Ctrl][=]** (Win) or **[command][=]** (Mac); to zoom out, you press **[Ctrl][−]** (Win) or **[command][−]** (Mac); and to return to 100% from any other zoom level, you press **[Ctrl][1]** (Win) or **[command][1]** (Mac).

Organizing Edge Animate Projects

An Edge Animate project consists of a number of files automatically generated by Edge Animate, including HTML (.html), JavaScript (.js), and Edge Animate (.ea) files. To keep your files organized, it's a good idea to save each Edge Animate project in its own folder. When you're working with multiple projects, this organization method makes it easy to identify which files are part of which project. This is especially important when sharing files with other developers or publishing them to the web.

Getting Started with Edge Animate

Figure 2 *Edge Animate welcome screen*

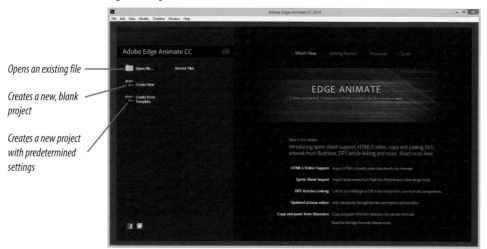

Opens an existing file

Creates a new, blank project

Creates a new project with predetermined settings

Figure 3 *Resizing panels*

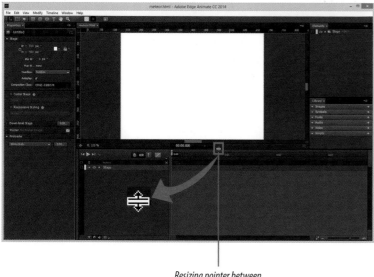

Resizing pointer between Stage and Timeline

Start Edge Animate and explore the workspace

1. Start Adobe Edge Animate **An**. The Edge Animate welcome screen is displayed, as shown in Figure 2.

2. Click **Create New** to open a new, blank project.

3. Click **File** on the menu bar, then click **Save**.

4. Navigate to the drive and folder where your Data Files for Chapter 1 are saved, open the **ursa** folder, type **ursa** as the file name, then click **Save**.

5. Click **Window** on the menu bar, point to **Workspace**, click **Reset "Default,"** then click **Yes** in the Reset Workspace dialog box.

   If another user had previously customized the Edge Animate workspace, the default settings for the workspace are now restored, so that your workspace layout matches the one shown in Figure 1.

6. On the Lessons panel tab, click the **Close button** . The Lessons panel closes, and the Stage and Timeline widen to occupy the space previously occupied by the Lessons panel.

7. Move the pointer over the black line between the Stage and the Timeline until it turns into ⬍, as shown in Figure 3, then click and drag down about half the height of the Timeline.

   Dragging the border between two panels changes their size. In this case, the Timeline shrinks and the Stage expands.

8. Click the **Library panel tab** to select the Library panel.

   When a panel is selected, it is surrounded by an orange outline.

   (continued)

9. Click the **Library panel tab** then drag the **Library panel tab** up over the Elements panel tab until a blue bar is displayed over the Elements panel tab as shown in Figure 4 then release the mouse button.

The tabs for the Elements and Library panels are now grouped, with the Library panel tab to the right or left of the Elements panel tab.

In a project with many items in both of these lists, you could move them into the same panel to allow you to easily see the contents of either list at once. You could also group them and reduce the size of the grouped panel to make more space for other panels in the workspace.

Note: If the panels do not appear grouped, repeat Step 9, making sure a blue rectangle overlaps the Elements panel tab before you release the mouse button.

10. Click **Window** on the menu bar, point to **Workspace**, click **Reset "Default,"** then click **Yes** in the Reset Workspace dialog box.

You can quickly undo any custom changes to the default workspace using the Reset "Default" command.

11. On the Lessons panel, click the **Close button** .

You started Edge Animate, created a new file, worked with panels, and restored the default workspace.

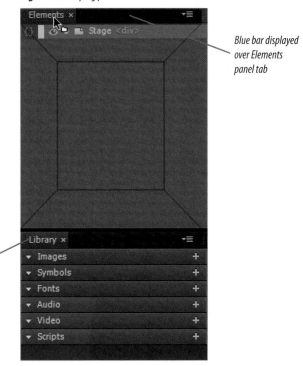

Figure 4 *Grouping panels*

Blue bar displayed over Elements panel tab

Library panel dragged up over Elements panel

Creating a Custom Workspace

If you find yourself switching between a few specific workspace layouts on a regular basis, you can save yourself the time it takes to rearrange them by saving each layout as a custom workspace. To create a custom workspace, first hide and resize panels as necessary until the workspace is set up the way you like. Then click Window on the menu bar, point to Workspace then click New Workspace. In the New Workspace dialog box, enter a descriptive name for the workspace, then click OK. From then on, when you open the Window menu and point to Workspace, you can simply click the name you assigned your custom workspace to instantly resize and rearrange the panels.

Figure 5 *Stage zoomed to 50%*

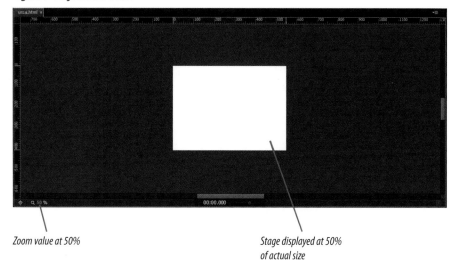

Zoom value at 50%

Stage displayed at 50%
of actual size

Figure 6 *Editing the Zoom value*

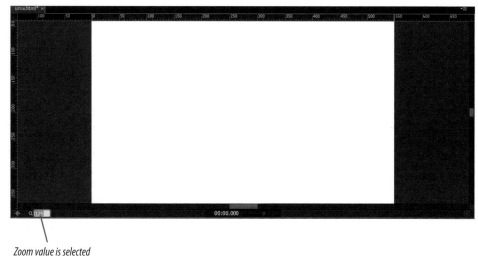

Zoom value is selected
and editable

Zoom the Stage

1. Click anywhere on the Stage, press **[Ctrl][−]**
   (Win) or **[command][−]** (Mac), then press
   [Ctrl][−] (Win) or **[command][−]** (Mac)
   again.

   The Stage zooms out to 75% and then to 50%, as
   shown in Figure 5.

2. Press **[Ctrl][=]** (Win) or **[command][=]** (Mac),
   and then press **[Ctrl][=]** (Win) or
   [command][=] (Mac) twice more.

   The Stage zooms in to 125%.

3. Click the Zoom value at the bottom-left corner of
   the Stage.

   The Zoom value becomes editable, as shown
   in Figure 6.

4. Type **75**, then press **[Enter]**.

   The Stage zooms out to 75%.

5. Press **[Ctrl][1]** (Win) or **[command][1]** (Mac).

   The Stage zoom returns to 100%.

You zoomed the Stage in and out.

LESSON 2

Open and Play an Edge Animate File
AND USE HELP

What You'll Do

 In this lesson, you will open an Edge Animate file, explore the Timeline, play an animation on the Stage, and access Edge Animate Help.

Opening an Animation in Edge Animate

Animations created with Edge Animate are saved as HTML (.html) and JavaScript (.js) files. Edge Animate also creates an additional file with the extension .an that stores information about the relationship between files in your project. However, you can open an existing web application in Edge Animate, and when you save it, Edge Animate will generate a .an file.

Any project that was created in Edge Animate, or that was previously opened in Edge Animate, has both a .html and a .an file. Selecting either file opens the project in Edge Animate.

Interacting with the Timeline

When you open a project in Edge Animate, the Stage shows you what the animation looks like at the moment it starts, and the Timeline shows the elements involved in the animation, such as images or text. For example, the animation shown in Figure 7 includes a text element and several images. Each element is shown on the Stage and is also listed on the Timeline. The left side of the Timeline lists the elements involved in the animation, and displays the CSS properties involved in the animation of each element. The right side of the Timeline indicates when in the animation each change occurs. The numbers at the top of the Timeline indicate the time elapsed since the start of the animation. The first digit is the number of minutes, followed by a colon and the number of seconds, including fractions of seconds. The starting point for any animation is 0:00, which means 0 minutes and 0 seconds. The 1.5 second mark on the Timeline would be indicated with 0:01.500. A yellow marker known as the **playhead** is displayed at the top of the Timeline to mark the current location. As you play an animation, the playhead moves to the right along the Timeline (that is, it moves forward in time), indicating the current point in time within the animation. You've probably interacted with a playhead when viewing a YouTube video or watching a movie online. If so, you know that you can drag it left or right to move backwards or forwards in the video, an action known as **scrubbing**. In Edge Animate, the contents of the Stage represent the animation at the position of the playhead.

Figure 7 *Edge Animate Timeline*

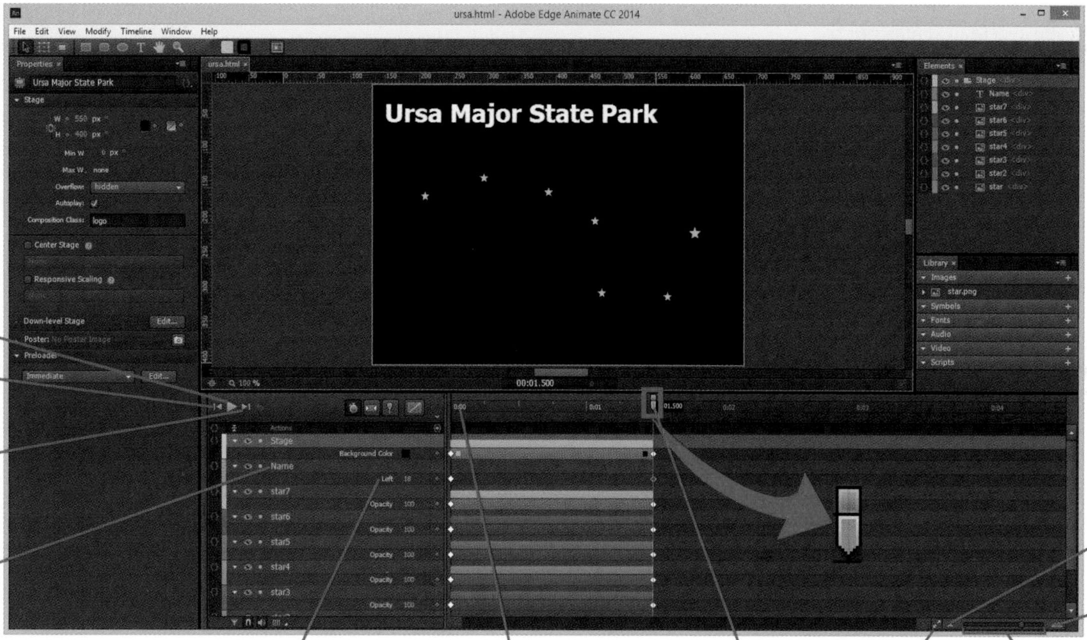
ursa.html - Adobe Edge Animate CC 2014
Ursa Major State Park
00:01.500
Play button
Go to Start button
Go to End button
Each row lists a single element involved in the animation
Rows below each element detail the CSS properties that are animated for that element
Start of Timeline is at 0:00
Playhead
Zoom Timeline to Fit button
Timeline zoom slider
Zoom Timeline Out button
Zoom Timeline In button

Dragging the playhead is not the only way to navigate through an animation. Figure 8 summarizes some other options.

Using Edge Animate Help

If you're having trouble remembering how to accomplish a task in Edge Animate, or just want to learn about a feature, you can click Help on the menu bar to access the Edge Animate Help system. As Figure 9 shows, the Edge Animate Help menu offers several options. Clicking Edge Animate Help opens current, online Help documents in a browser. The Edge Animate Community Forums option takes you to online forums hosted by Adobe where you can ask questions of other users, or search a library of previously answered questions posted by other members. Note that you need Internet access to take advantage of the Edge Animate Help system.

Figure 8 *Methods of Timeline navigation*

Goal	Keyboard Shortcut	Button
move to start	[Home] (Win) [fn][left arrow] (Mac)	Go to Start
move to end	[End] (Win) [fn][right arrow] (Mac)	Go to End
play	[Spacebar]	Play
zoom out	[−]	Zoom Timeline Out
zoom in	[=]	Zoom Timeline In
zoom to fit	[\]	Zoom Timeline to Fit
variable zoom		Zoom slider

© 2015 Cengage Learning®.

Figure 9 *Some Edge Animate Help commands*

Opens online Help documents

Opens online forums where you can ask, answer, and search questions

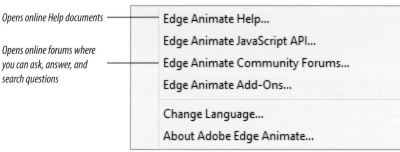

Edge Animate Help...

Edge Animate JavaScript API...

Edge Animate Community Forums...

Edge Animate Add-Ons...

Change Language...

About Adobe Edge Animate...

Edge Animate provides additional assistance in the form of tutorials, which are displayed by default on the Lessons panel. As shown in Figure 10, the Lessons panel lists several topics related to Edge Animate. When you click a topic, the Lessons panel displays a series of links that guide you through steps and explanations related to that topic. You can use these lessons to expand your Edge Animate skills or to brush up on specific topics.

QUICK TIP

If the Lessons panel is closed, you can open it by clicking Window on the menu bar, then clicking Lessons.

Figure 10 *Lessons panel*

Open a file in Edge Animate

1. Click **File** on the menu bar, then click **Open**.

2. Navigate to the drive and folder where your Data Files for Chapter 1 are saved, open the **meteor** folder, click the file with the name **meteor** and the file type of AN, then click **Open**.

TIP The file name may be shown as "meteor.an," or it may simply be shown as "meteor" with another column for file type displaying "AN".

The meteor file opens, with the contents at the start of the animation (a black background) displayed on the Stage. The yellow star to the left of the Stage is also part of the animation, as you'll see shortly when you play the animation. An arrow 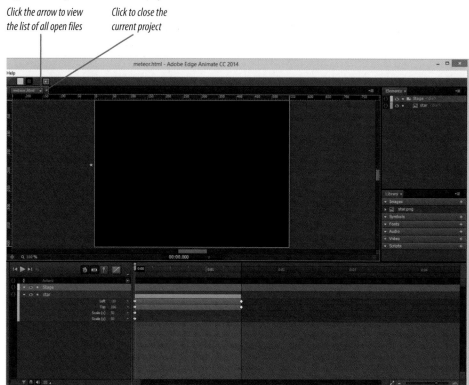 is now displayed to the right of the filename in the upper-left corner of the Stage, as shown in Figure 11. Depending on the size of your screen and your Edge Animate window, the Overflow area around the Stage may be smaller or larger than shown in the figure.

TIP The filename shown above the Stage always includes the extension .html, even if you opened the file by selecting the version with the extension .an (the Edge Animate file).

(continued)

Figure 11 *Stage for the meteor.html project*

Click the arrow to view the list of all open files

Click to close the current project

Figure 12 *Switching between open files*

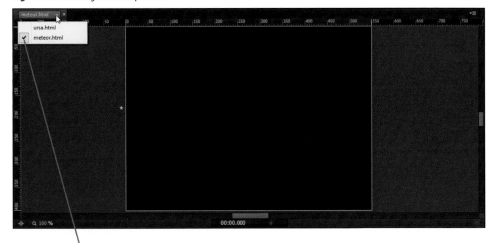

Check mark indicates the
currently displayed file

3. Click the **arrow** to the right of the filename on the Stage.

   As Figure 12 shows, a list is displayed containing the names of the two open files: meteor.html and ursa.html, the new project you created in the previous lesson. The check mark next to meteor.html indicates that it is currently displayed on the Stage.

4. Click **ursa.html**. The current view switches to the empty project you created.

5. Click the **Close button** next to the filename, in the upper-left corner of the Stage. The ursa.html project closes, the meteor.html file becomes the current file, and the arrow to the right of the filename is no longer displayed, indicating that only one project is open.

TIP If a dialog box opens asking if you'd like to save changes to the file, click No (Win) or Don't Save (Mac).

You opened a saved project, navigated between open projects, and closed a project.

Explore the Timeline and play an animation

1. On the Timeline, click the **Go to Start button**. The playhead moves to the start of the animation on the Timeline. The number 0:00 is displayed next to the playhead.

2. Click the **Play button**. The playhead automatically moves to the start of the animation then plays the animation on the Stage, stopping when it gets to the end.

3. Press **[Spacebar]**. The playhead returns to the start of the animation, and the animation plays all the way through once again.

(continued)

4. Click the **Zoom Timeline to Fit button** 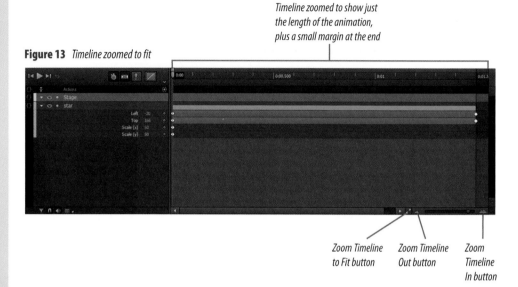.

The length of time represented on the Timeline can be shorter or longer than the length of the animation. When you click the Zoom Timeline to Fit button, the Timeline scales so the entire length of the animation is displayed, as shown in Figure 13.

5. Click the **Zoom Timeline Out button** .

The animation contents now take up a smaller portion of the Timeline.

6. Click the **Zoom Timeline In button** , then click the **Zoom Timeline In button** again. Only a portion of the animation length is now visible on the Timeline.

7. Click the **Zoom Timeline to Fit button** .
The entire length of the animation is displayed on the Timeline once again.

8. In the upper-left corner of the Timeline, click the **Go to End button** . The playhead moves to the end of the animation on the Timeline, and the number 0:01.500 is displayed next to it, as shown in Figure 14. This indicates that the animation ends after exactly 1.5 seconds.

9. Drag the **playhead** to the left.

As you drag the playhead, the time represented by its location is displayed in an adjacent black box. In addition, the current time is displayed below the Stage.

10. Drag the **playhead** to approximately the 0:01 mark on the Timeline.

You may notice that as you approach the 0:01 mark, the playhead is drawn to it. When it's

(continued)

Figure 13 *Timeline zoomed to fit*

Timeline zoomed to show just the length of the animation, plus a small margin at the end

Zoom Timeline to Fit button   Zoom Timeline Out button   Zoom Timeline In button

Figure 14 *Playhead moved to end of animation*

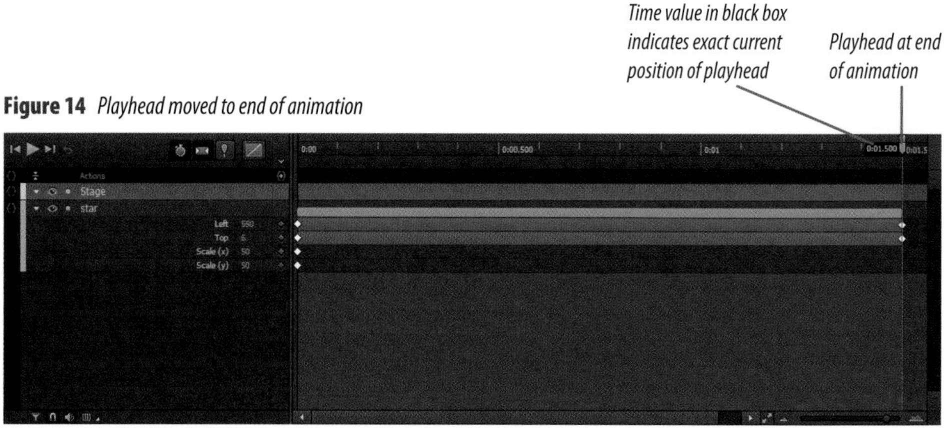

Time value in black box indicates exact current position of playhead   Playhead at end of animation

Getting Started with Edge Animate

Figure 15 *Edge Animate Help on adobe.com*

Figure 16 *Search results for "playhead"*

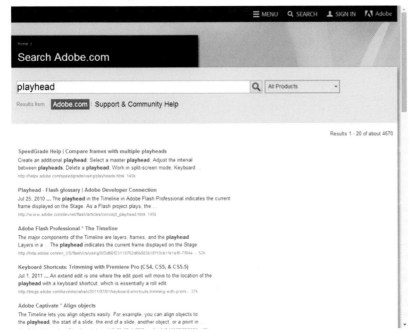

being dragged, the playhead is drawn to the numbered increments to make it easier to position it exactly. Notice also that as you drag the playhead, the Stage shows the state of the animation at the corresponding position in the Timeline.

You played an animation, you zoomed an animation on the Timeline, and you moved through an animation by dragging the playhead.

Use Edge Animate Help

1. Click **Help** on the menu bar to display the menu.

2. Click **Edge Animate Help**.

    A browser window opens, displaying the Edge Animate Help section of the Adobe website. Figure 15 shows the Help contents at the time this book was written. The Help page you see might look different.

TIP You must have an Internet connection to view the Edge Animate Help contents.

3. Click **Search**, in the Search box type **playhead**, then press **[Enter]**.

    A list of links to articles containing the word "playhead" is displayed. Figure 16 shows the contents of this page at the time this book was written. The page you see might look different.

4. Click one of the links, examine the article, then close the browser tab.

You accessed the Edge Animate Help system and you found Help documents on a specific subject.

LESSON 3

Set Properties and
ADD ELEMENTS

What You'll Do

 In this lesson, you will set properties for the Stage, import a graphic as an asset, add instances of the graphic to the Stage, and create a text element.

Setting Properties for an Element

Each item that you add to the Stage is represented in Edge Animate as an HTML element. Even the Stage itself is an element. When you select an element, the Properties panel displays the CSS properties for that element. When you move the pointer over the icon for a property value on the Properties panel, a tooltip displays "CSS:" followed by the property name, as shown in Figure 17. When you move the pointer over a property value, a tooltip displays the inline style code for that property and value, as shown in Figure 18.

Most properties have a numeric value that is displayed in orange on the Properties panel. To change the value of a property, you first click the property value. This selects the value and makes it editable. You can edit the existing value or type a new one, and then press Enter to finalize the change.

Figure 17 *Properties panel Tooltip for property icon*

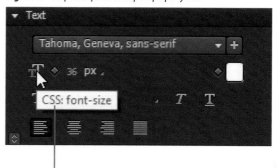

Tooltip shows CSS property name when pointer is over property icon

Getting Started with Edge Animate

Position Properties

When you place or move an element on the Stage, its position is described by the CSS properties Left and Top. The Left property specifies the distance of the left edge of the element from the left edge of the Stage. Likewise, the Top property specifies the distance of the top edge of the element from the top edge of the Stage. Edge Animate also describes position using the x, y coordinate system, where x corresponds to the Left property and y matches the Top property.

You view and change the position properties in the Position and Size section of the Properties panel. The Left property has the label X and the Top property has the label Y.

Size Properties

You use the CSS width and height properties to set the dimensions of an element on the Stage, or the Stage itself. In the Position and Size section of the Properties panel, the Width property has the label W and the Height property has the label H.

Color Properties

For some elements in an Edge Animate project, you can set a background color, while for others you can set a foreground color. The background color corresponds to the CSS background-color property, which is the color displayed behind any content in an element. For instance, the background color of the Stage is displayed behind any element on the Stage. For text elements, you can set a foreground color, which corresponds to the CSS color property. The foreground color is the color of the text itself.

Color settings are represented on the Properties panel with color chips, which are

Figure 18 *Properties panel Tooltip for property value*

Tooltip shows the code for the
CSS property and value when
the pointer is over the value

Understanding Image Dimension Values

If a colleague, such as a designer or another web developer, provides you with dimensions, they may simply give you two numbers with an x between them, such as 550 × 400. In this shorthand format, the first number is the width and the second number is the height, and the units are assumed to be pixels (px). Therefore, 550 × 400 means a width of 550px and a height of 400px.

---

squares of color representing the currently selected values, as shown in Figure 19. To change a foreground or background color, you click its color chip 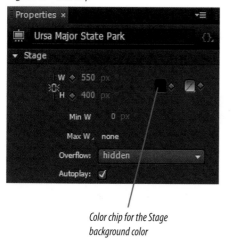 to open the color picker. As Figure 20 shows, the color picker allows you to select a color several different ways. You can drag the Saturation and brightness selector to choose variations of the current hue. You can also use the Hue, Lightness, and Alpha sliders to vary components of the current color.

The box at the bottom-left of the color picker displays a numerical representation of the currently selected color. By default, this is displayed in **RGBa format**, which specifies numerical values from 0-255 for the red, green, and blue components of the color, along with a transparency, or **alpha**, value between 0 (fully transparent) and 1

Figure 20 *The color picker*

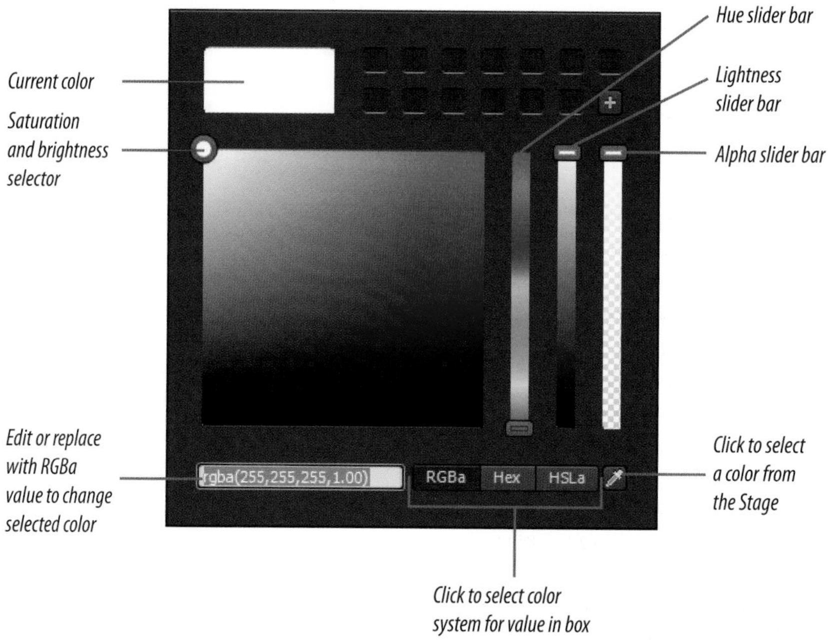

Hue slider bar

Current color

Lightness slider bar

Saturation and brightness selector

Alpha slider bar

Edit or replace with RGBa value to change selected color

rgba(255,255,255,1.00)   RGBa   Hex   HSLa

Click to select a color from the Stage

Click to select color system for value in box

Figure 19 *Color chip*

Properties ×

Ursa Major State Park

▼ Stage

W ◆ 550 px
H ◆ 400 px
Min W   0 px
Max W   none
Overflow: hidden
Autoplay: ✓

Color chip for the Stage background color

Using Other Color Models

You can also choose to view and enter color values using two other color models. The **hexadecimal**, or **hex**, system includes values for the red, green, and blue components of the color, but unlike RGBa, a hexadecimal value represents these values using the hexadecimal (base 16) numbering system. The hexadecimal system uses 16 possible digits instead of just 10, so hexadecimal numbers can include not only the digits 0-9 but also the letters a-f. The hexadecimal value for white is #ffffff. Note that the hexadecimal color system does not support alpha values.

The third color system supported by the color picker is HSLa. Instead of specifying values for the red, green, and blue components, **HSLa** specifies values for hue, saturation, lightness, and alpha. The HSLa representation for an opaque white is hsla(0,0%,100%,1.00).

To view the selected color as a hex value, you click the Hex button to the bottom right of the color picker. To view it as an HSLa value, you click the HSLa button. Before you enter a color value directly in the box, make sure the color model you want to use is selected.

Getting Started with Edge Animate

(fully opaque). For instance, the value rgba(255,255,255,1.0) represents the color white at full opacity. If you know the RGBa value of the color you want to use, you can enter it directly in the box.

Importing Assets

Any piece of external content that you incorporate into an Edge Animate project is known as an asset. Commonly used assets in animations include images, fonts, audio, and video. You can import an asset directly into the Library panel by using the Add button for the appropriate category. (For example, you could use the Add Image button to add an image asset.) Once you have added an asset to the Library panel, you can drag it directly from the panel to the Stage to place it in your project. You can also click File on the menu bar and then click Import to import an asset. Using this method adds the asset to the Library panel and automatically places the asset on the Stage.

Each asset on the Library panel represents a single file, but you can include that same asset multiple times in the same project. Each use of an asset is known as an **instance**, and each instance is a separate HTML element. To help you distinguish between instances of a single asset, Edge Animate assigns an ID value to each instance of an asset. This ID value consists of the asset's filename followed by a number, as shown in Figure 21.

Figure 21 *Instances of an asset*

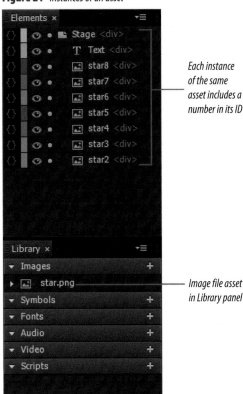

Each instance of the same asset includes a number in its ID

Image file asset in Library panel

Sampling a Color

The color picker also includes the Sample a color from the Stage button. When you click this button, the pointer changes to ⊕ when you move it over the Stage, and a ring of color surrounding the pointer changes to the color under the pointer crosshairs. When the pointer is over the color you want to use, you simply click to select that as the color in the color picker. This is an efficient way to sample a color from an image to use for text in your animation.

Creating Elements

The toolbar, shown in Figure 22, provides tools that you can use to create elements on the Stage or in the Overflow area. As you would expect, the Rectangle tool creates a rectangle shape. Likewise, the Rounded Rectangle tool creates a rectangle shape with rounded corners. You can use the Ellipse tool to create any oval shape, including a circle. You can use the Text tool to create text.

Formatting Text

You can use the Properties panel to set several properties that correspond to the CSS properties font-family, font-size, font-weight, font-style, text-decoration, and text-align, as shown in Figure 23. These properties are unique to text elements.

The Font Family list lets you choose the set of fonts you want browsers to use to display the text. The fonts available to a given browser depend on the fonts installed on that user's computer. By providing a list of fonts, rather than specifying a single font name, you give browsers alternatives in case your first choice of font isn't available.

QUICK TIP

By default, Edge Animate displays the font-size value in pixels. Every value is followed by an abbreviation for the units used. You can click the units abbreviation to choose another option—em or percent.

The Font Weight property takes a value between 100 and 900, with 900 being the boldest text, and 100 being the thinnest. The Font Style button *T* toggles italic formatting on or off, while the Text Decoration button T toggles underlining on or off. You can use the four Text Align buttons to left-align, center, right-align, or justify text.

Stacking Elements

Edge Animate treats each element on the stage as a separate layer. For example, in the meteor.html project, the black background is one layer, and the star is another. The various elements in an animation are stacked one on top of another on the Stage. By default, the first element you add to the Stage is on the bottom of the stack. Each time you add a new element, it lies on top of the elements you added earlier. This means a newer element may hide part of an element you added

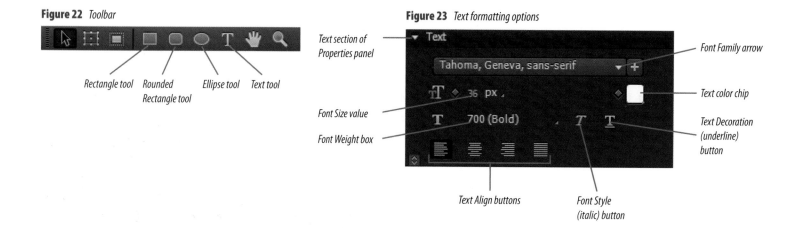

Figure 22 *Toolbar*

Rectangle tool   Rounded Rectangle tool   Ellipse tool   Text tool

Figure 23 *Text formatting options*

Text section of Properties panel
Font Size value
Font Weight box
Text Align buttons
Font Style (italic) button
Font Family arrow
Text color chip
Text Decoration (underline) button

Getting Started with Edge Animate

earlier. For example, in Figure 24 you can see what happens when a layer of text is below a red circle. In that case, the red circle obscures some of the text. If the layer of text is on top of the red circle, then all the text is legible, and it obscures some of the red circle.

The Elements panel contains one layer for each element in the animation in the order they are stacked on the Stage, as shown in Figure 25. The bottom layer on the Elements panel represents the element at the bottom of the stack, and the top layer is the element on top. You can change the stacking of elements on the Stage by dragging an element's name on the Elements panel to a different position in the stack.

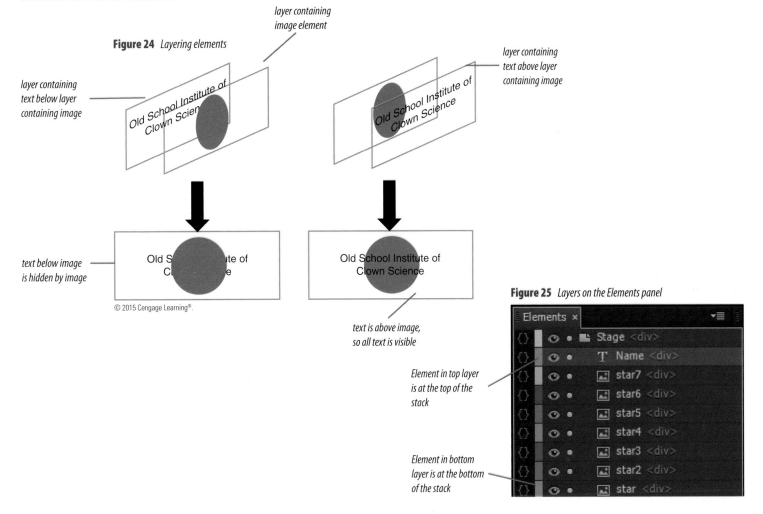

Figure 24 *Layering elements*

layer containing image element

layer containing text below layer containing image

layer containing text above layer containing image

text below image is hidden by image

© 2015 Cengage Learning®.

text is above image, so all text is visible

Old School Institute of Clown Science

Old School Institute of Clown Science

Figure 25 *Layers on the Elements panel*

Element in top layer is at the top of the stack

Element in bottom layer is at the bottom of the stack

Set properties

1. On the Stage, click the **Close button** 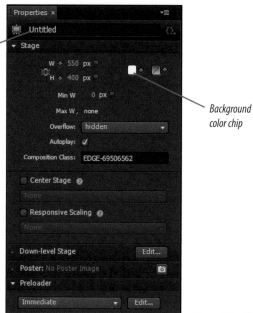 to close the meteor.html file, then, on the welcome screen, click **Open File**.

   TIP If a dialog box opens asking if you'd like to save changes to the meteor.html file, click No (Win) or Don't Save (Mac).

2. Navigate to the drive and folder where your Data Files for Chapter 1 are saved, open the **ursa** folder, click the file named **ursa** with a file type of AN, then click **Open**.

   The blank project you created in Lesson 2 opens. The Properties panel displays the default properties for the Stage, as shown in Figure 26. Because the Composition Class value on the Properties panel includes a random number generated by Edge Animate when you first create a file, your value may not match the one shown in Figure 26.

3. Click the **Title box**, double-click the text "Untitled" if necessary to select it, type **Ursa Major State Park**, then press **[Enter]**.

   The new title value, "Ursa Major State Park," will be displayed in the browser tab when the project is opened in a web browser.

4. Click the **background color chip** ▢.

   The color picker is displayed, as shown in Figure 27, with the numerical color value at the bottom-left selected by default.

5. Drag the **Saturation and brightness selector** around the Saturation and brightness box.

   The background color changes as you drag the selector to match the selected color.

6. Drag the **Hue slider** up and down, then repeat with the **Lightness slider** and the **Alpha slider**.

   (continued)

Figure 26 *Properties panel with default values*

Title box

Background color chip

Figure 27 *Color picker*

Currently selected color

Edit or replace with RGBa value to change selected color

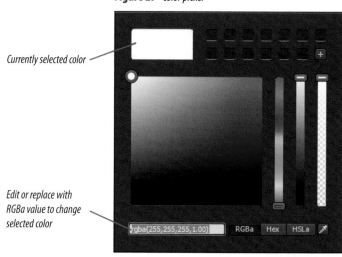

Getting Started with Edge Animate

Figure 28 *Image preview in Library panel*

Images header

Click to hide
image preview

Filename of
image added
to library

Image preview

Add Image button

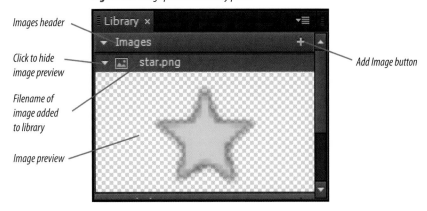

The Hue slider changes the selected color within the spectrum, the Lightness slider makes the selected color lighter or darker, and the Alpha slider makes the color more or less opaque.

7. With the color value at the bottom of the color picker selected, type **rgba(187,187,187,1.0)**, then press **[Enter]**.

   The color picker closes and the background color of the Stage changes to the light gray color specified by the RGBa value 187,187,187,1.0.

8. On the Properties panel, click the width value to select the number 550, type **800**, then press **[Enter]**.

9. Click the width value to select the number 800, type **550**, then press **[Enter]**. The Stage returns to its original width.

You changed the default values for project title and Stage background color.

Import an asset

1. On the Library panel, next to the Images header, click the **Add Image button** .

2. In the Import dialog box, navigate to the drive and folder where your Data Files for Chapter 1 are saved, open the **ursa** folder, then double-click the file named **star**.

   The dialog box closes and the filename "star.png" is displayed below the Images header on the Library panel.

3. On the Library panel, click next to the filename "star.png."

   As Figure 28 shows, a preview of the image is displayed.

4. Click next to "star.png" to hide the image preview.

You imported an image to the library.

Add image instances to the Stage

1. From the Library panel, drag the **star.png** filename to the Stage.

   The pointer changes to ⬚ and the current x and y coordinates of the top-left corner of the image are displayed above the pointer, as shown in Figure 29. The first value indicates the number of pixels from the left side of the Stage, and the second value is the number of pixels from the top of the Stage.

2. Drag the image to approximately the coordinates **63, 148**, then release the mouse button.

   As Figure 30 shows, the star image is displayed on the Stage at this location, and a row is added to the Timeline corresponding to this element. The white handles around the star tell you that the image is selected on the Stage. The property values shown in the Properties tab apply to this selected instance of the image.

3. In the Properties tab, under the Transform header, next to the Scale X icon ⬚, click the value **100** to select it, type **75**, then press **[Enter]**.

   The X value changes to 75%, indicating that the image is now scaled to 75% of its width. Because the width and height values are linked by default, the Y value changes automatically to 75% as well. The star instance on the Stage is reduced to 75% of its original size.

4. Repeat Steps 1-3 to place 4 additional instances of the star.png image at the following coordinates, and to scale the images: 152, 122; 248, 142; 316, 183; 326, 285; 427, 290.

   (continued)

Figure 29 *Dragging an image instance to the Stage*

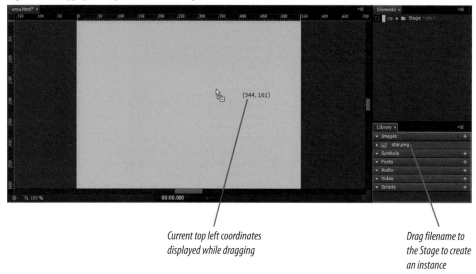

(344, 161)

Current top left coordinates
displayed while dragging

Drag filename to
the Stage to create
an instance

Figure 30 *Star image placed on the Stage*

Selected image
is surrounded by
white handles

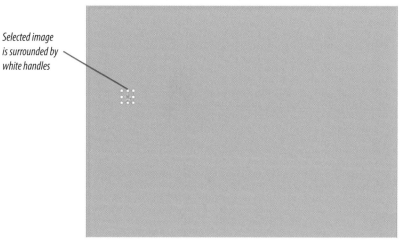

Getting Started with Edge Animate

Figure 31 *Seven instances of star image on the Stage*

Final star not
scaled to 75%

5. Repeat Steps 1 and 2 to place a final instance of
the star.png image at the coordinates 467, 200
without scaling it, then press **[Ctrl][S]** (Win) or
[command][S] (Mac) to save your changes. Your
project should match Figure 31.

You added image instances to the Stage.

Add text to the Stage and format it

1. On the toolbar, click the **Text tool** T , then click
in the middle of the Stage.

TIP   The exact position of the text doesn't matter at this
point. After you specify its properties you'll move it to
its final position.

2. In the Text box, type **Ursa Major State Park**,
then click a blank area of the Stage.

The text you typed is displayed on the Stage in
the default font, Arial.

3. If necessary, click the text element you just
created to select it.

4. The text is surrounded by a blue box, with white
handles, and the Properties panel displays
property options for the text element.

5. On the Properties panel, click in the **Title box**,
double-click to select the default value, type
Name, then press **[Enter]**.

TIP   By default, a text element is given the title "Text,"
followed by a number if the project contains more
than one text element. Replacing this default title
with a unique name makes it easier to identify
elements in the Timeline when you animate them.

(continued)

6. Below the Text section header, click the **font-family arrow**, then click **Tahoma, Geneva, sans-serif**.

7. Click the font-size value **24** to select it, type **36**, then press **[Enter]**. The text size changes from 24 pixels to 36 pixels.

8. Click the **text color chip** 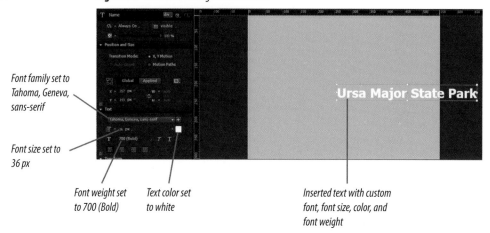, then in the color picker drag the **Saturation and brightness selector** to the top-left corner of the Saturation and brightness box, then press **[Enter]**. The text color changes to white.

TIP The text color chip is black by default, and is located just below and to the right of the font family box.

9. Click the **font-weight box**, then click **700 (Bold)**. Your project should match Figure 32.

10. Press **[Ctrl][S]** (Win) or **[command][S]** (Mac) to save your work.

You added text to the Stage and formatted it.

Reorder layers

1. On the Elements panel, click **Name layer**.

   The row representing the Name element is selected, as indicated by a slightly lighter gray background.

2. Drag the **Name layer** to the bottom of the list in the Elements box until a black line is displayed below the last instance of the star image in the list, as shown in Figure 33, then release the mouse button.

   The Name element, containing the text Ursa Major State Park, is now the bottom layer in the project.

(continued)

Figure 32 *Text added to Stage and formatted*

Font family set to Tahoma, Geneva, sans-serif

Font size set to 36 px

Font weight set to 700 (Bold)

Text color set to white

Inserted text with custom font, font size, color, and font weight

Figure 33 *Repositioning an element as the bottom layer*

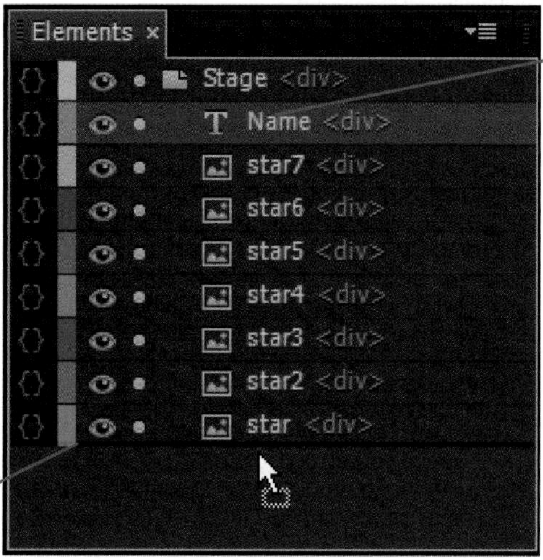

Name layer selected

Black line indicates new location of selected layer when mouse button is released

Figure 34 *Image instance on higher layer displayed over text*

*Overlapping image displayed
over text because text is the
bottom layer*

*Name layer containing
text moved to bottom
layer position*

Figure 35 *Image instance on lower layer hidden by text*

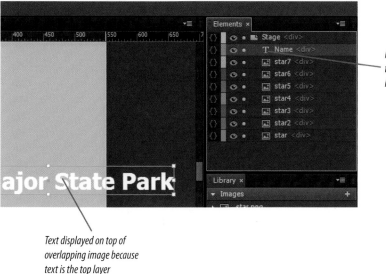

*Name layer containing
text moved to top
layer position*

*Text displayed on top of
overlapping image because
text is the top layer*

3. Click the text element on the Stage to select it, if necessary, then, if necessary, drag it until one of the stars overlaps one of the letters.

   Because the text element is the bottom layer, an image in a higher layer is displayed on top of it, as shown in Figure 34.

4. On the Elements panel, click the **Name layer** to select it, drag the selected layer to the top of the list in the Elements box until a black line is displayed just below the word "Stage", then release the mouse button. The text element is now the top layer. As Figure 35 shows, the star that was displayed on top of the text in the previous step is now hidden by the text.

5. Verify that the text element is selected on the Stage, then on the Properties panel, under the "Position and Size" heading, change the top value (labeled "X") to **18 px**, then change the left value (labeled "Y") to **18 px**.

   TIP   There are also values labeled "X" and "Y" below the "Transform" heading. Be sure to edit the values under the "Position and Size" heading.

   The text is now displayed in the top-left corner of the stage.

6. Press **[Ctrl][S]** (Win) or **[command][S]** (Mac) to save your work.

You changed the order of layers on the Stage.

Animate Elements
WITH THE TIMELINE

What You'll Do

 In this lesson, you will create an animation using keyframes.

Animating an Element

You can animate any element you add to the Stage or the Overflow area. An animation is essentially a change in one or more of an element's properties either instantly or over time. For example, in the meteor project you opened and viewed earlier, the Left property changes from −20px to 550px, and the Top property changes from 166px to 6px. These changes happen gradually over 1.5 seconds, an effect known as a transition. Alternatively, you could animate the star without a transition, which would result in the element jumping from one position to another rather than moving gradually between the two.

To create an animation with Edge Animate, you use keyframes. A **keyframe** specifies the value of a property at a specific time during an animation. An animation must include a minimum of two keyframes, and complex animations may use more. In a simple animation with two keyframes, the first keyframe indicates the state of the element when the animation starts, and the second indicates its state when the animation ends. When you create a keyframe, a diamond shape called a **keyframe mark** is added to the Timeline in a row for the element and property being modified, and located at the time in the animation that the change occurs. Figure 36 shows a keyframe mark for the Background Color property of the Stage at 0:00, the start of the animation, and a second keyframe mark for the same property at 0:01.500, the end of the animation.

You can animate anything in Edge Animate by following these six steps:

1. Move the playhead to the point on the Timeline when you want the animation to begin.
2. Set the starting value for the property you want to animate.
3. Insert a keyframe.
4. Move the playhead to the point on the Timeline when you want the animation to end.
5. Set the property's ending value.
6. Insert a keyframe.

Using this information, Edge Animate can create a gradual transition from the starting value to the ending value for each animated property. In that case, the property value will change gradually from the beginning of the animation to its end. Alternately, Edge Animate can change a property's value from the starting value to the ending value at a certain point in time, with no transition between the two. In that case, the property value will change abruptly when the animation reaches the second keyframe.

You can create a simple animation with just two keyframes that specify different values for the same property at different times on the Timeline. These two keyframes mark the start and the end of the animation. You can make a more complex animation by including more keyframes for the same property. In addition, you can animate multiple properties of an element, as well as properties for multiple elements, on the same Timeline.

Adding Keyframes

Once you move the playhead to the starting point for an animation and set the starting value for a property, the next step is to add a keyframe. The easiest way to insert a keyframe for the starting value is to click the Add Keyframe button ◆ next to the property name on the Properties panel. Creating a keyframe for a property of an element automatically adds a layer for that property to the Timeline, as shown in Figure 36.

After you move the playhead to the ending point for an animation and set the ending value for the property, you could click the property's Add Keyframe button ◆ to create the ending keyframe. However, it's easier to turn on Auto-Keyframe Mode, which causes Edge Animate to create an ending keyframe for a property automatically when you specify an ending value.

You can click the **Auto-Keyframe Mode button** ⏱ in the Timeline, as shown in Figure 37, to toggle Auto-Keyframe Mode on (which makes the button red) and off (which makes the button gray). To use Auto-Keyframe mode, first make sure the Auto-Keyframe Mode button is red, then drag the playhead to the point on the Timeline when you want

Figure 36 *Keyframe marks on the Timeline*

Property name displayed below relevant element name

Keyframe mark for the Background Color property of the Stage at 0:00

Keyframe mark for the Background Color property of the Stage at 0:01.500

the animation to end, and set the property's ending value. Edge Animate will then insert the ending keyframe automatically.

Creating Transitions

You can use Auto-Transition Mode to automatically create gradual transitions between a property's starting value and its ending value. You can toggle Auto-Transition mode on and off by clicking the **Auto-Transition Mode button**  on the Timeline (shown in Figure 37). When the button is green, Auto-Transition Mode is turned on, and Edge Animate inserts a gradual transition before any ending keyframe you insert. When the button is gray, Auto-Transition Mode is turned off. In that case, Edge Animate does not insert a transition before an ending keyframe, so an animated element is displayed with the initial property value until the ending keyframe, at which point the property value instantly changes to the ending value. When you want changes to occur little by little, Auto-Transition Mode creates a professional effect without requiring you to create complex code. When you simply want to change from one value to another, though, Auto-Transition Mode is unnecessary.

Figure 37 *Timeline tools*

Auto-Keyframe
Mode button

Auto-Transition
Mode button

> **QUICK TIP**
>
> In some situations, it can be easier to create the ending keyframe first, and then create the starting keyframe. Edge Animate doesn't care about the order in which you create keyframes, so it's totally fine to create keyframes starting at the end of an animation.

Making an Element Appear and Disappear

You can use three different properties to make an element seem to appear or disappear. An element's Opacity property controls how transparent the element is. Setting this to 0 makes an element totally transparent, and therefore effectively invisible on the Stage. By contrast, setting the Opacity property to 100 makes the element fully visible on the Stage. The values in between make the element increasingly less transparent as you go up from 1 to 99. Another property, the Display property, has only two options: on or off. Setting display to on makes an element visible on the Stage, and setting display to off makes it invisible. The Opacity property is useful for a transition when you want an element to become gradually visible or invisible, while the Display property is useful only without a transition, switching immediately from on to off or vice versa. A third way to animate the appearance or disappearance of an element is using the left or top properties, which are located below the Position and Size heading on the Properties panel and are labeled X and Y, respectively. When an element is positioned off the Stage in the Overflow area, by default it is invisible to users, but still part of the animation. You can change an element's position using a transition, so it slowly moves on or off the Stage, or you can use the Left or Top property without a transition, so the element appears or disappears instantaneously.

Fixing Mistakes

Like most applications, Edge Animate includes an Undo function that lets you roll back an error. To undo your most recent action, press [Ctrl][Z] (Win) or [command][Z] (Mac). You can undo several consecutive actions by pressing the key combination the appropriate number of times.

If you create a keyframe without meaning to, you can delete it immediately using the Undo function. If you realize the error later and can't use Undo, simply right-click (Win) or press and hold [command] while you click (Mac) the keyframe marker on the Timeline, and then on the menu that opens click Delete.

Getting Started with Edge Animate

Figure 38 *Background Color keyframe mark added*

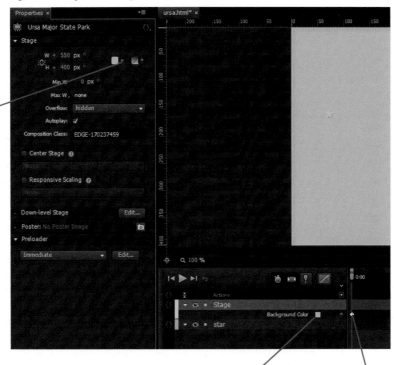

Add Keyframe for Background Color button

New Background Color row added below the label for the Stage layer

Keyframe mark added for Background Color at 0:00

Animate background color with keyframes

1. Click a blank area of the Stage.

   The Properties panel displays property values for the Stage itself.

2. Click the **Add Keyframe for Background Color button** ![button] to the right of the background color chip.

   On the Timeline, below the label for the Stage layer, a new row is added containing the text "Background Color," along with a keyframe mark at 0:00, as shown in Figure 38.

3. If necessary, click the **Auto-Keyframe Mode button** ![button] to turn it on, then if necessary, click the **Auto-Transition Mode button** ![button] to turn it on.

   When Auto-Keyframe Mode is on, the circle in the center of the button ![button] is red. Likewise, when Auto-Transition mode is on, the background of the icon on the button ![button] is green.

   TIP If you're unsure whether the Auto-Keyframe Mode button or the Auto-Transition Mode button is toggled on, hold the mouse pointer over the button for a second. A text box is displayed showing the name of the button. If the button is toggled on, the second line of the text box starts with the text "Enabled."

4. Drag the **playhead** ![playhead] to 0:01.500.

   (continued)

5. Click the **background color chip** ▢, then in the color picker, drag the **Saturation and brightness selector** to the bottom right of the Saturation and brightness box, as shown in Figure 39. The Stage background color changes to black.

6. Click a blank area of the Stage to close the color selection dialog box. A keyframe mark is automatically added to the Background Color row on the Timeline at the current time, 0:01.500, as shown in Figure 40.

7. Press **[Spacebar]**. The animation returns to the start and then plays. The gray background color gradually changes to black over the 1.5 seconds you specified.

8. Press **[Ctrl][S]** (Win) or **[command][S]** (Mac) to save your work.

You created and played a keyframe animation.

Animate opacity with keyframes

1. On the Timeline, click the **Go to Start button** ◁. The playhead moves to the start of the animation.

2. Click one of the stars on the Stage, press and hold **[Shift]**, click each of the remaining stars, then release **[Shift]**.

   All seven instances of the star image are selected on the Stage. In addition, the row in the Timeline associated with each instance changes to light gray.

   (continued)

Figure 39 *Black background color selected*

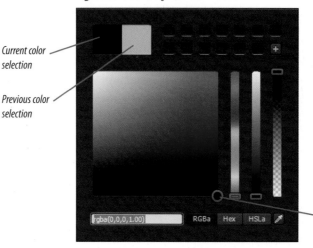

Current color selection

Previous color selection

Saturation and brightness selector moved to bottom right of Saturation and brightness box

Background color changed to black

Figure 40 *Ending keyframe added automatically*

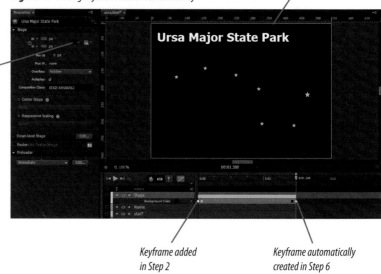

Add Keyframe for Background Color button

Keyframe added in Step 2

Keyframe automatically created in Step 6

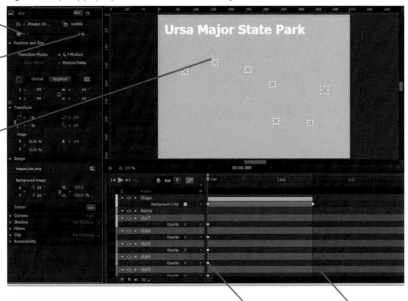

Figure 41 *Opacity property added to timeline for each image instance*

Add Keyframe
for Opacity
button

Opacity value
changed to 0

All star instances
selected
and totally
transparent

Keyframe added for
opacity property of
each image instance

Background of selected
elements in Timeline
changed to light gray

3. On the Properties panel, to the right of the Opacity icon ▨, click the opacity value of **100**, type **0**, then press **[Enter]**.

   The opacity value changes to 0%. Because this setting makes the stars totally transparent, the stars themselves are no longer visible on the Stage. Instead, you only see the blue square inside each set of white handles, indicating that the stars are still selected.

4. Next to the Opacity icon ▨, click the **Add Keyframe for Opacity button** ◈.

   The Opacity property is added to the Timeline for each of the seven instances of the star image and a keyframe is added for each, as shown in Figure 41.

5. On the Timeline, drag the **playhead** to 0:01.500.

   (continued)

6. With all seven instances of the star image still selected, click the opacity value of **0**, type **100**, then press **[Enter]**.

The star images are once again visible on the Stage, as they are now fully opaque. In addition, a keyframe is added automatically at the current time (0:01.500) for the Opacity property for each star image in the Timeline, as shown in Figure 42.

7. Click a blank area of the Stage to deselect the star instances, then press **[Spacebar]** to play the animation. In addition to the background color change you added in the previous steps, the stars fade in until they are totally opaque at the end of the animation.

You animated the Opacity property of multiple images.

Animate a property without a transition

1. On the Timeline, verify that the playhead is at the end of the animation (at 0:01.500).

2. On the Stage, click the text **Ursa Major State Park** to select it.

3. On the Properties panel, in the Position and Size section, to the right of the label X, click the **Add Keyframe for Left button** .

TIP Be sure to click the button next to the label X in the Position and Size section and not the one in the Transform section. If you're unsure, hold the mouse pointer over the button for a second before clicking it, and verify that the tooltip that Edge Animate displays reads "Add Keyframe for Left."

A row for the Left property is added to the Timeline below the Text element, and a keyframe is added for the Left property at the end of the animation, at 0:01.500 on the Timeline.

(continued)

Figure 42 *Fully opaque image instances with ending keyframes*

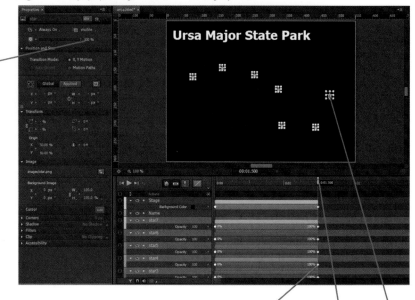

Opacity value changed to 100

Keyframe added for final opacity property of each image instance

Playhead at 0:01.500

Stars fully opaque

Getting Started with Edge Animate

Figure 43 *Keyframes created for text element*

Text element selected

Left value changed to -420

Add Keyframe for Left button

Playhead at 0:00

Keyframe added for starting Left value for Text element

Outline keyframe for ending Left value indicates immediate change

4. On the Timeline, click the **Go to Start button** [◄].

   The playhead moves to the start of the animation.

5. Click the **Auto-Transition Mode button** [⬛] to deactivate it.

   With Auto-Transition Mode off, any new changes you make in property values will be applied all at once when the animation hits the second keyframe, rather than gradually between the two keyframes.

6. Verify that the text element is still selected on the stage.

7. On the Properties panel, in the Position and Size section, click the left value **18**, which is just to the right of the Add Keyframe for Left button, type **-420**, then press **[Enter]**.

   The text element is repositioned off the Stage to the left, and a keyframe is added at 0:00 on the Timeline for the Left property of the Text element, as shown in Figure 43. Note that the keyframe for the Left property at the end of the animation changes from a solid diamond to an outline, indicating that the change happens all at once rather than with a transition. In the final animation, text positioned off the Stage will not be visible to viewers.

8. Press **[Spacebar]**. The text is not visible until the end of the animation, when it is displayed in its original position on the Stage.

9. Press **[Ctrl][S]** (Win) or **[command][S]** (Mac) to save your work.

You animated the Left property of text without a transition.

View Your Work
IN A BROWSER

What You'll Do

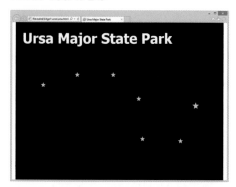

Ursa Major State Park

In this lesson, you will examine the files created for an Edge Animate project, you will set properties that affect the project's behavior and appearance in a browser, and you will open the project in your browser.

Understanding Edge Animate Project Files

In many Adobe Creative Suite applications, when you save your work, it's stored in a single file using a format specific to that application. For instance, Photoshop files are saved in the .ps format. Edge Animate saves files a little differently, however. When you create a project in Edge Animate and save it, several files are created. One is an Edge Animate specific file with the extension .an. At the same time, Edge Animate automatically saves the content of your project as a set of HTML (.html) and JavaScript (.js) files.

Because these files are created by default and updated automatically when you save changes, any project you work with and save in Edge Animate is automatically ready to be incorporated into a website or web application, and can be viewed immediately in a browser, with no exporting required.

Properties that Affect Appearance in a Browser

Although the effects of many Stage properties are visible within Edge Animate, some are apparent only when you view a project in a web browser. Figure 44 shows some of these properties on the Properties panel.

The **Autoplay property** affects whether an animation plays by default when a project opens in a browser. When you work with a file in Edge Animate, you can use the Timeline controls to play it from start to finish. However, when you open a project in a web browser, the Timeline is not available to start or stop the animation. To make an animation run when it loads in a browser, you need to enable the Autoplay property.

Two additional properties that affect the appearance of an animation in the browser are Center Stage and Responsive Scaling. By default, a browser displays an Edge Animate project in the top-left corner of the browser window, and at the dimensions specified for the Stage—550px by 400px in the case of ursa.html. You can toggle on the **Center Stage property** and then select whether you want the animation centered vertically, horizontally, or both ways. Likewise, you can toggle on the **Responsive Scaling property** and choose to scale the project to the browser window horizontally, vertically, or both ways.

Figure 44 *Properties that affect behavior and appearance in a browser*

Autoplay box

Center Stage box

Center Stage list

Responsive Scaling box

Responsive Scaling list

Options for Center Stage and Responsive Scaling properties

Examine the files saved for an Edge Animate project

1. Open File Explorer (Win) or Finder (Mac), navigate to the location of your Data Files for this chapter, then open the **ursa** folder.

2. Press **[Ctrl][Shift][6]** (Win) or **[command][F2]** (Mac) to view files and folders in a detailed list.

   Figure 45 shows the files in Windows File Explorer. The folder contains two subfolders, as well as files with the .js, .an, and .html extensions.

3. Open the **edge_includes folder**. This folder contains two .js files, which contain JavaScript code.

4. Open the **images folder**. This folder contains star.png, the image you imported to the Library panel. When you imported this asset, Edge Animate made a copy of the original file and placed it in this folder.

You examined the project files created by Edge Animate.

Figure 45 *Edge Animate project files in Windows Explorer*

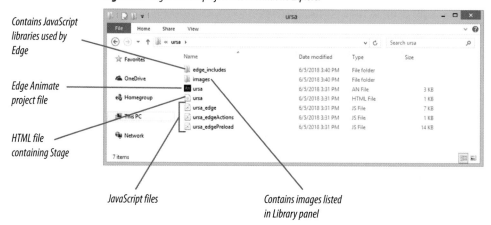

Contains JavaScript libraries used by Edge

Edge Animate project file

HTML file containing Stage

JavaScript files

Contains images listed in Library panel

Getting Started with Edge Animate

Figure 46 *Animation displayed in a browser window*

Animation displayed in top left corner of browser window

First frame of animation displayed without playing through

Animation displayed at fixed width and height

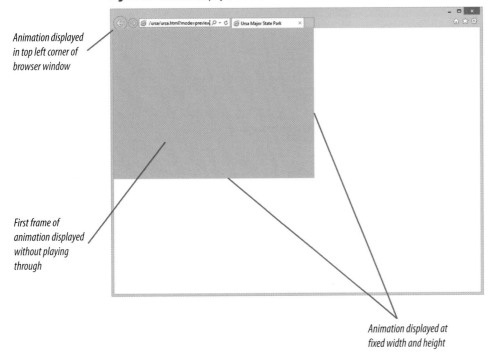

Open an Edge Animate project in your browser

1. In Edge Animate, click an empty part of the Stage.

2. On the Properties panel, click the **Autoplay box** to uncheck it, then press **[Ctrl][S]** (Win) or **[command][S]** (Mac) to save your changes.

3. Press **[Ctrl][Enter]** (Win) or **[command][Enter]** (Mac).

   Your animation opens in your default browser. As Figure 46 shows, the animation opens in the top-left corner of the browser window and shows just the beginning state, with the gray background.

   TIP In Internet Explorer, click the Allow Blocked Content button to allow the browser to load all the files for your animation.

4. Return to Edge Animate, then click a blank area of the Stage.

5. On the Properties panel, click the **Autoplay box** to check it.

   (continued)

6. Click the **Center Stage box** to select it, click the **Center Stage arrow** (to the right of the word "Horizontal"), then on the list that opens, click **Both**.

7. Click the **Responsive Scaling box** to select it, click the **Responsive Scaling arrow** (to the right of the word "width"), then on the list that opens, click **Both**. Your settings should match Figure 47.

(continued)

Figure 47 *Settings for browser display*

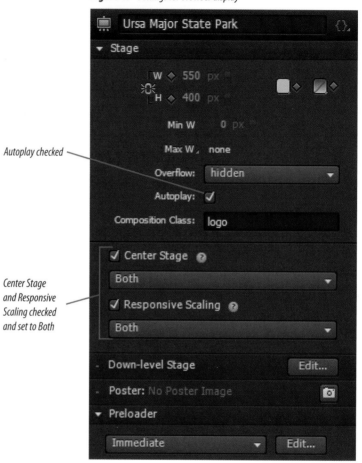

Autoplay checked

Center Stage and Responsive Scaling checked and set to Both

Getting Started with Edge Animate

Figure 48 *Animation in browser with final settings*

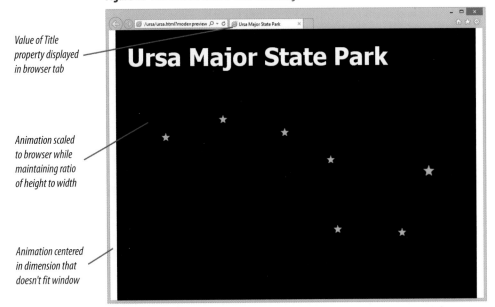

Value of Title
property displayed
in browser tab

Animation scaled
to browser while
maintaining ratio
of height to width

Animation centered
in dimension that
doesn't fit window

8. Press **[Ctrl][S]** (Win) or **[command][S]** (Mac) to save your work, return to ursa.html in your browser, then click the **Refresh** or **Reload button**.

As Figure 48 shows, the animation is now centered vertically and horizontally in the browser window, and scales to best fit the vertical and horizontal dimensions of the browser window while maintaining its own aspect ratio. In addition, the animation automatically plays through once when the page loads. Note that the value of the Title property is displayed in the browser tab.

You viewed an animation in your browser, and specified options for its behavior and appearance in the browser window.

Explore the Edge Animate workspace.

1. Start Edge Animate.
2. Open a new, blank project, then save it to the card folder on the drive and folder where your Data Files for Chapter 1 are saved with the file name **card**. *Note*: If your computer is configured to show file extensions, the filename may be displayed as card.html.
3. Reset the Default workspace, then close the Lessons panel.
4. Select the Properties panel, then widen it to about double its starting width.
5. Combine the Library and Elements panels into a single panel with two tabs.
6. Reset the Default workspace, then close the Lessons panel.

Open and play an Edge Animate file and use help.

1. Open the meteor file from the meteor folder.
2. Play the meteor animation on the Stage.
3. Switch to the card.html project.
4. Close the card.html project.

Set properties and add elements.

1. Close the meteor.html file, then from the card folder, open the card project.
2. On the Properties panel, change the Title value to **Happy Holidays**.
3. Change the background color to rgba(37,115,171,1.00).

4. Add the image snowflake (from the card folder) to the Library, then add the image bear (from the card folder) to the Library.
5. Drag the bear image from the Library to the bottom-right corner of the Stage, then drag to reposition as necessary so the bottom-left corner of the image is over the bottom-left corner of the Stage.
6. Place nine instances of the snowflake image on different parts of the Stage.
7. Scale two of the snowflakes to 25%, two to 50%, and three to 75%.
8. At the top of the Stage, add text that reads **Happy Holidays!**
9. Change the Title for the text you just inserted to **HappyHolidays**.
10. Change the font family of the text to Georgia, Times New Roman, Times, serif.
11. Change the font size to **48**.
12. Change the font color to rgba(255,86,16,1.00), then save your work.
13. Move the layer containing the text above the layers containing the snowflake images.

Animate elements with the Timeline.

1. Drag all nine snowflake instances and the text "Happy Holidays!" off the Stage on the left side.
2. Create a keyframe for the Left property for each of the nine snowflakes and for the text element.
3. At 0:00.500 (0.5 sec) on the Timeline, move one of the snowflake instances to its final position on the

stage to create a keyframe without a transition. (*Hint*: Be sure the Auto-Transition Mode button is inactive.)
4. At 0:01.000 (1.0 sec), move another snowflake instance to its final position on the Stage to create a keyframe without a transition.
5. Continue placing snowflakes on the Stage at half-second increments.
6. At 0:05.00 (5 sec), move the text "Happy Holidays!" to a position centered between the left and right sides of the Stage, without a transition.
7. At 0:00 on the Timeline, add a keyframe for the Stage background color. Create a transition to the color rgba(209,230,245,1.00) that ends at 0:05.00. (*Hint*: Be sure the Auto-Transition Mode button is active.)
8. Play the animation, and then save your work. The end of your animation should resemble Figure 49.

View your work in a browser.

1. In File Explorer (Win) or Finder (Mac), navigate to the drive and folder where your Data Files for Chapter 1 are saved, and open the card folder, then if necessary change the display to show a detailed list of the folder contents.
2. Examine the contents of the card folder, including any subfolders.
3. In Edge Animate, deselect the Autoplay option, save your changes, then open your animation in your browser. (*Hint*: In Internet Explorer, click the Allow Blocked Content button to allow the browser to load all the files for your animation.)

Getting Started with Edge Animate

4. Return to Edge Animate, then change the Stage properties so the animation autoplays in a browser, so it's centered vertically and horizontally in the browser window, and so it scales vertically and horizontally to the browser window.

5. Save your changes, return to card.html in your browser, click the Refresh or Reload button, then verify that the animation plays automatically, that it's centered vertically

and horizontally in the browser window, and that it scales to best fit the vertical and horizontal dimensions of the browser window while maintaining its own aspect ratio.

Figure 49 *Final state of Skills Review animation*

©iStock.com/myillo.

You're designing a banner ad for Mountain Airlines to advertise a current fare special. To attract viewers' attention, your plan calls for animating an image of a plane within the ad so it moves across the ad and appears to approach the viewer.

1. Create a new Edge Animate project and then save it with the name **fly** in the fly subfolder on the drive and folder where your Data Files for Chapter 1 are saved.
2. Change the Stage dimensions to 800px by 300px, and set the background color to a sky blue shade.
3. Near the top of the Stage, add the text **L.A. to Mammoth $259**, change the font family to one you like, change the font weight to make the text more noticeable, and then change the font size as appropriate so the text extends across the Stage.
4. Near the bottom of the Stage, add the text **Mountain Airlines**. Apply the same font family that you used for the text at the top of the Stage, and position the next text roughly centered between the left and right sides of the Stage. Italicize the airline name.
5. Import the image mountain.png from the fly folder into the Library panel. Drag an instance of the image onto the Stage to the left of the airline name, resizing and repositioning the text if necessary to create room.
6. Change the color of the text "Mountain Airlines" to 103,121,24,1.00.
7. Import the image plane.png from the fly folder to the Library panel. Drag an instance of the image onto the Stage. Scale the image to 20% of its original size, and then drag it to the Overflow area off the left side of the Stage.
8. Create a 5-second animation with transitions for the plane image, increasing the Left property to move the plane across the Stage, and increasing the width and height of the image to its full size. At the end of the animation, the image should be 100% of its original size, and only the tail should be visible in the bottom right corner of the Stage, as shown in Figure 50. (*Hint*: If necessary, use the Zoom Timeline buttons to adjust the amount of time visible on the Timeline.)
9. Save your work, play the animation in a browser, and ensure that it autoplays but is not centered or scaled.

Figure 50 *Sample Project Builder 1 at end of animation*

©iStock.com/mrjimbo.
Source: U.S. Customs and Border Protection.

You're responsible for maintaining the front page of the website for the Gasconade Beacon, a local news organization. A new feature story has just been cleared to go live on the site. You will create a banner to highlight the story, animating the background image to draw readers' attention.

1. Create a new Edge Animate project and then save it with the name **banner** in the banner subfolder on the drive and folder where your Data Files for Chapter 1 are saved.
2. Change the Stage dimensions to 600px by 100px.
3. Import the image red.png from the banner folder into the Library panel. Drag an instance of the image onto the Stage. Position the image so the top, left, and right sides align with the corresponding sides of the Stage. Half of the image should extend off the bottom of the Stage.
4. Near the top of the Stage, add the text **A new way to beat drought?**, change the font family to one you like, change the font weight to make the text more noticeable, and then change the font size as appropriate so the text extends across the stage.
5. Above the Stage, add the text **A Beacon exclusive by science reporter Becky Li**. Apply the same font family that you used for the text you added in the previous step, and change the font size so the text spans most of the width of the Stage. Change the font color to white.
6. Create a 2-second animation without a transition that moves the text you added in Step 5 from its position off the Stage to the bottom of the Stage.
7. Create a 2-second animation with a transition that shifts the red.png image up, so the bottom edge is even with the bottom of the Stage, and the top half of the image extends off the top of the Stage. At the end of your animation, all text should be visible on the Stage and the bottom half of the red.png image should be visible, as shown in Figure 51.
8. Save your work, play the animation in a browser, and ensure that it autoplays but is not centered or scaled.

Figure 51 *Sample Project Builder 2 at end of animation*

Source: National Atlas of the United States

One of the best ways to understand what an application like Edge Animate can do is to view projects created by professional developers. Adobe maintains a gallery of noteworthy content created with Edge Animate.

1. In a browser, open *http://html.adobe.com/edge/animate/showcase.html*, and then scroll down to explore the page. As shown in Figure 52, the page contains links you can click to view and download projects created with Edge Animate.
2. Select a project on the page that you'd like to explore, click its View button, and then observe what the project does upon opening. If necessary, refresh the page to view the animation again.
3. In a text editor, create a new document and answer the following questions:
   - What is the project's URL?
   - Which elements on the page look like they're images?
   - Focusing on one text element on the page, name all the aspects of text formatting that have been applied to the text (such as size or weight), and for each one, describe the setting (for instance, the font may be blue and look like standard-weight Arial).
   - Which elements on the page are animated when the page opens? For each element, describe which property or properties are involved, and whether the changes to each property involve a transition.
4. Repeat Steps 2 and 3 for a second project, then save your document.

Figure 52 *Design Project*

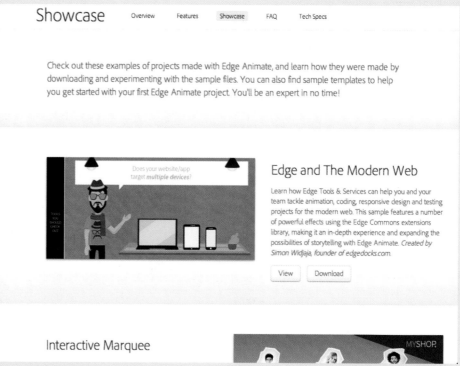

Adobe Systems Incorporated.

A common creative use of animation online is in greeting cards. Animated cards enhance scenes like those on printed greeting cards with movement. Create a new project in Edge Animate and use the images in the mansion folder where your Data Files are stored to create a scene that includes a house, the moon overhead, and a ghost flying above the ground. Add at least one text element to the project and format it. Animate at least three elements of the project, including at least one with a transition and one without. Create titles for the Stage and the text element. Figure 53 shows a sample project at the end of the animation. Save your project with the name **mansion.html** in the mansion folder on the drive and folder where your Data Files for Chapter 1 are saved.

Figure 53 *Sample Portfolio Project at end of animation*

©iStock.com/JohnBigl,
©iStock.com/ChrisGorgio,
Source: NASA.

CHAPTER 2 CREATING INTERACTIVE ANIMATIONS WITH EDGE ANIMATE

1. Draw shapes

2. Group elements

3. Specify a startup action

4. Specify events, actions, and targets for interaction

5. Examine code and test interactivity on desktop browsers

6. Test interactivity on a mobile device

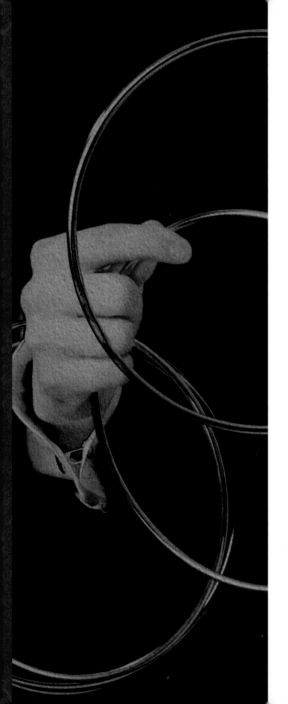

CREATING INTERACTIVE ANIMATIONS WITH EDGE ANIMATE

Introduction

So far you have focused on using Edge Animate to create non-interactive animations. In this chapter, you will learn how to create projects that respond to user actions. At their simplest, these animations let a user start and stop a simple, linear animation. However, learning how to create animations with user interaction opens the door for complex and highly creative projects such as video games and immersive media.

Web documents commonly integrate many small animations that are triggered by user interaction. One of the simplest is a **rollover effect**—or simply a **rollover**—which is a change in a page element in response to the user moving the mouse pointer over that element or over another element. Creating a rollover involves specifying the default appearance of the element that changes, which may be a set of CSS properties or an image, then specifying the changed CSS properties or new image that constitutes the appearance of the element in response to the rollover. Each of these appearances—the default and the rollover—is known as a **state**.

In a keyframe animation, elements change as time elapses. In contrast, an interactive animation responds to user actions. For this reason, you can create a simple interactive animation using a single point of time on the Edge Animate Timeline.

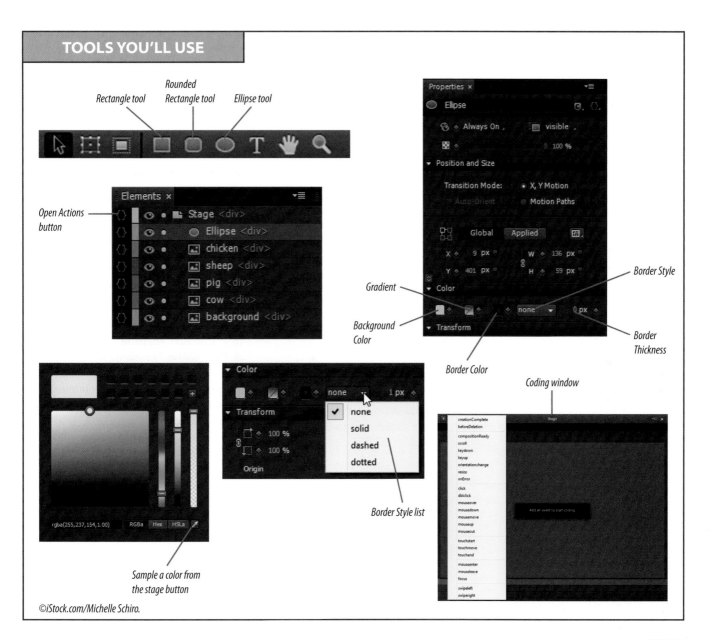

©iStock.com/Michelle Schiro.

Rectangle tool

Rounded Rectangle tool

Ellipse tool

Open Actions button

Elements ×

Stage <div>
Ellipse <div>
chicken <div>
sheep <div>
pig <div>
cow <div>
background <div>

Properties ×

Ellipse

Always On   visible

100 %

Position and Size

Transition Mode: X, Y Motion

Auto-Orient   Motion Paths

Global   Applied

X   9 px   W   136 px

Y   401 px   H   59 px

Color

Transform

Gradient

Background Color

Border Color

Border Style

Border Thickness

Color

none   1 px

Transform

100 %

100 %

Origin

none
solid
dashed
dotted

Border Style list

Coding window

rgba(255,237,154,1.00)   RGBa   Hex   HSLa

Sample a color from the stage button

creationComplete
beforeDeletion
compositionReady
scroll
keydown
keyup
orientationchange
resize
onError
click
dblclick
mouseover
mousedown
mousemove
mouseup
mouseout
touchstart
touchmove
touchend
mouseenter
mouseleave
focus
swipeleft
swiperight

Stage

Add an event to start coding

Draw SHAPES

What You'll Do

©iStock.com/Michelle Schiro.

 In this lesson, you will create an ellipse, set its properties, and duplicate it.

Using the Shape Tools

When your design calls for an element to be displayed over a background or another element, it's often helpful to create a border around the element. The border can help to visually distinguish the displayed element. Edge Animate does not allow you to specify borders for many web page elements, including text and images. However, you can create shapes in Edge Animate, then specify borders for those shapes.

As Figure 1 shows, the Edge Animate Toolbar includes three tools that you can use to create shapes. The **Rectangle tool** lets you create a rectangle shape. You can use the **Rounded Rectangle tool** to create a rectangle with rounded corners. Finally, you can create an ellipse or circle using the **Ellipse tool**.

You can add a border to a shape using the Color section of the Properties panel, as shown in Figure 2. Clicking the Border Color swatch displays a color selector that lets you select the border color just as you would select the stage background color or any other color in Edge Animate. You can choose a border style from the four choices in the Border Style list: none, solid, dashed, or dotted. Finally, you can set the thickness of the border, sometimes referred to as the **stroke**, by clicking the Border Thickness value and entering a new value.

To create the effect of a border around another element, such as a text element, you first create a shape of the appropriate dimensions, then set the appropriate border properties. Next, you move the text element over the shape, and ensure that the text layer is above the shape layer on the Elements panel. The text then appears to have a rectangular, rounded rectangular, or elliptical border. In addition, you can assign a color to the shape that's different from the shape's border color,

Figure 1 *Shape tools on the Tools panel*
©iStock.com/Michelle Schiro.

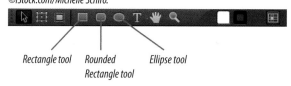

Rectangle tool   *Rounded Rectangle tool*   *Ellipse tool*

which gives the text element the appearance of a contrasting background color. Figure 3 illustrates the use of layers to add a border and a background color to text.

Duplicating Shapes

Sometimes you need to create multiple shapes that share the same dimensions. Instead of creating each individually, you can create one shape that matches your requirements then duplicate it to create new shapes with the same properties. Edge Animate offers multiple ways to duplicate a shape. You can right-click the shape then click Duplicate from the context menu. You can also select the shape to duplicate then press the [Ctrl][D] keyboard shortcut. After you create a duplicate shape, you can customize its properties just as you would for a shape you created using the shape tools on the Tools panel.

Figure 3 *Border and background added to text with a shape*

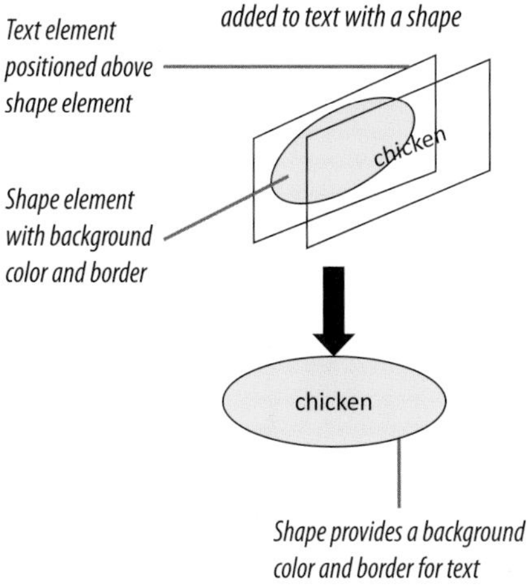

Text element positioned above shape element

Shape element with background color and border

chicken

chicken

Shape provides a background color and border for text

© 2015 Cengage Learning®.

Figure 2 *Color options on the Properties panel for a shape*

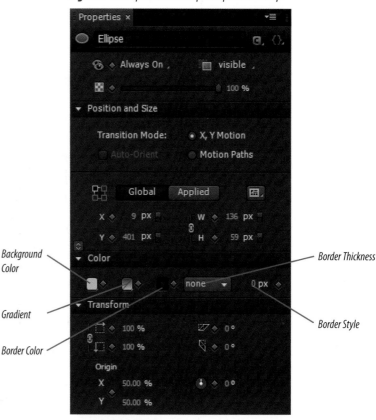

Background Color

Gradient

Border Color

Border Thickness

Border Style

©iStock.com/Michelle Schiro.

Drawing Squares and Circles

A square is a specific type of rectangle in which all four sides are the same length. Similarly, a circle is a type of ellipse in which the radius is the same all the way around. You can use the [Shift] key with the Rectangle tool and the Ellipse tool to draw perfect squares and circles, respectively. To create a square, click the Rectangle tool, press and hold the [Shift] key, click and drag to create your square, release the mouse button, then release the [Shift] key. Likewise, to create a circle, click the Ellipse tool, press and hold the [Shift] key, click and drag to create your circle, release the mouse button, then release the [Shift] key.

Create a shape

1. In Edge Animate, open the **farm.an** file from the farm folder where your Data Files are saved.

   The project contains a background image of a barn, along with images of a chicken, a cow, a pig, and a sheep.

2. If necessary, zoom the stage out until you can see all four animals, then click the **chicken**.

   Because the chicken is a separate image on its own layer, a blue border surrounds it, indicating that it's selected. In addition, the layer with the label "chicken" is selected on the Timeline and on the Elements panel, as shown in Figure 4.

3. Repeat Step 2 to select the **cow**, the **pig**, and the **sheep**, verifying that each is a separate image with its own layer.

4. On the Elements panel, click **Stage** to select the stage.

   Note that the dimensions of the stage are the same as the dimensions of the background image in the layer named background. For this reason, you can't select the stage directly by clicking it.

   (continued)

Figure 4 *Chicken image selected*

The selected element is surrounded by a blue border on the stage

The selected element is highlighted on the Elements panel

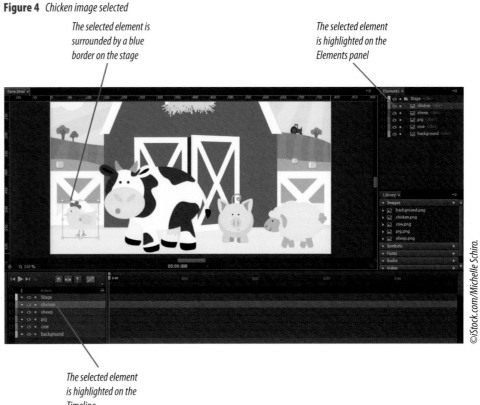

The selected element is highlighted on the Timeline

©iStock.com/Michelle Schira.

Creating Interactive Animations with Edge Animate

Figure 5 *Ellipse added above chicken*

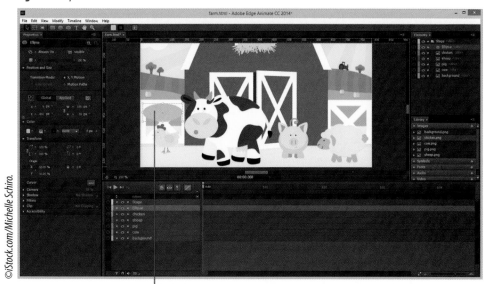

Ellipse added using
the Ellipse tool

5. In the Toolbar, click the **Ellipse tool** , then move the pointer to the stage, above the chicken, until the pointer changes to $+$.

6. Move the pointer just above the chicken and near the left edge of the stage, click and drag up and to the right until the pointer is just under the cow's ear, then release the mouse button.

As Figure 5 shows, an ellipse is displayed above the chicken.

TIP The ellipse shown in Figure 5 is gray and has no border. However, depending on recent activity on your computer, your ellipse may have a different color and may have a border. You'll customize the border and color in the following steps.

You used the Ellipse tool to create an ellipse.

Specify shape border properties

1. If necessary, click the ellipse you created to select it.

   The Properties panel displays properties for the ellipse.

2. In the Title box, position the insertion point to the left of the "E" in "Ellipse," which is the default layer name, type **Chicken**, then press **[Enter]**.

   The title is now ChickenEllipse.

3. On the Properties panel, in the Color section, click the **Border Style arrow**.

   The Border Style list is displayed, as shown in Figure 6.

   (continued)

Figure 6 *Border Style list*

Border Style list

Creating Interactive Animations with Edge Animate

Figure 7 *Solid black border added to ellipse*

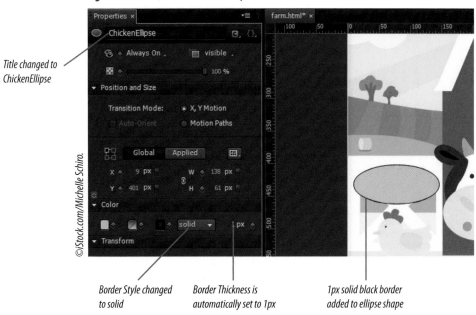

Title changed to ChickenEllipse

Border Style changed to solid

Border Thickness is automatically set to 1px

1px solid black border added to ellipse shape

Figure 8 *Sample a color from the stage pointer*

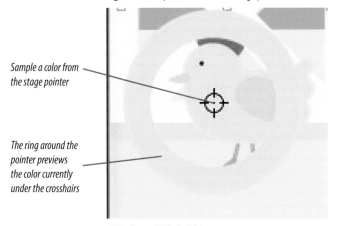

Sample a color from the stage pointer

The ring around the pointer previews the color currently under the crosshairs

4. On the Border Style list, click **solid**. The Border Thickness value automatically changes to 1px and a border is displayed around the ellipse, as shown in Figure 7.

Note that the border is black because this is the default border color. You can change this color using the Border Color swatch.

You added a solid black border to the ellipse.

Specify a shape background color

1. If necessary, click the ellipse to select it.

2. On the Properties panel, in the Color section, click the **Background Color swatch** ▢, click the **Sample a color from the stage button** 🖉, then move the pointer over the chicken until the pointer changes to ⊕ with a ring around it matching the color currently under the crosshairs, as shown in Figure 8.

(continued)

3. Move the pointer over a **light yellow area** of the chicken, then click.

The selected color changes to a value similar to rgba(255,237,154,1.00) and the ellipse changes to yellow, as shown in Figure 9.

You changed the color of the ellipse to yellow.

Duplicate a shape element

1. Right-click the **ellipse** to open the context menu, then click **Duplicate**.

A second ellipse with the same properties is created on a new layer with the name ChickenEllipseCopy.

TIP The new ellipse is placed exactly on top of the ellipse you created, so the only way to verify that the new ellipse has been created is to check the Elements panel or Timeline for a layer named ChickenEllipseCopy.

(continued)

Figure 9 *Yellow background color added to ellipse*

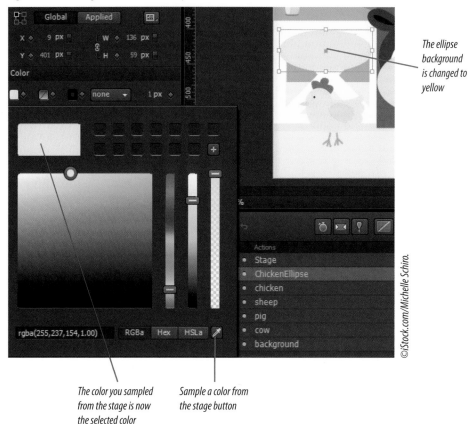

The ellipse background is changed to yellow

The color you sampled from the stage is now the selected color

Sample a color from the stage button

©iStock.com/Michelle Schiro.

Creating Interactive Animations with Edge Animate

Figure 10 *Duplicate ellipse positioned above cow*

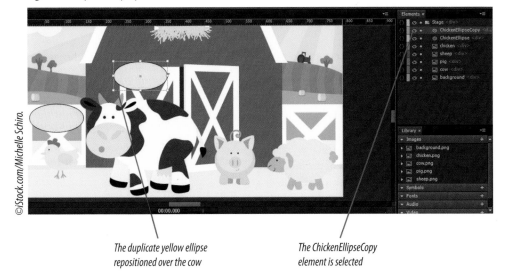

©iStock.com/Michelle Schiro.

The duplicate yellow ellipse
repositioned over the cow

The ChickenEllipseCopy
element is selected

Figure 11 *Duplicate ellipses added to the stage*

©iStock.com/Michelle Schiro.

2. On the Elements panel, verify that the ChickenEllipseCopy layer is selected,then drag the selected **ellipse** above the cow, as shown in Figure 10.

3. On the Properties panel, select the text in the Title box, type **CowEllipse**, then press **[Enter]**.

4. In the Color section of the Properties panel, click the **Background Color swatch** ☐, click the **Sample a color from the stage button** 🖋, click a **white part** of the cow, then press **[Enter]**.

   The background color of the CowEllipse shape is now white.

5. Repeat Steps 1-4 to create two more copies of the ChickenEllipse shape. One should be named **PigEllipse** and should have a background color that matches the lightest pink part of the pig image. The other should be named **SheepEllipse** and should have a background color that matches the lightest color of the sheep image.

   Your project should match Figure 11.

6. Save your changes to farm.html.

You created three duplicate ellipses.

Group ELEMENTS

What You'll Do

©iStock.com/Michelle Schiro.

 In this lesson, you will group the text and ellipse for each animal label into a single unit.

Grouping Elements

When your project contains elements that rely on each other—such as text and a border shape—you can work with them more easily by **grouping** them, which involves telling Edge Animate that you want to work with them as a single unit. To group elements in an Edge Animate project, you hold the [Shift] key, click each of the elements you want to group, release the [Shift] key, then press [Ctrl][G] (Windows) or [command][G] (Mac). The individual elements you grouped are still displayed on the Timeline and on the Elements panel, but they are indented beneath a new element that contains them. Edge Animate treats this new group element the same as any other element. Once you have created elements and placed them in relation to each other, grouping them makes it easier to work with them for tasks like moving them around the stage. Figure 12 shows grouped elements on the Elements panel.

QUICK TIP

When naming grouping elements, it's helpful to give them names that describe their contents. This makes it easier to ensure you're working with the right element later.

Figure 12 *Grouped elements on the Elements panel*

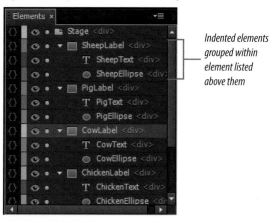

Indented elements grouped within element listed above them

©iStock.com/Michelle Schiro.

Creating Interactive Animations with Edge Animate

Figure 13 *Duplicate text element created*

©iStock.com/Michelle Schiro.

Duplicate ChickenText element

ChickenText element

"chicken" text is positioned over the ellipse above the chicken image

Duplicate "chicken" text element is positioned over the ellipse above the cow image

Create text labels

1. In the Toolbar, click the **Text tool** ⊤, click in the **yellow ellipse** above the chicken image, type **chicken**, then click the **blue sky** in the background image.

   The text "chicken" is displayed in the yellow ellipse.

2. With the "chicken" text element selected, select the contents of the Title box on the Properties panel, type **ChickenText**, then press **[Enter]**.

   The title of the layer is changed to "ChickenText."

3. Click the **font size value** to select it, type **30**, then press **[Enter]**. The text size changes to 30px.

4. If necessary, drag the text element to center it vertically and horizontally on the yellow ellipse.

TIP With a text element or any other element selected, you can also use the arrow keys to move the element in small increments.

5. With the "chicken" text element selected, press **[Ctrl][D]** (Win) or **[command][D]** (Mac) to duplicate it, then drag the duplicate on the white ellipse above the cow image.

   The duplicate is displayed on the Elements panel with the name "ChickenTextCopy," as shown in Figure 13.

TIP If the copy of the chicken text is invisible when placed on the white ellipse, locate the ChickenTextCopy layer on the Elements panel then drag it above the CowEllipse layer.

6. Double-click the text you just moved to select it in the ChickenTextCopy box, type **cow**, click the **blue sky** of the background image, then if necessary, drag the text "cow" so it's centered vertically and horizontally on the white ellipse.

(continued)

7. With the "cow" text element selected, click in the **Title box** on the Properties panel, edit the title to read **CowText**, then press **[Enter]**.

8. Repeat Steps 5-7 to create two additional duplicates of the ChickenText layer. Place one duplicate on the pink ellipse, change its text to **pig**, and change its title to **PigText**. Place the other duplicate on the gray ellipse, change its text to **sheep**, and change its title to **SheepText**.

Figure 14 shows the project with all the text added.

9. Save your changes to **farm.html**.

You layered a text element over each ellipse.

Group text labels and ellipses

1. On the Elements panel, click the **ChickenEllipse element**, press and hold **[Ctrl]** (Win) or **[command]** (Mac), click the **ChickenText element**, then release **[Ctrl]**(Win) or **[command]**(Mac).

Both the ChickenEllipse and ChickenText elements are selected on the Elements panel and on the stage.

2. Right-click the **ChickenText element** on the Elements panel, then click **Group elements in DIV**.

A new element named "Group" is added to the Elements panel, with the ChickenText and ChickenEllipse elements indented beneath it.

TIP When grouping elements, you can right-click any selected element.

3. On the Elements panel, double-click the label **Group**.

The label text is selected and editable, as shown in Figure 15.

(continued)

Figure 14 *Text labels added*

©iStock.com/Michelle Schira.

Figure 15 *Editing a group label*

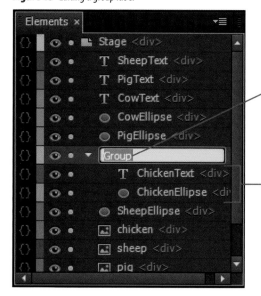

The name of the new element is selected and editable on the Elements panel

The ChickenText and ChickenEllipse elements are indented beneath the Group element, indicating that they are grouped within it

Figure 16 *Completed groups for all four labels*

©iStock.com/Michelle Schiro.

Four grouped elements created

4. Type **ChickenLabel** then press **[Enter]**.

The group name changes to "ChickenLabel."

5. Repeat Steps 1-4 to create groups named **CowLabel**, **PigLabel**, and **SheepLabel**.

Figure 16 shows the grouped labels on the Elements panel.

6. On the Elements panel, click the **ChickenLabel** group.

Note that when a group is selected on the Elements panel, all elements that are part of that group are selected on the stage.

7. Drag the **ChickenLabel group** anywhere on the stage.

Notice that whether you position the pointer over the ellipse or over the text when you start dragging, both grouped elements move together as a unit.

8. If necessary, return the ChickenLabel group to its position just above the chicken image, as shown in Figure 16.

You grouped text elements and shapes.

Specify a
STARTUP ACTION

What You'll Do

©iStock.com/Michelle Schiro.

In this lesson, you will use the compositionReady event to specify the actions you want your animation to perform when the animation first loads in a browser.

Understanding Events, Actions, and Targets

All web browsers are designed to respond to **events**, which are circumstances that occur in the browser. Events can be things that happen by default, such as a project loading, or they can be initiated by users with activities such as clicking or moving the mouse, or touching or swiping on a touchscreen. Edge Animate enables you to specify events that your animation, or elements of your animation, should respond to. For instance, you could specify that the animation should respond when a user clicks a certain element. When an event takes place, it is said to **fire**.

In addition to specifying an event that browsers should respond to, you also need to indicate what your animation should do when that event happens. To enable users to interact with an animation, you pair an event with an **action**, which is something that the animation can do. Common actions include starting or stopping the animation, moving to a specific point on the Timeline, or showing or hiding an element.

Some events are generated by specific elements—for instance, when you click a button on a web page, the button generates the event. The element that generates an event is known as the **source element**, or simply **source**.

Each action that you specify must include a **target**, which is the element on which the action is performed. In some cases, you want to perform an action on the same element that fires the event. For instance, if you want a button to change color when a user moves the mouse pointer over it, the source and target elements are the same. In other cases, you want an event fired on one element to initiate an action on another element. In this case, you simply specify the name of the element that the action should affect. Figure 17 illustrates the relationship between an event, action, source, and target.

QUICK TIP

An animation can incorporate many sets of events and actions. For instance, in an animation with two buttons, you could specify that clicking one button starts the animation and clicking the other button stops the animation.

Specifying Sources, Events, Actions, and Targets

Using events in your animations involves four steps:

1. Select a source element.
2. Specify an event that can affect that element, such as the user clicking the mouse button.
3. Indicate an action that the animation should perform in response to the specified event.
4. Identify a target for the indicated action.

At the left edge of each element on the Elements panel and in the Timeline is an Open Actions button ![icon], as shown in Figure 18. Clicking this button for an element specifies that you want that element to be the source of an event, and opens the coding window for that element, as shown in

Figure 17 *Relationship between event, action, source, and target*

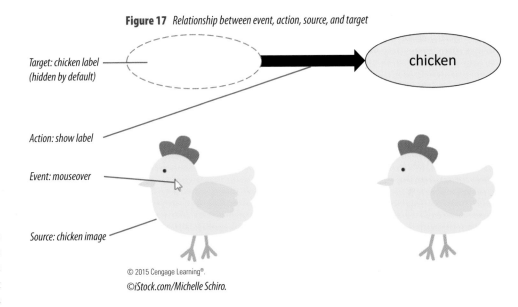

Target: chicken label (hidden by default)

Action: show label

Event: mouseover

Source: chicken image

chicken

© 2015 Cengage Learning®.
©iStock.com/Michelle Schiro.

Figure 18 *Locations of Open Actions buttons*

Each element on the Elements panel has an Open Actions button

Each element in the Timeline has an Open Actions button

©iStock.com/Michelle Schiro.

Figure 19. By default, the list of events available for the selected element is displayed. When you click an event, a tab for that event is added to the window. Each tab has three sections, as shown in Figure 20. The first of the three sections is a code pane, which is displayed at the top of the window. Whenever you add an element to the stage, Edge Animate writes the HTML code for that element to the project's .html file. In the same way, each time you specify an event and an action for an element, Edge Animate generates code that tells the browser what event to listen for and what action to take when that event fires. The only difference between these two types of code is that the code for an event and action is in **JavaScript**, a programming language that enables interactivity in web documents. The code pane displays the JavaScript code as it is generated. If you are experienced with writing JavaScript

Figure 19 *Coding window showing events list*

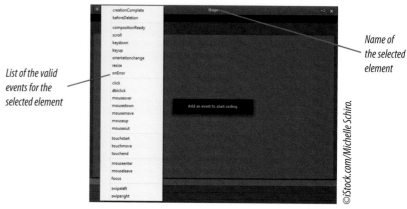

List of the valid events for the selected element

Name of the selected element

©iStock.com/Michelle Schira.

Figure 20 *Sections of coding window*

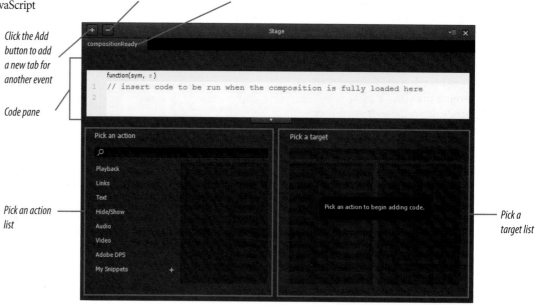

click the Remove button to delete the current tab

tab name is the event selected from the events list

Click the Add button to add a new tab for another event

Code pane

Pick an action list

Pick a target list

Creating Interactive Animations with Edge Animate

code, you can write and edit code directly in this pane. However, Edge Animate was created to be useful for developers with little or no coding experience, so instead of writing JavaScript code, you can instead use the Pick an action list and the Pick a target list, below the code pane, to specify an action and the element it should apply to. Edge Animate will then automatically generate the necessary JavaScript code and display it in the code pane.

Below the code pane are two additional sections: the Pick an action list and the Pick a target list. The Pick an action list displays categories of actions available for the selected element and event. When you click a category, a list of actions in that category is displayed to the right. Clicking an action has two results: code is added to the code pane, and a list of targets is displayed in the Pick a target list. At the top of the list of targets is a direct link to the element whose Open Actions button you clicked. Below it is a link to the stage, which you can click to either select the stage itself, or to view and navigate through the elements on the stage. Figure 21 shows the coding window with both an action and a target selected.

Once you have selected both an action and a target, the final step is to press Enter to finalize the JavaScript code generated from your selections. The code is displayed in color in the code pane.

QUICK TIP

The code in the code pane often starts with a JavaScript comment, which is displayed all in gray. If you scroll down in the code pane, you'll usually see code in multiple colors below the comment.

Because you can specify more than one action and target for any event, the element window remains open. To finish your work for the selected element, you simply click the Close button ☒.

QUICK TIP

The events list is displayed by default when the coding window opens. If you finish adding an event and action for a source element and want to add another event and action for the same source, you can click the Add button ➕ in the top-left corner to display the event list.

Using the compositionReady Event

Sometimes you'll want your animation to perform an action immediately after it is loaded by a browser. To do this, you use the **compositionReady event**, which fires when an animation is ready to play, but before autoplay starts (if you've enabled the Autoplay property). The compositionReady event is useful for tasks that need to happen before your animation is ready for user interaction. For instance, if you're creating a rollover effect that makes an element visible, you need that element to be hidden when the animation loads.

Figure 21 *Coding window with selected action and target*

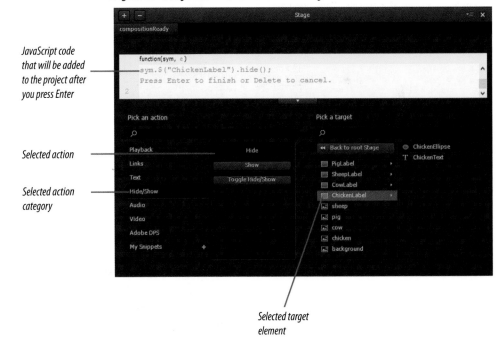

JavaScript code that will be added to the project after you press Enter

Selected action

Selected action category

Selected target element

Specify actions and targets for the compositionReady event

1. On the Elements panel, locate **Stage** in the list (you might need to scroll up to see it), then click the **Open Actions button** 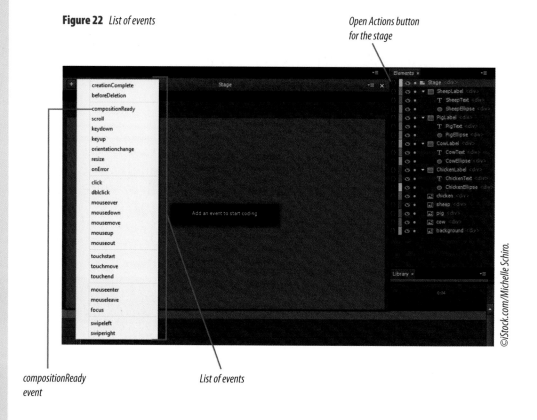 for the stage.

   The coding window for the stage opens, with the list of events displayed, as shown in Figure 22.

2. In the list of events, click **compositionReady**.

   A tab is added to the coding window with the name compositionReady. In addition, the code pane, Pick an action list, and Pick a target list are displayed.

   (continued)

Figure 22 *List of events*

Open Actions button for the stage

compositionReady event

List of events

©iStock.com/Michelle Schira.

Creating Interactive Animations with Edge Animate

Figure 23 *List of actions*

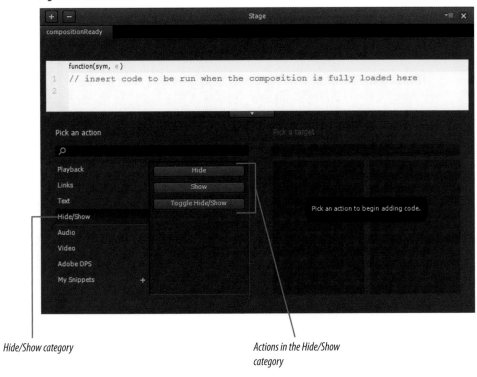

Hide/Show category

Actions in the Hide/Show
category

3. In the Pick an action list, click **Hide/Show**.

   A list of actions in the Hide/Show category is displayed to the right of the category list, as shown in Figure 23.

4. In the list of Hide/Show actions, click **Hide**.

   The target list is displayed in the Pick a target panel.

   (continued)

5. In the Pick a target list, click the lower instance of the word **Stage**.

A list of elements on the stage is displayed to the right of the word Stage, as shown in Figure 24.

6. Click **ChickenLabel**, then press **[Enter]**.

The JavaScript code for the event and action you specified is added to the coding panel.

TIP Depending on the size of your coding window, you may not be able to see the newly added code unless you scroll within the code pane.

7. Save your changes to the project.

Saving the project automatically closes the coding window. Remember that you can close the coding window manually by clicking its Close button ⊠.

8. Press **[Ctrl][Enter]** (Win) or **[command][Enter]** (Mac) to open the project in your default browser.

As a result of the hide action you specified for the ChickenLabel element, which was executed when the project loaded in the browser, the ChickenLabel element is no longer displayed.

TIP Notice that the label is not hidden in Edge Animate. Although you can preview a keyframe animation in Edge Animate, you can view the results of events only in a browser.

(continued)

Figure 24 *List of elements on the stage*

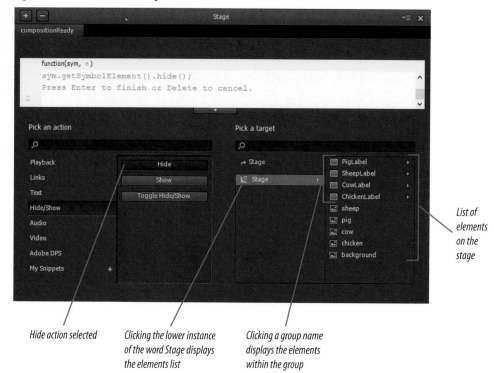

Hide action selected

Clicking the lower instance of the word Stage displays the elements list

Clicking a group name displays the elements within the group

List of elements on the stage

Creating Interactive Animations with Edge Animate

Figure 25 *Label elements hidden in browser*

All four labels
are hidden

©iStock.com/Michelle Schiro.

9. Return to Edge Animate, then click the **Open Actions button** ⬛ for the stage.

   The coding window opens again, with the compositionReady tab displayed.

10. Repeat Steps 3-6 three times to hide the **CowLabel**, **PigLabel**, and **SheepLabel** elements.

11. Save your changes to the project, then press **[Ctrl][Enter]** (Win) or **[command][Enter]** (Mac) to open the project in your default browser.

    As Figure 25 shows, all four labels are now hidden.

You used four actions and targets for the compositionReady event on the stage to hide the animal labels when the animation loads in a browser.

Specify Events, Actions,
AND TARGETS FOR INTERACTION

What You'll Do

©iStock.com/Michelle Schiro.

In this lesson, you will specify actions for the mouseover and mouseout events to enable the rollover effect on the four animal images.

Specifying Interactive Events

In the previous lesson, you used the compositionReady event to initiate actions when your animation loaded in the browser. Edge Animate provides access to many other events that browsers fire in response to the user performing an action with a mouse or with a mobile device. Table 1 describes some user-initiated events that an Edge Animate project can respond to.

TABLE 1: USER-INITIATED EVENTS	
User-Initiated Event	**Description**
orientationchange	The user changes the device orientation between portrait (device held so it's taller than it is wide) and landscape (device held so it's wider than it is tall)
click	The user clicks the left mouse button while the pointer is over the element
mouseover	The user moves the mouse pointer over the element
mousedown	The user presses the left mouse button while the pointer is over the element
mousemove	The user moves the mouse while the pointer is over the element and the left mouse button has been pressed
mouseup	The user releases the left mouse button while the pointer is over the element
mouseout	The user moves the mouse pointer off the element
touchstart	A finger or stylus touches the screen over the element
touchmove	A finger or stylus moves while touching the screen over the element
touchend	A finger or stylus stops touching the screen while over the element
mouseenter	The user moves the mouse pointer over the element
mouseleave	The user moves the mouse pointer off of the element
focus	The element becomes the current element (by clicking, touching, or keyboard navigation)
swipeleft	A finger touching the screen moves quickly to the left
swiperight	A finger touching the screen moves quickly to the right

Creating a Rollover Effect

A rollover effect has two parts: it starts in response to a user moving the mouse pointer over the source element, and ends when a user moves the mouse pointer off the source element. To create the first part of the rollover effect, you use the mouseover event, which fires when a user moves the mouse pointer over the source element. You create the second part of the rollover effect using the mouseout event, which fires when the user moves the mouse pointer off the source element. For each element with a rollover effect, you need to specify an action and a target for both events, as illustrated in Figure 26.

Although both the mouseover and mouseout events include the word "mouse" in their names, they are also supported on touch devices without mice, such as phones and tablets. On a touch device, touching an element fires its mouseover event, and touching a different element fires the original element's mouseout event.

Figure 26 *The two events needed for a rollover effect*

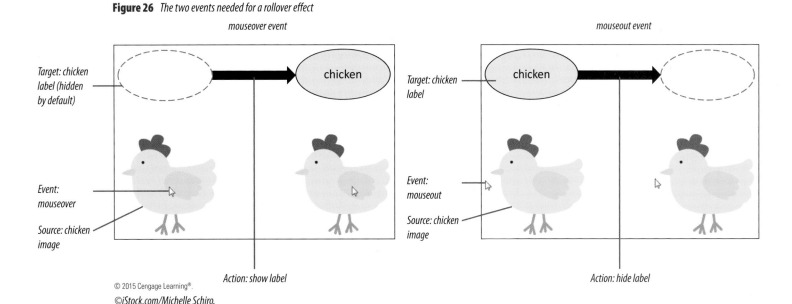

© 2015 Cengage Learning®.

©iStock.com/Michelle Schiro.

Add actions for the mouseover event

1. On the Elements panel, locate the chicken element in the list, then click the **Open Actions button** 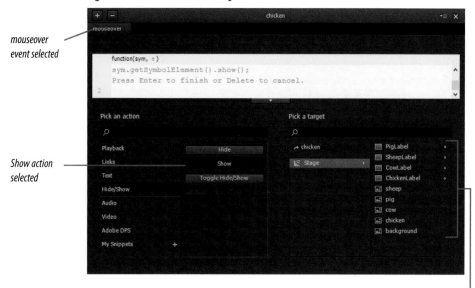 for the chicken element.

TIP Be sure not to click the Open Actions button for the ChickenLabel, ChickenText, or ChickenEllipse elements.

The coding window for the chicken element opens, with the list of events displayed.

2. In the list of events, click **mouseover**.

A tab named mouseover is added to the coding window. In addition, the code pane, Pick an action list, and Pick a target list are displayed.

3. In the Pick an action list, click **Hide/Show**, then in the list of Hide/Show actions, click **Show**.

The target list is displayed in the Pick a target panel.

4. In the Pick a target list, click **Stage**.

A list of elements on the stage is displayed to the right of the word "Stage," as shown in Figure 27.

5. Click **ChickenLabel**, press **[Enter]**, then in the code pane, scroll down.

The JavaScript code for the event and target you specified is added to the coding panel, as shown in Figure 28.

6. Save your changes to the project, then press **[Ctrl][Enter]** (Win) or **[command][Enter]** (Mac) to open the project in your default browser.

All four labels remain hidden.

(continued)

Figure 27 *List of elements on the stage*

mouseover event selected

Show action selected

List of elements on the stage

Creating Interactive Animations with Edge Animate

Figure 28 *Code created for the mouseover event on the chicken element*

JavaScript code for the show action on the ChickenLabel target

Scroll bar for the code pane

```
function(sym, e)
sym.$("ChickenLabel").show();
```

Pick an action

Playback
Links
Text
Hide/Show
Audio
Video
Adobe DPS
My Snippets

Pick a target

Pick an action to begin adding code.

Figure 29 *Chicken label displayed in response to mouseover event*

The ChickenLabel element is shown in response to the mouseover event on the chicken image

chicken

The mouseover event fires when the mouse pointer moves over the chicken image

©iStock.com/Michelle Schiro.

7. Move your mouse pointer over the chicken image.

    When you moved your mouse pointer over the chicken image element, the Show action you specified for that element was executed, causing the ChickenLabel element to be displayed, as shown in Figure 29.

8. Move your mouse pointer off the chicken image.

    Notice that the chicken label is still displayed. You'll fix this later.

9. Repeat Steps 1-5 for the **cow**, **pig**, and **sheep** elements to show the **CowLabel**, **PigLabel**, and **SheepLabel** elements, respectively.

10. Save your changes to the project, press **[Ctrl] [Enter]** (Win) or **[command][Enter]** (Mac) to open the project in your default browser, then move the mouse pointer over each animal.

    The label for each animal should be displayed when you move the mouse pointer over the animal, and should remain visible after you move the mouse pointer off of the animal.

TIP If an event does not produce the desired action, open the coding window for the source element, click the tab for the incorrect event, then click the Remove button ➖. This removes the code for the selected event, allowing you to redo the steps.

You added actions and targets for the mouseover event for the four animal images.

Add actions for the mouseout event

1. In Edge Animate, on the Elements panel, locate the chicken element in the list, then click the **Open Actions button** for the chicken element.

   TIP Be sure not to click the Open Actions button for the ChickenLabel, ChickenText, or ChickenEllipse elements.

   The coding window for the chicken element opens, with the list of events displayed.

2. Click the **Add button**, then in the list of events, click **mouseout**.

   A tab named mouseout is added to the coding window, as shown in Figure 30.

3. In the Pick an action list, click **Hide/Show**, then in the list of Hide/Show actions, click **Hide**.

   The target list is displayed in the Pick a target panel.

4. In the Pick a target list, click **Stage**.

   A list of elements on the stage is displayed to the right of the word Stage.

5. Click **ChickenLabel**, press **[Enter]**, then in the code pane, scroll down.

   The JavaScript code for the event and action you specified is added to the coding panel, as shown in Figure 31.

6. Save your changes to the project, then press **[Ctrl][Enter]** (Win) or **[command][Enter]** (Mac) to open the project in your default browser.

   All four labels remain hidden.

   (continued)

Figure 30 *mouseout tab added to coding window*

Add button

New mouseout tab added

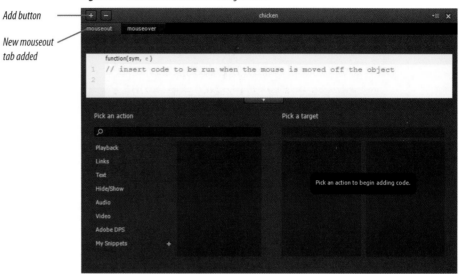

Figure 31 *Code created for the mouseout event*

New JavaScript code to hide the ChickenLabel element is added

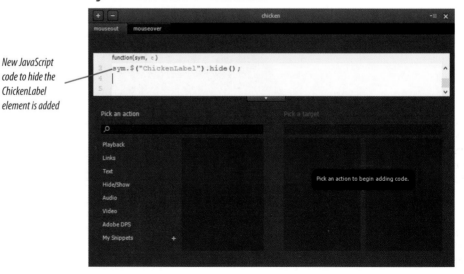

Creating Interactive Animations with Edge Animate

Figure 32 *Text label displayed in response to mouseover event*

The ChickenLabel
element is displayed
in response to the
mouseover event on
the chicken image

The mouse pointer
is over the chicken
image

©iStock.com/Michelle Schiro.

Figure 33 *Text label hidden in response to mouseout event*

The ChickenLabel
element is hidden
in response to the
mouseout event on
the chicken image

The mouse pointer
is off the chicken
image

©iStock.com/Michelle Schiro.

7. Move your mouse pointer over the chicken image until the chicken label is displayed, as shown in Figure 32.

8. Move your mouse pointer off the chicken image.

   When you moved your mouse pointer off the chicken image element, the Hide action you specified for that element was executed, causing the ChickenLabel element to disappear (hide), as shown in Figure 33.

9. Repeat Steps 1-5 for the **cow**, **pig**, and **sheep** elements to hide the **CowLabel**, **PigLabel**, and **SheepLabel** elements, respectively.

10. Save your changes to the project, press **[Ctrl] [Enter]** (Win) or **[command][Enter]** (Mac) to open the project in your default browser, then move the mouse pointer over and off of each animal.

    The label for each animal should be displayed when you move the mouse pointer over the animal, and should be hidden once again when you move the mouse pointer off of the animal.

You added actions and targets for the mouseout event for the four animal images.

Examine Code and Test Interactivity
ON DESKTOP BROWSERS

What You'll Do

In this lesson, you will view the JavaScript code for your project generated by Edge Animate, and you'll test your project in multiple desktop browsers.

Using the Code Panel

In addition to all the panels displayed by default in Edge Animate, one extra panel is hidden: the Code panel. You can open the Code panel by clicking the Window menu then clicking Code. You can also open the Code panel with the keyboard shortcut [Ctrl][E] (Win) or [command][E] (Mac).

As Figure 34 shows, the Code panel enables you to view the JavaScript code generated by Edge Animate for the current project. In this way, the Code panel is similar to the coding window you used in the last lesson to specify events, actions, and targets. The difference is that the left side of the Code panel lists each event and its corresponding source element, with the source element listed first, followed by a period, followed by the event. You can click any item in this list to see all

the relevant JavaScript code on the right side of the panel.

The Code panel also includes a Full Code button at the top right. You can click this button to view all the JavaScript code generated for your project in a single file.

The Code panel is most useful for experienced web developers who want to write or edit the project's JavaScript code directly. However, as you're learning how Edge Animate works and what it can do, it can be useful to examine the code generated by your projects to better understand how Edge Animate translates the selections you make into the code that runs in browsers.

Testing Animations on Desktop Browsers

Building an Edge Animate project and verifying that it works as you expect in a browser is an important step in creating a final product. However, testing your project in a variety of desktop browsers and on a range of mobile devices is an important next step in creating a product that works reliably for your target audience.

Edge Animate generates code that is designed to work on the current versions of all modern desktop browsers, including Chrome, Firefox,

Figure 34 *The Code panel*

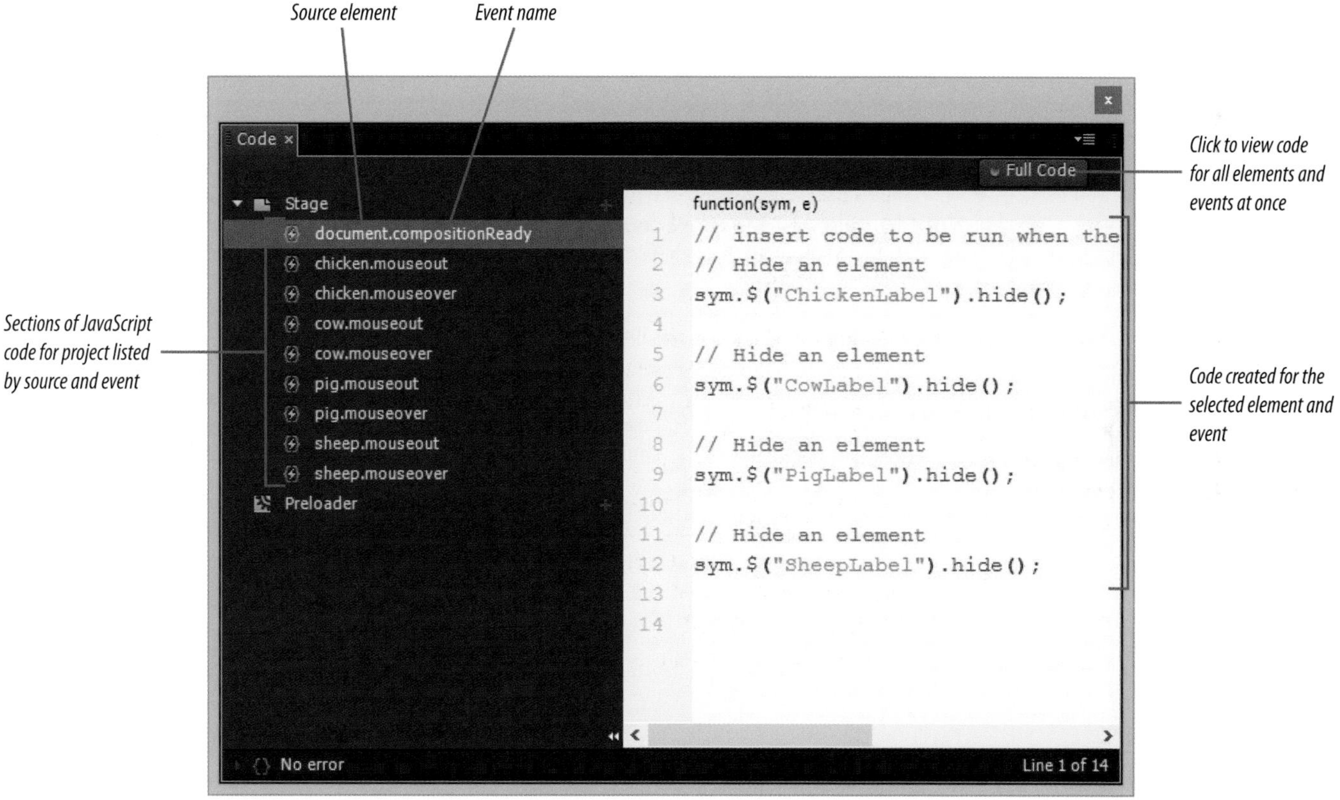

Source element

Event name

Sections of JavaScript code for project listed by source and event

Click to view code for all elements and events at once

Code created for the selected element and event

```
function(sym, e)
1    // insert code to be run when the
2    // Hide an element
3    sym.$("ChickenLabel").hide();
4
5    // Hide an element
6    sym.$("CowLabel").hide();
7
8    // Hide an element
9    sym.$("PigLabel").hide();
10
11   // Hide an element
12   sym.$("SheepLabel").hide();
13
14
```

and Internet Explorer. In addition, simpler animations may work on older desktop browsers that are still in significant use; chief among these is Internet Explorer 8.

Before creating an animation, it's important to understand which desktop browsers you expect your target audience to be using. If you need to support older browsers, it's important to be sure that the features you're implementing in Edge Animate are supported on those platforms. In addition, sometimes a project that you create with Edge Animate may not work as you expect in some browsers. To ensure that your project works as you expect on all of the browsers in use by your target audience, it's important to install all of those browsers on your testing machine and to test your animation on each of them to ensure it works as expected.

Basic Desktop Browsers for Testing

The vast majority of desktop web users access documents using the current versions of Chrome, Firefox, or Internet Explorer. To perform basic testing when developing content for the web, you should have access to all three of these browsers. Because a significant number of users still access the web with Internet Explorer 8, it can also be useful to have access to this browser as well. If you have browsing statistics on your target audience, you should test on all browsers that are used by significant portions of your audience; one common rule is that you should test on any browser used by at least 1 percent of your target audience.

Internet Explorer is available only for Windows. If you're using a Mac, you can't run Internet Explorer under Mac OS X. If you have access to a Windows computer, you can instead use that machine to test your projects on Internet Explorer. Alternatively, you can install Windows on your Mac as a virtual machine using software such as Parallels, VMWare Fusion, or VirtualBox.

Especially if your audience uses a large number of older browsers, it can be challenging to maintain installations of all necessary browsers on your own computer. You can instead use an online testing service such as *browserstack.com* or *saucelabs.com*, both of which allow you to interact with your content as it is rendered on any browser you specify.

Creating Interactive Animations with Edge Animate

Figure 35 *Initial view of the Code panel*

Figure 36 *JavaScript code for chicken.mouseout*

Code created for the
mouseout event on
the chicken element

View the final JavaScript code for a project

1. In Edge Animate, click the **Window menu**, then click **Code**.

   The Code panel is displayed, as shown in Figure 35. Because you specified actions for multiple events on several elements, these elements are listed twice in the list on the left side of the Code panel—once for each event you specified.

2. Click **chicken.mouseout**.

   The code for the mouseout event on the chicken element is displayed on the right side of the screen. This is the same code that was displayed on the Code panel on the mouseout tab in the coding window for the chicken event.

   (continued)

3. On the left side of the Code window, click **document.compositionReady**.

The code for the compositionReady event on the document element is displayed, as shown in Figure 37. This code includes all four of the actions you specified to be executed when the compositionReady event fires.

TIP The document element is the name assigned to the stage in JavaScript.

4. Click the **Close button** 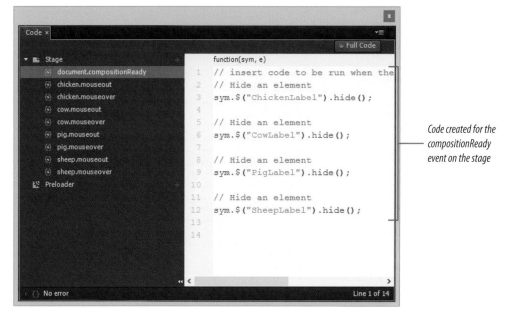 to close the Code panel.

You examined the JavaScript code for your project on the Code panel.

Test interactive features in Chrome, Firefox, and Internet Explorer

To complete the following steps, you should have access to current versions of Chrome, Firefox, and Internet Explorer.

1. In Edge Animate, with farm.html open, press **[Ctrl][Enter]** (Win) or **[command][Enter]** (Mac) to open the project in your default browser.

The project opens in your default browser. Depending on the configuration of your system, your default browser could be Chrome, Firefox, Internet Explorer, or another browser.

(continued)

Figure 37 *JavaScript code for document.compositionReady*

Code created for the compositionReady event on the stage

Creating Interactive Animations with Edge Animate

Figure 38 *URL selected in the Address bar*

Address bar

The URL for
the project
is selected

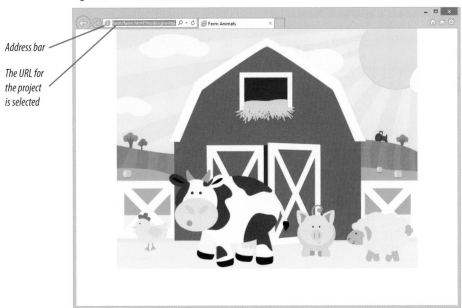

©iStock.com/Michelle Schiro. ©Microsoft Corporation.

2. In your default browser, move the mouse pointer over and off of each of the four animals and verify that the text label for each animal is displayed when the pointer is over the image and hidden when the pointer moves off the image.

3. In your browser's Address bar, select the **entire URL** of the project, as shown in Figure 38, then press **[Ctrl][C]** (Win) or **[command][C]** (Mac) to copy it to the Clipboard.

   Opening a file in your default browser from within Edge Animate uses Edge Animate's built in web server, which you'll learn more about in the next lesson. For now, just recognize that this is the reason that the URL starts with a set of numbers.

4. Open another browser, delete the contents of the Address bar, press **[Ctrl][V]** (Win) or **[command][V]** (Mac) to paste the address of your project into the Address bar, then press **[Enter]**.

   The project opens from the Edge Animate web server.

5. Move the mouse pointer over and off of each of the four animals and verify that the text label for each animal is displayed when the pointer is over the image and hidden when the pointer moves off the image.

6. Repeat Steps 4 and 5 with each remaining major browser until you have tested in all three major browsers.

You tested your project in current versions of all three major desktop browsers.

Test Interactivity on a
MOBILE DEVICE

What You'll Do

©iStock.com/Michelle Schiro.

 In this lesson, you will use Edge Inspect to test your project on a mobile device, and you'll enhance your project to better support touch devices.

Testing Projects on Mobile Devices

As people increasingly access the web using mobile devices, it's also important to test your content on the mobile devices used by your audience. Most users accessing the web on a mobile device use either Safari (on Apple iOS devices such as the iPhone and iPad) or Chrome (on Google Android devices such as Nexus and Galaxy series phones and tablets). Although it's unlikely that you'll physically own every device that your audience may use to access your content, you can start by testing on any mobile devices you have. In addition, by sharing devices with fellow students and colleagues, you may be able to access many of the most common devices.

On a desktop computer, you can open content in a browser from your computer's internal storage. However, to test your content on a mobile device, you generally need to first place that content on a **web server**, which is software that makes web content stored on a computer available to other computers. For testing purposes, it's common for web developers to install and configure a web server on their own computers. By doing this, you can make your content available to other devices on the same local wireless network.

Edge Animate includes its own rudimentary web server, so you don't need to install a separate web server to test Edge Animate projects on mobile devices.

Testing with Edge Inspect

The Adobe Edge suite includes a utility called Edge Inspect, which simplifies testing on mobile devices that you have access to. After you install Edge Inspect on your computer, you must also install Google Chrome; install a small, free application known as an **extension** within Google Chrome; and install a free Edge Inspect app on each mobile device that you want to test on. When all devices are configured and connected, you can open your content in Google Chrome, as shown in Figure 39 and see it rendered at the same time on each mobile device, as shown in Figure 40. You can also interact with the content on each mobile device while it's open, which lets you ensure that events and actions you specify work across devices as you intended.

Incorporating Touch Events

Events designed for use with a desktop computer, such as mouseover and mouseout, don't always work reliably with touchscreen

Creating Interactive Animations with Edge Animate

devices. For this reason, Edge Animate supports a set of events known as **touch events**, which are designed specifically for touchscreen devices. The **touchstart** event fires when a user touches an element, the **touchmove** event fires when a user moves the finger touching an element, and the **touchend** event fires when a user stops touching an element.

You can specify an action for a mouse event on an element while also specifying an action for a touch event on the same element. Browsers on non-touchscreen devices will never fire the touch event, and in most cases, touchscreen devices ignore any mouse event in favor of the touch event.

Figure 39 *Google Chrome desktop browser with Edge Inspect application*

Source: Google.

Figure 40 *Edge Inspect app on a mobile device*

Click to view list of desktop computers to connect to

The name of the computer the app is connected to

Mobile Edge Inspect app displays the same content shown in the desktop browser

Click the Edge Inspect icon to turn Edge Inspect on or connect to a mobile device

Edge Inspect configuration window

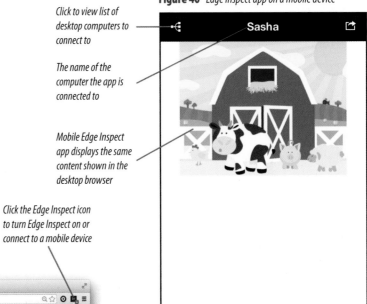

©iStock.com/Michelle Schiro.

Use Edge Inspect to test interactive features on a mobile device

Before you can complete the following steps, you need to install Adobe Edge Inspect, Google Chrome, and the Edge Inspect extension for Google Chrome on your desktop computer. You also need a mobile device with the Edge Inspect app installed. Both the desktop computer and the mobile device must be connected to the same local network. Instructions for installing Edge Inspect are available at *http://forums.adobe.com/docs/DOC-2535*.

1. On your desktop computer, start **Edge Inspect**, start **Google Chrome**, then ensure that the Edge Inspect extension for Chrome is installed.

2. On your mobile device, ensure that Edge Inspect is installed, then start **Edge Inspect**.

3. If necessary, in Google Chrome on your desktop computer, enter the **6-digit code** displayed on your mobile device, as shown in Figure 41.

    Entering this code connects the two devices, allowing the mobile device to display the content that's open in Google Chrome on the desktop computer.

4. In Edge Animate, press **[Ctrl][Enter]** (Win) or **[command][Enter]** (Mac) to open the farm. html project in your default browser using the Edge Animate web server.

    The project opens in your default browser.

    (continued)

Figure 41 *Entering the six-digit code to connect devices*

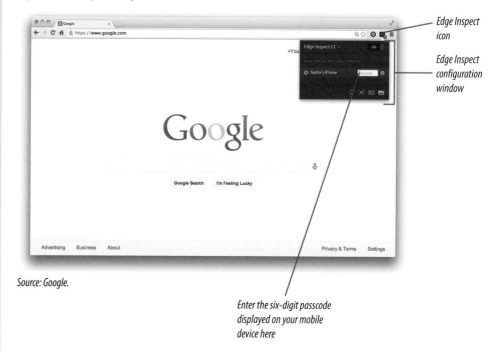

Source: Google.

Edge Inspect icon

Edge Inspect configuration window

Enter the six-digit passcode displayed on your mobile device here

Creating Interactive Animations with Edge Animate

Figure 42 *farm.html displayed on a mobile device with Edge Inspect*

The original document open in the desktop browser is displayed

©iStock.com/Michelle Schiro.

5. If your default browser is not Chrome, select the contents of the Address bar, press **[Ctrl][C]** (Win) or **[command][C]** (Mac), open Chrome, if necessary delete the contents of the Address bar, press **[Ctrl][V]** (Win) or **[command][V]** (Mac) to paste the address of the project, then press **[Enter]**.

The farm.html project opens in Chrome from the Edge Animate web server. Your content is displayed in Google Chrome as it was in the previous set of steps. It's also displayed on your mobile device, as shown in Figure 42.

6. On your mobile device, touch the **chicken image**.

The label "chicken" is displayed above the image, just like when you move the mouse pointer over the image in a desktop browser.

7. Touch the **cow image**.

Touching the cow image fires the mouseout event for the chicken image, hiding the chicken label, and fires the mouseover event for the cow image, showing the cow label.

8. Touch the **pig image**, then touch the **sheep image**.

Each touch fires the mouseout event on the previous image, as well as the mouseover event on the touched image.

9. On your mobile device, touch the **background image**.

On some devices, touching the screen outside of an element is equivalent to the mouseout event on that element, hiding the label. On other devices, however, this does not fire the mouseout event; in that case, the only way to hide one label is to touch another animal image.

You tested your project on a mobile device using Edge Inspect.

Specify an action for a touch event

The testing portion of these steps requires the same Edge Inspect installation described in the previous steps.

1. In Edge Animate, click the **Open Actions button** for the chicken element, if necessary click ➕, then in the list of events, click **touchstart**.

2. In the Pick an action pane, click **Hide/Show**, then in the list that is displayed, click **Toggle Hide/Show**.

   The Toggle Hide/Show action shows an element if it is hidden and hides and element if it is shown. Using this event will allow users to touch an image once to show the label, then touch it again to hide the label.

3. In the Pick a target pane, click **Stage**, click **ChickenLabel**, then press **[Enter]**.

   The code for the touchstart event is added to the code pane.

4. Save your changes to farm.html, return to Chrome, then press **[Ctrl][R]** (Win) or **[command][R]** (Mac) to reload the page with your changes.

TIP Reloading a document in Chrome also causes the document to reload in the Edge Inspect app on any connected mobile device.

5. Move the mouse pointer over the **chicken**, then move the mouse pointer off the **chicken**.

   The mouseover event still shows the label, and the mouseout event still hides it.

6. On your mobile device, touch the **chicken**.

   The label is displayed above the chicken, as shown in Figure 43.

(continued)

Figure 43 *Chicken label displayed in response to a touch*

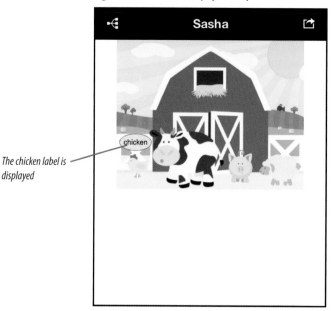

The chicken label is displayed

©iStock.com/Michelle Schiro.

Creating Interactive Animations with Edge Animate

Figure 44 *Chicken label hidden in response to second touch*

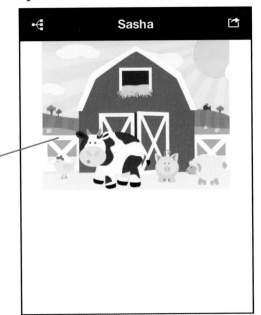

The chicken label is hidden without another animal's label being displayed

©iStock.com/Michelle Schiro.

7. Touch the **chicken** a second time.

Unlike when your project used only mouse events, the label is now hidden on all devices, as shown in Figure 44.

TIP If you touch an element twice in rapid succession, many devices interpret your action as a double-tap, which may zoom the screen instead of firing events on the element. Be sure to pause between your first and second taps.

8. Return to **Edge Animate**, then repeat Steps 1-3 for the **cow**, **pig**, and **sheep** images.

9. Save your changes to farm.html, return to Chrome, then press **[Ctrl][R]** (Win) or **[command][R]** (Mac) to reload the page with your changes.

10. Repeat Steps 6 and 7 for the **cow**, **pig**, and **sheep** images to verify that the label is displayed on the first touch and hidden on the second touch.

You specified actions for touch events and tested them on a mobile device using Edge Inspect.

Draw shapes and group elements.

1. In Edge Animate, open a new project, then set the stage dimensions to 480px (width) by 270px (height), and the stage background color to a light brown color such as rgba(199,184,164,1.00). Save the project with the name **gallery.html** to the gallery folder where you store your Data Files. Note that the gallery folder includes an images folder, so the five images in this folder are automatically added to the Library panel when you save your project.

2. Drag the file IMG_01.jpg from the Library panel to the stage, placing it so the image borders match the stage borders. On the Elements panel, change the name of the element to daisy. Repeat to stack the remaining images from the Library panel on the stage, using the following names for the elements:
   - IMG_02.jpg: **aster**
   - IMG_03.jpg: **oxalis**
   - IMG_04.jpg: **nasturtium**
   - IMG_05.jpg: **pricklypear**

3. In the bottom-left corner of the stage, use the Text tool to add the word **Daisy**. Set the font to Georgia, Times New Roman, Times, serif, and the size to 22px. Change the element name to **Daisy text**. Repeat to add the names **Aster**, **Oxalis**, **Nasturtium**, and **Prickly Pear** across the bottom of the stage, as shown in Figure 45.

4. Use the Rectangle tool to draw a rectangle that covers the word "Daisy." Use the Elements panel to change the stacking order so the word "Daisy" is visible over the rectangle you drew. Change the background color of the rectangle to a light green color. Add a 1px solid black border to the rectangle. Change the name of the rectangle element to **DaisyRectangle**.

5. Duplicate the DaisyRectangle element, drag the duplicate over the word "Aster," change the stacking order so the word "Aster" is visible over the duplicate rectangle, then adjust the size and position as necessary so the word fits within its borders. Change the name of the rectangle element to **AsterRectangle**. Repeat for the remaining three names, using the element names **OxalisRectangle**, **NasturtiumRectangle**, and **PricklyPearRectangle**.

6. Group each plant name with its background rectangle, then rename each group using the names **DaisyLabel**, **AsterLabel**, **OxalisLabel**, **NasturtiumLabel**, and **PricklyPearLabel**.

Specify a startup action.

1. Use the coding window for the stage to hide all five image elements (which you previously named daisy, aster, oxalis, nasturtium, and pricklypear) when the project loads in a browser.

2. Add the following text above the plant labels: **Move your mouse pointer over a plant name, or touch it, to view an image**. Use the font: Arial, Helvetica, sans-serif; the font size: 38px; the font color: white; and center the text horizontally. Rename the text element **InstructionText**, then reposition it as the bottommost layer in the project.

Figure 45 *Completed Skills Review*

Photo courtesy Sasha Vodnik.

Creating Interactive Animations with Edge Animate

3. Save your changes, open the project in your default browser, then verify that no images are displayed and that the instruction text is visible, as shown in Figure 46.

Specify events, actions, and targets for interaction.

1. Use the coding window for the DaisyLabel element to add actions and targets for three events: show the daisy element in response to the mouseover event, hide the daisy element in response to the mouseout event, and toggle the visibility of the daisy element in response to the touchstart event.
2. Repeat Step 1 for the remaining label elements, using the corresponding image elements as targets for all three events.
3. Save your changes.

Examine code and test interactivity on desktop browsers.

1. Open the project in your default browser.
2. Move the mouse pointer over the Daisy label and verify that an image is displayed. Move the mouse pointer to a blank area of the browser window and verify that the image is hidden and the instruction text is visible once again. Repeat for the four remaining labels.

3. Copy the complete address from the Address bar to the Clipboard, then use it to open the project in a current version of one of the three major browsers. Repeat the testing outlined in Step 2.
4. Repeat Step 3 for each of the remaining major browsers.

Test interactivity on a mobile device.

1. From Edge Animate, open the project in your default browser, then if necessary, copy the address and use it to open the project in Chrome.

2. On a mobile device, open Edge Inspect, connect to the desktop computer you're using for testing, then verify that the instruction text and labels are displayed.
3. Touch the Daisy label and verify that an image is displayed. Touch the Daisy label again and verify that the image is hidden and the instruction text is visible once again. Repeat for the four remaining labels.

Figure 46 *Default view of Skills Review project in a browser*

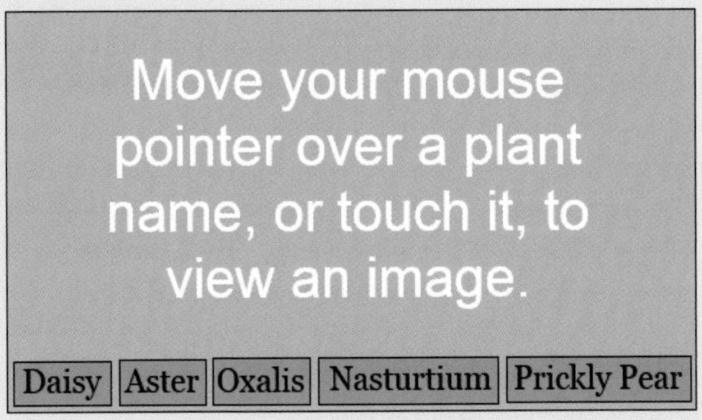

Move your mouse pointer over a plant name, or touch it, to view an image.

Daisy Aster Oxalis Nasturtium Prickly Pear

You're creating interactive menus for the Life on Rocks Wildlife Cruises website. The menus will display three main items by default, as shown in Figure 47. When a user moves the mouse pointer over a menu item, or touches it, a submenu of related options will be displayed, as shown in Figure 48. When the user moves the mouse pointer off the menu item, or touches that item again, the submenu will be hidden once again.

1. Create a new Edge Animate project then save it with the name **menus.html** in the folder named menus where you store your Data Files.

2. Along the top of the stage, create three text elements with the text **Cruises**, **Rates**, and **Directions**. Assign each element an appropriate title.

3. Create a rectangle element that covers the text "Directions," assign it a color of your choice, duplicate it twice, then move one copy over the word "Rates" and another copy over the word "Cruises." Rearrange how the elements are layered so all three text elements are displayed above their rectangles. Change the font color if necessary to contrast with the background color you chose. Assign each rectangle element an appropriate title, group it with its text element, then assign the group an appropriate title as well.

Figure 47 *Default view of Project Builder 1 in browser*

Figure 48 *Project Builder 1 with submenu displayed*

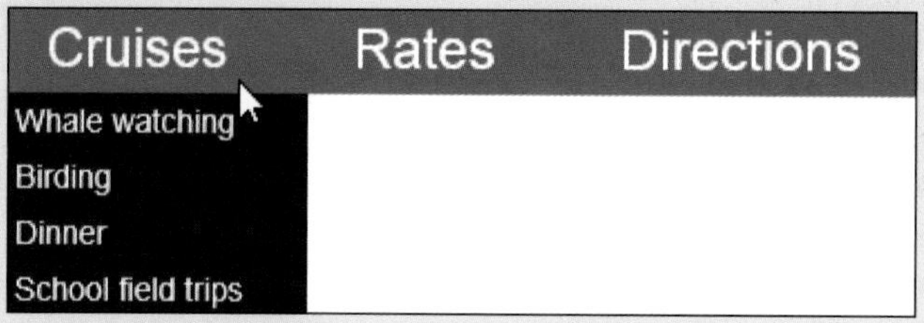

4. Create a text element for each of the 11 submenu items shown in Figure 49, arranging them as shown and assigning each element an appropriate title. Create a rectangle covering the "Whale watching" text that's the same width as the Cruises box, and assign it a different background color than the first three rectangles you created. Duplicate the new rectangle 10 times, moving one rectangle over each text label you created. Rearrange how the elements are layered so all three text elements are displayed above their rectangles. Change the font color if necessary to contrast with the background color you chose. Assign each rectangle element an appropriate title, group it with its text element, then assign the group an appropriate title as well.

5. On the Elements panel, select the four submenu items displayed under the Cruises option, group them, then assign the group the title **CruisesSubmenu**. Repeat for the options under the Rates option and the Directions option, using the titles **RatesSubmenu** and **DirectionsSubmenu**, respectively.

6. Specify actions that hide the three submenus when the project first loads in a browser.

7. Specify actions that show the CruisesSubmenu element when a user moves the mouse pointer over the Cruises option, hides it when a user moves the mouse pointer off the Cruises option, and toggles between showing and hiding it when a user touches the Cruises option on a touchscreen. Repeat for the Rates and Directions options.

8. Save your work and test your project in current versions of all three major desktop browsers. Working with classmates or friends if necessary, use Edge Inspect to test your project on at least one iOS (Apple) touchscreen device and one Android (Google) touchscreen device.

Figure 49 *Sample Project Builder 1 in Edge Animate*

Cruises	Rates	Directions
Whale watching	Children (0-17)	From the north
Birding	Adults	From the south
Dinner	Seniors (60+)	From the east
School field trips	Groups	

You're enhancing the website for the International Relations department at your school. You'll add quotes from three female Nobel Peace Prize laureates to the site using an interactive animation.

1. In Edge Animate, open the quotes.an file from the quotes folder where you store your Data Files. The file contains six text elements, including three elements containing the names of three Nobel Peace Prize laureates (along the left side of the stage), and three elements containing quotes from the laureates (layered on top of each other on the right).

2. Create a rectangle element that covers the name "Rigoberta Menchú Tum." If necessary, adjust the position and size of the rectangle so its top-left corner is in the top-left corner of the stage, its width is 204px, and its height is 43px. Assign a distinctive background color to the rectangle. Move the rectangle element under the text element, then assign the rectangle element an appropriate title.

3. Duplicate the rectangle you created in Step 2 twice, moving one duplicate over the second name and one over the third. Assign each a different distinctive background color, move each under its associated text element, and assign it an appropriate title. Group each of the three text elements with its associated rectangle, and assign each group an appropriate title.

4. Create a rectangle that covers the quotes on the right side of the stage. If necessary, adjust the position and size of the rectangle so its top-right corner is in the top-right corner of the stage, its width is 596px, and its height is 129px. Assign the same background color to the rectangle that you assigned to the rectangle for the name Rigoberta Menchú Tum. Move the rectangle under the text element with the title RMTQuoteText, then assign the rectangle element an appropriate title.

5. Duplicate the rectangle you created in Step 4 twice. Assign one the background color you used behind the name Wangari Muta Maathai, and the other the background color for the name Aung San Suu Kyi. Move each rectangle just below its associated text element on the Elements panel, and assign it an appropriate title. Group each of the three quotes with its associated rectangle, and assign the groups the titles **ASSKQuoteUnit**, **WMMQuoteUnit**, and **RMTQuoteUnit**. (*Hint*: If you have trouble identifying the element you're working with on the stage, you can temporarily set the Display property of other layers to Off while you're working with a layer, then display the other layers again when you're done.)

6. Specify actions that hide the WMMQuoteUnit and ASSKQuoteUnit groups when the project first loads in a browser. *Note*: You should not hide the group containing the RMTQuoteText element.

7. Specify actions that show the WMMQuoteUnit element when a user moves the mouse pointer over the group containing the WMMNameText element, hides it when a user moves the mouse pointer off the group containing the WMMNameText element, and toggles between showing and hiding it when a user touches the group containing the WMMNameText element on a touchscreen. Repeat for the ASSKQuoteUnit element and the group containing the ASSKNameText element.

8. Save your work and test your project in current versions of all three major desktop browsers. The project should display the Rigoberta Menchú Tum quote by default, as shown in Figure 50. Moving the mouse pointer over either of the other two names should show the associated quote, as shown in Figure 51. Working with classmates or friends if necessary, use Edge Inspect to test your project on at least one iOS (Apple) touchscreen device and one Android (Google) touchscreen device.

Figure 50 *Default view of Project Builder 2 in browser*

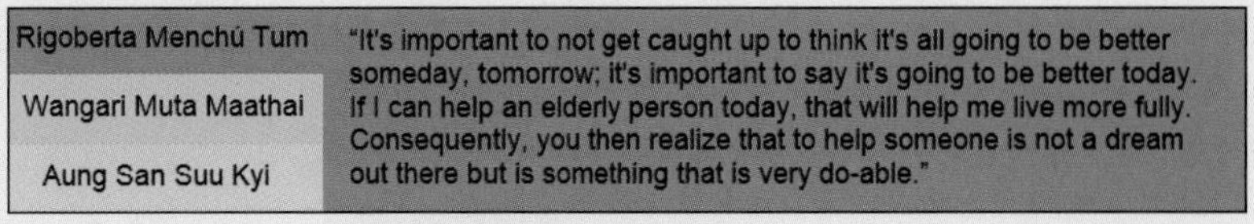

Rigoberta Menchú Tum	"It's important to not get caught up to think it's all going to be better someday, tomorrow; it's important to say it's going to be better today. If I can help an elderly person today, that will help me live more fully. Consequently, you then realize that to help someone is not a dream out there but is something that is very do-able."
Wangari Muta Maathai	
Aung San Suu Kyi	

Figure 51 *Project Builder 2 in use*

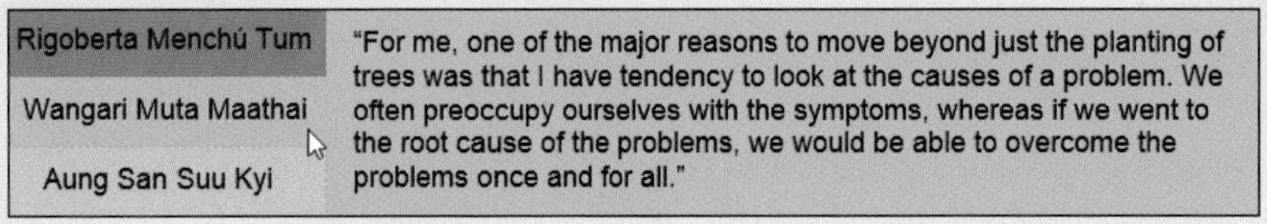

Rigoberta Menchú Tum	"For me, one of the major reasons to move beyond just the planting of trees was that I have tendency to look at the causes of a problem. We often preoccupy ourselves with the symptoms, whereas if we went to the root cause of the problems, we would be able to overcome the problems once and for all."
Wangari Muta Maathai	
Aung San Suu Kyi	

Many websites use rollover effects for a variety of purposes. For instance, NASA's page on solar system exploration includes a menu with rollover effects.

1. In a browser, open *http://solarsystem.nasa.gov/index.cfm* and explore the page.

2. Move your mouse pointer over different elements of the page to locate rollover effects. For instance, as shown in Figure 52, the menu items on the left side of the page show submenu items in response to a rollover.

3. Locate an example of a rollover on the page then, in a text editor, create a new document and answer the following questions:

   ■ Where on the page is the rollover? (Include any steps you had to take to navigate there, such as clicking a tab.)

   ■ What element or elements have the rollover? (Describe them.)

   ■ What changes happen to the page in response to the rollover?

4. Repeat Step 3 for two additional examples of rollovers on the page.

5. Save your document.

Figure 52 *Menu with rollovers on NASA Solar System Exploration page*

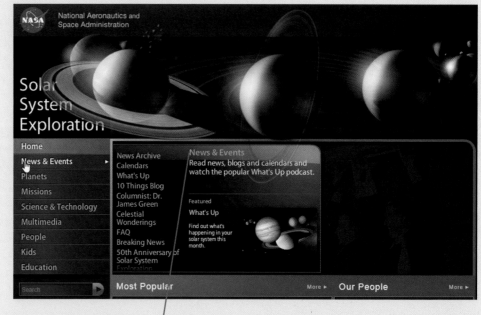

Source: NASA

News & Events information displayed in response to a rollover on the News & Events link in the navigation bar

One of the many uses of rollover effects is to provide additional information or resources related to an element on a web page. Open the keywords.an file from the keywords folder where your Data Files are stored. The project contains a text element containing text from this chapter. Add a rectangle element over the first instance of each of the following words: source element, event, action, and target. Apply a mostly transparent background color to each rectangle, such as rgba(241,241,47,0.23), so the words stand out but are still legible. Look up the definition of each of the four terms in this chapter, add the definition text to the project as a text element, then use the Rounded Rectangle tool to add a rounded rectangle with a contrasting color behind each definition. Title and group each definition and its rectangle. Specify actions that hide all four definition groups when the project loads in a browser; make each definition visible when a user moves the mouse pointer over the box highlighting the

term; hide each definition when a user moves the mouse pointer off the box highlighting the term; and toggle between showing and hiding each definition when a user touches the box highlighting the term. Figure 53 shows the rollover effect in action for a sample project.

Preview the project in current versions of all three major desktop browsers. Working with classmates or friends if necessary, use Edge Inspect to test your project on at least one iOS (Apple) touchscreen device and one Android (Google) touchscreen device.

Figure 53 *Sample Portfolio Project*

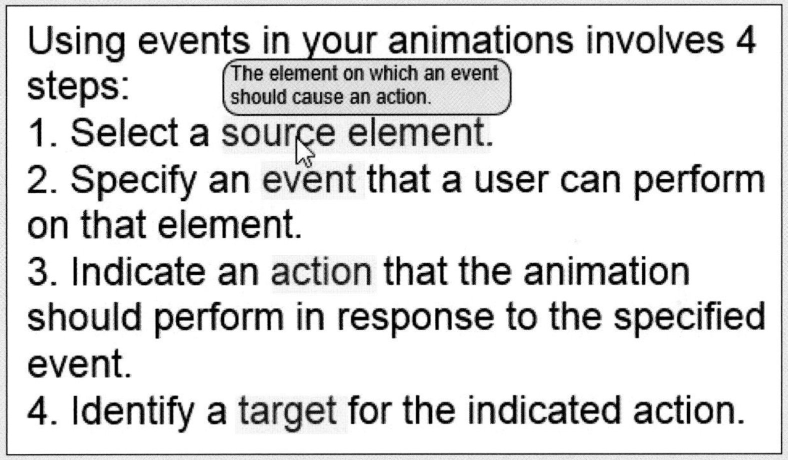

CHAPTER **1**

INTEGRATING ADOBE CC
WEB COLLECTION

1. Insert a Flash movie in Dreamweaver
2. Edit a Flash HTML5 Canvas document in Dreamweaver
3. Incorporate an Edge Animate composition into a Dreamweaver document
4. Export a sprite sheet from Flash and import it into Edge Animate

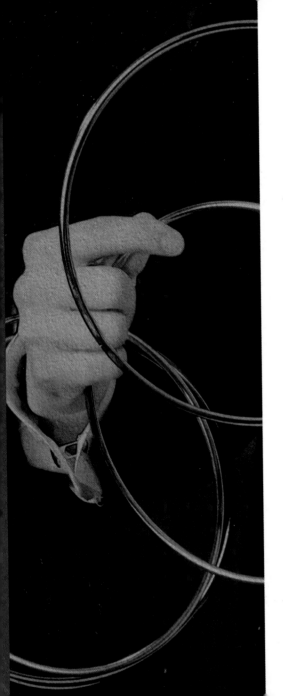

CHAPTER 1

INTEGRATING ADOBE CC
WEB COLLECTION

Introduction

As you've seen in the preceding chapters, each web development tool in Adobe Creative Cloud is optimized for certain uses. When creating web content in one application, you'll often find that you need to import or edit content created in another application. For example, although you can use Dreamweaver to position and style content in a web document, you may need to use other software to create some of that content. After you create a Flash movie in Flash Professional, you need to export it as an SWF file, open or create a web document in Dreamweaver, and place the SWF file in it before publishing the movie on the web. Edge Animate files are saved as HTML documents that you can publish to the web; however, in some cases you may want to apply a style sheet or specific styles, or add HTML elements to an Edge Animate composition. To do so, you can export the HTML document from Edge Animate into Dreamweaver, make

any changes or additions, then publish the document. In addition, if you have an existing Dreamweaver document into which you'd like to insert an Edge Animate composition, you can import the composition in Dreamweaver and place it in the existing web document.

In addition to publishing content, sometimes you may need to move content between Flash Professional and Edge Animate. Flash Professional allows you to export a symbol in a format used by Edge Animate. You can then import the symbol into Edge Animate and use the symbol in that application without needing to recreate it from scratch.

In web development and graphic design, the set of steps followed and the tools used to accomplish a specific task are sometimes collectively referred to as a **workflow**. In this chapter, you'll learn workflows for several common tasks that involve moving content between Dreamweaver, Flash, and Edge Animate.

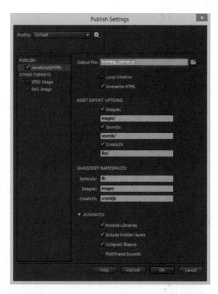

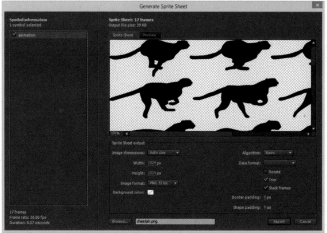

©iStock.com/Freder.

Insert a Flash Movie
IN DREAMWEAVER

What You'll Do

In this lesson, you will add a Flash movie to a Dreamweaver document and edit the movie within Dreamweaver.

Inserting a Flash Movie into a Dreamweaver Document

You can easily insert a Flash movie (an SWF file) into a Dreamweaver document. Doing so allows you to integrate your Flash movie into an existing web document, giving the movie context when you publish it on the web. To do this, set the insertion point where you want the movie to appear, and then use the Media command on the Insert menu to select Flash SWF as the media to insert. If the file is not in the root folder for the website, Dreamweaver will prompt you to indicate whether or not you would like to copy it into the root folder. It is recommended that you copy the file to the root folder, so that it is accessible when you publish the site. When the insert process is completed, a placeholder appears at the insertion point in the Dreamweaver document.

Using the Property Inspector with the Movie

When you click the placeholder to select it, the Dreamweaver Property inspector displays information about the movie, including the filename, as shown in Figure 1.

You can use the Property inspector to complete the following:

- Play and stop the Flash movie
- Set width and height dimensions
- Cause the movie to loop
- Reposition the placeholder in the document window

Figure 1 *The Property inspector with a movie selected*

Flash movie placeholder selected

Flash movie properties

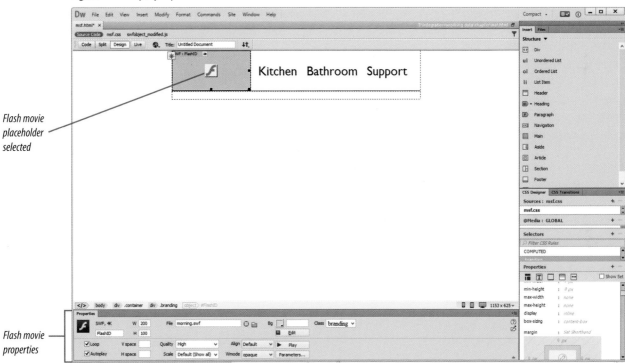

Insert a Flash movie into Dreamweaver

1. Start Dreamweaver.

2. Open the **IC1_1.html** file from the Lessons folder in your Data Files for this chapter, then save a copy with the name **msf_flash.html** to the same location.

   The document contains a navigation bar with an empty div element to its left, as shown in Figure 2.

3. Click in the top-left corner of the empty div element to position the insertion pointer within it. Ensure you are in the .branding div by verifying .branding is present on the status bar.

4. Click **Insert** on the menu bar, point to **Media**, click **Flash SWF**, then if necessary click **Nest**.

5. If necessary, navigate to the location of your Data Files for this chapter, open the **Lessons** folder, click **morning.swf**, then click **OK** (Win) or **Open** (Mac).

6. In the Object Tag Accessibility Attributes dialog box, type **Morning Star Faucets** in the Title box, then click **OK**.

   A Flash movie placeholder is inserted at the location of the insertion line, as shown in Figure 3. On some systems, the layout of the navigation bar elements may not match the figure.

   TIP If the placeholder is not displayed in the empty div, click Edit on the Menu bar, click Undo, then repeat Steps 3-6, being sure the .branding div is selected in Step 3.

7. Save your work.

   TIP If a Copy Dependent Files message box appears, click OK.

You inserted a Flash movie into a Dreamweaver document and copied the Flash movie to the root folder of the website.

Figure 2 *Structure of the msf_flash.html document*

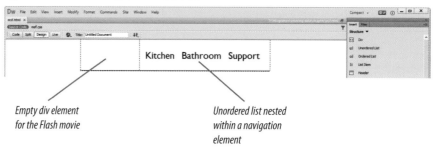

Empty div element for the Flash movie

Unordered list nested within a navigation element

Figure 3 *The Flash movie placeholder*

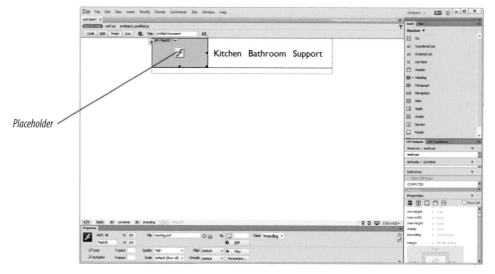

Placeholder

Figure 4 *Changing the movie dimensions*

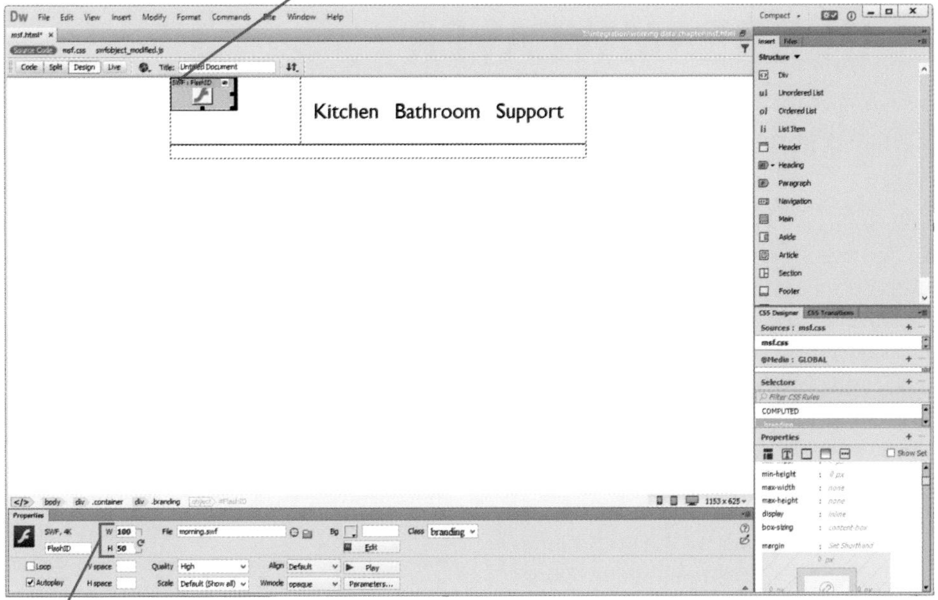

*The placeholder size changes
to match the new dimensions*

*Width and Height
properties changed*

Play a Flash movie and change its properties within Dreamweaver

1. Click the Flash movie placeholder to select it (if necessary).

2. Click the **Play button** on the Property inspector.

   TIP If Dreamweaver doesn't display a Play button, press [F12] (Win) or [fn][F12] (Mac) to preview the document in your default browser, then skip to Step 4.

3. Click the **Stop button** on the Property inspector.

4. Click the **Loop check box** on the Property inspector to uncheck it.

5. Double-click the **Width box (W)**, type **100**, then press **[Tab]**.

6. In the **Height box (H)**, type **50**, then press **[Enter]**. Your screen should resemble Figure 4.

7. Click the **Play button** on the Property inspector, view the resized movie, then click the **Stop button**.

8. Click the **Reset size button** on the Property inspector to restore the previous setting.

9. Save your work, then close all open files in Dreamweaver.

You played a Flash movie and changed its properties in Dreamweaver by turning off the Loop option, then changing and resetting the movie height.

Edit a Flash HTML5 Canvas Document
IN DREAMWEAVER

What You'll Do

In this lesson, you will use Dreamweaver to edit an HTML5 Canvas document exported from Flash.

Creating an HTML5 Canvas Document in Flash

You've seen in the preceding chapters that you can save a Flash movie as an HTML5 Canvas document instead of an ActionScript 3 document. Creating content as a HTML5 Canvas document enables users to view and interact with your content without needing a browser plugin, widening your audience to include mobile device users. Once you've created HTML5 Canvas content, the next step is to publish the movie as JavaScript and HTML files. Publishing an HTML5 Canvas document offers different publishing options than an ActionScript 3 document. Figure 5 shows the Publish Settings window in Flash for an HTML5 Canvas document.

Working with an HTML5 Canvas Document in Dreamweaver

After you set publishing settings and publish an HTML5 Canvas document from Flash, the published movie is saved as an HTML file along with one or more associated JavaScript files. You can then open the published HTML file in Dreamweaver and work with it as you would any other HTML file.

When you open an HTML5 Canvas document in Dreamweaver, a placeholder appears in place of the canvas element. When you click the placeholder to select it, the Dreamweaver Property inspector displays limited options for the object, as shown in Figure 6.

You can only use the Property inspector to change the default ID value assigned to the object and to change the object's width and height.

Because an HTML5 Canvas document is a standard HTML document, you can work with it in Dreamweaver just as you would any other HTML document. You can add elements to the document, add CSS sources, and edit styles.

Figure 5 *The Publish Settings window for an HTML5 Canvas document*

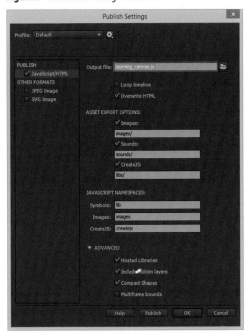

Figure 6 *The Property inspector with an HTML5 Canvas object selected*

HTML5 Canvas object placeholder

HTML5 Canvas object properties

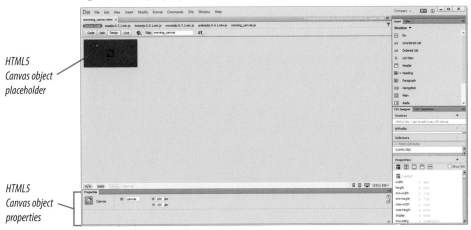

Lesson 2   Edit a Flash HTML5 Canvas Document in Dreamweaver

Publish an HTML5 Canvas document

1. In Flash, open the **IC1_2.fla** file from the Lessons folder in your Data Files for this chapter, then save a copy with the name **morning_canvas.fla** to the same location.

   The document contains the same animation as in the morning.swf file you worked with in the previous lesson, but saved as an HTML5 Canvas document.

2. Click **File** on the menu bar, then click **Publish Settings**.

3. In the Publish Settings window, ensure that the JavaScript/HTML box is the only checked box in the left column.

4. In the right column, if necessary click the **Loop timeline box** to uncheck it.

5. Click the **Publish button**, then when the Publishing window closes, click the **OK button**.

TIP The Output panel may display one or more warning messages during publishing. For more complex HTML5 Canvas documents, these messages may be useful if the published project doesn't work as expected. However, for this simple HTML5 Canvas document, you can safely ignore these messages.

6. Save your changes, then close morning_canvas.fla.

7. In File Explorer (Win) or Finder (Mac), navigate to the Lessons folder in the location of your Data Files for this chapter.

   Flash has generated the files morning_canvas .html and morning_canvas.js in the same directory as the morning_canvas.fla file, along with an images folder containing the image file (star.png) used in the animation. Figure 7

   (continued)

Figure 7 *The published files in File Explorer*

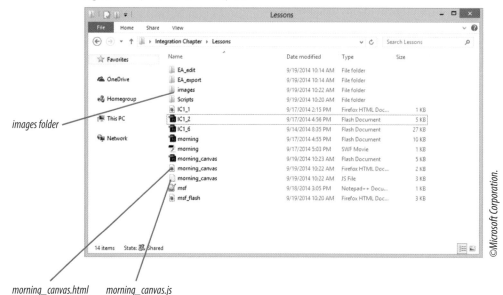

images folder

morning_canvas.html   *morning_canvas.js*

©Microsoft Corporation.

Integrating Adobe CC Web Collection

Figure 8 *Dreamweaver document containing an HTML5 Canvas object*

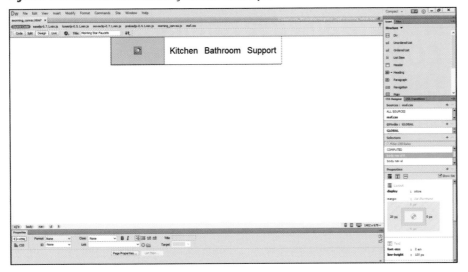

Figure 9 *HTML document containing the canvas object in a browser*

HTML5 Canvas
object

shows the published files in File Explorer, with descriptions of the file types in the Type column.

You published an HTML5 Canvas document as a collection of HTML, JavaScript, and image files.

Edit a document containing a canvas object

1. In Dreamweaver, open the **morning_canvas .html** file from the Lessons folder in your Data Files for this chapter.

   The document contains a placeholder for the animation.

2. In the Title box, change the value to **Morning Star Faucets**.

3. Remove the inline background color from the body element.

4. Attach the msf.css style sheet, which is located in the Lessons folder.

5. Position the insertion point to the right of the placeholder, then insert a navigation element.

6. Within the navigation element, add an unordered list element, then add the following three list items: **Kitchen**, **Bathroom**, **Support**.

   Your project should match Figure 8.

7. Save your changes, then preview your document in a browser.

   The animation runs once when you first open the page. As Figure 9 shows, the appearance of this page is almost identical to the one from the previous lesson.

8. Return to Dreamweaver, then close all open files.

You opened an HTML document containing a canvas object in Dreamweaver, added elements to the document, modified styles, and viewed the result in a browser.

Incorporate an Edge Animate
COMPOSITION INTO A
DREAMWEAVER DOCUMENT

What You'll Do

In this lesson, you will export an Edge Animate composition and use Dreamweaver to add it to a web document.

Editing an Edge Animate Project in Dreamweaver

Just as you can incorporate animations created with Flash into Dreamweaver documents, you can also work with Edge Animate animations in Dreamweaver. Two workflows are available for accessing Edge Animate content in Dreamweaver. Because an Edge Animate project is saved as an HTML file by default, the first option is simply to open the HTML file in Dreamweaver and change, style, and add elements. This workflow is similar to working with an HTML5 Canvas document exported from Flash. When you open an HTML document created in Edge Animate in Dreamweaver, the animation itself is represented by an empty placeholder, as shown in Figure 10. This workflow makes the most sense when you don't have an existing template or page layout that you want to insert the Edge Animate composition into. Using this workflow, you can simply add elements and styles to the HTML file generated by Edge Animate.

Importing an Edge Animate Animation into a Dreamweaver Document

You can also use a second workflow to work with content generated in Edge Animate in Dreamweaver. Edge Animate enables you to export a project as an **OAM file**, which contains all the files that make up an Edge Animate composition. You can import that OAM file into some other Adobe applications, including Dreamweaver. To export an Edge Animate project in OAM format, you click select Animate Deployment Package as the Publish Target in the Publish Settings window.

To import an OAM file in Dreamweaver, you click Insert on the menu bar, point to Media, then click Edge Animate Composition. As with a Flash SWF file, the animation is placed at the location of the insertion point and a placeholder is displayed, as shown in Figure 11.

> **QUICK TIP**
>
> The Edge Animate placeholder may appear larger in Dreamweaver than its eventual appearance in a browser. When in doubt, save your work and preview the document in a browser to verify the appearance of the Edge Animate composition in the web page.

Figure 10 *Empty placeholder in Edge Animate composition open in Dreamweaver*

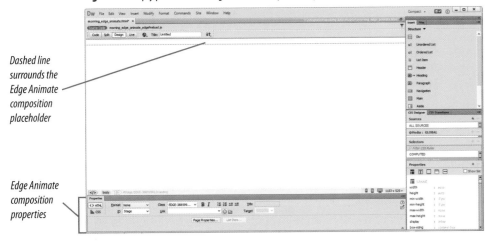

Dashed line surrounds the Edge Animate composition placeholder

Edge Animate composition properties

Figure 11 *HTML document containing Edge Animate animation in browser*

Morning Star Faucets ★ Kitchen Bathroom Support

The Effects of Editing an Edge Animate Project in Dreamweaver

Even after you edit an Edge Animate HTML file in Dreamweaver, you can reopen the file in Edge Animate and work with it there. All the elements that you place on the Stage in Edge Animate are placed within a div element with the ID value stage. If you add other elements to an Edge Animate HTML file, you should be sure to add them outside of the stage element. If you reopen the HTML file in Edge Animate after adding elements outside the Stage, the added elements are displayed on the Elements panel but are grayed out, indicating that you can't work with them.

Note that if you attach an external style sheet to an Edge Animate HTML file in Dreamweaver, and then reopen the HTML file in Edge Animate and resave it, the association with the external style sheet is lost. For this reason, it's generally best to finish all your Edge Animate work before opening an Edge Animate HTML file in Dreamweaver. If you need to continue work on an Edge Animate presentation at the same time you're working on the document that will contain it in Dreamweaver, it's less complicated to keep the two documents separate and to import the final Edge Animate animation into the Dreamweaver document.

Edit an Edge Animate project in Dreamweaver

1. In Dreamweaver, open the **IC1_3.html** file from the EA_edit folder within the Lessons folder in your Data Files for this chapter, then save a copy with the name **morning_edge_animate.html** to the same location. As Figure 10 shows, the animation is represented by an empty placeholder.

TIP Be sure not to open the files in the EA_export folder, which you will use later in this lesson.

2. In the Title box, type **Morning Star Faucets**.

3. Remove the inline margin property values from the body element.

4. Attach the msf.css style sheet, which is located in the EA_edit folder, to the morning_edge_animate.html document.

5. Position the insertion point to the right of the placeholder, then insert a navigation element.

6. Within the navigation element, add an unordered list element, then add the following three list items: **Kitchen**, **Bathroom**, **Support**.

7. Save your changes, then preview your document in a browser.

   The animation runs once when you first open the page. As Figure 11 shows, the appearance of this page is almost identical to those from the previous lessons.

8. Return to Dreamweaver, then close all open files.

You opened an Edge Animate HTML document in Dreamweaver, added elements to the document, modified styles, and viewed the result in a browser.

Export an Edge Animate project in OAM format

1. In Edge Animate, open the **IC1_4.html** file from the EA_export folder within the Lessons folder in your Data Files for this chapter, then save a copy with the name **morning_edge_animate.html** to the same location.

TIP Be sure not to open the files in the EA_edit folder, which you used in the previous set of steps.

The document contains the same animation as in the previous lessons, but created in Edge Animate.

2. Click **File** on the menu bar, then click **Publish Settings**.

3. In the Publish Settings dialog box, click the **Web box** to uncheck it, then click the **Animate Deployment Package box** to check it.

Your Publish Settings dialog box should match Figure 12.

4. Click **Publish**.

5. Save your changes to morning_edge_animate .html, then close the file.

You exported an Edge Animate project as an OAM file.

Figure 12 *Edge Animate Publish Settings dialog box*

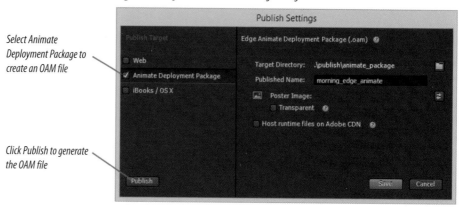

Select Animate Deployment Package to create an OAM file

Click Publish to generate the OAM file

Figure 13 *Edge Animate placeholder in Dreamweaver document*

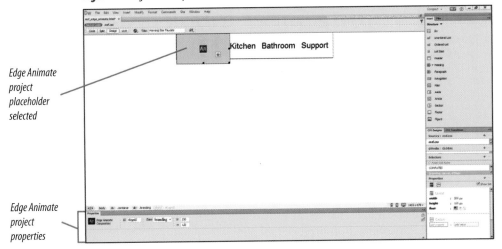

Edge Animate
project
placeholder
selected

Edge Animate
project
properties

Figure 14 *HTML document containing inserted OAM file in browser*

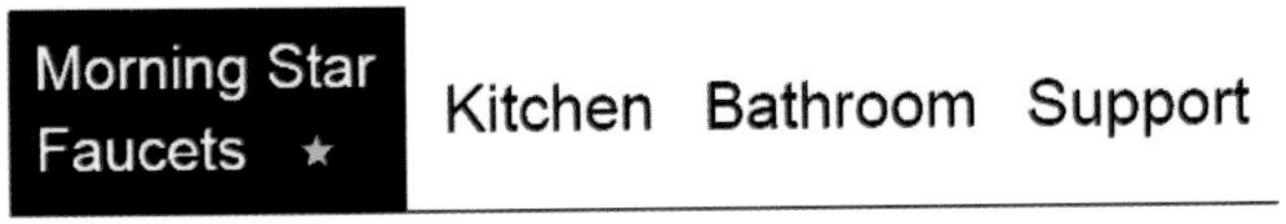

Morning Star Faucets ★   Kitchen   Bathroom   Support

Insert an Edge Animate OAM file into Dreamweaver

1. In Dreamweaver, open the **IC1_5.html** file from the EA_export folder within the Lessons folder in your Data Files for this chapter, then save a copy with the name **msf_edge_animate.html** to the same location.

   The document contains a navigation bar with an empty div element to its left.

2. In the empty div element, click in the top-left corner to position the insertion point within it.

3. Click **Insert** on the menu bar, point to **Media**, click **Edge Animate Composition**, then if necessary click **Nest**.

4. Navigate to the location of your Data Files for this chapter, open the **Lessons** folder, open the **EA_export** folder, open the **publish** folder, open the **animate_package** folder, click **morning_edge_animate.oam**, then click **OK** (Win) or **Open** (Mac).

   The Edge Animate composition is inserted and a placeholder is displayed, as shown in Figure 13.

5. Save your changes, then preview the **msf_edge_animate.html** file in a browser.

   The animation runs once when you first open the page. As Figure 14 shows, the appearance of this page is almost identical to those from the previous lessons.

6. Return to Dreamweaver, then close all open files.

You inserted an OAM file containing an Edge Animate composition into a Dreamweaver document.

Export a Sprite Sheet from Flash AND IMPORT IT INTO EDGE ANIMATE

What You'll Do

©iStock.com/Freder.

In this lesson, you will use Flash to create a sprite sheet, and you will import the sprite sheet into an Edge Animate project.

Exporting Sprite Sheets from Flash

You can export a symbol from Flash and then import it into Edge Animate. This enables developers who are more familiar with the Flash interface to create symbols in Flash and then export them to Edge Animate to use when creating animations. It also provides an easy way for developers who have existing content in Flash format to generate web standard versions of the content. A Flash symbol is exported as a **sprite sheet**, which is a single image file that contains a representation of each frame of the animation.

To export a symbol from Flash, you right-click the symbol on the Library panel, then click Generate Sprite Sheet. In the Generate Sprite Sheet dialog box, you can set options for the sprite sheet. For a sprite sheet that you'll import into Edge Animate, you select Edge Animate as the Data Format. When you click Export, Flash generates not only an image file but also a file with the extension .eas, which contains information about the sprite sheet that Edge Animate can use to automate the import process.

Importing Sprite Sheets into Edge Animate

To import the sprite sheet into Edge Animate, you click File on the menu bar, then click Import Spritesheet. In the Select sprite sheet image dialog box, you navigate to the location of the sprite sheet, select it, then click Open. In the Define Sprite Tiles dialog box, you check the Load an EAS file box, as shown in Figure 15. Checking this box indicates that your sprite sheet file is accompanied by a Flash-generated file that describes the size and location of each frame. Finally, you click Import. The Flash symbol is displayed in the Symbol section of the Edge Animate Library panel.

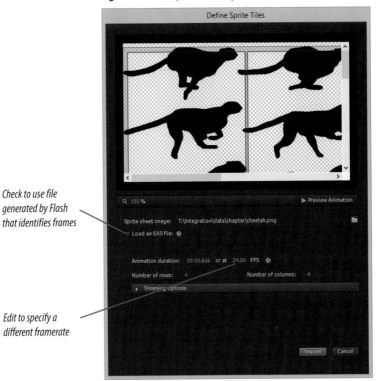

Figure 15 *Define Sprite Tiles dialog box*

Check to use file generated by Flash that identifies frames

Edit to specify a different framerate

©iStock.com/Freder.

QUICK TIP

Regardless of the original framerate of a Flash symbol, Edge Animate imports a sprite sheet with a framerate of 24 FPS (frames per second) by default. You can change this value while importing a sprite sheet in Edge Animate. In the Define Sprite Tiles dialog box, the editable FPS value is displayed to the right of the animation duration.

Understanding Sprite Sheets

HTML documents often include a number of images, including logos, photos, and design graphics. Because of the process that goes on behind the scenes as files associated with a web page are downloaded to a browser, each additional image slows down the loading of the page out of proportion with its file size. For this reason, developers routinely combine all the images used in a web page into a single image file, known as a sprite sheet. A sprite sheet allows all the images for a page to be downloaded at once, which reduces the amount of time it takes to download the page. Instead of using img elements to place images from a sprite sheet, developers set the sprite sheet graphic as the background for a div or other block element, then set properties for the div that show only the relevant part of the sprite sheet as the background. Edge Animate automates this process for you when you import a sprite sheet with an associated EAS file, which indicates the size and position in the sprite sheet of each individual image.

Export a sprite sheet from Flash

1. In Flash, open the **IC1_6.fla** file from the Lessons folder in your Data Files for this chapter, then save a copy as **cheetah.fla** to the same location.

2. On the Library panel, double-click the **animation symbol** to open it, click the canvas, then press **[Enter]** to play the symbol.

   The animation shows the outline of a leopard running. As the Timeline in Figure 16 shows, the animation is made up of numerous frames.

3. On the Library panel, right-click (Win) or hold **[command]** and click (Mac) the **animation symbol**, then on the context menu, click **Generate Sprite Sheet**.

   The Generate Sprite Sheet dialog box opens, as shown in Figure 17.

4. Click the **Image format arrow**, then click **PNG 8 bit**.

5. Click the **Data format arrow**, then click **Edge Animate**.

6. If necessary, click the **Browse button**, navigate to the Lessons folder within your Data Files for this chapter, then click **Save**.

7. Click **Export**.

8. Save your changes, then close cheetah.fla.

You exported a Flash symbol as a sprite sheet with an accompanying file to make it easier to import it into Edge Animate.

Figure 16 *Timeline for cheetah animation*

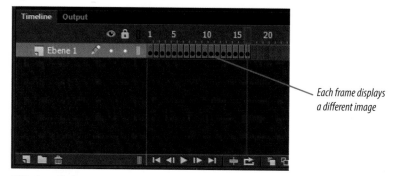

©iStock.com/Freder.

Each frame displays a different image

Figure 17 *Generate Sprite Sheet dialog box*

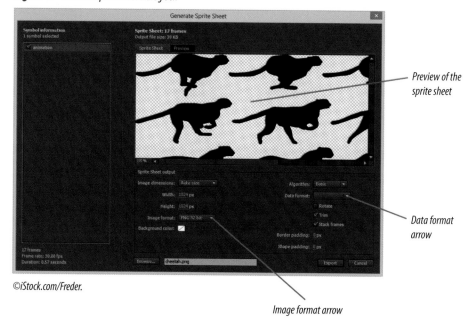

©iStock.com/Freder.

Preview of the sprite sheet

Data format arrow

Image format arrow

Figure 18 *Cheetah symbol imported into Edge Animate composition*

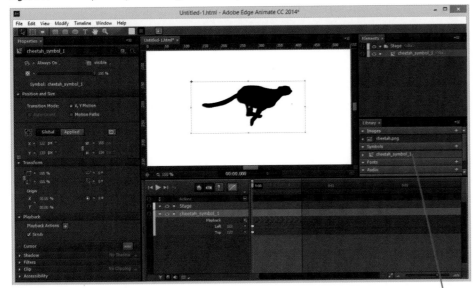

©iStock.com/Freder.

Cheetah sprite sheet
imported to the
library as a symbol

1. In Edge Animate, create a new composition, then save it as **cheetah.html** to the Lessons folder in your Data Files for this chapter.

2. Click **File** on the menu bar, then click **Import Spritesheet**.

3. In the Select sprite sheet image dialog box, navigate to the Lessons folder in your Data Files for this chapter, click **cheetah.png**, then click **Open**.

4. In the Define Sprite Tiles dialog box, click the **Load an EAS file box** to check it, then click **Import**.

   The cheetah symbol is added to the Symbols section of the Library panel with the name cheetah_symbol_1.

5. Drag the **cheetah_symbol_1** symbol from the Library panel to the Stage.

   The cheetah outline is displayed on the Stage, as shown in Figure 18. Don't worry if you symbol is in a different position than the one shown in the figure.

6. Press **[Spacebar]**.

   The animation plays just as it did in Flash.

7. Save your changes to cheetah.html.

You imported a sprite sheet into Edge Animate as a symbol, added it to a composition, and played it.

Insert a Flash movie in Dreamweaver.

1. In Dreamweaver, open the IC1_7.html file from the SkillsReview folder in your Data Files for this chapter, then save a copy with the name **tks.html** to the same location.
2. Within the empty div element at the top of the document, insert the tks.swf movie, specifying a title of **Treetop Kitchen Supply**.
3. Play the movie (or preview the document in a browser), clicking OK if asked to copy dependent files.
4. Resize the Flash movie to 450px by 75px, then turn off looping for the movie.
5. Play or preview the resized movie, then reset the movie size to the default.
6. Save your work, then close all open files in Dreamweaver.

Edit a Flash HTML5 Canvas document in Dreamweaver.

1. In Flash, open the IC1_8.fla file from the SkillsReview folder in your Data Files for this chapter, then save a copy with the name **tks_canvas.fla** to the same location.
2. Publish JavaScript and HTML files based on this document, with the resulting animation playing only once.
3. Save your changes, then close tks_canvas.fla.
4. In Dreamweaver, open the tks_canvas.html file from the SkillsReview folder within your Data Files for this chapter.

5. Set the document title to **Treetop Kitchen Supply**, remove the inline background color from the body element, then attach the tks.css style sheet to the document.
6. Position the insertion point to the right of the placeholder, then insert a navigation element. Within the navigation element, add an unordered list element, then add the following four list items: **Cooking**, **Baking**, **Serving**, **Decor**.
7. Save your changes, then preview your document in a browser. Verify that the animation runs just once, and that the document matches Figure 19.
8. Close all open files in Dreamweaver.

Incorporate an Edge Animate composition into a Dreamweaver document.

1. In Dreamweaver, open the IC1_9.html file from the EA_edit folder within the SkillsReview folder in your Data Files for this chapter, then save a copy with the name **tks_edge_animate.html** to the same location.
2. Change the document's title value to **Treetop Kitchen Supply**, remove the inline margin property values from the body element, then attach the tks.css style sheet to the document.
3. Position the insertion point to the right of the placeholder, then insert a navigation element. Within the navigation element, add an unordered

list element, then add the following four list items: **Cooking**, **Baking**, **Serving**, **Decor**.
4. Save your changes, then preview your document in a browser. Verify that the animation runs just once, and that the document matches Figure 19.
5. Close all open files in Dreamweaver.
6. In Edge Animate, open the IC1_10.html file from the EA_export folder within the SkillsReview folder in your Data Files for this chapter, then save a copy with the name **tks_edge_animate.html** to the same location.
7. Publish the presentation as an OAM file, save your changes to tks_edge_animate.html, then close the file.
8. In Dreamweaver, open the IC1_11.html file from the EA_export folder within the SkillsReview folder in your Data Files for this chapter, then save a copy with the name **tks.html** to the same location.
9. Insert the OAM file you exported within the empty div element at the top of the document. (*Hint*: The OAM file is located at the following path: EA_export > publish > animate_package.)
10. Save your changes, then preview the tks.html file in a browser. Verify that the animation runs just once, and that the document matches Figure 19.
11. Return to Dreamweaver, then close all open files.

Export a sprite sheet from Flash and import it into Edge Animate.

1. In Flash, open the IC1_12.fla file from the SkillsReview folder in your Data Files for this chapter, then save a copy as **cat.fla** to the same location.

2. Using the Library panel, play the animation symbol, then generate a sprite sheet based on the symbol, specifying an image format of PNG 8 bit and a data format of Edge Animate, and saving the sprite sheet to the SkillsReview folder within your Data Files for this chapter.

3. Save your changes, then close cat.fla.

4. In Edge Animate, create a new composition, then save it as **cat.html** to the SkillsReview folder in your Data Files for this chapter.

5. Import the cat.png sprite sheet, loading the accompanying EAS file during the import. Place the resulting symbol on the Stage and play it.

6. Save your changes to cat.html, then close the file.

Figure 19 *Completed Skills Review*

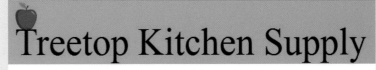

©iStock.com/bortonia.

You are creating an online banner advertisement for a "Managing Your Money" seminar presented by the Tortoiseshell Federal Credit Union. Along with text and a background, the ad will include a looping animation of a spinning coin. You will use Dreamweaver to insert a Flash version of the ad into a web page. You will also export an animated symbol from a Flash project as a sprite sheet and import it into an Edge Animate version of the ad. Finally, you'll generate an HTML/JavaScript version of the ad with Edge Animate and insert this into a web page. Figure 20 shows the final ad inserted into the provided sample web page.

1. In Dreamweaver, open the IC1_13.html file from the PB1 folder in your Data Files for this chapter, then save a copy with the name **testsite_flash.html** to the same location.
2. In the empty div element to the right of the placeholder text for Article 1, insert tfcu.swf from the PB1 folder, with the accessibility title **Tortoiseshell Federal Credit Union "Managing Your Money" seminar**. Ensure the animation loops. Save your work, then test the document in a browser.
3. In Flash, open the IC1_14.fla file from the PB1 folder in your Data Files for this chapter, then save a copy to the same location with the name **tfcu.fla**. Generate a sprite sheet for Edge Animate based on the animation symbol, saving it to the same location.

4. In Edge Animate, open the IC1_15.html file from the tfcu_EA directory within the PB1 directory in the Data Files for this chapter. Save a copy to the same location with the name **tfcu_edge_animate.html**. Import the tfcu.png sprite sheet, then place the tfcu_symbol_1 symbol in the top-right corner of the Stage. Publish an OAM file of the tfcu_edge_animate project.
5. In Dreamweaver, open the IC1_16.html file from the tfcu_EA directory within the PB1 directory in the Data Files for this chapter, then save a copy with the name **testsite_EA.html** to the same location.
6. In the empty div element below the heading "Article 1 Heading," insert the tfcu_edge_animate.oam file you published. (*Hint*: The document is saved within the PB1 folder in your Data Files at the path tfcu_EA > publish > animate_package.) Save your work, then test the document in a browser.

Figure 20 *Completed Project Builder 1*

Test Website

Article 1 Heading

Lorem ipsum dolor sit amet, consectetur adipiscing...

Article 2 Heading

Lorem ipsum dolor sit amet, consectetur adipiscing...

Article 3 Heading

Lorem ipsum dolor sit amet, consectetur adipiscing...

Article 4 Heading

Lorem ipsum dolor sit amet, consectetur adipiscing...

Article 1 Heading

Lorem ipsum dolor sit amet, consectetur adipiscing elit. Aliquam sit amet fermentum eros. Mauris ac urna sollicitudin, iaculis tellus gravida, blandit dui. Curabitur eget odio condimentum, mollis lectus accumsan, varius tortor. Maecenas vitae malesuada ipsum. Integer tempor ipsum nec magna ornare, ut egestas nunc porta. Curabitur ac risus fermentum, porta tortor sit amet, varius tortor. Nunc neque enim, pharetra et quam in, bibendum rhoncus erat. Etiam non porttitor enim, id congue urna. Integer dignissim vitae odio ac venenatis. Fusce at felis pretium, bibendum mauris et, dapibus urn;a. Sed pulvinar commodo sem, sit amet luctus erat tincidunt at. Duis sodales massa sit amet est sodales lobortis vel eu eros. Morbi id eros nec massa consequat ultricies ac quis tortor. Nam purus mauris, aliquet id lacus sed, placerat blandit est.

Managing Your Money

a FREE seminar presented by

Tortoiseshell Federal Credit Union

©iStock/yurakr.

You are creating a website for a new organization called the Acton Film Archive. Before you start designing and building the site, your team members would like to see sample HTML documents containing a film clip embedded as a Flash animation, as an HTML5 canvas object, and as an HTML/JavaScript animation. You will use one of the first moving pictures, a looping animation of a bison walking created by Eadweard Muybridge, as the sample movie. You will insert a Flash file into an HTML file, you will export a Flash HTML5 Canvas version of the movie, you will create a sprite sheet of the film and import it into Edge Animate, and you will publish an HTML/JavaScript version of the clip and place it in another HTML document. Figure 21 shows the final appearance of the documents you will create.

1. In Dreamweaver, open IC1_17.html from the PB2 directory in your Data Files for this chapter, then save a copy with the name **afa_flash.html** to the same location. In the empty div element below the navigation element, insert the bison.swf file with the accessibility title **"Movie by Eadweard Muybridge of bison walking"**. Ensure that the movie does not loop. Save your changes and preview the document in a browser.

2. In Flash, open IC1_18.fla from the PB2 directory in your Data Files for this chapter, then save a copy with the name **afa_canvas.fla** to the same location. Publish the movie with looping disabled.

3. In Dreamweaver, open afa_canvas.html from the PB2 directory in your Data Files for this chapter. Remove the inline style for the body element, then attach the afa.css style sheet from the same directory. Enclose the canvas element in a div element with the class value movie. Enclose the div element with an article element. Above the article element, add a navigation element. Within the navigation element, insert an unordered list with three list items containing the text **About, Schedule**, and **Donate**, respectively. Above the navigation element, insert a header element. Within the header element, insert an h1 element containing the text Acton Film Archive. Save your changes, then preview afa_canvas.html in a browser.

4. In Flash, open IC1_19.fla from the PB2 directory in your Data Files for this chapter, then save a copy with the name **bison.fla** to the same location. Generate a sprite sheet from the animation symbol. The sprite sheet

should be compatible with Edge Animate, and should be saved to the same directory as the bison.fla file.

5. In Edge Animate, open IC1_20.html from the bison_EA folder within the PB2 folder, then save a copy with the name **bison_edge_animate.html** to the same location. Import the bison.png sprite sheet from the PB2 directory, changing the FPS value to 10. (*Hint*: In the Define Sprite Tiles window, to the right of the Animation duration value, change the default value of 24.00 to 10.) Place the bison_symbol_1 symbol on the Stage, then publish the project as an OAM file.

6. In Dreamweaver, open IC1_21.html from the bison_EA folder within the PB2 folder, then save a copy with the name **afa_edge_animate.html** to the same location. In the empty div element below the navigation element, insert the bison_edge_animate.oam file. Save your changes and preview the document in a browser.

Figure 21 *Completed Project Builder 2*

Acton Film Archive

About   Schedule   Donate

Source: http://www.muybridge.org/Other/Animal-Lovomotion-Vol-11 -WILD/15860622_8nj5Vb#!i=1426200947&k=7Qpxxwb

Web developers decide between using Flash movies, HTML5 canvas objects, and HTML/JavaScript animations based on a number of factors.

1. In a text editor, create a new document, save it as **Integration Design Project** in the DP directory in your Data Files for this chapter. Enter your name and today's date at the top of the document, then use the document to record your answers to the questions in the following steps.

2. Open Flash and Edge Animate and compare the interfaces. Based on your experience using the two tools, list one or more advantages of creating a Flash HTML 5 Canvas document rather than using Edge Animate, and one or more advantages of using Edge Animate.

3. From the Lessons folder in your Data Files for this chapter, open msf_flash.html, morning_canvas .html, and morning_edge_animate.html (from the EA_export folder) in Google Chrome. Use Edge Inspect to view each document on an iOS device, and on an Android device. Record the make and model of each device, and describe whether the animation in each document works on the device. In addition, for each document, describe any differences in each animation between a specific device and the desktop.

4. Use a search engine to locate articles about developers who've created websites or applications using Flash movies, Flash canvas objects, or Edge Animate, such as *http://blogs.adobe.com/flashpro/ category/html5/*, shown in Figure 22, which includes articles describing developers' experiences building canvas objects with Flash. List at least one URL for each file format, along with a sentence summarizing what you learned from the article.

5. Based on your answers to the previous questions, if you were designing a website for a personal project that included animation, which of the three formats would you choose, and why?

Figure 22 *Adobe Flash Professional Team Blog HTML5 category*

Adobe Systems Incorporated.

This is a continuation of the Portfolio Project you developed in Dreamweaver Chapters 1-6. No Data Files are supplied. You are building this website from chapter to chapter, so you must do each Portfolio Project assignment in each Dreamweaver chapter to complete this project.

1. Design a simple animation that fits into your existing website and helps it fulfill its purpose.
2. Build the animation using Flash, and publish it as a Flash movie.
3. Convert the Flash project to a Flash HTML5 Canvas document, then publish it.
4. Recreate the animation in Edge Animate.
5. If the Flash animation includes a frame-by-frame animation, convert it to a symbol, export a sprite sheet, then import the sprite sheet into Edge Animate and use the resulting symbol in the Edge Animate animation.
6. Create three copies of your Dreamweaver site, changing one of the directory names to include the word "flash," another to include "canvas," and the third to include "edge_animate."
7. Incorporate the Flash movie into the first website, the Flash canvas object into the second, and the Edge Animate composition into the third.
8. Test all three websites in a desktop browser and verify that the appearance of all three is the same.
9. Review the checklist in Figure 23 and make any necessary changes.

Figure 23 *Portfolio Project checklist*

Website Checklist

1. Have you created Flash movie, Flash HTML5 Canvas, and Edge Animate versions of the animation?
2. If necessary, have you exported a sprite sheet from Flash and imported it into Edge Animate?
3. Have you created three copies of your website and assigned the containing folders the appropriate names?
4. Have you incorporated all three animation formats into their respective websites?
5. Have you tested all three websites in a desktop browser?

Read the following information carefully.

Find out from your instructor the location where you will store your files.

- To complete many of the chapters in this book, you need to use the Data Files provided on Cengage Brain. To access the Data Files on Cengage Brain:
  1. Open your browser and go to http://www.cengagebrain.com
  2. Type the author, title, or ISBN of this book in the Search window. (The ISBN is listed on the back cover.)
  3. Click the book title in the list of search results.
  4. When the book's main page opens, click the Access Now button under Free Materials.
  5. To download Data Files, select a chapter number and then click on the Data Files link on the left navigation bar to download and unzip the files.

- Your instructor will tell you where to save the Data Files and where to store the files you create and modify.
- All the Data Files are organized in folders named after the software application and the chapter in which they are used. For instance, all Chapter 1 Data Files for Dreamweaver are stored in the Dreamweaver zip file in the chapter_1 folder. You should leave all the Data Files in these folders; do not move any Data File out of the folder in which it is originally stored.

Copy and organize your Data Files.

- Copy the folders that contain the Data Files to a USB storage drive, network folder, hard drive, or other storage device.
- For the Dreamweaver files, as you build each website, the exercises in this book will guide you to copy the Data Files you need from the appropriate Data Files folder to the folder where you are storing

the website. Your Data Files should always remain intact because you are copying (and not moving) them to the website.
- For the Dreamweaver files, because you will be building a website from one chapter to the next, sometimes you will need to use a Data File that is already contained in the website you are working on.

Find and keep track of your Data Files and completed files.

- Use the **Data File Supplied** column to make sure you have the files you need before starting the chapter or exercise indicated in the **Chapter** column.
- Use the **Student Creates File** column to find out the filename you use when saving your new file for the exercise.
- The **Used In** column tells you the lesson or end of chapter exercise where you will use the file.

ADOBE DREAMWEAVER CC			
Chapter	**Data File Supplied**	**Student Creates File**	**Used In**
Chapter 1	boilerplate.css		Lesson 2
	dw1_1.html		
	striped_styles.css		
	assets/pool.jpg		
	assets/su_banner.gif		
	assets/su_logo.gif		
	boilerplate.css		Lesson 4
	dw1_2.html	index.html	
	respond.min.js	activities.html	
	su_styles.css	cafe.html	
	assets/su_banner.gif	cruises.html	
	assets/su_logo.gif	fishing.html	
		index.html	
		spa.html	
	bb_styles.css		Skills Review
	blooms_styles.css		

ADOBE DREAMWEAVER CC			
Chapter	**Data File Supplied**	**Student Creates File**	**Used In**
Chapter 1, continued	boilerplate.css		
	dw1_3.html	annuals.html	Skills Review
	dw1_4.html	index.html	
	respond.min.js		
	assets/blooms_banner.jpg	newsletter.html	
	assets/blooms_banner_tablet.jpg	perennials.html	
	assets/blooms_logo.jpg	plants.html	
	assets/tulips.jpg	tips.html	
		water_plants.html	
		workshops.html	
	boilerplate.css	argentina.html	Project Builder 1
	dw1_5.html	catalog.html	
	tripsmart_styles.css	egypt.html	
	assets/tripsmart_banner.jpg	index.html	
	assets/tripsmart_logo.gif	newsletter.html	

ADOBE DREAMWEAVER CC			
Chapter	**Data File Supplied**	**Student Creates File**	**Used In**
Chapter 1, continued		services.html	
		tours.html	
	boilerplate.css	adults.html	Project Builder 2
	cc_styles.css	catering.html	
	dw1_6.html	children.html	
	assets/cc_banner.jpg	classes.html	
	asets/cc_banner_tablet.gif	index.html	
	assets/cc_logo.gif	recipes.html	
		shop.html	
	none		Design Project
	none		Portfolio Project
Chapter 2	spa.txt		Lesson 2
	assets/sea_spa_logo.png		
	gardening_tips.txt		Skills Review
	assets/butterfly.jpg		

ADOBE DREAMWEAVER CC			
Chapter	**Data File Supplied**	**Student Creates File**	**Used In**
Chapter 2, continued	none		Project Builder 1
	none		Project Builder 2
	none		Design Project
	none		Portfolio Project
Chapter 3	questions.txt		Lesson 1
	none		Skills Review
	dw3_1.html		Project Builder 1
	assets/tripsmart_banner.jpg		
	dw3_2.html		Project Builder 2
	assets/cc_banner.jpg		
	assets/pie.jpg		
	none		Design Project
	none		Portfolio Project
Chapter 4	dw4_1.html		Lesson 1
	assets/club_house.jpg		
	assets/water.jpg		Lesson 3

ADOBE DREAMWEAVER CC			
Chapter	**Data File Supplied**	**Student Creates File**	**Used In**
Chapter 4, continued	starfish.ico		Lesson 4
	assets/map_large.jpg		
	assets/map_small.jpg		
	dw4_2.html		Skills Review
	flower.ico		
	assets/lady_in_red.jpg		
	assets/rose.jpg		
	assets/two_roses.jpg		
	assets/two_roses_large.jpg		
	airplane.ico		Project Builder 1
	dw4_3.html		
	assets/nile.jpg		
	assets/statues.jpg		
	dw4_4.html		Project Builder 2
	assets/cc_banner_mobile.jpg		
	assets/peruvian_glass.jpg		
	none		Design Project
	none		Portfolio Project

ADOBE DREAMWEAVER CC			
Chapter	**Data File Supplied**	**Student Creates File**	**Used In**
Chapter 5	dw5_1.html		Lesson 1
	assets/family_sunset.jpg		
	assets/su_banner.gif		
	assets/two_dolphins_small.jpg		
	dw5_2.html		Lesson 2
	assets/transparent.gif		Lesson 4
	dw5_3.html		Lesson 5
	dw5_4.html		
	assets/boats.jpg		
	assets/fisherman.jpg		
	dw5_5.html		Skills Review
	dw5_6.html		
	dw5_7.html		
	dw5_8.html		
	assets/blooms_banner.jpg		
	assets/coleus.jpg		
	assets/fiber_optic_grass.jpg		
	assets/plants.jpg		

ADOBE DREAMWEAVER CC			
Chapter	**Data File Supplied**	**Student Creates File**	**Used In**
Chapter 5, continued	assets/ruby_grass.jpg		
	assets/trees.jpg		
	assets/water_lily.jpg		
	dw5_9.html		Project Builder 1
	dw5_10.html		
	dw5_11.html		
	assets/glacier.jpg		
	assets/iguazu_falls.jpg		
	assets/patagonia.jpg		
	assets/ride_to_temple.jpg		
	assets/tripsmart_banner.jpg		
	dw5_12.html		Project Builder 2
	dw5_13.html		
	dw5_14.html		
	assets/children_cooking.jpg		
	assets/egyptian_lunch.jpg		
	assets/egyptian_traditional_dessert.jpg		
	none		Design Project
	none		Portfolio Project

ADOBE DREAMWEAVER CC			
Chapter	**Data File Supplied**	**Student Creates File**	**Used In**
Chapter 6	cafe.txt		Lesson 3
	assets/club_house_oceanside.jpg		
	assets/shrimp_bisque.jpg		Lesson 5
	composting.txt		Skills Review
	assets/pink_rose.jpg		
	assets/shade_garden.jpg		
	hiking.txt		Project Builder 1
	assets/three_hikers.jpg		
	marshmallows.txt		Project Builder 2
	assets/marshmallows.jpg		
	none		Design Project
	none		Portfolio Project
Chapter 7	none	The Striped Umbrella.ste	Lesson 5
	none	Blooms & Bulbs.ste	Skills Review
	none	TripSmart.ste	Project Builder 1
	none	Carolyne's Creations.ste	Project Builder 2
	none		Design Project
	none		Portfolio Project

ADOBE FLASH CC			
Chapter	**Data File Supplied**	**Student Creates New File**	**Used In**
Chapter 1	fl1_1.fla		Lesson 2
	*demoMovie.fla	demoMovieBanner	
		tween.fla	Lesson 3
	*tween.fla	tweenEffects.fla	
	*tween.fla	layers.fla	Lesson 4
	fl1_2.fla		Lesson 5
	car3.gif		
	fl1_3.fla		Skills Review
	GrayBkDrop.bmp		
		demonstration.fla	Project Builder 1
	fl1_4.fla		Project Builder 2
		dpc1.doc	Design Project

*Created in a previous Lesson or Skills Review in current chapter.

Note: Because of the number of files generated in the Flash chapters, the "Student Creates New File" column lists only the files the student creates from scratch.

ADOBE FLASH CC			
Chapter	**Data File Supplied**	**Student Creates New File**	**Used In**
Chapter 2	fl2_1.fla		Lesson 1
	fl2_2.fla		Lesson 2
	fl2_3.fla		
		textObjects.fla	Lesson 3
	fl2_4.fla		Lesson 4
	fl2_5.fla		Lesson 5
	fl2_6.fla		Skills Review
	beachBall.png		
	logo.png	odysseyTours2.fla	Project Builder 1
		The JazzClub2.fla	Project Builder 2
		dcp2.doc	Design Project
		portfolio2.fla	Portfolio Project

ADOBE FLASH CC			
Chapter	**Data File Supplied**	**Student Creates New File**	**Used In**
Chapter 3	fl3_1.fla		Lesson 1
	fl3_2.fla		
	fl3_3.fla		Lesson 2
	fl3_4.fla		Lesson 3
	fl3_5.fla		
	fl3_6.fla		Lesson 4
	fl3_7.fla		
	fl3_8.fla		
	fl3_9.fla		Lesson 5
	fl3_10.fla		Lesson 6
	*textAn.fla	rallySnd.fla	Lesson 7
	beep.wav		
	CarSnd.wav		
	fl3_11.fla		Skills Review
	fl3_12.fla		
		odysseyTours3.fla	Project Builder 1
	fl3_13.fla		Project Builder 2
		dpc3.doc	Design Project
	**portfolio2.fla	portfolio3.fla	Portfolio Project

**Created in a previous chapter.

ADOBE FLASH CC			
Chapter	**Data File Supplied**	**Student Creates New File**	**Used In**
Chapter 4	fl4_1.fla		Lesson 1
	Game36.png		
	Game48.png		
	Game72.png		
		AccelBall-sim.fla	Lesson 2
	fl4_2.fla		
	fl4_3.fla		Lesson 3
	*phoneF.fla	tabletF.fla	
		accel.fla	Lesson 4
	*accel.fla	accelDragonfly.fla	
	dragonfly-bkgrnd.fla		
		accelHit.fla	
		WildHorses.fla	Lesson 5
	*WildHorses.fla	WildHorsesZoom.fla	
	NobleEye.jpg		
	WildBlue.jpg		
	WildGold.jpg		
	fl4_4.fla		Skills Review
		odysseyTours4.fla	Project Builder 1

*Created in a previous Lesson or Skills Review in current chapter.

ADOBE FLASH CC			
Chapter	Data File Supplied	Student Creates New File	Used In
Chapter 4, continued	Arc de Triomphe.jpg	swipePrototype.fla	Project Builder 2
	Eiffel Tower.jpg		
	NotreDame.jpg		
		dpc4.doc	Design Project
	fl4_5.fla		Portfolio Project
	math.swf		
	shirt.swf		
	shirt2.swf		
Chapter 5	safari.flv	bannerAd.fla	Lesson 1
	fl5_1.html		
	fl5_2.fla		
	fl5_3.fla		Lesson 2
	sky-image.png	zodiacSigns.fla	
	scorpio-image.png		
	fl5_4.fla		Lesson 3
	countICON48.png		
		AIRWinSamp.fla	Lesson 4
	fl5_5.fla		
	fireworks.mp4		Skills Review

ADOBE FLASH CC			
Chapter	**Data File Supplied**	**Student Creates New File**	**Used In**
Chapter 5, continued	fl5_6.html		
	*skillsDemo5A.swf		
	fl5_7.fla		
	fl5_8.fla		
	*skillsDemo5C.fla	skillsDemo5CCVS.fla	
	AE-backdrop.jpg	skillsDemo5D.fla	
	moonB.png		
	star.png		
	ufo.png		
	fl5_9.fla		
	fl5_10.fla		
	mGame48.png		
	fl5_11.fla		Project Builder 1
	matchG48icon.png		
	GameBackground.png	customGame.fla	Project Builder 2
		dpc5.doc	Design Project
	fl5_12.fla		Portfolio Project
	*portfolio5.fla	portfolio5CVS.fla	

*Created in a previous Lesson or Skills Review in current chapter.

ADOBE EDGE ANIMATE CC			
Chapter	**Data File Supplied**	**Student Creates New File**	**Used In**
Chapter 1		ursa/ursa.html	Lesson 1
	meteor/meteor.an		Lesson 2
	meteor/meteor.html		Lesson 2
	ursa/star.png		Lesson 3
	card/bear.png		Skills Review
	card/snowflake.png		Skills Review
		card/card.html	Skills Review
	fly/mountain.png		Project Builder 1
	fly/plane.png		Project Builder 1
		fly/fly.html	Project Builder 1
	banner/red.png		Project Builder 2
		banner/banner.html	Project Builder 2
	mansion/ghost.png		Portfolio Project
	mansion/house.png		Portfolio Project
	mansion/moon.png		Portfolio Project
		mansion/mansion.html	Portfolio Project

ADOBE EDGE ANIMATE CC			
Chapter	Data File Supplied	Student Creates New File	Used In
Chapter 2	farm/farm.an		Chapter
	farm/farm.html		Chapter
	gallery/images/IMG_01.jpg		Skills Review
	gallery/images/IMG_02.jpg		Skills Review
	gallery/images/IMG_03.jpg		Skills Review
	gallery/images/IMG_04.jpg		Skills Review
	gallery/images/IMG_05.jpg		Skills Review
		gallery/gallery.html	Skills Review
		menus/menus.html	Project Builder 1
	quotes/quotes.an		Project Builder 2
	quotes/quotes.html		Project Builder 2
	keywords/keywords.an		Portfolio Project
	keywords/keywords.html		Portfolio Project

ADOBE CC WEB COLLECTION INTEGRATION			
Chapter	**Data File Supplied**	**Student Creates New File**	**Used In**
Chapter 1	Lessons/IC1_1.html	Lessons/msf_flash.html	Lesson 1
	Lessons/morning.swf		Lesson 1
	Lessons/IC1_2.fla	Lessons/morning_canvas.fla	Lesson 2
	Lessons/msf.css		Lessons 2-3
	Lessons/EA_Edit/IC1_3.html	Lessons/EA_Edit/morning_edge_animate.html	Lesson 3
	Lessons/EA_Export/IC1_4.html	Lessons/EA_Export/morning_edge_animate.html	Lesson 3
		Lessons/EA_Export/publish/animate_package/morning_edge_animate.oam	Lesson 3
	Lessons/EA_Export/IC1_5.html	Lessons/EA_Export/msf_edge_animate.html	Lesson 3
	Lessons/IC1_6.fla	Lessons/cheetah.fla	Lesson 4
		Lessons/cheetah.png	Lesson 4
		Lessons/cheetah.eas	Lesson 4
		Lessons/cheetah.html	Lesson 4
	SkillsReview/IC1_7.html	SkillsReview/tks.html	Skills Review
	SkillsReview/tks.swf		Skills Review
	SkillsReview/IC1_8.fla	SkillsReview/tks_canvas.fla	Skills Review
		SkillsReview/tks_canvas.html	Skills Review

ADOBE CC WEB COLLECTION INTEGRATION

Chapter	Data File Supplied	Student Creates New File	Used In
Chapter 1, continued	SkillsReview/tks.css		Skills Review
	SkillsReview/EA_edit/IC1_9.html	SkillsReview/EA_edit/tks_edge_animate.html	Skills Review
	SkillsReview/EA_export/IC1_10.html	SkillsReview/EA_export/tks_edge_animate.html	Skills Review
		SkillsReview/EA_Export/publish/animate_package/tks_edge_animate.oam	Skills Review
	SkillsReview/EA_export/IC1_11.html	SkillsReview/EA_export/tks.html	Skills Review
	SkillsReview/IC1_12.fla	SkillsReview/cat.fla	Skills Review
		SkillsReview/cat.png	Skills Review
		SkillsReview/cat.eas	Skills Review
		SkillsReview/cat.html	Skills Review
	PB1/IC1_13.html	PB1/testsite_flash.html	Project Builder 1
	PB1/tfcu.swf		Project Builder 1
	PB1/IC1_14.fla	PB1/tfcu.fla	Project Builder 1
		tfcu.png	Project Builder 1
		tfcu.eas	Project Builder 1
	PB1/tfcu_EA/IC1_15.html	PB1/tfcu_EA/tfcu_edge_animate.html	Project Builder 1

ADOBE CC WEB COLLECTION INTEGRATION			
Chapter	**Data File Supplied**	**Student Creates New File**	**Used In**
Chapter 1, continued		PB1/tfcu_EA/publish/animate_ package/tfcu_edge_animate.oam	Project Builder 1
	PB1/tfcu_EA/IC1_16.html	PB1/tfcu_EA/testsite_EA.html	Project Builder 1
	PB2/IC1_17.html	PB2/afa_flash.html	Project Builder 2
	PB2/bison.swf		Project Builder 2
	PB2/IC1_18.fla	PB2/afa_canvas.fla	Project Builder 2
		PB2/afa_canvas.html	Project Builder 2
	PB2/afa.css		Project Builder 2
	PB2/IC1_19.fla	PB2/bison.fla	Project Builder 2
		PB2/bison.png	Project Builder 2
		PB2/bison.eas	Project Builder 2
	PB2/bison_EA/IC1_20.html	PB2/bison_EA/bison_edge_ animate.html	Project Builder 2
		PB2/bison_EA/publish/animate_ package/bison_edge_animate .oam	Project Builder 2
	PB2/bison_EA/IC1_21.html	afa_edge_animate.html	Project Builder 2
		DP/Integration Design Project	Design Project

A

Absolute path
A path containing an external link that references a link on a web page outside of the current website, and includes the protocol "http" and the URL, or address, of the web page.

Accelerometer
A built-in feature of mobile devices that causes objects on the screen to move in response to the movement of the device.

Actions panel
In Flash, the panel where you create and edit ActionScript code for an object or a frame.

ActionScript
The Adobe Flash scripting language used by developers to add interactivity to movies, control objects, exchange data, and create complex animations.

ActionScript 3.0 (AS3)
The version of Flash ActionScript that is based on Object Oriented Programming (OOP) standards that provides a way to organize code (a set of instructions).

Adobe Flash CC
A development tool that allows you to create compelling interactive experiences, often by using animation.

Adobe Media Encoder CC
A tool used to output video in a variety of video file formats.

AIR (Adobe Integrated Runtime)
A Flash technology used to create applications that can be played without a browser. An AIR app can be displayed on mobile devices, on stand-alone computers, on the Internet, and even on television sets.

AIR for Android
A feature of Flash that allows you to publish Flash FLA files so that they run on Android devices (smartphones and tablets).

AIR for iOS
A feature of Flash that allows you to publish Flash FLA files so that they run on iOS devices (iPhones and iPads).

Align
Position an image on a web page or on the Stage in relation to other elements on the page or on the Stage.

Alpha
In Edge Animate, the degree of a color's transparency, specified as a value between 0 and 1 (in Edge Animate) or 0 and 100 (in Flash).

Animation
The perception of motion caused by the rapid display of a series of still images.

AP div tag
A div that is assigned a fixed (absolute) position on a web page.

AP element
The container that an AP div tag creates on a page. *See also* AP div tag.

Apache web server
A public domain, open source web server that is available using several different operating systems, including UNIX and Windows.

Application bar (Win)
In Dreamweaver, the toolbar located above the Document window that includes menu names, a Workspace switcher, and other application commands.

Applications, or apps
Products such as interactive games, tutorials, demonstrations, business and informational programs that can be incorporated in a website, deployed on a desktop computer or delivered on a mobile device.

Assets
In Dreamweaver and Edge Animate, files that are not web pages, such as images, audio files, and video clips. In Flash, associated files and objects available for use with a project.

Assets panel
A panel that contains eight categories of assets, such as images, used in a website. Selecting a category button displays a list of those assets.

Auto format
A button in the Actions panel that, when clicked, formats the code in accordance with ActionScript formatting conventions.

Auto-Keyframe Mode button
The button that controls whether Edge Animate creates an ending keyframe for a property automatically when you specify an ending value.

Auto-Transition Mode button
The button that controls whether Edge Animate inserts a gradual transition before any ending keyframe you insert.

————————— **B** —————————

Background color
A color that fills an entire web page, frame, table, cell, or CSS layout block.

Background image
A graphic file used in place of a background color.

Balance
In screen design, the distribution of optical weight in the layout. Optical weight is the ability of an object to attract the viewer's eye, as determined by the object's size, shape, color, and other factors.

Banner
An image that generally appears across the top or down the side of a web page and can incorporate a company's logo, contact information, and links to the other pages in the site.

BaseCamp
A web-based project collaboration tool used by many companies.

Bitmap image
An image based on pixels, rather than mathematical formulas. Also referred to as a raster image.

Blog
A website where the website owner regularly posts commentaries and opinions on various topics.

Blue drop zone
See Drop zone.

Body
The part of a web page that appears in a browser window. It contains all of the page content that is visible to users, such as text, images, and links.

Border
An outline that surrounds a cell, a table, or a CSS layout block.

Breadcrumb trail
A list of links that provides a path from the initial page opened in a website to the page being currently viewed.

Break apart
The process of breaking apart text to place each character in a separate text block. Also, the process of separating groups, instances, and bitmaps into ungrouped, editable elements.

Broken link
A link that cannot find the intended destination file for the link.

Browser
See web browser.

Browser-native animations
Animations created with HTML, CSS, and JavaScript.

Bullet
A small dot or similar icon preceding unordered list items. *See also* Bulleted list.

Bulleted list
An unordered list that uses bullets. *See also* Bullet.

Button symbol
Object on the Stage that is used to provide interactivity, such as jumping to another frame on the Timeline.

————————— **C** —————————

Cascading Style Sheet
A set of formatting attributes used to format web pages to provide a consistent presentation for content across a website.

Cell
A small box within a table that is used to hold text or graphics. Cells are arranged horizontally in rows and vertically in columns.

Cell padding
The distance between the cell content and the cell walls in a table.

Cell spacing
The distance between cells in a table.

Cell walls
The edges surrounding a cell in a table.

Center Stage property
The property in Edge Animate that you use to center an animation vertically and/or horizontally.

Child page
A page at a lower level in a web hierarchy that links to a page at a higher level, called a parent page.

Class type
A type of style that can contain a combination of formatting attributes that can be applied to a block of text or other page elements. Custom style names begin with a period (.). Also called a custom type.

Clean HTML code
Code that does what it is supposed to do without using unnecessary instructions, which take up memory.

Cloak
To exclude from certain processes, such as being transferred to a remote site.

Code hint
An auto-complete feature that displays lists of tags that appear as you type in Code view.

Code Inspector
A separate floating window that displays the current page in Code view.

Code Snippets
Predefined blocks of ActionScript 3.0 and HTML5 Canvas code that provide a quick way to insert AS3 code into the Script pane.

Code view
The Dreamweaver view that shows the underlying HTML code for a page; use this view to read or edit the code.

Coding toolbar
A toolbar that contains buttons you can use when working in Code view.

Column
Table cells arranged vertically.

Comment
Gray, non-executable tags preceded by "/*" that tell a browser to skip over the code that follows it until it gets to an ending comment tag.

CompositionReady event
The EdgeAnimate event that fires when an animation is ready to play, but before autoplay starts.

Compound type
A type of style that is used to format a selection.

Controller
A window that provides the playback controls for a movie.

Coordinate
The position of a pixel on the Stage as measured across (X coordinate) and down (Y coordinate) the Stage.

Copyright
A legal protection for the particular and tangible expression of an idea; the right of an author or creator of a work to copy, distribute, and modify a thing, idea, or image; a type of intellectual property.

CSS layout block
A section of a web page defined and formatted using a Cascading Style Sheet.

CSS Layout Box Model
CSS layout blocks defined as rectangular boxes of content with margins, padding, and borders.

CSS page layout
A method of positioning objects on web pages through the use of containers formatted with CSS. *See also* Cascading Style Sheets.

—————— **D** ——————

Data type
The kind of data used to populate a variable. For example a variable assigned a Number data type can only accept numeric characters.

Debug
To find and correct coding errors.

Default font
The font a browser uses to display link text if no other font is assigned.

Default link color
The color a browser uses to display text if no other color is assigned.

Delimited file
A database, word processing, or spreadsheet file that has been saved as a text file with data separated with delimiters such as commas or tabs.

Delimiter
A comma, tab, colon, semicolon, or similar character that separates tabular data.

Deliverables
Products that will be provided to the client at the product completion such as pages or graphic elements.

Dependent file
A file that another file needs to be complete, such as an image or style sheet.

Deprecated
Term used to describe code that is no longer within the current standard and in danger of becoming obsolete.

Derivative work
An adaptation of another work, such as a movie version of a book; a new, original product that includes content from a previously existing work.

Description
A short summary that resides in the head section of a web page and describes the website content. *See also* Head content.

Design Note
A separate file in a website file structure that contains additional information about a page file or a graphic file.

Design view
The Dreamweaver view that shows the page similar to how it would appear in a browser and is primarily used for creating and designing a web page.

Digital Certificate
Electronic form used to verify the identity of an application developer.

Div tag
An HTML tag that is used to format and position web page elements.

Dock
A collection of panels or buttons surrounded by a dark gray bar. The arrows in the dock are used to maximize and minimize the panels.

Document
A Flash file which, by default, is given the .fla file extension.

Document toolbar
A toolbar that contains buttons and drop-down menus for changing the current work mode, checking browser compatibility, previewing web pages, debugging web pages, choosing visual aids, and viewing file management options.

Document window
The large area under the Document toolbar in the Dreamweaver workspace where you create and edit web pages.

DOM (Document Object Model)
A convention that represents the order and type of elements on a page.

Domain name
An IP address expressed in letters instead of numbers, usually reflecting the name of the business represented by the website; also referred to as a URL.

Download
The process of transferring files from a remote site to a local site.

Dreamweaver workspace
The entire window, from the Application bar (Win) or Menu bar (Mac) at the top of the window, to the status bar at the bottom border of the program window; the area in the Dreamweaver program window that includes all of the menus, panels, buttons, inspectors, and panes that you use to create and maintain websites.

Drop zone
A blue outline area that indicates where a panel can be moved.

Dynamic text field
A text box created on the Stage with the Text tool that displays information derived from variables.

——————— **E** ———————

Element Quick View
A visual representation of the DOM structure for a page.

Elements panel
The panel in Edge Animate that lists all the HTML elements that are part of the current file, arranged hierarchically based on their nesting in the file.

Ellipse tool
The Edge Animate tool that lets you create an ellipse or a circle.

Embedded style
A style whose code is located in the head section of an individual page. Also called an internal style.

Embedded style sheet
See Embedded style.

Embedded video
A video file that has been imported into a Flash document and becomes part of the SWF file.

Event Listener
ActionScript 3.0 code that "listens" to "hear" when an event occurs. For example, a button object might listen for a mouse click.

Event sound
A sound that plays independently of the Timeline. The sound starts in the keyframe to which it is added, but it can continue playing even after a movie ends. An event sound must download completely before it begins playing.

Events
Circumstances that occur in the browser; for example, when a page finishes loading, or a when a user clicks the left mouse button.

Export
To save data that was created in Dreamweaver in a special file format so that you can open it in another software program.

Extension
A small application you can install within a web browser.

External link
A link that connects to a web page in another website or to an e-mail address.

External style sheet
Collection of styles stored in a separate file that controls the formatting of content on a web page. External style sheets have a .css file extension.

——————— **F** ———————

Facebook
A social networking site that let users interact as an online community through the sharing of text, images, and videos.

Fair use
A part of copyright law that allows a user to make a copy of all or part of a work, even if permission has not been granted.

Favicon
Short for favorites icon, a small image that represents a website and appears in the address bar of many browsers.

File Transfer Protocol (FTP)
The process of uploading and downloading files to and from a remote site.

Files panel
A window similar to File Explorer (Windows) or Finder (Macintosh), where Dreamweaver displays and manages files and folders. The Files panel contains a list of all the folders and files in a website.

Filters
Special effects, such as drop shadows, that can be applied to text using options on the Filters area in the Properties panel.

Fire
To occur; when an event takes place, it is said to fire.

Flash
See Adobe Flash CC.

Flash Player
A free plugin program from Adobe that allows Flash movies (.swf formats) to be viewed on a computer.

Flowchart
A visual representation of how the contents in an application or a website are organized and how various screens are linked.

Fluid grid layout
A system for designing layouts that will adapt to multiple screen sizes.

Fluid Grid Layout guides
Visual aids that show you the number of columns used in Mobile, Tablet, and Desktop views.

Focus group
A marketing tool that asks a group of people for feedback about a product, such as the impact of a television ad or the effectiveness of a website design.

Font stack
See Font-combination.

Font-combination
A set of font choices that specifies which fonts a browser should use to display text, such as Arial, Helvetica, sans serif. Also known as a font stack. Font combinations that a user creates are called custom font stacks.

Frame-by-frame animation
An animation created by specifying the object that is to appear in each frame of a sequence of frames (also called a frame animation).

Frames
Individual cells that make up the Timeline in Flash.

FTP
See File Transfer Protocol.

———————— **G** ————————

GIF
Acronym for Graphics Interchange Format file. A type of file format used for images placed on web pages that can support both transparency and animation.

Google Video Chat
A video sharing community hosted by Google.

GPS
Acronym for Global Positioning System; a device used to track your position through a global satellite navigation system.

Gradient
A color fill that makes a gradual transition from one color to another causing the colors to blend into one another.

Graphic
A picture or design element that adds visual interest to a page.

Graphic symbols
In Flash objects, such as drawings, that are converted to symbols and stored in the Library panel. A graphic symbol is the original object. An instance (copy) of a symbol can be made by dragging the symbol from the Library to the Stage.

Grid
Horizontal and vertical lines that fill the page or Stage and are used to align page elements or objects.

Group
To organize Edge Animate elements within another element in order to work with them as a single unit.

Guide
A horizontal or vertical line that you drag from the rulers onto the page or Stage to help you align objects.

Guide layers
Layers used to align objects on the Stage.

H

Head content
The part of a web page that includes the page title that appears in the title bar of the browser, as well as meta tags, which are HTML codes that include information about the page, such as keywords and descriptions, and are not visible in the browser.

Hex
See hexadecimal.

Hex triplet
A color value expressed with three characters that represents the amount of red, green, and blue present in a color. Also known as an RGB triplet.

Hexadecimal
A color system that represents values for the red, green, and blue components of a color using the hexadecimal (base 16) numbering system.

Hexadecimal RGB value
A six-character value that represents the amount of red, green, and blue in a color and is based on the Base 16 number system. If expressed in three characters instead of six, it's called an RGB triplet or a hex triplet.

History panel
A panel that contains a record of each action performed during an editing session, and allows you to undo actions; up to 1000 levels of Undo are available through the History panel (20 levels by default).

Home page
The first page that is displayed when users go to a website.

Hotspot
A selectable area on an image that, when selected, links to a different location on the page or to another web page.

HSLa
A color system that specifies values for hue, saturation, lightness, and alpha.

HTML
Stands for Hypertext Markup Language, the language web developers use to create web pages.

HTML5 Canvas
An element used in web development that defines a region of a web page used to display multimedia content such as graphics, animations and interactive video created using JavaScript.

HUD
An acronym for Heads up Display; a mini-toolbar with tools for editing a div tag.

Hyperlink
An image or text element on a web page that users select to display another location on the page, another web page on the same website, or a web page on a different website; also known as a link.

I

ID type
A type of CSS rule that is used to redefine an HTML tag.

Image
A graphic such as a photograph or a piece of artwork on a web page; images in a website are known as assets.

Image map
An image that has one or more specially-designated areas, each of which serves as a link.

Import
To bring data created in one software application into another application.

In-app messages
Messages that appear within an application to suggest tips for boosting workflow productivity.

Increment action
An ActionScript operator, indicated by ++ (two plus signs), that adds 1 unit to a variable or expression.

Inherit
A property that specifies that the property and value are applied from a parent container.

Inheritance
The CSS governing principle that allows for the properties of a parent container to be used to format the content in a child container. Also refers to the properties of device size selectors: global (mobile) selectors govern tablet and desktop size selectors; tablet size selectors govern desktop size selectors.

Inline style
A style whose code is placed within the body tags of a web page.

In-product messages
Messages that appear within Dreamweaver to suggest tips for Dreamweaver integration with other Creative Cloud apps.

Input text field
A text field created on the Stage with the Text tool that takes information entered by a user and stores it as a variable.

Insert panel
In Dreamweaver, a panel with eight categories of buttons for creating and inserting objects displayed as a drop-down menu: Common, Structure, Media, Form, jQuery Mobile, jQuery UI, Templates, and Favorites. Also called the Insert bar.

Instance
Each use of an asset.

Instances
Editable copies of symbols that are placed on the Stage.

Intellectual property
A product resulting from human creativity, such as movies, songs, designs, and the like.

Internal link
A link to a web page within the same website.

Internal style sheet
A style sheet whose code is saved within the code of a web page, rather than in an external file. Also called an embedded style.

Internet Service Provider (ISP)
A service to which you subscribe to be able to connect to the Internet with your computer.

Inter-screen unity
Refers to the design that viewers encounter as they navigate from one screen to another, and that provides consistency throughout the application.

Intra-screen unity
Refers to how the various screen objects relate and how they all fit in.

IP address
An assigned series of numbers, separated by periods, that designates an address on the Internet.

Item
A link in a menu bar.

──────────── J ────────────

JavaScript
A programming language that is commonly used to create interactive effects on web pages.

JPEG or JPG
A graphics file format that is especially useful for photographic images. JPEG graphics are viewable on the web.

──────────── K ────────────

Keyframe
In Flash, a frame that signifies a change in a movie, such as the end of an animation. In Edge Animate, part of an animation that specifies the value of a property as a specific time during the animation.

Keyframe mark
A diamond shape added to the timeline when you create a keyframe in Edge Animate.

Keyword
In Dreamweaver, a word that relates to the content of a website and resides in the head section of a web page.

──────────── L ────────────

LAN
Acronym for Local Area Network, a network that is not connected to the Internet.

Layers
In Flash, rows on the Timeline that are used to organize objects and that allow the stacking of objects on the Stage.

Lessons panel
The panel in Edge Animate that contains links to a set of introductory tutorials that explain how to use Edge Animate.

Library panel
In Flash, the panel that contains the objects (graphics, buttons, sounds, movie clips, etc.) that are used in a Flash movie. In Edge Animate, the panel that lists all assets available for use with your project.

Licensing agreement
The permission given by a copyright holder that conveys the right to use the copyright holder's work.

Line break
Places a new text line without creating a new paragraph.

Link
See Hyperlink.

Live view
A Dreamweaver view that displays an open document as if you were viewing it in a browser, with interactive elements active and functioning.

Local root folder
See Local site folder.

Local site folder
A folder on a hard drive, Flash drive, or floppy disk that holds all the files and folders for a website; also called the local root folder.

──────────── M ────────────

Mailto: link
An e-mail address formatted as a link that opens the default mail program with a blank, addressed message.

Main Timeline
The primary Timeline for a Flash movie that is displayed when you start a new Flash document.

Marquee
Created when you drag the Selection tool pointer around an entire object to select it.

Mask layer
In Flash, a layer used to cover up the objects on another layer(s) and, at the same time, create a window through which you can view various objects on the other layer.

Match.com
A social networking site that lets users share information in order to establish relationships.

Media queries
A Dreamweaver feature that uses files that specify set parameters for displaying pages on separate devices, such as tablets or smartphones.

Mega menu
A type of menu that uses sub-menus to group related pages under a main menu item.

Menu bar
In Adobe CC, a bar across the top of the program window that is located under the program title bar and lists the names of the menus that contain commands. Also, an area on a web page that contains links to the main pages of a website; also called a navigation bar.

Merge cells
To combine multiple adjacent cells in a table into one cell.

Merge Drawing Model
A drawing mode that causes overlapping drawings (objects) to merge so that a change in the top object, such as moving it, may affect the object beneath it.

Meta tag
An HTML code that resides in the head section of a web page and includes information about the page, such as keywords and descriptions. *See also* Head content.

Mobile Content Simulator
A feature in Flash that allows you to test mobile applications. The simulator displays the application as it would appear on a mobile phone and allows you to use events and gestures, such as swipe and zoom, to see how the application reacts.

Morphing
The animation process of changing one object into another, sometimes unrelated, object. For example, animating a car to change into a bus.

Motion guide
Feature that allows you to draw a path and attach motion-tweened animations to the path. A motion guide has its own layer.

Motion path
A dotted line on the Stage that represents the path the object takes from the beginning frame to the ending frame of a motion tween.

Motion presets
Pre-built animations that can be applied to objects in Flash. For example, applying a bouncing effect to a ball.

Motion span
See tween span.

Motion tweening
The process used in Flash to automatically fill in the frames between keyframes in an animation that changes the properties of an object such as the position, size, or color. Motion tweening works on symbols and groups.

Movement
In screen design, the way the viewer's eye moves through the objects on the screen.

Movie clip symbol
An object, often animated, that is stored as a single, reusable symbol in the Library panel. It has its own Timeline, independent of the main Timeline.

MP4
A video file format commonly used on the web.

N

Native animations
See browser-native animations.

Navigation bar
See Menu bar.

Navigation structure
A set of text or graphic links usually organized in rows or columns that users can select to navigate between pages of a website. *See also* Menu bar.

Nested table
A table within a table.

Nesting
Including another symbol within a symbol, such as nesting a graphic symbol, button, or another movie clip symbol within a movie clip symbol.

No right-click script
JavaScript code that will block users from displaying the shortcut menu when they right-click an image on a web page.

Number variable
In ActionScript, a variable type that contains a number with which you can use arithmetic operators, such as addition and subtraction. To create a number variable use the Number data type.

Numbered list
See Ordered list.

O

Object Drawing Model
A drawing mode that allows you to overlap objects, which are then kept separate, so that changes in one object do not affect another object. You must break apart these objects before being able to select their stroke and fills.

Objects
Items, such as drawings and text, that are placed on the Stage and can be edited and manipulated.

Onion skin
In Flash, a feature that displays the outlines of an animated object so that the positions of the object in a series of frames can be viewed all at once.

Online community
Social website you can join, such as Facebook and Twitter, where you can communicate with others by posting messages or media content such as images or videos.

Opacity
Degree of transparency; PNG files have varying degrees of opacity.

Ordered list
A list of items that are placed in a specific order and preceded by numbers or letters; sometimes called a numbered list.

Orphaned file
Files that are not linked to any pages in the website.

Overflow area
The gray area surrounding the Edge Animate stage.

———————— P ————————

Panel
A tabbed window in Adobe CC that displays information on a particular topic or contains related commands. In Flash, panels are use to view, organize and modify objects and features in a movie.

Panel groups
Sets of related panels that are grouped together and displayed through the Window menu; also known as Panel sets and Tab groups.

Parent page
A page at a higher level in a web hierarchy that links to other pages on a lower level, called child pages.

Pasteboard
The gray area surrounding the Flash Stage where objects can be placed and manipulated. Neither the Pasteboard nor objects placed on it appear in the movie unless the objects move onto the Stage during the playing of the movie.

Path
The location of a file in relation to its place in the folder structure of the website.

Permissions process
The process to obtain permission to use content legally.

Persistence of vision
The phenomenon of the eye capturing and holding an image for one-tenth of a second before processing another image. This enables the rapid display of a series of still images to give the impression of motion and creates an animation.

Pinterest
A social networking site that lets users interact as an online community through the sharing of crafts, recipes, and other items of interest.

Pixel
Each dot in a bitmap graphic. Pixels have an exact position on the screen and a precise color.

Playhead
In Flash, the indicator specifying which frame is playing in the Timeline of a Flash movie. In Edge Animate, the yellow marker displayed at the top of the timeline to mark the current location.

PNG
The acronym for Portable Network Graphics File, a file format used for images placed on web pages;

capable of showing millions of colors but is small in file size. PNG is the native file format in Fireworks.

Podcast
"Pod" is an acronym for Programming On Demand, in which users can download and play digitally broadcasted files using devices such as computers or MP3 players.

Point of contact
A place on a web page that provides users with a means of contacting the company.

Portable Network Graphics (PNG)
A graphics file format developed specifically for images that are to be used on the web.

POUR
The acronym for Perceivable, Operable, Understandable, and Robust; guidelines for building accessible websites.

POWDER
The acronym for Protocol for Web Description Resources; an evaluation system for web pages developed with the World Wide Web Consortium (W3C) that provides summary information about a website.

Properties pane
The bottom pane of the CSS Designer panel when it is shown as a single column or the right side when it is expanded into two columns; lists a selected rule's properties.

Properties panel
In Flash, the panel that displays the properties of the selected object, such as size and color, on the Stage or the selected frame. The Properties panel can be used to edit selected properties. In Edge Animate, the panel that displays CSS properties and their values for the element currently selected on the stage, or for the stage itself if no element is selected.

Property
An attribute of an object such as its size or color.

Property inspector
In Dreamweaver, a panel that displays the properties of a selected web page object; its contents vary according to the object currently selected.

Protocol for Web Description Resources
See POWDER.

Public domain
Work that is no longer protected by copyright; anyone can use it for any purpose.

Publish
In Dreamweaver, to make a website available for viewing on the Internet or on an intranet by transferring the files to a web server. In Flash, the process used to generate the files necessary for delivering Flash movies on the web, such as SWF, AIR and HTML5 Canvas files.

————— **Q** —————

QuickTime
A file format used for movies and animations that requires a QuickTime Player.

————— **R** —————

Raster image
An image based on pixels, rather than mathematical formulas. Also referred to as a bitmap image.

Really Simple Syndication
See RSS.

Rectangle tool
The Edge Animate and Flash tool that lets you create a rectangle shape.

Registration point
The point on an object that is used to position the object on the Stage using ActionScript code.

Related file
A file that is linked to a document and is necessary for the document to display and function correctly.

Related Files toolbar
A toolbar located below an open document's filename tab that displays the names of any related files.

Relative path
A path used with an internal link to reference a web page or graphic file within the website.

Remote server
A web server that hosts websites and is not directly connected to the computer housing the local site.

Remote site
A website that has been published to a remote server. *See also* Remote server.

Rendering
The way fonts are drawn on a screen.

Responsive design
Using style sheets and media queries to control how pages look on different devices, such as tablets and smartphones.

Responsive Scaling property
The property in Edge Animate that you use to scale a project to the browser window horizontally and/or vertically.

RGBa format
A color format that specifies numerical values from 0-255 for the red, green, and blue

components of the color, along with an alpha value between 0 (fully transparent) and 1 (fully opaque).

Rich media content
Attractive and engaging images, interactive elements, video, or animations.

Rollover or Rollover effect
A special effect that changes the appearance of an element in a web page in response to the user moving the mouse pointer over that element or over another element.

Root folder
See Local site folder.

Rounded Rectangle tool
The Edge Animate tool that lets you create a rectangle with rounded corners.

Row
Table cells arranged horizontally.

RDS
Acronym for Remote Development Services; provides access control to web servers using Cold Fusion.

RSS
Acronym for Really Simple Syndication, a method websites use to distribute news stories, information about upcoming events, and announcements, known as an RSS Feed.

RSS feed
A way to distribute news stories through websites. *See also* RSS.

Rule
A set of formatting attributes that define styles in a Cascading Style Sheet.

Rule of thirds
A design principle that entails dividing a page into nine squares and then placing the page elements of most interest on the intersections of the grid lines.

Rulers
On screen markers that help you precisely measure and position an object. Rulers can be displayed using the View menu.

 S

Scene
A Timeline designated for a specific part of the movie. Scenes are a way to organize long movies by dividing the movie into sections.

Scope creep
A situation that occurs when impromptu changes or additions are made to a project without corresponding increases in the schedule or budget.

Screen readers
Devices used by persons with visual impairments to convert written text on a computer monitor to spoken words.

Scrubbing
Dragging the playhead left or right to move backwards or forwards in a video or on the Flash timeline.

Secure FTP (SFTP)
A method for transferring files with encryption to protect the file content, user names, and passwords.

Selector
The name of the tag to which style declarations have been assigned.

Semantic markup
Coding to emphasize meaning.

Set up a site
To specify a website's name and the location of the local site folder using the Dreamweaver Manage Sites dialog box.

(SFTP)
See Secure FTP.

Shape hints
Indicators used to control the shape of a complex object as it changes appearance during an animation.

Shape tweening
The process of animating an object so that its shape changes. Shape tweening requires editable graphics.

Show Code and Design views
A combination of Code view and Design view; the best view for correcting errors.

Site definition
Important information about a website, including its URL, preferences that you've specified, and other secure information, such as login and password information; you can export a site definition to another location using the Export command.

Site map
A graphical representation or a directory listing of how web pages relate to each other within a website.

Skype
A video sharing application.

Slider
The small indicator on the left side of the History panel that you can drag to undo or redo one or more actions.

Smart object
An image layer that stores image data from raster or vector images.

Social networking
The grouping of individual web users who connect and interact with other users in online communities.

Source
See source element.

Source element
The element that generates an event.

Specifications
A list of what will be included in each screen including the arrangement of each element and the functionality of each object (for example, what happens when you click the button labeled Skip Intro).

Split a cell
To divide table cells into multiple cells.

Stage
In Flash, the area of the Flash workspace that contains the objects that are part of the movie and that will be seen by the viewers. In Edge Animate, the area of the Edge Animate workspace that displays the animation you are working on.

Standard toolbar
A toolbar that contains buttons you use to execute frequently used commands that are also available on the File and Edit menus.

State
In a browser, the condition of an item in a menu bar in relation to the pointer. In Edge Animate, each of the possible appearances of an element in a rollover effect.

Status bar
In Dreamweaver, the bar that appears at the bottom of the Dreamweaver document window; the left end of the status bar displays the tag selector, which shows the HTML tags being used at the insertion point location. The right end displays the window size and estimated download time for the page displayed.

Step
Each task performed in the History panel.

Storyboard
A series of sketches that illustrate the sequence of events in an animation.

Streaming video
The process of delivering video content using a constant connection established with a Flash Communication Server.

Stroke
The thickness of an element's border.

Symbols
The basic building blocks of a Flash application. There are three types: graphic, button, and movie clip.

Synchronize
A Dreamweaver command that compares the names, dates, and times on all files on a local and remote site, then transfers only the files that have changed since the last upload.

—————— **T** ——————

Table
Grids of rows and columns that can be used either to hold tabular data on a web page or as a basic design tool for data placement.

Table caption
Text at the top of a table that describes the table contents; read by screen readers.

Table header
Text placed at the top or sides of a table on a web page; read by screen readers to help provide accessibility for table content.

Tag (HTML)
The individual pieces of code that specify the appearance for page content when viewed in a browser.

Tag selector
The left side of the status bar that displays HTML tags used at the insertion point location.

Tag type
A style type used to redefine an HTML tag.

Target
In Dreamweaver, the location on a web page that the browser displays when users select an internal link. In Edge Animate, the element on which an action is performed.

Template
A web page that contains the basic layout for each page in the site, including the location of a company logo, banner, and navigation links.

Templates
Pre-developed FLA files that can be used as starting points for an application.

Terms of use
The rules that a copyright owner uses to establish how users may use his or her work.

Thumbnail image
A small version of a larger image.

Tiled image
A small graphic that repeats across and down a web page, appearing as individual squares or rectangles.

Timeline
In Flash, the component used to organize and control the movie's contents over time by specifying when each object appears on the Stage. In Edge Animate, a horizontal panel that lets you visualize the length and components of an animation.

Toolbar
The bar in Edge Animate that contains buttons that let you create and select elements such as rectangles, rounded rectangles, ellipses, and text elements.

Tools panel
The component of Flash that contains a set of tools used to draw, select, and edit graphics and text. It is divided into four sections.

Touch and Gesture Events
In Flash, features of mobile device applications such as drag, swipe, and zoom. In Edge Animate, events that are designed specifically for touchscreen devices.

Touchend
An event that fires when a user stops touching an element.

Touchmove
An event that fires when a user moves the finger touching an element.

Touchstart
An event that fires when a user touches an element.

Tracing image
An image that is placed in the background of a web page as a guide to create page elements on top of it, similar to the way tracing paper is used.

Trademark

An indicator that protects an image, word, slogan, symbol, or design used to identify goods or services.

Transformation point

The point used to orient an object as it is being animated. For example, a rotating object will rotate around the transformation point. Also, the point of an object that snaps to a motion guide.

Tumblr

A blog where users can post and share text, photos, music, and videos.

Tween span

The number of frames in a motion tween.

Tweening

The process of filling the in-between frames in an animation.

Tweet

A short message posted on the Twitter website that is no more than 140 characters.

Twitter

A website where viewers can post short messages up to 140 characters long, called "tweets."

Typekit

A repository of over a thousand font families that you can use in web and print projects.

--------------- U ---------------

Uniform Resource Locator (URL)

An address that determines a route on the Internet or to a web page. *See also* Domain name.

Unity

Intra-screen unity refers to how the various screen objects relate in screen design. Inter-screen unity refers to the design that viewers encounter as they navigate from one screen to another.

Unordered list

A lists of items that do not need to be placed in a specific order and are usually preceded by bullets.

Unvisited link

A link that the user has not yet selected, or visited. The default color for unvisited links is blue.

Upload

The process of transferring files from a local drive to a web server.

URL

See Uniform Resource Locator.

--------------- V ---------------

Validate markup

To submit files to the W3C Validation Service so it can search through the code to look for errors that could occur with different language versions, such as HTML5.

Variable

A container that holds information, such as numbers, and is used in ActionScript code.

Vector graphic

An image calculated and stored according to mathematical formulas rather than pixels, resulting in a smaller file size and the ability to resize the image without a loss in quality.

Vidcast

See Vodcast.

View

A choice for displaying page content in the Document window; Dreamweaver has three working views: Design view, Code view, and Show Code and Design views.

Visited link

A link that has been previously selected, or visited. The default color for visited links is purple.

Vodcast

Short for Video podcast; also called a vidcast.

VPAT

Acronym for Voluntary Product Accessibility Template; a document that lists how an app such as Dreamweaver complies with Section 508 provisions and information on how people with disabilities use assistive devices to navigate the Internet.

--------------- W ---------------

WAVE

Acronym for Web Accessibility Evaluation Tool; used to evaluate website accessibility.

Web 2.0

The evolution of web applications that facilitate and promote information sharing among Internet users.

Web 3.0

The next generation of the web where browsers can handle multiple searches simultaneously.

Web browser

A program, such as Microsoft Internet Explorer, Apple Safari, Google Chrome, or Mozilla Firefox, that displays web content.

Web cam

A web camera used for video conferencing with a high-speed Internet connection.

Web server

A computer dedicated to hosting websites; it is connected to the Internet and configured with software to handle requests from browsers. Also, software that makes web content stored on a computer available to other computers.

WebDav

Acronym for Web-based Distributed Authoring and Versioning, a type of connection used with the WebDav protocol, such as a website residing on an Apache web server.

Website

A group of related web pages that are linked together and share a common interface and design.

White space

An area on a web page that is not filled with text or graphics; not necessarily white.

Wiki

Named for the Hawaiian word for "quick," a site where a user can use simple editing tools to contribute to and edit the site's content.

Wikipedia

An online encyclopedia that allows users to contribute to site content.

Wireframe

A prototype that represents every page and its contents in a website. Like a flowchart or storyboard, a wireframe shows the relationship of each page in the site to all the other pages.

Workspace

In Flash, the customizable area where you work with documents, movies, tools, and panels. In Edge Animate, the screen that contains all the menus, toolbars, panels, and other items you need to create animations.

Workspace switcher

A drop-down menu located on the right side of the Menu bar that allows you to change the workspace layout.

———————— **X** ————————

XHTML

The acronym for eXtensible HyperText Markup Language, the current standard language used to create web pages.

XML

Acronym for Extensible Markup Language, a type of language that is used to develop customized tags to store information.

XSL

Acronym for Extensible Stylesheet Language, which is similar to CSS; the XSL style sheet information formats containers created with XML.

XSLT

Acronym for Extensible Stylesheet Language Transformations; interprets the code in an XSL file to transform an XML document, much like style sheet files transform HTML files.

———————— **Y** ————————

YouTube

A website where you can upload and share videos.

indenting text, keyboard shortcut, DW 3–31
inherited styles, DW 3–23
Ink Bottle tool, FLASH 2–5
inline styles, DW 3–10
in-product messages, DW 1–8
Insert Date dialog box, DW 2–31
Insert Navigation command, DW 5–16—17
Insert Navigation dialog box, DW 2–22
Insert panel, DW 1–4
inserting Flash movies in Dreamweaver, INT 1–4—INT 1–7
    changing movie's properties, INT 1–7
    playing movies within Dreamweaver, INT 1–7
    Property inspector, INT 1–4—INT 1–5
instances, EDGE 1–21, FLASH 2–30
    adding to Stage, EDGE 1–26—EDGE 1–27
    breaking apart, FLASH 2–35
    creating, FLASH 2–32
    editing, FLASH 2–32
    giving symbols instance names, FLASH 2–41
intellectual property, DW 7–36
interactive design guidelines, FLASH 1–48
interactive events, specifying, EDGE 2–24—EDGE 2–25
interactivity, testing on mobile devices, EDGE 2–36—EDGE 2–41
internal links, DW 5–2
    creating, DW 5–DW 4—5, DW 5–8
    to IDs, creating, DW 5–10—12, DW 5–14—15
internal selectors, moving to external style sheets, DW 4–23—24
internal style(s), DW 3–10
internal style sheets, DW 3–20
Internet Service Providers (ISPs), DW 1–21
inter-screen unity, FLASH 1–48
intra-screen unity, FLASH 1–48
iOS devices, apps. *See* mobile applications
IP addresses, DW 1–22
ISPs (Internet Service Providers), DW 1–21
italics, keyboard shortcut, DW 3–31
item(s), menu bars, DW 5–16, DW 5–19—20
Item Preview window, FLASH 1–41

JavaScript, EDGE 2–18
    viewing code, EDGE 2–33—EDGE 2–34
JavaScript (.js) format, animations, EDGE 1–10
JavaScript functions, DW 2–27
JPEG (Joint Photographic Experts Group), DW 4–4

keyboard shortcuts. *See also* Power User Shortcuts
    resetting, DW 2–26
    undoing and redoing steps, DW 2–26
Keyboard Shortcuts dialog box, DW 1–11
keyframe(s), EDGE 1–30, FLASH 1–18, FLASH 1–33
    adding, EDGE 1–31—EDGE 1–32
    animating background color, EDGE 1–33—EDGE 1–34
    animating opacity with, EDGE 1–34—EDGE 1–36
    property, FLASH 3–6
keyframe marks, EDGE 1–30
keywords, DW 2–4
    entering, DW 2–7
    web pages, DW 2–7

Languages tab settings, mobile applications, FLASH 4–8
LANs (local area networks), DW 7–15
Lasso tool, FLASH 2–4, FLASH 2–6
layers, FLASH 1–5, FLASH 1–32—FLASH 1–33
    adding, FLASH 1–35
    changing names, FLASH 1–37
    elements, EDGE 1–22—EDGE 1–23
    mask. *See* mask layers
    masked, creating, FLASH 3–45
    reordering, EDGE 1–28—EDGE 1–29
layout
    web pages. *See* Fluid Grid Layout(s); page layouts
    workspace, choosing, DW 1–10
Learn & Support / Dreamweaver Help web page, DW 1–13
legal issues, DW 7–36—39
    copyright, DW 7–36—37
    downloaded media, DW 7–36
    fair use, DW 7–37
    intellectual property, DW 7–36
    licensing agreements, DW 7–37—38
    obtaining permission or license, DW 7–38
    posting copyright notices, DW 7–38—39
    proper use of work, DW 7–37
Lessons panel, EDGE 1–6, EDGE 1–13
Library panel, EDGE 1–6, FLASH 1–5, FLASH 1–40—FLASH 1–43
    creating folders, FLASH 1–42
    organizing items within folders, FLASH 1–43
licenses, obtaining, DW 7–38
licensing agreements, DW 7–37—38
line breaks, keyboard shortcut, DW 2–29

Line tool, FLASH 2–5, FLASH 2–14—FLASH 2–15
link(s), DW 1–12
    adding to web pages, DW 2–20, DW 2–23
    broken. *See* broken links
    case-sensitive, DW 5–8
    checking, keyboard shortcut, DW 5–33
    default color, DW 2–5
    default colors, DW 2–5
    external. *See* external links
    internal. *See* internal links
    keyboard shortcut for creating, DW 5–33
    to larger image, DW 4–26, DW 4–28
    mailto:, DW 2–20, DW 2–24—25
    managing, DW 5–30—33
    menu bars, DW 2–20—21, DW 2–22
    removing, keyboard shortcut, DW 5–33
    targets, DW 5–10
    to, Creative Cloud files, sending, CC 1–10
    unvisited, DW 2–5
    viewing in Assets panel, DW 5–9
    visited, DW 2–5
    WCAG accessibility guidelines, DW 2–21
Link Checker panel, DW 7–4, DW 7–6
linking Microsoft Office documents, DW 2–18
list(s)
    bulleted, DW 3–4, DW 3–5
    definition, DW 3–5
    ordered (numbered), DW 3–5, DW 3–8—9
    unordered, DW 3–DW 4—5, DW 3–6—7
Live view, DW 1–5, DW 1–7
    viewing and editing pages, DW 1–7
local area networks (LANs), DW 7–15
local folders, setting up web server connection, DW 7–18
local root folders, DW 1–24
local site folders, DW 1–20, DW 1–24
    creating, DW 1–23

Magic Wand tool, FLASH 2–4
mailto: links, DW 2–20, DW 2–24—25
Manage Fonts dialog box, DW 3–25
marquees, FLASH 1–18—FLASH 1–19
mask layers, FLASH 3–40—FLASH 3–47
    creating, FLASH 3–44—FLASH 3–45
    frame-by-frame animations, FLASH 3–43

scope creep, DW 1–21

screen design guidelines, FLASH 1–47—FLASH 1–48

screen readers, DW 4–15

scrubbing, EDGE 1–11

Secure FTP (SFTP), DW 7–15

selecting

    all, keyboard shortcut, DW 2–29

    cells, keyboard shortcut, DW 6–36

    frames, FLASH 3–27

    images for responsive design, DW 4–5

    objects, FLASH 2–6

    templates, FLASH 5–28—FLASH 5–29

Selection tool, FLASH 2–4, FLASH 2–6

selectors

    adding to style sheets, DW 3–18—19

    applying, DW 4–12

    background-image, editing, DW 4–25

    CSS Designer, DW 3–10

    CSS menu bar, editing, DW 5–23—25

    global class, DW 4–8—9

    tablet size, DW 4–10—11

semantic web, coding for, DW 3–6

servers. *See* web server(s)

SFTP (Secure FTP), DW 7–15

shape(s)

    creating, EDGE 2–6—EDGE 2–7

    drawing, EDGE 2–4—EDGE 2–11

    duplicating, EDGE 2–5, EDGE 2–10—EDGE 2–11

    specifying background color, EDGE 2–9—EDGE 2–10

    specifying border properties, EDGE 2–8—EDGE 2–9

shape hints, shape tweening, FLASH 3–29, FLASH 3–33

shape tools, EDGE 2–4—EDGE 2–5

shape tweening, FLASH 3–28—FLASH 3–33

    adjusting rate of change, FLASH 3–32

    creating animations, FLASH 3–30

    creating morphing effect, FLASH 3–28—FLASH 3–29, FLASH 3–31

    Properties panel options, FLASH 3–29

    shape hints, FLASH 3–29, FLASH 3–33

sharing, Creative Cloud files, CC 1–10

shortcut(s), FLASH 1–15

shortcut keys. *See* Power User Shortcuts

Show Code and Design views, DW 1–6

showing

    Code Inspector, keyboard shortcut, DW 2–29

    panels, keyboard shortcut, DW 1–33

Signature tab settings, AIR applications, FLASH 5–24

simplicity, advantages, DW 2–2

Site button, DW 4–7

site definitions, DW 7–32—35

    exporting, DW 7–32, DW 7–33

    importing, DW 7–32, DW 7–34

    viewing imported sites, DW 7–35

site reports, DW 7–DW 4—5

site root-relative paths, DW 5–5

Site Setup dialog box, DW 7–14—15

size properties, EDGE 1–19

skewing

    objects, FLASH 2–8

    text, FLASH 2–25

skins, FLASH 5–8

Skype, DW 5–35

slider, History panel, DW 2–26

Smart Objects, DW 4–18

smartphones, resizing applications for, FLASH 4–22

social networking, DW 5–2, DW 5–34

sound, adding to movies, FLASH 3–48—FLASH 3–50

source(s), specifying, EDGE 2–17—EDGE 2–19, EDGE 2–20—EDGE 2–23

source elements, EDGE 2–16

space, adding to images, DW 4–17

specifications, applications, FLASH 1–47

spell checking, DW 2–19

    keyboard shortcut, DW 2–29

splitting table cells, DW 6–26, DW 6–27, DW 6–28

    keyboard shortcut, DW 6–36

sprite sheets

    exporting from Flash, INT 1–16, INT 1–18

    importing into Edge Animate, INT 1–16—INT 1–17, INT 1–19

squares, drawing, EDGE 2–5

stacking, elements, EDGE 1–22—EDGE 1–23

Stage, EDGE 1–4—EDGE 1–5, FLASH 1–4, FLASH 1–11

    adding instances, EDGE 1–26—EDGE 1–27

    adding text, EDGE 1–27—EDGE 1–28

    making elements appear and disappear, EDGE 1–32

positioning objects on, FLASH 2–16—FLASH 2–17, FLASH 2–18—FLASH 2–19

    zooming, EDGE 1–9

Standard toolbar, DW 1–5

starting

    Dreamweaver. *See* starting Dreamweaver

    Edge Animate, EDGE 1–7

    Flash, FLASH 1–9

starting Dreamweaver

    Macintosh, DW 1–8

    Windows, DW 1–7

startup actions, EDGE 2–16—EDGE 2–23

    compositionReady event, EDGE 2–19

    specifying sources, events, actions, and targets, EDGE 2–17—EDGE 2–19, EDGE 2–20—EDGE 2–23

states, DW 5–16, EDGE 2–2

    buttons, FLASH 2–36

status bar, DW 1–6

step(s), History panel, DW 2–26

Step Backward One Frame command, FLASH 1–13

Step Forward One Frame command, FLASH 1–13

stop action, assigning to frames, FLASH 2–45

storing images, DW 4–21

storyboards, FLASH 1–48—FLASH 1–49

Stroke Color tool, FLASH 2–5

structure of website, planning, DW 1–19—20

style(s)

    converting, DW 3–29

    embedded. *See* embedded styles

    external, DW 3–10

    inherited, DW 3–23

    inline. *See* inline styles

    internal (embedded), DW 3–10

    managing with CSS Designer, DW 3–11

style sheets. *See also* Cascading Style Sheets (CSSs); external style sheets

    advantages, DW 3–11

    internal, DW 3–20

    moving styles between, DW 3–32

    responsive design, DW 2–33—34

Subselection tool, FLASH 2–4

Subversion control, DW 7–23

Swap Colors tool, FLASH 2–5

swapping objects, Accelerometer, FLASH 4–31—FLASH 4–32